Brookings Papers

ON ECONOMIC ACTIVITY

FALL 2019

JANICE EBERLY

JAMES H. STOCK

Editors

BROOKINGS INSTITUTION PRESS
Washington, D.C.

Brookings Papers
ON ECONOMIC ACTIVITY

FALL 2019

This journal is printed in black and white but is available online in color. The numbered graphical figures in a paper may contain colored elements (lines, dots, bars, and areas) to which the paper's text refers. To see these colored elements, please consult the online versions of the papers at https://www.brookings.edu/project/brookings-papers-on-economic-activity/.

PURPOSE   The *Brookings Papers on Economic Activity* publishes research on current issues in macroeconomics, broadly defined. The journal emphasizes rigorous analysis that has an empirical orientation, takes real-world institutions seriously, and is relevant to economic policy. Papers are presented and discussed at conferences held twice each year, and the papers and discussant remarks from each conference are published in the journal several months later. Research findings are described in a clear and accessible style to maximize their impact on economic understanding and economic policymaking; the intended audience includes analysts from universities, governments, and businesses. Topics covered by the journal include fiscal and monetary policy, consumption and saving behavior, business investment, housing, asset pricing, labor markets, wage and price setting, business cycles, long-run economic growth, the distribution of income and wealth, international capital flows and exchange rates, international trade and development, and the macroeconomic implications of health costs, energy supply and demand, environmental issues, and the education system.

We would like to thank the supporters of the *Brookings Papers on Economic Activity* conference and journal, including the Alfred P. Sloan Foundation; BlackRock Financial Management, Inc.; the National Science Foundation, under Grant No. 1756544; and State Farm Mutual Automobile Insurance Company.

The papers and discussant remarks reflect the views of the authors and not necessarily the views of the funding organizations or the staff members, officers, or trustees of the Brookings Institution.

CALL FOR PAPERS   Most papers that appear in the *Brookings Papers on Economic Activity* are solicited by the editors, but the editors also consider submitted proposals. Editorial decisions are generally made about a year in advance of each conference. Therefore, proposals should be received by December 1 for the following fall conference and by June 1 for the following spring conference. Proposals can be submitted at http://connect.brookings.edu/submit-your-paper-to-bpea.

ACCESSING THE JOURNAL   All past editions of the *Brookings Papers on Economic Activity*—along with appendix materials, data, and programs used to generate results—are made freely available for download at www.brookings.edu/past-bpea-editions. To purchase subscriptions or single copies, visit www.brookings.edu/press, or contact the Brookings Institution Press at (866) 698-0010 or P.O. Box 465, Hanover, PA 17331-0465. Brookings periodicals are available online through both the Online Computer Library Center (contact the OCLC subscription department at (800) 848-5878) and Project Muse (http://muse.jhu.edu). Archived issues of the *Brookings Papers on Economic Activity* are also available through JSTOR (www.jstor.org).

Michael T. Kiley *Federal Reserve Board of Governors*
Aaron Klein *Brookings Institution*
Jeffrey Kling *Congressional Budget Office*
Narayana Kocherlakota *University of Rochester*
Wojciech Kopczuk *Columbia University*
M. Ayhan Kose *The World Bank*
Ed Lazear *Stanford University*
Hervé Le Bihan *Banque de France*
Nellie Liang *Brookings Institution*
John Lipsky *Johns Hopkins University (SAIS)*
Christos Makridis *Sloan School of Management,*
    Massachusetts Institute of Technology
N. Gregory Mankiw *Harvard University*
Victoria Marone *Northwestern University*
Julien Matheron *Banque de France*
Mark Mazur *Urban-Brookings Tax Policy Center*
Warwick McKibbin *Australian National University*
Karel Mertens *Federal Reserve Bank of Dallas*
Frederic Mishkin *Columbia University*
Adele C. Morris *Brookings Institution*
Matthew J. Notowidigdo *Northwestern University*
Ryan Nunn *Brookings Institution*
Tom Orlik *Bloomberg*
Matea Pender, *The College Board*
George Perry *Brookings Institution*
Jonathan Pingle *BlackRock*
Eswar Prasad *Brookings Institution*
Valerie Ramey *University of California, San Diego*
David H. Romer *University of California, Berkeley*
John Sabelhaus *Washington Center for Equitable Growth*
Bruce Sacerdote *Dartmouth College*
Emmanuel Saez *University of California, Berkeley*
Claudia Sahm *Washington Center for Equitable Growth*
Brian Scholl *U.S. Securities and Exchange Commission*
Jay Shambaugh *Brookings Institution*
Louise Sheiner *Brookings Institution*
Tara Sinclair *George Washington University*
Jonathan Skinner *Dartmouth College*
Luminita Stevens *University of Maryland*
James H. Stock *Harvard University*
Michael Strain *American Enterprise Institute*
Federico Sturzenegger *Universidad de San Andrés*
Phillip Swagel *Congressional Budget Office*
Marzie Taheri Sanjani *International Monetary Fund*
Andrés Velasco *London School of Economics and Political Science*
Stan Veuger *American Enterprise Institute*
Alan Viard *American Enterprise Institute*
Ivan Vidangos *Federal Reserve Board of Governors*
Alice Volz *Federal Reserve Board of Governors*
Hilary Waldron *Social Security Administration*
William L. Wascher *Federal Reserve Board of Governors*
David Wessel *Brookings Institution*
David W. Wilcox *Peterson Institute for International Economics*
Justin Wolfers *University of Michigan*

Janet Yellen *Brookings Institution*
Jeromin Zettelmeyer *Peterson Institute for International Economics*
Gabriel Zucman *University of California, Berkeley*

Francisca P. Alba *Brookings Institution*
Siobhan Drummond *Brookings Institution*
Stephanie K. Holzbauer *Brookings Institution*
Mary E. King *Brookings Institution*

CRAIG GARTHWAITE
Northwestern University

ZEYNAL KARACA
Agency for Healthcare Research and Quality

JOHN GRAVES
Vanderbilt University

VICTORIA MARONE
Northwestern University

TAL GROSS
Boston University

MATTHEW J. NOTOWIDIGDO
Northwestern University

All Medicaid Expansions Are Not Created Equal: The Geography and Targeting of the Affordable Care Act

ABSTRACT   We use comprehensive patient-level discharge data to study the effect of Medicaid on the use of hospital services. Our analysis relies on cross-state variation in the Affordable Care Act's Medicaid expansion, along with within-state variation across zip codes in exposure to the expansion. We find that the Medicaid expansion increased Medicaid visits and decreased uninsured visits. The net effect is positive for all visits, suggesting that those who gain coverage through Medicaid consume more hospital services than they would if they remained uninsured. The increase in emergency department visits is largely accounted for by "deferrable" medical conditions. Those who gained coverage under the Medicaid expansion appear to be those who had

Conflict of Interest Disclosure: Craig Garthwaite is the Herman R. Smith Research Professor at the Kellogg School of Management at Northwestern University; John Graves is an associate professor at Vanderbilt University School of Medicine; Tal Gross is associate professor of markets, public policy, and law at the Questrom School of Business at Boston University; Zeynal Karaca is a senior economist and program director for market analytics and research at the Agency for Healthcare Research and Quality; Victoria Marone is a doctoral candidate at Northwestern University; Matthew J. Notowidigdo is an associate professor of economics and of strategy at the Weinberg College of Arts and Sciences at Northwestern University. Beyond these affiliations, the authors did not receive financial support from any firm or person for this paper or from any firm or person with a financial or political interest in this paper. None of the authors of this paper are currently officers, directors, or board members of any organization with an interest in this paper. Beyond the Agency for Healthcare Research and Quality, whose data are utilized in this paper, no outside party had the right to review this paper before circulation. The views expressed in this paper are those of the authors and do not necessarily reflect any of the institutions affiliated with the authors.

1

relatively high need for hospital services, suggesting that the expansion was well targeted. Lastly, we find significant heterogeneity across Medicaid expansion states in the effects of the expansion, with some states experiencing a large increase in total utilization and other states experiencing little change. Increases in hospital utilization were larger in Medicaid expansion states that had more residents gaining coverage and lower pre-expansion levels of uncompensated hospital care costs.

The United States health care sector is often described as a market-based system driven by private firms. The government nevertheless plays an enormous role. As of 2018, nearly half of all U.S. health care expenditures came from the public sector—primarily through Medicare and Medicaid but also through the subsidization of employer-sponsored health insurance via the tax code. Medicare has covered the elderly (65 and over) population in the United States since its creation in 1965, and growth in program enrollment has been driven primarily by shifting demographics. Medicaid, by contrast, has grown from a program that initially targeted the indigent and the disabled to a far more generous program that currently provides coverage to over 70 million Americans (Rudowitz, Hinton, and Antonisse 2018).

Expansion of Medicaid eligibility can be thought of as a reflection of society's evolving beliefs about social insurance. Historically, Medicaid enrollees needed to be both low-income and in a particular category in order to qualify for coverage. Coverage was extended to pregnant women and their children in the 1980s and then to relatively higher-income children in the 1990s through the State Children's Health Insurance Program (SCHIP). Throughout the 1990s and 2000s, states used federal waivers to expand Medicaid to additional categories of low-income individuals. These expansions mostly covered parents, but in only a few states were low-income childless adults covered (Long, Zuckerman, and Graves 2006). This focus on categorical eligibility was partly motivated by a belief that individuals in these specific groups were in particular need of assistance and that limiting the eligibility criteria to include only those groups could increase the target efficiency of Medicaid spending.

The largest and most controversial expansion occurred with the implementation of the Affordable Care Act (ACA) in 2014. For those earning below 138 percent of the federal poverty level (approximately $16,600 for an individual in 2019), the ACA fundamentally changed the concept of Medicaid eligibility. It did so by stripping away categorical requirements, along with considerations over nonincome assets, for the purposes of determining program eligibility for the under-65 population. Instead, the law transformed Medicaid into an entitlement with new eligibility criteria based on a current monthly modified adjusted gross income (MAGI) standard.[1]

Expansion of Medicaid eligibility to a greater fraction of the low-income population was driven by a variety of motivations. Certainly, policymakers were motivated by the desire to ensure some baseline level of access to health care. As such, the expansions reflected the preferences of the electorate over what this baseline level of access entails.[2] That said, policymakers were also motivated by questions regarding the efficiency of the health care sector. Specifically, policymakers and advocates for the ACA routinely noted that lack of access to formal insurance results in health care being provided in more-expensive settings than would otherwise be necessary (for example, primary care services provided in emergency departments).

Finally, federal lawmakers have also shown a preference for establishing a baseline of access to health care across states. While Medicaid has always been a state-administered program, federal expansions have progressively raised the floor of who would be covered in all states. States have always had—and many have exercised—the right to exceed that floor and provide more generous social insurance. In this way, federal Medicaid policy serves as a safety net that reflects the nation's preferences for a compromise, maintaining a minimum level of access but allowing for variation above that minimum across states.

The ACA represents the largest reform of the health care sector since the creation of the Great Society programs in the 1960s. But nearly a decade after the ACA's adoption, approximately 10 percent of the non-elderly population remains formally uninsured. This persistence of uninsurance stems, in part, from a 2012 Supreme Court decision that allowed states to refrain from implementing the ACA's Medicaid expansion. In 2014, when the expansion was fully implemented with 100 percent federal financing,

1. Categorical eligibility determinations are still used within non-expansion states and within the entire Medicaid program to determine the share of state versus federal financing. Moreover, asset tests can still be used for eligibility determinations of individuals over age 65.

2. In 2013, President Obama defended the ACA and cited both its social insurance benefits and increased access to health care: "In the wealthiest nation on Earth, no one should go broke just because they get sick. In the United States, health care is not a privilege for the fortunate few, it is a right" (Wilson and Wiggins 2013).

only twenty-four states elected to expand Medicaid. Over the next three years, an additional seven states adopted expansions. Currently, thirty-six states have expanded their Medicaid programs under the (nearly full) federal financing and authority granted by the ACA. Research has shown that state expansion decisions have a meaningful impact on access to formal insurance. As of 2018, the share of the population without insurance was 16.1 percent in non-expansion states compared to 7.5 percent in expansion states (Haley and others 2018).

While the decision over whether to expand Medicaid is clearly an important one, a variety of other policy decisions have contributed to an ongoing lack of universal coverage in the United States. These include features of the ACA as well as differences in implementation decisions both within and across states. Lack of universal coverage has led to a variety of calls to further expand the social safety net for health care. These policies range from expansions of the existing ACA framework to a single-payer system that covers the entire nation.

Evaluating the efficacy of an expanded social insurance system requires careful consideration of the impact of previous expansions. In this paper, we examine the effects of the ACA using a large data set maintained by the Agency for Healthcare Research and Quality (AHRQ) that covers the near universe of hospitalizations in twenty states. In each of those states, shown in figure 1, we have data from 2012 to 2015 covering all outpatient and inpatient emergency department visits as well as inpatient hospitalizations that initiated in the emergency department.[3] As we consider the ACA, three natural questions arise that can inform both the design of future expansion efforts as well as help with understanding broader economic effects of existing social insurance programs.

First, did the ACA's expansion of Medicaid lead to a more efficient utilization of health care? In particular, did those who became newly insured through Medicaid decrease their use of emergency departments? To answer this question, we use several identification strategies to examine overall and state-level impacts of the Medicaid expansion on emergency department use. We find consistent evidence across those identification strategies that Medicaid coverage increased the use of hospital services.

---

3. The data encompass about 95 percent of all discharges in each state. Healthcare Cost and Utilization Project (HCUP) databases do not include federal hospitals (for example, Veterans Affairs, Department of Defense, and Indian Health Service hospitals), long-term hospitals, psychiatric hospitals, alcohol/chemical dependency treatment facilities, and hospital units within institutions such as prisons.

Figure 1. Map of States in Analysis Sample

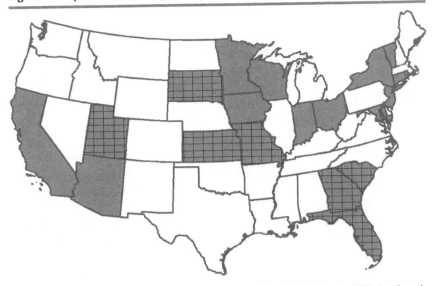

Source: Authors' calculations based on Healthcare Cost and Utilization Project (HCUP) data from the Agency for Healthcare Research and Quality (AHRQ).

Note: The sample includes twenty states: thirteen expansion states and seven non-expansion states. The non-expansion states are indicated with a grid pattern in this map and all of the maps that follow.

The estimates rule out large declines in the use of emergency departments as a result of Medicaid expansions.

Second, did the expansion and transformation of Medicaid meet the goal of providing access to health care for those who most needed it? This is often described as the "target efficiency" of social insurance: the degree to which those who gain coverage are those who most need the assistance. To examine the target efficiency of the ACA we examine the use of health care for the newly insured compared to those who remain ineligible for the expanded program. We find that those gaining access to Medicaid in expansion states had greater pre-expansion utilization of health care than those who remained uninsured. This suggests that the expansion of Medicaid based on income, rather than specific categories of need, successfully targeted the remaining uninsured with greater pre-expansion use of medical services. Looking at non-expansion states, we see an increase in private insurance driven by the creation of the ACA marketplaces. In this setting, we find that those who purchased private insurance were also those with the greatest use of medical services. This suggests that the subsidized marketplaces, even though they required contributions from enrollees, provided coverage to those with a greater demand for health care services.

Finally, we examine heterogeneity in the impact of the expansion across states. At a minimum, the decision of some states not to expand Medicaid created variation in the social safety net across states. We investigate other sources of heterogeneity in the effects of the ACA across states. This variation extends beyond simply the question of take-up (that is, how much of the eligible population signed up for formal insurance) and also reflects differences in the increase in the use of hospital services among the newly insured. This heterogeneity should generate some caution in generalizing results from previous state expansions to other settings. It also provides some explanation for the heterogeneity in the existing litera-ture on the relationship between Medicaid coverage and hospitalizations. Across all the states in our sample, we find that the ACA Medicaid expan-sion resulted in an increase in the use of hospital services. In a number of states, however, the estimated effect is small and statistically indistinguish-able from zero. We also examine heterogeneity in the target efficiency of the expansions, finding that the degree to which the expansions could target those with the greatest need for medical services varied meaning-fully across states.

I. Medicaid Expansions and Use of Hospital Services

Concerns about access to health care have resulted in regulations that make the sale of health care fundamentally different from other sectors of the economy. For instance, hospital emergency departments are required by law to stabilize anyone with an emergency condition regardless of their ability to pay.[4] This creates several economic frictions. First, hospitals are effectively required to serve as "insurers of last resort" for care not paid for directly by patients or explicitly financed via public or private insurance (Garthwaite, Gross, and Notowidigdo 2018).[5] Second, since only hospitals with emergency departments are covered by this mandate, some conditions

---

4. The Emergency Medical Treatment and Active Labor Act (EMTALA) introduced this requirement in 1983.

5. While hospitals do receive supplementary funding to account for these expenses, the degree to which these fully reimburse hospitals is unclear. For example, Garthwaite, Gross, and Notowidigdo (2018) find that hospitals bear the brunt of the costs of marginal uninsured patients through lower profits.

Table 1. Average Utilization Rate by Type of Visit and Insurance Status

	Uninsured	Medicaid	Private
Type of visit			
Inpatient hospital visit (not originating in emergency department)	0.009	0.046	0.026
Inpatient hospital visit (originating in emergency department)	0.026	0.049	0.018
Outpatient emergency department visit	0.357	0.364	0.138
Total visits (hospital plus emergency department visits)	0.391	0.459	0.181
Share of total visits			
Inpatient hospital visit (not originating in emergency department)	2.2%	10.0%	14.1%
Inpatient hospital visit (originating in emergency department)	6.6%	10.7%	9.9%
Outpatient emergency department visit	91.2%	79.4%	76.0%
Ratio of outpatient emergency department visits/ inpatient visits			
Not originating in emergency department	42.0	7.9	5.4
Originating in emergency department	13.8	7.4	7.6
Share of inpatient visits originating in emergency department	75.3%	51.6%	41.3%

Source: Authors' calculations.

Note: Data are 2013 estimates (for all states in the sample) of average utilization by insurance status and type of visit. Diagnosis-related group (DRG) population estimates were used to calculate utilization rate: the total number of visits divided by population with that insurance status.

may be treated in the relatively high marginal cost setting of the hospital emergency department when they could be more efficiently treated in other, lower-cost settings. Third, the uninsured are often unable to gain access to routine, preventive primary care and expensive pharmaceuticals. Thus, there is a concern that medical conditions that could have been managed early and at a lower cost instead develop into acute episodes that end up costing the entire system more than they would if there were more widespread insurance coverage.

Differences in the ability to access health care can be seen in the data. Table 1 describes the use of hospital services by insurance status before the ACA. In our data, only 2.2 percent of the hospital visits for the uninsured were inpatient stays that did not originate in the emergency department. This is far less than the share for Medicaid patients (10 percent) and the privately insured (14.1 percent). Relatedly, three-quarters of the inpatient visits for the uninsured began in the emergency department. The corresponding numbers for Medicaid recipients and the privately insured are much lower, 52 and 41 percent, respectively. Overall, those with private insurance had the lowest use of hospital services, which likely reflects the fact that those with private coverage are relatively healthy.[6]

These estimates suggest that while the uninsured do have access to health care through the emergency department, there are legitimate concerns that they lack access to more discretionary and expensive health care services. Those concerns are often called the "access motive" for health insurance. The access motive argues that consumers need health insurance for reasons that extend beyond the need to smooth consumption across different states of the world, that is, the traditional economic rationale for insurance. Rather, an additional primary benefit of health insurance is to maintain *access* to health care for liquidity-constrained populations (Nyman 1998; Besanko, Dranove, and Garthwaite 2016).

The access motive was cited by many policymakers in support of the ACA. For example, Speaker of the House Nancy Pelosi argued that "the uninsured will get coverage, no longer left to the emergency room for medical care" (Blase 2016). On the opposite side of the aisle, Rick Snyder, the Republican governor of Michigan, argued: "Uninsured citizens often turn to emergency rooms . . . leading to crowded emergency rooms, longer wait times and higher costs. By expanding Medicaid, those without insurance will have access to primary care, lowering costs and improving overall health" (Kliff 2014).

As is often the case, economic research on this topic is less clear than what one would infer from the statements of activists and policymakers. It is true that the uninsured often face barriers to care outside of the emergency department. That said, care at the emergency department for the uninsured can be quite costly to the uninsured themselves. While hospitals are required to stabilize emergency patients regardless of their ability to pay, they are allowed to (and often do) bill for these services. Existing evidence suggests that hospitals do not recover all—or even most—of the costs of providing this service, but they do exact meaningful financial and psychic costs on those from whom they attempt to collect (Mahoney 2015). Nonprofit hospitals enjoy tax-exempt status because they provide community benefit, including charity care to the uninsured. But even nonprofit hospitals have been shown to go to

---

6. Despite some erroneous commentary in the popular press, it is wrong to consider this higher use of medical services by Medicaid recipients as a causal effect of Medicaid decreasing people's health.

great lengths—including litigation and wage garnishment—to recover unpaid bills.[7]

As a result, health insurance decreases the cost of accessing the emergency department, and this could create a moral hazard response that results in more emergency department visits. The moral hazard effect could be exacerbated by both perceived and real transaction costs. These costs derive from the need to separately secure office-based appointments, lab tests, and other complementary services outside of the emergency setting. This requires identifying providers that accept Medicaid as a form of payment and have availability for appointments—a process that can be time consuming. By comparison, nearly all hospital-based emergency departments accept Medicaid as payment, offer a wide spectrum of services under one roof, and have minimal differential cost-sharing requirements for Medicaid patients. In addition, it is unclear whether emergency department services are a complement or a substitute for primary care or whether that relationship might vary by insurance status.

Numerous studies have found clear evidence that Medicaid coverage tends to increase health care consumption in general and emergency department visits in particular. The Oregon health insurance experiment found that low-income, uninsured people who gain health insurance coverage through Medicaid are 40 percent more likely to visit an emergency department (Taubman and others 2014). That finding matches the conclusions of work by Nikpay and others (2017); Anderson, Dobkin, and Gross (2012, 2013); Card, Dobkin, and Maestas (2008); Dresden and others (2017); DeLeire and others (2013); Garthwaite and others (2017); Smulowitz and others (2014); and Heavrin and others (2011).

These studies have shown that insurance coverage increases the likelihood of an emergency department visit. But the literature is not entirely uniform on this point. Antwi et al. (2015), Hernandez-Boussard and others (2014), and Sommers and others (2016) all conclude that expansions of Medicaid actually *decrease* the risk of an emergency department visit. In particular, Miller (2012) finds that the Massachusetts health care reform—which nearly eliminated the uninsured population in that state—decreased emergency department visits overall.

---

7. For example, a recent investigation by *ProPublica* found that Methodist Le Bonheur Healthcare in Memphis brought thousands of lawsuits for unpaid medical bills in recent years (Thomas 2019), and the *New York Times* published a similar investigation into the collection efforts of nonprofit hospitals back in 2004 (Cohn 2004). Such practices have led some politicians to discuss trying to "rein in" nonprofit hospitals that bring lawsuits and garnish wages (Armour 2019).

Some of the disagreement across these studies may be driven by general equilibrium effects in the provision of medical services. For example, in a more heavily insured population, primary care physicians or other outpatient facilities may change their business practices to accommodate the new payer mix in ways that change the use of emergency department facilities (Richards, Nikpay, and Graves 2016). This could explain why two of the studies of the market-wide change in Massachusetts produced estimates that were different from the general thrust of the literature.

By changing both the quantity and setting of health care consumed, expansions of Medicaid can have meaningful economy-wide impacts. To the extent that expansion leads to lower health care spending, this can free up economic resources for more efficient uses in other parts of the economy. In addition, to the extent that more efficient provision of health care can increase the underlying health of the population, it could also increase labor force productivity for those affected. Both of these channels suggest meaningful macroeconomic impacts from changes to Medicaid.

Determining the broader economic impact of Medicaid is even more important given the current uneven geographic access to the ACA Medicaid expansion. As of mid-2019, thirteen states have still not expanded their programs. In the next section, we describe the specifics of the ACA Medicaid expansion, which underlies our various identification strategies.

II. Background on the ACA Medicaid Expansion

Of primary importance to the questions in this paper, the ACA increased access to health insurance through both a large expansion of Medicaid for low-income populations and the creation of a series of state-based insurance marketplaces where individuals could purchase non-group insurance. Individuals purchasing insurance in these state-based marketplaces could not be denied coverage for preexisting medical conditions, and their premiums could vary only by smoking status, across geographic rating areas determined by the state, and by age (with the ratio of premiums across age groups not to exceed 3:1). In order to combat adverse selection, individuals were mandated to purchase insurance or pay a penalty on their income taxes.[8]

Legal residents who earn less than 138 percent of the federal poverty level are eligible for Medicaid. Those who earn between 100 and 400 percent

---

8. The individual mandate was effectively eliminated as part of a congressional reform of the federal tax system in 2017.

of the federal poverty level and who aren't otherwise Medicaid-eligible qualify for federal subsidies that limit marketplace plan premiums to a fixed percentage of the enrollee's income. Those earning between 138 and 250 percent of the federal poverty level receive additional subsidies that limit their exposure to cost sharing (for example, deductibles, copayments, and coinsurance). Those who earn more than 400 percent of the federal poverty level, and those under 100 percent, can still purchase insurance on the marketplace but they are required to pay the entire premium.

The ACA was exceptionally controversial and attracted large amounts of litigation. In the summer of 2012, the U.S. Supreme Court upheld the constitutionality of the ACA's individual mandate. However, the court also allowed states to opt out of the act's expansion of Medicaid to 138 percent of the federal poverty level.

For those living in states that did not expand Medicaid, access to formal health insurance effectively depends on family income. Those who earn between 100 and 138 percent of the federal poverty level can purchase heavily subsidized insurance on the marketplace. These individuals also receive generous cost-sharing subsidies that make their coverage more similar to Medicaid—though Medicaid could be a preferred coverage vehicle given its even lower cost-sharing requirements, zero-dollar premiums (in some states), and broader range of benefits than traditionally covered by private plans (for example, transportation services).

Residents in non-expansion states who earn less than 100 percent of the federal poverty level fall into a coverage gap. These residents earn too much money to qualify for their state's relatively parsimonious and categorically based Medicaid program and too little to qualify for subsidies on the ACA marketplaces. According to the Kaiser Family Foundation, this has resulted in approximately 2.3 million residents who lack access to health insurance based solely on their state of residence (Garfield, Orgera, and Damico 2020). Nearly half of these residents live in either Florida or Texas and over 90 percent live in the southern United States. Given the state-based nature of decisions about the ACA, the potential economic benefits of the increased social insurance and the economic opportunities that it might provide can impact the economic growth of different geographies. In addition, the uneven implementation of Medicaid expansion under the ACA raises concerns over equity. To a greater degree than in the past, Americans' access to health care often depends on the state in which they reside.

The number of people in the coverage gap meant that the share of the uninsured population fell faster in expansion states compared to non-expansion states. For example, in the first quarter of 2018, the share of uninsured in non-expansion states was 16.1 percent compared to 7.5 percent in expansion states (Haley and others 2018). In addition to having a higher share of uninsured, the composition of the insured market also differed based on a state's Medicaid expansion decision. In expansion states, those between 100 and 138 percent of poverty enrolled in Medicaid. However, in non-expansion states these individuals had access to heavily subsidized insurance through the marketplaces. Thus, one would expect the share with private insurance to be different across these states after the implementation of the ACA.

III. Data

The primary databases used in our empirical analysis are the State Emergency Department Databases (SEDD) and the State Inpatient Databases (SID). The databases are part of the Healthcare Cost and Utilization Project (HCUP) and are maintained by the Agency for Healthcare Research and Quality (AHRQ).

The SID and the SEDD are both made up of state-specific files. Each state-specific file covers a near census of hospital and emergency department visits for a given calendar year. The databases are detailed and comprehensive; they are well suited to studying state-level policy changes. Our analysis focuses on the following twenty states: Arizona, California, Connecticut, Florida, Georgia, Iowa, Indiana, Kansas, Maryland, Minnesota, Missouri, New Jersey, New York, Ohio, Rhode Island, South Carolina, South Dakota, Utah, Vermont, and Wisconsin.[9] These states cover 51 percent of the U.S. population and 55 percent of the Medicaid population and include both expansion and non-expansion states.[10]

The SID contains about 97 percent of all inpatient hospitalizations in participating states, while the SEDD contains more than 95 percent of emergency department encounters. Both databases contain clinical information

9. We selected this sample of states based on conversations with AHRQ staff. We excluded states that did not have consistent measurement and categorization of payer categories during this time period or did not have patient zip code information that is necessary for our county- and zip code–level analysis.

10. Data sources for these calculations are the U.S. Census Bureau American FactFinder (https://factfinder.census.gov/faces/tableservices/jsf/pages/productview.xhtml?pid=PEP_2018_ PEPANNRES&src=pt) and the Centers for Medicare and Medicaid Services enrollment data (https://data.medicaid.gov/Enrollment/2018-12-Updated-applications-eligibility-determina/ gy72-q4z9/data).

(for example, length of stay, primary and secondary diagnoses) and non-clinical information (for example, age, gender, race, total charges) on all patients, including individuals covered by Medicare, Medicaid, or private insurance, as well as those who are uninsured.[11] In this paper, we focus on the primary diagnosis code, since it allows us to categorize hospitalizations into deferrable versus nondeferrable visits.

We follow Mulcahy and others (2013) and Garthwaite and others (2017) in identifying deferrable and nondeferrable visits. Deferrable visits are those for which, as indicated by a panel of physicians, the patient likely has some discretion as to when to present to a professional. By contrast, nondeferrable visits are hospital visits for one of twelve conditions that have been identified by a panel of physicians as likely to require immediate medical treatment regardless of insurance coverage or financing. For instance, an intracerebral hemorrhage is classified as nondeferrable—patients with this condition would almost certainly present at an emergency department regardless of their insurance status.[12]

Most important for our purposes, we also observe each patient's insurance coverage (Medicare, Medicaid, private) as well as whether the patient was uninsured. Lastly, we observe the patient's zip code of residence, and we observe hospital identifiers in both databases, which we merge to hospital-level characteristics using survey data from the American Hospital Association (AHA).

We process the SID and SEDD state-specific files by first restricting the data to 2012–2015. We then collapse the data into counts of visits by the following variables: patient zip code, year, month, indicator functions for deferrable conditions, insurance status, and age group (under 18, 18–64, and age 65 and above).[13] The collapsed data can then be used for difference-in-differences and event study analyses, and most of our empirical models use either raw counts of visits or the natural logarithm of those counts.

---

11. We categorize patients as uninsured if they are labeled as self-pay, no charge, or no expected payment source in the data.

12. Nondeferrable conditions include fracture, poison or toxic effects, dislocation, intracranial injury, appendicitis, foreign body, internal injury, ectopic pregnancy with rupture, crush injury, bowel obstruction, blood-vessel injury, and other nondiscretionary conditions.

13. We use patient zip code information to exclude out-of-state patients; these visits represent a small share of all visits. We also exclude the fourth quarter of 2015, because this is when HCUP switched from International Classification of Diseases, Ninth Revision (ICD-9) to ICD-10 for diagnostic code variables; excluding this quarter helps to maintain comparability across time. We have data covering the first quarter of 2012 through the third quarter of 2015 for all states except for Utah, where we drop all of 2015 because of missing data.

Our secondary data come from several other sources. We collect information on state-level uncompensated care costs (per uninsured individual) by merging AHA data on hospital-level uncompensated care costs with Current Population Survey (CPS) data that allow us to measure the size of the uninsured population in each state in 2013.[14] We calculate the share of the uninsured population eligible for the Medicaid expansion in each county using estimates from the Small Area Health Insurance Estimates (SAHIE) program. Finally, we combine these data with county-level enrollment totals for public and private sources of insurance from Decision Resources Group (DRG), a market research firm. We also draw on longitudinal data on health insurance coverage from waves 1 and 2 of the 2014 Survey of Income and Program Participation (SIPP). As explained below, we use these supplementary data sources to estimate county-based measures of the share of the pre–Medicaid expansion uninsured population who transitioned to Medicaid coverage after the expansions.

IV. The Effects of the ACA Medicaid Expansion on Hospitalizations and Emergency Department Visits

In order to estimate the effects of the ACA expansion, we exploit the decision by states as to whether or not to expand Medicaid. Figure 2 presents a simple time series of hospital encounters across states that either expanded Medicaid or did not. The top panel of the figure presents trends by insurance status for all hospital discharges, and the bottom panel presents the same for scheduled inpatient visits.[15] Each panel consists of two separate figures: one for non-expansion states and one for states that did expand Medicaid in January 2014. Then, in the same vein, figure 3 presents those plots for inpatient emergency discharges and outpatient emergency discharges.

Across all types of hospital encounters, a basic pattern is unchanged. Medicaid expansion states saw a decrease in uninsured visits and a corresponding increase in Medicaid visits. By contrast, we observe only a slight increase in Medicaid-covered visits in non-expansion states, possibly

---

14. Garthwaite, Gross, and Notowidigdo (2018) describe the AHA and CPS data in more detail.

15. By "scheduled inpatient visits," we mean overnight stays in the hospital that do not involve the emergency department. By "emergent inpatient visits," we mean overnight stays in the hospital in which the patient is admitted through the emergency department.

Figure 2. Total Discharges in Sample States, by Payer Category and State Treatment Status

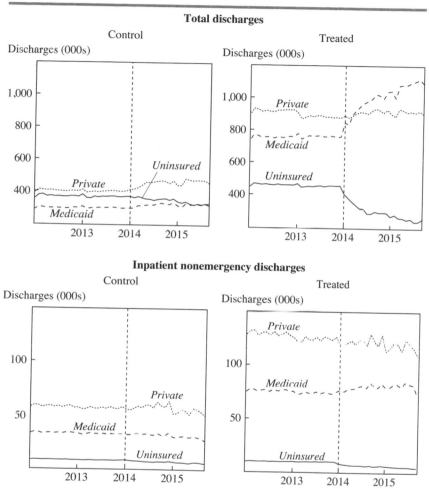

Source: Authors' calculations.

Note: Total discharges include hospital and emergency department combined; inpatient nonemergency discharges are shown for the expansion (treated) and non-expansion (control) states. The monthly totals are aggregated across expansion and non-expansion states separately, with month fixed effects residualized out to remove seasonality; the trends are reported separately for three insurance types: Medicaid, private, and uninsured. The data are monthly totals, and the time period spans January 2012 through September 2015.

Figure 3. Emergency Department Discharges in Sample States, by Payer Category and State Treatment Status

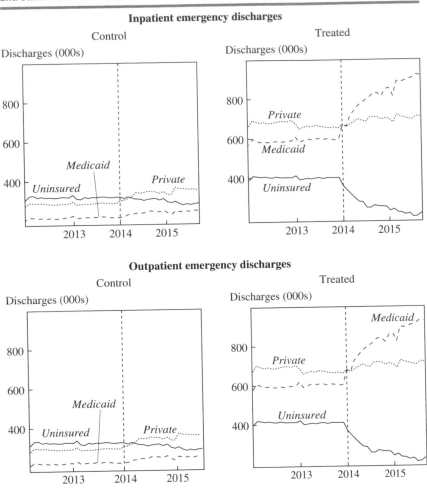

Source: Authors' calculations.

Note: The monthly totals are aggregated across expansion and non-expansion states separately, with month fixed effects residualized out to remove seasonality; the trends are reported separately for Medicaid, private, and uninsured. The data are monthly totals, and the time period spans January 2012 through September 2015.

Figure 4. Total Discharges in Sample States, Combining Medicaid and Uninsured

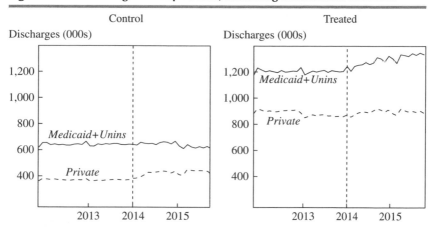

Source: Authors' calculations.

Notes: Total discharges include hospital and emergency department combined; inpatient nonemergency discharges are shown for the expansion (treated) and non-expansion (control) states. The monthly totals are aggregated across expansion and non-expansion states separately, with month fixed effects residualized out to remove seasonality. The trends are reported separately for two insurance types: Medicaid and uninsured (combined) and private. The data are monthly totals, and the time period spans January 2012 through September 2015.

driven by the welcome mat effect.[16] These patterns in the data are what we would expect given states' decisions over the Medicaid expansion.

Figure 4 combines the Medicaid and uninsured visits into one category. Looking at the treatment states, this figure provides evidence of an increase in the use of hospital services following the expansion.

Figure 5 describes the share of visits by insurance category—and the growing importance of Medicaid in expansion states. Together, figures 4 and 5 present another intriguing and perhaps less expected pattern. We observe a moderate increase in private discharges in non-expansion states and yet no such increase in Medicaid expansion states. One explanation is that private visits differentially increased in non-expansion states as a result of the presence of individual marketplace subsidies for individuals at 100–138 percent of the federal poverty level in non-expansion states

---

16. The "welcome mat effect" refers to the tendency for Medicaid enrollment to increase among previously eligible (but unenrolled) individuals as a consequence of broad outreach and enrollment efforts for the ACA's insurance exchanges. Even in states that did not expand Medicaid, the attention and advertising involved in the rollout of the ACA may have led those who were already eligible for Medicaid to sign up for preexisting Medicaid programs.

Figure 5. Share of Total Discharges by Type of Insurance

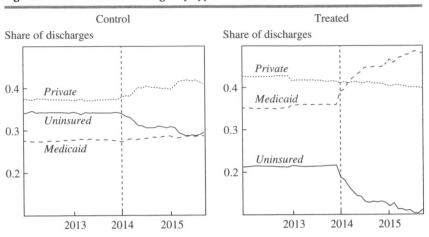

Source: Authors' calculations.

Note: The share of total discharges by insurance type (Medicaid, Private, Uninsured) for expansion (treated) and non-expansion (control) states is based on the residualized discharges reported in figures 3 and 4.

but not in expansion states (individuals in expansion states would have been enrolled in Medicaid instead). A portion of the population targeted for Medicaid expansion (that is, those under 138 percent) thus received access to more affordable marketplace coverage when no Medicaid option was made available. Below, we provide further evidence for this explanation with enrollment data.

This presents an interesting economic point and an econometric complication. Of economic interest, this suggests that low-income residents (100–138 percent of the federal poverty level) in non-expansion states are more likely to be covered by private rather than public coverage. Future work should examine the impact of this difference on access to health care and on health outcomes, as differences in utilization mediated by type of coverage (for example, Medicaid or heavily subsidized private insurance) could inform current policy debates over whether to expand further via public or private modes of coverage. Unfortunately, we were unable to quantify these impacts in our data because we lacked measures of individual income to identify patients in this narrow income range.

Econometrically, this dynamic complicates a simple difference-in-differences approach because the non-expansion states still saw increases in coverage among an overlapping share of the low-income population (those at 100–138 percent of the federal poverty level). This complication extends to the wide and growing body of research on the ACA as well. In essence, the estimated effect of Medicaid expansion is the differential effect of Medicaid for those below 100 percent of the federal poverty level plus the effect of differences in mode of coverage for those between 100 and 138 percent. The effect of differences in mode of coverage on utilization is likely not insubstantial. In a recent study, among those at 100–138 percent of the federal poverty level, adults in expansion states had differentially lower out-of-pocket spending (−$344) and a lower probability of having a high spending burden (−4.1 percentage points) as compared to those in non-expansion states (Blavin and others 2018). We discuss this issue further in section IV.B, first by examining the effect of the expansion on private coverage and then by studying within-state variation in exposure to the expansion.

Regardless, these raw time-series figures suggest a natural starting point to study the effects of Medicaid expansion. We next explore standard difference-in-differences regressions that assess the degree to which Medicaid expansion affected the magnitude and coverage profile of hospital utilization. As discussed below, we account for this increase in private coverage in non-expansion states. We then examine a triple difference specification that attempts to overcome the potential bias from the differential impact of the ACA on private insurance coverage in the non-expansion states.

IV.A. Difference-in-Differences Estimates

To isolate the effect of the Medicaid expansion, we calculate utilization for each zip code, year, and month. We estimate the following regression model:

$$(1) \qquad Y_{ist} = \beta \times Post_{st} + \alpha_i + \alpha_t + \alpha_s \times t + \varepsilon_{ist}.$$

Here, we study outcome Y_{ist} for zip code i in state s and year-month t. The variable $Post_{st}$ indicates whether the state has expanded Medicaid, α_i are zip code–specific fixed effects, α_t are year-month-specific fixed effects. In addition, we include a state-specific linear time trend, $\alpha_s \times t$.

Such a regression approach relies on the standard parallel trends assumption, which is that trends in hospital utilization would have evolved along parallel paths in expansion states relative to non-expansion states if not for the expansion itself. We evaluate the validity of this assumption by examining trends in raw data in the years leading up to the reform as well as the pre-expansion coefficients from event study specifications.

Figure 6. Event Study Estimates, Total Discharges

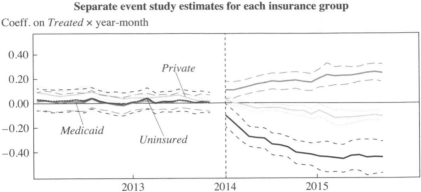

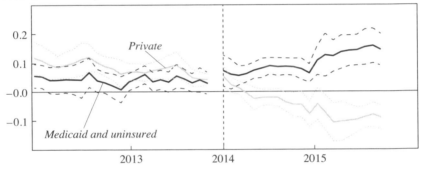

Source: Authors' calculations.

Notes: Data report event study estimates analogous to the difference-in-differences estimates. The standard errors are clustered by state and year-month. Each event study coefficient (for each insurance type) is relative to December 2013 (the omitted year-month).

Figures 6 through 8 present event study estimates for a variety of outcomes. First, the top panel of figure 6 presents event study estimates for all hospital discharges and each type of insurance. Each point represents the difference in total discharges in Medicaid expansion states versus nonexpansion states with the associated confidence interval plotted by dashed lines. The figure suggests that, after 2014, there was a clear increase in Medicaid visits and a decrease in uninsured visits. Importantly, the 2014 change does not seem to be driven by a preexisting trend. In that sense, the figure supports the parallel trends assumption that underlies the regression estimates in equation (1).

In order to examine whether the expansion increased utilization, we next consider combinations of visits for patients with various types of insurance. The bottom panel of figure 6 presents similar event studies, but with Medicaid-plus-uninsured hospital discharges plotted alongside private visits. The estimates suggest a clear increase in Medicaid-plus-uninsured visits. Again, that change appears to be sudden and not explained by pre-2014 trends. However, it is also clear that there was a *decrease* in private hospital discharges. Given the aggregate trends described above (and depicted in figures 4 and 5) this differential decline is likely driven by the *increase* in private coverage in non-expansion states as low-income individuals became eligible for heavily subsidized marketplace coverage.[17] In expansion states, individuals with income that qualifies them for Medicaid coverage would likely prefer that to marketplace coverage because Medicaid provides superior financial protection. Therefore, these estimates likely reflect an actual treatment of the ACA on insurance access for low-income individuals in non-expansion states. This increase should provide caution for interpreting other studies comparing expansion and non-expansion states that do not account for differential use of the ACA marketplaces by individuals earning between 100 and 138 percent of the federal poverty level.

Next, figure 7 presents event study estimates separately for the three types of hospital discharges: scheduled inpatient, inpatient emergency, and outpatient emergency.[18] The three panels of figure 7 suggest decreases in uninsured visits, increases in Medicaid visits, and smaller decreases in private visits with a smaller effect for inpatient discharges. That smaller effect for inpatient visits is unsurprising given that relatively few uninsured patients have scheduled inpatient visits and those visits tend to be less discretionary. Recall that hospitals are only required to provide care regardless of the ability to pay for patients in the emergency room; they are not required to provide scheduled inpatient visits to the uninsured. Finally, figure 8 presents the same analysis but focuses on the sum of Medicaid and uninsured visits. Like the bottom panel of figure 6, figure 8 suggests a net increase in Medicaid-plus-uninsured visits and a decrease in private visits across all types of discharges.

17. Given that the decline in private hospital discharges appears to be driven by an *increase* in private admissions in the non-expansion states, we do not believe that it demonstrates a crowding out of private coverage by public coverage in the expansion states.

18. Emergency department visits come in two types. Outpatient emergency department visits are medical encounters that begin and end in the emergency department and the patient is never admitted to the hospital. Inpatient emergency department visits are medical encounters that begin in the emergency department and the patient is subsequently admitted to the hospital. Inpatient visits are hospitalizations that do not originate in the emergency department.

Figure 7. Event Study Estimates by Type of Encounter (Each Insurance Type Estimated Separately)

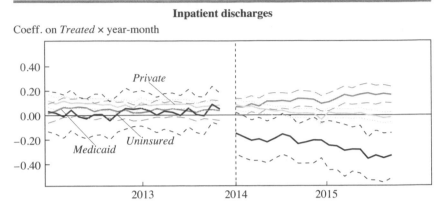

Inpatient discharges

Coeff. on *Treated* × year-month

Inpatient emergency discharges

Coeff. on *Treated* × year-month

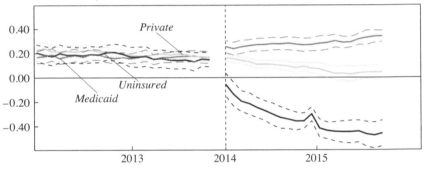

Outpatient emergency discharges

Coeff. on *Treated* × year-month

Source: Authors' calculations.

Note: Data report event study estimates analogous to the difference-in-differences estimates. The standard errors are clustered by state and year-month. Each event study coefficient (for each insurance type) is relative to December 2013 (the omitted year-month).

Figure 8. Event Study Estimates by Type of Encounter (Medicaid plus Uninsured)

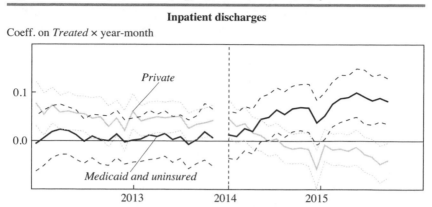

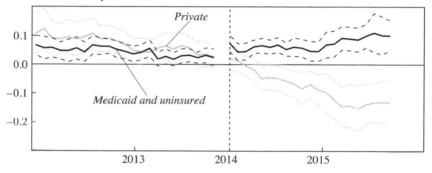

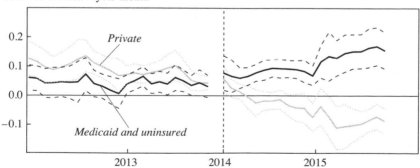

Source: Authors' calculations.

Note: Data report event study estimates analogous to the difference-in-differences estimates. The standard errors are clustered by state and year-month. Each event study coefficient (for each insurance type) is relative to December 2013 (the omitted year-month).

In order to provide a sense of the magnitude of the effect, we also estimate the regression specification above. The top part of table 2 presents this approach for all types of hospital encounters, with the dependent variable being the number of visits in levels. Each cell presents estimates from a separate regression, with the main $Post_{st}$ coefficient tabulated. Column (1) suggests that Medicaid expansion led to roughly 10,000 more Medicaid-covered hospitalizations and roughly 7,000 fewer uninsured hospitalizations. Those point estimates, in combination, suggest that the increase in Medicaid visits was larger than the decrease in uninsured visits. The second part of table 2 presents estimates in which the logarithm of hospitalizations is the outcome of interest; Medicaid visits increase by roughly 14 percent and uninsured visits decrease by roughly 25 percent.[19]

To further study that comparison, the table also presents estimates for the sum of Medicaid and uninsured visits and for the sum of Medicaid, uninsured, and privately covered visits. The estimates suggest an increase in both of these groupings, though the estimate for all visits is less precisely estimated and more sensitive to the specification. This pattern suggests that Medicaid coverage leads to an increase, rather than a decrease, in utilization.

To better understand the dynamics of the effect of expanding Medicaid on utilization, we separate hospital encounters by category. Columns (2) through (4) suggest a roughly similar pattern for scheduled inpatient visits, inpatient visits that originated in the emergency department, and emergency department visits, respectively. In all cases, we see a statistically significant decrease in uninsured visits, combined with an increase in Medicaid visits. All types of encounters seem to increase on net: the increase in Medicaid visits is larger than the decrease in uninsured visits. When we consider all visits (Medicaid, uninsured, private) the effect is still positive and relatively large but is not statistically significant in all specifications.

Finally, table 2 offers insight into which *types* of hospital encounters became more common. Column (5) presents estimates with deferrable hospital visits as the outcome of interest, and column (6) presents estimates with nondeferrable hospital visits as the outcome of interest. Following Garthwaite and others (2017), we focus on deferrable and nondeferrable visits as a way to disentangle changes in coverage rates from changes in the propensity to visit the hospital.

---

19. It is important to remember that these percentage changes are from meaningfully different bases and therefore the magnitudes should not be directly compared. This is why the net effect of the smaller percentage Medicaid change is still an increase in overall use for the Medicaid and uninsured population.

Table 2. Difference-in-Differences Estimates at the Level of the Zip Code

	(1) All visits	(2) Scheduled inpatient visits	(3) Emergency inpatient visits	(4) Emergency outpatient visits	(5) Deferrable visits	(6) Nondeferrable visits
Number of visits						
Medicaid	9.812	0.343	1.037	8.431	9.371	0.441
	(1.208)***	(0.084)***	(0.114)***	(1.088)***	(1.149)***	(0.071)***
Private	-1.221	-0.051	-0.141	-1.029	-1.090	-0.131
	(0.783)	(0.087)	(0.101)	(0.671)	(0.743)	(0.070)*
Uninsured	-6.932	-0.142	-0.692	-6.099	-6.451	-0.482
	(0.909)***	(0.035)***	(0.085)***	(0.827)***	(0.863)***	(0.060)***
Medicaid plus uninsured	2.879	0.202	0.345	2.333	2.920	-0.041
	(1.081)***	(0.088)**	(0.104)***	(0.973)**	(1.048)***	(0.066)
Medicaid plus uninsured plus private	1.659	0.150	0.204	1.304	1.830	-0.172
	(1.389)	(0.136)	(0.149)	(1.267)	(1.337)	(0.119)
Logarithm of visits						
Medicaid	0.132	0.042	0.115	0.141	0.131	0.126
	(0.017)***	(0.012)***	(0.014)***	(0.018)***	(0.017)***	(0.017)***
Private	-0.025	-0.002	-0.026	-0.029	-0.024	-0.029
	(0.009)***	(0.008)	(0.011)**	(0.010)***	(0.009)***	(0.016)*
Uninsured	-0.223	-0.107	-0.335	-0.209	-0.219	-0.209
	(0.024)***	(0.024)***	(0.027)***	(0.024)***	(0.024)***	(0.021)***
Medicaid plus uninsured	0.031	0.026	0.035	0.030	0.032	-0.001
	(0.010)***	(0.011)**	(0.008)***	(0.011)***	(0.010)***	(0.014)
Medicaid plus uninsured plus private	0.010	0.010	0.010	0.010	0.012	-0.016
	(0.007)	(0.006)	(0.006)*	(0.008)	(0.007)*	(0.014)

Source: Authors' calculations.

Note: Each cell presents the estimates of the key difference-in-differences coefficient for a separate regression. The sample consists of zip code by year by month counts of hospitalizations; there are 18,643 zip codes and 45 months (January 2012 through September 2015) for a total of $N = 838,935$ observations per payer and type of hospital visit. When logarithm of visits is the dependent variable, we add 1 to the number of visits. Standard errors in parentheses are clustered on state and year-month. Zip code–specific fixed effects, year-month-specific fixed effects, and zip code–specific time trends not shown.

The two columns suggest similar relative drops in uninsured visits for either category, with roughly similar relative increases in Medicaid-covered visits. However, the regressions suggest a clear increase in Medicaid-plus-uninsured visits for deferrable encounters and no such increase for non-deferrable encounters. That pattern of results is easy to rationalize. The types of visits that are most discretionary are deferrable visits. So it is unsurprising that we see a net increase in those types of visits. Nondeferrable visits, by contrast, are visits that likely must occur regardless of insurance status.[20]

IV.B. Triple Difference Estimates

A concern with the difference-in-differences approach above is that there may be a variety of state-level factors that are correlated with the Medicaid expansion decision which could bias the estimates. For example, differential exposure to subsidized coverage in the ACA marketplaces for those at 100–138 percent of the federal poverty level may make it hard to assess the effect of the Medicaid expansion on the overall use of hospital services. This may contribute to the relatively small and imprecise estimates of the effect of insurance on the overall use of hospital services.

To address these concerns and provide a more reliable estimate of the effect of the ACA Medicaid expansion, we next explore within-state variation in the share of each zip code that was made newly eligible for Medicaid as a result of the expansion. Given that the ACA was based on a single income standard (that is, earnings below 138 percent of the federal poverty line) there is a large amount of variation in the share of each zip code that gained Medicaid eligibility. To measure that variation, we use a zip code–level measure of new Medicaid eligibility adapted from the work of Dranove, Garthwaite, and Ody (2016).[21]

Figure 9 shows the variation across states in this measure. The top map shows variation across expansion states in the overall share of each population made newly eligible, with larger increases in eligibility in California and Ohio and relatively smaller increases in Indiana and Iowa. The bottom

---

20. In addition, regulations require hospitals to treat all patients with an emergency condition regardless of ability to pay.

21. This measure was generated using a combination of data from the Brookings Institution on zip code income, the Current Population Survey, and Kaiser Family Foundation income limits for eligibility. The measure is intended to calculate the share of a zip code that would have been made newly eligible for Medicaid as a result of the ACA expansion based on income and the state's preexisting income limits and the distribution of income in the zip code. More details can be found in footnotes 11–14 in Dranove, Garthwaite, and Ody (2016).

Figure 9. Share of Population Treated by Medicaid Expansion

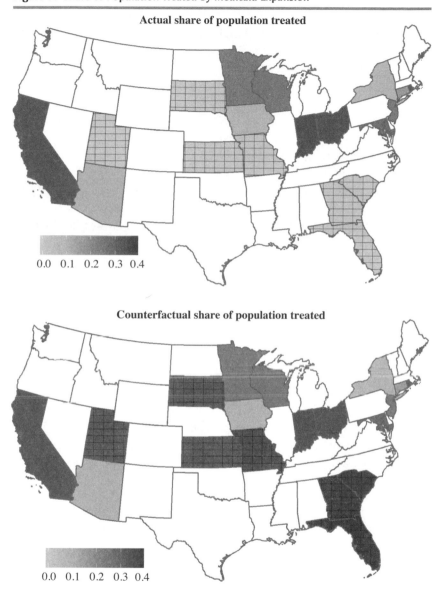

Source: Authors' calculations.

Note: The top map shows the actual share of the population treated by the Medicaid expansion, with non-expansion states all set to zero, since these states chose not to expand Medicaid. The bottom map shows the counterfactual share of population that would have been treated by the Medicaid expansion in the non-expansion states (had they expanded), using the same gradient for scale. Vermont is excluded from this map because we do not have information on the share treated but is in the analysis sample for difference-in-differences results (though not in triple difference results that use the share treated).

map shows the counterfactual population share that would have been made newly eligible in non-expansion states; this map shows that all of the non-expansion states would have had high treatment intensity compared to the expansion states (that is, much closer to the large increases in California and Ohio than the other expansion states in our sample).

Figure 10 illustrates the within-state variation (across zip codes) for two expansion states, Minnesota and New Jersey (the zip code maps for the remaining expansion states are available in the online appendix). The maps show that some zip codes had relatively small changes in eligibility, while other zip codes had increases in eligibility of more than 30–40 percent.

Using this within-state variation, we implement a triple difference specification that allows the effect of the Medicaid expansion to vary by the share of newly eligible in each zip code. This approach allows us to control for other features of the marketplace or the ACA (other than the Medicaid expansion) that differentially impacted zip codes with a greater share of their residents made eligible. Additionally, we are able to include state-year-month fixed effects in all specifications, which can account for confounding state-level shocks that are correlated with expansion and non-expansion status. We estimate the following regression model:

$$(2) \qquad Y_{ist} = \beta \times Post_{st} \times ShareEligible_i + \alpha_i + ShareEligible_i$$
$$\times \alpha_t + \alpha_s \times \alpha_t + \varepsilon_{ist}.$$

As with the difference-in-differences model above, we study outcome Y_{ist} for zip code i in state s and year t. The variable $Post_{st}$ indicates whether the state has expanded Medicaid, α_i are zip code–specific fixed effects. The *ShareEligible* variable is the estimate of the share of the zip code's population that was made newly eligible for the ACA in expansion states and the share that would have been made eligible in non-expansion states. In the spirit of a triple difference model, this variable is interacted with a full set of year-month-specific fixed effects, α_t, and the regression model also includes a full set of state-year-month-specific fixed effects.

Figure 11 presents event study estimates from such a triple difference specification.[22] The top panel presents estimates for each type of insurance. Prior to the expansion, the pattern of the estimated coefficients for all

---

22. The event study estimates are based on the same estimation equation except that the $Post_{st}$ variable is replaced with a full set of event time dummy variables for each month, excluding December 2013 (which is the normalized reference month in all of our event study figures).

Figure 10. In-State Variation in Share of Population Treated by Expansion

Source: Authors' calculations.
Note: These are two of the twelve expansion states in our sample for which we have information on the share treated by expansion; analogous maps for the remaining expansion states are in the online appendix, figure A7.

Figure 11. Triple Difference Event Studies

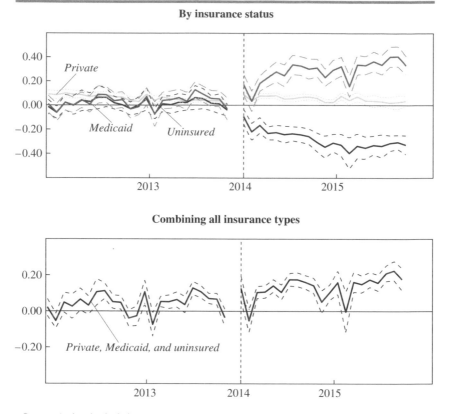

Source: Authors' calculations.
Note: The vertical axis reports event study coefficients in log-linear regression models. The confidence intervals are based on standard errors clustered by state and year-month.

insurance types is broadly flat and generally statistically insignificant. After the expansion, there is an immediate change in utilization by insurance status, with Medicaid visits surging and uninsured visits declining. Unlike the negative estimates of the difference-in-differences specification above, we observe no meaningful changes in the number of privately covered visits.

The bottom panel of figure 11 presents triple difference event study coefficients for the combined outcome of Medicaid, uninsured, and privately insured visits. Similar to the estimates by category, prior to the expansion, these estimates are broadly flat and near zero. After the expansion, the estimates suggest a gradual, positive, and statistically significant post-expansion increase in hospital visits. That pattern is consistent with individuals gaining access to insurance and changing their use of medical services, rather than simply a mechanical reclassification of existing behavior, although more research is needed to understand the mechanism driving this gradual increase.

To explore the precise magnitude of the change depicted in these event study figures, table 3 presents triple difference regression estimates. Considering the overall use of hospital services, column (1) suggests that the Medicaid expansion caused an increase in the number of hospital visits. To interpret the magnitude of the coefficient, consider that the average zip code in our sample had 24 percent of its residents made eligible for Medicaid. Based on the estimates in table 3, this implies a change in utilization of approximately 1.9 percent (0.080 coefficient for Medicaid plus uninsured for log visit outcome, multiplied by 24 percent).[23] Understanding the treatment on the treated—that is, the implied effect for those who actually gained coverage—involves considering the impact of the Medicaid expansion on the share of the population with coverage. If we consider the overall population (that is, the Medicaid, uninsured, and private) the increase in the share of the population with coverage is approximately 3.75 percent.[24] This implies an increase in the use of hospital services of approximately 50 percent.

Given that most of the privately insured population was largely unaffected by the expansion, this treatment-on-the-treated estimate likely overestimates the change in the use of hospital services. If, instead, we consider the change in insurance status for the population most directly affected by the expansion (that is, the Medicaid and uninsured population), the implied change in the use of hospital services is much smaller and likely a more accurate estimate of the actual change in behavior. The expansion is associated with a 9.6 percentage point increase in the share of the Medicaid and uninsured population with insurance coverage. This implies an increase in the use of hospital services by each newly insured person of approximately 20 percent.

Columns (5) and (6) of table 3 estimate the change in utilization by the type of visit. These estimates show that the overall increase in hospital visits was almost entirely driven by outpatient emergency department visits

23. We reach a similar conclusion whether we rely on the Medicaid plus uninsured specification or the Medicaid plus uninsured plus private specification.

24. This is based on authors' estimates in the SIPP of the expansion increasing the Medicaid population by 15 percent off of a base of 25 percent.

Table 3. Triple Difference Estimates at the Level of the Zip Code

	(1) All visits	(2) Scheduled inpatient visits	(3) Emergency inpatient visits	(4) Emergency outpatient visits	(5) Deferrable visits	(6) Nondeferrable visits
A. Number of visits						
Medicaid	0.539	0.003	0.039	0.500	0.516	0.023
	(0.029)***	(0.002)	(0.003)***	(0.027)***	(0.028)***	(0.001)***
Private	0.010	0.000	−0.006	0.016	0.008	0.002
	(0.012)	(0.001)	(0.001)***	(0.011)	(0.012)	(0.001)**
Uninsured	−0.449	−0.011	−0.052	−0.388	−0.428	−0.021
	(0.025)***	(0.002)***	(0.003)***	(0.022)***	(0.024)***	(0.001)***
Medicaid plus uninsured	0.191	−0.005	−0.001	0.196	0.183	0.007
	(0.027)***	(0.002)**	(0.004)	(0.025)***	(0.026)***	(0.001)***
Medicaid plus uninsured plus private	0.167	−0.003	−0.007	0.175	0.159	0.008
	(0.031)***	(0.002)	(0.004)*	(0.028)***	(0.030)***	(0.001)***
B. Logarithm of visits						
Medicaid	0.240	0.002	0.035	0.249	0.235	0.022
	(0.013)***	(0.002)	(0.003)***	(0.014)***	(0.013)***	(0.001)***
Private	0.004	0.000	−0.006	0.009	0.003	0.002
	(0.008)	(0.001)	(0.001)***	(0.008)	(0.008)	(0.001)**
Uninsured	−0.302	−0.011	−0.050	−0.268	−0.292	−0.020
	(0.015)***	(0.002)***	(0.003)***	(0.014)***	(0.015)***	(0.001)***
Medicaid plus uninsured	0.080	−0.004	0.000	0.091	0.079	0.007
	(0.011)***	(0.002)**	(0.003)	(0.012)***	(0.011)***	(0.001)***
Medicaid plus uninsured plus private	0.079	−0.002	−0.004	0.087	0.078	0.007
	(0.011)***	(0.002)	(0.003)	(0.011)***	(0.011)***	(0.001)***

Source: Authors' calculations.

Note: Each cell presents the estimates of the key triple difference coefficient for a separate regression. The key variable on the right-hand side is the interaction between a post–January 2014 indicator for states expanding Medicaid during the sample period and share eligible for Medicaid as a result of the ACA. Share eligible is calculated for both expansion and non-expansion states. The sample consists of zip code by year by month counts of hospitalizations; see table 1 for more details. The sample excludes all zip codes in Vermont in all regressions. There are 18,643 zip codes and 45 months (January 2012 through September 2015) for a total of $N = 838{,}935$ observations per payer and type of hospital visit. When logarithm of visits is the dependent variable, we add 1 to the number of visits. Standard errors in parentheses are clustered on state and year-month. Zip code–specific fixed effects, year-month–specific fixed effects, and zip code–specific time trends not shown. The average share of the population treated in expansion states is 0.24.

for deferrable conditions. This pattern of estimates is intuitive. Medicaid expansion effectively lowers the price of an emergency department visit for the patient, and so we would expect an increase in visits for those that are discretionary. Online appendix figure A5 presents the corresponding event studies for these outcomes. These again suggest that the increase in outpatient emergency department visits was gradual in the post-expansion months and not a sharp reclassification.

VARIATION IN THE NUMBER OF RESIDENTS TRANSITIONING TO MEDICAID
The triple difference estimates result from the combination of two mechanisms. First, there is a mechanical effect: visits that would have occurred without any policy change are now categorized as a Medicaid visit rather than an uninsured visit. Second, there is an increase in use by those who gained coverage. This second effect likely operates through several channels, including a reduction in the price of a hospital visit, a greater ability of insured patients to access nonemergency hospital services, and the potential that hospitals are a complement, rather than a substitute, for physician and outpatient services.

Given Medicaid's retroactive coverage, the mechanical transition of uninsured to Medicaid visits can happen without any action by the newly eligible. After all, if those individuals have a medical shock that requires the use of hospital services, they (or the hospital) can sign up for Medicaid at that point. The behavioral effect, however, likely requires that an individual is actually aware of their new Medicaid coverage in order to change their consumption of medical services.

To examine this second point, we turn to an analysis that examines within-state changes in hospital encounters based on county-level estimates of the number of residents who shifted from uninsured status to Medicaid. This analysis is motivated by the hypothesis that the changes in health care utilization we observe were driven by those who actually obtained coverage rather than simply those who were made eligible. We therefore seek to measure the size of the transition population and to exploit variation across counties in that number to estimate the direct effect of Medicaid on the use of health care services. Again, exploiting this source of variation allows us to estimate the effect both in the entire sample and in a sample consisting of only counties in Medicaid expansion states.

The triple difference analysis above examines the relationship between the outcome (hospital utilization) and the expansion dose, the fraction of the population that could enroll in Medicaid. However, to facilitate interpretation in terms of utilization rates per person, we develop estimates of the response, the number of uninsured individuals who actually took up the

Figure 12. Correlation between Number of Uninsured-to-Medicaid Transitions and 2013–2015 Change in Medicaid and Uninsured Visits

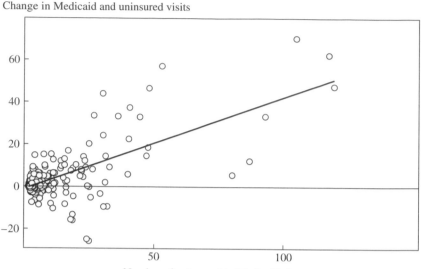

Change in Medicaid and uninsured visits

Number of uninsured-to-Medicaid changes

Source: Authors' calculations.

Notes: The scatter plot excludes the two largest counties in the sample for readability, but these counties are included in some of the columns in table 4. The slope of the regression line is 0.40 (with a standard error of 0.02), which means that each uninsured-to-Medicaid change in a county is associated with an additional 0.40 visits.

Medicaid coverage for which they were newly eligible. We derive these county-level measures from three data sources: (1) county-specific estimates of the number of insured and uninsured residents in 2013 from the Census Bureau; (2) county-level measures of Medicaid and private coverage enrollment in 2013 from DRG; and (3) a model of insurance transitions fitted to a large nationally representative longitudinal (January 2013 to December 2014) panel of monthly insurance coverage among 44,227 individuals in the SIPP.[25] Using those data, we construct a measure for each county of the number of uninsured residents who actually enrolled in Medicaid. This procedure follows the work of Graves and others (2020) and Graves, Hatfield, and McWilliams (2020).

Figure 12 summarizes the relationship between this measure and a measure of the change in health care utilization before and after the expansion

---

25. We also utilize the Census Bureau's 2015 Small Area Health Insurance Estimates (SAHIE) in a validation exercise, as described below.

from the HCUP data. Specifically, we limit the data to the eleven Medicaid expansion states in the main sample. The figure plots the association between the change in total Medicaid and uninsured visits from 2013 to 2015 for each county and the number of uninsured-to-Medicaid transitions in that county during the same time period. The figure demonstrates a positive relationship.

Building on figure 12, table 4 reports analogous regression results, quantifying the magnitude of the association. Table 4 presents regressions in which the outcome of interest is the difference in Medicaid-plus-uninsured visits between the 12 months after Medicaid expansion and the 12 months before. Column (1) presents a simple regression in which the only variable on the right-hand side is the measure, described above, of the number of county residents who shifted from uninsured status to being Medicaid covered. The coefficient on that variable is 0.32, suggesting that each county resident who gained Medicaid was associated with approximately one-third of a visit.

Columns (2) through (4) probe the robustness of this finding. The regression in column (2) adds controls for state-specific fixed effects in order to isolate within-state variation in uninsured-to-Medicaid transitions, and the regression in column (3) adds a control for the number of visits consumed by the county's residents in the pre-expansion period. Column (4) includes a control for the size of the county's Medicaid enrollment before expansion. In all cases, the key coefficient on the proxy for the number of uninsured-to-Medicaid transitions remains roughly 0.3. Columns (5) through (8) present similar results from analogous specifications that exclude the largest counties. Since the regression is in first differences and in levels, including the largest counties substantially increases precision, but the inclusion of those counties does not entirely drive the results.

Online appendix table A1 reports results which address the fact that we likely measure each county's number of uninsured-to-Medicaid transitions with error. Given that potential measurement error, we instrument for the uninsured-to-Medicaid transitions with the change in the uninsured population before and after Medicaid expansion. The IV estimates in online appendix table A1 are very similar in magnitude to the estimates in table 4.[26] Finally, online appendix table A2 replicates table 4, but with

---

26. Additionally, online appendix table A2 reports results using the DRG-based estimate rather than the SIPP-based population estimate. That table presents fairly similar results to those in table 4 using this alternative estimate of population transitioning from being uninsured to being on Medicaid.

Table 4. Heterogeneity across Counties in Number of Uninsured Who Transitioned to Medicaid

	Full sample				Exclude largest counties			
	(1)	*(2)*	*(3)*	*(4)*	*(5)*	*(6)*	*(7)*	*(8)*
Number of uninsured who transitioned to Medicaid	0.321 (0.016)***	0.318 (0.016)***	0.302 (0.051)***	0.359 (0.061)***	0.326 (0.045)***	0.327 (0.048)***	0.323 (0.098)***	0.347 (0.103)***
Total encounters July 2012–June 2013			0.007 (0.021)	0.034 (0.027)			0.001 (0.025)	0.017 (0.039)
Initial number of uninsured residents				−0.023 (0.017)				−0.012 (0.024)
State fixed effects		✓	✓	✓		✓	✓	✓
N	553	553	553	553	551	551	551	551
R^2	0.816	0.835	0.835	0.840	0.537	0.589	0.589	0.592

Source: Authors' calculations.

Note: Each column presents regression estimates where the dependent variable is the 2013–2015 change in the total number of Medicaid and emergency department visits combined). The sample consists of counties in the eleven ACA Medicaid expansion states we study. The key variable on the right-hand side is the number of uninsured individuals who transitioned to Medicaid. The columns report results from alternative specifications, and the last four columns exclude the two largest counties in the sample. Robust standard errors are reported in parentheses.

the outcome of interest being the combined total of Medicaid, uninsured, and private visits. Those estimates are quite similar to those in tables 4 and online appendix table A1, which suggests that changes in private visits are not biasing our conclusions about the net effect of the expansion on Medicaid-plus-uninsured visits.

This estimated increase is larger in magnitude than our preferred triple difference estimate. This is understandable given that this is likely an overestimate of the true increase in use resulting from the expansion. While we are able to accurately measure the share of the population that actively transitions to Medicaid, any individuals who become newly eligible as a result of the expansion but do not sign up for coverage would not be accounted for in our transition measure. Visits by these individuals, however, would largely be categorized as a Medicaid visit in the hospital data because these individuals are retroactively eligible for coverage and Medicaid therefore paid for the visit. Thus, the measure of the increased use of hospital services based on the transition measure will overstate the true increase in use by those who take up Medicaid coverage. That said, this upward bias is likely small and therefore the fact that this estimate is similar to the triple difference estimate provides additional support for the fact that insurance expansions increase rather than decrease the use of hospital services.

V. How Target Efficient Was the ACA Medicaid Expansion?

One of the goals of publicly provided insurance is to provide assistance for those with the highest unmet need for health care coverage. The ACA attempted to meet this goal through both the expansion of Medicaid and the creation of heavily subsidized insurance marketplaces. This section examines how well targeted these policies were toward those with the highest unmet need for health insurance.[27]

V.A. The Target Efficiency of Medicaid Expansions

Historically, Medicaid has been a program of categorical eligibility with benefits provided to low-income groups that were perceived to have high unmet need for health care. For example, Medicaid was available for low-income individuals who were disabled or pregnant—two groups with higher-than-average medical spending. The ACA expansion did not

---

27. Note that this is not the same as unmet need for health care. We lack data on underlying health status and instead have data on the use of health care services.

target particular groups but instead made coverage available to everyone earning below 138 percent of the federal poverty level. That feature of the expansion led to a concern that the program would fail to provide coverage to those with the highest demand for health care. This would decrease the proverbial "bang for the buck" of the program.

To examine the target efficiency of the ACA Medicaid expansion, we focus on counties in the thirteen expansion states listed in section III. In each of these counties, we calculate average utilization by dividing total uninsured visits by an estimate of the uninsured population from 2012 to 2014. We then perform the same calculation for the Medicaid population, dividing utilization by enrollment in each year. Finally, we do the same calculation for the privately insured.

Table 5 reports the results of these calculations. The first row shows an average of 0.355 visits (combining hospital visits and emergency department visits) per uninsured individual in the pre-ACA period. After the ACA, this average drops to 0.237 in 2014, a decline of 33.2 percent. These averages are based on simple unweighted means across the counties in the sample; the last two columns suggest a similar pattern when taking a weighted average across counties based on pre-ACA county population. This weighting causes little substantive change in the estimates. The decline in average utilization for the uninsured is consistent with the hypothesis that those who move from uninsured status to Medicaid have higher-than-average utilization in the pre-ACA period. As a result, removing them from the uninsured population leads to a reduction in the average utilization rate for the uninsured population in the post-ACA period. These estimates thus suggest that the ACA was broadly target efficient.

The data for the Medicaid population in table 5 also suggest that *pre-ACA* Medicaid expansions were not particularly target efficient compared to earlier categorical expansions. After the ACA expansion, the visits per Medicaid enrollee increases. This suggests that the newly insured also had a greater use of hospital services than those who were made eligible for Medicaid through prior expansions. In other words, Medicaid under categorical eligibility was not more target efficient, on average, than a system with eligibility based solely on income.

A concern with this analysis is that these changes in utilization rates might be driven by broader trends over time unrelated to the ACA. For that reason, table 5 presents the same calculations for non-expansion states. Reassuringly, the bottom three rows of table 5 suggest relatively small changes in utilization rates for non-expansion states. This suggests that the changes in expansion states were not driven by preexisting trends.

Table 5. Average Utilization Rate for Uninsured and Medicaid Populations, Before and After ACA Medicaid Expansion

	Average utilization rate across counties				Weighted average utilization rate			
	(1) *2012*	*(2)* *2013*	*(3)* *2014*	*(4)* *% change, 2012–14*	*(5)* *2012*	*(6)* *2013*	*(7)* *2014*	*(8)* *% change, 2012–14*
Expansion states								
Uninsured population	0.355	0.355	0.237	−33.2%	0.358	0.352	0.249	−30.4%
Medicaid population	0.553	0.535	0.683	+23.5%	0.459	0.464	0.582	+26.8%
Private population	0.199	0.191	0.199	+0.0%	0.190	0.183	0.188	−1.1%
Non-expansion states								
Uninsured population	0.433	0.430	0.419	−3.2%	0.462	0.462	0.445	−3.7%
Medicaid population	0.388	0.383	0.403	+3.9%	0.432	0.439	0.468	+8.3%
Private population	0.191	0.189	0.206	+7.9%	0.178	0.179	0.200	+12.4%

Source: Authors' calculations.

Note: Each cell presents estimates of average utilization (total hospital plus emergency department visits divided by total population). Columns (1) through (3) report average utilization by calculating averages in each county and then calculating (unweighted) averages across the counties in the expansion state sample. Columns (5) through (7) present weighted averages, weighting by the pre-ACA population.

V.B. Target Efficiency of the ACA Marketplaces

The results above ought to be interpreted with one important institutional detail in mind. Unlike private insurance, Medicaid coverage is retroactive, that is, enrollees can receive coverage for medical expenses that occurred prior to their enrollment. Hospital billing departments often facilitate this enrollment in order to secure coverage for emergency services. There are thus two types of new Medicaid enrollees: those who enrolled in Medicaid ahead of their hospitalization and those who enrolled afterward. The former likely value Medicaid more than the latter, since they enrolled soon after becoming eligible. But we cannot separate those two types of Medicaid enrollees in the data. Therefore, it is difficult for us to estimate enrollees' valuation of Medicaid. The results, however, do speak to the Medicaid expansion's target efficiency. The expansion's target efficiency is based on society's preference for providing health insurance to those who most need health care. Estimating the need for health care across subpopulations does not involve enrollees' valuation of Medicaid and so is an object we can pursue in the data.

An additional question is whether those who gained access to insurance as a result of the ACA were truly those who valued it most as opposed to simply those who consumed the most hospital services. An individual's valuation of Medicaid may not match their use of health care if they bore little cost for the uncompensated use of hospital care when they were uninsured. A number of recent papers have examined the willingness to pay for individuals who gain access to subsidized health insurance. For example, Finkelstein, Hendren, and Shepard (2019) and Finkelstein, Hendren, and Luttmer (2019) examine whether individuals value publicly provided insurance greater than the cost of the coverage.[28] These papers are consistent with the work of Garthwaite, Gross, and Notowidigdo (2018) and other studies which demonstrate that hospitals provide substantial

---

28. Finkelstein, Hendren, and Luttmer (2019) calibrate a stylized model of the demand for health insurance using results from the Oregon health insurance experiment and conclude that the average willingness to pay for Medicaid is quite low (on the order of 20 percent of costs). Finkelstein, Hendren, and Shepard (2019) estimate demand for public health insurance using a regression discontinuity (RD) approach, where the out-of-pocket premium varies with household income. They show how to translate the RD estimate into a revealed preference measure of demand for public health insurance and also conclude that demand is low on average. The existence of hospital uncompensated care, free health care clinics, and other charity care in the health care system is one possible explanation for the low estimated willingness to pay in both settings.

uncompensated care and that this may crowd out demand for formal health insurance.

The creation of the ACA marketplaces in non-expansion states can shed further light on this issue. Standard economic theory suggests that the least healthy will value health insurance the most, holding constant risk preferences and other demand-side factors. This, in turn, suggests that the least healthy uninsured ought to be those most eager to transition onto formal insurance when they become eligible for subsidized coverage. While everyone below the income threshold becomes eligible for Medicaid without taking any action, those who were ineligible for expanded Medicaid needed proactively to sign up for coverage in the ACA marketplaces during an open enrollment period.[29]

Given these facts about the enrollment process, we can use data from non-expansion states to examine whether those who signed up on the ACA marketplaces were healthier on average than those who remained uninsured. The data for the non-expansion states in table 5 present the change in the use of hospital services in non-expansion states by insurance status. The utilization rate for uninsured residents of non-expansion states declined, while the utilization rate for the privately insured increased. This pattern suggests that those who purchased insurance used more medical services than those who previously lacked coverage and further, that many state residents were previously uninsured and had a high valuation of insurance but were kept from coverage by either a preexisting condition or a lack of financial resources.[30]

It should be noted that a firm conclusion on whether the ACA's expansion of coverage via marketplaces is target efficient is much more difficult to pin down. Viewed one way, if the marketplaces attracted individuals with the highest health care needs, then this pattern of results might lead us to believe that the expansion was target efficient. But this observation is also consistent with a standard adverse selection story. Viewed another way,

29. Even those who did not proactively sign up for Medicaid could join the program retroactively. Hospitals can help those individuals enroll in Medicaid even after they receive treatment. Regarding the ACA's marketplaces, open enrollment periods are required in order to avoid adverse selection. Absent a change in life circumstances (birth, death, change in employer-provided coverage), individuals can only enroll in coverage during open enrollment periods.

30. The table also suggests a slight increase in utilization among Medicaid enrollees. Given that there was no change in Medicaid eligibility in these states, the increase in use for Medicaid enrollees could be the result of a change in the use of hospital services for those who signed up for Medicaid as a result of the welcome effect.

then, the consequent rise in private insurance premiums to cover higher costs induced by adverse selection (and moral hazard) could price out higher-income (unsubsidized) people with high health care needs. Indeed, enrollment data since 2014 demonstrate that as marketplace premiums have increased, enrollment in the unsubsidized (greater than 400 percent of the federal poverty level) income range has shrunk—the marketplaces are now effectively concentrated to those in the subsidized income range. As of February 2019, for example, 87 percent of marketplace enrollees received premium assistance (that is, had income 100–400 percent of the federal poverty level).[31] Whether or not the policy was target efficient is therefore an open question that is highly dependent on society's preferences for redistribution *away* from higher-income people with health care needs and toward lower-income people with high health care needs.

VI. How Did the Effects of the ACA Medicaid Expansion Vary across States?

The estimates above suggest that Medicaid coverage increases hospital and emergency department visits and that the Medicaid expansion was generally well targeted, that is, those gaining coverage had greater demand for hospital services than those who remained uninsured. That said, an important feature of Medicaid is that the program is jointly funded by federal and state governments but is solely administered by the states. Prior to the ACA expansion, states made a number of different decisions about the operation and generosity of their Medicaid programs that could affect the impact of the expansion. In addition, Medicaid works in concert with a variety of other supply-side features of the health care market that vary across states.

The combination of these supply- and demand-side factors could result in heterogeneous effects of the expansion on the increased use of hospital services and the target efficiency of the policy. This section investigates state-level heterogeneity on both of these dimensions. We first document a wide amount of state-level heterogeneity in the magnitude of the effect of Medicaid expansion on utilization. We then investigate potential explanations for that heterogeneity by correlating state-specific estimates with characteristics of each state and expansion. Finally, we examine how the

---

31. See Kaiser Family Foundation, "Marketplace Effectuated Enrollment and Financial Assistance," https://www.kff.org/other/state-indicator/effectuated-marketplace-enrollment-and-financial-assistance/.

target efficiency of the program varied across both expansion and non-expansion states.

VI.A. Heterogeneity in the Use of Hospital Services

We first estimate the effects of Medicaid expansion on hospital utilization for every state. This exercise is different from simply estimating the change in the take-up of Medicaid across states. Unlike private insurance, individuals are able to sign up for Medicaid at any point within the year, and they have retroactive eligibility that allows them to apply Medicaid to medical events that happen prior to enrollment. Given that we use administrative—as opposed to survey—data, the uninsured in our data must be those who are likely ineligible for Medicaid and did not enroll for private insurance during open enrollment. Therefore, changes in overall utilization in the data reflect differences in the take-up decision across states to the extent that such enrollment in insurance has an impact on the decision to seek treatment at the hospital. Our results above suggest that enrollment in insurance does have a causal effect on utilization. Differences across states in the increase in utilization that is correlated with differences in state take-up would further support these estimates and demonstrate that gaining insurance increases the use of hospital services.

Given that Medicaid is administered at the state level, the program's operations differ somewhat across states. Even among the states that chose to expand Medicaid, a variety of operational decisions likely affected the success of these expansions at decreasing the share of uninsured and increasing the take-up of Medicaid. While most research has focused on the binary state-level decision of whether or not to expand Medicaid to adults under the ACA, states faced many additional decisions once they decided to expand Medicaid. For example, states could choose whether or not to set up state-based marketplaces or whether to rely on the federal marketplace. Similarly, states decided whether their marketplaces had the authority to enroll eligible applicants in Medicaid or the Children's Health Insurance Program (CHIP). The so-called no wrong door policy in the ACA required all marketplaces to assess whether applicants are eligible for Medicaid or CHIP but only required state-based marketplaces to go through and actually enroll publicly eligible applicants (Skinner 2012). In other words, if states decided to rely on the federal exchange rather than set up their own state-level exchange, they could defer that enrollment authority to state Medicaid agencies.

As a result, the ultimate effect of Medicaid expansion on the take-up of Medicaid could have been shaped by these other state-level decisions.

To the extent that enrollment has a causal impact on the utilization of health care services, these decisions would then affect utilization. All Medicaid expansions, in other words, are not created equal.

Hudson and Moriya (2018) suggest that a key factor in determining Medicaid take-up is not whether the state's marketplace was a state-based exchange or a "federally facilitated" exchange but rather whether the exchange had the authority to enroll individuals who had been determined to be eligible for Medicaid. The key factor is marketplace enrollment authority, because otherwise Medicaid-eligible applicants would have to leave the marketplace and seek out state Medicaid agencies themselves, a process that invariably involved fewer state residents gaining Medicaid coverage.

Of course, variation in the effect of the Medicaid expansion on utilization likely reflects far more than differences in take-up. For example, variation could also be driven by the underlying demand for health care by low-income individuals and the access to care for the uninsured prior to the expansion. Some states arranged generous financing for uncompensated care which may have affected whether the uninsured could have regularly visited hospitals and emergency departments prior to the Medicaid expansion. By contrast, if the uncompensated-care financing pool was less generous or nonexistent, then hospitals may have discouraged visits from the uninsured in ways that did not violate the Emergency Medical Treatment and Active Labor Act. For instance, hospitals may have aggressively billed self-pay patients, partially to discourage visits from the uninsured. The availability of uncompensated care may influence the decision to sign up for Medicaid (Finkelstein, Mahoney, and Notowidigdo 2018). However, in our context even those who do not sign up for Medicaid would appear as a Medicaid visit in the data if they were eligible for the expansion.

To investigate these issues empirically, we augment the main difference-in-differences specification above by interacting the key difference-in-differences coefficient with a full set of indicator functions for each state that expanded Medicaid. This amounts to a fully nonparametric specification of state-level treatment-effect heterogeneity, continuing to use the non-expansion states as controls. The results of these augmented difference-in-differences results are first presented in maps in figures 13 through 15. Since the non-expansion states are used as controls, they are normalized to zero in each map. The gradient scale in each map shows the difference in each expansion state relative to average non-expansion states, with darker shades indicating larger changes. For example, the top map in figure 13 shows larger changes in uninsured visits in Ohio and Iowa and

Figure 13. State Heterogeneity in Effect of Medicaid Expansion on Uninsured Visits and Medicaid Visits

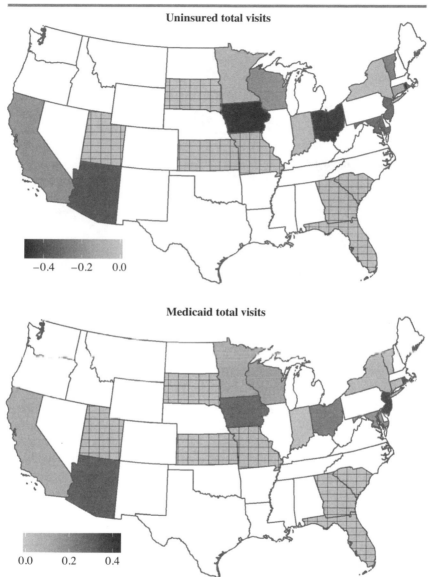

Source: Authors' calculations.

Note: The top map shows the state-specific estimates of the effect of the Medicaid expansion on uninsured total visits relative to non-expansion states (which are normalized to zero). The bottom map reports analogous estimates for Medicaid total visits.

Figure 14. State Heterogeneity in Effect of Medicaid Expansion on Uninsured plus Medicaid Visits

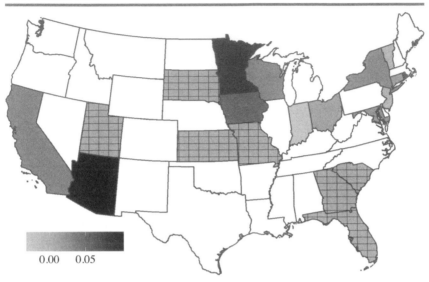

Source: Authors' calculations.
Note: The map shows the state-specific estimates of the effect of the Medicaid expansion on combined Medicaid and uninsured visits relative to non-expansion states (which are normalized to zero).

relatively smaller changes in New York (relative to non-expansion states), and the bottom map shows a similar geographic pattern for changes in Medicaid visits. Figure 14 reports the combined Medicaid and uninsured visits. Figure 15 then breaks out Medicaid visits by type of encounter, and these maps show greater geographic variation for outpatient emergency visits relative to scheduled inpatient visits. This implies that the small average effect for scheduled inpatient visits reported in tables 1 and 2 is broadly replicated across each state. By contrast, the significant increase in Medicaid visits and decrease in uninsured visits (on average across expansion states) masks considerable heterogeneity across the expansion states in our sample.

Figure 16 presents the point estimates from these specifications. The dotted line plots the cross-state average estimate, an equal-weighted average across eleven expansion states.[32] On average, Medicaid expansion

32. We exclude Vermont and Indiana (which are expansion states in our main analysis sample) because we do not have all of the explanatory variables in the analysis that follows.

Figure 15. State Heterogeneity in Effect of Medicaid Expansion, by Type of Encounter

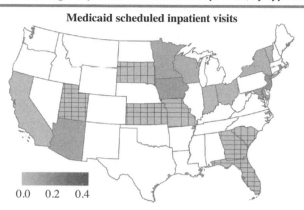

Medicaid scheduled inpatient visits

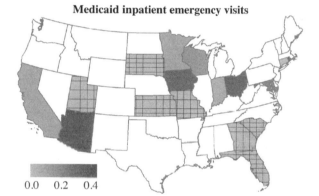

Medicaid inpatient emergency visits

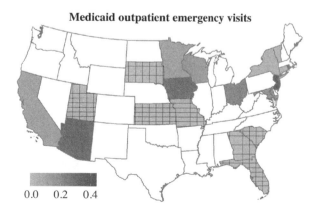

Medicaid outpatient emergency visits

Source: Authors' calculations.
Note: The maps show the state-specific estimates of the effect of the Medicaid expansion on Medicaid visits (for each category of visits: scheduled inpatient visits, inpatient emergency visits, and outpatient emergency visits), relative to non-expansion states (which are normalized to zero).

Figure 16. State-Specific Heterogeneity in the Estimated Effect of ACA Medicaid Expansion on Combined Medicaid plus Uninsured Encounters

Coefficient on *Year ≥ 2014*

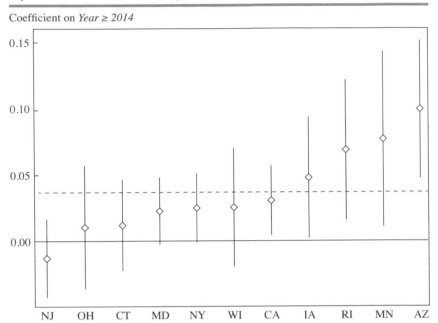

Source: Authors' calculations.

Note: State-specific difference-in-differences estimates of the effect of the ACA Medicaid expansion on total encounters (hospital and emergency department visits) combining Medicaid visits and uninsured visits are shown. The dotted line is the average. State-specific estimates include 95 percent confidence intervals based on standard errors clustered by state and year-month.

is associated with an increase in the total number of visits of roughly 4 percent. Interestingly, the effects of Medicaid expansion vary considerably across the expansion states in our sample. In Minnesota and Arizona, the difference-in-differences coefficient is roughly 10 percent, while in New Jersey and Connecticut the estimates are close to zero and are not statistically significant. In other words, some states that expanded Medicaid saw no meaningful change in visits. Additionally, we can reject the null hypothesis that all of the state-specific estimates are the same, which provides an initial piece of evidence of meaningful state-level heterogeneity in the effects of the Medicaid expansion.

To investigate the source of that heterogeneity, consider whether or not states implemented their own exchanges. Among the states in figure 16, California, Maryland, New York, Rhode Island, and Minnesota created their own marketplaces. The remaining states relied on the federal marketplace

Figure 17. Correlation between State-Specific Estimates of the Effect of ACA Medicaid Expansion on Medicaid Encounters and Effect of ACA Medicaid Expansion on Uninsured Encounters

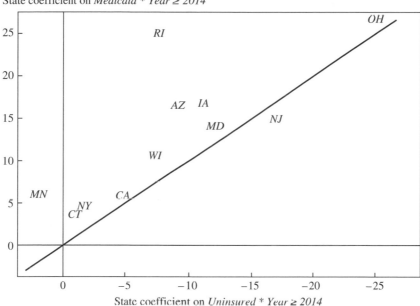

State coefficient on *Medicaid * Year ≥ 2014*

State coefficient on *Uninsured * Year ≥ 2014*

Source: Authors' calculations.
Notes: All states above the 45-degree line (solid line) have larger increases in Medicaid visits than they have decreases in uninsured visits.

or had a federal-state partnership. New Jersey is the only state that used the federal exchange but allowed the federal marketplace to make a Medicaid eligibility determination, as all the state-based exchanges would have done (Rosenbaum and others 2016). Thus, the four states in figure 16 with the lowest Medicaid-plus-uninsured utilization effects allowed exchanges to determine eligibility, as opposed to assessing potential eligibility and then referring individuals to state Medicaid agencies.

To further explore state-level heterogeneity, we separately estimate an effect on Medicaid and an effect on uninsured emergency department visits for each state. Figure 17 plots the state-specific effects, with the effect on uninsured visits along the horizontal axis and the effect on Medicaid visits along the vertical axis. The figure suggests a natural correlation: states that experienced the largest decreases in uninsured visits after expansion saw the largest increases in Medicaid visits. The two patterns are nearly mirror images of each other. To facilitate comparison, the figure includes a 45-degree line.

Lastly, we account for state-level heterogeneity by regressing the state-level estimates on four state-specific variables. The first is the measure of the number of individuals that likely transitioned from uninsured status to Medicaid as a result of the expansion. We aggregate these county-level estimates to construct a state-level estimate of the number of state residents transitioning from being uninsured to being on Medicaid.

The second variable is a measure of which states were more "treated" by the Medicaid expansion, based on the share of the adult population that was made newly eligible (that is, the dose measure in the SIPP transition model, described in section IV.B). For example, in New York only about 7 percent of the adult population was made eligible for Medicaid through the Medicaid expansion, while in Ohio and Rhode Island that share was closer to 33 percent. Given Medicaid's retroactive eligibility, if any of these newly eligible individuals sought hospital treatment after the expansion they would be classified as a Medicaid patient.

The third variable we explore is a state-level measure of the total uncompensated hospital care costs per uninsured adult. This measure is constructed following Garthwaite, Gross, and Notowidigdo (2018), who study the relationship between Medicaid eligibility and uncompensated hospital care costs. We interpret this variable as reflecting a combination of the preexisting generosity of uncompensated care in the state (across hospitals) as well as the latent demand for health care among the uninsured. In other words, high spending on the uninsured by hospitals (as measured by uncompensated costs—costs for which the hospitals are not directly compensated) can arise because the uninsured are particularly sick in that state and also because the hospitals provide more uncompensated care than other states (perhaps because of the state's generous uncompensated care policies toward hospitals). For states where uncompensated care is constrained by the willingness of hospitals to treat uninsured people (that is, where uncompensated care per capita was low), an insurance expansion could increase total utilization.

The final variable we construct is a binary indicator variable for whether the state's exchange allowed for Medicaid eligibility determination. We hypothesize, following Hudson and Moriya (2018), that exchanges that directly enrolled Medicaid-eligible applicants would lead to higher Medicaid enrollments and thus larger impacts on hospital visits.

Table 6 reports the estimates from this regression for the outcome of Medicaid plus uninsured visits, total visits combining hospital visits and

Table 6. State-Level Heterogeneity in Effects of ACA Medicaid Expansion

	(1)	(2)	(3)	(4)	(5)
Number of individuals changing from uninsured to Medicaid	4.99 (1.43) (3.494)				3.88 (1.33) (2.921)
Share of adult population newly eligible for Medicaid		−8.69 (8.60) (1.010)			−1.11 (5.91) (0.188)
State-wide hospital uncompensated care costs per uninsured individual, 2010			−2.52 (0.79) (3.181)		−2.10 (0.70) (2.990)
Federal or state health insurance exchange eligibility determination indicator				−1.44 (1.56) (0.923)	−0.97 (1.09) (0.885)
OLS regression weighted by inverse of the standard error of state-specific difference-in-differences estimate	✓	✓	✓	✓	✓
N (no. of states)	11	11	11	11	11
R^2	0.24	0.10	0.55	0.09	0.72

Source: Authors' calculations.

Note: The dependent variable is the state-specific estimate of Medicaid expansion on total inpatient and emergency department visits, Medicaid plus uninsured. Regressions are shown for state-specific difference-in-differences estimates of Medicaid expansion on four variables to explore whether they predict the magnitude of the state-specific effect of expansion. Weighted OLS regressions are used for efficiency, where the weight is the inverse of the standard error of state-specific difference-in-differences estimate. Robust standard errors are reported in parentheses.

emergency department encounters. Columns (1) to (4) each present a specification including only one of the four state-specific variables; column (5) presents a specification that includes all of the variables. The only statistically significant predictors of variation across states are the size of the population that took up insurance and the amount of uncompensated care prior to the expansion.

The negative coefficient on uncompensated care suggests that in places where there was a lot of uncompensated care before the expansion there was a smaller increase in total hospital encounters as a result of the expansion. This suggests that a large amount of uncompensated care prior to expansion represents high utilization by the uninsured prior to the expansion. If the degree of implicit insurance via uncompensated care was relatively higher in states with high levels of uncompensated care, we might expect that the uninsured transitioning to Medicaid would not have increased utilization as much following expansion of explicit insurance through Medicaid.

We also find that in places where take-up was higher, there was a greater increase in total hospital encounters. This is consistent with the results in section IV and further suggests that gaining insurance increases the use of hospital services.

VI.B. Heterogeneity in the Target Efficiency of the ACA Expansion

A variety of factors may have led to variation in the target efficiency of the Medicaid expansion across states. Some states had built more-generous Medicaid programs before the ACA. States also varied in the share of their population that is low income and in the underlying health status of their uninsured populations. All of these factors could lead to meaningful variation in the target efficiency of the expansion.

To examine that potential variation, we study the relationship between changes in utilization and features of each state's pre-expansion market. If we observe a decline in utilization by the uninsured, then that suggests that the expansion was largely target efficient, in that those who gained coverage had a greater need for health care prior to the expansion. Conversely, if we observe an increase in the utilization by Medicaid patients, then that suggests that the pre-expansion Medicaid system was not particularly target efficient.

Figure 18 examines the relationship between the decrease in the size of a state's uninsured population and the change in hospital visits for the uninsured, Medicaid, and privately insured populations. The top panel shows that states which experienced a greater decline in the size of their uninsured populations saw larger decreases in utilization for the uninsured. This suggests that larger expansions appear to be more target efficient. That is, those gaining insurance had a greater demand for health care than those who remained uninsured.

The middle panel of figure 18 shows that states with the largest declines in their uninsured population were also those with the largest increases in the use for hospital services in the post-expansion Medicaid program. This suggests that state decisions about the generosity of the existing Medicaid program appear to have resulted in a set of uninsured residents that had a higher demand for hospital services than those who were able to qualify for social insurance. Whether or not this was optimal is a question of how much value state residents placed on access to care for various groups. It does, however, suggest that if the metric is providing formal insurance for individuals who would still otherwise consume a large amount of hospital services, then some of these existing programs were not accomplishing that goal.

Figure 18. State Heterogeneity in Targeting

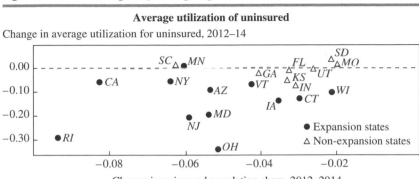

Average utilization of uninsured

Change in average utilization for uninsured, 2012–14

Change in uninsured population share, 2012–2014

Average utilization of Medicaid

Change in average utilization for Medicaid, 2012–14

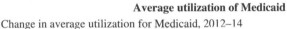

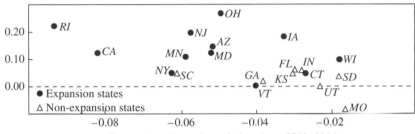

Change in uninsured population share, 2012–2014

Average utilization of private

Change in average utilization for private, 2012–14

Change in uninsured population share, 2012–2014

Source: Authors' calculations.

Note: Data show the association between change in average utilization (for uninsured, Medicaid, and private) and the change in the share uninsured. Both are calculated as long differences between 2012 and 2014. The top panel shows that the larger reduction in average utilization among the uninsured in expansion states (relative to non-expansion states) masks considerable heterogeneity across expansion states. The pattern for average utilization for Medicaid is similar, with more variation along the vertical axis for expansion states relative to non-expansion states (middle panel). The bottom panel shows more variation in non-expansion states (in contrast to the other two).

Finally, the bottom panel of figure 18 depicts the change in the use of hospital services by the privately insured based on the change in the share uninsured. Non-expansion states are marked with triangles and show a clear pattern where states with larger declines in the share of uninsured had greater increases in the post-expansion use of hospital services by the privately insured. This suggests that the ACA marketplaces provided access to health insurance for enrollees with a greater demand for hospital services than the set of patients with prior insurance prior to the expansion.

Further evidence of target efficiency can be seen in the top panel of figure 19, which shows that states which had the highest use of hospital services for the uninsured prior to the expansion also had the largest declines in the use of hospital services by the uninsured after the expansion. While some of this relationship may be mechanical, that is, those states also had the greatest potential for a decline in hospital visits, this figure suggests that overall the expansion provided coverage for uninsured residents with the greatest demand for hospital services. This can also be seen in the bottom panel of figure 19, where states with the greatest amount of uncompensated care prior to the expansion also saw the largest declines in the use of hospital services by the remaining uninsured.

VII. The Broader Economic Impacts of Variation in the Social Safety Net

Our results demonstrate that the ACA Medicaid expansion resulted in meaningful changes in the access to and utilization of health care services. In addition, we demonstrate that there is meaningful variation in the impact of this expansion across states. This results not just from the state-level decision to expand Medicaid but is also a function of both state decisions to support the ACA and the preexisting market conditions for the uninsured.

Given the growing importance of the social safety net, this can have a variety of impacts that extend well beyond health care utilization but could lead to regional variation in a variety of economic outcomes. This includes, but is not limited to, changes in labor market structure, the market for entrepreneurs, and underlying productivity and income.

In order to understand how variation in the expansion could affect broader economic outcomes, we next summarize the relevant literature in various areas where a differential impact of Medicaid could help to shape and drive economic growth.

Figure 19. Exploring State Heterogeneity in Changes in the Average Utilization for Uninsured

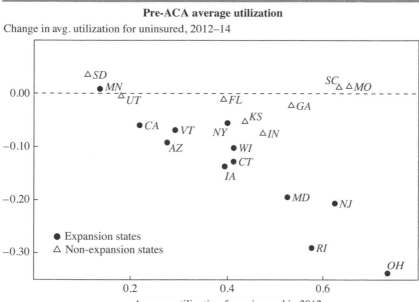

Pre-ACA average utilization

Change in avg. utilization for uninsured, 2012–14

Average utilization for uninsured in 2012

Uncompensated care costs per uninsured

Change in avg. utilization for uninsured, 2012–14

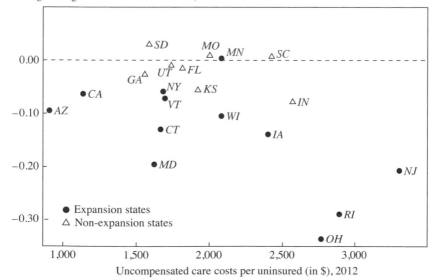

Uncompensated care costs per uninsured (in $), 2012

Source: Authors' calculations.

VII.A. *Effects of Medicaid on Health*

An important contributor to economic growth and productivity is the underlying health of the population. An important question then is how does health insurance coverage affect health itself? Unfortunately, this question is not easily answered. Studies on health insurance and health need to overcome several empirical challenges in order to credibly capture the health effects of insurance. First, they need to exploit plausibly exogenous variation in health insurance, given that the insured population differs from the uninsured population. Second, credible studies need to quantify health, an outcome that is arguably multidimensional and that evolves slowly over time. A small body of research literature has overcome those challenges—the paucity of studies is remarkable given the importance of the topic.[33]

First, several studies have evaluated the health effects of Medicare. Finkelstein and McKnight (2008) studied the introduction of Medicare in 1965 and found no effect of the program on aggregate death rates. Card, Dobkin, and Maestas (2008) focused on emergency hospital visits by patients who just barely qualified for Medicare based on its age 65 threshold versus patients who were too young to qualify for Medicare. Within that particular sample, the authors found a large effect of Medicare coverage on short-term mortality.

Most of the other work on this topic has focused on Medicaid. The Oregon health insurance experiment found that Medicaid coverage improved self-reported physical and mental health and increased the diagnosis of diabetes and the use of diabetes medication.[34] Other research has focused on Medicaid expansions before the ACA and expansions that were part of the ACA. Sommers, Baicker, and Epstein (2012) study state-by-state Medicaid expansions through a difference-in-differences framework and find a clear reduction in mortality rates after expansion. Additional research by Sommers and others (2015) and Miller and

33. We focus here on the effect of health insurance on the health of adults. A related literature has studied the health of children (Dafny and Gruber 2005) and also the long-term impacts of providing children with health insurance (Wherry and others 2017; Goodman-Bacon 2016).

34. The evidence from the Oregon health insurance experiment on blood pressure and other physical outcomes did not find statistically significant health improvements, although there exists some debate regarding the study's statistical power for some of these outcomes (see, for example, "Effects of Medicaid on Clinical Outcome" (letter to the editor), *New England Journal of Medicine,* August 8, 2013, https://www.nejm.org/doi/full/10.1056/NEJMc1306867).

Wherry (2017) demonstrates that the ACA's Medicaid expansions led to an improvement in self-reported health. Finally, a recent working paper has found that the Medicaid expansion led to a decrease in mortality for eligible Americans in expansion states compared to non-expansion states (Miller and others 2019).

All in all, these studies tend to find that health insurance coverage leads to improvements in health. That said, relatively few studies exist in this area, and several studies of the ACA expansion have found no effect (Mazurenko and others 2018). Moreover, the majority of studies focus on the short-run impacts of health insurance, which may be very different from the long-run impacts. Health, after all, is a stock variable (Grossman 1972), which suggests treatment effects that change over time.

Nevertheless, the research suggests that health insurance coverage reduces mortality, improves self-reported health, and improves some short-run markers of good health. One analysis found that Medicaid costs between $327,000 to $867,000 for every life it saves (Sommers 2017). Those estimates of the program are based solely on the effect of Medicaid on mortality, ignoring its other benefits, and suggest that Medicaid is likely a cost-effective use of government funds. To the extent that our estimates demonstrate a meaningfully different impact of the ACA expansion across states, this would lead to different impacts of the expansions on health.

VII.B. Labor Market Effects of Medicaid

Historically, most Americans have faced a remarkably tight link between health insurance coverage and employment. They could find affordable health insurance coverage by working for a large employer but would lose that coverage if they stopped working or moved to a smaller firm. As a result, expanded access to health insurance could potentially have a large effect on the labor market, allowing workers to leave their jobs without fear of losing their health insurance coverage.

To date, several studies have demonstrated a significant relationship between insurance coverage and labor supply. Garthwaite, Gross, and Notowidigdo (2014) studied a large Medicaid disenrollment in Tennessee in 2005, during which approximately 170,000 Tennessee residents lost Medicaid coverage. The authors found large increases in labor supply as a result and argued that those who lost Medicaid coverage entered the labor market in order to regain health insurance coverage. Similarly, Dague, DeLeire, and Leininger (2017) studied Wisconsin residents who were allowed onto Medicaid and found that those new Medicaid recipients became much less likely to seek employment. Kim (2016) found that

Connecticut's early expansion of Medicaid under the ACA led to a reduction in the employment rate.

At the same time, other studies have not found such a clear link between Medicaid coverage and the labor market. Leung and Mas (2018) found that the 2014 expansion of Medicaid did not meaningfully affect employment. Similarly, participants in the Oregon health insurance experiment who gained Medicaid did not become more or less likely to work (Baicker and others 2014).

This literature is thus divided between studies that have found a significant effect of Medicaid coverage on labor supply and studies that have not. One important issue in evaluating this gap in the literature is the degree to which the studies in question isolate workers who highly value health insurance. Basic economic theory suggests that the workers who value health insurance the most will be those who enter the labor market to retain access to health insurance. For instance, those who are HIV positive, who are diabetic, or who suffer from other chronic conditions find it extremely costly to be without health insurance. Such workers are difficult to isolate in the national surveys that are often used to measure employment rates and so may not have been captured by some of the previous research.

Beyond the extensive margin of labor supply, broader access to health insurance could plausibly increase entrepreneurship. Without the ACA, aspiring entrepreneurs may be locked into work for large employers. A reform that makes health insurance cheaper for small businesses and individuals might eliminate that barrier for aspiring entrepreneurs (Fairlie, Kapur, and Gates 2011).

In addition, there is a case to be made that health insurance coverage may directly increase the productivity of its beneficiaries. To begin with, there is evidence that medical treatment can increase labor supply and productivity. Berndt and others (1998) found that the treatment of clinical depression led to an increase in a self-reported composite measure of workplace performance. Garthwaite (2012) studied the removal of Vioxx from the market, a drug commonly used to treat arthritis at the time. His results suggest that a large share of Americans left the labor market once their arthritis was no longer treated. More generally, Chen and Goldman (2018) performed a meta-analysis of randomized clinical trials that evaluated the effect of medical care on productivity. The authors found that, for many disease categories, randomized trials have uncovered large productivity effects, in some cases greater than 25 percent.

So if medical care improves productivity, then health insurance, by increasing access to medical care, may also boost productivity. To our knowledge, there exists no direct evidence for such an effect, that is, no studies have demonstrated that individuals who are given health insurance experience increases in their labor market productivity, but such a hypothesis appears warranted based on previous research. Furthermore, to the extent that these broad labor supply effects vary with the magnitude of the expansion, the variation that we identify could have meaningful economic impacts.

VII.C. Longer-Run Effects of Health Insurance Coverage

The majority of the research described here focuses on the short-run impact of health insurance coverage across a variety of outcomes. The typical study relies on a difference-in-differences regression or instrumental variables strategy that isolates the effect of health insurance over, at most, several years. It is much more challenging to study effects that evolve over decades. And yet, in the context of health insurance, longer-run effects might be very different from what we observe over only a year or two. Health is a stock variable, and so cumulative access to health care over decades can lead to dramatic consequences later (Grossman 1972).

Several studies have compiled suggestive evidence on precisely such a dynamic. Brown, Kowalski, and Lurie (2019), Miller and Wherry (2017), and Goodman-Bacon (2019) all study childhood Medicaid coverage and adult outcomes. The studies consider children who were born in particular states and particular years such that they enjoyed Medicaid coverage through their childhoods and compare them to similar children who were not covered by Medicaid. The authors then study health outcomes years later and find dramatic benefits of childhood Medicaid coverage. Adults who were covered by Medicaid as children earn more, are less likely to be disabled, and are more likely to be employed. Related work by Cohodes and others (2016) suggests that childhood Medicaid coverage also leads to increases in educational attainment. Brown, Kowalski, and Lurie (2019) estimate that the federal government recovers 57 percent of the cost of Medicaid coverage through increased tax revenue years later. Overall, we view these studies as suggestive of meaningful longer-run effects of Medicaid coverage, although more research is needed to uncover a fuller picture.

VII.D. Economic Transfers between States

Medicaid is administered by state governments but is jointly financed by federal and state governments. The amount of money from the federal government is dictated by each state's federal medical assistance percentage (FMAP). In 2012, the average FMAP was 60 percent: for every dollar of Medicaid spending, 60 percent came from the federal rather than the state government. This average masks a great deal of variation, because each state's FMAP is determined based on the state's average personal income. States that have lower average incomes receive more federal assistance. By statute, the FMAP cannot fall below a floor of 50 percent. In fiscal year 2020, this FMAP floor applied to Alaska, California, Colorado, Connecticut, Maryland, Massachusetts, Minnesota, New Hampshire, New Jersey, New York, Virginia, Washington, and Wyoming. Many states have FMAPs well above this floor. For example, the following states had an FMAP above 70 percent: Arizona, Idaho, South Carolina, Arkansas, Kentucky, Alabama, New Mexico, West Virginia, and Mississippi.

Expansions of Medicaid have often involved enhanced FMAPs that provide more-generous federal support for the newly eligible population. For example, under the State Children's Health Insurance Program (SCHIP), states received an enhanced FMAP that ranged from 76.5 to 95 percent in fiscal year 2020. These enhanced FMAPs continued with the ACA Medicaid expansion, where the federal government pays a constant 90 percent of costs across all states regardless of the state's income.

This generous contribution combined with variation in both the expansion decision and the impact of the expansions has meaningfully shifted the distribution of transfers across states. Table 7 contains data from the Medicaid and CHIP Payment and Access Commission (MACPAC) on funding sources and enrollment for Medicaid programs by a state's expansion status. Unsurprisingly, these data show that the average expansion state had a much larger increase in Medicaid enrollment than the average non-expansion state. That said, non-expansion states also saw a nontrivial increase in the size of their Medicaid population. This is a combination of economic conditions and the welcome mat effect described in section IV, where publicity about Medicaid and the ACA individual mandate increased enrollment. Importantly, some of the increase in expansion states is also likely the result of this welcome mat effect.

These new enrollees resulted in greater spending for both sets of states. However, for expansion states there was also a meaningful increase in the share of spending coming from the federal government. This was likely driven by the more generous sharing of costs for the newly eligible cohort. In non-expansion states the share paid by the federal government was largely flat. Looking at spending per enrollee, the average expansion state saw its own spending per enrollee drop by 18 percent from 2012 to

Table 7. Characteristics of the States' Medicaid Programs

	Expansion states	*Non-expansion states*
Mean enrollment before expansion	1,164,453	1,175,039
Mean enrollment after expansion	1,667,961	1,443,135
% change in enrollment	43%	23%
Mean federal funding before expansion (in thousands)	$5,613.59	$5,339.85
Mean federal funding after expansion (in thousands)	$8,288.20	$6,466.15
Mean state funding before expansion (in thousands)	$4,479.41	$3,196.46
Mean state funding after expansion (in thousands)	$4,776.03	$3,829.69
% increase in total spending	29%	21%
Pre-expansion federal share	56%	63%
Post-expansion federal share	63%	63%
Average state spending per enrollee, 2012	$3,592.68	$2,720.30
Average state spending per enrollee, 2016	$2,962.78	$2,653.73
Decline in state spending per enrollee	−18%	−2%

Source: Authors' calculations.

2016. Non-expansion states saw a decline of only 2 percent over the same time period.

An economically meaningful fraction of Medicaid spending simply replaces uncompensated care that would have been provided by hospitals in that state (Garthwaite, Gross, and Notowidigdo 2018). In addition, the increased use of hospital services resulting from the ACA expansion represents an infusion of federal sources into state economics. To the extent this infusion exceeds the state's contribution to federal taxation, this shift in the distribution of federal spending could have economically meaningful effects on regional economic output. Future work should examine the potential fiscal and economic ramifications of this effect on regional economic development.

VIII. Conclusion

The United States social insurance system has meaningfully expanded over the past two decades and yet a nontrivial fraction of the United States population remains uninsured. The uninsured population is not evenly distributed across the country. Much of this variation results from state differences in decisions to adopt (mostly) federally financed social insurance programs. As we consider expanding the social safety net further to address the remaining uninsured, it is important to have a full under-standing of both the impact of the ACA and variation in its impact across the country.

This paper's results lead to three main conclusions. First, the paper provides evidence that the market-wide impact of the ACA has been to increase the use of hospital services. That increase primarily occurred through outpatient visits to the emergency department for conditions that might have been deferrable and treatable outside of the emergency department. Our preferred estimate suggests an approximately 20 percent increase in the use of the hospital for the newly insured.

It is unclear whether or not that increase in emergency department visits is socially efficient. On the one hand, emergency departments are believed to be especially expensive venues to treat deferrable conditions. An increase in emergency department visits for such conditions thus indicates an inefficient use of resources, since those patients could have been treated in lower-cost settings. On the other hand, it is unclear whether the emergency department is truly a higher-cost setting. If the higher utilization is completely accounted for in slack capacity of the emergency department, the marginal costs could be quite low. However, the presence of a large number of potential uninsured patients could distort the fixed cost decision of the hospital for the optimal size of its emergency department, which means that evaluating economic costs using only the marginal cost may not be appropriate. In addition, other studies on health insurance, catalogued above, suggest that insurance coverage decreases mortality rates. It is difficult to assess whether that decrease in mortality rates is driven by the increase in utilization, but such a mechanism is, at the very least, plausible. In that case, the increased spending on hospital services likely increases social welfare. More research is needed to assess both the true increased economic costs from this increased utilization and whether those costs are greater than the societal benefits.

Second, beyond the increase in utilization, this paper also demonstrates variation in the impact of the ACA across states. The results suggest that some of that variation can be explained by the size of the expansion and the preexisting levels of uncompensated hospital care. There is room for more work unpacking the mechanism behind how a uniform federal policy can have such different effects across the country. Still, these estimates should raise broad concerns about the ability to generalize from a single setting to the entire nation. The variation that we estimate demonstrates that even small differences in the implementation of a uniform policy can cause meaningfully different outcomes. Beyond demonstrating important questions about external validity, this variation is something that policymakers may hope to harness as they attempt to develop a nationwide health care safety net. Given the important economic impact of health insurance, failing to understand and plan for this variation could lead to meaningfully different regional economic impacts from federal policies. For this reason, we believe that far more research is needed to understand the mechanisms underlying our results. These mechanisms could be useful policy levers for elected officials as they attempt to develop a robust social safety net.[35]

Finally, we also study the target efficiency of the Medicaid expansion, the degree to which it gave coverage to those who most needed it. The estimates suggest that the existing safety net's policy of categorical eligibility was not more target efficient than the Medicaid expansion. As federal policymakers consider the optimal size and nature of the safety net it may be necessary to more clearly account for the degree to which existing market features can drive the efficiency of federal spending.

Taken together, this paper's estimates lead to several implications for policy. First, the results clearly suggest that the ACA's Medicaid expansions increased hospital utilization, including use of the emergency department. That finding should inform analysts seeking to predict the cost of future expansions. Moreover, if policymakers plan to expand coverage in areas with little excess supply of health care, then they should also consider complementary policies to expand the capacity of the local health care system. Second, policymakers should view evidence of state-specific heterogeneity as perhaps suggesting that some federal laws should leave room for state-by-state customization. Health care is a fundamentally local product, and thus markets for health care act very differently across the country. Finally, this paper's estimates suggest that the ACA Medicaid expansion was well targeted. To the extent that policymakers are worried about targeting in a social insurance program that is available based only on income, our estimates should decrease these concerns.

---

35. Another implication of this across-state heterogeneity is that it may affect the interpretation of future difference-in-differences studies of the ACA. Those future studies will be carried out over longer time periods, particularly as other states choose to expand Medicaid. Recent research emphasizes that difference-in-differences studies with variation in treatment timing need to be interpreted carefully when there is treatment-effect heterogeneity (Goodman-Bacon 2018), and so the results above imply that future researchers need to pay close attention to state-level heterogeneity when comparing results across studies that are estimated in different time periods or sets of expansion and non-expansion states.

ACKNOWLEDGMENTS   The views expressed are those of the authors and do not necessarily reflect those of the Agency for Healthcare Research and Quality (AHRQ), the U.S. Department of Health and Human Services, or the National Institute on Aging. No official endorsement by any agency of the federal or state governments is intended or should be inferred. This research was supported in part by a P30 grant from the National Institute on Aging to the NBER Center for Aging and Health Research (P30AG012810) and by a R01 grant (Graves) from the National Cancer Institute (R01HG009694). We thank Janet Eberly, Amy Finkelstein, and Jonathan Skinner for their detailed feedback, and we thank Julie Hudson and Asako Moriya for helpful comments. Eliana Buckner and Peter Nam provided superb research assistance. We are grateful to Herbert Wong for his assistance and guidance throughout this project. We also acknowledge the Healthcare Cost and Utilization Project (HCUP) Partners. The academic coauthors on this paper received access to the database through a HCUP Contractor agreement. All of the analysis occurred on a secure server that was set up and made available to the academic collaborators for this project for the duration of the study.

References

Anderson, Michael L., Carlos Dobkin, and Tal Gross. 2012. "The Effect of Health Insurance Coverage on the Use of Medical Services." *American Economic Journal: Economic Policy* 4, no. 1: 1–27. https://doi.org/10.1257/pol.4.1.1.

Anderson, Michael L., Carlos Dobkin, and Tal Gross. 2013. "The Effect of Health Insurance on Emergency Department Visits: Evidence from an Age-Based Eligibility Threshold." *Review of Economics and Statistics* 96, no. 1: 189–95. https://doi.org/10.1162/REST_a_00378.

Antwi, Yaa Akosa, Asako S. Moriya, Kosali Simon, and Benjamin D. Sommers. "Changes in Emergency Department Use among Young Adults after the Patient Protection and Affordable Care Act's Dependent Coverage Provision." *Annals of Emergency Medicine* 65, no. 6: 664–72.

Armour, Stephanie. 2019. "When Patients Can't Pay, Many Hospitals Are Suing." *Wall Street Journal*, June 25. https://www.wsj.com/articles/nonprofit-hospitals-criticized-for-debt-collection-tactics-11561467600.

Baicker, Katherine, Amy Finkelstein, Jae Song, and Sarah L. Taubman. 2014. "The Impact of Medicaid on Labor Market Activity and Program Participation: Evidence from the Oregon Health Insurance Experiment." *American Economic Review* 104, no. 5: 322–28. https://doi.org/10.1257/aer.104.5.322.

Berndt, Ernst R., Stan N. Finkelstein, Paul E. Greenberg, Robert H. Howland, Alison Keith, A. John Rush, James Russell, and Martin B. Keller. 1998. "Workplace Performance Effects from Chronic Depression and Its Treatment." *Journal of Health Economics* 17, no. 5: 511–35.

Besanko, David, David Dranove, and Craig Garthwaite. 2016. "Insurance and the High Prices of Pharmaceuticals." Working Paper 22353. Cambridge, Mass.: National Bureau of Economic Research. https://www.nber.org/papers/w22353.

Blase, Brian. 2016. "Medicaid Expansion Causes Surge in ER Visits." *Forbes*, October 20. https://www.forbes.com/sites/theapothecary/2016/10/20/medicaid-expansion-causes-surge-in-er-visits/.

Blavin, Fredric, Michael Karpman, Genevieve M. Kenney, and Benjamin D. Sommers. 2018. "Medicaid versus Marketplace Coverage for Near-Poor Adults: Effects on Out-of-Pocket Spending and Coverage." *Health Affairs* 37, no. 2 (2018): 299–307.

Brown, David, Amanda Kowalski, and Ithai Lurie. 2019. "Long-Term Impacts of Childhood Medicaid Expansions on Outcomes in Adulthood." *Review of Economic Studies*. https://doi.org/10.1093/restud/rdz039.

Card, David, Carlos Dobkin, and Nicole Maestas. 2008. "The Impact of Nearly Universal Insurance Coverage on Health Care Utilization: Evidence from Medicare." *American Economic Review* 98, no. 5: 2242–58. https://doi.org/10.1257/aer.98.5.2242.

Chen, Alice, and Dana Goldman. 2018. "Productivity Benefits of Medical Care: Evidence from US-Based Randomized Clinical Trials." *Value in Health* 21, no. 8: 905–10.

Cohodes, Sarah R., Daniel S. Grossman, Samuel A. Kleiner, and Michael F. Lovenheim. 2016. "The Effect of Child Health Insurance Access on Schooling: Evidence from Public Insurance Expansions." *Journal of Human Resources* 51, no. 3: 727–59.

Cohn, Jonathan. 2004. "Uncharitable?" *New York Times*, December 19. https://www.nytimes.com/2004/12/19/magazine/uncharitable.html.

Dafny, Leemore, and Jonathan Gruber. 2005. "Public Insurance and Child Hospitalizations: Access and Efficiency Effects." *Journal of Public Economics* 89, no. 1: 109–29. https://doi.org/10.1016/j.jpubeco.2003.05.004.

Dague, Laura, Thomas DeLeire, and Lindsey Leininger. 2017. "The Effect of Public Insurance Coverage for Childless Adults on Labor Supply." *American Economic Journal: Economic Policy* 9, no. 2: 124–54. https://doi.org/10.1257/pol.20150059.

DeLeire, Thomas, Laura Dague, Lindsey Leininger, Kristen Voskuil, and Donna Friedsam. 2013. "Wisconsin Experience Indicates That Expanding Public Insurance to Low-Income Childless Adults Has Health Care Impacts." *Health Affairs* 32, no. 6: 1037–45.

Dranove, David, Craig Garthwaite, and Christopher Ody. 2016. "Uncompensated Care Decreased at Hospitals in Medicaid Expansion States but Not at Hospitals in Nonexpansion States." *Health Affairs* 35, no. 8: 1471–79.

Dresden, Scott M., Emilie S. Powell, Raymond Kang, Megan McHugh, Andrew J. Cooper, and Joe Feinglass. 2017. "Increased Emergency Department Use in Illinois after Implementation of the Patient Protection and Affordable Care Act." *Annals of Emergency Medicine* 69, no. 2: 172–80. https://doi.org/10.1016/j.annemergmed.2016.06.026.

Fairlie, Robert W., Kanika Kapur, and Susan Gates. 2011. "Is Employer-Based Health Insurance a Barrier to Entrepreneurship?" *Journal of Health Economics* 30, no. 1: 146–62. https://doi.org/10.1016/j.jhealeco.2010.09.003.

Finkelstein, Amy, Nathaniel Hendren, and Erzo F. P. Luttmer. 2019. "The Value of Medicaid: Interpreting Results from the Oregon Health Insurance Experiment." *Journal of Political Economy* 127, no. 6: 2836–74.

Finkelstein, Amy, Nathaniel Hendren, and Mark Shepard. 2019. "Subsidizing Health Insurance for Low-Income Adults: Evidence from Massachusetts." *American Economic Review* 109, no. 4: 1530–67. https://doi.org/10.1257/aer.20171455.

Finkelstein, Amy, Neale Mahoney, and Matthew J. Notowidigdo. 2018. "What Does (Formal) Health Insurance Do, and for Whom?" *Annual Review of Economics* 10:261–86. https://doi.org/10.1146/annurev-economics-080217-053608.

Finkelstein, Amy, and Robin McKnight. 2008. "What Did Medicare Do? The Initial Impact of Medicare on Mortality and Out of Pocket Medical Spending." *Journal of Public Economics* 92, no. 7: 1644–68.

Garfield, Rachel, Kendal Orgera, and Anthony Damico. 2020. "The Coverage Gap: Uninsured Poor Adults in States That Do Not Expand Medicaid." Issue

Brief. Kaiser Family Foundation. https://www.kff.org/medicaid/issue-brief/the-coverage-gap-uninsured-poor-adults-in-states-that-do-not-expand-medicaid/.

Garthwaite, Craig L. 2012. "The Economic Benefits of Pharmaceutical Innovations: The Case of Cox-2 Inhibitors." *American Economic Journal: Applied Economics* 4, no. 3: 116–37. https://doi.org/10.1257/app.4.3.116.

Garthwaite, Craig, Tal Gross, and Matthew J. Notowidigdo. 2014. "Public Health Insurance, Labor Supply, and Employment Lock." *Quarterly Journal of Economics* 129, no. 2: 653–96.

Garthwaite, Craig, Tal Gross, and Matthew J. Notowidigdo. 2018. "Hospitals as Insurers of Last Resort." *American Economic Journal: Applied Economics* 10, no. 1: 1–39. https://doi.org/10.1257/app.20150581.

Garthwaite, Craig, Tal Gross, Matthew Notowidigdo, and John A. Graves. 2017. "Insurance Expansion and Hospital Emergency Department Access: Evidence from the Affordable Care Act." *Annals of Internal Medicine* 166, no. 3: 172–79. https://doi.org/10.7326/M16-0086.

Goodman-Bacon, Andrew. 2016. "The Long-Run Effects of Childhood Insurance Coverage: Medicaid Implementation, Adult Health, and Labor Market Outcomes." Working Paper 22899. Cambridge, Mass.: National Bureau of Economic Research. https://www.nber.org/papers/w22899.

Goodman-Bacon, Andrew. 2018. "Difference-in-Differences with Variation in Treatment Timing." Working Paper 25018. Cambridge, Mass.: National Bureau of Economic Research. https://www.nber.org/papers/w25018.

Graves, John, Laura Hatfield, William J. Blot, Nancy Keating, and J. Michael McWilliams. 2020. "Medicaid Expansion Slowed Rates of Health Decline for Low-Income Adults in Southern States." *Health Affairs* 39, no. 1:67–76. https://doi.org/10.1377/hlthaff.2019.00929.

Graves, John, Laura Hatfield, and J. Michael McWilliams. 2020. "Difference-in-Difference Estimation for Transitions in Discrete Outcomes: Insurance Transitions after the Affordable Care Act's Medicaid Expansion." Working Paper.

Grossman, Michael. 1972. "On the Concept of Health Capital and the Demand for Health." *Journal of Political Economy* 80, no. 2: 223–55.

Haley, Jennifer, Stephen Zuckerman, Michael Karpman, Sharon Long, Lea Bart, and Joshua Aarons. 2018. "Adults' Uninsurance Rates Increased by 2018, Especially in States That Did Not Expand Medicaid—Leaving Gaps in Coverage, Access, and Affordability." Blog post, September 6, Health Affairs, Bethesda. https://www.healthaffairs.org/do/10.1377/hblog20180924.928969/full/.

Heavrin, Benjamin S., Rongwei Fu, Jin H. Han, Alan B. Storrow, and Robert A. Lowe. 2011. "An Evaluation of Statewide Emergency Department Utilization Following Tennessee Medicaid Disenrollment." *Academic Emergency Medicine* 18, no. 11: 1121–28. https://doi.org/10.1111/j.1553-2712.2011.01204.x.

Hernandez-Boussard, Tina, Carson S. Burns, N. Ewen Wang, Laurence C. Baker, and Benjamin A. Goldstein. 2014. "The Affordable Care Act Reduces Emergency

Department Use by Young Adults: Evidence from Three States." *Health Affairs* 33, no. 9: 1648–54.

Hudson, Julie L., and Asako S. Moriya. 2018. "Association between Marketplace Policy and Public Coverage among Medicaid or Children's Health Insurance Program–Eligible Children and Parents." *JAMA Pediatrics* 172, no. 9: 881–82. https://doi.org/10.1001/jamapediatrics.2018.1497.

Kim, Daeho. 2016. "Health Insurance and Labor Supply: Evidence from the Affordable Care Act Early Medicaid Expansion in Connecticut." Working Paper. https://doi.org/10.2139/ssrn.2785938.

Kliff, Sarah. 2014. "Study: Expanding Medicaid Doesn't Reduce ER Trips. It Increases Them." *Washington Post*, January 2. https://www.washingtonpost.com/news/wonk/wp/2014/01/02/study-expanding-medicaid-doesnt-reduce-er-trips-it-increases-them/.

Leung, Pauline, and Alexandre Mas. 2018. "Employment Effects of the Affordable Care Act Medicaid Expansions." *Industrial Relations* 57, no. 2: 206–34. https://doi.org/10.1111/irel.12207.

Long, Sharon K., Stephen Zuckerman, and John A. Graves. 2006. "Are Adults Benefiting from State Coverage Expansions? Public Coverage Does Increase as a Result of States' Program Expansions, but Sometimes at the Expense of Private Coverage." *Health Affairs* 25, suppl. 1: W1–W14. https://doi.org/10.1377/hlthaff.25.w1.

Mahoney, Neale. 2015. "Bankruptcy as Implicit Health Insurance." *American Economic Review* 105, no. 2: 710–46. https://doi.org/10.1257/aer.20131408.

Mazurenko, Olena, Casey P. Balio, Rajender Agarwal, Aaron E. Carroll, and Nir Menachemi. 2018. "The Effects of Medicaid Expansion under the ACA: A Systematic Review." *Health Affairs* 37, no. 6: 944–50.

Miller, Sarah. 2012. "The Effect of Insurance on Emergency Room Visits: An Analysis of the 2006 Massachusetts Health Reform." *Journal of Public Economics* 96, nos. 11–12: 893–908. https://doi.org/10.1016/j.jpubeco.2012.07.004.

Miller, Sarah, and Laura Wherry. 2017. "Health and Access to Care during the First Two Years of the ACA Medicaid Expansions." *New England Journal of Medicine* 376: 947–56.

Miller, Sarah, Sean Altekruse, Norman Johnson, and Laura R. Wherry. 2019. "Medicaid and Mortality: New Evidence from Linked Survey and Administrative Data." Working Paper 26081. Cambridge, Mass.: National Bureau of Economic Research.

Mulcahy, Andrew, Katherine Harris, Kenneth Finegold, Arthur Kellermann, Laurel Edelman, and Benjamin D. Sommers. 2013. "Insurance Coverage of Emergency Care for Young Adults under Health Reform." *New England Journal of Medicine* 368, no. 22: 2105–12. https://doi.org/10.1056/NEJMsa1212779.

Nikpay, Sayeh, Seth Freedman, Helen Levy, and Tom Buchmueller. 2017. "Effect of the Affordable Care Act Medicaid Expansion on Emergency Department Visits: Evidence from State-Level Emergency Department Databases."

Annals of Emergency Medicine 70, no. 2: 215–25.e6. https://doi.org/10.1016/j.annemergmed.2017.03.023.

Nyman, John A. 1998. "Theory of Health Insurance." *Journal of Health Administration Education* 16, no. 1: 41–66.

Richards, Michael R., Sayeh S. Nikpay, and John A. Graves. 2016. "The Growing Integration of Physician Practices: With a Medicaid Side Effect." *Medical Care* 54, no. 7: 714–18. https://doi.org/10.1097/MLR.0000000000000546.

Rosenbaum, Sara, Sara Schmucker, Sara Rothenberg, and Rachel Gunsalus. 2016. "Streamlining Medicaid Enrollment: The Role of the Health Insurance Marketplaces and the Impact of State Policies." Issue Brief 1869, vol. 8. Washington: Commonwealth Fund. https://www.commonwealthfund.org/publications/issue-briefs/2016/mar/streamlining-medicaid-enrollment-role-health-insurance.

Rudowitz, Robin, Elizabeth Hinton, and Larisa Antonisse. 2018. "Medicaid Enrollment and Spending Growth: FY 2018 and 2019." Blog post, October 25, Kaiser Family Foundation. https://www.kff.org/medicaid/issue-brief/medicaid-enrollment-spending-growth-fy-2018-2019/.

Skinner, Jonathan. 2012. "Causes and Consequences of Regional Variations in Health Care." In *Handbook of Health Economics*, vol. 2, edited by Mark V. Pauly, Thomas G. Mcguire, and Pedro P. Barros. Waltham, Mass.: Elsevier. https://doi.org/10.1016/B978-0-444-53592-4.00002-5.

Smulowitz, Peter B., James O'Malley, Xiaowen Yang, and Bruce E. Landon. 2014. "Increased Use of the Emergency Department after Health Care Reform in Massachusetts." *Annals of Emergency Medicine* 64, no. 2: 107–15, 115.c1-3. https://doi.org/10.1016/j.annemergmed.2014.02.011.

Sommers, Benjamin D. 2017. "State Medicaid Expansions and Mortality, Revisited: A Cost-Benefit Analysis." *American Journal of Health Economics* 3, no. 5: 392–421. https://doi.org/10.1162/ajhe_a_00080.

Sommers, Benjamin D., Katherine Baicker, and Arnold M. Epstein. 2012. "Mortality and Access to Care among Adults after State Medicaid Expansions." *New England Journal of Medicine* 367, no. 11: 1025–34. https://doi.org/10.1056/NEJMsa1202099.

Sommers, Benjamin D., Robert J. Blendon, E. John Orav, and Arnold M. Epstein. 2016. "Changes in Utilization and Health among Low-Income Adults after Medicaid Expansion or Expanded Private Insurance." *JAMA Internal Medicine* 176, no. 10: 1501–9. https://doi.org/10.1001/jamainternmed.2016.4419.

Sommers, Benjamin D., Munira Z. Gunja, Kenneth Finegold, and Thomas Musco. 2015. "Changes in Self-Reported Insurance Coverage, Access to Care, and Health under the Affordable Care Act." *JAMA* 314, no. 4: 366–74. https://doi.org/10.1001/jama.2015.8421.

Taubman, Sarah L., Heidi L. Allen, Bill J. Wright, Katherine Baicker, and Amy Finkelstein. 2014. "Medicaid Increases Emergency-Department Use: Evidence from Oregon's Health Insurance Experiment." *Science* 343, no. 6168: 263–68. https://doi.org/10.1126/science.1246183.

Thomas, Wendi C. 2019. "The Nonprofit Hospital That Makes Millions, Owns a Collection Agency and Relentlessly Sues the Poor." *ProPublica*, June 27. https://www.propublica.org/article/methodist-le-bonheur-healthcare-sues-poor-medical-debt.

Wherry, Laura R., Sarah Miller, Robert Kaestner, and Bruce D. Meyer. 2017. "Childhood Medicaid Coverage and Later-Life Health Care Utilization." *Review of Economics and Statistics* 100, no. 2: 287–302. https://doi.org/10.1162/REST_a_00677.

Wilson, Scott, and Ovetta Wiggins. 2013. "Obama Defends Health-Care Law, Calls Coverage 'a Right.'" *Washington Post*, September 26. https://www.washington post.com/politics/obama-defends-health-care-law-calling-health-insurance-a-right/2013/09/26/9e1d946e-26b8-11e3-b75d-5b7f66349852_story.html.

Comments and Discussion

COMMENT BY
AMY FINKELSTEIN   This is an extremely nice paper which brings fan-
tastic, novel national data to bear on a question that is simultaneously both
timely and perennial: How do health insurance expansions affect health
care utilization? To study this, the authors take advantage of a rich database
that covers essentially all hospital admissions and emergency room visits
in about half of the states. They use these data to study the impact of the
expansion of Medicaid under the Affordable Care Act (ACA) to previously
ineligible low-income adults. Their empirical strategy leverages the fact
that some states expanded Medicaid—the public health insurance program
for low-income adults—while others did not. They find that the Medicaid
expansions increased both hospital admissions and emergency room visits
but that effects were quite heterogeneous across states. The heterogeneity
of impacts across states is intriguing—and highly related to a rich existing Dartmouth Atlas Project literature documenting substantial geographic
variation in health care provision across the United States. My fellow discussant covers this aspect of the work very well. I will instead confine my
remarks to two sets of comments.

My first set of comments takes a step back from the paper to provide some perspective. Readers not deeply steeped in health care policy
debates would be forgiven for asking: Why, in 2019, is it still a question
whether health insurance increases health care utilization? Health insurance by design lowers the price individuals pay for their medical care;
isn't it pretty well established that demand curves tend to slope down?
My comments here are designed to help place the current paper in the
larger context.

My second set of comments offers some speculations on where we might
go next. Here I draw on recent research (much of which is conducted by

combinations of the current authors) that suggests that the *direct* effects of Medicaid expansions on the newly insured may be only part of the story of the total impact of Medicaid; there are also substantial *indirect* beneficiaries of Medicaid expansions which warrant further investigation.

DIRECT EFFECTS OF MEDICAID EXPANSIONS ON HEALTH CARE USE: DEMAND CURVES SLOPE DOWN

Theories. Health insurance, by design, lowers the price individuals pay for their medical care. One might think it therefore obvious that health insurance increases use of health care, that is, that the demand curve for medical care slopes downward. Yet, in the context of health care, there are (at least) two other views.

One view is rooted in the notion that health care is not like other goods; it is determined by needs, not by economic factors. Or, as an economist might put it, the demand for health care is completely inelastic with respect to its price. Malcolm Gladwell has forcefully articulated this view in a 2005 *New Yorker* article tellingly entitled "The Moral-Hazard Myth" (Gladwell 2005). He writes: "The moral-hazard argument makes sense . . . only if we consume health care in the same way that we consume other consumer goods, and to [some] economists . . . this assumption is plainly absurd. We go to the doctor grudgingly, only because we're sick." According to this view, health insurance will not change health care use.

A second view holds that health insurance will actually *reduce* health care use: demand for health care slopes up! This view is rooted in two related hypotheses. One is the conjecture that health insurance will improve people's health by increasing timely and effective medical care (for example, preventive care or better management of chronic conditions) and that this improved health will in turn reduce health care utilization. Another version focuses on the idea that health insurance will make the provision of health care more efficient, thus reducing health care spending. In particular, although most health care providers in the United States can choose whether or not to see patients, emergency rooms cannot; the Emergency Medical Treatment and Active Labor Act (EMTALA) requires hospitals to provide emergency medical treatment to all patients.

There is therefore widespread speculation that one of the benefits of providing health insurance to previously uninsured individuals is to get them out of the expensive emergency room and into cheaper primary care. Indeed, this has become a leitmotif of advocates of expanding health insurance coverage in the United States. For example, in making the case that Michigan should expand Medicaid coverage under the ACA, Republican governor Rick Snyder's policy team argued: "Today, uninsured citizens often turn to emergency rooms for non-urgent care because they don't have access to primary care doctors—leading to crowded emergency rooms, longer wait times and higher cost. By expanding Medicaid, those without insurance will have access to primary care, lowering costs and improving overall health" (Michigan State 2013).

Evidence. With this set of theories by way of background we can put this part of the paper in perspective: it is yet another in a long line of papers providing compelling evidence that in health care, as with most goods, demand curves slope down. And yet, despite a large body of existing evidence on this point, the preceding discussion illustrates how timely and well-crafted papers such as this one are unfortunately still needed to hammer yet more nails into this coffin.

An enormous body of empirical literature has provided compelling empirical evidence that health insurance increases health care spending. There have been, to date, three randomized evaluations of health insurance coverage in the United States, all of which focus on non-elderly populations, primarily adults, and all of which find that health insurance increases health care spending. The first was the famous RAND health insurance experiment of the 1970s, which randomly assigned different cost sharing provisions (that is, copays and deductibles) across about 2,000 non-elderly families for three to five years (Newhouse 1993; Aron-Dine, Einav, and Finkelstein 2013). Second, the 2008 Oregon health insurance experiment randomly assigned Medicaid for about two years to about 10,000 uninsured adults below the federal poverty line (Finkelstein and others 2012; Baicker and Finkelstein 2013; Baicker and others 2013; Baicker and others 2014; Taubman and others 2014; Finkelstein and others 2016). Finally, the 2007–2009 Accelerated Benefits Demonstration randomly assigned public health insurance to about 1,000 uninsured adults on Social Security disability insurance during their two-year waiting period for Medicare (Michalopoulos and others 2011).

In addition to the evidence from randomized evaluations, there is a wealth of evidence from quasi-experimental studies that health insurance increases health care spending. These studies exploit variation in health insurance coverage arising from, among other things, the introduction of Medicare coverage for the elderly both in calendar time (1965) and over the life cycle (at age 65), the staggered introduction of Medicaid coverage by states in the 1960s, the staggered expansions by states of Medicaid coverage to low-income women and children in the 1980s and 1990s, the more recent Medicaid expansions under the ACA, and the sharp change in health insurance coverage when individuals enter the famous "donut hole" for prescription drug coverage in Medicare Part D. Einav and Finkelstein (2018) and Finkelstein, Mahoney, and Notowidigdo (2018) provide a more detailed discussion of this quasi-experimental literature.

According to a 2015 survey by the IGM Economic Experts Panel, only 7 percent of economists surveyed agree with the statement "expanding health insurance to more people through the ACA's public subsidies and Medicaid expansion will reduce total healthcare spending in the economy"—and none strongly agree (IGM Forum 2015). Unfortunately, despite the overwhelming empirical evidence and the near consensus among economic experts that health insurance expansions increase health care spending, the general public is not yet convinced. I am grateful to Garthwaite and his colleagues for being willing to undertake the important but often thankless task of continuing to beat this dead horse.

INDIRECT EFFECTS OF MEDICAID EXPANSIONS

Providers of uncompensated care. Compared to the copious existing evidence on the direct impacts of Medicaid expansions on the recipients, there is relatively little evidence on what is likely as important a group of beneficiaries: those actors who were previously covering the costs of providing care to the low-income uninsured. This is an important direction for further work, as it likely affects both the economic impact and politics of public health insurance expansions.

The history and policies of health insurance in the United States strongly hint at the existence of substantial indirect beneficiaries beyond those newly covered by insurance. For example, the first wide-scale formal health insurance plans in the United States, the Blue Cross hospital insurance plans, were created during the Great Depression to provide financial help not only to patients but also to the hospitals that served them. As one hospital executive from the time recalled, "I could remember the difficulties we had then, trying to keep our doors open. . . . People brought chickens in and meat to pay their bills. They would paint or do work around the hospital of some kind" (Cunningham and Cunningham 1997, 9–10). In more recent times, hospitals have been an important lobbying force for Medicaid expansions under the ACA, and against their subsequent repeal, arguing that increases in the number of uninsured patients would be financially devastating (Ollove 2013; Goldstein 2016).

The uninsured receive substantial implicit insurance (Mahoney 2015; Dobkin and others 2018). Estimates suggest that the uninsured pay only

20–35 cents per dollar of expenditures on their medical care (Coughlin and others 2014; Hadley and others 2008; Finkelstein, Hendren, and Luttmer 2019). This implicit insurance arises due to a host of factors. For example, the federal EMTALA requires hospitals to provide emergency care on credit and prohibits them from delaying treatment to inquire about insurance status or means of payment. As a matter of practice, many hospitals report providing nonemergency medical care on credit as well (IRS 2007). Nonprofit hospitals—which constitute approximately 70 percent of all hospitals—are required to provide a community benefit in exchange for federal, state, and local tax exemptions; charity care, along with medical research and teaching, is one way that hospitals can fulfill this requirement (U.S. Government Accountability Office 2008; Nicholson and others 2000). In addition, a number of states have charity care pools that redistribute funding to hospitals based on the volume of uncompensated care (Dranove, Garthwaite, and Ody 2016). Finally, even when medical providers wish to seek payment for medical services, a number of factors limit their recovery rates, generating ex post charity care—that is, bad debt. The uninsured have disproportionately low incomes, and many have very few assets (Mahoney 2015); as a result, medical providers typically recover only about 10–20 percent of bills submitted to uninsured individuals (LeCuyer and Singhal 2007).

As a result, when the previously uninsured are covered by a Medicaid expansion, those who were previously bearing the cost of informally insuring the uninsured also benefit. An open and challenging question concerns the economic incidence of this informal insurance. But we have some suggestive evidence already.

In the first instance, implicit insurance for the uninsured seems to be directly financed by hospitals and the public sector. For example, Garthwaite, Gross, and Notowidigdo (2018) estimate that each uninsured individual costs hospitals approximately $800 per year in uncompensated care costs. Likewise there is evidence that states that expanded Medicaid under the ACA experienced a decline in hospital uncompensated care costs relative to nonexpansion states (Dranove, Garthwaite, and Ody 2016). There are also a number of ways the public sector pays for implicit insurance, including federal disproportionate share hospital (DSH) payments and state uncompensated care pools that provide funding to hospitals that face bad debt from unpaid medical bills and funding shortfalls due to providing uncompensated care to the uninsured seeking emergency medical treatment (Hadley and others 2008). As a result, formal health insurance expansions are also accompanied by a reduction of such public funding (Rudowitz 2013; Kolstad and Kowalski 2012).

The ultimate economic incidence of changes in implicit insurance payments due to formal health insurance is conceptually complicated and empirically elusive. The list of potentially affected parties is long and includes shareholders (at for-profit hospitals), buyers (insurance companies and patients), suppliers (for example, employees and prescription drug and medical device manufacturers), hospital competitors (community health clinics), and local, state, and federal governments. Interestingly, many policymakers either implicitly or explicitly assume that hospitals simply pass on uncompensated care costs to privately insured patients. For example, the text of the ACA (42 U.S.C. 18091) states, "to pay for [uncompensated care], health care providers pass on the cost to private insurers, which pass on the cost to families. This cost-shifting increases family premiums by on average over $1,000 a year. By significantly reducing the number of the uninsured, the requirement, together with the other provisions of this Act, will lower health insurance premiums." Cost shifting was also cited by Chief Justice Roberts in the Supreme Court decision upholding the ACA' s constitutionality (*National Federation of Independent Business v. Sebelius*, 567 U.S. 1, 2012). Despite this widespread assumption of substantial cost shifting, there is limited empirical evidence of the ability of hospitals to actually pass on uncompensated care costs. Garthwaite, Gross, and Notowidigdo (2018) show that increases in the uninsurance rate are associated with a decline in hospital operating (profit) margins. This indicates that hospitals are not able to fully pass on increased uncompensated care costs, at least over the relatively short time horizon that Garthwaite and others examine.

The previously insured. Finally, but relatedly, another group of actors potentially affected by health insurance expansions are the previously insured. Market-wide expansions in insurance coverage may well have general equilibrium effects on those whose insurance is not affected. Here, however, the sign of any such effects is theoretically unclear, and the empirical evidence is limited.

On the one hand, if the supply of health care inputs is upward sloping, an expansion of health insurance to one group—and with it increased demand for health care by that group—may reduce care for the previously uninsured. This seems particularly plausible for physicians, where supply is constrained by the American Medical Association's determination of the number of residency slots. Consistent with this, Garthwaite

(2012) finds that the expansion of public health insurance for low-income children in the 1990s reduced the amount of time physicians spent per office visit.

On the other hand, by expanding aggregate demand for (and use of) health care, health insurance expansions may stimulate increased supply of health care inputs. Consistent with this, I found that the introduction of Medicare in 1965 increased hospital construction and the adoption of new medical technologies (Finkelstein 2007). Other work from the pharmaceutical industry indicates that increases in market size (such as presumably occur through health insurance expansions) increase research and development on new drugs (Finkelstein 2004; Acemoglu and Linn 2004; Yin 2008).

CONCLUSION The impact of health insurance on health care spending by the newly insured has been well studied and the verdict is clear: health insurance increases health care spending. There is no free lunch. Garthwaite and his colleagues drive home this point forcefully.

Equally important, however, is the impact of health insurance on other actors, including those who were implicitly or explicitly subsidizing care provision for the previously uninsured and the previously insured whose own care may be affected—even if their insurance nominally remains the same—by the changes in the market for health care. These are more subtle issues on which both economic theory and economic evidence is not definitive. Moreover, they have important implications for both the politics of health insurance reform and its economic impacts. Hopefully we will see more work on these important and challenging issues going forward.

REFERENCES FOR THE FINKELSTEIN COMMENT

Acemoglu, D., and J. Linn. 2004. "Market Size in Innovation: Theory and Evidence from the Pharmaceutical Industry." *Quarterly Journal of Economics* 119, no. 3: 1049–90.

Aron-Dine, Aviva, Liran Einav, and Amy Finkelstein. 2013. "The RAND Health Insurance Experiment, Three Decades Later." *Journal of Economic Perspectives* 27, no. 1: 197–222.

Baicker, Katherine, and Amy Finkelstein. 2013. "Effects of Medicaid on Clinical Outcomes: Reply to Letters." *New England Journal of Medicine* 369, no. 6: 581–83.

Baicker, Katherine, Amy Finkelstein, Jae Song, and Sarah L. Taubman. 2014. "The Impact of Medicaid on Labor Market Activity and Program Participation: Evidence from the Oregon Health Insurance Experiment." *American Economic Review* 104, no. 5: 322–28.

Baicker, Katherine, Sarah L. Taubman, Heidi L. Allen, Mira Bernstein, Jonathan H. Gruber, Joseph P. Newhouse, Eric C. Schneider, Bill J. Wright, Alan M. Zaslabsky, and Amy Finkelstein. 2013. "The Oregon Experiment—Effects of Medicaid on Clinical Outcomes." *New England Journal of Medicine* 386, no. 18: 1713–22.

Coughlin, Teresa A., John Holahan, Kyle Caswell, and Megan McGrath. 2014. *Uncompensated Care for the Uninsured in 2013: A Detailed Examination.* Washington: Henry J. Kaiser Family Foundation. https://www.kff.org/uninsured/report/uncompensated-care-for-the-uninsured-in-2013-a-detailed-examination/.

Cunningham, Robert, III, and Robert M. Cunningham Jr. 1997. *The Blues: A History of the Blue Cross and Blue Shield System.* DeKalb, Ill.: Northern Illinois University Press.

Dobkin, Carlos, Amy Finkelstein, Raymond Kluender, and Matthew J. Notowidigdo. 2018. "The Economic Consequences of Hospital Admissions." *American Economic Review* 108, no. 2: 308–52.

Dranove, David, Craig Garthwaite, and Christopher Ody. 2016. "Uncompensated Care Decreased at Hospitals in Medicaid Expansion States but Not at Hospitals in Nonexpansion States." *Health Affairs* 35, no. 8: 1471–79.

Einav, Liran, and Amy Finkelstein. 2018. "Moral Hazard in Health Insurance: What We Know and How We Know It." *Journal of the European Economic Association* 16, no. 4: 957–82.

Finkelstein, Amy. 2004. "Static and Dynamic Effect of Health Policy: Evidence from the Vaccine Industry." *Quarterly Journal of Economics* 119, no. 2: 527–64.

Finkelstein, Amy. 2007. "The Aggregate Effects of Health Insurance: Evidence from the Introduction of Medicare." *Quarterly Journal of Economics* 122, no. 1: 1–37.

Finkelstein Amy, Nathaniel Hendren, and Erzo F. P. Luttmer. 2019. "The Value of Medicaid: Interpreting Results from the Oregon Health Insurance Experiment." *Journal of Political Economy* 127, no. 6: 2836–74.

Finkelstein, Amy, Neale Mahoney, and Matthew J. Notowidigdo. 2018. "What Does (Formal) Health Insurance Do, and For Whom?" *Annual Review of Economics* 10:261–86.

Finkelstein, Amy, Sarah L. Taubman, Heidi L. Allen, Bill J. Wright, and Katherine Baicker. 2016. "Effect of Medicaid Coverage on ED Use—Further Evidence from Oregon's Experiment." *New England Journal of Medicine* 375, no. 16: 1505–7.

Finkelstein, Amy, Sarah L. Taubman, Bill J. Wright, Mira Bernstein, Jonathan Gruber, Joseph P. Newhouse, Heidi L. Allen, and Katherine Baicker. 2012. "The Oregon Health Insurance Experiment: Evidence from the First Year." *Quarterly Journal of Economics* 127, no. 3: 1057–1106.

Garthwaite, Craig L. 2012. "The Doctor Might See You Now: Supply Side Effects of Public Health Insurance Expansions." *American Economic Journal: Economic Policy* 4, no. 3: 190–217.

Garthwaite Craig L., Tal Gross, and Matthew J. Notowidigdo. 2018. "Hospitals as Insurers of Last Resort." *American Economic Journal: Applied Economics* 10, no. 1: 1–39.

Gladwell, Malcolm. 2005. "The Moral-Hazard Myth." *New Yorker*, August 29. https://www.newyorker.com/magazine/2005/08/29/the-moral-hazard-myth.

Goldstein, Amy. 2016. "Hospitals Warn Trump, Congress of Massive Losses with Affordable Care Act Repeal." *Washington Post*, December 6. https://www.washingtonpost.com/national/health-science/hospitals-warn-trump-congress-of-massive-losses-with-affordable-care-act-repeal/2016/12/06/3de2f7de-bbd8-11e6-91ee-1adddfe36cbe_story.html.

Hadley, Jack, John Holahan, Teresa Coughlin, and Dawn Miller. 2008. "Covering the Uninsured in 2008: Current Costs, Sources of Payment, and Incremental Costs." *Health Affairs* 27, no. s1: 399–415.

Initiative on Global Markets (IGM) Forum. 2015. "Health Insurance Subsidies." Chicago Booth, October 5. http://www.igmchicago.org/surveys/health-insurance-subsidies.

Internal Revenue Service (IRS). 2007. *Hospital Compliance Project: Interim Report.* https://www.irs.gov/pub/irs-tege/eo_interim_hospital_report_072007.pdf.

Kolstad, Jonathan T., and Amanda E. Kowalski. 2012. "The Impact of Health Care Reform on Hospital and Preventive Care: Evidence of Massachusetts." *Journal of Public Economics* 96, nos. 11–12: 909–29.

LeCuyer, Nick A., and Shubham Singhal. 2007. "Overhauling the US Health Care Payment System." *McKinsey Quarterly.* https://healthcare.mckinsey.com/overhauling-us-healthcare-payment-system.

Mahoney, Neale. 2015. "Bankruptcy as Implicit Health Insurance." *American Economic Review* 105, no. 2: 710–46.

Michalopoulos, Charles, David Wittenburg, Dina A. R. Israel, Jennifer Schore, Anne Warren, Aparajita Zutshi, Stephen Freedman, and Lisa Schwartz. 2011. *The Accelerated Benefits Demonstration and Evaluation Project: Impacts on Health and Employment at Twelve Months.* New York: MDRC. https://www.mdrc.org/publication/accelerated-benefits-demonstration-and-evaluation-project.

Michigan State. 2013. "Facts about Medicaid Expansion: Improving Care, Saving Money." https://www.michigan.gov/documents/snyder/Medicaid_expansion_-_factsheet_final_2-6-13_410658_7.pdf.

Newhouse, Joseph P. 1993. *Free for All?* Cambridge, Mass.: Harvard University Press.

Nicholson, Sean, Mark V. Pauly, Lawton R. Burns, Agnieshka Baumritter, and David A. Asch. 2000. "Measuring Community Benefits Provided by For-Profit and Nonprofit Hospitals." *Health Affairs* 19, no. 6: 168–77.

Ollove, Michael. 2013. "Hospitals Press States to Expand Medicaid." *Kaiser Health News*, April 17. https://khn.org/newshospitals-lobby-for-medicaid-expansion-states/.

Rudowitz, Robin. 2013. "How Do Medicaid Disproportionate Share Hospital (DSH) Payments Change under the ACA?" Issue Brief. Washington: Kaiser Commission on Medicaid and the Uninsured, Henry J. Kaiser Family Foundation. https://www.kff.org/medicaid/issue-brief/how-do-medicaid-disproportionate-share-hospital-dsh-payments-change-under-the-aca/.

Taubman, Sarah L., Heidi L. Allen, Bill J. Wright, Katherine Baicker, and Amy Finkelstein. 2014. "Medicaid Increases Emergency-Department Use: Evidence from Oregon's Health Insurance Experiment." *Science* 343, no. 6168: 263–68.

U.S. Government Accountability Office. 2008. *Nonprofit Hospitals: Variation in Standards and Guidance Limits Comparison of How Hospitals Meet Community Benefit Requirements.* GAO-08-880. Washington: U.S. Government Accountability Office.

Yin, Wesley. 2008. "Market Incentives and Pharmaceutical Innovation." *Journal of Health Economics* 27:1060–77.

COMMENT BY

JONATHAN SKINNER   In considering the legacy of the Patient Protection and Affordable Care Act (ACA), the expansion of the Medicaid program will likely rank as one of the most important changes, if not the most important change, in the provision of U.S. health care. By fiscal year 2017, Medicaid and CHIP (the Children's Health Insurance Program) enrolled 73.7 million people, an increase of 35 percent above the 54.5 million enrolled in fiscal year 2010, at the outset of the ACA.[1] Yet aside from the Oregon experiment, which took place in a single state prior to the ACA expansions (Finkelstein and others 2012; Baicker and others 2013), we know little about the detailed impact of this great experiment. It is for this reason that this paper by Garthwaite and his colleagues is a welcome study that considers the Medicaid expansion across a wide sample of states and captures the impact of the expansion on emergency room admissions, the differential impact on discretionary versus nondiscretionary admissions, and the extent to which the expansions have targeted the sickest patients. The study is notable for using a wide range of data sources and a very strong triple difference identification strategy that avoids serious biases inherent in the conventional difference-in-differences approaches.

While my fellow discussant, Amy Finkelstein, addresses the larger questions regarding the demand curve for health care, I will focus here

1. Medicaid and CHIP Payment and Access Commission (MACPAC), Exhibit 10: Medicaid Enrollment and Total Spending Levels and Annual Growth, https://www.macpac.gov/publication/medicaid-enrollment-and-total-spending-levels-and-annual-growth/.

on the authors' finding that when it comes to Medicaid, all states are not alike. Despite the uniform size of the federal subsidy—with states paying almost nothing for the new enrollees under the expansion—the authors find heterogeneity in both how enrollment rates increased and by how much utilization changed. The idea that there might be variability across states in their response to health insurance expansion under the ACA is not new given that many states opted out of the expansion entirely, but what is surprising here is the heterogeneity even among states that chose to sign up.[2] In these comments, I therefore expand on the authors' finding of heterogeneity at both the *micro* level—that the level of Medicaid reimbursement rates matters in encouraging providers to see newly enrolled patients—and at the *macro* level—how variations in state-level responses undermine the redistributive macroeconomic goals of federal health policy. I consider each in turn.

A MICRO-LEVEL PERSPECTIVE The authors consider a variety of state-level policies that could explain the heterogeneity across states in the extent to which hospital discharges and emergency department (ED) visits responded to Medicaid expansions. But there may be another salient factor that could help to explain the variability in Medicaid expansion: the reimbursement rates paid to Medicaid providers. There are well-known differences across states in how well they compensate providers for services to Medicaid enrollees (Alexander and Schnell 2019). Figure 1 illustrates the theoretical impact of such differences on the expansionary effect of a given Medicaid expansion. The key assumption is an upward-sloping supply curve for Medicaid utilization rates; an increase in the reimbursement rate leads to a higher level of utilization per Medicaid enrollee. Initially, the supply curve is given by S for a restricted group of Medicaid enrollees. After Medicaid expansion, a greater number of previously unreimbursed patients became eligible for Medicaid, leading to a larger number of Medicaid visits supplied by physicians at a given price. Thus the Medicaid expansion shifts the supply curve of Medicaid services over to S' at a fixed price. Considering first a generous price P', the increase in utilization rates is given by the difference between U and U^*. By contrast, when the price is lower, at P, the expansionary effect (shown by the smaller arrow) is considerably less. While one must take care in making inferences about log changes in utilization (given that, at P, the initial level of utilization is also lower),

---

2. Kowalski (2016) has considered the potential for heterogeneity in the pre-ACA Oregon and Massachusetts expansions based on patient types; and Kowalski (2014) finds substantial state-level heterogeneity in the expansion of health insurance exchanges.

Figure 1. A Hypothetical Association between the Medicaid Reimbursement Rate and the Impact of Medicaid Expansion on Utilization

Medicaid reimbursement rate

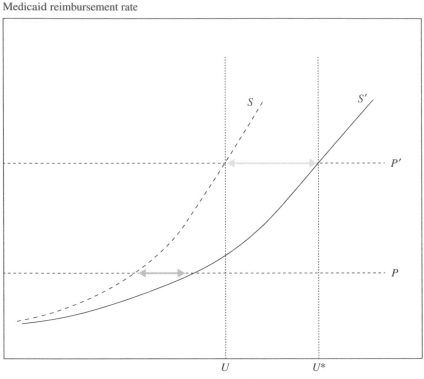

Health care quantity

Source: Author's calculations.

Note: The graph illustrates a hypothetical case demonstrating how the Medicaid reimbursement rate might affect the size of a given Medicaid expansion. The expansion is shown by a shift in the supply curve from S to S' as a larger number of patients become eligible for Medicaid services. As drawn it shows the difference in health care quantity that occurs when the price is high P' (the difference between U and U^*) versus the much smaller expansionary effect occurring at the lower price P (shown by the gap between S and S').

the fraction of uninsured affected by the expansion will be larger the higher is the newly available Medicaid reimbursement rate.

Is there any empirical support for this proposition? Alexander and Schnell (2019) compiled state-level measures of Medicaid reimbursement rates for a new patient physician evaluation. They kindly provided data by state prior to 2013 for Medicaid reimbursement rates relative to the corresponding Medicare reimbursement rate; I refer to the Medicaid/Medicare ratio as the "reimbursement gap" or a proxy for the Medicaid price paid for

Figure 2. The Association between the Medicaid Reimbursement Rate for an Office Visit and the Change in Medicaid and Uninsured Hospital Admissions, by State

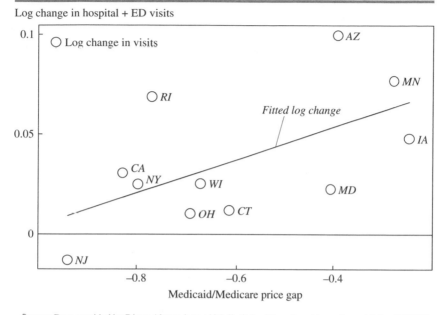

Log change in hospital + ED visits

Source: Data provided by Diane Alexander and Molly Schnell based on Alexander and Schnell (2019).
Note: Data for price differentials are for an office visit relative (in log terms) to the Medicare reimbursement rate, while the quantity change is also in log terms for total (Medicaid plus uninsured) hospital admissions plus emergency department (ED) visits.

hospital and ED visits. As I do not have direct measures of reimbursement rates for hospitalizations and ED visits, I must assume that states that pay their physicians generously feel the same largess when it comes to hospital and ED visits.[3]

Figure 2 considers the association between the reimbursement gap (Alexander and Schnell 2019) and the log change in hospital and ED visits for the combined group of uninsured and Medicaid insured (from the current authors). There is a strong positive correlation of $\rho = 0.59$,

3. A key focus of Alexander and Schnell (2019) is the *change* in the reimbursement rate. Under the ACA, Medicaid physician reimbursement rates were set equal to Medicare reimbursement for 2013–14; subsequently, some states restored the previous reimbursement rates while others maintained parity with Medicare. The authors use these changes to identify the supply curve. However, prices paid for hospital and ED visits were not affected by this policy change, and thus I use the pre-2013 data as a proxy for what Medicaid is assumed to have continued to pay during the period of analysis.

and the result holds up even after adjusting for commensurate changes in Medicaid enrollment.[4]

While these are correlations and cannot be interpreted as causal, the pattern estimated by the authors and by Alexander and Schnell (2019) points toward a general principle regarding state-administered Medicaid programs. Even though the federal government may pay the lion's share of the expenses, every state runs its programs with varying degrees of generosity, eligibility, provider engagement, and patient populations. So perhaps it is not altogether surprising that even among states that did expand Medicaid coverage, the overall impact on enrollment (and likely benefits) varied so much.

A MACRO-LEVEL PERSPECTIVE ON MEDICAID (AND MEDICARE) The United States spends more than $3 trillion on health care, with approximately one-third financed through the Medicare and Medicaid programs; these two programs in turn account for nearly one-quarter of all federal spending.[5] Federal health transfers are a highly progressive avenue for redistribution to states with larger elderly or disabled populations or, more importantly, for states with a larger fraction of their populations at or near the poverty level. The reason is straightforward: a larger fraction of residents should be eligible for Medicaid, the federal government pays a much higher fraction of Medicaid payments in lower-income states (among those previously enrolled in Medicaid), and federal tax outflows are much smaller in magnitude for low-income states (Feenberg and Skinner 2000).

The heterogeneity in the responsiveness of state Medicaid programs to the ACA expansions might therefore have macroeconomic effects, as well as affecting the progressivity of federal government transfers across states. To assess whether these macroeconomic effects are substantial, I draw on the National Health Expenditures database in conjunction with data from MACPAC (2015) and the Kaiser Family Foundation to calculate the state-level per capita inflow of federal funds arising from Medicaid, and

---

4. The p-value for the simple bivariate regression is 0.057, although it is likely to be biased because the data from Garthwaite and his colleagues were from their triple difference regression estimates. The multivariate regression explaining the log expansion in hospital discharges plus ED visits ($N = 11$) was $.053 + 0.226 *$ (percentage increase in Medicaid enrollment) [s.e. $= 0.176] + 0.083 *$ (reimbursement gap) [s.e. $= 0.036$].

5. According to the Center for Budget and Policy Priorities, health care spending is about 25 percent of total federal spending, but that figure includes exchange subsidies and children's health insurance (CHIP); see "Policy Basics: Where Do Our Federal Tax Dollars Go?," http://goo.gl/ZgeQBo.

Medicaid plus Medicare combined.[6] Because the direct recipients of these federal transfers are health care providers—health care professionals and hospital systems—I consider federal flows based on where the provider is located, rather than where the patient lives.[7] Unfortunately, the state-level National Health Expenditures were available only through 2014, so I just have one year of data following the Medicaid expansion.

In considering the change over time in federal funds, there were not large differences across states in the Garthwaite sample with regard to changes in federal inflows through Medicaid; New Jersey (at the low end of increased utilization) experienced an increase of $202 per capita in Medicaid transfers, while Minnesota (at the high end) gained $342. However, the story is quite different when one expands the sample to all states, including those that failed to expand Medicaid.

Figure 3 shows per capita federal flows from Medicaid and Medicare (in constant 2014 dollars) for three states. During much of the 2000s, Kansas and Oregon received about the same per capita federal dollars, but the two states diverged in the late 2000s when Oregon began an early expansion of its Medicaid program.[8] Following an enthusiastic response to the ACA Medicaid expansion, these factors combined (along with increases in Medicare spending) led to a sharp increase of roughly $1,000 in federal health spending for every person in Oregon between 2008 and 2014. By contrast, Kansas eschewed the expansion, and its federal inflows declined slightly in real terms during the same period. These are large and continued macroeconomic inflows for Oregon; if applied at the national level, it would be equivalent to more than a $300 billion expansionary policy. And it is perhaps coincidental that during 2008–18, Oregon's annual real GDP growth rate exceeded Kansas's growth rate by 0.4 percent.[9]

The endogeneity of state responses to federal policy may ultimately challenge the progressive structure of federal spending across regions. This can be seen again in figure 3 by comparing federal per capita spending in Louisiana and Oregon. In 2018, Oregon's median family income

6. This calculation requires applying the average federal matching rates to state-level Medicaid payments; the calculation becomes more complicated in 2014 when new Medicaid enrollees experienced a much higher match rate. See MACPAC (2015, 45–46); and the Kaiser Family Foundation, Federal Medical Assistance Percentage (FMAP) for Medicaid and Multiplier.

7. I am grateful to Victor Fuchs for suggesting this approach.

8. As in Finkelstein and others (2012).

9. Based on the difference in real per capita GDP by state; www.statistica.com.

Figure 3. Per Capita Federal Medicare plus Medicaid Transfers, 2004–14, by Selected States

U.S. dollars

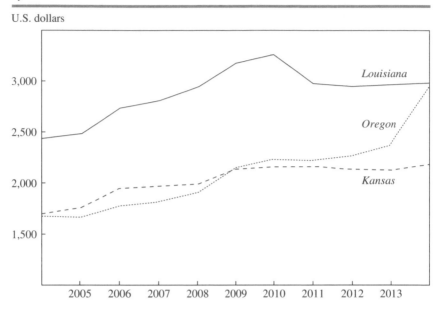

Sources: Health Expenditures by State of Provider, 2017, Centers for Medicare and Medicaid Services, https://www.cms.gov/Research-Statistics-Data-and-Systems/Statistics-Trends-and-Reports/National HealthExpendData; share data from the Kaiser Family Foundation, Federal Medical Assistance Percentage (FMAP) for Medicaid and Multiplier, 2019, and from the Medicaid and CHIP Payment and Access Commission (MACPAC) Report, Exhibit 10: Medicaid Enrollment and Total Spending Levels and Annual Growth (posted December 4, 2018).

Note: Federal Medicare plus Medicaid transfers are defined as state-level Medicare reimbursements plus the federal share of Medicaid payments, based on the residence of the provider (not the enrollee).

was 25 percent higher than in Louisiana.[10] For most of the 2000s, there were correspondingly greater federal transfers to Louisiana compared to Oregon. Like Kansas, Louisiana did not expand Medicaid, and so its federal support remained roughly constant, but Oregon's efforts to expand coverage, as noted earlier, turned on the federal money tap, so by 2014, Oregon was receiving about the same federal health spending on a per capita basis as Louisiana. While the net federal health care transfers—after

10. Based on American Community Survey data from 2018 on median family income (in Oregon, $77,655, and in Louisiana, $61,847); https://data.census.gov/cedsci/table?g= 0100000US.04000.001&tid=ACSST1Y2018.S1901&hidePreview=false&vintage=2018&t= Income%20%28Households,%20Families,%20Individuals%29&cid=S1901_C01_001E.

accounting for federal taxes—are still presumably in Louisiana's favor, the impact of the ACA is still one that may have reduced the progressivity of government transfers across regions. And while the ACA was successful in reducing disparities in health insurance coverage at the micro level by race, income, and marital status (Courtemanche and others 2019), it may be contributing to increasing divergence in regional income over time (Ganong and Shoag 2017).

In sum, the study by Garthwaite and his colleagues has given us an important first look at the variability in how the Medicaid program can have widely disparate effects depending on state-level characteristics of policies, patients, and providers. As federal policy on health care continues to evolve—whether toward block grants to states or toward a stronger federal role in Medicare expansions—the issues raised in this paper will only become more important.

REFERENCES FOR THE SKINNER COMMENT

Alexander, Diane, and Molly Schnell. 2019. "The Impacts of Physician Payments on Patient Access, Use, and Health." Working Paper 26095. Cambridge, Mass.: National Bureau of Economic Research. https://www.nber.org/papers/w26095.

Baicker, Katherine, Sarah L. Taubman, Heidi L. Allen, Mira Bernstein, Jonathan H. Gruber, Joseph P. Newhouse, Eric C. Schneider, Bill J. Wright, Alan M. Zaslabsky, and Amy Finkelstein. 2013. "The Oregon Experiment—Effects of Medicaid on Clinical Outcomes." *New England Journal of Medicine* 386, no. 18: 1713–22.

Courtemanche, Charles J., Ishtiaque Fazlul, James Marton, Benjamin D. Ukert, Aaron Yelowitz, and Daniela Zapata. 2019. "The Impact of the ACA on Insurance Coverage Disparities after Four Years." Working Paper 26157. Cambridge, Mass.: National Bureau of Economic Research. https://www.nber.org/papers/w26157.

Feenberg, Daniel R., and Jonathan Skinner. 2000. "Federal Medicare Transfers across States: A Lifetime Perspective." *National Tax Journal* 52, no. 3: 713–32.

Finkelstein, Amy, Sarah L. Taubman, Bill J. Wright, Mira Bernstein, Jonathan Gruber, Joseph P. Newhouse, Heidi L. Allen, and Katherine Baicker. 2012. "The Oregon Health Insurance Experiment: Evidence from the First Year." *Quarterly Journal of Economics* 127, no. 3: 1057–1106.

Ganong, Peter, and Daniel Shoag. 2017. "Why Has Regional Income Convergence in the US Declined?" *Journal of Urban Economics* 102:76–90.

Kowalski, Amanda E. 2014. "The Early Impact of the Affordable Care Act State-by-State." *Brookings Papers on Economic Activity*, Fall, 277–333.

Kowalski, Amanda E. 2016. "Doing More When You're Running LATE: Applying Marginal Treatment Effect Methods to Examine Treatment Effect Heterogeneity in Experiments." Working Paper 22363. Cambridge, Mass.: National Bureau of Economic Research. https://www.nber.org/papers/w22363.

Medicaid and CHIP Payment and Access Commission (MACPAC). 2015. *MACPACStats: Medicaid and CHIP Data Book.* https://www.macpac.gov/wp-content/uploads/2015/11/MACStats-Medicaid-and-CHIP-Data-Book-December-2015.pdf.

GENERAL DISCUSSION   Caroline Hoxby wondered whether it was possible to get person-level data to explore the hypothesis that once people receive Medicaid (or any type of health care) they will make more use of primary care.

John Haltiwanger noted that it was likely that Medicaid expansions and the Affordable Care Act (ACA) changed the composition of where people get their care. This possibility, along with the large heterogeneity in productivity across hospitals, is likely to have affected the productivity of the health care sector. He asked the authors to comment on this possible phenomenon.

Ed Lazear observed that a major problem with health care is that people use the wrong amount on the margin. He pondered what would happen if—when instituting a new program, like Medicaid—the amount of doctor visits increased and the amount of emergency room (ER) visits decreased to zero. Although the number of ER visits is zero in this scenario, he commented, it is complicated by the fact that people are using more services. He noted that one advantage of the ER is that it is unpleasant, which could serve as another way to price the services; he asked the authors to remark on whether they thought this consequence had any social value.

Henry Aaron asked the authors to comment on the policy implications of their paper.

James Stock stated that a macroeconomic reason a policymaker might pursue a Medicaid expansion is its possible effect on the economy. He noted that the authors' findings showed there was no increase in the incomes of the people who became insured due to a Medicaid expansion and asked the authors to comment on the implications of this finding.

William Brainard noted a recent experience when he took a friend to the doctor and they were immediately sent to the ER. The ER then kept this person for several days, but never admitted them. The ER personnel called this special designation "observational." He wondered how many institutions have this observational category and how this might affect the results of the paper.

Jason Furman remarked that one defense of the emergency department proposition is the cross-price effect. The paper shows—in line with other research—that there is no cross-price effect. He pointed out, however, that a more sophisticated defense of this proposition is that although Medicaid expansions increase use, they also include a whole bunch of other delivery system reforms, like accountable care organizations (ACOs) and better payment mechanisms that keep people out of the emergency room. He queried the authors to comment on this sophisticated defense and whether the state variation is at all related to these differences.

Craig Garthwaite responded that there aren't any fine-grain primary care data, although there are survey data. The survey data could be used to figure out whether people make more use of primary care once they receive Medicaid. He observed that this question is related to whether primary care services and inpatient emergency department (ED) visits are complements or substitutes. For example, one could find that Medicaid coverage increases the use of physicians, which then increases ED visits. He remarked that the answer to this question of primary care use affects the interpretation of their paper's findings, rather than the findings themselves.

John Graves added that there are ways to get at the primary care data question indirectly, for example, ambulatory care sensitive hospitalization data which can be filtered by International Classification of Diseases, Ninth Revision (ICD-9) codes. He commented that although these measures allow researchers to get around the lack of data—especially for the uninsured—they are noisy.

Craig Garthwaite explained that the existing data on Medicaid recipients' use of physicians are of poor quality. Generally, the data are mostly from Medicaid managed care organizations, which means they are within-firm data. Moreover, since the data are post-insurance, they do not include information about the uninsured. In addition, since physicians are not required to provide care to the uninsured by law, they provide relatively little uncompensated care compared to hospitals. Indeed, a paper by Gruber finds that physicians provide negative uncompensated care since they charge the uninsured such high prices, which makes up for any losses from those who don't pay.[1]

In response to Haltiwanger's question, Garthwaite noted that there are currently two reinsurance program designs, each of which affects productivity differently. First, he noted, there are market-based mechanisms (like Medicaid) which provide health insurance to the individual. Under this design, patients can receive care wherever they want, which implies

---

1. Jonathan Gruber and David Rodriguez, "How Much Uncompensated Care Do Doctors Provide?," *Journal of Health Economics* 26:1151–69, https://economics.mit.edu/files/6423.

that some people might switch from public to private facilities. Second, the government can directly pay certain hospitals to provide care to the uninsured. Although in this type of program the uninsured can't receive care wherever they want, allocated hospitals are able to remain open even though they are providing a large amount of uncompensated care. He noted that the United States already has programs that do this—such as the disproportionate share program (DSH). DSH funds provide an additional supplement to hospitals based on how many uninsured people they treat. All in all, this implies that the United States has two reinsurance programs. He commented that it is important to discuss which of these programs is the most efficient way to provide care to the uninsured. For example, maybe it is most efficient to have the uninsured receive care in the lowest marginal cost setting possible, which would allow more people to receive care.

In response to Lazear's question, Garthwaite made it clear that he and his coauthors do not hold the normative view that ED use is bad. He remarked, however, that increased demand does require constructing newer and larger ED facilities. Building new, larger facilities could be wasteful if the types of conditions being treated in such facilities could be handled in a lower fixed and marginal cost setting.

He stated that the paper does discuss the effect of Medicaid on incomes and added that the literature shows that there are some economic benefits to Medicaid beneficiaries in the long term. However, he noted that seeing an effect in the data in the short term depends on the channel. If, for example, giving people more income increases their human capital, which in turn increases their productivity, he would expect this effect to be realized later than the eight to nine years currently observed in the data.

In response to Brainard's question, Garthwaite noted that a patient classified under an observational status would show up as an outpatient ED visit in their data set. He said that since hospitals do a large amount of outpatient ED visits, he doesn't believe this classification would affect any of their results.

He stated that he doesn't believe the development of Medicaid ACOs would have much of an effect on their results, since there aren't many facilities, although there might be some general spillover effects. He noted that there are more Medicare ACOs and that the best data on these types of organizations show that they have had little effect. He mentioned, however, that research shows that physician-led ACOs have been more successful. He said that these physician-led organizations have more of an effect because they are built around the right incentives; indeed, a physician can reduce a hospital visit and share in some of the savings. If a hospital, however, reduces hospital visits, it loses money.

John Graves remarked on Amy Finkelstein's presentation where she made the comment that knowing one state Medicaid program means that you only know one state Medicaid program. He said that Tennessee's TennCare program has been particularly out-front in terms of adopting bundle payments and other alternative payment models. However, this is specific to Tennessee and he wasn't sure what the effect would be in the aggregate.

Zeynal Karaca responded to Aaron's question about policy implications and Hoxby's question on physician data. In terms of policy implications, he noted a key takeaway from their paper was the heterogeneity across states. In terms of physician data, he noted that his agency—the Agency for Healthcare Research and Quality (AHRQ)—is currently working on a physician database. However, like other commenters, he mentioned that the collection of this type of data is quite challenging and is very expensive. He specified that whether the AHRQ ends up producing the data will depend on appropriation of funding in their budget.

Amy Finkelstein responded to Lazear's comment on the implicit assumption that ED is bad. She remarked that just because the ER is expensive doesn't mean it has a greater social cost. Indeed, if an emergency room must be staffed for 24 hours, the social marginal cost of a doctor's time at 4:00 a.m. might be quite low, even though it is billed at a high rate. Along these lines, she added that the question of whether triage is being handled efficiently within the emergency room is an important question about which there exists little evidence.

Finkelstein noted that she wrote a paper with Erzo Luttmer and Nathaniel Hendren that analyzes the social welfare of the Oregon experiments.[2] The paper compares the costs and benefits of the Oregon program. She stated that the costs of the program—such as direct public spending and increased medical care—were easy to measure. She remarked, on the other hand, that benefits were difficult to measure as they are typically traded in a poorly functioning market. This problem meant that they couldn't use standard demand tools. Instead, they calibrate a utility model and estimate the welfare benefits. Their results show that low-income uninsured individuals

---

2. Amy Finkelstein, Nathaniel Hendren, and Erzo F. P. Luttmer, "The Value of Medicaid: Interpreting Results from the Oregon Health Insurance Experiment," *Journal of Political Economy* 127, no. 6: 2836–74, https://scholar.harvard.edu/hendren/publications/value-medicaid-interpreting-results-oregon-health-insurance-experiment.

prefer cash to a Medicaid transfer. In addition, Finkelstein mentioned another paper she wrote with Hendren and Shepard that estimates the demand curve for Medicaid using a product traded on the Massachusetts health insurance exchange.[3] Similarly, in this paper, she and her colleagues find that willingness to pay for Medicaid was well below cost. She perceived these results to explain low program take-up. Furthermore, she stated that these results imply that Medicaid is not a very effective redistributive program; indeed, Medicaid is paying for the care that was being previously paid for by hospitals to the low-income uninsured.

Jonathan Skinner remarked on Aaron's question about policy implications. He observed that his most important takeaway was that health insurance program designs for those who are low-income should be the reverse of a block grant. He noted that, in an ideal world, Medicaid should be an entirely federally funded program with federal rules. He asked those in the room to image what Medicare would look like today if states paid for half of it. In such a situation, he postulated, there would be an enormous amount of inequality. The fact that Louisiana is shutting down their Medicaid out of failure to pay while Oregon has taken advantage of Medicaid expansion policies and has lots of money as a result is direct evidence, to him, that redistribution is not happening.

Garthwaite ended the discussion by mentioning what he took to be the most important policy implication. He stated that the federal government should look carefully at how they distribute non-Medicaid money. For example, there might be other ways through supplemental payments to inject money in non-expansion states for low-income people. He noted that some states like New Jersey and California have low reimbursement rates, while Alabama and Mississippi have high reimbursement rates. Although slightly counterintuitive, he specified that while these southern states substantially limit Medicaid eligibility, doctor visits for the small amount who are eligible are reimbursed at a high rate. All in all, he noted that policymakers should look more carefully at payment rules; changing such rules could be an important redistributive method and reduce inequalities in Medicaid access.

3. Amy Finkelstein, Nathaniel Hendren, and Mark Shepard, "Subsidizing Health Insurance for Low-Income Adults: Evidence from Massachusetts," *American Economic Review* 109, no. 4: 1530–67.

CHRISTOPHER AVERY
Harvard University

MATEA PENDER
The College Board

JESSICA HOWELL
The College Board

BRUCE SACERDOTE
Dartmouth College

Policies and Payoffs to Addressing America's College Graduation Deficit

ABSTRACT   We consider four distinct policy levers available to states for raising bachelor's degree completion rates in the United States through their public colleges and universities. We simulate these policies using elasticities from the existing literature and a matched College Board/National Student Clearinghouse data set on enrollment and degree completion. Increasing spending at public colleges and targeted elimination of tuition and fees at four-year public colleges with an income cutoff are projected to be the most effective of these policies in terms of cost per additional bachelor's degree. Reducing tuition and fees at public colleges and a distinct policy of moving students to the best available in state public college (BISPO) are next best on a cost-benefit basis. Free community college policies are significantly less cost-effective at raising bachelor's degree completion, though such policies do improve other outcomes. Reducing community college tuition and fees to zero does lead to more associate degrees, though students are drawn away from the four-year sector in the process. Low-income students see the smallest gains from free community college policies since these students already face very low net prices of attendance.

Conflict of Interest Disclosure: Christopher Avery is the Roy E. Larsen Professor of Public Policy at the Kennedy School of Government at Harvard University; Jessica Howell is the Vice President of Research at the College Board; Matea Pender is a policy research scientist at the College Board; and Bruce Sacerdote is the Richard S. Braddock 1963 Professor in Economics at Dartmouth College. Beyond these affiliations, the authors did not receive financial support from any firm or person for this paper or from any firm or person with a financial or political interest in this paper. They are currently not an officer, director, or board member of any organization with an interest in this paper. Beyond the College Board, no outside party had the right to review this paper before circulation. The views and opinions expressed in this article are those of the authors and do not necessarily reflect the policies of the College Board.

D espite the substantial economic returns to completing a college degree, the United States is situated in the middle of the pack within Organisation for Economic Cooperation and Development (OECD) countries for the fraction of high school students who complete a four-year college degree.[1] Most of the gap between the United States and the leading countries stems not from a failure of U.S. students to enter postsecondary education but rather from the high number of U.S. students who enter college or university but do not complete a four-year degree. We focus on the role of public colleges in promoting or inhibiting college completion in the United States because of their substantial market share: 42 percent of students enrolled in college attend four-year public colleges, and approximately three-quarters of students attend either two-year or four-year public colleges.[2] Nearly 15 million students are enrolled in public colleges in the United States, yet there are three distinct constraints that limit the impact of public colleges in helping these students achieve their degree completion goals.

First, funding plans for public colleges have shifted over time to emphasize tuition revenues rather than state support in the form of public subsidies. For two decades or more the average levels of tuition and fees at public colleges have increased at rates that outpace inflation and that also outpace increases at private colleges (Ma and others 2019, fig. 4b). Although government funding has generally increased over time as well, the net cost of public colleges has also increased over time, and this increase in net cost has likely contributed to the contemporaneous increase in student loans (Ma and others 2019, figs. 8 and 9). Students from low-income backgrounds have typically been underrepresented at selective public colleges, even after accounting for correlation between income and academic qualifications (see, for example, Pallais and Turner 2006). Although the vast majority of low-income students pay less than $5,000 per year in tuition and fees at public institutions (Ma and others 2019, fig. 11), recent evidence suggests it is an economic hardship for Pell Grant–eligible students to attend most flagship public universities (Debaum and Warwick 2019).

A second potential limitation of public colleges is that students at public institutions take longer, on average, to complete degrees and also complete bachelor's degrees at lower rates than students at comparable private

---

1. See OECD Data, Graduation rate, https://data.oecd.org/eduatt/graduation-rate.htm#indicator-chart.

2. National Center for Education Statistics, Digest of Education Statistics, table 303.25; https://nces.ed.gov/programs/digest/d13/tables/dt13_303.25.asp. See figure 3 for more details.

colleges. The average time to degree for those completing a bachelor's degree is 4.6 years at public colleges compared to 4.2 years at private colleges.[3] One possible explanation for these differentials is that per student instructional spending is lower, on average, at public colleges than at comparable private colleges.[4]

Finally, there may be structural differences in the supply of public colleges and universities across states that have an impact on student choices and postsecondary outcomes. Since students are broadly tied to in-state public colleges, students who reside in states with relatively small populations often do not have access to an in-state public college that matches their academic qualifications. Hillman and Weichman (2016) expand this observation to the local level, noting that 57.4 percent of freshmen attending four-year public colleges travel less than 50 miles from home to college. In many states, the supply of seats in four-year public colleges is less than the number of students with sufficient academic credentials for admission, further exacerbating the matching process for students who hope to stay closer to home and pay in-state tuition. The inevitable result of this imbalance between supply and demand at the state level is "undermatching," as defined by Smith, Pender, and Howell (2013, 247) to occur "when a student's academic credentials permit them access to a college or university that is more selective than the postsecondary alternative they actually choose." Undermatching has been linked to lower rates of degree completion, particularly among students from under-resourced backgrounds (Bowen, Chingos, and McPherson 2009; Roderick and others 2008; Smith, Pender, and Howell 2013).

In this paper, we consider policies designed to address each of these constraints. We simulate the effects of four separate policies: (1) eliminating tuition for two-year public colleges (aligned to free community college proposals that have gained considerable prominence in recent policy discussions); (2) reducing tuition at all four-year public colleges; (3) increasing funding for four-year public institutions to reduce the gap in spending between the otherwise comparable public and private colleges in the same

---

3. Authors' calculations from results provided by Shapiro and others (2017).

4. See Mitchell, Leachman, and Masterson (2017). It is also possible that selection of students into the public versus private sector may account for some portion of these differences in graduation rates and time to completion; we conducted exploratory regression analysis of graduation rates (with a single college as the unit of observation) and continued to find large and significant differences in graduation rates after controlling for observable differences in the average characteristics of students enrolling at public versus private colleges.

state; and (4) eliminating undermatching by relaxing institutional capacity constraints so that it is possible for currently undermatched students to attend the best in-state public option (BISPO) to which they could be admitted. We consider two versions of the BISPO policy: one where all undermatched students are moved to more appropriate four-year colleges and another, likely more realistic, where we assume that colleges face supply constraints and may not be able to accommodate the number of new students required to eliminate undermatching.

We compare the efficacy of these four policy changes using the primary metric of projected expenditure per additional bachelor's degree since the policies vary considerably in cost.[5] This summer, two states have taken well-publicized stands related to our simulations: Illinois launched Illinois Commitment, which covers the cost of tuition and fees at the flagship public university, University of Illinois, for students from families with less than $61,000 in income.[6] By contrast, the state of Alaska enacted a new budget that cuts funding to its university system by more than 40 percent; after subsequent negotiations, the state agreed to reduce the budget cuts by half and to spread them over three years (Harris 2019).

We evaluate the four different policy changes with micro-level simulations using data on PSAT and SAT takers who graduated from high school in spring 2007. In our simulations, students respond to the differing policies by potentially changing educational sector (that is, not enrolled, two-year public, four-year public, and so on), potentially changing institutions, and potentially changing the likelihood of obtaining associate and bachelor's degrees. To capture these student-level responses, we use micro elasticities taken from the literature. Our key elasticities include parameters that describe the enrollment and graduation responses to free community college policies, to tuition cuts, and to increases in per student spending.

These policy changes have potentially important macroeconomic implications because two of the important challenges facing the U.S. economy are relatively stagnant levels of GDP and productivity growth in combination with inequality in the distribution of gains (Piketty and Saez 2003). Since 2010, real GDP per capita growth has averaged 1.5 percent, which is meaningfully less than the 2.0 plus growth of earlier decades.[7] Of greater

---

5. We recognize that bachelor's degree attainment is only one measure of success for college entrants. We also consider associate degree attainment and a projection of expected earnings based on Chetty and others' (2017) mobility report cards by institution.

6. See University of Illinois, Illinois Commitment, https://osfa.illinois.edu/types-of-aid/other-aid/illinois-commitment/.

7. Authors' calculations from BEA data via FRED.

concern is the fact that median household incomes and mean wages have both grown by less than 1 percent per year since 1985 (Shambaugh and others 2017; Sacerdote 2017).[8] Investments in human capital, and in college degrees in particular, are among the most likely ways to create income growth (Goldin and Katz 2018; Oreopoulos and Petronijevic 2013; Dynarski 2008). There is considerable debate about whether returns to college measured at the micro level have relevance for macroeconomics (Bils and Klenow 2000; Barro and Sala-i-Martin 1998), but it is at least plausible that increases in bachelor's degree completion rates could increase growth at the national level.[9]

The paper proceeds as follows. Section I expands on the points raised in this introduction to present a detailed set of stylized facts about public colleges. Section II reviews past literature, emphasizing studies that are relevant to the four policy simulations we conduct. Section III provides details of the data used in our simulation analysis. Section IV provides technical details of the simulation. Section V reports our results. Section VI concludes.

I. Key Facts

I.A. Fact 1. The United States Has a Problematic College Graduation Rate

As shown in figure 1, the proportion of 25-to-29-year-olds in the United States who have completed college degrees has grown steadily but somewhat slowly over time. In the March 1995 Current Population Survey, 24.7 percent of 25-to-29-year-olds had completed a bachelor's degree and 33.0 percent completed either an associate or a bachelor's degree. Two decades later, in the March 2017 Current Population Survey, these numbers had increased, as 35.7 percent of 25-to-29-year-olds had completed a bachelor's degree and 46.1 percent had completed either an associate or a bachelor's degree.

---

8. Measurement of inflation (Broda and Weinstein 2008; Costa 2001), of transfers (Meyer and Sullivan 2009), and of household size (Aguiar and Bils 2015) make a big difference to this conclusion but don't necessarily overturn it.

9. Observational data suggest a clear positive correlation between educational attainment and many positive attributes connected to growth. More-educated people are healthier, less likely to be on public assistance, more engaged in civic activities, and more likely to promote education in the next generation. See tables 2.12 to 2.23 in Ma, Pender, and Weltch (2016).

Figure 1. Proportion of U.S. 25-to-29-Year-Olds with College Degrees, over Time (Selected Years)

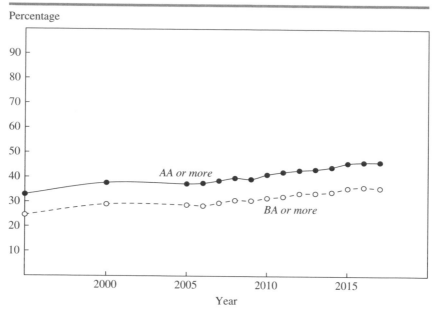

Percentage

Source: National Center for Education Statistics, Digest of Education Statistics, 2017, table 104.20, https://nces.ed.gov/programs/digest/d17/tables/dt17_104.20.asp.

Figure 2 illustrates similar increases in college enrollment for recent high school graduates over time. In 1975, only about half of those graduating from high school enrolled in college; today, approximately 70 percent of high school graduates go on to either a two-year or four-year college. Although enrollment in two-year colleges has fallen somewhat since the end of the financial crisis, enrollment in four-year colleges in the United States is presently at an all-time high and nearly half (46 percent) of students enroll in a four-year college in the year after high school graduation.[10] But as these numbers indicate, only about half of recent high school graduates who go on directly to college complete a bachelor's degree and approximately one-third of them do not complete either an associate degree or a bachelor's degree within six years of high school graduation.

10. National Center for Education Statistics, Digest of Education Statistics, table 302.10, https://nces.ed.gov/programs/digest/d16/tables/dt16_302.10.asp.

Figure 2. Proportion of Recent U.S. High School Graduates Enrolling in College, Over Time

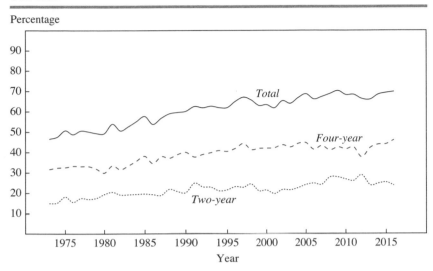

Source: National Center for Education Statistics, Digest of Education Statistics, 2017, table 302.10, https://nces.ed.gov/programs/digest/d17/tables/dt17_302.10.asp.

I.B. Fact 2. Public Colleges Serve the Majority of Students

While private colleges outnumber public colleges, especially in popular rankings and lists of the most selective institutions, public colleges are important because they serve as the default option for most high school graduates. Figure 3 documents the distribution of current college students by control (public, private not-for-profit, for-profit) and level (two-year or four-year). Nearly three-quarters of all college students are enrolled in public institutions, with 42 percent enrolled in four-year public colleges and 31 percent enrolled in two-year public colleges. By contrast, only 20 percent of college students attend four-year private colleges and less than 1 percent of them attend a two-year private college. While for-profit institutions, have been the focus of many media stories and policy debates, they play a relatively limited role for recent high school graduates. As also shown in figure 3, about 2 percent of college students age 18 to 21 attend for-profit colleges, whereas 7 percent of all college students (and 11 percent of college students older than 21) attend for-profit colleges.

We provide further descriptive statistics using data from the College Board database, noting that the units in figure 4 are not directly comparable

Figure 3. Institutional Type for College Students in 1990 and 2015

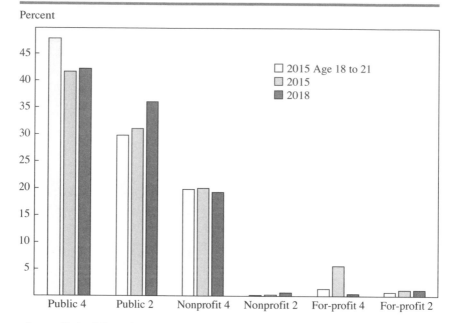

Source: National Center for Education Statistics, Digest of Education Statistics, 2017, tables 303.25 and 303.55, https://nces.ed.gov/programs/digest/d17/tables/dt17_303.25.asp and https://nces.ed.gov/programs/digest/d17/tables/dt17_303.55.asp, respectively.

to the units in figure 3 because figure 4 also includes high school graduates who do not enroll in college. As shown in figure 4, approximately half of students with combined math and verbal SAT scores between 1000 and 1390 enroll in four-year public colleges.[11] Enrollment in four-year private colleges is highly correlated with standardized test scores. More than half of the high school graduates in the right tail of the distribution with combined SAT scores from 1400 to 1600 enroll in four-year private colleges.

Figures 5a and 5b compare the enrollment patterns by SAT score for students from families with incomes below $40,000 and students with family income above $100,000. Perhaps surprisingly, there does not appear to be very much difference in the enrollment rates in four-year public colleges for high-income versus low-income students by SAT category. In each subgroup, for example, approximately half of students with

11. We calculate estimated SAT score for students who only took PSAT (see notes in figure 4).

Figure 4. Choice of Program by SAT/PSAT Score

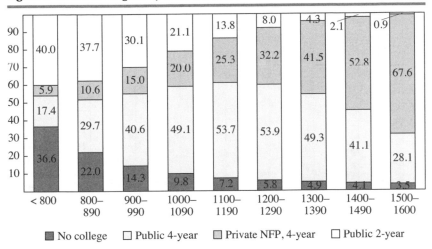

Source: College Board Data matched to National Student Clearinghouse, Cohort 2007.
Note: We include PSAT/SAT takers regardless of the timing of the college enrollment (approximately 2 million students). We exclude a small number of students who enrolled in for-profit sector or nonprofit two-year institutions (30K), and we also exclude students who do not have reported or predicted income (300K). We calculate predicted SAT score for students who only took PSAT. We do this by finding average SAT by PSAT bins (each section separately) for students who took both PSAT and SAT.

combined math and verbal SAT scores between 1000 and 1390 enroll in four-year public colleges. One important difference in enrollment patterns is that a much larger proportion of low-income students enroll in two-year public colleges or do not enroll in college compared to high-income students (except perhaps for students at the very top of the SAT distribution).

I.C. Fact 3. Graduation Rates Are Lower at Public than at Private Colleges

One concern about public colleges is that their graduation rates are lower than those at private colleges.[12] Figure 6 shows the six-year graduation rates by range of PSAT/SAT score for individual students in the high school graduating class of 2007. In the lower ranges of SAT scores, high-income students have the highest six-year bachelor's degree completion rates, with little difference between the graduation rates for those at four-year

12. National Center for Education Statistics, Digest of Education Statistics, table 326.10, https://nces.ed.gov/programs/digest/d17/tables/dt17_326.10.asp.

Figure 5a. Choice of Program by SAT/PSAT Score for Low-Income Students

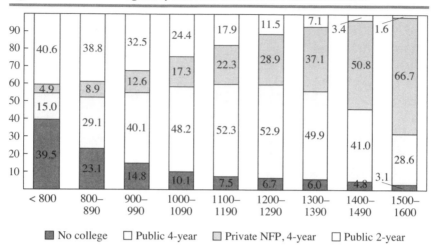

Source: College Board Data matched to National Student Clearinghouse, Cohort 2007.
Note: We include PSAT/SAT takers regardless of the timing of the college enrollment (approximately 2 million students). We exclude a small number of students who enrolled in for-profit sector or nonprofit two-year institutions (30K), and we also exclude students who do not have reported or predicted income (300K). We calculate predicted SAT score for students who took only PSAT by finding average SAT by PSAT bins (each section separately) for students who took both PSAT and SAT.

Figure 5b. Choice of Program by SAT/PSAT for High-Income Students

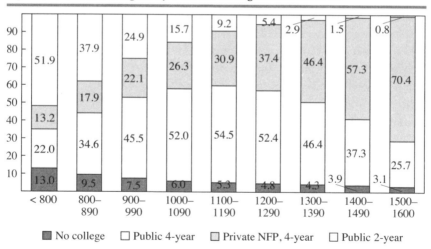

Source: College Board Data matched to National Student Clearinghouse, Cohort 2007.
Note: We include PSAT/SAT takers regardless of the timing of the college enrollment (approximately 2 million students). We exclude a small number of students who enrolled in for-profit sector or nonprofit two-year institutions (30K), and we also exclude students who do not have reported or predicted income (300K). We calculate predicted SAT score for students who took only PSAT by finding average SAT by PSAT bins (each section separately) for students who took both PSAT and SAT.

Figure 6. Six-Year Bachelor's Degree Completion Rates by SAT/PSAT Score, Family Income, and Institution Sector

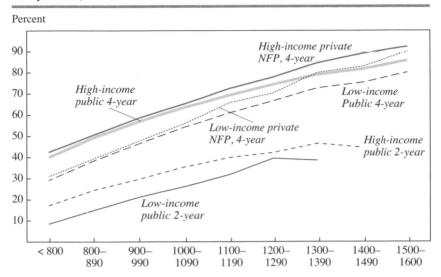

Source: College Board data matched to National Student Clearinghouse (NSC).

Note: The sample includes PSAT/SAT takers in the 2007 high school graduating cohort who enrolled in public or private nonprofit colleges on time (within 180 days of graduating from high school). Low-income category includes students with family income of less than $40,000; high-income refers to students with family income of $100,000 or more. Six-year bachelor's degree completion rate from first institution attended is calculated among students who first enroll in four-year sector. Otherwise, for students who first enroll in two-year sector, NSC tracks bachelor's degree completion at first four institutions a student attended. We calculate estimated SAT score for students who only took PSAT.

private versus public colleges. In the middle ranges of SAT scores, from 1000–1090 to 1300–1390, where figure 4 shows that approximately half of students enroll in four-year public colleges, graduation rates for private and public colleges gradually diverge. As shown in figure 6, low-income students enrolled at four-year private colleges actually have higher graduation rates than high-income students enrolled at four-year public colleges. Figure 6 also illustrates a striking differential between bachelor's degree completion rates for students enrolling at two-year versus four-year colleges within each SAT category.[13]

13. The positive outcome reported in figure 6 is six-year bachelor's degree completion from first college for students who initially enroll at a four-year college, while for other students the positive outcome is completion at any of the four-year colleges that the National Student Clearinghouse tracks. So this measure is skewed, if anything, toward underestimating the difference in bachelor's degree completion rates for those starting at a four-year college by comparison to students in the same SAT category who start at a two-year college.

I.D. Fact 4. Graduation Rates Are Particularly Low at Two-Year Public Colleges

Less than 25 percent of recent high school graduates who enroll in two-year public colleges complete an associate degree within three years. By contrast, approximately 60 percent of high school graduates who enroll in two-year private colleges complete an associate degree within three years.[14] (The two-year private sector is quite small, covering only about 1 percent of recent high school graduates.) A total of 37.5 percent of recent high school graduates who enroll in two-year colleges complete a degree within six years of high school graduation, with 14.7 percent of them completing bachelor's degrees in that time. The average length of time to completion of first degree for those starting at a two-year public college is not very different from those starting at a four-year public college.[15]

I.E. Fact 5. Public Colleges Have Increased in Price over Time

If higher education is to be the engine of social mobility, it is critical for public colleges to be affordable for all students. One challenge to this ideal is the fact that tuition and fees have been steadily rising at all institutions but especially at public institutions. In constant 2019 dollars, tuition and fees at four-year public colleges more than doubled from $3,760 in 1990–91 to $10,440 in 2019–20, corresponding to an annual rate of increase more than 4 percent above and beyond the rate of inflation (Ma and others 2019, fig. 9). In comparison, tuition and fees at four-year private and two-year public colleges also increased steadily, but at a lower rate (between 2 percent and 3 percent per year) above and beyond the rate of inflation. Of course, it is important to consider not just sticker prices but net price. Using its annual survey of colleges, the College Board shows that net tuition, fees, and room and board at four-year public colleges has risen from $9,070 in 1999–00 to $15,380 in 2019–20 (all in 2019 dollars; Ma and others 2019, fig. 9).

I.F. Fact 6. Enrollment in Public College Has Expanded over Time, but Could Expand Even More

Two phenomena have led to increased absolute enrollment of recent high school graduates over time. First, after a brief decline at the end of the baby boom, the number of high school graduates has been increasing

---

14. National Center for Education Statistics, Digest of Education Statistics, table 326.20, https://nces.ed.gov/programs/digest/d18/tables/dt18_326.20.asp.

15. Authors' calculations based on data from appendix C in Shapiro and others (2017).

steadily from about 2.3 to 2.5 million per year in the early 1990s to about 3.2 million students per year from 2010 to 2016.[16] Second, as shown in figure 2, the proportion of high school graduates enrolling in college has increased to nearly 70 percent in recent years. To accommodate these increases in demand, some new colleges have opened and many existing colleges, especially public colleges, have expanded their class sizes (Kelly 2016).

These recent trends indicate that the capacity of seats for entering freshmen at many colleges is somewhat fluid and this makes it difficult to pinpoint a specific capacity constraint at (say) four-year public colleges. At any moment in time, there are substantially more students who graduate from high school each year with the academic qualifications for colleges of a given level of selectivity than the number who actually enroll at a college at least that selective. It is not clear, however, whether this apparent discrepancy in numbers indicates limited supply or limited demand for seats at four-year public colleges.

Geographic constraints may also be important to this discussion. Due to considerations of critical mass, the nearest public college to many households is a two-year rather than a four-year college. Similarly, since there is typically only one flagship public college per state, some households are located closer to a four-year public college that is not the flagship public college. Thus, the predilection for many students to choose a college that is proximate to their high school provides a systemic reason for a certain amount of undermatching.

The top panel of figure 7 shows that a small number of SAT-taking states—notably California, Texas, New York, and Florida—stand out in the number of undermatched students, though as shown in the bottom panel, those states do not especially stand out in terms of the percentage of undermatched students. Interestingly, these states are often lauded for the breadth and strength of their public college systems—in particular, their flagship public colleges are competitive with highly selective private colleges, meaning that even high-achieving students in these states tend to have a matched college option. In California, constraints on in-state enrollment are fairly explicit and are closely tied to negotiations over year-by-year state budgets. In the University of California system, for instance, some colleges systematically respond to negative budget shocks by reducing the number of seats for in-state students in the next year's class

---

16. National Center for Education Statistics, Digest of Education Statistics, https://nces. ed.gov/programs/digest/d17/tables/dt17_219.10.asp.

Figure 7. The Number and Proportion of Undermatched Students by State

Number

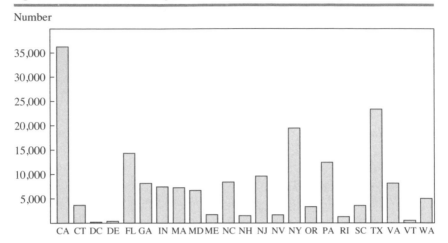

Percentage

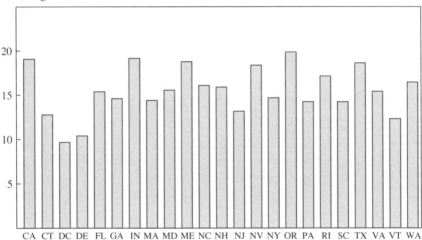

Source: College Board data matched to National Student Clearinghouse.

Note: Includes only students who enrolled in college on time (within 180 days of graduating from high school) and in states where the College Board has high PSAT/SAT coverage. Colleges are classified as a reach, match, safety, or undermatch following the definition established in Hoxby and Avery (2013) and used in Hoxby and Turner (2013). Essentially, the percentile of a student's SAT score is compared to the percentile associated with the average SAT score among students enrolled at their chosen college. If that difference is within five percentile points of zero in either direction, the student-college combination is considered an academic match. Lower academic-match colleges ("safety schools") are those with average SAT percentiles 5 to 15 points below the student's SAT percentile, while academic reaches are colleges with average SAT percentiles more than 5 points above the student's SAT percentile. We classify students as undermatched if they enroll in a college where their own SAT percentile is more than 15 points higher than the percentile of the college's average SAT. Institutions with admission rate of less than or equal to 20 percent are always considered reach colleges. For colleges that do not report average SAT/ACT in IPEDS, we calculate average SAT using a cohort of 2007 SAT takers.

(Leal 2015). The California State University (CSU) system has created a new designation of an "impacted" campus, as described on its website: "As you get ready to apply to the CSU, you may find that a campus or undergraduate major you're considering is 'impacted,' meaning there are more applications from qualified applicants than there are available spaces."[17] Seven CSU institutions (Cal Poly San Luis Obispo, Fresno State, CSU Fullerton, CSU Long Beach, Cal State Los Angeles, San Diego State, and San Jose State) are "impacted" at the campus level.

I.G. Fact 7. The Cost-Benefit Trade-off for Marginal College Students Is Unclear

The wage premium for a bachelor's degree has always been sufficient to make college an appealing financial investment—at least for those who are relatively likely to complete the degree (Avery and Turner 2012).[18] The cost-benefit computation for today's marginal college student, who might enroll at a two-year public college or a nonselective or less-selective four-year college, is not so clear (Athreya and Eberly forthcoming; Benson, Esteva, and Levy 2015). The trade-off between enrolling in college or entering the workforce may well turn on potential differences between marginal and average completion rates (Denning 2017) and the wage gains from magnitude of gains for attending "some college," which is still in question in the recent literature (Kane and Rouse 1999; Reynolds 2012; Mountjoy 2019). Further, an expected value calculation downplays the costs of a negative outcome, as students who do not complete college are several times more likely to default on student loans than those who do complete degrees (Baum 2016), and there may be long-lasting effects on consumption in general for those who enroll in college but do not complete a degree (Athreya and Eberly forthcoming). Given these considerations, it seems much more plausible to attempt to increase bachelor's degree completion rates with policies that target increases in completion rates for inframarginal college students rather than policies that attempt to increase college enrollment.

17. California State University, "Impaction at the CSU," accessed January 3, 2019, https://www2.calstate.edu/attend/impaction-at-the-csu.
18. See Ma, Pender, and Welch (2019), especially figure 2.1, for more recent estimates of average wages by postsecondary attainment. See also Zimmerman (2014) and Goodman, Hurwitz, and Smith (2017) for causal estimates of the value of enrolling at a four-year rather than a two-year public college.

II. Related Literature

The twin phenomena that many students begin college but do not graduate and that well less than half of adults in the United States have a bachelor's degree have been the object of study in the academic literature for quite some time. Turner (2004), Bound, Lovenheim, and Turner (2010), and Bowen, Chingos, and McPherson (2009) documented the fact that aggregate college completion rates were low and apparently stagnating. Denning, Eide, and Warnick (2019) observe that college completion rates have increased, though not dramatically, in recent years.

One specific strand of related literature focuses on the connection between college costs and college enrollment as well as completion. Dynarski (2000) and Cornwell, Mustard, and Sridhar (2006) found positive effects of the Georgia HOPE (merit) scholarship on college enrollment. Dynarski (2008) expanded this analysis to other state merit aid programs, estimating that these programs increase both college enrollment and completion, with effects being particularly strong for women. Many papers consider the effect of other policies that changed college prices or aid levels, typically finding a positive and significant effect of reduction in net costs on college enrollment (Dynarski 2003; Denning 2017).

A growing set of more recent studies uses regression discontinuity strategies to demonstrate a formal link between financial aid and college persistence and completion. Bettinger and others (2019) study the impacts of the California Cal Grant using discontinuities in program eligibility at high school GPA and income thresholds, finding that Cal Grant eligibility raises bachelor's degree attainment by 3–4 percentage points. Scott-Clayton (2011) examines the West Virginia Promise Scholarship and uses ACT score thresholds to calculate the scholarship's impact. She finds that Promise receipt raises four-year bachelor's degree completion by 6–7 percent. Scott-Clayton and Zafar (2019) find that the West Virginia Promise Scholarship has an impact on earnings, though in this study effects on college graduation fade out as a cohort progresses through college. Castleman and Long (2016) find a positive and significant effect of the Florida Student Assistance Grant (FSAG) on both enrollment and completion; their analysis is distinct because the eligibility for the program was determined by a cutoff in expected family contribution rather than academic attainment.

A second specific strand of related literature considers unequal outcomes by demographic background. Ellwood and Kane (2000) provided descriptive evidence to suggest that family income and academic achievement in high school were broadly equivalent predictors of college enrollment. Roderick and others (2008) and Bowen, Chingos, and McPherson (2009) introduced the concept of "undermatching," finding that low-income students are disproportionately likely not to enroll at one of the most selective colleges where they would likely be admitted.[19] Hoxby and Avery (2013) noted that many high-achieving, low-income students do not apply to the most selective schools. Hoxby and Turner (2013) followed this work by testing an intervention designed to widen the choice set of these low-income, high-achieving students and potentially lead to better matches between students and schools.

A growing set of more recent studies finds a causal link between undermatching and graduation: a quasi-randomly assigned student tends to adopt the graduation rate of her assigned college. Zimmerman (2014) and Goodman, Hurwitz, and Smith (2017) use regression discontinuity methods to compare the effects of college choice on students at the margin of two-year versus four-year college enrollment, finding large positive effects of four-year colleges by comparison to two-year colleges in promoting degree completion.

A different set of studies finds positive effects of attending a more selective four-year college rather than a less selective one. Hoekstra (2009) shows that students just over the margin of admission to a flagship four-year public college have earnings that are 20 percent greater than the earnings of similar students who just missed admission. In contrast, Cohodes and Goodman (2014) study students induced to attend an in-state public college by winning Massachusetts's John and Abigail Adams Scholarship. These students adopt the lower graduation of Massachusetts's public colleges relative to the more selective private colleges attended by students who just missed eligibility for the Adams Scholarship. Using a regression discontinuity in high school GPA to qualify to participate in the Bottom Line after-school guidance program, Castleman and Goodman (2018) and Barr and Castleman (2017) find that students counseled to apply to a set of selective four-year institutions have higher persistence than peers who did not receive the counseling.

A third strand of the literature considers the effects of state funding for public colleges on students. Bound and others (2019) find that public colleges respond to reductions in state appropriations by increasing the

---

19. See Smith, Pender, and Howell (2013) and Dillon and Smith (2017) for assessments of the prevalence of undermatching at the national level.

share of out-of-state students, particularly international students, if possible. As a result, the most selective four-year public institutions are implicitly insured against funding declines, but a perhaps unanticipated consequence of these funding cuts is a reduction in the proportion of in-state students at those institutions. Less selective public universities have diminished capacity to increase tuition revenue, so those colleges tend to reduce student services in response to funding cuts. Deming and Walters (2017) and Bound and others (2019) conclude that reductions in state funding lead to reductions in graduation rates at public colleges; Chakrabarti, Gorton, and Lovenheim (2018) find that reductions in state funding lead to significant reductions in measures of student financial success beyond age 30. Deming and Walters (2017) particularly find that spending on student support is linked to increased graduation rates.[20]

Several previous studies have conducted analyses related to the simulations we carry out below. Dynarski (2008) and Denning, Marx, and Turner (2018) estimate the social welfare effects of increases in grant aid.[21] Chingos (2012) and Howell and Pender (2016) simulate the effects of changes in enrollment across campuses to address undermatching of low-income students. Chingos (2012) takes the supply of college seats as fixed, so the reallocation of some low-income students to more selective colleges in that simulation requires a corresponding reallocation of other students to less selective colleges; it is not surprising that this approach is estimated to produce only second-order effects on bachelor's degree completion. Howell and Pender (2016) is the only one of these papers to conduct a simulation based on individual-level data. As in our simulations related to undermatching, Howell and Pender (2016) allow for expansion of seats at both public and private four-year colleges, but their analysis is primarily limited to undermatching and reallocation of low-income students to more selective colleges. Mayer and others (2015) conduct randomized evaluations of six different performance-based scholarship programs targeted to low-income students, estimating that these programs increase completion rates by 3.3 percentage points on average.

---

20. See also Clotfelter, Hemelt, and Ladd (2018) and Evans and others (2017) for related evidence that one-on-one guidance, academic or otherwise, can promote college completion.
21. See Deming and Walters (2017) for a detailed proposal for a dramatically expanded federal college grant program.

III. Data Description and Empirical Approach

The data come from a comprehensive merge of College Board data with National Student Clearinghouse data. Our study uses the entire 2007 cohort of students who took the SAT or PSAT (2.3 million students); this was the most recent cohort for which six-year graduation data were available at the time that we started this project.[22] We do not have data from the ACT and note that our sample is primarily applicable for states where the SAT is the most common college entrance exam. The sample includes PSAT takers as well as SAT takers, so it is not limited, even in ACT states, to students who intend to apply to selective schools. While selection into the sample likely limits our ability to make inferences about all college-bound seniors, it is much less of an issue in sixteen states, primarily those on the East Coast, where our data include 90 percent or more of all graduating high school seniors.[23]

Information on student demographic characteristics, including race or ethnicity, gender, family income, and parent's education, comes from the Student Data Questionnaire completed by students when they register for the SAT. We have self-reported information about family income for about 40 percent of the students in the sample (we are missing this information for students who took only the PSAT and for students who took the SAT but omitted an answer to this question). We use the method described in Howell and Pender (2016) to impute family income for the remaining students in the sample.

The National Student Clearinghouse (NSC) collects data from 3,600 participating colleges and universities, which represents 98 percent of enrolled students across the country. Participating institutions provide the NSC with student-level data on enrollment by semester, graduation date, degree earned, and duration of studies. For-profit colleges tend to be under-represented in the NSC data, particularly for the time period covered by

22. The sample includes PSAT/SAT takers in the 2007 high school graduating cohort who enrolled in nonprofit public or private colleges on time (within 180 days of graduating from high school) and have income data. We calculate estimated SAT score for students who took only PSAT. We do this by finding average SAT by PSAT bins (each section separately) for students who took both PSAT and SAT.

23. Very high coverage states include Georgia, Maryland, Delaware, Maine, the District of Columbia, Rhode Island, South Carolina, Florida, Nevada, New Jersey, North Carolina, Virginia, Massachusetts, Connecticut, New York, and Indiana. Coverage in Texas is roughly 88 percent.

our data (Dynarski, Hemelt, and Hyman 2015), but, as described above in our discussion of fact 2, only about 2 percent of recent high school graduates actually attend for-profit colleges.[24] We focus our analysis on those students who enroll in a two-year public, four-year public, or nonprofit four-year private college within six months of graduating from high school. Our main indicator for college graduation is bachelor's degree attainment within six years.[25]

Institutional net price data are from the Integrated Postsecondary Education Data System (IPEDS). For each of the undermatched students in our data set we estimate net price at both the chosen institution and the rematched institution. The IPEDS data provide institution-level information on the average SAT scores of students entering college in 2007–8 and instructional and total spending per student. We use these to estimate the total costs (that is, state, federal, and student) of moving a student from college A (an academic undermatch) to college B (an academic match).

Table 1 contains basic summary statistics on our sample. The sample is 45 percent male, 11 percent black, and 11 percent Hispanic. Sixteen percent of the students are from families with income less than $40,000 per year. Average SAT score in the sample is 1029.[26]

Table 2 provides summary statistics on students' initial college enrollment choice. Sixteen percent of students are undermatched, meaning these students have an SAT score percentile more than 15 percentile points greater than the average score percentile of students at the college in which they enroll. Fourteen percent of students enroll at a safety school, meaning a school with an average score within 5 to 15 percentile points below the student's own score. Academic match schools are those with an average SAT score that is within plus or minus 5 percentile points of the student's own score. Reach schools are those that have average SATs more than 5 percentile points above the student's score. Seventy-eight percent of students enroll in-state and 76 percent enroll at a two- or four-year public college. Twenty-six percent of enrollments are at two-year colleges.

24. Our reference for overall enrollment at for-profit colleges is the Digest of Education Statistics, which in turn references the Integrated Postsecondary Data System, which is distinct from NSC data.

25. Six-year bachelor's degree completion rate from first institution attended is calculated among students who first enrolled in a four-year sector. Otherwise, for students who first enrolled in a two-year sector, NSC tracks bachelor's degree completion at first four institutions a student attended.

26. The College Board redesigned the SAT and PSAT assessments in 2015. Our sample includes students who took these assessments prior to the substantial redesign.

Table 1. Summary Statistics Simulation Sample: 2007 Cohort

	Mean	SD	Min.	Max.
n = 1,388,012				
Student demographic characteristics				
Gender				
Male	0.449	0.497	0	1
Race/ethnicity				
White	0.659	0.474	0	1
Black	0.105	0.307	0	1
Hispanic	0.106	0.307	0	1
Asian	0.078	0.268	0	1
Other	0.052	0.222	0	1
Family income				
>$40K	0.160	0.366	0	1
$40K–70K	0.267	0.442	0	1
$70K–100k	0.350	0.477	0	1
>$100k	0.224	0.417	0	1
Parent's education				
HS or less	0.101	0.302	0	1
Some college	0.183	0.386	0	1
Bachelor's or higher	0.423	0.494	0	1
Missing	0.293	0.455	0	1
Student academic characteristics				
PSAT or SAT score/100	10.29	1.93	4	16
PSAT taker	0.849	0.358	0	1
SAT taker	0.781	0.414	0	1
Number of days between HS graduation and college entrance	73.85	10.60	0	179

Source: College Board Data matched to National Student Clearinghouse.

IV. Methodology

We conduct four different simulations of policy changes designed to promote bachelor's degree completion at public colleges. Two of these policies are tied to absolute goals and necessarily have different total (or per student) costs: (1) eliminating tuition at two-year colleges; and (2) ensuring sufficient supply of seats at selective public colleges to eliminate undermatching within a state. The other two policies—(3) reducing tuition and (4) increasing funding for academic support—could be calibrated to match the cost of any other policy. Since the first two policies are not equal in costs, we chose round number targets for the reduction in tuition and for the increase in funding in our simulations. We use cost-benefit ratios as the standard for comparison of the efficacies of these four policies with regard to bachelor's degree completion rates (the focus of the paper)

Table 2. College Characteristics by Initial Enrollment Choice: 2007 Cohort

	Mean	*SD*	*Min.*	*Max.*
Percentage graduating within six years	0.502	0.500	0	1
Academic alignment with first college				
Undermatch	0.164	0.370	0	1
Safety	0.136	0.342	0	1
Match	0.247	0.431	0	1
Reach	0.453	0.498	0	1
Enrolled in-state	0.778	0.415	0	1
Enrolled in public two-year or four-year college	0.757	0.429	0	1
First college characteristics				
Average college SAT/ACT				
≥ 1300	0.059	0.236	0	1
1200–1290	0.100	0.299	0	1
1100–1190	0.230	0.421	0	1
1000–1090	0.212	0.409	0	1
< 1000	0.137	0.343	0	1
Two-year	0.263	0.440	0	1
Number of full-time first-time undergraduates (100s)	22.998	18.597	0.07	75.88
Tuition and fees, 2007–08 ($k)	10.035	10.049	0.48	39.24
Net tuition and fees ($)	5,856	6,505	−3,294	29,737
Number receiving any financial aid	1,694	1,469	6	6,523
Percentage receiving any financial aid	73.755	18.286	14	100
Instruction expenses per FTE ($k)	8.263	6.960	0	78.381
Size				
< 5K	0.210	0.407	0	1
5–10K	0.183	0.387	0	1
10–20K	0.245	0.430	0	1
> 20K	0.361	0.480	0	1
Urbanicity				
City	0.564	0.496	0	1
Suburban	0.228	0.419	0	1
Town	0.130	0.336	0	1
Rural	0.079	0.270	0	1
Region				
New England	0.079	0.270	0	1
Mideast United States	0.220	0.414	0	
Great Lakes	0.122	0.327	0	1
Plains	0.041	0.199	0	1
Southeast	0.251	0.434	0	1
Southwest	0.098	0.297	0	1
Rocky Mountains	0.025	0.155	0	1
Far West	0.164	0.370	0	1

Source: College Board Data matched to National Student Clearinghouse.

and projected median income. We also consider the effects of the policy of eliminating tuition at two-year colleges on the left tail of the income distribution.

Our primary goal is to produce a broad-brush ranking of the four policy options to see if any policy seems to dramatically outperform or underperform the others. Since there are multiple sources of underlying uncertainty in each case, we do not attempt to produce confidence intervals for any of our cost-benefit measures.[27] Instead, we provide bounds in terms of underlying elasticities to provide context for assessing the magnitude of differences in our results, that is, how much would our underlying elasticity values have to change for each pairwise cost-benefit comparison to reverse in order?

IV.A. Identifying Elasticity Values

Each policy either changes enrollment patterns (directly or indirectly through changes in prices), improves graduation rates conditional on enrollment at a particular college, or both. Our simulations use a set of elasticities to quantify the separate effects of each aspect of these policies. We use recent empirical studies to guide our choices for these elasticity values. We summarize our modeling choices in this section; see online appendix C for more details about how and why we chose these particular values for the elasticities. Below we discuss the degree to which our chosen elasticities may not apply to the marginal students in our hypothetical national-level policy. In particular, the marginal students in our simulations may have lower academic ability and smaller graduation elasticities than some of the students in well-identified studies in the existing literature.

ELASTICITIES FOR TUITION CHANGES AT THE TWO-YEAR ENROLLMENT MARGIN Several states have eliminated tuition for two-year public colleges. While it is too early to assess the long-term effects of these policies, recent difference-in-differences analyses provide estimates of enrollment effects of changes in price for two-year colleges in Oregon (Gurantz 2019; Cox and others 2018) and Tennessee (Carruthers 2019; Carruthers, Fox, and Jepsen 2018; Tennessee Higher Education Commission 2019). We use the average implied elasticities from these two states to identify the price elasticities for enrollment at two margins: (1) four-year college versus two-year public college and (2) no college versus two-year public college.

---

27. In our Monte Carlo simulations, draws in which elasticities are all set at the most extreme values in the literature imply massive high or low benefits to the policies. Thus, the confidence intervals on our estimated benefits are very wide until we are willing to hone in on what we think are the most credible elasticity estimates in the literature.

The results reported by Carruthers (2019) imply an elasticity of .265 for the movement of not enrolled students into the two-year public sector. By contrast, the results reported by Gurantz (2019) imply an elasticity of .135. We average these two numbers and use an elasticity of .20. To estimate the elasticity of four-year students to enroll in two-year public institutions with respect to the two-year price, we again average results from the two studies and arrive at an elasticity of .075.[28] We think of these elasticities as being roughly the ones we want to use for our national simulation. That is to say that these two states have implemented policies similar to what a national-level policy would be like, so we think of the Carruthers (2019) and Gurantz (2019) studies as studying students at the same margin as those in our simulation.

ELASTICITIES FOR TUITION CHANGES ON FOUR-YEAR ENROLLMENT We consider a range of studies—the Cal Grant (Bettinger and others 2019), Social Security benefits (Dynarski 2003), the Florida Student Assistance Grant (Castleman and Long 2016), and the West Virginia Promise Scholarship (Deming and Walters 2017; Scott Clayton 2011)—to inform our choice of price elasticity of enrollment at the no college/four-year public college margin. These studies are not precisely comparable; several of them study policies with eligibility requirements and so pertain to students with particular and distinct characteristics.

We summarize many of the papers in this literature in online appendix A. The modal finding in this literature is that $1,000 in aid (translated to 2019 dollars) raises enrollment in four-year colleges by 2–3 percentage points. We took five of the most well-identified studies in the literature (the five listed above) and translated the findings into elasticities of enrollment with respect to price of between 0 and 9 percent; a 100 percent drop in the price of four-year public colleges increases enrollment by 0–9 percent of baseline enrollment. For example, Castleman and Long (2016) study a 57 percent tuition subsidy in Florida. This leads to increased four-year enrollment of 3.2 percentage points on a base of 61 percentage points. The implied elasticity of enrollment with respect to price is $(.032/.61)/.57 = .09$. We use an elasticity of .07 for our simulations.

We use results from Bettinger and others (2019) to identify the price elasticity of enrollment for switching from four-year private college to four-year public college in a response to a change in the relative price of

---

28. Technically we mean price elasticities of −.265, −.135, −.20, and so forth. Most of the literature and our simulations are estimating the positive impacts of price reductions, which is why we are reporting positive elasticities with respect to a price cut.

the two. The logic is that Cal Grant eligibility is a large reduction in the relative cost of attending a private in-state school and the discontinuity in eligibility identifies the impact of that price change. We also considered the results of Cohodes and Goodman (2014), which finds a larger price elasticity at the four-year private/four-year public margin, as well as Castleman and Long (2016), which estimates a price elasticity close to zero at this enrollment margin. Results from the Cal Grant study imply a price elasticity of switching from four-year private to four-year public of .22, while results from the FSAG study imply a price elasticity of 0 and the Adams Scholarship evidence implies an elasticity of 1.45. We combine these estimates into our preferred elasticity of .50.

ELASTICITIES FOR PRICE CHANGES ON COMPLETION RATES Carruthers, Fox, and Jepsen (2018) estimate that eliminating community college tuition increased the completion rate for associate degrees by 1 percentage point for students in Knox County, Tennessee, on an intention-to-treat basis; this estimate is drawn from their analysis of the results of Knox Achieves, the predecessor to the statewide program, Tennessee Promise, which is currently active. This is from a base of 4 percentage points of people earning an associate degree and would imply an elasticity of .25. But most of this increase likely stems from the additional 5 percentage points of the cohort attending community college, as opposed to a price effect on graduation holding community college attendance constant. Denning (2017) finds an elasticity of zero for the effect of community college tuition on associate degree completion. For our simulations we use a modest elasticity of .05.

We use Bettinger and others (2019) for our estimate of the elasticity of bachelor's degree completion with respect to community college tuition for students already enrolled in community college. In online appendix B, Bettinger and others (2019) find a 3 percentage point impact on bachelor's degree attainment for students intending to enroll in community college at the time they file the Cal Grant application. The 3 percentage point effect averages across the income and GPA discontinuities studied. The Cal Grant is essentially a 100 percent price cut on all tuition and fees (both two- and four-year institutions across four years of funding). We assume that the community college portion of the tuition cut represents only 10 percent of the total complete tuition cut that such bachelor's degree–bound community college students experience. Hence a community college tuition price cut would have one-tenth the impact on bachelor's degree attainment that the full Cal Grant program has for community college students. The 3 percentage point impact for the Cal Grant in bachelor's degree completion is on a base of 36 percentage points. This implies an elasticity of bachelor's degree completion with respect to community college tuition of $(.03/.36)/10 = .008$.

We use the overall estimated effect of the Cal Grant on bachelor's degree completion rates—an increase of 4.6 or 3.0 percentage points across all sectors for an offer of a 100 percent reduction in price in any sector (again on an intention-to-treat basis)—to estimate the change in bachelor's degree completion rates conditional on enrollment.[29] Since the 3.0 and 4.6 percentage point graduation rate increases are on a base of 46 percentage points, this implies an average elasticity of graduation with respect to price of $[(.03 + .046)/(2 \times .46)]/1 = .08$.

ELASTICITIES FOR FUNDING/SPENDING CHANGES We draw elasticities for the effect of changes in funding for public colleges from Deming and Walters (2017). This paper has among the most credible estimates to date of the effects from changes in spending at public colleges. The authors' instrument for spending per student uses state budget shocks and legislated tuition caps and freezes.

We assume that changes in spending that result from increases in funding are concentrated in the most efficient use (academic support), as identified by Deming and Walters (2017), for promoting bachelor's degree completion. We use the spending/enrollment elasticities implied by the estimates from Deming and Walters's (2017) tables 3 and 4. Specifically, we use an enrollment elasticity of spending of 1.05 for two-year public and 0.66 for four-year public colleges, and a degree completion elasticity of spending of 1.46 for associate degrees at two-year public colleges and 0.46 for bachelor's degrees at four-year public colleges.[30] Deming and Walters (2017) make the point that since these bachelor's degree attainments are two years after the shock (as opposed to four or more years after), these elasticities likely represent the impacts of spending shocks on persistence and graduation for already enrolled students. This is exactly the elasticity we want for our simulation.

---

29. Carruthers, Fox, and Jepsen (2018) estimate a negative net effect of Knox Achieves on bachelor's degree completion but do not attempt to disentangle the separate effects of (1) increased enrollment at two-year colleges, drawing students both from four-year college and noncollege options; (2) the effect of the elimination of community college tuition on graduation rates for students. The elasticity values we use for bachelor's degree completion rates are broadly consistent with their findings.

30. These estimates may seem unexpectedly large given that students would likely have little information about funding and spending changes at public colleges. One possibility is that admissions officers respond to spending increases by accepting more applicants, perhaps surmising that the funding increase will allow the college to serve more students.

EFFECTS OF EDUCATIONAL ATTAINMENT ON INCOME We use a background value of 9 percent return per year of education; this estimate is within the range of 6–10 percent suggested by the review study by Gunderson and Oreopoulos (2010). We further assume that students who enroll but do not attain a particular degree complete 50 percent of the years of education required for the degree—one year for those enrolling at two-year colleges and two years of postsecondary education for those enrolling at four-year colleges.

IV.B. Details of the Simulations

Our price- or spending-based policy simulations (free community college, increased spending at public colleges, and lower tuition at four-year public colleges) use three basic steps: (1) Students always start with their actual institutional choice and actual degree(s) earned. (2) We then add the relevant policy shock, which lowers tuition and fees or increases spending. The shock leads each student to have some (modest) probability that they switch across educational sectors within their home state. A sector is defined as not enrolled, two-year public, four-year public, or four-year private. (3) We then compute expected outcomes in the new sector.

For each student we estimate a probability of switching sectors. This estimate is the interaction of the general price elasticity for that switch (for example, not enrolled to enrolled in two-year public) taken from the literature *and* a student-specific probability of choosing that sector. The latter comes from an ordinary least squares (OLS) regression using our full data set and actual outcomes. For example, every student has their own predicted probability of choosing the two year public sector given state of residence, family income, SAT scores, gender, race, and age. The tuition elasticity for not enrolled students to switch to two-year public colleges is .2, which is the average elasticity estimated from the Oregon and Tennessee policies. This .2 estimate is then scaled up or down (in a mean preserving way) for each not enrolled student given the student's propensity to choose a two-year public college.

The probability of bachelor's degree or associate degree attainment can vary for two reasons. First, each policy affects graduation probability, holding institution constant via lowering price (or raising spending). Second, each policy can also affect associate degree or bachelor's degree attainment by altering the probability that a student is in a given sector.[31]

---

31. We also include the second-order effect that students can switch sectors and face the new (more favorable) price or spending per student regime in that sector.

Each student has a probability (predicted value) of obtaining a bachelor's (or associate) degree given an educational sector. These predicted values come from OLS regressions in which we predict a student's outcome for each sector given state, SAT scores, family income, race, age, and gender.

We predict earnings for students at baseline and given the policy shock. We predict earnings conditional on choosing a given educational sector using an OLS regression and all student characteristics including home state. Baseline earnings are simply the medians from Chetty and others (2017), who calculate median earnings for students who begin their educational career at a given institution (or no institution). These earnings are then modified in the simulation because sector may change under the new policy or graduation probability may change even given the original institution.

Given the probability of changing sectors and the new graduation probabilities (both at the old institution and the new sector), we can then calculate outcomes under the new policy. The outcomes are the probabilistic blend of the student's original outcome, which inherently gets the most weight, the probability that the student switches to a different sector, and the student's predicted outcomes for that new sector.[32] We also include the effects on attainment and earnings that stem from higher graduation probabilities, holding institution/sector constant.

When students change sectors, they are assigned an estimated graduation probability and estimated earnings which are specific to the student's state, test scores, and demographics. For price and spending simulations (other than BISPO), we do not assign the student to a specific new institution but rather give the predicted outcomes, which are a student-specific amalgam across institutions the student might attend within that sector.

A given policy shock can have very different price change implications for students with different characteristics (for example, high- versus low-income students; student in California versus Texas). We estimate a student-specific net cost of attendance at both the actual initial school choice and at a potential new choice of educational sector in response to a given policy change. We perform this calculation using IPEDS data and the student's state and family income. For the initial institution chosen we use the average net price faced by students at that institution with the same family income. We use the IPEDS figure for that institution and family income category. For prices a student faces in other educational sectors

---

32. We assume that students who originally attained a particular degree will attain at least that same degree if they do not change colleges as a result of a particular policy.

(for example, two-year public, four-year public) after the policy shock, we assume that the student faces the average net price (post policy shock) in the sector within the student's state and family income category. These average prices are weighted by the number of students in that state-sector-income category.

As mentioned above, the marginal student in our national simulations likely differs from the marginal student in the best identified studies in the literature. For example, nearly all of the students in the Cal Grant study are college bound and 46 percent of that sample completes a bachelor's degree. Our simulations deal with this mismatch in two ways. First we are not imposing that our marginal entrants have the average level of bachelor's degree attainment. Rather our predicted graduation probabilities are specific to the student and are estimates (via OLS) using all available demographics and SAT/PSAT scores. Hence our marginal students are already estimated to have significantly lower probabilities of bachelor's degree completion than average students. The elasticities in the simulation are applied to these lower probabilities. Furthermore we have robustness checks in which we assume that the actual price elasticities with respect to graduation are half of our preferred elasticity estimates from the literature.

V. Results

We report results for a given set of outcomes for each of our simulations: cost per student, enrollment, degree completion, and projected median income. For each student we have the results in practice from the College Board and National Student Clearinghouse data *and* simulated outcomes for these same variables. We report both actual and simulated averages for these variables for each of the four policy shocks that we consider.

V.A. Free Community College

We first consider a policy that eliminates tuition at two-year public colleges. We maintain enrollments at specific colleges for students who do not change colleges as a result of this policy. If a student is induced by the policy to switch to the two-year sector, we assign that student to a (fictitious) college with the average characteristics of all two-year public colleges in the student's home state. There are three mechanisms by which the policy affects projected outcomes: (1) it increases degree completion probabilities (both associate and bachelor's) for students who enrolled originally at two-year public colleges; (2) it induces some students who would not have enrolled to enroll at two-year public colleges; and (3) it induces some students to switch from four-year to two-year colleges, thereby increasing their chances of competing an associate degree, but reducing their chances of completing a bachelor's degree.

As shown in table 3a, our simulation yields a 6.5 percentage point increase in enrollment at two-year colleges, from 27.5 to 34 percent of high school graduates, along with a corresponding 3.3 percentage point decrease in enrollment at four-year colleges. Since the net change in enrollment at four-year colleges is roughly half the magnitude of the net change in enrollment at two-year colleges, the number of students who move from four-year to two-year colleges is roughly equal to the number of students who move from no college to a two-year college in this simulation.

We project a bachelor's degree completion rate of less than 10 percent for students who did not enroll in the baseline case and who are induced to enroll in a two-year college as a result of this policy. This relatively low completion rate reflects the fact that students at the margin between no college and two-year college tend to have less than average academic credentials. But we also project a reduction in bachelor's degree completion rate of approximately 40 percentage points for students induced to move from a four-year to a two-year public college as a result of the policy. Combining these effects, we find a net increase in the percentage of students completing an associate degree along with a slightly smaller reduction in the percentage of students completing a bachelor's degree. In the full sample of students, these two effects roughly offset each other with regard to earning potential; we project minimal change in median income overall.

The cost per year of this policy is relatively low (about $566 per student enrolling in a two-year public college and approximately $200 per high school graduate) both because tuition levels are much lower in two-year colleges than in four-year colleges and because students (for example, those receiving Pell Grants) pay less than full tuition in any case.[33] As shown in table 3a, we project little to no effect of the policy for low-income students, because those students typically qualify for Pell Grants and often already have zero net cost for attending a two-year public college.

Our choice of bachelor's degree completion rates and median income as outcome measures is not wholly appropriate for evaluating a free community college policy because that policy is targeted, in large part,

---

33. The free college policy that has been enacted in most states is a "last dollar" policy, whereby there is still a list price for enrolling in a two-year public college and the state covers only the remaining cost of attendance after accounting for all other sources of aid for a student.

Table 3a. Simulation of Free Community College Policy on Enrollments, Graduation, and Earnings

	All students			Low-income students		
	N	Mean	SD	N	Mean	SD
Net tuition and fees original ($)	1,806,094	4697.06	5873.76	291,567	614.31	1848.18
Net tuition, fees, room and board original ($)	1,805,428	13034.60	7328.89	291,353	11063.20	6058.95
Size of community college subsidy ($)	629,182	566.71	799.05	131,896		
Size of community college subsidy including zeroes ($)	2,291,621	201.46	480.88	390,728		
Start at two-year institution	2,291,621	0.275	0.447	390,728	0.338	0.473
Start at four-year institution	2,291,621	0.521	0.500	390,728	0.414	0.493
Not enrolled	2,291,621	0.204	0.403	390,728	0.248	0.432
Start at two-year institution new	2,291,621	0.340	0.412	390,728	0.365	0.458
Start at four-year institution new	2,291,621	0.488	0.469	390,728	0.402	0.479
Not enrolled new	2,291,621	0.172	0.343	390,728	0.233	0.409
Obtain bachelor's degree within six years original	2,291,621	0.386	0.487	390,728	0.250	0.433
Obtain bachelor's degree within six years new	2,291,621	0.376	0.464	390,728	0.247	0.424
Obtain associate degree within four years original	2,291,621	0.058	0.233	390,728	0.065	0.247
Obtain associate degree within four years new	2,291,621	0.070	0.229	390,728	0.071	0.245
Expected median income original ($)	1,986,342	36209.7	15734.7	338,991	32704.5	14095.2
Expected median income new ($)	1,986,342	36147.5	14744.8	338,991	32738.5	13669.6

Source: College Board Data matched to National Student Clearinghouse.

Note: Using the entire cohort of SAT/PSAT takers, we simulate the impacts of free community college on student choices and outcomes. We show outcomes for all students and for low-income students (family income <$40k). Predicted earnings and graduation vary at the student level and are dependent on student demographics, state, and test scores. Elasticities of enrollment and graduation with respect to the price of community college are taken from the literature as described in the text and summarized in online appendix C.

Table 3b. Simulation of Free Community College Policy: Detailed Results
for Educational Attainment

Attainment level	Original (actual outcome)	Free community college (projected outcome)
Percentage of students in the sample at each level of educational attainment		
No college	20.4	17.2
Some college, no degree	35.2	38.2
Associate degree	5.8	7.0
Bachelor's degree	38.6	37.6
Cumulative distribution for educational attainment		
No college	20.4	17.2
Some college, no degree	55.6	55.4
Associate degree	61.4	62.4
Bachelor's degree	100	100

Source: College Board Data matched to National Student Clearinghouse.

to students who would not otherwise attend college. The issue is that substantial improvements in outcomes for these students might not have any effect on either median income or bachelor's degree completion. Table 3b reports the partial and cumulative distributions for educational attainment to highlight the likely distributional effects of the free community college policy. Of particular importance, we project that the free community college policy yields a 3.2 percentage point reduction (from 20.4 percent to 17.2 percent) for not attending college and a corresponding 3 percentage point increase (from 35.2 percent to 38.2 percent) for attending college but not receiving a degree. Thus, we might expect this projected shift from "No college" to "Some college, no degree" to influence outcomes somewhat below the median, perhaps around the 20th to 30th percentile of the income distribution. From this perspective, a possible positive effect of the free community college policy is that students who are prompted to enroll by this policy but who do not earn any degree might still derive higher lifetime incomes as a result of their time in college.

A counterweight to this view is the fact that our simulations also do not include a provision to account for any lasting effects of student debt. Baum (2016) and others observe that default rates are especially high for student borrowers who spend a year or less in college. Some students may need to borrow to enroll even if community college is free; it is not certain that these students would benefit financially from attending community college but not completing a degree.

Since our sample consists of PSAT/SAT takers, it may tend to exclude less academically oriented students who disproportionately opt out of taking either of these standardized tests. For this reason, there could be an even greater absolute response to a free community college policy than is indicated in our simulations, as students who are excluded from our data are relatively unlikely to enroll in college. The direction of this selection effect on our cost-benefit estimates is not clear, as these students who are omitted from the sample are also presumably relatively unlikely to complete college if they are induced to enroll by a policy intervention. In any case, the results of our simulations remain qualitatively consistent with descriptive statistics provided in early analyses of the Oregon program and Tennessee Promise (Gurantz 2019; Carruthers, Fox, and Jepsen 2018), and as discussed above, our data cover at least 90 percent of high school graduates in sixteen states.

An important point raised by our discussants is that explicitly advertising community college as *free* can have larger effects than a similar-sized price subsidy (for example, the Pell Grant) that is more complex, requires an application, has a set of requirements, and may not cover all of tuition and fees. We agree; our simulation is calibrated to the Tennessee and Oregon shocks where an advertised promise of free community college was put in place. Our other tuition reduction simulations are not as closely matched to an actual state policy.

Another important point raised by our discussants is that our analysis does not account for the effect of free community college on students who would otherwise enroll in a for-profit college. In fact, students at community colleges have somewhat better job prospects than do students at for-profit colleges, while graduation rates and default rates on loans are quite similar for community colleges and for-profit colleges (Looney and Yannelis 2015). Given the small proportion (about 2 percent) of recent high school graduates who enroll in for-profit colleges, these aggregate results suggest that our results would not change much if we were able to identify and include all students who enrolled at for-profit colleges in our analysis.

V.B. Reduced Tuition at Four-Year Colleges

We consider two policies that reduce tuition and fees at four-year public colleges. The first is a 10 percent reduction in tuition and fees for all students. The second policy eliminates tuition and fees at four-year public colleges for students with family income less than $60,000; this second policy is inspired by Illinois Commitment, which uses a similar threshold but only includes the flagship state college (whereas our analysis considers a policy that extends to all in-state four-year public colleges).

Reductions in tuition and fees at four-year public colleges affect long-term outcomes through two channels: first, by improving graduation rates for students who enrolled in a four-year public college in the baseline case; and second, by inducing some students to change plans and enroll in the four-year public sector. We assume that there is a single four-year public college option for students not already enrolling at a particular four-year public college; this single fictitious college has the average characteristics of the four-year public colleges in the state.[34] As a result, students face a price change in the four-year sector that is specific to the student's state and income level.

As shown in table 4a, our simulation of a 10 percent reduction in tuition and fees yields a 1.2 percentage point increase in enrollment at four-year public colleges and a .2 percentage point decrease in enrollment at two-year public colleges. The biggest projected effect on enrollment, however, is a shift of students from four-year private to four-year public colleges. The overall result is a modest increase of .3 percentage points in bachelor's degree completion; one reason that this increase is not larger is that students induced to change from four-year private to four-year public colleges typically reduce their chances of graduation by doing so (Cohodes and Goodman 2014). At the same time, the cost of the reduction in tuition and fees is not that large. As with the elimination of tuition at two-year colleges, the average cost per student affected by the change is not that large, on the order of about $400 per year in 2007 dollars (less than $200 per year after averaging over all students).

As shown in table 4b, our simulation of elimination of tuition and fees at four-year public colleges for students from families with income below $60,000 yields a 3.1 percentage point increase in enrollment at four-year public colleges and a .8 percentage point decrease in enrollment at two-year public colleges. We project lower-income students (with family income less than $40,000) to exhibit a substantial response to this policy, with a 4.0 percentage point increase in enrollment at four-year colleges, a 9.1 percentage point increase in enrollment at four-year public colleges, and a net increase of 2.9 percentage points in bachelor's degree completion. The

---

34. We made a specific choice not to assume that a student who moves into the four-year sector enrolls at the college that best matches their academic credentials, as this assumption would implicitly incorporate elements of the fourth policy that we consider—eliminating undermatching.

Table 4a. Simulation of Reduced Tuition at Public Four-Year Colleges: Impacts on Enrollments, Graduation, and Earnings

	All students			Low-income students		
	N	*Mean*	*SD*	*N*	*Mean*	*SD*
Net tuition and fees original ($)	1,806,094	4697.06	5873.76	291,567	614.31	1848.18
Net tuition, fees, room and board original ($)	1,805,428	13034.58	7328.89	291,353	11063.22	6058.95
Reduction in tuition at public four years ($)	781,811	399.10	340.83	115,840	18.45	69.95
Reduction in tuition at public four years including zeroes ($)	2,291,621	188.44	270.14	390,728	7.52	39.64
Start at two-year institution	2,291,621	0.275	0.447	390,728	0.338	0.473
Start at four-year institution	2,291,621	0.521	0.500	390,728	0.414	0.493
Start at four-year public institution	2,291,621	0.348	0.476	390,728	0.302	0.459
Not enrolled	2,291,621	0.204	0.403	390,728	0.248	0.432
Start at two-year institution new	2,291,621	0.273	0.443	390,728	0.336	0.470
Start at four-year institution new	2,291,621	0.525	0.496	390,728	0.418	0.489
Start at four-year public institution new	2,291,621	0.360	0.468	390,728	0.311	0.453
Not enrolled new	2,291,621	0.202	0.400	390,728	0.246	0.429
Obtain bachelor's degree within six years original	2,291,621	0.386	0.487	390,728	0.250	0.433
New bachelor's degree rate within six years	2,291,621	0.389	0.484	390,728	0.253	0.430
Expected median income original ($)	1,986,342	36209.7	15734.7	338,991	32704.5	14095.2
Expected median income new ($)	1,986,342	36147.5	14744.8	338,991	32738.5	13669.6

Source: College Board Data matched to National Student Clearinghouse.

Note: We simulate the impacts of a 10 percent cut in tuition and fees at each four-year public college. Responses of enrollment and graduation to tuition and fees are taken from estimates in the literature as detailed in online appendix C and the text.

Table 4b. Simulation of Zero Tuition for Students with Family Income Less than $60,000 at Public Four-Year Colleges: Impacts on Enrollments, Graduation, and Earnings

	All students			Low-income students		
	N	Mean	SD	N	Mean	SD
Net tuition and fees original ($)	1,806,094	4697.06	5873.76	291,567	614.31	1848.18
Net tuition, fees, room and board original ($)	1,805,428	13034.58	7328.89	291,353	11063.22	6058.95
Reduction in tuition at public four years ($)	228,361	1973.85	2885.09	115,840	184.54	699.52
Reduction in tuition at public four years including zeroes ($)	2,291,621	264.38	1131.04	390,728	75.23	396.43
Start at two-year institution	2,291,621	0.275	0.447	390,728	0.338	0.473
Start at four-year institution	2,291,621	0.521	0.500	390,728	0.414	0.493
Start at four-year public institution	2,291,621	0.348	0.476	390,728	0.302	0.459
Not enrolled	2,291,621	0.204	0.403	390,728	0.248	0.432
Start at two-year institution new	2,291,621	0.267	0.435	390,728	0.315	0.441
Start at four-year institution new	2,291,621	0.534	0.487	390,728	0.454	0.460
Start at four-year public institution new	2,291,621	0.379	0.464	390,728	0.393	0.422
Not enrolled new	2,291,621	0.198	0.393	390,728	0.231	0.403
Obtain bachelor's degree within six years original	2,291,621	0.386	0.487	390,728	0.250	0.433
New bachelor's degree rate within six years	2,291,621	0.396	0.478	390,728	0.279	0.412
Expected median income original ($)	1,941,617	36531.64	15707.45	335,738	32807.91	14095.85
Expected median income new ($)	1,941,617	36528.11	15545.98	335,738	32818.77	13974.90

Source: College Board Data matched to National Student Clearinghouse.
Note: We simulate the impacts of going to zero tuition and fees at each four-year public college for students with family income of less than $60,000 per year. Responses of enrollment and graduation to tuition and fees are taken from estimates in the literature as detailed in online appendix C and the text.

result of the simulation is that about 10 percent of high school graduates would enroll in a four-year public college, with an average cost (averaging over all students) of about $260 per year, a 30–40 percent increase over a universal reduction of 10 percent in tuition and fees.

V.C. Increased Spending at Public Colleges

Our third policy is an increase in state funding. We first calculate the gap in spending per student between each four-year public institution and the average of the four-year private institutions in the same state. We then increase spending at each four-year public college to remove 10 percent of the spending gap between that specific four-year public college and the average of in-state private colleges. For community colleges we simply raise per student spending by 10 percent of that institution's spending.[35] We assume that the increase in funding is directed in the manner observed in historical analysis by Deming and Walters (2017). By definition, this policy increases completion rates for students conditional on enrollment at a particular college. It also induces movement both into college and across the two-year/four-year college margin.

As shown in table 5, our simulation yields a .7 percentage point increase in enrollment at four-year colleges and a .4 percentage point increase in enrollment at two-year public colleges. The policy primarily changes outcomes, however, by increasing completion rates at public colleges conditional on enrollment. The overall result is an increase of 1.1 percentage points in bachelor's degree completion, combining the effects of students enrolling in two-year and four-year public colleges, as bachelor's degree completion rates increase for students who enroll at any type of public college in response to this policy. The cost of the policy is approximately $360 per student, averaging over students who enroll in some college, and approximately $280 per student, averaging over all students in the sample.

V.D. Best Available In-State Public College (BISPO)

Our last policy is a reallocation of students who are currently undermatched to an academically matched in-state four-year public college. We refer to this policy as BISPO, using the acronym for "best in-state public option"; we specifically consider a counterfactual world where

---

35. We note that comparably selective four-year private colleges have always exhibited higher levels of spending than four-year public colleges, so we consider a policy that increases spending at four-year public colleges, but only to the point of reducing a fraction of this gap in spending.

Table 5. Simulation of Increased per Student Spending at Public Four-Year and Two-Year Colleges: Impacts on Enrollments, Graduation, and Earnings

	All students			Low-income students		
	N	Mean	SD	N	Mean	SD
Net tuition and fees original ($)	1,806,094	4,697	5873.76	291,567	614.314	1848.18
Net tuition, fees, room and board original ($)	1,805,428	13034.6	7328.89	291,353	11063.2	6058.95
Spending boost per student ($)	1,764,494	364.104	765.736	282,942	477.485	898.807
Spending boost per student including zeroes ($)	2,291,621	284.791	687.899	390,728	352.754	791.687
Start at two-year institution	2,291,621	0.275	0.447	390,728	0.338	0.473
Start at four-year institution	2,291,621	0.521	0.5	390,728	0.414	0.493
Not enrolled	2,291,621	0.204	0.403	390,728	0.248	0.432
Start at two-year institution new	2,291,621	0.279	0.444	390,728	0.344	0.47
Start at four-year institution new	2,291,621	0.528	0.493	390,728	0.424	0.485
Not enrolled new	2,291,621	0.193	0.382	390,728	0.232	0.406
Obtain bachelor's degree within six years original	2,291,621	0.386	0.487	390,728	0.25	0.433
New bachelor's degree rate within six years	2,291,621	0.397	0.486	390,728	0.263	0.434
Expected median income original ($)	1,941,617	36531.64	15707.45	335,738	32807.91	14095.85
Expected median income new ($)	1,941,617	36566.61	15413.46	335,738	32919.03	13095.01

Source: College Board Data matched to National Student Clearinghouse.

Note: We simulate the impacts of raising per student spending on outcomes. At each public four-year institution, we raise spending by 30 percent of the gap between that institution and the average per student spending at in-state private institutions. At two-year institutions, we raise spending by 20 percent of the current level. Elasticities of enrollment and graduation with respect to spending are taken from Deming and Walters (2017). We show outcomes for all students and for low-income students (family income <$40k). Predicted earnings and graduation vary at the student level and are dependent on student demographics, state, and test scores.

(some) undermatched students change colleges and enroll at a specific matched public college in their home state. Following Hoxby and Avery (2013), we define any student as undermatched if enrolled at a college with median SAT composite score at least 15 national percentile points below a student's own composite SAT score. By this definition, approximately 16 percent of the students in our sample are undermatched. We include some students at two-year colleges in our definition of undermatch but exclude students who do not enroll in college. Eliminating undermatching requires a switch of many students from less selective to more selective public colleges and thus incurs increased costs, since the less selective colleges are generally characterized by relatively low expenditures per student. We assume that expenditure per student is held constant for each public college in response to enrollment changes, and thus that the underlying probability of graduation for a particular student at a particular college is not affected by this policy.

A related challenge is that the policy of eliminating undermatching requires an increase in the number of seats at some public colleges. We run our simulation with and without constraints on the supply of seats at any given college. To estimate an upper bound on enrollment at a given public institution, we use IPEDS data on full-time undergraduate enrollment at that institution from 2002 to 2017. We calculate the annual standard deviation of log(full-time enrollment) for each school and impose that enrollment can grow by no more than one standard deviation in our reallocation. Almost all (93 percent) of undermatched students have an in-state public college that is a better match, but only about half of them can be moved under the limited supply scenario. We focus on the results for the limited supply case because changes of college under the unlimited supply assumption requires unrealistic expansions in a few states, such as California and New York, where the public college system is already overburdened.

As shown in table 6, our simulation of the limited supply policy yields an overall 3.2 percentage point increase in enrollment at four-year public colleges. This stems in part from a 1.9 percentage point increase in enrollment at four-year public colleges from movement of students who are undermatched at two-year colleges. Many more students change from a less selective four-year college to a more selective four-year college. The net result is an increase of 1 percentage point in bachelor's degree completion, with an original bachelor's degree completion rate of 34.2 percent and new bachelor's degree completion rate of 35.2 percent. We project a slightly larger increase of 1.2 percentage points in bachelor's degree completion rates for low-income students, consistent with the observation

Table 6. Simulation of BISPO Impacts on Enrollments, Graduation, and Earnings

	All students			Low-income students		
	N	Mean	SD	N	Mean	SD
Obtain bachelor's degree within six years original	2,308,129	0.342	0.314	398,085	0.223	0.263
New bachelor's degree rate within six years	2,307,979	0.352	0.317	398,041	0.235	0.272
Net cost of attendance	1,529,297	$16,526	$8,606	269,668	$10,580	$5,974
New net cost of attendance	1,545,919	$16,582	$8,474	272,633	$10,563	$5,828
Instructional spending per FTE original	1,841,825	$7,658	$6,770	301,327	$6,354	$5,171
Instructional spending per FTE new	1,841,825	$7,824	$6,780	301,327	$6,576	$5,257
Total expenditures per FTE original	1,841,825	$20,130	$17,352	301,327	$16,956	$14,033
Total expenditures per FTE new	1,841,825	$20,711	$17,480	301,327	$17,672	$14,389
Start at two-year institution	2,308,129	0.274	0.446	398,085	0.336	0.472
Start at four-year institution	2,308,129	0.524	0.499	398,085	0.421	0.494
Not enrolled	2,308,129	0.202	0.401	398,085	0.243	0.429
Start at four-year public institution	2,308,129	0.343	0.475	398,085	0.295	0.456
Start at two-year institution new	2,308,129	0.247	0.431	398,085	0.304	0.460
Start at four-year institution new	2,308,129	0.551	0.497	398,085	0.453	0.498
Not enrolled new	2,308,129	0.202	0.402	398,085	0.243	0.429
Start at four-year public institution new	2,308,129	0.375	0.484	398,085	0.334	0.472
Expected median income original	1,996,778	$36,078	$15,760	344,192	$32,519	$14,084
Expected median income new	1,999,027	$36,646	$15,931	345,678	$33,322	$14,588

Source: College Board Data matched to National Student Clearinghouse.

Note: We simulate the impacts of moving undermatched students to better in-state public institutions. We assume a constraint of an increase of no more than one standard deviation in cohort size at any public institution. We show outcomes for all students and for low-income students (family income <$40k). Predicted earnings and graduation vary at the student level and are dependent on student demographics, state, and test scores.

that low-income students are disproportionately likely to undermatch in the baseline case.

The reallocation of students in this scenario increases costs in two ways. First, it yields direct increases in instructional spending per student, a total of $166 per student. More generally, it yields increases in spending in other areas as well, a total of $581 per student overall, averaging across the entire sample. We use the larger figure of $581 in increased expenditures per student. The unlimited supply scenario (included in table 8 but not reported in detail here) approximately doubles the increase in bachelor's degree completion as a result of a BISPO policy, but at approximately three times the cost of the limited supply scenario. As this result suggests, the states that are most constrained in enrollment of undermatched students are also states with relatively large expenses per student at their most selective public colleges.

VI. Discussion and Conclusion

Table 7a provides a decomposition analysis of the effects of these policies on different subpopulations of students based on their current college choices. Since we are considering interventions with different costs per student, it is not necessarily meaningful to compare the absolute magnitudes of the interventions for a given subgroup. Instead, this table highlights the relative merits of each policy as well as the subgroups of students most affected.

As shown in table 7a, we project that a free community college policy would induce many students to change their choice of college, with about 15 percent of students who would otherwise not enroll in any college and about 6–7 percent of students who would enroll in a four-year college switching to a two-year college. As shown in table 7b, the effects on bachelor's degree completion are naturally mixed, but on balance negative in the simulation; that is, we project the policy to change outcomes both positively and negatively for different subpopulations of students.

The other policies are projected to have broadly positive effects on bachelor's degree completion for all of these subgroups of students based on choice of college in practice. As shown in table 7b, we project that the policies of increasing funding or reducing tuition at four-year public colleges would especially improve bachelor's degree completion rates for students who enroll in four-year public colleges under the status quo. At the same time, we project these two policies to have similarly positive effects on students who would otherwise not have enrolled at any

Table 7a. Decomposition Analysis of Effects of the Different Interventions: Change in Four-Year Public College Enrollment

Baseline enrollment choice	Free two-year college (%)	Reduced public college tuition (%)	Targeted elimination of public college tuition and fees (%)	Increased funding for public colleges (%)	BISPO with limited supply (%)
Not enrolled	+15.5[a]	+0.7	+2.6	+3.4	X
Enrolled in two-year college	X	+0.7	+2.8	0	+9.8
Enrolled in four-year public college	−6.8	X	X	X	X
Enrolled in four-year private college	−5.8	+5.0[b]	+10.5[b]	X	+3.1

Source: College Board Data matched to National Student Clearinghouse.

Notes: A value of "X" in a given cell indicates that, by assumption (or design), this policy has no effect on four-year college enrollment for this subgroup of students. By assumption, our simulations of BISPO policies do not affect the choices or outcomes of students who did not enroll in college in the baseline case.

a. Our simulation estimates that a free two-year college program would induce 15.5 percent of the students who did not previously enroll to enroll at a two-year college.

b. With both reduced public college tuition and targeted elimination of tuition and fees at four-year public colleges, our simulation estimates that 5.0 percent of the students who previously enrolled at a four-year private college would switch to a four-year public college.

Table 7b. Decomposition Analysis of Effects of the Different Interventions: Change in Probability of Completing a Bachelor's Degree

Baseline enrollment choice	Free two-year college (%)	Reduced public college tuition (%)	Targeted elimination of public college tuition and fees (%)	Increased funding for public colleges (%)	BISPO with limited supply (%)
Not enrolled	+1.5	+0.4	+1.3	+2.1	X
Enrolled in two-year college	+0.1	+0.2	+0.7	+0.1	+3.0
Enrolled in four-year public college	−2.8	+0.5	+1.5	+1.8	+0.4
Enrolled in four-year private college	−2.4	+0.1	+0.2	0	+0.3

Source: College Board Data matched to National Student Clearinghouse.

Note: A value of "X" in a given cell indicates that, by assumption (or design), this policy has no effect on four-year college enrollment for this subgroup of students. By assumption, our simulations of BISPO policies do not affect the choices or outcomes of students who did not enroll in college in the baseline case.

Table 8. Projected Cost-Benefit Ratios for Each Simulated Policy

	Cost per student-year ($)	Change in bachelor's degree completion rate	Cost per additional bachelor's degree ($)
Free community college	151.6	−.010	NA
Reduced four-year tuition and fees	187.5	+ .003	269,875
Targeted elimination of four-year tuition and fees	264.4	+ .010	114,068
Increased spending at public colleges	280.9	+ .010	121,293
BISPO limited supply	581	+ .010	250,876
BISPO unlimited supply	1,545	+ .019	351,122
	Cost per student-year ($)	Change in median income per year ($)	Cost per additional $ in median income
Free community college	151.6	−61	NA
Reduced four-year tuition and fees	187.5	+ 320	2.53
Targeted elimination of four-year tuition and fees	264.4	+ 357	3.20
Increased spending at public colleges	280.9	+ 676	1.79
BISPO limited supply	581	+ 568	4.42
BISPO unlimited supply	1,545.0	+ 1,445	4.62

Source: Authors' calculations.

Note: We compute cost-benefit ratios for projected increases in bachelor's degree completion and median income that result from each policy. Tables 3 through 6 report costs in per-year units of 2007 dollars. We convert 2007 dollars to 2019 dollars using a 1.27 multiplier and convert per-year to lifetime costs using an estimate of 3.4 years of enrollment per student who enrolls in a four-year college. This estimate is based on the rough averages that 60 percent of students who enroll initially in a four-year college complete a bachelor's degree, with an average of 4.6 years of enrollment per student who completes a bachelor's degree and an average of 1.5 years of enrollment per student who does not complete a bachelor's degree.

college—highlighting the fact that we assume positive elasticities for new enrollment of students in response to each of these policies. By contrast, BISPO has a much greater effect on students currently enrolled in two-year public colleges than any other group of students, thereby highlighting the policy importance of undermatching at the margin of two-year versus four-year enrollment.

We present cost-benefit comparisons for these policies in table 8. Tables 3 through 6 present changes in outcomes and cost per student of each policy in 2007 dollars for a single year. The tables provide the cost averaged over *all* students (including students affected and unaffected by the policy) for a single year. The tables also contain the average change in the bachelor's degree rate computed across all students. To turn these numbers into a cost per additional bachelor's degree, we need to multiply the annual cost by the average years spent in college and then divide by the increase in the bachelor's degree completion rate. The average number of years of enrollment is 3.4 for students starting at four-year institutions. Finally we scale up our cost per bachelor's degree from 2007 dollars to present-day dollars with a 1.27 multiplier.[36]

Free community college stands out among these four policies, as it is the only one that produces ambiguous results. On the one hand, it increases the proportion of high school graduates who complete a postsecondary degree, but it does so at the expense of bachelor's degrees. With this background, it is interesting that this policy has gained so much traction in recent practice. On the positive side, with about 70 percent of high school graduates proceeding immediately to college, free community college is one of relatively few policies that both increase funding for public colleges and also target the lowest quartile of students in terms of academic achievement and future earning potential. Even so, the design of most free community college policies excludes students from lowest-income families as these students would already be eligible for Pell Grants that would cover most, if not all, of tuition cost for community college.

Another important effect of the free community college policy that is not incorporated in our cost-benefit analysis for degree completion is the fact that the predominant effect of the policy is to induce students who would otherwise not enroll to complete some time in college without attaining a degree. It is unclear whether the positive effects of exposure to the college environment and acquisition of skills in college courses outweigh the opportunity costs of time enrolled and the subsequent (potential) costs of repaying student loans for these students.

While there is a great deal of uncertainty surrounding each estimate from our simulation, we interpret these results as providing strong evidence that a free community college policy is a poor vehicle for promoting bachelor's degree completion. To have a neutral effect on bachelor's

36. We use the Bureau of Labor Statistics' CPI inflation calculator to derive this multiplier; see http://data.bls.gov/cgi-bin/cpicalc.pl. It could be argued that we should use a larger multiplier to convert 2007 college costs into present-day college costs given that tuition and fees have outpaced inflation during that time. For example, Ma and others (2019, fig. 9) report a 35 percent increase in published prices for four-year public colleges from 2008 to 2018 in 2018 dollars, but they also report a 30 percent increase in grant aid in 2018 dollars during that time period. The choice of this multiplier affects only the absolute values of these estimated cost-benefit ratios, not the relative rankings of the four policies.

degree completion, a free community college policy would need to attract approximately four new students who would otherwise not have enrolled in any college for each student who moves from a four-year college to a two-year college in response to the policy. Yet, in practice, this rate has been observed to be approximately one to one. We conducted an alternative simulation (not reported here) to consider the extreme case where no student moved from a four-year college to a two-year college in response to a free community college policy; we project that the cost-benefit result for the policy would be approximately equal to that of reduced four-year tuition, and still not comparable to the result of increasing spending at public colleges. To reiterate the conclusion of Athreya and Eberly (forthcoming), increasing college enrollment is not an attractive route for increasing bachelor's degree completion at this point.

Reducing tuition is projected to have positive results, but at about twice the cost per degree of increasing spending at public colleges. On average reducing tuition yields a cost per additional bachelor's degree of $270,000. The success of this policy on a cost-benefit basis is limited by two main structural factors. First, the tuition discount applies to many inframarginal students who completed bachelor's degrees at public colleges in the baseline case.[37] Second, reduced tuition at four-year public colleges induces some students to switch from four-year private to four-year public colleges with lower expenditure per student and lower graduation rates. Thus, while the policy increases bachelor's degree completion rates for students already enrolled at four-year public colleges and who are induced to enroll at a four-year college as a result of the policy, it is projected to reduce bachelor's degree completion rates for those who respond by switching from four-year private to four-year public colleges.

Targeted elimination of tuition and fees at four-year public colleges with an income threshold is projected to be much more efficient than partial reduction in tuition and fees for all students in terms of the cost per additional bachelor's degree. The cost per additional bachelor's degree is $114,000. This result stems, at least in part, from our use of elasticities in modeling, which in turn imply relatively large proportional responses to the elimination of tuition and fees (because these are "zero prices"). This modeling choice accords with the point Dynarski and others (2019) make about the high impact of advertising college as free. As shown in table 7b, we project

---

37. As such, we could consider the tuition discount to these inframarginal students as a transfer payment from the government, which would have benefits for those students, but not of the sort that we are prioritizing in this analysis.

this policy to produce a substantial response in terms of enrollment and completion for low-income students at relatively minimal cost. Interestingly, the simulation indicates a similar change in median income to the partial reduction in tuition and fees for all students. The combination of these results suggests that increases in degree completion especially affect incomes for students who are below the median income level (with and without the change in policy).

Some current proposals combine tuition reductions at two-year and four-year public colleges. While we do not explicitly consider hybrid policies of this sort, we believe that a weighted average of the results of the individual policies gives a reasonably accurate approximation of a more involved simulation. For example, we project the negative effect of free community college on bachelor's degree completion to be about 3.7 times as large as the positive effect of a 10 percent tuition reduction at four-year public colleges. Thus, a policy that combines free community college with a 30–40 percent tuition reduction at four-year public colleges would likely be projected to be nearly neutral in terms of its effect on bachelor's degree completion.

The BISPO policy is projected to have effects on the same order as, or slightly worse than, reducing college tuition. BISPO with limited supply expansion costs roughly $250,000 per additional bachelor's degree. This is approximately twice the cost of increased spending at public colleges ($121,000 per bachelor's degree). In essence, the comparison of BISPO and increased spending policies is a question of relative efficiency within the public college system on a state-by-state basis. Is it more cost-effective to produce bachelor's degrees by moving students to high-cost institutions with high graduation rates or to increase expenditures at lower-cost institutions? Our simulations suggest, in fact, that investments in the lower-cost institutions produce higher relative returns; this result may reflect the observation that more selective public colleges have a broader mission than simply educating undergraduates.

To test this further, we have tried subdividing our sample of students into quartiles of the bachelor's degree completion rate of their starting institution. Because of IPEDS data limitations, we can do this only for students who begin at a four-year institution. These results confirm our intuition that there is a lot of bang for the buck in increasing spending or lowering tuition for students at less expensive, lower-performing public institutions.

Consider the policy of boosting spending at four-year public institutions. Students who begin at four-year public institutions in the bottom quartile of bachelor's degree completion rates see increased rates of 2.7 percentage points and the cost per additional bachelor's degree is $156,000. Students in top quartile institutions see only a .1 percentage point increase in the bachelor's degree completion rate and the cost per bachelor's degree is $323,000. Note that because this is only for the subset of students starting in four-year public institutions, these outcomes will not add up to the average outcome of the policy for all students.

A similar result obtains for the policy of free tuition and fees for students with family incomes of less than $60,000. Students from bottom quartile public institutions see increases in the bachelor's degree completion rate of 1.9 percentage points at a cost per bachelor's degree of $94,000. Students from top quartile institutions see a smaller increase in the bachelor's degree completion rate (1.2 pp) and a larger cost per bachelor's degree at $248,000. This higher cost stems from the higher costs of attendance at the higher-performing institutions. Overall these results suggest that there is significant value in increased spending or free tuition at the four-year public colleges with lower bachelor's degree completion rates.

VI.A. Limitations of the Simulations

We believe that it is important to highlight a number of limitations to our approach. In particular, the results of each simulation are dependent on point estimates of one or more crucial elasticities. While we make an effort to choose estimates of these elasticity values that correspond to the consensus of well-designed studies in recent literature, the estimates in the prior literature are typically local estimates that pertain to the context of the program studied and may not necessarily generalize to the broad distributions of students in the College Board sample. Further, we acknowledge that we have to draw on modest amounts of evidence in the choice of some parameters. For example, we have the luxury of observing initial evidence from two separate statewide programs (Tennessee and Oregon) to assess the enrollment effects of a free community college, but even then, these programs are quite young and may not yet be producing stable results.

The BISPO policy is distinct from the others because it specifically defines the college choices of individual students, and thus its results are not dependent on the choice of enrollment elasticity values at any margin. Yet the results of the BISPO policy still rely on the critical assumption that graduation rates will not change after the implementation of reasonably large-scale movements of students to new colleges. Beyond this specific example, there is some possibility that unmodeled general equilibrium effects to any of these individual policy interventions could affect the results of those interventions.

DECISIONS BY MARGINAL STUDENTS   As shown in table 7b, we project largest or near-largest increases in bachelor's degree completion in response to the two highest-ranked policies from the group of students who would not otherwise enroll in any college. We reiterate the fact that projected results for this subgroup are especially uncertain. First, our sample may under-weight this group relative to its true size, as students who do not enroll in college are relatively unlikely to take PSAT/SAT and thus are unusually likely to be excluded from the sample. Second, our elasticity estimates for this subgroup may not adequately account for selection bias: these students may be unusually unlikely to enroll in college in response to a change in incentives or may not be as likely to complete a bachelor's degree conditional on enrollment as would be suggested by our quantitative predictions. It is not clear whether the net effect of these issues is positive or negative in terms of the evaluation of the effects of these policies.

The above discussion highlights the problems of identifying elasticities for the marginal college entrant in our simulations. As one robustness check, we rerun our simulations, cutting the graduation responses to the policies in half. Interestingly we still find that boosting spending and cutting tuition for families with less than $60,000 in income are still highly cost effective. The cost per additional bachelor's degree for the spending boost policy rises to $133,000 and the cost per additional bachelor's degree for the income-targeted free tuition policy rises to $126,000.

ROBUSTNESS ANALYSIS WITH VARYING ELASTICITY VALUES   As we note above in footnote 35 we believe that it would be difficult to identify meaningful confidence intervals for any of the results of interest, such as the cost-benefit ratios for each policy, given the dependence of the results on the choices of more than one elasticity value. The resulting estimates are somewhat delicate. What we can do is report how much our point elasticities would have to change in order to flip our broad conclusions about the merits of free community college and increased spending at public colleges. Consider first the free community college policy. The Achilles' heel of that policy is the tendency to draw students away from four-year options and into two-year public colleges. Based on the Tennessee and Oregon policy shocks, we estimate the propensity of four-year college students to switch to two-year public colleges to have a price elasticity (with respect to the two-year tuition price) of .075. This is the midpoint between the Tennessee and Oregon estimates. To eliminate the negative bachelor's degree graduation effects of the policy (and also the negative earnings impacts of the policy), we need to drop this elasticity to .025. This creates bachelor's degree impacts of zero while raising associate degrees and expected earnings. To justify this elasticity one needs to believe that the impact of free community college is half or less than the elasticity observed in Tennessee (which had the smaller elasticity). We think that such an elasticity is certainly plausible, though it is outside the confidence intervals from the studies of both existing shocks.

A similar question is whether the cost per additional bachelor's degree of increased spending per student is truly half the cost per bachelor's degree of reducing tuition. We address this question by checking the robustness of our finding to different elasticities of enrollment in four-year public colleges and bachelor's degree attainment with respect to four-year tuition and fees. Our simulations show that the impacts of the policy on bachelor's degree attainment are roughly proportional to the changes in elasticities that we posit. In short, if we cut all of the elasticities in half, the positive impacts are roughly halved. So if the impacts of increased spending at four-year public colleges as estimated by Deming and Walters (2017) are too high by a factor of two, the benefits are roughly halved. With smaller elasticities we estimated the cost per bachelor's degree of increased spending at $212,000 per additional bachelor's degree which is quite similar to cost per additional bachelor's degree of cutting tuition or matching students with their best in-state public option (in the limited supply scenario).

With this background, we emphasize the broad distinction between free community college, which is estimated to have a negative effect on bachelor's degree completion and the other policies, which seem almost necessarily to have positive effects.[38]

VI.B. Broad Conclusions

The cost benefit ratio for increased spending at public colleges and for targeted elimination of tuition and fees at public colleges—approximately $121,000 in 2019 dollars per additional bachelor's degree—is roughly equivalent to that of the most positive results demonstrated in the prior literature.[39] The cost-benefit results for reducing tuition and the BISPO

38. The possible exception to this is tuition reduction at four-year colleges; see Cohodes and Goodman (2014).

39. For example, Barr (2015) for the GI Bill, Bettinger and others (2019) for the Cal Grant, and Scott-Clayton (2011) for the West Virginia Promise Scholarship. Castleman and Long (2016) produce a much lower estimate of $28,000 per additional bachelor's degree for the FSAG program, but this appears to be anomalously low in the context of the estimated effects of similar programs in other states.

policy are about 2.5–3 times as high but still seem within reason as plausible policy options. It is notable that the reduced tuition option appears to be much less effective on a cost-benefit basis than a more targeted approach as well as the more specific aid programs studied in previous papers. From the perspective of targeting, most of the policies that we study are necessarily scattershot in their approach as they are designed (in some sense) to apply to all students. This observation suggests that the cost-benefit ranking of the programs as given by the point estimates in table 8 reflects the degree to which they successfully target the marginal students with greatest propensity to improve their educational outcomes.

The actual cost (in terms of tuition and fees) for sending a single student through a public college to bachelor's degree completion is roughly $22,800. We estimate this in two ways. The mean net tuition and fees in our data is $3,990 in 2007 dollars. Once we adjust this to 2019 dollars and calculate the average number of years in school to complete, we obtain $3,990 \times 1.27 \times 4.5 \approx \$22,800$. If we instead use the College Board's *Trends in College Pricing 2018*, we obtain an estimate of $3,780 \times 4.5 \approx \$17,000$. Naturally the cost of creating additional bachelor's degrees via price or spending subsidies exceeds the actual cost of sending the single marginal student through college. In fact our results suggest that even for a successful policy like eliminating tuition for families with less than $60,000 in annual income, for each $1 spent on a marginal student who is induced to complete a bachelor's degree, an additional $5 is spent on each inframarginal student.

The policies we study also vary in the degree to which they benefit low-income students. An interesting paradox is that some policies that appear to focus on low-income students may have the opposite effect. The usual explanation for this paradox is that Pell Grants cover some or all of tuition costs for low-income students. As a result, even seemingly targeted programs, such as tuition reductions with an income threshold, tend to benefit the near-poor much more than those who already qualify for Pell Grants.

In general, we view the cost-benefit estimates of table 8 as presenting the clear message that it is important and likely cost effective to increase spending on one or more policies to increase completion of four-year bachelor's degrees. But it is imperative to avoid the temptation of enacting low-cost policies that are politically viable but that do not take on the systemic problems in current practice that limit completion rates. Reducing or eliminating tuition at two-year public colleges may seem superficially attractive and also inexpensive, but this policy only indirectly addresses the challenge of low completion rates at two-year colleges. Similarly, a policy that reduces tuition but simultaneously cuts expenditures to compensate for lost tuition revenue cannot be expected to have a substantive effect on student outcomes.

ACKNOWLEDGMENTS   Corresponding author: Department of Economics, Dartmouth College, 6106 Rockefeller, Hanover NH 03755. bruce.sacerdote@dartmouth.edu. Jaclyn Eagle and Carolyn Zhou provided outstanding research assistance. We are grateful to the National Science Foundation for generous support.

References

Aguiar, Mark, and Mark Bils. 2015. "Has Consumption Inequality Mirrored Income Inequality?" *American Economic Review* 105, no. 9: 2725–56.

Athreya, Karthik B., and Janice C. Eberly. Forthcoming. "Risk, the College Premium, and Aggregate Human Capital Investment." *American Economic Journal: Macroeconomics*.

Avery, Christopher, and Sarah Turner. 2012. "Student Loans: Do College Students Borrow Too Much or Not Enough?" *Journal of Economic Perspectives* 26, no. 1: 165–92.

Barr, Andrew. 2015. "From the Battlefield to the Schoolyard: The Short-Term Impact of the Post-9/11 GI Bill." *Journal of Human Resources* 50, no. 3: 580–613.

Barr, Andrew, and Benjamin Castleman. 2017. "The Bottom Line on College Counseling." Working Paper. http://people.tamu.edu/~abarr/BL_shell_10_17_2017.pdf.

Barro, Robert J., and Xavier Sala-i-Martin. 1998. *Economic Growth*. Cambridge, Mass.: MIT Press.

Baum, Sandy. 2016. *Student Debt: Rhetoric and Reality of Higher Education Financing*. London: Palgrave Pivot Publishing.

Benson, Alan, Raimundo Esteva, and Frank Levy. 2015. "Dropouts, Taxes, and Risk: The Economic Return to College under Realistic Assumptions." Working Paper. https://papers.ssrn.com/sol3/papers.cfm?abstract_id=2325657.

Bettinger, Eric, Oded Gurantz, Laura Kawano, Bruce Sacerdote, and Michael Stevens. 2019. "The Long-Run Impacts of Financial Aid: Evidence from California's Cal Grant." *American Economic Journal: Economic Policy* 11, no. 1: 64–94.

Bils, Mark, and Peter J. Klenow. 2000. "Does Schooling Cause Growth?" *American Economic Review* 90, no. 5: 1160–83.

Bound, John, Breno Braga, Gaurav Khanna, and Sarah Turner. 2019. "Public Universities: The Supply Side of Building a Skilled Workforce." Working Paper 25945. Cambridge, Mass.: National Bureau of Economic Research. https://www.nber.org/papers/w25945.

Bound, John, Michael F. Lovenheim, and Sarah Turner. 2010. "Why Have College Completion Rates Declined? An Analysis of Changing Student Preparation and Collegiate Resources." *American Economic Journal: Applied Economics* 2, no. 3: 129–57.

Bowen, William G., Matthew M. Chingos, and Michael S. McPherson. 2009. *Crossing the Finish Line: Completing College at America's Public Universities*. Princeton, N.J.: Princeton University Press.

Broda, Christian Miguel, and David E. Weinstein. 2008. *Prices, Poverty, and Inequality: Why Americans Are Better Off than You Think*. Washington: American Enterprise Institute.

Carruthers, Celeste K. 2019. "Five Things to Know about the Tennessee Promise Scholarship." Blog post, May 6, Brookings Institution. https://www.brookings.

edu/blog/brown-center-chalkboard/2019/05/06/five-things-to-know-about-the-tennessee-promise-scholarship/.

Carruthers, Celeste K., William F. Fox, and Christopher Jepsen. 2018. "Promise Kept? Free Community College and Attainment in Tennessee." Working Paper.

Castleman, Benjamin L., and Joshua Goodman. 2018. "Intensive College Counseling and the Enrollment and Persistence of Low Income Students." *Education Finance and Policy* 13, no. 1: 19–41.

Castleman, Benjamin L., and Bridget Terry Long. 2016. "Looking beyond Enrollment: The Causal Effect of Need-Based Grants on College Access, Persistence, and Graduation." *Journal of Labor Economics* 34, no. 4: 1023–73.

Chakrabarti, Rajashri, Nicole Gorton, and Michael F. Lovenheim. 2018. "The Effect of State Funding for Postsecondary Education on Long-Run Student Outcomes." Paper presented at the IZA World Labor Conference, Institute of Labor Economics, Berlin, June 28–29.

Chetty, Raj, John N. Friedman, Emmanuel Saez, Nicholas Turner, and Danny Yagan. 2017. "Mobility Report Cards: The Role of Colleges in Intergenerational Mobility." Working Paper 23618. Cambridge, Mass.: National Bureau of Economic Research. https://www.nber.org/papers/w23618.

Chingos, Matthew M. 2012. "Graduation Rates at America's Universities: What We Know and What We Need to Know." In *Getting to Graduation: The Completion Agenda in American Higher Education*, edited by Andrew P. Kelly and Mark Schneider. Baltimore: Johns Hopkins University Press.

Clotfelter, Charles T., Steven W. Hemelt, and Helen F. Ladd. 2018. "Multifaceted Aid for Low-Income Students and College Outcomes: Evidence from North Carolina." *Economic Inquiry* 56, no. 1: 278–303.

Cohodes, Sarah R., and Joshua S. Goodman. 2014. "Merit Aid, College Quality, and College Completion: Massachusetts' Adams Scholarship as an In-Kind Subsidy." *American Economic Journal: Applied Economics* 6, no. 4:, 251–85.

Cornwell, Christopher, David B. Mustard, and Deepa J. Sridhar. 2006. "The Enrollment Effects of Merit-Based Financial Aid: Evidence from Georgia's HOPE Program." *Journal of Labor Economics* 24, no. 4: 761–86.

Costa, Dora L. 2001. "Estimating Real Income in the United States from 1888 to 1994: Correcting CPI Bias Using Engel Curves." *Journal of Political Economy* 109, no. 6: 1288–1310.

Cox, Amy G., Elizabeth Martinez, Shiyan Tao, Balaji Rajaram, Betsey Simpkins, Olga Levadnaya, Vern Mayfield, Amy Keir, and Dean Crews. 2018. *Senate Bill 81(2015): The Oregon Promise—Report from Year 3*. Salem, Ore.: Oregon Higher Education Coordinating Commission. https://www.oregon.gov/highered/research/Documents/Reports/SB-81-Oregon-Promise-2018.pdf.

Debaum, Bill, and Carrie Warwick. 2019. *The Growing Gap: Public Higher Education's Declining Affordability for Low-Income Students*. Washington: National College Access Network. https://collegeaccess.org/page/affordability.

Deming, David J., and Christopher R. Walters. 2017. "The Impacts of Price and Spending Subsidies on U.S. Postsecondary Attainment." Working Paper 23726.

Cambridge, Mass.: National Bureau of Economic Research. https://www.nber.org/papers/w23736.

Denning, Jeffrey T. 2017. "College on the Cheap: Consequences of Community College Tuition Reductions." *American Economic Journal: Economic Policy* 9, no. 2: 155–88.

Denning, Jeffrey T., Eric R. Eide, and Merrill Warnick. 2019. "Why Have College Completion Rates Increased?" Working Paper 12411. Bonn: Institute of Labor Economics. http://ftp.iza.org/dp12411.pdf.

Denning, Jeffrey T., Benjamin M. Marx, and Lesley J. Turner. 2018. "Welfare Effects of Changes in College Pricing." Working Paper. https://drive.google.com/file/d/1NadO0AEMmVVlJ1AlMxTOjZY0hKTzGQOa/view.

Dillon, Eleanor Wiske, and Jeffrey A. Smith. 2017. "Determinants of the Match between Student Ability and College Quality." *Journal of Labor Economics* 35, no. 1: 45–66.

Dynarski, Susan M. 2000. "Hope for Whom? Financial Aid for the Middle Class and Its Impact on College Attendance." *National Tax Journal* 53, no. 3: 629–62.

Dynarski, Susan M. 2003. "Does Aid Matter? Measuring the Effect of Student Aid on College Attendance and Completion." *American Economic Review* 93, no. 1: 279–88.

Dynarski, Susan M. 2008. "Building the Stock of College-Educated Labor." *Journal of Human Resources* 43, no. 3: 576–610.

Dynarski, Susan M., Steven W. Hemelt, and Joshua M. Hyman. 2015. "The Missing Manual: Using National Student Clearinghouse Data to Track Post-secondary Outcomes." *Educational Evaluation and Policy Analysis* 37, no. 1: 53S–79S.

Dynarski, Susan M., C. J. Libassi, Katherine Michelmore, and Stephanie Owen. 2018. *Closing the Gap: The Effect of a Targeted, Tuition-Free Promise on College Choices of High-Achieving, Low-Income Students*. Working Paper 25349. Cambridge, Mass.: National Bureau of Economic Research.

Ellwood, David T., and Thomas J. Kane. 2000. "Who Is Getting a College Education? Family Background and the Growing Gaps in Enrollment." In *Securing the Future: Investing in Children from Birth to College*, edited by Sheldon Danziger and Jane Waldfogel. New York: Russell Sage Foundation.

Evans, William N., Melissa S. Kearney, Brendan C. Perry, and James X. Sullivan. 2017. "Increasing Community College Completion Rates among Low-Income Students: Evidence from a Randomized Controlled Trial Evaluation of a Case Management Intervention." Working Paper 24150. Cambridge, Mass.: National Bureau of Economic Research. https://www.nber.org/papers/w24150.

Goldin, Claudia, and Lawrence F. Katz. 2018. "The Race between Education and Technology." In *Inequality in the 21st Century*, edited by David B. Grusky and Jasmine Hill. New York: Routledge.

Goodman, Joshua, Michael Hurwitz, and Jonathan Smith. 2017. "Access to 4-Year Public Colleges and Degree Completion." *Journal of Labor Economics* 35, no. 3: 829–67.

Gunderson, Morley, and Philip Oreopoulos. 2010. "Returns to Education in Developed Countries." In *International Encyclopedia of Education*, edited by Penelope Peterson, Eva Baker, and Barry McGaw. Amsterdam: Elsevier Science.

Gurantz, Oded. 2019. "What Does Free Community College Buy? Early Impacts from the Oregon Promise." *Journal of Policy Analysis and Management* 39, no. 1: 11–35.

Harris, Adam. 2019. "Alaska Still Hasn't Saved Its Universities." *Atlantic,* August 15. https://www.theatlantic.com/education/archive/2019/08/alaskas-higher-education-system-still-trouble/596191/.

Hillman, Nicholas, and Taylor Weichman. 2016. *Education Deserts: The Continued Significance of "Place" in the Twenty-First Century.* Washington: American Council on Education. https://www.acenet.edu/Documents/Education-Deserts-The-Continued-Significance-of-Place-in-the-Twenty-First-Century.pdf.

Hoekstra, Mark. 2009. "The Effect of Attending the Flagship State University on Earnings: A Discontinuity-Based Approach." *Review of Economics and Statistics* 91, no. 4: 717–24.

Howell, Jessica S., and Matea Pender. 2016. "The Costs and Benefits of Enrolling in an Academically Matched College." *Economics of Education Review* 51: 152–68.

Hoxby, Caroline, and Christopher Avery. 2013. "The Missing 'One-Offs': The Hidden Supply of High-Achieving Low-Income Students." *Brookings Papers on Economic Activity*, Spring, 1–66.

Hoxby, Caroline, and Sarah Turner. 2013. "Expanding College Opportunities for High-Achieving, Low-Income Students." Working Paper 12-014. Stanford, Calif.: Stanford Institute for Economic Policy Research. https://siepr.stanford.edu/research/publications/expanding-college-opportunities-high-achieving-low-income-students.

Kane, Thomas J., and Cecelia Elena Rouse. 1999. "The Community College: Educating Students at the Margin between College and Work." *Journal of Economic Perspectives* 13, no. 1: 63–84.

Kelly, Andrew. 2016. "The Supply Side of College Match: Where Are the Seats?" In *Matching Students to Opportunity*, edited by Andrew P. Kelly, Jessica S. Howell, and Carolyn Sattin-Bajaj. Cambridge, Mass.: Harvard Education Press.

Leal, Fermin. 2015. "UC Aiming to Add 10,000 More In-State Undergrad Students by 2018." Blog post, November 10, EdSource. https://edsource.org/2015/uc-aiming-to-add-10000-more-in-state-undergrad-students-by-2018/90321.

Looney, Adam, and Constantine Yannelis. 2015. "A Crisis in Student Loans? How Changes in the Characteristics of Borrowers and the Institutions They Attended Contributed to Rising Loan Defaults." *Brookings Papers on Economic Activity*, Fall, 1–89.

Ma, Jennifer, Sandy Baum, Matea Pender, and C. J. Libassi. 2019. *Trends in College Pricing 2019*. New York: College Board. https://research.collegeboard.org/trends/college-pricing.

Ma, Jennifer, Matea Pender, and Meredith Weltch. 2016. *Education Pays 2016: The Benefits of Higher Education for Individuals and Society.* New York: College Board. https://research.collegeboard.org/trends/education-pays/resource-library.

Mayer, Alexander, Reshma Patel, Timothy Rudd, and Alyssa Ratledge. 2015. *Designing Scholarships to Improve College Success: Final Report on the Performance-Based Scholarship Demonstration.* New York: MDRC. https://www.mdrc.org/publication/designing-scholarships-improve-college-success.

Meyer, Bruce D., and James X. Sullivan. 2009. "Five Decades of Consumption and Income Poverty." Working Paper 14827. Cambridge, Mass.: National Bureau of Economic Research.

Mitchell, Michael, Michael Leachman, and Kathleen Masterson. 2017. *A Lost Decade in Higher Education Funding: States Have Driven Up Tuition and Reduced Quality.* Washington: Center on Budget and Policy Priorities. https://www.cbpp.org/research/a-lost-decade-in-higher-education-funding-state-cuts-have-driven-up-tuition-and-reduced.

Mountjoy, Jack. 2019. "Community Colleges and Upward Mobility." Working Paper. https://sites.google.com/site/jackmountjoyeconomics/.

Oreopoulos, Philip, and Uros Petronijevic. 2013. "Making College Worth It: A Review of the Returns to Higher Education." *The Future of Children* 23, no. 1: 41–65.

Pallais, Amanda, and Sarah Turner. 2006. "Opportunities for Low Income Students at Top Colleges and Universities: Policy Initiatives and the Distribution of Students." *National Tax Journal* 59, no. 2: 357–86.

Piketty, Thomas, and Emmanuel Saez. 2003. "Income Inequality in the United States, 1913–1998 (updated through 2012)." *Quarterly Journal of Economics* 118, no. 1: 1–41.

Reynolds, C. Lockwood. 2012. "Where to Attend? Estimating the Effects of Beginning College at a Two-Year Institution." *Economics of Education Review* 31, no. 4: 345–62.

Roderick, Melissa, Jenny Nagaoka, Vanessa Coca, and Eliza Moeller. 2008. *From High School to the Future: Potholes on the Road to College.* Chicago: Consortium on Chicago School Research. https://consortium.uchicago.edu/sites/default/files/2018-10/CCSR_Potholes_Report.pdf.

Sacerdote, Bruce. 2017. "Fifty Years of Growth in American Consumption, Income, and Wages." Working Paper 23292. Cambridge, Mass.: National Bureau of Economic Research. https://www.nber.org/papers/w23292.

Scott-Clayton, Judith. 2011. "On Money and Motivation: A Quasi-Experimental Analysis of Financial Incentives for College Achievement." *Journal of Human Resources* 46, no. 3: 614–46.

Scott-Clayton, Judith, and Basit Zafar. 2019. "Financial Aid, Debt Management, and Socioeconomic Outcomes: Post-College Effects of Merit-Based Aid." *Journal of Public Economics* 170: 68–82.

Shambaugh, Jay, Ryan Nunn, Patrick Liu, and Greg Nantz. 2017. *Thirteen Facts about Wage Growth.* Washington: The Hamilton Project. https://www.brookings.edu/research/thirteen-facts-about-wage-growth/.

Shapiro, Doug, Afet Dundar, Faye Huie, Phoebe Khasiala Wakhungu, Xin Yuan, Angel Nathan, and Aysesha Bhimdiwali. 2017. *Completing College: A National View of Student Completion Rates—Fall 2011 Cohort*. Report no. 14. Herndon, Va.: National Student Clearinghouse Research Center. https://nscresearchcenter. org/wp-content/uploads/SignatureReport14_Final.pdf.

Smith, Jonathan, Matea Pender, and Jessica Howell. 2013. "The Full Extent of Student-College Academic Undermatch." *Economics of Education Review* 32: 247–61.

Tennessee Higher Education Commission (THEC). 2019. *Tennessee Higher Education Fact Book 2018–19*. https://www.tn.gov/content/dam/tn/thec/bureau/ research/other-research/factbook/2018%2019%20Fact%20Book%20Suppressed %20Final.pdf.

Turner, Sarah. 2004. "Going to College and Finishing College: Explaining Different Educational Outcomes." In *Proceedings of College Choices: The Economics of Where to Go, When to Go, and How to Pay For It*, edited by Caroline Hoxby. Chicago: University of Chicago Press.

Zimmerman, Seth D. 2014. "The Returns to College Admission for Academically Marginal Students." *Journal of Labor Economics* 32, no. 4: 711–54.

Comments and Discussion

COMMENT BY
SUSAN M. DYNARSKI This paper presents a timely and thorough analysis of policies to increase the supply of college graduates. The authors analyze a number of options for increasing the production of baccalaureate degrees in the United States, from free college to improving the quality of public postsecondary institutions.

Degrees matter in the labor market. The earnings of workers with some college credits but no bachelor's degree look more like those of high school graduates than college graduates (Autor 2014). The bachelor's degree is a clear dividing line in the earnings distribution. Expanding the supply of college graduates holds the promise of both reducing income inequality and increasing worker productivity (Goldin and Katz 2010).

The divide is even starker when we consider historical growth in earnings. For nearly half a century, earnings growth has been concentrated among those who have at least a bachelor's degree. The fastest growth of all is among those with advanced degrees, such as a master's in business or medicine. The earnings of workers without a bachelor's degree have either stagnated or dropped, depending on the deflator used (Autor 2014).

Yet the United States has stumbled in increasing the supply of college graduates. College entry has grown rapidly, with 70 percent of high school graduates now heading to college. Almost all of them intend to earn a degree (Jacob and Wilder 2011), but many of them will drop out before reaching that goal. Six years after starting college, just about half of students have earned a bachelor's degree.

The United States has a much higher college dropout rate than other developed countries. In part, this is because our postsecondary system is far more open than most. Our nonselective schools, including community colleges, give students who want to try out college the opportunity to

150

fail. By contrast, in many countries, colleges—especially those that grant baccalaureate degrees—are open only to the very top performers in secondary school (OECD 2019).

The optimal dropout rate is certainly not zero. Students learn about themselves and about college when they matriculate, and for some the right decision is to leave (Manski 1989; Stange 2012). But it is also certain that the optimal dropout rate is not as high as 50 percent. There is room for improving the degree production of U.S. colleges, and this paper examines paths to that end.

THE GOAL OF THE PAPER It is important to understand what the paper does and does not set out to do. The authors examine the effect of a set of policies on the production of bachelor's degrees. The goal of the paper is to predict which policy will most efficiently increase the supply of bachelor's degrees, that is, which policy delivers the biggest baccalaureate bang for the buck.

The paper does *not* attempt a social welfare analysis of the four policies it examines. The paper does not tell us which policy is best because that depends on one's policy goals and distributional preferences. The paper's metric of policy success is efficient production of baccalaureate degrees.

Making community college free has little impact on baccalaureate production, the authors conclude, and so that policy ranks low in this particular horse race. In a different horse race—one focusing on boosting earnings at the bottom of the distribution or reducing student debt burdens—free community college might well move up in the rankings.

THE ELASTICITIES The paper uses a simulation model to estimate the effect of each policy on the supply of bachelor's degrees. The authors calibrate the model using parameters from a growing body of well-identified evidence that estimates the causal impact of a range of postsecondary policies on educational attainment. They do a heroic job of converting parameter estimates from multiple methodologies, settings, and policies into a set of elasticities that they apply in the simulation model.

The elasticities are at the heart of the authors' findings. They are used to predict how efficiently a given policy will convert dollars into baccalaureate degrees. The authors survey a broad range of research in pursuit of estimates that will help them predict the effectiveness of postsecondary policies. There are no perfect matches between the existing evidence and the proposed policies. There never are, of course. The important question is whether gaps in the evidence produce any serious blind spots in our policy predictions.

First, what we know.

We have pretty strong evidence that getting students enrolled in colleges with better resources will increase the likelihood those students will graduate (Hoekstra 2009; Zimmerman 2014; Dillon and Smith 2018). In the past it was unclear whether selection was the whole story, with better students going to better colleges. But we have compelling evidence that at least some of the correlation is causal. Expanding the supply of strong four-year colleges will almost certainly boost the production of baccalaureate degrees. We also have solid evidence that reducing the price of four-year colleges gets more students to attend college and graduate with a bachelor's degree (Page and Scott-Clayton 2016; Dynarski 2000; Cornwell, Mustard, and Sridhar 2006; Dynarski 2008; Dynarski 2003; Bettinger and others 2019; Scott-Clayton 2011; Scott-Clayton and Zafar 2019; Castleman and Long 2016).

All of this evidence provides a strong foundation for the simulations that estimate the effect on baccalaureate production of investing in four-year public colleges and reducing the price of those colleges.

Second, what we don't know.

We have a relatively weak understanding of how policy changes in the community college sector affect the production of baccalaureate degrees.

Do cheaper community colleges divert students from four-year colleges, thereby reducing the production of bachelor's degrees? Or do they so widen the pipeline of students entering postsecondary education, some of whom transfer to four-year colleges, that they increase the production of bachelor's degrees (Rouse 1995)? Which causal channel dominates determines whether making community college free will increase or decrease the supply of bachelor's degrees.

Which causal channel dominates also depends heavily on the institutional context, which varies from state to state (Kane and Rouse 1999). We have evidence on these questions from a couple of states, but the institutional context is so important here that the external validity of this evidence is likely very limited. California has a robust community college system and a robust state university system, and legislation governs students' ability to transfer credits between the two. Michigan has no community college system or state university system, and credit transfers depend on the existence and extent of pairwise articulation agreements between each community college and university. Evidence on the effect of free college in Michigan is unlikely to validly extrapolate to California, and vice versa.

THE POWER OF ZERO Demand elasticities have a straightforward functional form. A given percentage change in price charged is predicted to produce a given percentage change in quantity purchased.

Prices in postsecondary education are anything but straightforward. The price a student pays is a function not just of tuition prices but of financial aid provided by the federal and state governments, as well as colleges themselves. The sticker price is a poor predictor of this net price, especially for low-income students who qualify for need-based grants. As the authors rightly point out, in almost every state, the net price of community college is already zero for low-income students, since federal Pell Grants more than cover tuition costs. They conclude that free community college initiatives will have little effect on the schooling choices of low-income students because their net price is unchanged.

But a growing body of evidence shows that students don't know of or respond to the aid for which they are theoretically eligible (Bettinger and others 2012; Dynarski and Scott-Clayton 2006). The aid system in the United States is complicated and opaque, and students can't respond to a price subsidy they don't know about. A policy that prominently sets community college tuition to zero may well boost the enrollment of students who, in principle, already faced a net price of zero.

In Michigan, an initiative promised upfront the free tuition for which students would be eligible, *in expectation*, after they completed the financial aid process (Dynarski and others 2018). From a purely financial perspective, there was zero change in college prices for these students. An elasticity analysis would predict zero change in demand. Yet students who got this offer were three times as likely to apply as students who did not. The implication is that a "free college" program may have a much larger effect on educational attainment than an elasticity would predict.

REFERENCES FOR THE DYNARSKI COMMENT

Autor, David H. 2014. "Skills, Education, and the Rise of Earnings Inequality among the 'Other 99 Percent.'" *Science* 344, no. 6186: 843–51.

Bettinger, Eric P., Oded Gurantz, Laura Kawano, Bruce Sacerdote, and Michael Stevens. 2019. "The Long-Run Impacts of Financial Aid: Evidence from California's Cal Grant." *American Economic Journal: Economic Policy* 11, no. 1: 64–94.

Bettinger, Eric P., Bridget Terry Long, Philip Oreopoulos, and Lisa Sanbonmatsu. 2012. "The Role of Application Assistance and Information in College Decisions: Results from the H&R Block FAFSA Experiment." *Quarterly Journal of Economics* 127, no. 3: 1205–42.

Castleman, Benjamin L., and Bridget Terry Long. 2016. "Looking beyond Enrollment: The Causal Effect of Need-Based Grants on College Access, Persistence, and Graduation." *Journal of Labor Economics* 34, no. 4: 1023–73.

Cornwell, Christopher, David B. Mustard, and Deepa J. Sridhar. 2006. "The Enrollment Effects of Merit-Based Financial Aid: Evidence from Georgia's HOPE Program." *Journal of Labor Economics* 24, no. 4: 761–86.

Dillon, Eleanor Wiske, and Jeffrey A. Smith. 2018. "The Consequences of Academic Match between Students and Colleges." Working Paper 25069. Cambridge, Mass.: National Bureau of Economic Research. https://www.nber.org/papers/w25069.

Dynarski, Susan M. 2000. "Hope for Whom? Financial Aid for the Middle Class and Its Impact on College Attendance." *National Tax Journal* 53, no. 3: 629–62.

Dynarski, Susan M. 2003. "Does Aid Matter? Measuring the Effect of Student Aid on College Attendance and Completion." *American Economic Review* 93, no. 1: 279–88.

Dynarski, Susan M. 2008. "Building the Stock of College-Educated Labor." *Journal of Human Resources* 43, no. 3: 576–610.

Dynarski, Susan M., C. J. Libassi, Katherine Michelmore, and Stephanie Owen. 2018. "Closing the Gap: The Effect of a Targeted, Tuition-Free Promise on College Choices of High-Achieving, Low-Income Students." Working Paper 25349. Cambridge, Mass.: National Bureau of Economic Research. https://www.nber.org/papers/w25349.

Dynarski, Susan M., and Judith E. Scott-Clayton. 2006. "Cost of Complexity in Federal Student Aid: Lessons from Optimal Tax Theory and Behavioral Economics." *National Tax Journal* 59, no. 2: 319–56.

Goldin, Claudia, and Lawrence F. Katz. 2010. *The Race between Education and Technology.* Cambridge, Mass.: Harvard University Press.

Hoekstra, Mark. 2009. "The Effect of Attending the Flagship State University on Earnings: A Discontinuity-Based Approach." *Review of Economics and Statistics* 91, no. 4: 717–24.

Jacob, B. A., and Tamara Wilder. 2011. "Educational Expectations and Attainment." In *Whither Opportunity? Rising Inequality and the Uncertain Life Chances of Low-Income Children,* edited by Greg J. Duncan and Richard J. Murnane. New York: Russell Sage Press.

Kane, Thomas J., and Cecilia Elena Rouse. 1999. "The Community College: Educating Students at the Margin between College and Work." *Journal of Economic Perspectives* 13, no. 1: 63–84.

Manski, Charles F. 1989. "Schooling as Experimentation: A Reappraisal of the Postsecondary Dropout Phenomenon." *Economics of Education Review* 8, no. 4: 305–12.

OECD. 2019. *Education at a Glance 2019: OECD Indicators.* Paris: OECD Publishing. https://doi.org/10.1787/f8d7880d-en.

Page, Lindsay C., and Judith Scott-Clayton. 2016. "Improving College Access in the United States: Barriers and Policy Responses." *Economics of Education Review* 51:4–22.

Rouse, Cecilia. 1995. "Democratization or Diversion? The Effect of Community Colleges on Educational Attainment." *Journal of Business and Economic Statistics* 13, no. 2: 217–24.

Scott-Clayton, Judith. 2011. "The Causal Effect of Federal Work-Study Participation: Quasi-Experimental Evidence from West Virginia." *Educational Evaluation and Policy Analysis* 33, no. 4: 506–27.

Scott-Clayton, Judith, and Basit Zafar. 2019. "Financial Aid, Debt Management, and Socioeconomic Outcomes: Post-College Effects of Merit-Based Aid." *Journal of Public Economics* 170:68–82.

Stange, Kevin M. 2012. "An Empirical Investigation of the Option Value of College Enrollment." *American Economic Journal: Applied Economics* 4, no. 1: 49–84.

Zimmerman, Seth D. 2014. "The Returns to College Admission for Academically Marginal Students." *Journal of Labor Economics* 32, no. 4: 711–54.

COMMENT BY

CAROLINE HOXBY   Once, in the not too distant past, I sat down with a governor of the state of New Jersey to discuss higher education policy. The governor turned to boasting about the state's New Jersey Student Tuition Assistance Reward Scholarship (NJ STARS) program which, according to the governor, was increasing the state's share of students who obtained high-quality baccalaureate degrees, thereby making the state a more attractive location for employers who needed skilled workers.

My immediate thought was that NJ STARS was one of the most ill-conceived policies ever implemented in American higher education. Any serious economist of higher education would recognize, as soon as he or she learned how the program worked, that NJ STARS was unlikely to produce the intended effect. Worse, the program was at least somewhat likely, if not very likely, to produce the *opposite* of the intended effect. Since I did not know the governor well, I tried to explain these points in a tactful manner.

Briefly, NJ STARS offers a college scholarship to New Jersey's highest achieving students (those in the top 15 percent), but only if the student begins postsecondary education at his or her local two-year public college. After two years there, if the student is interested in transferring to a four-year public college and has accumulated all the necessary credits with strong grades, he or she can apply to transfer and receive some additional scholarship benefits.[1]

---

1. The source is "NJ STARS Fact Sheet for 2019 High School Graduates" (Higher Education Student Assistance Authority 2019).

NJ STARS is ill-conceived for two main reasons that should be obvious to any economist of higher education. First, the state's highest-achieving students are precisely those who are best prepared for the curriculum offered by four-year institutions. Most of them, in the absence of the program, would be among the most likely to attain a baccalaureate degree creditably and on time so long as they initiated their postsecondary education at a four-year school—which the vast majority of them would do. However, if the same students were induced to start their postsecondary education at a two-year school, the evidence suggests that they would be less likely to attain a baccalaureate degree at all or would attain it more slowly.[2] Through this channel, the share of students attaining a high-quality baccalaureate degree in the state would be likely to fall—exactly the opposite of the intended effect.

Now, some might argue that this negative channel would likely apply mainly to middle- or higher-income students whose families could afford tuition in the absence of the scholarship. According to this argument, the scholarship might induce *poor* high achievers, who might otherwise fail to enroll at all, to attend at least a two-year school. Might not this potentially positive effect offset the aforementioned expected negative effect? Unfortunately, here again, NJ STARS was ill-conceived. Poor students were already qualified for the federal Pell Grant which covered most costs at the state's two-year schools. So, in fact, the NJ STARS scholarship had little value for poor students initiating their education at such institutions. Thus the positive channel was likely to be moribund.

In my meeting, I tried to walk the governor and the governor's aides through these points but with little success. They could not keep track of the moving parts. Students induced to begin at two-year colleges being less likely to graduate from four-year colleges? Two-year college tuition already being paid for poor students by Pell Grants? It was all too confusing. Who could possibly know about these effects or understand the interactions? In any case, NJ STARS was already in place and had developed its own brand of policy inertia.

I begin my discussion of "Policies and Payoffs to Addressing America's College Graduation Deficit" by Christopher Avery, Jessica Howell, Matea Pender, and Bruce Sacerdote with this long anecdote for a reason. As I read their paper, I realized that it was exactly what I had needed in my conversation with the governor. While the paper has limitations, noted below, what it does well is produce plausible answers to policy

2. See, for instance, Long and Kurlaender (2008).

questions along the lines of "Is a program like NJ STARS likely to generate its intended effects?" Specifically, the paper sets up a "machine" for answering such questions. It cannot produce answers of the same quality that one could obtain by conducting a very credible evaluation of the program itself   an evaluation that would probably require randomized assignment of the scholarship, something anathema to most policymakers. But the advantage of the authors' machine is that it can answer questions before an actual program is put in place and has the opportunity to develop the inertia that makes evaluation difficult. There are some questions that the authors' machine cannot answer and the inputs to the machine might be improved in the future, but for a range of questions one can crank the handle and their machine will produce reasonable predictions.

WHAT THE PAPER DOES The authors do a good job of explaining what they attempt to do and how the attempt is made. Nevertheless, it may help readers understand what the paper does if I consider how I might run NJ STARS through the machine. In the anecdote above, I implicitly relied on certain information to predict the most basic effects of the program:

1. Which students would be induced by the program to switch from four-year to two-year schools when initiating their postsecondary education? From which four-year schools would they switch? From selective public schools? From nonprofit private schools?

2. Which students (if any) would be induced by the program to switch from no college to at least some postsecondary education?

3. What would be the family incomes of the students who switched from four-year to two-year schools? Of the students (if any) who switched from no college to at least some postsecondary education?

4. What would be the causal effect of all this induced switching on the receipt of baccalaureate degrees, quality-adjusted (since four-year colleges differ substantially)? What would be the causal effect on the receipt of two-year degrees? On how quickly degrees were obtained?

If I had wanted to produce a fuller accounting of the likely effects of the program on the state of New Jersey, I would have needed some additional information:

5. How much would costs change vis-à-vis having no program in place? Would the cost of a four-year degree fall (since it would be more likely to have started at a cheaper two-year school) or rise (since it might take longer to obtain or be less likely to be obtained at all)? Similar cost questions arise for two-year degrees.

6. How would cost changes be split between families and taxpayers? Would there be distributional effects?

7. How would prospective students' earnings change? Would changes in lifetime discounted earnings likely produce a reasonable return on social investment?

8. Since the program would be unlikely to affect poorer and richer students equally, would there be distributional effects of the program—redistribution from poorer to richer students, say?

9. Would the program affect the supply side of postsecondary education, especially the supply of private, as opposed to public, college education?

10. Would the program affect migration of prospective students out of state?

11. Would the program alter the incentives of students to be high achievers? If so, which students would be affected?

The authors attempt to tackle, to at least some degree, the first seven of the questions posed above. They also discuss, much more lightly, some of the remaining questions. They take on these questions by deploying data on individual students who appear in the College Board's data and applying to these students estimates of the answers to the questions posed above. Thus, if they were evaluating NJ STARS, they would take existing estimates from the economics literature on the extent to which a scholarship would induce switching from four-year to two-year institutions. They would apply it to their student data in an attempt to answer the first question posed above. And, they would proceed in that manner through the remaining questions that they attempt to tackle. Eventually, they would gather up the results from all of the questions and attempt to answer questions along the lines of "Did NJ STARS increase quality-adjusted baccalaureate degree attainment?" and "What was the return on investment of the NJ STARS program, from society's point of view (that is, including taxpayer-funded costs and students' future earnings)?"

Of course, the authors do not consider NJ STARS; that is just my evocative example. However, they do consider several policies that are highly relevant to current policy debates. In particular, they consider free community college, reductions in the tuition of four-year public colleges, higher spending at public colleges, and the speculative idea of moving students to what the authors call the "best available in-state public college." (It is unclear how the last of these options would be implemented, but it is an interesting thought experiment.)

THE STRENGTHS OF THE AUTHORS' MACHINE There are two features that are indispensable to the working of the authors' machine. First, they have fairly rich data on individual students so that, when they apply estimates from the literature, they can—for instance—differentiate between the effects for high-achieving and low-achieving students or between the effects for high-income and low-income students. Second, the authors use estimates of the effects ("estimated parameters") that are credibly causal. This last feature is absolutely crucial because all of the questions posed above are causal questions. Identification strategies that do not produce credibly causal estimates are likely to produce biased answers to the questions.

For instance, consider that—without the inducement of an NJ STARS-like program—it is anomalous for high achievers to commence college at a two-year school rather than a four-year school.[3] Thus, when we observe high achievers at a two-year school, we might reasonably infer that some unobserved factor (such as the need to live at home to support a disabled family member) has caused them to make an unusual choice. One cannot simply take the outcomes of current high achievers at two-year schools and assume that those outcomes would apply to high achievers induced to attend two-year schools by some policy. One needs to have a credibly causal estimate of how high achievers' outcomes change when they are induced by a scholarship, financial aid, or some other tuition policy to attend a two-year school.

This is just one example of the sort of credibly causal parameter estimate the authors need. They need a good number of others, and a lot of their work for this paper went into scouring the literature and making careful decisions about the estimates to use. This work is somewhat hidden because much of it appears only in appendices. Nevertheless, it matters greatly.

Summing up, the strength of the authors' machine is that it allows them credibly to distinguish effects among different types of students and among different types of schools. Even if we should not put much faith in the exact estimates produced by the machine, it tends to reveal the key forces and the basic magnitudes of those forces. For instance, it reveals that free community college has at best ambiguous effects on degree completion: fewer baccalaureate degrees somewhat offset by more associate degrees. It also reveals that free community college conveys few benefits to low-income students because financial aid already covers most of their tuition and fees at two-year public schools.

3. The source is my calculations based on College Board, ACT, and National Student Clearinghouse data. These data are described in detail in Hoxby and Avery (2013). These data are the best source and also have the benefit of being largely aligned with the data used in the paper on which this is a comment. (The difference is that ACT data were not available to the authors of the paper under discussion. This point is discussed below.) Another calculation that I made to confirm this fact is based on the High School Longitudinal Study (HSLS), the most recent NCES longitudinal data set.

THE LIMITATIONS OF THE AUTHORS' MACHINE So far, I have emphasized the machine's strengths and its usefulness. What are its limitations? First, the machine is only as good as the parameter estimates fed into it. There are a few reasons why the estimates are problematic. Some of the estimates are based on fairly weak empirical strategies, even if they are among the best available. On many causal questions, there just is not a convincing, recent study that has produced reasonably precise estimates. Also, the estimates used are frequently local to some population: a single state or even a single county; a group of students near some peculiar policy threshold such as a test score cutoff. Some of the estimates are generated by evaluations of idiosyncratic policies that are only modestly related to the far more general policies considered by the authors. Furthermore, the estimates used are often noisy, and the authors' machine is not built to account for all of the potential sources of error. In short, since the estimates have a variety of problems, I encourage the reader to view the findings as a good starting place and as a showing of the main forces, not as precise predictions.

To be clear, the problems associated with the parameter estimates could be remedied over time as new, more credible, more applicable estimates are produced by researchers. Thus, this is not a fundamental limitation of the authors' machine: it is an opportunity for future improvements. While I would not task the authors with revising their paper as each new estimate is released, I would not be surprised if another scholar comes along in the future and—starting from the authors' work—revises their evaluations or evaluates additional policies that may be under consideration at that future time.

A more serious limitation is that the data that the authors use are not representative of possible college students in the United States. This is for several reasons. Although about 80 percent of students in current U.S. high school cohorts will eventually enroll in some postsecondary school, only about 44 percent of them take one of the College Board tests (the PSAT or SAT).[4] This is partly because some students take one of the ACT tests instead

---

4. The source for the 80 percent number is my calculations based on projecting detailed educational attainment of 30-year-olds using the American Community Survey from 2000 to 2018 (Ruggles and others 2019) along with the percentages of the population of 18- to 24-year-olds from the same birth cohorts who were enrolled in various levels of school from National Center for Education Statistics, Digest of Education Statistics, table 103.20 (Snyder, de Brey, and Dillow 2019). The sources for the approximate rates of College Board test taking are *2014–15 College-Bound High School Sophomores: Summary Report* (College Board 2015) and *2016 College Bound Seniors: Total Group Profile Report* (College Board 2016).

(PLAN, the PreACT, or ACT) and partly because about a third of students take neither a College Board nor an ACT test.[5] Moreover, the students who are missing from the authors' data are by no means a random sample.

Why? States located in the middle of the country tend to be severely underrepresented in the authors' data because those states tend to contract with ACT.[6] In such states, it is typically only those students who aspire to attend a very selective out-of-state college who take the SAT in addition to the ACT. The result of this limitation is that the authors' findings are local to states that are not dominated by ACT. The findings are also somewhat skewed toward the behavior of high-achieving students who are not too concerned about attending close to home. These are issues that could potentially be addressed by future authors who have access to ACT as well as College Board data.

Moreover, students who are less well prepared for college tend not to take a College Board test or any college aptitude examination. We know this from studies of what occurs when a school district or state makes the SAT or ACT mandatory.[7] The students who are shifted from being non–test takers to test takers are very disproportionately low achievers. When testing is not mandatory, students who would end up with top decile scores are almost certain to take a test anyway while students who would end up with bottom decile scores are almost certain *not* to take one. Between the top and bottom deciles, the probability that a student takes a test—when it is not mandatory—declines monotonically. This

---

5. Because some students take both College Board and ACT tests, it is hard to determine exactly how many students are tested by at least one of the organizations. However, in the cohorts relevant to the paper, the ACT tested about 32 percent of students and about 15 percent of students took both organizations' tests. Thus, a reasonable estimate is that 61 to 66 percent of students in recent cohorts are tested by one of the two organizations. Another way to calculate a similar number is to focus on sophomores, many of whom are required to take an ACT or College Board test even as the tests for juniors and seniors are optional. Also, compared to seniors, sophomores who take an ACT test are less likely to take a College Board test and vice versa. Thus, sophomores are less likely to be double-counted in the test-taking rate. The sophomore-focused reports are *2014-15 College-Bound High School Sophomores: Summary Report* (College Board 2015) and *Building Momentum: The Condition of Progress toward College Readiness* (ACT 2016).

6. States that are dominated by ACT as opposed to the College Board change every year as the two organizations write new contracts. However, ACT is more likely to be dominant in states that are in the middle of the country, and the College Board is more likely to be dominant in coastal states. For instance, in recent years that are reflected in the authors' data for this paper, the following states have been ACT-dominant states: Alabama, Arkansas, Hawaii, Kentucky, Illinois, Louisiana, Michigan, Mississippi, Missouri, Montana, Nebraska, Nevada, North Carolina, North Dakota, South Carolina, Utah, Wisconsin, and Wyoming.

7. See Klasik (2013), Bulman (2015), and Hyman (2017).

limitation of the data has serious consequences for the usefulness of the authors' machine, as described in the next section. Before that discussion, though, let me briefly note some other limitations of the exercise.

In my experience, the income measures contained in the College Board data are poor in accuracy. Many students do not report their family income at all in the Student Data Questionnaire, a survey that they are asked to fill out before taking the SAT. Students who do answer the question often give replies that appear implausible when we compare their replies to tax data and American Community Survey data. None of this is really surprising: many students may have only a vague idea of their family income, especially as they are asked to report it before their parents have filled out the Free Application for Federal Student Aid (FAFSA). Nevertheless, using inaccurate income data is obviously a problem for evaluating policies that change the availability of financial aid or the level of tuition.

On a related note, nearly all of the policies that the authors consider have consequences for the regressivity or progressivity of government policy. For instance, policies that reduce tuition or increase funding at selective public universities may be regressive because affluent students are substantially more likely to be well qualified for admission there. If those same affluent students end up with higher earnings in consequence, those earnings will also affect the income distribution. Despite the fact that so many Americans are currently interested in income inequality, and therefore in the regressivity or progressivity of policies, the paper does not give much attention to such issues. This inattention may be a reflection of the low accuracy of the income data: the necessary calculations might well push the data beyond their capacities.

For-profit institutions play a larger role in American higher education with each passing year. In 2017, they accounted for 7 percent of postsecondary enrollment, about 2.2 million students.[8] The University of Phoenix alone enrolls about 180,000 students, at least half of whom make use of one of the federal grant or subsidized loan programs. An additional and large share make use of the tax benefits for tuition and fees.[9] Thus, we

---

8. See the National Center for Education Statistics, Digest of Education Statistics, table 303.20 (Snyder, de Brey, and Dillow 2019).

9. The source is my calculations based on the institution-level data from the Integrated Postsecondary Education Data System, micro data for 2017–18 (National Center for Education Statistics 2019). The calculation of "at least half" includes veterans benefits but, notably, does not include federal tax benefits for tuition and fees. Were the tax benefits to be included as well, nearly all students at the University of Phoenix would be found to receive some federal aid (see Hoxby 2018).

should be deeply interested in how policies play out in these institutions. Yet the authors do not include for-profit institutions in their study. This is probably because such institutions are very underrepresented in the College Board data for the reasons described above. Regardless of the reason, omitting for-profit institutions is problematic. For instance, during the Great Recession, enrollment in nonselective colleges surged since opportunity costs were low, owing to the weak labor market. Much of the increase in enrollment occurred at for-profit institutions since community colleges, apparently, could not expand rapidly enough.[10] This suggests that community colleges and for-profit schools are fairly close substitutes. Thus, a policy like free community college might have a profound effect on for-profit enrollment.

The elasticity estimates that the authors use are drawn from partial equilibrium studies whereas the policies they consider would induce general equilibrium effects. For instance, making community college free or reducing public colleges' tuition would also certainly affect students' preparation for college, the tuition charged by for-profit institutions, and the supply of nonprofit colleges. There is not much that the authors can do about the gap between partial equilibrium estimates and general equilibrium consequences. To their credit, they discuss general equilibrium issues coherently. Nevertheless, the gap exists and is a limitation.

THE ELEPHANT IN THE ROOM I began these comments with an anecdote about NJ STARS, a program for high-achieving students who are well prepared for very selective colleges. This was deliberate because the authors' machine is ideally suited for answering questions about programs like NJ STARS. However, it is much less well suited for answering questions about some of the policies that the authors actually consider—especially, but not only, free community college.

Why is this? When I consider any of the policies that the authors consider, one of my primary concerns—often my dominant concern—is whether students who will fail in college and who would be better off pursuing some other activity (vocational training, a job in which they would gain skills, the military, and so on) will be induced to enroll, often ending up with no degree, wasting valuable time, and sometimes ending up with loans that they cannot repay. The evidence indicates that a large share of American students are not prepared for college and are likely to drop out because they are unable to do the work.[11] The lack of college preparedness

10. See, for example, Deming, Goldin, and Katz (2013).
11. Some of the best evidence comes from Stinebrickner and Stinebrickner (2012).

among students is the elephant in the room in all debates about U.S. post-secondary education. Many of the things that go wrong in American higher education—the high dropout rate, the student loan crisis, the flourishing of shady institutions that deceive students or illegally receive federal aid—have origins in the country's failure to turn out high school students who are prepared for college.

The most widely used definition of *college-ready* is not arbitrary but, instead, empirical. The ACT, for instance, defines it as "the knowledge and skills a student needs to enroll in and succeed in credit-bearing first-year courses at a postsecondary institution (such as a two- or four-year college, trade school, or technical school) without the need for remediation" (ACT, n.d.). The ACT determines its threshold for college-readiness by examining which students fail to pass introductory classes and fail to get the grades to continue in academic standing as postsecondary students. Since the institutions used to set the threshold include two-year colleges, trade schools, and technical schools, the standard is not high.

The ACT and other organizations regularly recheck their thresholds for college readiness using evidence on college success so the thresholds vary slightly over the years. However, they tend to be close to the "proficient" threshold used by the National Assessment of Educational Progress (NAEP), the only test mandated to be taken at very regular intervals by a repre-sentative sample of American students.[12] In the most recent assessments of twelfth graders, 25 percent were rated as proficient in math, 22 percent proficient in science, 37 percent proficient in reading, and 27 percent profi-cient in writing.[13] In fact, since about 10 percent of students leave high school before the twelfth grade and therefore cannot be tested, the college-readiness rates are even lower than the above numbers suggest. For instance, the percentage of American students (as opposed to twelfth graders) who are college-ready in math is about 22.5 percent. Since about half of the students who have left before the twelfth grade will eventually earn the General Educational Development (GED) certificate and thus be eligible to enroll in college, their (lack of) college readiness matters too.[14]

---

12. In the states where 100 percent of high school graduates take the ACT, about the same percentage of students are rated as college-ready based on the ACT as are rated proficient based on the NAEP. Compare *The Condition of College and Career Readiness 2019: National* (ACT 2019, 14) to *Digest of Education Statistics 2018* (Snyder, de Brey, and Dillow 2019, 155).

13. The most recent assessments for twelfth graders in math, science, and reading were in 2015. The most recent assessment in writing was in 2011. See table 221.20 in *Digest of Education Statistics 2018* (Snyder, de Brey, and Dillow 2019, 155).

14. The source is my calculation based on the American Community Survey, 2000 to 2018.

Since the late 1970s, when twelfth graders first took NAEP tests, their proficiency has remained strikingly similar to the latest results, just mentioned.[15] Yet, in the late 1970s, only about 50 percent of the population eventually enrolled in postsecondary education.[16] In other words, in those days, the share of students who were college-ready was less, but not grossly less, than the share who would eventually enroll. Today, even though current students are no more likely to be college-ready than 1970s students, a reasonable projection is that about 80 percent of today's students will eventually enroll in postsecondary education.[17] This means at least 55 percent of enrollees will probably lack adequate preparation in one or more core subjects. Put another way, marginally prepared students are now not the exception: they are the rule. No one should be surprised, therefore, that the United States has a remarkably low percentage of postsecondary students who complete (within 150 percent of the normal time required) the degree that is their goal when they enroll.

Like many other economists, my assessment is that the United States needs to induce an ever-increasing share of its population to gain the skills we associate with higher education. That is just the way the economy is evolving, owing to forces from trade and technology. However, my assessment is about the need for skills, while many policies seem only to have induced a larger share of students to enroll in postsecondary education regardless of whether they were prepared and regardless of whether they were likely to acquire skills. Over the past few decades, U.S. colleges have dug deeper and deeper into the ranks of students who are only marginally prepared. These marginally prepared students are the "swing" students—the students whose conduct ultimately dominates how most policy innovations have worked out.

It is tempting for scholars to focus on fairly high-achieving students, like those in the NJ STARS program or those who are overrepresented in the College Board data. But we ought instead to be focused on marginally prepared students when we evaluate many policy innovations like free community college or reduced tuition at public colleges. Because marginally prepared students are woefully underrepresented in the College Board data, the authors' machine is not designed to allow us to focus on these crucial students. Thus the machine can deliver meaningful findings on

15. Source: author's analysis of the NAEP data available for interactive analysis (Data Explorer) on the NCES website.

16. The source is my calculation based on the detailed educational attainment of 30-year-olds in the 5 percent micro data sample of the 1980 Census of Population and Housing.

17. See note 4.

some important questions in higher education but, on other questions, it cannot. This is the elephant in the room.

SUMMING UP Despite my discussion of limitations and the elephant in the room, I plan to rely on the key findings in this paper, at least as regards their signs and general magnitudes (as opposed to the point estimates) for the sort of questions that the authors' machine answers well. That is a compliment to their work. And should I encounter another governor of New Jersey, I might just have a copy of the paper ready to hand over in order to back up my analysis.

REFERENCES FOR THE HOXBY COMMENT

ACT. 2016. *Building Momentum: The Condition of Progress toward College Readiness.* Iowa City, IA: ACT. http://www.act.org/content/act/en/research/reports/act-publications/building-momentum-condition-of-progress-toward-college-readiness.html.

ACT. 2019. *The Condition of College and Career Readiness 2019: National.* Iowa City, IA: ACT. http://www.act.org/content/dam/act/unsecured/documents/cccr-2019/National-CCCR-2019.pdf.

ACT. n.d. "PLAN Overview." https://www.act.org/content/dam/act/unsecured/documents/Plan-CommunicationText.pdf.

Bulman, George. 2015. "The Effect of Access to College Assessments on Enrollment and Attainment." *American Economic Journal: Applied Economics* 7, no. 4: 1–36.

College Board. 2015. *2014–15 College-Bound High School Sophomores: Summary Report.* New York: College Board.

College Board. 2016. *2016 College-Bound Seniors: Total Group Profile Report.* New York: College Board. https://reports.collegeboard.org/pdf/total-group-2016.pdf.

Deming, David James, Claudia D. Goldin, and Lawrence F. Katz. 2013. "For-Profit Colleges." Scholarly Article 12553738. Cambridge, Mass.: Harvard University Department of Economics.

Higher Education Student Assistance Authority (HESAA) of New Jersey. 2019. "NJ STARS Fact Sheet for 2019 High School Graduates." https://www.hesaa.org/Documents/FactSheets/NJSTARS/FactSheetfor2019HSGrad.pdf.

Hoxby, Caroline M. 2018. "Online Postsecondary Education and the Higher Education Tax Benefits: An Analysis with Implications for Tax Administration." In *Tax Policy and the Economy*, edited by Robert A. Moffitt. Chicago: University of Chicago Press.

Hoxby, Caroline, and Christopher Avery. 2013. "The Missing 'One-Offs': The Hidden Supply of High-Achieving Low-Income Students." *Brookings Papers on Economic Activity*, Spring, 1–66.

Hyman, Joshua. 2017. "ACT for All: The Effect of Mandatory College Entrance Exams on Postsecondary Attainment and Choice." *Education Finance and Policy* 12, no. 3 (Summer): 281–311.

Klasik, Daniel. 2013. "The ACT of Enrollment: The College Enrollment Effects of State-Required College Entrance Exam Testing." *Educational Researcher* 42, no. 3: 151–60.

Long, Bridget Terry, and Michal Kurlaender. 2008. "Do Community Colleges Provide a Viable Pathway to a Baccalaureate Degree?" Working Paper 14367. Cambridge, Mass.: National Bureau of Economic Research.

National Center for Education Statistics. 2019. *Integrated Postsecondary Education Data System*. Washington: U.S. Department of Education.

Ruggles, Steven, Sarah Flood, Ronald Goeken, Josiah Grover, Erin Meyer, Jose Pacas, and Matthew Sobek. 2019. *Integrated Public Use Microdata Series: Version 9.0* [data set]. Minneapolis: University of Minnesota. https://doi.org/10.18128/D010.V9.0.

Snyder, Thomas D., Cristobal de Brey, and Sally A. Dillow. 2019. *Digest of Education Statistics 2018*. NCES 2020-009. Washington: Institute of Education Sciences, National Center for Education Statistics, U.S. Department of Education. https://nces.ed.gov/pubs2020/2020009.pdf.

Stinebrickner, Todd, and Ralph Stinebrickner. 2012. "Learning about Academic Ability and the College Dropout Decision." *Journal of Labor Economics* 30, no. 4: 707–48.

GENERAL DISCUSSION   Drawing off Caroline Hoxby's concern about the authors' limited engagement with low levels of college preparation among high school students, Bob Gordon began by raising the additional concern that even among students who complete their college credential, many struggle to find a job that requires a college education. He noted that between 40 and 45 percent of graduates from a four-year college are underemployed and reiterated the importance of this finding, namely, that it highlights a discrepancy between the value of a college education as measured by median income and the value of a college education for those who end up in the bottom quarter of the income distribution, as those who struggle the most to find a college-level job are most often those who had the lowest levels of college preparation. Therefore, he concluded, measuring college outcomes by median income biases many of the estimates in this paper because the returns to a college education are overstated for the marginal individual who is moving from a two-year college to a four-year college.

Justin Wolfers offered two observations. First, certain institutions are better at graduating students than others. Consequently, one could imagine an entirely different approach to state education policy in which states with weak college systems stop offering postsecondary training altogether and instead send their students to states with postsecondary systems that produce superior outcomes. Second, the central, high-level concern addressed in the paper is the impact of additional money on higher education. Therefore, while the authors' analysis using elasticities is informative, Wolfers argued, an important piece of information left relatively unaddressed is the supply-side effect of the various policies outlined in the paper.

Harry Holzer urged the authors to place greater emphasis in the paper on outcomes besides bachelor's degree attainment, particularly associate degree and certificate attainment at community colleges; these institutions, he noted, are radically under-resourced despite supporting a large number of disadvantaged students. He agreed with the authors' argument that providing significantly more funding to community colleges would have a positive effect but also acknowledged its limited feasibility given the fiscal reality of state budgets. Giving these budgetary constraints, Holzer encouraged participants to consider where money spent would have the greatest impact. In this case, he argued that occupational programs with strong labor market value are among the most optimal targets for limited state appropriations.

Ed Lazear wondered about the role of forgivable loans in boosting college retention and completion rates. Drawing off his time on a Stanford University financial aid committee, Lazear raised the point that even if students are not financially needy, the majority of their assets may be relatively illiquid, which raises the question of whether these students should be receiving forgivable loans or tuition waivers. Lazear cited data he had gathered with colleagues that examined the differential effects of forgivable loans and tuition waivers on the probability that a student would accept admission to Stanford over Harvard. Results indicated that the forgivable loan affected behavior in nearly the same way as the grant. In light of this finding, Lazear concluded that examining forgivable loans as a viable practice may be worthwhile.

Robert Hall remarked that there is a fundamental policy design issue surrounding higher education reform that is neglected both in this paper and in the broader policy arena, namely, increasing barriers of entry into the middle class. He noted that a once-poor family loses their earned income tax credit (EITC) upon moving into the middle class, along with their ability to acquire need-based postsecondary assistance, particularly Pell Grants. Problems of this sort, he concluded, must be considered in any substantive conversation about America's graduation deficit.

Richard Cooper challenged the stated objective of the paper by posing the following two questions: Why do we as a society care about the number of bachelor's degrees? And why should that number be a focus of public policy at all? Supporting his inquiries, he remarked that a bachelor's degree surely holds market value, but because students are aware of this, post-secondary degree attainment is a private issue, not a social one. Following up on these comments, Cooper raised another concern about the paper—its disproportionate focus on the United States. Eighteen-year-olds in all rich countries face the same issues that American 18-year-olds face, he noted, and it is important when addressing this subject as a whole to draw on the experience of Western Europe.

Jason Furman advised the authors to work toward specific point estimates for the policies outlined in their paper, as opposed to general trends. He recommended starting by examining the effect of these policies on tuition, in particular, how the incidence of higher tuition rates would be distributed and how schools would allocate the additional funds. Furman also raised the question of how these policies are likely to affect the general equilibrium, that is, how much of the resulting effect is likely to be due to signaling, as opposed to a real increase in earnings. He concluded with the remark that he does not view the absence of precise point estimates as detracting from Hoxby's conclusions about the paper, only that their addition is important in future versions of the paper.

Ben Friedman raised the point that there is an unusual discontinuity in conversations about education: it is assumed that grades 11 and 12 should be provided for free, but that does not extend to grades 13 and 14. This logical disconnect, Friedman argued, bears directly on Hoxby's comment about students' low levels of college preparation. Indeed, students' performance in grade 13 will surely depend, to a certain extent, on their experience in grade 12. Friedman concluded that, while not a criticism of the paper, the literature would surely be helped if the authors' analysis was presented such that a sharp discontinuity did not exist between everything preceding grade 12 and everything following it.

Christopher Avery thanked the participants for their comments and assured them that he and his coauthors would do their best to incorporate them into the next version of the paper. Avery addressed Holzer's comment about free community colleges first. He emphasized that while those of us who study the economics of education may have a sense that free community college is bad, that is not necessarily the case among policymakers. A central objective of this paper, therefore, was to present the evidence that free community college is problematic in a clear and transparent way in the hopes of introducing that concept into the policy debate. A second important message, Avery continued, is that more spending is going to improve student outcomes. While the magnitude of this effect may vary depending on how funds are allocated, more financial resources will have a positive effect on students.

In response to Furman's remarks about the generality of the model, and specifically whether it is revenue neutral, Avery stated that while revenue neutrality will be a useful extension of the model for future editions of the paper, the use of a non-neutral revenue model was intentional, as it eliminated corresponding outflows of money from the system and allowed estimates to be interpreted directly.

On Friedman's comment about the logical discontinuity in the consideration of grades 13 and 14 relative to grades 11 and 12, Avery noted that the higher education discourse has begun to eliminate the distinction between those two groups. He spoke specifically about Goldrick-Rab's book on the merits of free community college in which she outlines the importance of thinking about grades 13 and 14 the same way we would grades 11 and 12.[1] This is a sentiment that is becoming widely shared, Avery continued. Nevertheless, he and his coauthors decided to uphold the distinction precisely because levels of preparation for anything after grade 12 are extremely heterogeneous across students.

With respect to Lazear's remark about elasticities, Avery stated that while the Harvard versus Stanford elasticity was well-measured, certain elasticities are not applicable outside of certain contexts. Indeed, robust methodology does not render a finding universally useful.

Moving on to Susan Dynarski's remarks about the importance of considering the distributional effects of various policies, and particularly free community college, Avery responded that he and his coauthors struggled to decide on the appropriate amount of information to provide on each policy. Based on her comments, however, a useful next step may be to add in distributional detail and kernel density income estimates for the free community college policy. However, it may be unwise to provide this much detail for all of the policies, Avery noted, as it may overwhelm the reader.

Avery commented that Dynarski and Hoxby made somewhat contradictory points on the topic of pushing more students into two-year colleges. On the one hand, Dynarski spoke about the positive returns to any subbaccalaureate degree and even enrolling in a two-year college. On the other hand, Hoxby strongly emphasized that the marginal student enrolled in

---

1. Sara Goldrick-Rab, *Paying the Price: College Costs, Financial Aid, and the Betrayal of the American Dream* (Chicago: University of Chicago Press, 2016).

these institutions is likely to be underprepared and drop out prematurely. In response to these conflicting ideas, Avery responded that it's extremely difficult to judge what will occur out of sample. Pushing more students into two-year colleges has the potential to provide benefits by exposing them to new experiences and fostering intellectual interests. However, it may also impose unnecessary costs, including emotional and financial hardship. There are experiments being conducted in real time in Tennessee and Oregon that will provide us with rich information on this topic down the road, but we just don't know that much right now, Avery concluded.

In response to Hoxby and Dynarski's comments about the regressivity of free college proposals, Avery remarked that it is important first to understand why free college proposals are so popular. The answer is fairly simple: free college proposals sound great, and they are not that expensive. As a last dollar program, he explained, free college would require students to use all available federal funding before any tuition assistance is applied. Consequently, for students who already have their tuition covered by, say, Pell Grants, the federal government would not be required to provide any additional funds. Therefore, as Dynarski claimed, these policies are fundamentally regressive. Avery concluded by stating that he believes the policies are popular precisely because they are regressive.

On the topic of adequate representation of for-profit colleges in the data, Matea Pender clarified, first and foremost, that their sample was not composed solely of individuals who took the SAT, as that is a highly selective group composed largely of college-bound students. Instead, the sample included both SAT and PSAT takers, as the latter group is far less self-selecting and contains low-achieving students who end up attending sub-baccalaureate institutions. In addition to the initial clarification, Pender added that because their data were linked to other college outcomes, the authors had an empirically based estimate of what it means to be "college ready" based on a certain probability of students getting a C in their first semester courses in college. The authors were then able to use that estimate in their simulations as a sensitivity analysis. Indeed, they could simply condition on those who were academically ready for the opportunity they were being moved into to see how much some of the estimates were reduced.

Responding to Hoxby's remark about the limitations of the authors' in-sample elasticities, Bruce Sacerdote agreed with her critique but provided the one caveat that the state-level policies in Tennessee and Oregon are quite young and not representative of the United States. Sacerdote also offered a clarification on his earlier remarks, stating that earning a bachelor's degree was not the only outcome of interest. Associate degrees were considered, too. One of the advantages of working with a micro data set, he continued, is that it is possible to use a more granular outcome measure, particularly credits earned, as opposed to degree attainment. While the authors did not make this choice, it could be an interesting extension to their work. Sacerdote concluded by stating his desire for U.S. Treasury data that would allow him to examine the effects of various policies on students' income, a measure that is perhaps more important than degree completion.

Returning to Holzer's comment, Avery offered a final thought on the topic of what students should be studying. He noted that there have been concerted efforts to push students into programs that will help them acquire lucrative employment following graduation, namely, occupational programs. The central policy challenge, however, is that the vast majority of students who enroll in two-year colleges intend to transfer to a four-year university. Consequently, many are resistant to pursuing programs that are not conducive to transfer, despite transfer prospects being weak for many students. This is a public policy problem that will need to be addressed behaviorally and instrumentally, Avery concluded.

In response to Cooper's question about why we care about the number of bachelor's degrees, Avery acknowledged that this is a challenging question to answer and that he will try to address it in future versions of the paper.

Similarly, Avery responded to Gordon's comment about signaling by acknowledging that attempting to isolate the human capital value of education from its signaling value is a fundamental challenge in labor economics and is difficult for the authors to address at this time.

Avery then thanked the participants for pushing him to consider the "bang for the buck" associated with various policies. Looking at the costs of these proposals relative to other social programs in education, namely Head Start, will be an objective of future versions of this paper.

In response to the question about supply, Pender concluded with the remark that while supply concerns constitute a separate paper and a separate problem, he does not disagree with the premise that fixing bad colleges by replicating good colleges is an objective to pursue.

PHILIPPE ANDRADE
Federal Reserve Bank of Boston

JORDI GALÍ
Centre de Recerca en Economia Internacional

HERVÉ LE BIHAN
Banque de France

JULIEN MATHERON
Banque de France

The Optimal Inflation Target and the Natural Rate of Interest

ABSTRACT   We study how changes in the steady-state real interest rate (henceforth r^*) affect the optimal inflation target in a New Keynesian dynamic stochastic general equilibrium (DSGE) model with trend inflation and a lower bound on the nominal interest rate. In this setup, a lower r^* increases the probability of hitting the lower bound. That effect can be counteracted by an increase in the inflation target, but the resulting higher steady-state inflation has a welfare cost in and of itself. We use an estimated DSGE model to quantify that trade-off and determine the implied optimal inflation target, conditional on the monetary policy rule in place before the financial crisis. The relation between r^* and the optimal inflation target is downward sloping. While the increase in the optimal inflation rate is in general smaller than the decline in r^*, in the currently empirically relevant region the slope of the relation is found to be close to -1. That slope is robust to allowing for parameter uncertainty. Under

Conflict of Interest Disclosure: Philippe Andrade is a senior economist and policy adviser at the Federal Reserve Bank of Boston; Jordi Galí is a senior researcher at the Centre de Recerca en Economia Internacional (CREI), a professor at Universitat Pompeu Fabra, and a research professor at the Barcelona Graduate School of Economics, as well as an academic consultant to Sveriges Riksbank and a member of the Research Council of the Deutsche Bundesbank; Hervé Le Bihan is Deputy Director for the Directorate of Monetary and Financial Studies at the Banque de France; Julien Matheron is a senior research adviser for the Directorate of Monetary and Financial Studies at the Banque de France. Beyond these affiliations, the authors did not receive financial support from any firm or person for this paper or from any firm or person with a financial or political interest in this paper. None of the authors are currently officers, directors, or board members of any organization with an interest in this paper. No outside party had the right to review this paper before circulation. The views expressed in this paper are those of the authors, and do not necessarily reflect those of the aforementioned institutions affiliated with the authors.

makeup strategies such as price level targeting, the optimal inflation target is significantly lower and less sensitive to r^*.

A recent but sizable literature has pointed to a permanent—or at least very persistent—decline in the natural rate of interest in advanced economies (Holston, Laubach, and Williams 2017; Laubach and Williams 2016). Various likely sources of that decline have been discussed, including a lower trend growth rate of productivity (Gordon 2015), demographic factors (Eggertsson, Mehrotra, and Robbins 2019), or an enhanced preference for safe and liquid assets (Caballero and Farhi 2018; Del Negro and others 2017; Summers 2014).

A lower steady-state real interest rate matters for monetary policy. Given average inflation, a lower steady-state real interest rate will cause the nominal interest rate to hit its zero lower bound (ZLB) more frequently, hampering the ability of monetary policy to stabilize the economy, bringing about more frequent (and potentially protracted) episodes of recession and below-target inflation. The low interest rate environment is a key factor behind the Federal Reserve's current review of its monetary policy (Clarida 2019; Fuhrer and others 2018).[1]

In the face of that risk several prominent economists have forcefully argued in favor of raising the inflation target.[2] Since a lower natural rate of interest is conducive to a higher ZLB incidence, one would expect a higher inflation target to be desirable as, other things being equal, a higher inflation target increases the steady-state nominal interest rate and reduces the ZLB incidence. But the answer to the practical question of how much should the target be increased is not obvious. Indeed, the benefit of providing a better hedge against hitting the ZLB, which is an infrequent event, comes at the cost of higher steady-state inflation which induces *permanent* costs, as recently argued by Bernanke (2016), among others. The answer to this question thus requires us to assess how the trade-off between the incidence of the ZLB and the welfare cost induced by steady-state inflation is modified when the natural rate of interest decreases. While the decrease in the natural rate of interest has been emphasized in the recent literature, such assessment has received surprisingly little attention.

---

1. Note that the numerical value of the inflation target is not part of that review.
2. See, among others, Ball (2014), Blanchard, Dell'Ariccia, and Mauro (2010), and, with qualifications, Williams (2016).

The present paper contributes to this debate by asking four questions. First, to what extent does a lower steady-state real interest rate (r^*) call for a higher optimal inflation target (π^*)? Second, does the source of decline in r^* matter? Third, how does parameter uncertainty affect the (r^*, π^*) curve? Fourth, to what extent do the strategy and rules followed by the central bank alter the relation between r^* and π^*? We focus on the U.S. economy but the issues we investigate equally apply to other advanced economies— in particular the euro area—because the decline in r^* appears to be a global phenomenon (Brand, Bielecki, and Penalver 2019; Del Negro and others 2019; Rachel and Summers 2019).[3]

We provide answers to these questions using a structural, empirically estimated, macroeconomic model. Our main findings can be summarized as follows: (1) The relation between r^* and π^* is downward sloping, *but not necessarily, in general, one-for-one*. (2) In the vicinity of the pre-crisis values for r^*, the slope of the (r^*, π^*) locus is close to −1, though slightly below in absolute value; the relation is largely robust to the underlying source of variation in r^* for a plausible range of r^* values. (3) The slope of the (r^*, π^*) locus remains close to −1 when the central bank is uncertain about the parameters of the model characterizing the economy, including r^*. (4) The slope of the curve is also robust to various alteration of the monetary policy rule but not to the adoption of rules such as price level targeting, which involve a credible commitment to making up for past deviations from the inflation target.

Our results are obtained from extensive simulations of a New Keynesian dynamic stochastic general equilibrium (DSGE) model estimated for the United States over a Great Moderation sample.[4] The framework features: (1) price stickiness and partial indexation of prices to trend inflation, (2) wage stickiness and partial indexation of wages to both inflation and productivity, and (3) a ZLB constraint on the nominal interest rate. The first two features imply the presence of potentially substantial costs associated with nonzero steady-state inflation. The third feature warrants a strictly positive inflation rate in order to mitigate the incidence and adverse effects of the ZLB. To our knowledge, these three features have not been jointly taken into account in previous analyses of optimal inflation.

---

3. We will provide a comparable analysis for the euro area in a work in progress, "Should the ECB Adjust Its Strategy in the Face of a Lower Natural Rate of Interest?"

4. In Andrade, Le Bihan, Galí, and Matheron (2020), we show that very similar results obtain in a model estimated with euro area data.

Our analysis focuses on the trade-off between the costs attached to the probability of hitting the ZLB and the costs induced by a positive steady-state inflation rate for a given monetary policy strategy. In the baseline, monetary policy follows an inertial interest rate rule estimated using pre-crisis data. Importantly, the specification of the policy rule implies that interest rates remain low for long after the end of a ZLB episode and that private agents expect the central bank to do so. This implies that some monetary accommodation can be provided despite the ZLB constraint. This specification can thus be seen as a parsimonious way to factor in the effects of nonconventional policies that the Fed implemented during the ZLB period in our analysis.

According to our simulations, the optimal inflation target obtained when the policymaker is assumed to know the economy's parameters with certainty (and taken to correspond to the mean of the posterior distribution) is around 2 percent (in annual terms). This result is obtained in an environment with a relatively low probability—around 6 percent—of hitting the ZLB when the target for the inflation rate is set at the historical mean of inflation and given the size of the shocks estimated on our Great Moderation sample. Our simulations also show that a 100 basis point drop of r^* from its estimated 2.5 percent pre-crisis level will almost double the probability of hitting the ZLB if the monetary authority keeps its inflation target unchanged. The optimal reaction of the central bank is to increase the inflation target by about 99 basis points. This optimal reaction limits the increase in the probability of hitting the ZLB to a mere half of a percentage point.

This optimal adjustment is robust to a set of alternative scenarios. It does not depend on the cause (productivity, demography, or safe assets) underlying such a structural decline. It also remains close to one for one when we consider alternative assumptions regarding key structural parameters: structural shocks with higher variance, alternative markups in the goods and labor market, and different degrees of indexation to trend inflation. Strikingly, while the level of the locus can be significantly affected by those changes—these alternative scenarios call for an optimal inflation target that would have been close to or above 2 percent before the crisis—overall the slope of the (r^*, π^*) relation remains close to −1 in the vicinity of the pre-crisis parameter region.

More generally, one may wonder how a central bank should adjust its optimal inflation target when it is uncertain about the true values of structural parameters describing the economy. A notable feature of our approach is that we perform a full-blown Bayesian estimation of the model. This allows us not only to assess the uncertainty surrounding π^* but also to derive an optimal inflation target taking into account the parameter uncertainty facing the policymaker, including uncertainty with regard to the determinants of the steady-state real interest rate. When that parameter uncertainty is allowed for, the optimal inflation target value increases significantly, to 2.4 percent. The higher optimal target under parameter uncertainty reflects the fact that the loss function is asymmetric, so that choosing an inflation target that is lower than the optimal one is more costly than choosing an inflation target that is above. In spite of the higher level, it remains true that a Bayesian-theoretic optimal inflation target rises by about 90 basis points in response to a downward shift of the distribution in r^* by 100 basis points.

Finally, we study how potential changes in the monetary policy rule or strategy affect the (r^*, π^*) relation. We consider a number of different cases: (1) defining the inflation target in terms of average realized inflation as opposed to a parameter in the rule; (2) a central bank constrained by an effective lower bound on the policy rate that can be below zero; (3) a central bank with a lower or higher smoothing parameter in the interest rate policy rule; (4) a monetary policy rule with a smoothing component that involves the lagged actual policy rate instead of the lagged shadow rate; and (5) a central bank targeting the price level rather than the inflation rate. All these changes have an impact on the level of π^* for any given level of r^*. Yet only in the case of higher interest rate smoothing and price level targeting do we find a noticeable change in the slope of the (r^*, π^*) relation. In these two cases, the relation is much less steep, illustrating the strength of makeup strategies to overturn the ZLB. However, as we discuss in the conclusion, an important caveat is that this result is obtained under the joint assumption of rational expectations, perfect information, and full credibility of the commitment.

The remainder of the paper is organized as follows. Section I describes our baseline model. Section II discusses how the model is estimated and simulated, as well as how the welfare-based optimal inflation target is computed. Section III is devoted to the analysis of the (r^*, π^*) relation under the baseline estimates as well as for a set of alternative parameters. Section IV presents and discusses this locus under parameter uncertainty. Section V investigates the (r^*, π^*) under alternative monetary policy rules and strategies. Finally section VI summarizes and concludes.

RELATED LITERATURE To our knowledge no paper has systematically investigated the (r^*, π^*) relation. Coibion, Gorodnichenko, and Wieland (2012), followed up by Dordal-i-Carreras and others (2016), and Kiley and Roberts (2017), are the papers most closely related to ours, as they study optimal inflation in quantitative setups that account for the ZLB. However, the analyses by Coibion, Gorodnichenko, and Wieland (2012) assume a constant steady-state natural rate of interest, so a key difference is our focus on eliciting the relation between the steady-state real interest rate and optimal inflation. Other differences are that we estimate, rather than calibrate, the model, and that we allow for wage rigidity in the form of infrequent, staggered, wage adjustments. A distinctive feature with respect to Kiley and Roberts (2017) is that we use a model-consistent, micro-founded loss function to compute optimal inflation.

A series of papers assessed the probability that the U.S. economy hit the ZLB for a given inflation target. Interestingly, our own assessment of this pre-crisis ZLB incidence falls in the ballpark of available estimates, for example, Chung and others (2012). As we show, when the inflation target is not adjusted, but allowing for post–Great Moderation shocks, we also get post-crisis probability of hitting the ZLB that is comparable to the ones obtained in recent related studies such as Chung and others (2019).

In the New Keynesian setup that we consider, agents have rational expectations and make decisions that are forward-looking: they fully understand that the central bank's inability to lower the policy further will lead to a deflation which magnifies the contractionary demand shocks that were responsible for driving the economy to the ZLB in the first place. One concern may be that this framework makes the ZLB too destabilizing, hence overweighing the benefits of a positive inflation target. However, this is partially offset by the fact that rational expectations and forward-looking decisions also make the lower for longer monetary policies that we consider at the end of the trap very effective, which limits the length and width of ZLB episodes. Chung and others (2019) illustrate that ZLB episodes can also be very costly in setups featuring agents that are less forward-looking, such as the FRB/US model (one of the Federal Reserve's models of the U.S. economy).

Our assessment of the (welfare) cost of inflation also critically relies on our assumptions of a Calvo mechanism for price and wage setting. Among the recent papers on ZLB, Blanco (forthcoming) studies optimal inflation in a state-dependent pricing model, that is, a menu cost model. In this setup, optimal inflation is typically positive and higher than with time-dependent pricing. Indeed, as in our analysis, positive inflation hedges the economy against the detrimental effects of the ZLB.[5] In addition, as shown

---

5. By contrast, see Burstein and Hellwig (2008) for a similar exercise under menu costs without ZLB, which leads to negative optimal inflation rate.

by Nakamura and others (2018), the presence of state-dependent pricing weakens considerably the positive relationship between inflation and price dispersion, thus reducing the costs of inflation. Nakamura and others (2018) further argue that menu costs are a more plausible mechanism for pricing frictions.[6] Two points are, however, worth making. First, in the range of values for the inflation target that we consider, the difference between the welfare cost in a Calvo model and in a menu cost model is less dramatic than with a 10 percent or higher inflation rate, as documented by Nakamura and others (2018). Second, most recent empirical analyses of price setting show that there is a mass of small price changes in the data that cannot be rationalized by a menu cost model. To fit the micro data, much of this recent literature typically introduces a random opportunity of price change, hence a Calvo component, in the menu cost model (Alvarez, Le Bihan, and Lippi 2016). In such an augmented menu cost model, the distinction with the assessment taken from the Calvo model is bound to be attenuated.

Our paper is also connected to the voluminous literature on monetary policy under uncertainty (Levin and others 2006; Williams 2013), although to our knowledge this literature has not investigated the impact of uncertainty on the determination of the optimal inflation target.

Other relevant references, albeit ones that put little or no emphasis on the ZLB, are the following. An early literature focuses on sticky prices and monetary frictions. In such a context, as shown by Khan, King, and Wolman (2003) and Schmitt-Grohé and Uribe (2010), the optimal rate of inflation should be slightly negative. Similarly, a negative optimal inflation would result from an environment with trend productivity growth and prices and wages both sticky, as shown by Amano and others (2009). In this kind of environment, moving from a 2 percent to a 4 percent inflation target would be extremely costly, as suggested by Ascari, Phaneuf, and Sims (2018). By contrast, adding search and matching frictions to the setup, Carlsson and Westermark (2016) show that optimal inflation can be positive. Bilbiie, Fujiwara, and Ghironi (2014) find positive optimal inflation can be an outcome in a sticky-price model with endogenous entry and product variety. Somewhat related, Adam and Weber (2019) show that, even without any ZLB concern, optimal inflation might be positive in the context of a model with heterogeneous firms and systematic firm-level productivity trends.

---

6. They document that the cross-sector dispersion in the size of price changes is similar in the current low inflation period as in the high inflation period of the late 1970s. If Calvo were the relevant pricing frictions, the dispersion in size of price changes should have been much larger in the high inflation period than today.

Finally, Lepetit (2018) shows that optimal inflation can be different from zero when profits and utility flows are discounted at different rates, as is generally the case in overlapping generation models. In a parameterized example of the latter, he shows the optimal steady-state inflation is significantly above zero.

I. The Model

We use a relatively standard medium-scale New Keynesian model as a framework of reference. Crucially, the model features elements that generate a cost to inflation: (1) nominal rigidities, in the form of staggered price and wage setting; (2) less than perfect price (and wage) indexation to past or trend inflation; and (3) trend productivity growth, to which wages are imperfectly indexed.

As is well known, staggered price setting generates a positive relation between deviations from zero inflation and price dispersion (with the resulting inefficient allocation of resources). Also, and ceteris paribus, price inflation induces (nominal) wage inflation, which in turn triggers inefficient wage dispersion in the presence of staggered wage setting. Partial indexation also magnifies the costs of nonzero price (or wage) inflation as compared to a setup where price and wages fully catch up with trend inflation (Ascari and Sbordone 2014). Finally the lack of a systematic indexation of wages to productivity also induces an inefficient wage dispersion.

At the same time, there are benefits associated to a positive inflation rate, as interest rates are subject to a ZLB constraint. In particular, and given the steady-state real interest rate, the incidence of binding ZLB episodes and the associated macroeconomic volatility should decline with the average rate of inflation.

Overall, the model we use, and the implied trade-off between costs and benefits of steady-state inflation, are close to those considered by Coibion, Gorodnichenko, and Wieland (2012). However we assume Calvo-style sticky wages, in addition to sticky prices.[7]

I.A. Households

The economy is inhabited by a continuum of measure one of infinitely lived, identical households. The representative household is composed of a

---

7. In their robustness analysis, Coibion, Gorodnichenko, and Wieland (2012) consider downward nominal wage rigidity, which entails different mechanisms than with Calvo-style rigidities.

continuum of workers, each specialized in a particular labor type indexed by $h \in [0,1]$. The representative household's objective is to maximize an intertemporal welfare function

$$(1) \qquad \mathbb{E}_t \sum_{s=0}^{\infty} \beta^s \left\{ e^{\zeta_{g,t+s}} \log\left(C_{t+s} - \eta C_{t+s-1}\right) - \frac{\chi}{1+v} \int_0^1 N_{t+s}(h)^{1+v} dh \right\},$$

where $\beta \equiv e^{-\rho}$ is the discount factor (ρ being the discount rate), $\mathbb{E}_t\{\cdot\}$ is the expectation operator conditional on information available at time t, C_t is consumption, and $N_t(h)$ is the supply of labor of type h. The utility function features habit formation, with degree of habits h. The inverse Frisch elasticity of labor supply is v, and χ is a scale parameter for labor disutility. The utility derived from consumption is subject to a preference shock $\zeta_{g,t}$.

The representative household maximizes equation (1) subject to the sequence of constraints

$$P_t C_t + e^{\zeta_{q,t}} Q_t B_t \le \int_0^1 W_t(h) N_t(h) \, dh + B_{t-1} - T_t + D_t,$$

where P_t is the aggregate price level, $W_t(h)$ is the nominal wage rate associated with labor of type h, $e^{\zeta_{q,t}} Q_t$ is the price at t of a one-period nominal bond paying one unit of currency in the next period, where $\zeta_{q,t}$ is a "risk-premium" shock, B_t is the quantity of such bonds acquired at t, T_t denotes lump-sum taxes, and D_t stands for the dividends rebated to the households by monopolistic firms.

I.B. Firms and Price Setting

The final good is produced by perfectly competitive firms according to the Dixit-Stiglitz production function

$$Y_t = \left(\int_0^1 Y_t(f)^{(\theta_p-1)/\theta_p} df \right)^{\theta_p/(\theta_p-1)},$$

where Y_t is the quantity of final good produced at t, $Y_t(f)$ is the input of intermediate good f, and θ_p the elasticity of substitution between any two intermediate goods. The zero-profit condition yields the relation

$$P_t = \left(\int_0^1 P_t(f)^{1-\theta_p} df \right)^{1/(1-\theta_p)}.$$

Intermediate goods are produced by monopolistic firms, each specialized in a particular good $f \in [0, 1]$. Firm f has technology

$$Y_t(f) = Z_t L_t(f)^{1/\phi},$$

where $L_t(f)$ is the input of aggregate labor, $1/\phi$ is the elasticity of production with respect to aggregate labor, and Z_t is an index of aggregate productivity. The latter evolves according to

$$Z_t = Z_{t-1} e^{\mu_z + \zeta_{z,t}},$$

where μ_z is the average growth rate of productivity. Thus, technology is characterized by a unit root in the model.

Intermediate goods producers are subject to nominal rigidities à la Calvo. Formally, firms face a constant probability α_p of not being able to reoptimize prices. In the event that firm f is not drawn to reoptimize at t, it rescales its price according to the indexation rule

$$P_t(f) = (\Pi_{t-1})^{\gamma_p} P_{t-1}(f),$$

where $\Pi_t \equiv P_t/P_{t-1}$, Π is the associated steady-state value and $0 \leq \gamma_p < 1$. Thus, in case firm f is not drawn to reoptimize, it mechanically rescales its price by past inflation. Importantly, however, we assume that the degree of indexation is less than perfect since $\gamma_p < 1$. One obvious drawback of the Calvo setup is that the probability of price reoptimization is assumed to be invariant, inter alia to the long-run inflation rate. Drawing from the logic of menu cost models, the Calvo parameter of price stickiness could be expected to endogenously decrease when trend inflation rises. However, in the range of values for trend inflation that we will consider, available microeconomic evidence, such as that summarized in Golosov and Lucas (2007), suggests there is no significant correlation between the frequency of price change and trend inflation.

If drawn to reoptimize in period t, a firm chooses P_t^* in order to maximize

$$\mathbb{E}_t \sum_{s=0}^{\infty} (\beta \alpha_p)^s \Lambda_{t+s} \left\{ (1 + \tau_{p,t+s}) \frac{V_{t,t+s}^p P_t^*}{P_{t+s}} Y_{t,t+s} - \frac{W_{t+s}}{P_{t+s}} \left(\frac{Y_{t,t+s}}{Z_{t+s}} \right)^{\phi} \right\},$$

where Λ_t denotes the marginal utility of wealth, $\tau_{p,t}$ is a sales subsidy paid to firms and financed via a lump-sum tax on households, and $Y_{t,t+s}$ is the demand function that a monopolist who last revised its price at t faces at $t + s$. It obeys

$$Y_{i,t+s} = \left(\frac{V^p_{t,t+s} P^*_t}{P_{t+s}} \right)^{-\theta_p} Y_{t+s},$$

where $V^p_{t,t+s}$ reflects the compounded effects of price indexation to past inflation

$$V^p_{t,t+s} = \prod_{j=t}^{t+s-1} (\Pi_j)^{\gamma_p}.$$

We further assume that

$$1 + \tau_{p,t} = (1 + \tau_p) e^{-\zeta_{u,t}},$$

with $\zeta_{u,t}$ appearing in the system as a cost-push shock. Furthermore, we set τ_p so as to neutralize the steady-state distortion induced by price markups.

I.C. Aggregate Labor and Wage Setting

There is a continuum of perfectly competitive labor-aggregating firms that mix the specialized labor types according to the CES technology

$$N_t = \left(\int_0^1 N_t(h)^{(\theta_w - 1)/\theta_w} dh \right)^{\theta_w/(\theta_w - 1)},$$

where N_t is the quantity of aggregate labor and $N_t(h)$ is the input of labor of type h, and where θ_w denotes the elasticity of substitution between any two labor types. Aggregate labor N_t is then used as an input in the production of intermediate goods. Equilibrium in the labor market thus requires

$$N_t = \int_0^1 L_t(f) \, df.$$

Here, it is important to notice the difference between $L_t(f)$, the demand for aggregate labor emanating from firm f, and $N_t(h)$, the supply of labor of type h by the representative household.

The zero-profit condition yields the relation

$$W_t = \left(\int_0^1 W_t(h)^{1-\theta_w} dh \right)^{1/(1-\theta_w)},$$

where W_t is the nominal wage paid to aggregate labor while $W_t(h)$ is the nominal wage paid to labor of type h.

Mirroring prices, we assume that wages are subject to nominal rigidities, à la Calvo, in the manner of Erceg, Henderson, and Levin (2000). Formally, unions face a constant probability α_w of not being able to reoptimize wages. In the event that union h is not drawn to reoptimize at t, it rescales its wage according to the indexation rule

$$W_t(h) = e^{\gamma_z \mu_z} \left(\Pi_{t-1}\right)^{\gamma_w} W_{t-1}(h),$$

where, as before, wages are indexed to past inflation. However, we assume that the degree of indexation is here, too, less than perfect by imposing $0 \leq \gamma_w < 1$. In addition, nominal wages are also indexed to average productivity growth with indexation degree $0 \leq \gamma_z < 1$.

If drawn to reoptimize in period t, a union chooses W_t^* in order to maximize

$$\mathbb{E}_t \sum_{s=0}^{\infty} (\beta \alpha_w)^s \left\{ (1 + \tau_w) \Lambda_{t+s} \frac{V_{t,t+s}^w W_t^*}{P_{t+s}} N_{t,t+s} - \frac{\chi}{1+v} N_{t,t+s}^{1+v} \right\},$$

where the demand function at $t + s$ facing a union who last revised its wage at t obeys

$$N_{t,t+s} = \left(\frac{V_{t,t+s}^w W_t^*}{W_{t+s}} \right)^{-\theta_w} N_{t+s},$$

and where $V_{t,t+s}^w$ reflects the compounded effects of wage indexation to past inflation and average productivity growth

$$V_{t,t+s}^w = e^{\gamma_z \mu_z (t+s)} \prod_{j=t}^{t+s-1} \left(\Pi_j\right)^{\gamma_w}.$$

Furthermore, we set τ_w so as to neutralize the steady-state distortion induced by wage markups.

I.D. Monetary Policy and the ZLB

Monetary policy in so-called normal times is assumed to be given by an inertial Taylor-like interest rate rule

(2) $$\hat{\imath}_t = \rho_i \hat{\imath}_{t-1} + (1 - \rho_i)(a_\pi \hat{\pi}_t + a_y \hat{x}_t) + \zeta_{R,t},$$

where $i_t \equiv -\log(Q_t)$, with $\hat{\imath}_t$ denoting the associated deviation from steady state, that is, $\hat{\imath}_t \equiv i_t - i$. Also, $\pi_t \equiv \log\Pi_t$, $\hat{\pi}_t \equiv \pi_t - \pi$ is the gap between inflation and its target, and $\hat{x}_t \equiv \log(Y_t/Y_t^n)$ where Y_t^n is the efficient level of output, defined as the level of output that would prevail in an economy with flexible prices and wages and no cost-push shocks. Finally, $\zeta_{R,t}$ is a monetary policy shock.

Importantly, we interpret π as the central bank target for change in the price index. An annual inflation target of 2 percent would thus imply $\pi = 2/400 = 0.005$, as the model will be parameterized and estimated with quarterly data. Note that the inflation target thus defined may differ from average inflation.

Crucially for our purposes, the nominal interest rate i_t is subject to a ZLB constraint:

$$i_t \geq 0.$$

The steady-state level of the real interest rate is defined by $r^* \equiv i - \pi$. Given logarithmic utility, it is related to technology and preference parameters according to $r^* = \rho + \mu_r$. Combining these elements, it is convenient to write the ZLB constraint in terms of deviations from steady state

(3) $$\hat{\imath}_t \geq -(\mu_z + \rho + \pi).$$

The rule effectively implemented is given by:

(4) $$\hat{\imath}_t = \max\{\hat{\imath}_t^n, -(\mu_z + \rho + \pi)\},$$

where

(5) $$\hat{\imath}_t^n = \rho_i \hat{\imath}_{t-1}^n + (1 - \rho_i)(a_\pi \hat{\pi}_t + a_y \hat{x}_t) + \zeta_{R,t},$$

with i_t^n denoting the shadow or notional rate, that is, the one that would be effective in the absence of the ZLB constraint. Thus the lagged rate that matters is the lagged notional interest rate, rather than the lagged actual rate. In making that assumption we follow Coibion, Gorodnichenko, and Wieland (2012) and a large share of the recent literature.

Before proceeding, several remarks are in order. First, note that realized inflation might be on average below the target π as a consequence of ZLB episodes, that is, $\mathbb{E}\{\pi_t\} < \pi$. In such instances of ZLB, monetary policy fails to deliver the appropriate degree of accommodation, resulting in a more severe recession and lower inflation than in an economy with no ZLB constraint.[8]

Second, we assume the central bank policy is characterized by a simple interest rate rule rather than a Ramsey-like fully optimal policy of the type studied, for example, by Khan, King, and Wolman (2003) or Schmitt-Grohé and Uribe (2010). Such rules have been shown to be a good empirical characterization of the behavior of central banks in the last decades.[9] Moreover, two features in our setup—the inertia in the monetary policy rule and the use of a lagged notional rate rather than a lagged actual rate— render the policy more persistent and thus closer to a Ramsey-like fully optimal interest rate rule. In particular the dependence on the lagged notional rate $\hat{\imath}_t^n$ results in the nominal interest rate $\hat{\imath}_t$ being lower for longer in the aftermath of ZLB episodes (as $\hat{\imath}_t^n$ will stay negative for a protracted period). In section V, we study how alternative strategies of lower for longer affect the (r^*, π^*) relation.

As equation (3) makes clear, μ_z, ρ, π enter symmetrically in the ZLB constraint. Put another way, for given structural parameters and a given process for $\hat{\imath}_t$, the probability of hitting the ZLB would remain unchanged if productivity growth or the discount rate decline by 1 percent and the inflation target is increased by a commensurate amount at the same time. Based on these observations, one may be tempted to argue that in response to a permanent decline in μ_z or ρ, the optimal inflation target π^* must necessarily change by the same amount (with a negative sign).

The previous conjecture is, however, incorrect. The reasons for this are twofold. First, any change in μ_z (or ρ) also translates into a change in the coefficients of the equilibrium dynamic system. It turns out that this effect is nonnegligible since, as our later results imply, after a 1 percentage point decline in r^* the inflation target has to be raised by more than 1 percent in order to keep the probability of hitting the ZLB unchanged. Second, because there are welfare costs associated with increasing the inflation target, the policymaker would also have to balance the benefits of keeping the incidence of ZLB episodes constant with the additional costs in terms

---

8. For convenience, table A.1 in the online appendix summarizes the various notions of optimal inflation and long-run or target inflation considered in this paper.

9. See, for example, Clarida, Galí, and Gertler (1998).

of extra price dispersion and inefficient resource allocation. These costs can be substantial and may more than offset the benefits of holding the probability of ZLB constant. Assessing these forces is precisely this paper's endeavor.

II. Estimation and Simulations

In the present section we discuss how the model is estimated and simulated, as well as how the welfare-based optimal inflation target is computed.

II.A. Estimation without a Lower Bound on Nominal Interest Rates

We estimate the model using data for a pre-crisis period over which the ZLB constraint is not binding. This enables us to use the linear version of the model.[10]

ESTIMATION PROCEDURE Because the model has a stochastic trend, we first induce stationarity by dividing trending variables by Z_t. The resulting system is then log-linearized in the neighborhood of its deterministic steady state.[11] We append to the system a set of equations describing the dynamics of the structural shocks, namely,

$$\zeta_{k,t} = \rho_k \zeta_{k,t-1} + \sigma_k \epsilon_{k,t}, \quad \epsilon_{k,t} \sim N(0,1)$$

for $k \in \{R, g, u, q, z\}$.

Absent the ZLB constraint, the model can be solved and cast into the usual linear transition and observation equations:

$$s_t = \mathcal{T}(\theta)s_{t-1} + \mathcal{R}(\theta)\epsilon_t,$$

$$x_t = \mathcal{M}(\theta) + \mathcal{H}(\theta)s_t,$$

with s_t a vector collecting the model's state variables, x_t a vector of observable variables, and ϵ_t a vector of innovations to the shock processes $\epsilon_t = (\epsilon_{R,t}, \epsilon_{g,t}, \epsilon_{u,t}, \epsilon_{q,t}, \epsilon_{z,t})'$. The solution coefficients are regrouped in the conformable matrices $\mathcal{T}(\theta)$, $\mathcal{R}(\theta)$, $\mathcal{M}(\theta)$, and $\mathcal{H}(\theta)$ which depend on the vector of structural parameters θ.

---

10. See Gust and others (2017) and Lindé, Maih, and Wouters (2017) for alternative methods that deal with the ZLB constraint at the estimation stage.
11. See the online appendix for further details.

The sample of observable variables is $X_T \equiv \{x_t\}_{t=1}^{T}$ with

$$
x_t = \begin{bmatrix} \Delta\log(\mathrm{GDP}_t), \\ \Delta\log(\mathrm{GDPDeflator}_t), \\ \Delta\log(\mathrm{Wages}_t), \\ \mathrm{ShortTermInterestRate}_t \end{bmatrix}',
$$

where the short-term nominal interest rate is the effective federal funds rate. We use a sample of quarterly data covering the period 1985:Q2–2008:Q3.[12] This choice is guided by two objectives. First, this sample strikes a balance between size and the concern of having a homogeneous monetary policy regime over the period considered. The sample covers the Volcker and post-Volcker period, arguably one of relative homogeneity of monetary policy. Second, we use a sample that coincides more or less with the so-called Great Moderation. Over the latter we expect smaller shocks to hit the economy. In principle, this will lead to a conservative assessment of the effects of the more stringent ZLB constraint due to lower real interest rates.

The parameters ϕ, θ_p, and θ_w are calibrated prior to estimation. The parameter θ_p is set to 6, resulting in a steady-state price markup of 20 percent. Similarly, the parameter θ_w is set to 3, resulting in a wage markup of 50 percent. These numbers fall into the arguably large ballpark of available values used in the literature. In a robustness section, we investigate the sensitivity of our results to these parameters. The parameter ϕ is set to 1/0.7. Given the assumed subsidy correcting the steady-state price markup distortion, this results in a steady-state labor share of 70 percent.

We rely on a full-system Bayesian estimation approach to estimate the remaining model parameters. After having cast the dynamic system in the state-space representation for the set of observable variables, we use the Kalman filter to measure the likelihood of the observed variables. We then form the joint posterior distribution of the structural parameters by combining the likelihood function $p(X_T|\theta)$ with a joint density characterizing some prior beliefs $p(\theta)$. The joint posterior distribution thus obeys

$$
p(\theta|X_T) \propto p(X_T|\theta)p(\theta).
$$

Given the specification of the model, the joint posterior distribution cannot be recovered analytically but may be computed numerically, using a

---

12. The data are obtained from the Federal Reserve Economic Data (FRED) database. GDP is expressed in per capita terms.

Table 1. Estimation Results

Parameter	Prior shape	Prior mean	Prior std.	Posterior mean	Posterior std.	Low	High
ρ	Normal	0.20	0.05	0.19	0.05	0.11	0.27
μ_z	Normal	0.44	0.05	0.43	0.04	0.36	0.50
π^*	Normal	0.61	0.05	0.62	0.05	0.54	0.69
α_p	Beta	0.66	0.05	0.67	0.03	0.61	0.73
α_w	Beta	0.66	0.05	0.50	0.05	0.43	0.58
γ_p	Beta	0.50	0.15	0.20	0.07	0.08	0.32
γ_w	Beta	0.50	0.15	0.44	0.16	0.21	0.68
γ_z	Beta	0.50	0.15	0.50	0.18	0.26	0.75
η	Beta	0.70	0.15	0.80	0.03	0.75	0.85
v	Gamma	1.00	0.20	0.73	0.15	0.47	0.97
a_p	Gamma	2.00	0.15	2.13	0.15	1.89	2.38
a_y	Gamma	0.50	0.05	0.50	0.05	0.42	0.58
ρ_{TR}	Beta	0.85	0.10	0.85	0.02	0.82	0.89
σ_z	Inverse Gamma	0.25	1.00	1.06	0.22	0.74	1.38
σ_R	Inverse Gamma	0.25	1.00	0.10	0.01	0.09	0.11
σ_q	Inverse Gamma	0.25	1.00	0.39	0.11	0.16	0.61
σ_g	Inverse Gamma	0.25	1.00	0.23	0.04	0.16	0.29
σ_u	Inverse Gamma	0.25	1.00	0.24	0.05	0.06	0.46
ρ_R	Beta	0.25	0.10	0.51	0.06	0.41	0.61
ρ_z	Beta	0.25	0.10	0.27	0.13	0.09	0.45
ρ_g	Beta	0.85	0.10	0.98	0.01	0.97	1.00
ρ_q	Beta	0.85	0.10	0.88	0.04	0.80	0.95
ρ_u	Beta	0.80	0.10	0.80	0.10	0.65	0.96

Source: Authors' calculations.
Note: "Low" and "High" denote the bounds of the 90 percent probability interval for the posterior distribution.

Markov chain Monte Carlo (MCMC) sampling approach. More specifically, we rely on the Metropolis-Hastings algorithm to obtain a random draw of size 1,000,000 from the joint posterior distribution of the parameters.

ESTIMATION RESULTS Table 1 reports the parameter's postulated priors (type of distribution, mean, and standard error) and estimation results, that is, the posterior mean and standard deviation, together with the bounds of the 90 percent probability interval for each parameter.

For the parameters π, μ_z and ρ, we impose Gaussian prior distributions. The parameters governing the latter are chosen so that the model steady-state values match the mean values of inflation, real per capita GDP growth, and the real interest rate in our U.S. sample. Our choice of priors for the other parameters are standard. In particular, we use beta distributions for parameters in [0,1], gamma distributions for positive parameters, and inverse gamma distributions for the standard error of the structural shocks.

Most of our estimated parameters are in line with the calibration adopted by Coibion, Gorodnichenko, and Wieland (2012), with important qualifications. First, we obtain a slightly higher degree of price rigidity than theirs (0.67 versus 0.55). Second, our specification of monetary policy is different from theirs. In particular, they allow for two lags of the nominal interest rate in the monetary policy rule while we have only one lag. However, we can compare the overall degree of interest rate smoothing in the two setups. To this end, abstracting from the other elements of the rule, we simply focus on the sum of autoregressive coefficients. It amounts to 0.92 in their calibration while the degree of smoothing in our setup has a mean posterior value of 0.85. While this might not seem to be a striking difference, it is useful to cast these figures in terms of half-life of convergence in the context of an autoregressive model of order 1. Our value implies twice as small a half-life than theirs. Third, our monetary policy shock and our shocks to demand have approximately twice as small an unconditional standard deviation as theirs. Finally, we estimate the degree of indexation to past inflation rather than setting it to zero as in Coibion, Gorodnichenko, and Wieland (2012). We find small though nonzero degrees of indexation to past inflation. This will translate into a higher tolerance for inflation in our subsequent analysis of the optimal inflation target. This is because a higher indexation helps to mitigate the distortions induced by a higher inflation target. However, it turns out that, given these estimates, this effect is quantitatively small.

Properties of the estimated model, such as the response to a monetary policy shock, are standard (see online appendix, section B; online appendix, section C, illustrates the lower for longer property embedded in the policy rule).

II.B. Computing the Optimal Inflation Target

Next we show how the optimal inflation target is computed.

SIMULATIONS WITH A ZLB CONSTRAINT The model becomes nonlinear when one allows the ZLB constraint to bind. The solution method we implement follows the approach developed by Bodenstein, Erceg, and Guerrieri (2009) and Guerrieri and Iacoviello (2015). The approach can be described as follows. There are two regimes: the no-ZLB regime $k = n$ and the ZLB regime $k = e$, and the canonical representation of the system in each regime is

$$\mathbb{E}_t\left\{\mathcal{A}^{(k)}s_{t+1} + \mathcal{B}^{(k)}s_t + C^{(k)}s_{t-1} + \mathcal{D}^{(k)}\epsilon_t\right\} + f^{(k)} = 0,$$

where s_t is a vector collecting all the model's variables, $\mathcal{A}^{(k)}$, $\mathcal{B}^{(k)}$, $C^{(k)}$, and $\mathcal{D}^{(k)}$ are conformable matrices, and $f^{(k)}$ is a vector of constants. In the no-ZLB regime, the vector $f^{(n)}$ is filled with zeros. In the ZLB regime, the row of $f^{(e)}$ associated with i_t is equal to $\mu_z + \rho + \pi$. Similarly, the rows of the system matrices associated with i_t in the no-ZLB regime correspond to the coefficients of the interest rate rule while in the ZLB regime, the coefficient associated with i_t is equal to 1 and all the other coefficients are set to zero.

In each period t, given an initial state vector s_{t-1} and vector stochastic innovations ϵ_t, we simulate the model under perfect foresight (that is, assuming that no further shocks hit the economy) over the next N periods, for N sufficiently large. In case this particular draw is not conducive to a ZLB episode, we find s_t using the linear solution stated above. In contrast, if this draw leads to a ZLB episode, we postulate integers $N_e < N$ and $N_x < N$ such that the ZLB is reached at time $t + N_e$ and left at time $t + N_x$. In this case, we solve the model by backward induction. We obtain the time varying solution

$$s_{t+q} = d_{t+q} + \mathcal{T}_{t+q}s_{t+q-1} + \mathcal{R}_{t+q}\epsilon_{t+q},$$

with $\epsilon_{t+q} = 0$ for $q > 0$ and where, for $q \in \{N_e, \ldots, N_x - 1\}$,

$$\mathcal{T}_{t+q} = -\left(\mathcal{A}^{(e)}\mathcal{T}_{t+q+1} + \mathcal{B}^{(e)}\right)^{-1} C^{(e)},$$

$$\mathcal{R}_{t+q} = -\left(\mathcal{A}^{(e)}\mathcal{T}_{t+q+1} + \mathcal{B}^{(e)}\right)^{-1} \mathcal{D}^{(e)},$$

$$d_{t+q} = -\left(\mathcal{A}^{(e)}\mathcal{T}_{t+q+1} + \mathcal{B}^{(e)}\right)^{-1} \left(\mathcal{A}^{(e)}d_{t+q+1} + f^{(e)}\right)$$

and, for $q \in \{0, \ldots, N_e - 1\}$,

$$\mathcal{T}_{t+q} = -\left(\mathcal{A}^{(n)}\mathcal{T}_{t+q+1} + \mathcal{B}^{(n)}\right)^{-1} C^{(n)},$$

$$\mathcal{R}_{t+q} = -\left(\mathcal{A}^{(n)}\mathcal{T}_{t+q+1} + \mathcal{B}^{(n)}\right)^{-1} \mathcal{D}^{(n)},$$

$$d_{t+q} = -\left(\mathcal{A}^{(n)}\mathcal{T}_{t+q+1} + \mathcal{B}^{(n)}\right)^{-1} \left(\mathcal{A}^{(n)}d_{t+q+1} + f^{(n)}\right),$$

using $\mathcal{T}_{t+N_x} = \mathcal{T}$, $\mathcal{R}_{t+N_x} = \mathcal{R}$ and d_{t+N_x} set to a column filled with zeros as initial conditions of the backward recursion.

We then check that given the obtained solution, the system hits the ZLB at $t + N_e$ and leaves the ZLB at $t + N_x$. Otherwise, we shift N_e or N_x forward or backward by one period and start all over again until convergence. Once convergence has been reached, we use the resulting matrices to compute s_t and repeat the process for all the simulation periods.

Our approach is thus similar to the one used by Coibion, Gorodnichenko, and Wieland (2012) in their study of the optimal inflation target in a New Keynesian setup.[13]

A shortcoming of this approach is that the agents in the model are assumed to believe that the ZLB will not bind again in the future, once the current ZLB episode comes to an end. This may bias estimates, as explained by Gust and others (2017), even when, as in our case, estimation is performed on a pre-ZLB period. The scope of this concern is, however, dampened by the fact that in the pre-crisis environment there is evidence that even experts severely underestimated the probability of the ZLB occurring (Chung and others 2012).[14]

A WELFARE-BASED OPTIMAL INFLATION TARGET A second-order approximation of the household expected utility derived from the structural model is used to quantify welfare, in a similar manner as in Woodford (2003), assuming a small steady-state inflation rate. As detailed in the online appendix, this second-order approximation is given by:

$$U_0 = -\frac{1}{2}\frac{1-\beta\eta}{1-\eta}\mathbb{E}_0\sum_{t=0}^{\infty}\left\{\beta^t\lambda_y\left[\hat{x}_t - \delta\hat{x}_{t-1} + (1-\delta)\bar{x}\right]^2\right.$$
$$+\lambda_p\left[(1-\gamma_p)\pi + \hat{\pi}_t - \gamma_p\hat{\pi}_{t-1}\right]^2$$
$$+\lambda_w\left[(1-\gamma_z)\mu_z + (1-\gamma_w)\pi + \hat{\pi}_{w,t} - \gamma_w\hat{\pi}_{t-1}\right]^2\right\}$$
$$+ \text{t.i.p} + O\left(\|\zeta,\pi\|^3\right),$$

where t.i.p collects terms that are independent of monetary policy and $O(\|\zeta, \pi\|^3)$ denotes residual terms of order 3, with $\|\zeta, \pi\|$ denoting a bound on

13. In practice we combine the implementation of the Bodenstein, Erceg, and Guerrieri (2009) algorithm developed by Coibion, Gorodnichenko, and Wieland (2012) with the solution algorithm and the parser from Dynare. Our implementation is in the spirit of Guerrieri and Iacoviello (2015), resulting in a less user-friendly yet faster suite of programs.

14. Global solution methods, such as advocated and implemented by Gust and others (2017), are in principle more accurate. However, given the size of our model and the large set of inflation targets and real interest rates that we need to consider (and given that these have to be considered for each and every parameter configuration in our simulations), a global solution would be computationally prohibitive.

the amplitude of exogenous shocks and the inflation target. Parameters λ_y, λ_p, and λ_w are effectively weights on an output gap term, a price inflation term, and a wage inflation term. Parameter δ fulfills $0 \le \delta \le 1$. The parameter $\bar{x}$ is the log ratio of steady-state output to efficient output; $\bar{x}$ is zero either when trend inflation and trend productivity growth are zero or when indexation is full, and negative otherwise (in which case, output is inefficiently low). Finally, λ_y, λ_p, λ_w, δ, and $\bar{x}$ are functions of the structural parameters θ.

We let $\mathcal{W}(\pi; \theta)$ denote this welfare criterion to emphasize that welfare depends on the inflation target π together with the rest of the structural parameters θ. Two cases are considered concerning the latter. In the baseline case, the structural parameters θ are fixed at reference values and taken to be known with certainty by the policymaker. In an alternative exercise, the policymaker maximizes welfare while recognizing the uncertainty associated with the model's parameters.

The optimal inflation target associated with a given vector of parameters θ, $\pi^*(\theta)$ is approximated via numerical simulations of the model allowing for an occasionally binding ZLB constraint, using the algorithm outlined above.[15] The optimal inflation rate associated to a given vector of parameters θ is then obtained as the one maximizing the welfare function, that is:

$$\pi^*(\theta) \equiv \arg\max_{\pi} \mathcal{W}(\pi; \theta).$$

Given parameter estimates at the posterior mean, we can compute the weight on output and wage inflation relative to inflation, that is, λ_y/λ_p and λ_w/λ_p. These relative weights are respectively equal to 0.22 and 0.10.[16] Note these values are in the ballpark of values obtained in analyses of optimal inflation based on welfare criteria.

---

15. More precisely, a sample of size $T = 100{,}000$ of innovations $\{\epsilon_t\}_{t=1}^{T}$ is drawn from a Gaussian distribution (we also allow for a burn in the sample of 200 points that we later discard). We use these shocks to simulate the model for given parameter vector θ. The welfare function $\mathcal{W}(\pi; \theta)$ is approximated by replacing expectations with sample averages. The procedure is repeated for each of $K = 51$ inflation targets on the grid $\{\pi^{(k)}\}_{k=1}^{K}$ ranging from $\pi = \left(\dfrac{0.5}{4}\right)$ percent to $\pi = \left(\dfrac{5}{4}\right)$ percent (expressed in quarterly rates). Importantly, we use the exact same sequence of shocks $\{\epsilon_t\}_{t=1}^{T}$ in each and every simulation over the inflation grid.

16. The absolute value of λ_p is found to be 130.52. See the online appendix for equations stating the formulas for lambdap, lambdaw, and lambdax.

Figure 1. Welfare and the Inflation Target

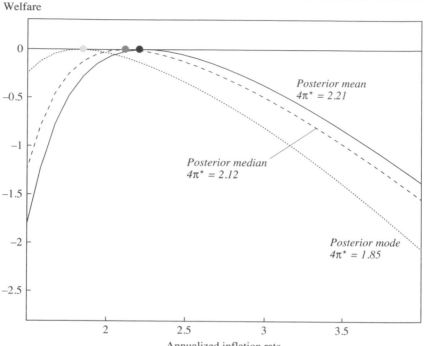

Welfare

Source: Authors' calculations.
Note: Solid line indicates parameters set at the posterior mean; dashed line indicates parameters set at the posterior median; dotted line indicates parameters set at the posterior mode. The equation $\pi^* \equiv \log(\Pi^*)$ pertains. In all cases, the welfare functions are normalized so as to peak at zero.

II.C. Some Properties of the Loss Function and the Optimal Inflation Target in the Estimated Model

This section presents selected properties of the model related to the optimal inflation target. Figure 1 displays the welfare function—expressed as losses relative to the maximum social welfare—associated with three natural benchmarks for the parameter vector θ: the posterior mean (dark line), the median (medium line), and the mode (light line). For convenience, the peak of each welfare function is identified with a dot. Also, to facilitate interpretations, the inflation targets are expressed in annualized percentage rates.

As figure 1 illustrates, the U.S. optimal inflation target is close to 2 percent and varies between 1.85 percent and 2.21 percent depending on which indicator of central tendency (mean, mode, or median) is selected. This

Figure 2. Probability of ZLB

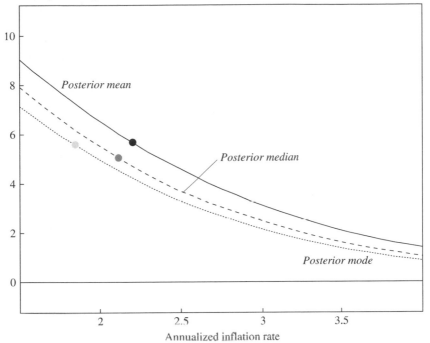

Probability of hitting ZLB

Annualized inflation rate

Source: Authors' calculations.
Note: Solid line indicates parameters set at the posterior mean; dashed line indicates parameters set at the posterior median; dotted line indicates parameters set at the posterior mode. The equation $\iota^* = \log(\Pi^*)$ pertains.

range of values is consistent with those of Coibion, Gorodnichenko, and Wieland (2012) even though in the present paper it is derived from an estimated model over a much shorter sample.[17] Importantly, while the larger shocks in Coibion, Gorodnichenko, and Wieland (2012) ceteris paribus induce larger inflation targets, the high degree of interest rate smoothing in their analysis works in the other direction (as documented in section V).

To complement these illustrative results, figure 2 displays the probability of reaching the ZLB as a function of the annualized inflation target (again, with the parameter vector θ evaluated at the posterior mean, median,

17. Coibion, Gorodnichenko, and Wieland (2012) calibrate their model on a post-WWII, pre–Great Recession U.S. sample. By contrast, we use a Great Moderation sample.

and mode). For convenience, the dot in each curve marks the corresponding optimal inflation target.

The probability of hitting the ZLB associated to these positive optimal inflation targets is relatively low, at about 6 percent. This result, as anticipated above, is the mere reflection of our choice of a Great Moderation sample. At the same time, our model is able to predict a fairly spread-out distribution of ZLB episode durations, with a significant fraction of ZLB episodes lasting more than, say, five years (see figure D.1 in the online appendix). Given the existence of a single ZLB episode in the recent history, we do not attempt here to take a stand on what is a relevant distribution of ZLB episodes.[18]

A property of our model, as noticed by Kiley (2019), is that ZLB episodes are rather costly, compared to other studies. This property reflects the absence in our model of ad hoc stabilizing devices sometimes present in other papers concerned with the ZLB, such as emergency fiscal packages or exogenous caps on the maximum duration of ZLB episodes, as in Kiley and Roberts (2017) and in Williams (2009). Allowing for such devices would mechanically reduce the severity of ZLB episodes in our framework, resulting in a lower optimal inflation target.

III. The Optimal Inflation Target and the Steady-State Real Interest Rate

The focus of this section is to investigate how the monetary authority should adjust its optimal inflation target π^* in response to changes in the steady-state real interest rate, r^*.[19] Intuitively, with a lower r^* the ZLB is bound to bind more often, so one would expect a higher inflation target should be desirable in that case. But the answer to the practical question of how much should the target be increased is not obvious. Indeed, the benefit of providing a better hedge against hitting the ZLB, which is an infrequent event, comes at a cost of higher steady-state inflation which induces permanent costs, as argued by Bernanke (2016).

To start with, we compute the relation linking the optimal inflation target to the steady-state real interest rate, based on simulations of the estimated

18 See Dordal-i-Carreras and others (2016) for further analysis in that direction.

19. Note our exercise here is different from assessing what would be the optimal response to a time-varying steady state—a specification consistent with econometric work like that of Holston, Laubach, and Williams (2017). Our exercise is arguably consistent with secular stagnation—understood as a permanently lower real rate of interest—while doing without having to assume a unit root process in the real rate of interest.

model and ignoring parameter uncertainty. We show that the link between π^* and r^* depends to some extent on the factor underlying a variation in r^*, that is, a change in the discount rate ρ or a change in the growth rate of technology μ_z. In our setup the first scenario roughly captures the "taste for safe asset" and "aging population" rationales for secular stagnation, while the second one captures the "decline in technological progress" rationale. Subsequently, we investigate how the relation between the optimal inflation target and the steady-state real interest rate depends on various features of the monetary policy framework, as well as on the size of shocks or on the steady-state price and wage markups.

III.A. The Baseline (r^*, π^*) Relation

To characterize the link between r^* and π^*, the following simulation exercise is conducted. The structural parameter vector θ is fixed at its posterior mean, $\bar{\theta}$, with the exception of μ_z and ρ. These two parameters are varied—each in turn, keeping the other parameter, μ_z or ρ, fixed at its baseline posterior mean value (namely, 1.72 percent and 0.76 percent, respectively, in annualized terms). For both μ_z and ρ, we consider values on a grid ranging from 0.4 percent to 10 percent in annualized percentage terms. The model is then simulated for each possible value of μ_z or ρ and various values of inflation targets π using the same procedure as before.[20] The optimal value π^* associated to each value of r^* is obtained as the one maximizing the welfare criterion $\mathcal{W}(\pi; \theta)$.

We finally obtain two curves. The first one links the optimal inflation target π^* to the steady-state real interest rate r^* for various growth rates of technology μ_z: $\pi^*[r^*(\mu_z)]$, where the notation $r^*(\mu_z)$ highlights that the steady-state real interest rate varies as μ_z varies. The second one links the optimal inflation target π^* to the steady-state real interest rate r^* for various discount rates ρ: $\pi^*[r^*(\rho)]$. Here, the notation $r^*(\rho)$ highlights that the steady-state real interest rate varies as ρ varies.[21]

Figure 3 depicts the (r^*, π^*) relations thus obtained. The round dots correspond to the case when the steady-state real interest rate r^* varies

---

20. In particular, we use the same sequence of shocks $\{\epsilon_t\}_{t=1}^{T}$ as used in the computation implemented in the baseline exercises of section II.B. Here again, we start from the same grid of inflation targets for all the possible values of μ_z or ρ. Then, for each value of μ_z or ρ, we refine the inflation grid over successive passes until the optimal inflation target associated with a particular value of μ_z or ρ proves insensitive to the grid.

21. In the online appendix, figures G.1 and G.2 report similar results at the posterior mode and at the posterior median. Figure H.1 documents the relation in terms of the optimal nominal interest rate.

Figure 3. Optimal Inflation Rate as a Function of the Steady-State Real Interest Rate (at the Posterior Mean)

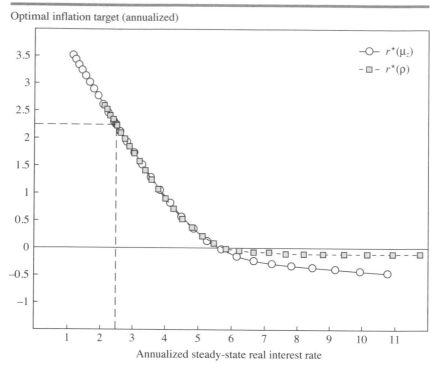

Source: Authors' calculations.

Note: The round dots correspond to the (r^*, π^*) locus when r^* varies with μ_z; the square dots correspond to the (r^*, π^*) locus when r^* varies with ρ.

with μ_z. The square dots correspond to the case when the steady-state real interest rate r^* varies with ρ. For convenience, both the real interest rate and the associated optimal inflation target are expressed in annualized percentage rates. The dashed gray lines indicate the benchmark result corresponding to the optimal inflation target at the posterior mean of the structural parameter distribution.

These results are complemented with figure 4 which shows the relation between r^* and the probability of hitting the ZLB, *evaluated at the optimal inflation target*. As with figure 3, round dots correspond to the case when r^* varies with μ_z, while square dots correspond to the case when it varies with ρ.[22]

---

22. Figure E.1 in the online appendix shows the relation between r^* and the nominal interest rate when the inflation target is set at its optimal value.

Figure 4. Relation between Probability of ZLB at Optimal Inflation and r^* (at the Posterior Mean)

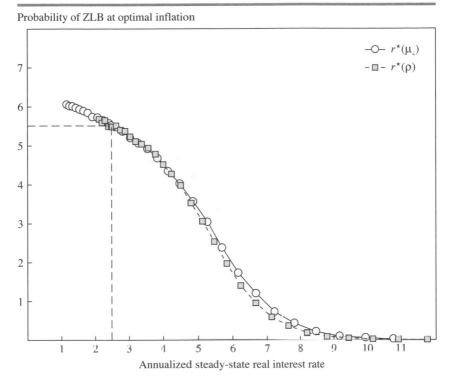

Probability of ZLB at optimal inflation

Annualized steady-state real interest rate

Source: Authors' calculations.

Note: The round dots correspond to the (r^*, π^*) locus when r^* varies with μ_z; the square dots correspond to the (r^*, π^*) locus when r^* varies with ρ.

As expected, the relation in figure 3 is decreasing. However, the slope varies with the value of r^*. The slope is relatively large in absolute value—although smaller than 1—for moderate values of r^* (say, below 4 percent). The slope declines in absolute value as r^* increases: lowering the inflation target to compensate for an increase in r^* becomes less and less desirable. This reflects the fact that, as r^* increases, the probability of hitting the ZLB becomes smaller and smaller. For very large r^* values, the probability becomes almost zero, as figure 4 shows.

At some point, the optimal inflation target becomes insensitive to changes in r^* when the latter originate from changes in the discount rate ρ. In this case, the inflation target stabilizes at a slightly negative value in order to lower the nominal wage inflation rate required to support positive productivity growth, given the imperfect indexation of nominal wages to productivity. At the steady state, the real wage must grow at a rate of μ_z. It is optimal to obtain this steady-state growth as the result of a moderate nominal wage increase and a moderate price *decrease*, rather than as the result of a zero price inflation and a consequently larger nominal wage inflation.[23]

The previous tension is even more apparent when r^* varies with μ_z since, in this case, the effects of imperfect indexation of wages to productivity are magnified given that a higher μ_z calls for a higher growth in the real wage, which is optimally attained through greater price deflation, as well as a higher wage inflation. Notice, however, that even in this case, the optimal inflation target becomes less sensitive to changes in r^* for very large values of r^*, typically above 6 percent.

For low values of r^*, on the other hand, the slope of the curve is steeper. In particular, in the empirically relevant region, the relation is not far from one to one. More precisely, it shows that, starting from the posterior mean estimate of θ, a 100 basis point decline in r^* should lead to an over 99 basis point increase in π^*. Importantly, this increase in the optimal inflation target is virtually the same no matter the underlying factor causing the change in r^*: a drop in potential growth, μ_z, or a decrease in the discount factor, ρ. At the same time, the ZLB incidence evaluated at the optimal inflation rate also increases when the real rate decreases. At some point, the speed at which this probability increases slows down, reflecting that the social planner would choose to increase the inflation target as needed so as to avoid a higher ZLB incidence.

Figure 5 shows how the probability of ZLB changes as a function of r^*, holding the inflation target constant. We first set the inflation target at its optimal baseline value (that is, the value computed at the posterior mean, 2.21 percent). This is reported as the square dots. Similarly, we also compute an analog relation assuming, this time, that the inflation target is held constant at the optimal value consistent with a steady-state real interest rate 1 percentage point lower (thus, inflation is set to 3.20). Here again, the other parameters are set at their posterior mean. This corresponds to the

---

23. For very large r^*, as a rough approximation, we can ignore the effects of shocks and assume that the ZLB is a zero-mass event. Assuming also a negligible difference between steady-state and efficient outputs and letting λp and λ_w denote the weights attached to price dispersion and wage dispersion, respectively, in the approximated welfare function, the optimal inflation obeys $\pi^* \approx -\lambda_w (1 - \gamma_z)(1 - \gamma_w)/[\lambda_p (1 - \gamma_p)^2 + \lambda_w (1 - \gamma_w)^2]\mu_z$. Given the low values of λ_w resulting from our estimation, it is not surprising that π^* is negative but close to zero. See Amano and others (2009) for a similar point in the context of a model abstracting from ZLB issues.

Figure 5. Relation between Probability of ZLB and r^* (at the Posterior Mean)

Probability of ZLB

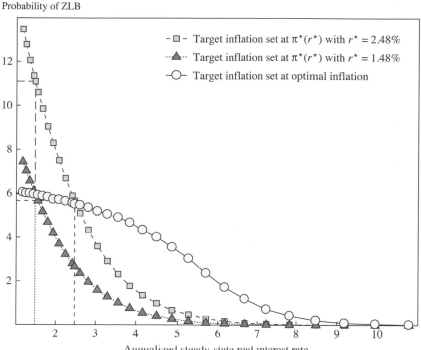

Annualized steady-state real interest rate

Source: Authors' calculations.
Note: The square dots correspond to the relation linking r^* and the probability of ZLB, holding the optimal inflation target π^* at the baseline value. The triangle dots correspond the same relation when the optimal inflation target π^* is set at the value consistent with a steady-state real interest rate one percentage point lower. The round dots correspond to the probability of ZLB obtained under the optimal inflation target π^* associated with a given value of r^*.

triangle dots in the figure. For convenience, we also report the the probability of hitting the ZLB as a function of r^* conditional on adjusting optimally the inflation target, as in figure 4. This corresponds to the round dots.

Consider first the square-dot curve. At the level of the real interest rate prevailing before the permanent decline, assuming that the central bank sets its target to the associated optimal level, the probability of reaching the ZLB would be slightly below 6 percent. Imagine now that the real interest rate experiences a decline of 100 basis points. Keeping the inflation target at the same level as prior to the shock, the probability of reaching the ZLB would now climb up to approximately 11 percent. However, the change in the optimal inflation target brings the probability of reaching the ZLB back to approximately 6 percent. Thus, the social planner would almost neutralize the effects of the natural rate decline on the probability of hitting the ZLB.

Finally we investigate whether the trade-off analyzed above translates into meaningful welfare costs, measured in terms of foregone per period consumption. Results are reported in the online appendix, section F. It turns out that, under sufficiently low r^* values, agents faced with a 1 percentage point decline in the steady-state real interest rates would require up to a 1.5 percentage point increase in consumption to be as well off under the former optimal inflation target (that is, 2.21 percent) as under the optimal target associated with the lower real interest rate (3.20 percent in this case). In other words, the welfare costs of not adjusting the target in the face of a decline in r^* are substantial.

III.B. Robustness to Alternative Structural Assumptions

In this section, we investigate the robustness of the (r^*, π^*) relation to altering (or modifying) some structural features of the environment. We consider several relevant dimensions: the case of larger shocks, alternative calibrations for the steady-state price and wage markup, and changes in the degree of price and wage indexation.[24]

LARGER SHOCKS As argued before, the model is estimated using data from the Great Moderation period. One may legitimately argue that the decline in the real interest rate resulting from the secular stagnation has come hand in hand with larger shocks, as the Great Recession suggests. To address this concern, we simulate the model assuming that demand shocks have a standard deviation 30 percent larger than estimated.

We conduct this exercise assuming that changes in average productivity growth μ_z are the only driver of changes in the natural rate. Apart from σ_q and σ_g, which are rescaled, all the other parameters are frozen at their posterior mean. Given this setup, the optimal inflation target is 3.7 percent as opposed to 2.21 percent conditional on the baseline value of r^*. Also, under the alternative shock configuration, the probability of hitting the ZLB is 5.3 percent, as opposed to 5.5 percent in the baseline. These probabilities may seem low, especially in the case of large shocks which we argue capture Great Recession-like shocks. However they are particularly low because the inflation target is chosen optimally in this setup. In particular, in the larger shocks case, the increase in the inflation target is large enough

---

24. Robustness to altering the monetary policy rule is assessed further in section V.

to offset the impact of larger shocks in terms of ZLB incidence. When instead we keep the inflation target unchanged, the probability of hitting the ZLB rises to 18 percent in the face of a 1 percent decline in r^*.[25] In that case, these ZLB probabilities come close to the probabilities reported by Kiley and Roberts (2017) in the case of their DSGE model (albeit they find a higher probability of ZLB, of the order of 30 percent when using the FRB/US model), or by Chung and others (2019).[26]

Figure 6 reports the (r^*, π^*) relation under larger demand shocks (square dots) and compares the outcome with the baseline relation (round dots).[27] Interestingly, the (r^*, π^*) locus has essentially the same slope in the low r^* region. Here again, we find a slope close to -1. However, the curve is somewhat steeper in the high r^* region and shifted up, compared to the baseline scenario. This reflects that under larger demand shocks, even at very high levels of the natural rate, a drop in the latter is conducive to more frequent ZLB episodes. The social planner is then willing to increase the inflation target at a higher pace than in the baseline scenario and generically sets the inflation target at higher levels to hedge the economy against ZLB episodes.

ALTERNATIVE MARKUPS The optimal level of inflation in our setup depends on the elasticities of substitution among intermediate goods, θ_p, and among labor types, θ_w, since those parameters determine the extent to which the price and wage dispersion induced by inflation is translated into an inefficient allocation of resources. These parameters have been calibrated, as they cannot be identified from time-series data and a log-linearized version of the model.

In our calibration, the baseline value for the elasticity of substitution θ_p is 6, leading to a steady-state price markup of 20 percent. While this value is in line with common textbook parameterizations (Galí 2015), and is close to the baseline value obtained in Hall (2018) and in Christiano, Eichenbaum, and Evans (2005), there is considerable uncertainty in the empirical literature about the level of markups. For example, some estimates in Basu and Fernald (1997) and Traina (2015) point to possibly much smaller values, while Autor and others (forthcoming), De Loecker

---

25. See the online appendix, section I, in which such counterfactual probabilities of ZLB are reported.

26. In addition to per period probability of ZLB, these authors also put forward and emphasize the probability that a ZLB event occurs in the next decade. By construction this number is a larger one, and the mapping between the two numbers is not fully straightforward.

27. We obtain this figure using the same procedure as outlined before. Here again, we run several passes with successively refined inflation grids.

Figure 6. Optimal Inflation Rate as a Function of the Steady-State Real Interest Rate with Larger Demand Shocks

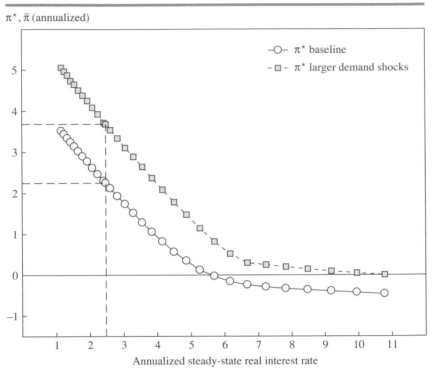

$\pi^*, \bar{\pi}$ (annualized)

Annualized steady-state real interest rate

Source: Authors' calculations.

Note: The round dots correspond to the baseline scenario wherein all the structural parameters are set at their posterior mean $\bar{\theta}$. The square dots correspond to the counterfactual simulation with σ_q and σ_g set to twice their baseline value.

and Eeckhout (2017), and Farhi and Gourio (2018) suggest substantially larger figures. To investigate the robustness of our results, we redo our main simulation exercise, this time setting θ_p to a value as large as 10 or as low as 3. These values largely encompass the range of available empirical estimates.

Similarly, for the wage markup, there is arguably even scarcer evidence, and in any case considerable uncertainty around our baseline parameterization, given by θ_w set to 3. Here again, so as to cover a broad range of plausible estimates, we run alternatives exercises, setting in turn θ_w to 8 and θ_w to 1.5. Results are reported in figure 7 in the case of robustness with respect to the price markup and in figure 8 with respect to the wage markup.

The main takeaway from these figures is that our key result is by and large preserved. That is, in the empirically relevant region (for levels of

Figure 7. Optimal Inflation Rate as a Function of the Steady-State Real Interest Rate with Alternative θ_p

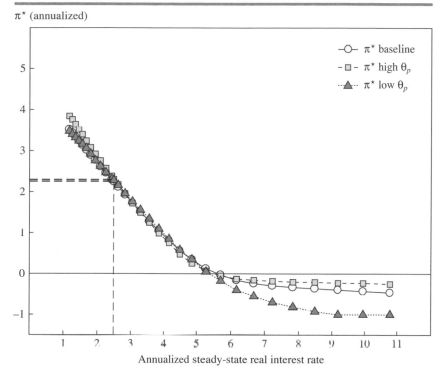

π^* (annualized)

Annualized steady-state real interest rate

Source: Authors' calculations.

Note: The round dots correspond to the baseline scenario wherein all the structural parameters are set at their posterior mean $\bar{\theta}$. The square dots correspond to the counterfactual simulation with θ_p set to 10. The triangle dots correspond to the counterfactual simulation with θ_p set to 3.

r^* lower than, say, 4 percent), the slope of the (r^*, π^*) curve is only very mildly affected when changing the elasticity of substitution of goods or labor types.

Another noticeable result of this robustness exercise is that, by contrast, in the region with high steady-state real interest rates (say, r^* larger than 5 percent) the value of the optimal inflation target and the slope of the curve of interest are more sensitive to the value of θ_p or θ_w. To see why, first notice that, in this region, the ZLB is essentially irrelevant so the standard welfare cost of inflation setup applies. With less substitution across goods, a given level of price dispersion induced by inflation leads to smaller output dispersion (as is clear, for instance, in the polar case of complementary goods, which leads to no output dispersion across firms at all). The effect

Figure 8. Optimal Inflation Rate as a Function of the Steady-State Real Interest Rate with Alternative θ_w

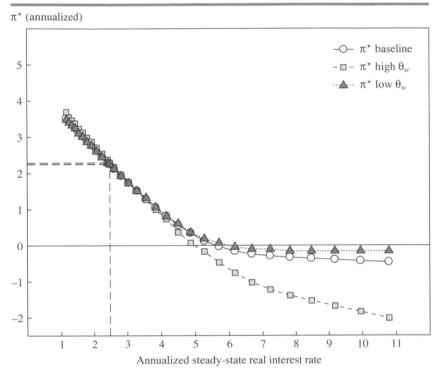

π^* (annualized)

Annualized steady-state real interest rate

Source: Authors' calculations.

Note: The round dots correspond to the baseline scenario wherein all the structural parameters are set at their posterior mean $\bar{\theta}$. The square dots correspond to the counterfactual simulation with θ_w set to 8. The triangle dots correspond to the counterfactual simulation with θ_w set to 1.5.

of θ_p on output dispersion is apparent from the formulas in our online appendix or in textbook derivations of output dispersion, for example, chapter 3 in Galí (2015). Thus, with a low substitution (that is, a low θ_p), the welfare loss due to inflation (or deflation) is smaller. Therefore a lower θ_p allows for an inflation target farther away from zero, insofar as there are motives for a nonzero steady-state inflation. Such a mechanism explains why, in figure 7, optimal inflation is more negative with lower substitution.

Interestingly, when we consider robustness with respect to parameter θ_w, the ranking of the corresponding curves is reversed (see figure 8). That is, a larger θ_w induces a larger inflation target in absolute value. The reason is that, with a larger substitution across labor types, a given nominal wage growth generates dispersion of quantities across types of labor that turns out to be particularly costly. In that case, it is optimal that the burden of adjustment of real wages to growth is borne not by nominal wages but rather by nominal prices (thus leading to a more pronounced deflation).[28]

ALTERNATIVE DEGREES OF INDEXATION The degree of indexation of price and wage is an important determinant of the cost of inflation. In our empirical estimate the degrees of indexation are moderate: 0.22 for prices and 0.44 for wages at the posterior mean. It is worthwhile examining the sensitivity of our results to the degree of indexation. Indeed, some existing macro estimates find or impose a much larger degree of indexation (Christiano, Eichenbaum, and Evans 2005). By contrast, existing micro studies hardly find any evidence of indexation. In this robustness exercise, we consider in turn a zero indexation case, a high indexation case (setting γ_p and γ_w to 0.7), and a very high indexation case (setting γ_p and γ_w to 0.9). The last two configurations are arguably unrealistic. Results are presented in figure 9. In the absence of indexation, results are similar to those under our estimated indexation levels. For the high indexation case (γ_p and γ_w equal to 0.7), the results differ from the baseline only for relatively large values of the steady-state real interest rate.

In the very high indexation case, the position and shape of the curve are substantially affected: the curve is nearly a decreasing straight line. Indeed, for a very large indexation degree the welfare cost of inflation (or deflation) is substantially reduced. As a result, it is optimal to allow for a sizable trend deflation when the natural rate is large as a result of large productivity growth. However, we can note that in the empirically relevant region, that is, for r^* below 2 percent, the local slope of the curve is similar whatever the degree of indexation.

IV. The Effect of Parameter Uncertainty

In this section we investigate the impact of parameter uncertainty on the relation between the optimal inflation target and the steady-state real interest rate. Specifically, we analyze how a Bayesian-theoretic optimal inflation target reacts to a downward shift in the *distribution* of the steady-state real interest rate.

---

28. This can be illustrated again in the approximated welfare function, ignoring the effects of shocks. Then the optimal inflation obeys $\pi^* \approx -(\lambda_w (1 - \gamma_z)(1 - \gamma_w)/[\lambda p (1 - \gamma_p)^2 + \lambda_w (1 - \gamma_w)^2]) \mu_z$. The inflation target is a decreasing function of λ_w, thus of θ_w.

Figure 9. Optimal Inflation Rate as a Function of the Steady-State Real Interest Rate with Alternative Indexation Degrees

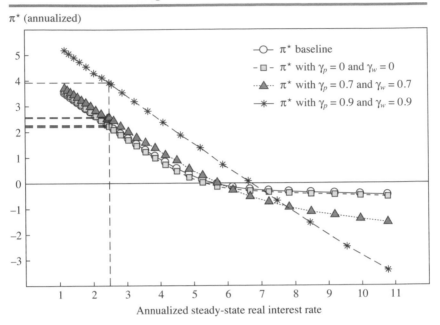

Source: Authors' calculations.

Note: The round dots correspond to the baseline scenario wherein all the structural parameters are set at their posterior mean $\bar{\theta}$. The square dots correspond to the counterfactual simulation with $\gamma_p = \gamma_w = 0$. The triangle dots correspond to the counterfactual simulation with $\gamma_p = \gamma_w = 0.7$. The star dots correspond to the counterfactual simulation with $\gamma_p = \gamma_w = 0.9$.

IV.A. A Bayesian-Theoretic Optimal Inflation Target

The location of the loss function $W(\pi; \theta)$ evidently depends on the vector of parameters θ describing the economy. As a result of estimation uncertainty around θ, the optimal inflation rate $\pi^*(\theta)$ will be subject to uncertainty. Further, a policymaker may wish to take into account the uncertainty surrounding θ when determining the optimal inflation target. A relevant feature of the welfare functions in our setup is that, in general, and as shown above, they are markedly asymmetric: adopting an inflation target 1 percentage point below the optimal value generates welfare losses larger than setting it 1 percentage point above. As a result, the certainty equivalence does not hold. A policymaker maximizing expected welfare while recognizing the uncertainty will choose an inflation target differing from that corresponding to the case where θ is set to its expected value and taken to be known with certainty, as in our baseline analysis.

Formally, the estimated posterior distribution of parameters $p(\theta|X_T)$ can be exploited to quantify the impact of parameter uncertainty on the optimal inflation target and to compute a Bayesian-theoretic optimal inflation target. We define the latter as the inflation target π^{**} which maximizes the expected welfare not only over the realizations of shocks but also over the realizations of parameters:[29]

$$\pi^{**} \equiv \arg\max_{\pi} \int_{\theta} \mathcal{W}(\pi; \theta) \, p(\theta|X_T) \mathrm{d}\theta.$$

We interpret the spread between the optimal Bayesian inflation target and the certainty-equivalent optimal inflation target at the posterior mean $\bar{\theta}$ as a measure of how uncertainty about the parameter values affects optimal inflation. Given the nature of the asymmetry in the welfare function, the spread will turn out to be positive: a Bayesian policymaker will tend to choose a higher inflation target than a policymaker taking θ to be known and equal to the mean of its distribution. A higher inflation target indeed acts as a buffer to hedge against particularly detrimental parameter values (either because they lead to more frequent ZLB episodes or because they lead to particularly acute inflation distortions). We define

$$\mathrm{Spr}(\theta) = \pi^{**} - \pi^{*}(\theta)$$

and assess below $\mathrm{Spr}(\bar{\theta})$.

IV.B. Results

According to the simulation exercise, $\pi^{**} = 2.40$ percent. This robust optimal inflation target is higher than the value obtained with θ set at its

---

29. This Bayesian inflation target is recovered from simulating the model under a ZLB constraint using the exact same sequence of shocks $\{\epsilon_t\}_{t=1}^{T}$ with $T = 100{,}000$ as in the previous subsection (together with the same burn-in sample) and combining it with N draws of parameters $\{\theta_j\}_{j=1}^{N}$ from the estimated posterior distribution $p(\theta|X_T)$, with $N = 500$. As in the previous section, the social welfare function $\mathcal{W}(\pi; \theta)$ is evaluated for each draw of θ over a grid of inflation targets $\{\pi^{(k)}\}_{k=1}^{K}$. The Bayesian welfare criterion is then computed as the average welfare across parameter draws. Here, we start with the same inflation grid as before and then run several passes. In the first pass, we identify the inflation target maximizing the Bayesian welfare criterion. We then set a finer grid of $K = 51$ inflation targets around this value. We repeat this process several times with successively finer grids of inflation targets until the identified optimal inflation target proves insensitive to the grid. In this particular exercise, some parameter draws for θ lead to convergence failure in the algorithm implementing the ZLB. These draws are discarded.

central tendency. As expected, a Bayesian policymaker chooses a higher inflation target to hedge against particularly harmful states of the world (that is, parameter draws) where the frequency of hitting the ZLB is high.

Assessing how a change in $r*$ affects $\pi**$ for every value of $r*$ is not possible, due to the computational cost involved. Such a reaction is thus investigated for a particular scenario: it is assumed that the economy starts from the posterior distribution of parameters $p(\theta|X_T)$ and that, everything else being constant, the mean of $r*$ decreases by 100 basis points. Such a 1 percentage point decline is chosen mainly for illustrative purposes. Yet, it is of a comparable order of magnitude, although somewhat smaller in absolute value, than recent estimates of the drop of the natural rate after the crisis, such as Laubach and Williams (2016) and Holston, Laubach, and Williams (2017). The counterfactual exercise considered can therefore be seen as a relatively conservative characterization of the shift in the steady-state real interest rate. Figure 10 depicts the counterfactual shift in the distribution of $r*$ that is considered.

The Bayesian-theoretic optimal inflation target corresponding to the counterfactual lower distribution of $r*$ is obtained from a simulation exercise that relies on the same procedure as before.[30] Given a draw in the posterior of parameter vector θ, the value of the steady-state real interest rate is computed using the expression implied by the postulated structural model $r* (\theta) = \rho(\theta) + \mu_z(\theta)$. From this particular draw, a counterfactual lower steady-state real interest rate, $r*(\theta_\Delta)$, is obtained by shifting the long-run growth component of the model μ_z downward by 1 percentage point (in annualized terms). The welfare function $\mathcal{W}(\pi; \theta_\Delta)$ is then evaluated. Since there are no other changes than this shift in the mean value of μ_z in the distribution of the structural parameters, we can characterize the counterfactual distribution $p(\theta_\Delta|X_T)$ as a simple transformation of the estimated posterior $p(\theta|X_T)$. The counterfactual Bayesian-theoretic optimal inflation target is then obtained as

$$\pi_\Delta^{**} \equiv \arg\max_{\pi} \int_{\theta_\Delta} \mathcal{W}(\pi; \theta_\Delta) \, p(\theta_\Delta|X_T) d\theta_\Delta .$$

Figure 11 illustrates the counterfactual change in optimal inflation target obtained when the mean of the distibution of the steady-state real interest rate declines by 100 basis points. The simulation exercise returns a value

---

30. Again, we use the same sequence of shocks and the same parameter draws as in section II.B.

Figure 10. Posterior Distributions of r^* and Counterfactual r^*

PDF

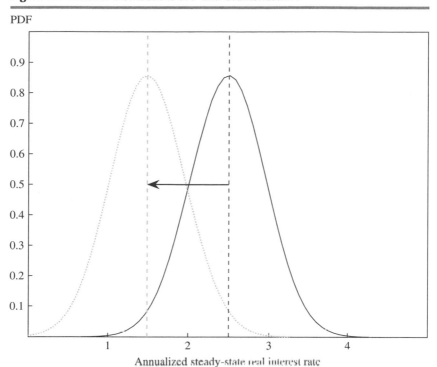

Annualized steady-state real interest rate

Source: Authors' calculations.
Note: The curves indicate PDFs of r^* (baseline solid and counterfactual dotted); the dashed vertical lines indicate mean value of r^*.

of $\pi_\Delta^{**} = 3.30$ percent, that is, 90 basis points higher than the optimal value under uncertainty obtained with the posterior distribution of parameters in the pre-crisis sample $\pi_\Delta^{**} = 2.40$ percent.[31]

Thus, in our setup, a monetary authority that is concerned about the uncertainty surrounding the parameters driving the costs and benefits of the inflation chooses a higher optimal inflation target. However, the reaction of this optimal inflation target following a drop in the mean r^* is hardly altered: a 100 basis point decrease in the steady-state real interest rate calls for a roughly 90 basis point increase in the optimal inflation target, in the vicinity of pre-crisis parameter estimates.

31. Figure J.1 in the online appendix shows how the posterior distribution of π^* is shifted after the permanent decline in the mean of r^*.

Figure 11. Expected Bayesian Welfare in Baseline and Counterfactual

Welfare (normalized)

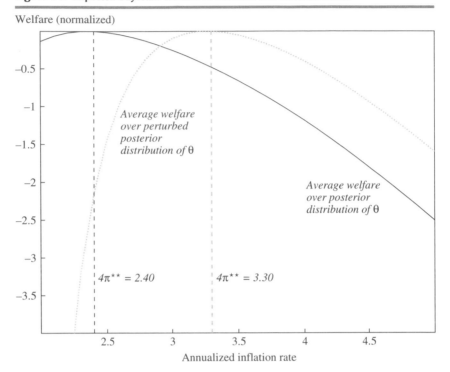

Source: Authors' calculations.
Note: Solid line is the curve $\mathbb{E}_\theta(W(\pi, \theta))$; dotted line is the curve $\mathbb{E}_\theta(W(\pi, \theta))$ with lower r^*.

IV.C. A Known Reaction Function

Here we study the consequences of the (plausible) assumption that the central bank actually knows the coefficients of its interest rate rule with certainty. More specifically we repeat the same simulation exercise as in the previous subsection but with parameters a_π, a_y, and ρ_i in the reaction function (equation 2) taken to be known with certainty. In practice we fix these three parameters at their posterior mean instead of sampling them from their posterior distribution. This is arguably the relevant approach from the point of view of the policymaker.[32] Note, however, that all the other parameters are subject to uncertainty from the standpoint of the central bank.

32. In practice, long-run inflation targets are seldom reconsidered while the rotation in monetary policy committees happens at a higher frequency. From this viewpoint, our baseline assumption of uncertainty on all the monetary policy rule parameters is not necessarily unwarranted.

Figure 12. Expected Bayesian Welfare

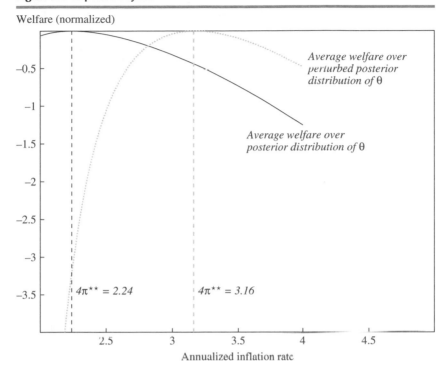

Welfare (normalized)

Average welfare over perturbed posterior distribution of θ

Average welfare over posterior distribution of θ

$4\pi^{**} = 2.24$ $4\pi^{**} = 3.16$

Annualized inflation rate

Source: Authors' calculations.

Note: The solid line indicates curve $\mathbb{E}_\theta(\mathcal{W}(\pi, \theta))$; the dotted line indicates curve $\mathbb{E}_\theta(\mathcal{W}(\pi, 0))$ with lower r^*. In each case, ρ_i, a_π, and a_y are frozen at their posterior mean values.

Figure 12 presents the Bayesian-theoretic optimal inflation targets obtained when simulating the model at the initial posteriors and after a -100 basis point level shift in the posterior distribution of the long-run growth rate μ_z and, hence, the steady-state real interest rate r^*. According to these simulations, the inflation target should initially be $\pi^{**} = 2.24$ percent. After the counterfactual change in the distribution of r^* considered, π^{**} should be increased to 3.16 percent, again in the ballpark of a 90 basis point increase in π^* in response to a 100 basis point downward shift in the distribution of r^*.

V. Alternative Monetary Policy Rules and Environments

In the present section we study the optimal adjustment of the inflation target in response to a change in the steady-state real interest rate under five alternative assumptions regarding monetary policy: setting the inflation target in terms of average realized inflation; an effective lower bound on the policy rate that can be below zero; alternative degrees of smoothing in the policy rule; a central bank with no lower for longer strategy; and a price level targeting rule. For simplicity, throughout this section we ignore the role of uncertainty and treat the model parameters as known.

V.A. Average vs. Target Inflation

As emphasized in recent works (Hills, Nakata, and Schmidt 2016; Kiley and Roberts 2017), when the probability of hitting the ZLB is nonnegligible, realized inflation is on average significantly lower than the inflation rate that the central bank targets in the interest rate rule (and which would correspond to steady-state inflation in the absence of shocks or in a linear model). This results from the fact that anytime the ZLB is binding (a recurrent event), the central bank effectively loses its ability to stabilize inflation around the target. Knowing this, it may be relevant to assess the central bank's outcomes and set the corresponding target in terms of the effective average realized inflation. In this section, we investigate whether measuring the inflation target in this alternative way matters.

To this end, the analysis of the (r^*, π^*) relation in section II.B is complemented here with the analysis of the relation between r^* and the average realized inflation rate $\mathbb{E}\{\pi_t\}$ obtained when simulating the model for various values of r^* and the associated optimal inflation target π^*. In the interest of brevity, the calculations are presented only in the case when the source of variation in the natural interest rate is the change in average productivity growth μ_z.

Figure 13 illustrates the difference between the (r^*, π^*) curve (round dots) and the $(r^*, \mathbb{E}\{\pi_t\})$ curve (square dots). The overall shape of the curve is unchanged. Unsurprisingly, both curves are identical when r^* is high enough. In this case, the ZLB is (almost) not binding and average realized inflation does not differ much from π^*. A spread between the two emerges for very low values of r^*. There, for low values of the natural rate, the ZLB incidence is higher and, as a result, average realized inflation becomes indeed lower than the optimal inflation target. However, that spread remains limited, less than 10 basis points. The reason is that the implied optimal inflation target is sufficiently high to prevent the ZLB from binding too frequently, thus limiting the extent to which average realized inflation and π^* can differ.

Unreported simulation results show that the gap between π^* and average realized inflation becomes more substantial when the inflation target is below its optimal value. For instance, mean inflation is roughly zero when

Figure 13. Average Realized Inflation and Optimal Inflation

$\pi^*, \bar{\pi}$ (annualized)

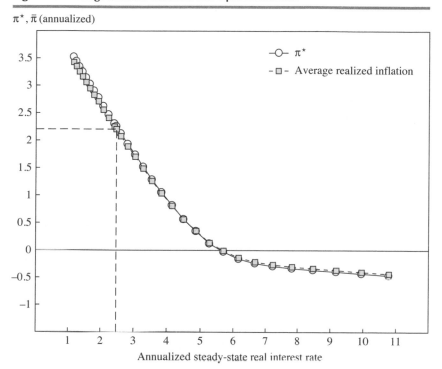

Annualized steady-state real interest rate

Source: Authors' calculations.

Note: The round dots correspond to the optimal inflation target π^* associated to a given value of r^*. The square dots correspond to the average realized inflation associated to a given value of r^*.

the central bank adopts a 1 percent inflation target in an economy where the optimal inflation target is $\pi^* = 2$ percent.

V.B. A Negative Effective Lower Bound

The recent experience of many advanced economies (including the euro area) points to an effective lower bound (ELB) for the nominal interest rate below zero. For instance, the ECB's deposit facility rate, which gears the overnight money market rate because of excess liquidity, was set at a negative value of −10 basis points in June 2014 and has been further lowered down to −40 basis points in March 2016.[33]

---

33. In September 2019, the rate on the deposit facility was lowered to −0.5 percent.

Figure 14. Optimal Inflation Rate as a Function of the Steady-State Real Interest Rate with a Negative ELB

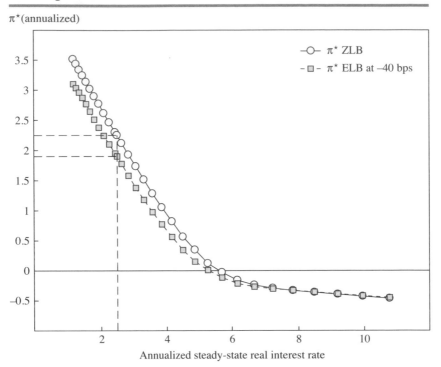

π^*(annualized)

Source: Authors' calculations.

Note: The round dots correspond to the optimal inflation target π^* associated with a given value of r^* in the baseline scenario. The square dots correspond to the average realized inflation associated with a given value of r^* under an ELB set at minus 50 basis points.

We use the estimated model to evaluate the implications of a negative ELB in the United States. More precisely, we set the lower bound on the nominal rate i_t so that

$$i_t \geq e,$$

and we set e to −40 basis points (in annual terms) instead of zero. Results are presented in figure 14. As expected, the (r^*, π^*) locus is shifted downward, though by somewhat less than 40 basis points. Importantly, its slope remains identical to the baseline case: around the baseline value for the real interest rate, a 100 basis point downward shift in the distribution of r^* calls for around a 90 basis point increase in π^*.

V.C. Alternative Degrees of Interest Rate Smoothing

Our analysis is conditional on a specific reaction function of the central bank, described in our setup by the set of parameters a_π, a_y, and ρ_i. Among these parameters, the smoothing parameter, ρ_i, has a key influence on the probability of being in a ZLB regime. A higher smoothing has two effects in our model. The first effect—through standard monetary policy rule inertia—is to reduce the speed at which interest rates are raised when the economy exits the lower bound regime since the current rate inherits the past values of the effective nominal rate. The second effect comes from the fact that the smoothing applies to the notional rate i_t^n that would prevail absent the lower bound constraint (see equation 5) while the effective nominal interest rate is the maximum of zero and the notional rate (see equation 4). Thus the interest rate inherits the past negative values of the notional nominal rate. So, a higher smoothing results in maintaining the effective interest rate at zero for an extended period of time beyond that implied by the macroeconomic shocks that initially brought the economy to the zero lower bound constraint. Such a monetary policy strategy introduces history dependence whereby, in the instance of a ZLB episode, the central bank is committed to keep rates lower for longer. As this reaction function is known to the agents in the model, this commitment to future accommodation, through generating higher expected inflation and output, helps with exiting the trap (or even avoiding entering it).

Through both effects, a higher degree of smoothing thus reinforces the history dependence of monetary policy and tends to shorten the length of ZLB episodes and the probability of hitting the ZLB constraint. Everything else equal, one should therefore expect a lower optimal inflation rate for higher values of the smoothing parameters. This property of the model is illustrated in figure 15 which depicts the (r^*, π^*) relation under three possible values of the smoothing parameter ρ_i. The value used under our baseline scenario, that is, posterior mean estimates, is 0.85. We also consider two alternative settings: a higher value of $\rho_i = 0.95$, which is close to the inertia of the central bank reaction function in Coibion, Gorodnichenko, and Wieland (2012), and a lower value of $\rho_i = 0.8$. These two values arguably encompass the existing empirical uncertainty on the degree of smoothing, as they stand outside the 90 percent probability interval of our posterior parameter estimates.

Figure 15. Optimal Inflation Rate as a Function of the Steady-State Real Interest Rate with Alternative ρ_i

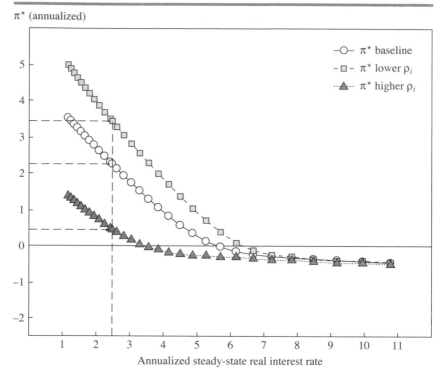

Source: Authors' calculations.
Note: The round dots correspond to the baseline scenario wherein all the structural parameters are set at their posterior mean $\bar{\theta}$. The square dots correspond to the counterfactual simulation with ρ_i set to 0.8. The triangle dots correspond to the counterfactual simulation with ρ_i set to 0.95.

The effect of a higher interest rate smoothing is to shift the (r^*, π^*) curve downward except for high values of r^* for which the probability of hitting the ZLB is close to zero and the optimal inflation target is slightly negative. Under this strategy, the pre-crisis optimal inflation rate would be close to 0.5 percent in the United States.[34] Conversely, a lower interest rate

34. This is not inconsistent with the result in Coibion, Gorodnichenko, and Wieland (2012), who report an optimal inflation target of 1.5 percent under their baseline calibration on U.S. post-WWII data. Indeed, the variance of their underlying shocks is higher than in our baseline, which is based on Great Moderation estimates. As discussed above, a higher variance of shocks induces more frequent ZLB episodes; hence, it calls for a higher optimal inflation target.

smoothing shifts the (r^*, π^*) curve upward, even for relatively high values of r^*, because the probability of being in a ZLB regime increases under this strategy. With a lower ρ_i, the pre-crisis optimal inflation rate would be close to 3.5 percent.

As for the slope of the (r^*, π^*) curve, in the empirically relevant region (that is, for values close to the baseline estimates), it is much less affected than the level of this locus. It is, however, more affected in this exercise than in other robustness experiments considered above. A very large smoothing parameter, due to its effect outlined above on the probability of ZLB, somewhat alleviates the extent to which an increase in the inflation target is needed. The slope is indeed close to –0.7 in that case. For a strategy associated with a low smoothing parameter, the slope is close to –1, so closer to the benchmark case. For large values of r^*, the degree of smoothing is irrelevant.

V.D. More Traditional Specifications of the Policy Rule

We also considered the case of a monetary policy rule featuring no shadow rate (that is, no lower for longer feature), as well as of a simple nonintertial Taylor rule. Results are reported in figures 16 and 17. In the first case, the lagged interest rate is the lagged actual rate. As soon as the liftoff occurs after a ZLB episode, the interest rate follows a standard path, so monetary policy does not retain the memory of having been constrained for some periods by the ZLB (unlike under our baseline specification). In the second case, there is no inertia at all, but we use a four-quarter inflation rate as in the standard Taylor (1993) rule and its implementation in Kiley and Roberts (2017). In both cases, the overall degree of monetary policy inertia decreases, and so the stabilization property of the policy rule is weaker in our forward-looking model, materializing in more frequent ZLB episodes. As a result, the optimal inflation rate is in both cases larger than in the baseline for realistic values of the real interest rate. Also the optimal inflation rate is positive for a wider range of values of r^*. However, in both variants the slope of the (r^*, π^*) is similar to that of our baseline curve around the sample value of r^*.

V.E. A Price Level Targeting Rule

We finally consider that the rule effectively implemented by the central bank reacts to deviations of the (log) price level $\hat{p}_t = \hat{p}_{t-1} + \hat{\pi}_t$ to a targeted path, instead of the gap $\hat{\pi}_t$ between the inflation rate and its

Figure 16. Optimal Inflation Rate as a Function of the Steady-State Real Interest Rate with Simple Standard Taylor Rule

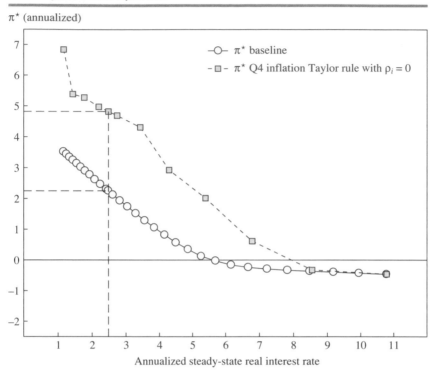

Source: Authors' calculations.

Note: The round dots correspond to the baseline scenario. The square dots correspond to the counterfactual simulation with simple standard Taylor rule used. Parameters of the rules on inflation and output gap are the same as in the baseline, but there is no inertia and year-on-year inflation is used.

target. Formally, we assume that the central bank sets the policy rate according to the following rule:

$$\hat{\imath}_t^{plt} = \rho_i \hat{\imath}_{t-1}^{plt} + (1 - \rho_i)(a_p \hat{p}_t + a_y \hat{x}_t) + \zeta_{R,t}$$

with $\hat{\imath}_t = \max\{\hat{\imath}_t^{plt}, -(\mu_z + \rho + \pi)\}$.

We perform the same exercises as before, focusing on the case in which average productivity growth μ_z is the driver of changes in the natural rate. We consider two values for a_p: .1 and .5. All the other parameters of the model are set to their posterior mean.

Figure 18 reports the (r^*, π^*) relation obtained under these two alternative scenarios. A striking feature of that new curve is that the optimal

Figure 17. Optimal Inflation Rate as a Function of the Steady-State Real Interest Rate with "No Shadow Rate" Rule

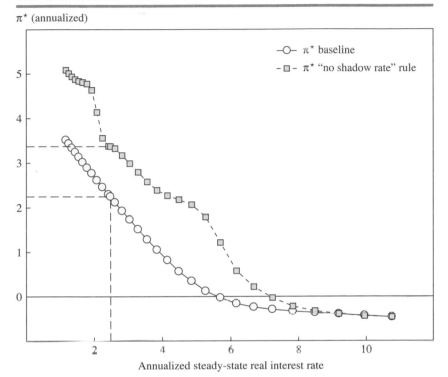

π* (annualized)

Annualized steady-state real interest rate

Source: Authors' calculations.
Note: The round dots correspond to the baseline scenario. The square dots correspond to the counter-factual noninertial policy rule used.

inflation target lies then between 0 percent and 1 percent as opposed to 2.21 percent in the baseline. Price level targeting makes the commitment to make up for past inflation undershooting (or overshooting) even stronger than what can be obtained when increasing the smoothing parameters in a rule which targets inflation instead. This commitment stabilizes inflation expectations so that both the probability of hitting the zero lower bound and the average length of such episodes are reduced. As a consequence, there is no incentive to bear the costs of a positive steady-state inflation and the optimal inflation target is close to zero. This holds whether the central bank reacts aggressively or not to the price level deviating from its targeted path.

Another striking result is that the (r^*, π^*) relation is much flatter in the vicinity of the pre-crisis level for r^* than under alternative inflation

Figure 18. Optimal Inflation Rate as a Function of the Steady-State Real Interest Rate with Price Level Targeting Strategy

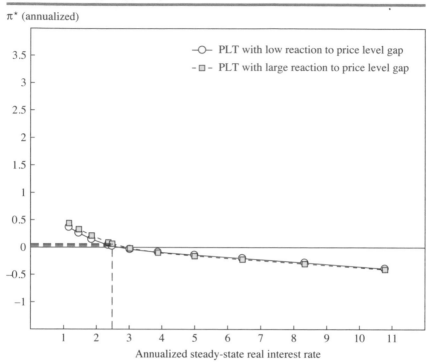

Source: Authors' calculations.
Note: Simulations obtained under the price level targeting policy rule given in equation 7. The round (square) dots correspond to the scenario wherein $\alpha_p = .1$ (.5). All the other structural parameters are set at their posterior mean $\bar{\theta}$.

targeting monetary policy strategies. The slope is close to −0.3 instead of the [−1, −0.7] range obtained previously. A price level targeting strategy thus allows the costs of the ZLB to be kept small even if the natural rate of interest dropped by, say, 1 percent compared to the pre-crisis regime.

VI. Summary and Conclusions

In this paper, we have assessed how changes in the steady-state natural interest rate (r^*) translate into changes in the optimal inflation target in a model subject to the ZLB. Our main finding is that, starting from pre-crisis values, a 1 percentage point decline in r^* should be accommodated by an increase in the optimal inflation target between 0.9 and 1 percentage point.

Table 2. Effect of a Decline in r^* under Alternative Notions of Optimal Inflation

	Baseline	Lower r*	Δ
Mean of π^*	2.00	3.00	1.00
Median of π^*	1.96	2.90	.94
π^* at posterior mean	2.21	3.20	.99
π^* at posterior median	2.12	3.11	.99
π^{**}	2.40	3.30	.90
π^{**}, frozen MP	2.24	3.16	.92
Average realized inflation at posterior mean	2.20	3.19	.99
π^* at posterior mean, ELB −40 bp	1.90	2.83	.93
Average realized inflation at posterior mean, ELB −40 bp	1.86	2.77	.91
π^* at posterior mean, higher ρ_i	0.44	1.13	.69
π^* at posterior mean, price level targeting	0.06	0.32	.26

Source: Authors' calculations.
Note: All figures are in annualized percentage rate.

For convenience, table 2 recapitulates our results. Overall, across the different concepts of optimal inflation considered in this paper, the level of optimal inflation does vary. However, it is a very robust finding that the slope of the (r^*, π^*) relation is close to −1 in the vicinity of the pre-crisis value of steady-state real interest rates.

In our analysis, we have considered adjusting the inflation target as the only option at the policymaker's disposal, while preserving all other elements of the monetary policy strategy. In reality policymakers have a larger set of options. As a matter of fact, recent discussions revolving around monetary policy in the new normal have suggested that the various nonconventional measures—forward guidance on interest rates and large-scale asset purchases—used in the aftermath of the Great Recession could feature permanently in the policy toolbox. In particular, unconventional monetary policies could represent useful second-best instruments when the ZLB is reached, as advocated by Reifschneider (2016), Swanson (2018), and Sims and Wu (2019).[35] By implying a low for long interest rate at the end of a liquidity trap, the monetary policy rule that we consider in our exercise accounts, at least partially, for the effect of nonconventional policies that were implemented at the ZLB. But more aggressive non-conventional packages could be considered as alternative strategies. Beyond these monetary policy measures, fiscal policies could also play a significant

---

35. See also Eberly, Stock, and Wright (2019) and Chung and others (2019) for recent work documenting the effectiveness of such instruments.

role, as emphasized by Correia and others (2013). As a result, the ZLB might be less stringent a constraint in a practical policy context than in our analysis, as argued in Debortoli, Galí, and Gambetti (forthcoming). However, the efficacy and the costs of these policies should also be part of the analysis. The complete comparison of these policy trade-offs goes beyond the scope of the present paper.

An alternative would consist of a change of the monetary policy strategy, for example, adopting variants of the price level targeting strategy, as recently advocated by Williams (2016) and Bernanke, Kiley, and Roberts (2019). Our exercise emphasizes that, when the central bank follows a strategy of making up for past inflation deviations from target, the case for increasing the inflation target is much reduced. Nevertheless, these results are obtained under the assumption that private agents believe and understand the commitment of the central bank to deviate from its inflation target in order to compensate for previous deviations. This is a debatable assumption. Andrade and others (2019) show that the lower for longer guidance on future interest rates that the Federal Open Market Committee gave during the recent ZLB episode was interpreted differently by private agents, including professional forecasters: some viewed it as good news of a commitment to future accommodation, and some viewed it as bad news that the lowflation will last longer. As they emphasize, lower for longer policies are much less effective in practice than implied by theoretical models with perfect credibility, full information, and rational expectations. They can even be detrimental if the bad signals prevail.

We have discussed the potential desirability of a higher inflation target, abstracting from the challenges of implementing an eventual transition to the new objective. In the current lowflation environment, increasing the inflation target in reaction to a drop in the steady-state value of the real interest rate might raise some credibility issues. However, a move toward makeup strategies would as well raise substantial credibility issues, as these imply an arguably time-inconsistent commitment to deviate from the inflation target once it has been reached.

Finally, our analysis has also abstracted from forces identified in the literature as warranting a small, positive inflation target, irrespective of ZLB issues, as emphasized in, for example, Bernanke and others (1999) and Kiley, Mauskopf, and Wilcox (2007). The first argument is grounded on measurement issues, following the finding from the 1996 Boskin report that the consumer price index did probably overestimate inflation in the United States by more than 1 percentage point in the early 1990s. The second argument is rooted in downward nominal rigidities. In an economy where there are such downward rigidities (for example, in nominal wages) a positive inflation rate can help "grease the wheel" of the labor market by facilitating relative price adjustments. Symmetrically, we also abstracted from forces calling for lower inflation targets. The most obvious is the so-called Friedman (1969) rule, according to which average inflation should be equal to minus the steady-state real interest rate, hence be *negative*, in order to minimize loss of resources or utility and the distortionary wedge between cash and credit goods (for example, consumption and leisure) induced by a nonzero nominal interest rate. Presumably, these and several other factors were taken into account when an inflation target of 2 percent was chosen. But an estimate of r^* was, undoubtedly, one of the key factors in that choice. Accordingly, the current reassessment of r^* by the Federal Reserve and other central banks would seem to call for a simultaneous reassessment of the optimal inflation target.

ACKNOWLEDGMENTS   Andrade: philippe.andrade@bos.frb.org. Galí: jgali@crei.cat. Le Bihan: herve.lebihan@banque-france.fr. Matheron: julien. matheron@banque-france.fr. We thank Janice Eberly, James Stock and our discussants, Mike Kiley and Luminita Stevens, for their comments and suggestions. We also thank Olivier Blanchard, Olivier Coibion, Isabel Correia, Kevin Lansing, Kemal Ozhan, Argia Sbordone, Ruf Wouters, and Johannes Wieland, as well as participants at several conferences and seminars, for comments and discussions on an earlier draft. The views expressed herein are those of the authors and do not necessarily reflect those of the Banque de France, the Eurosystem, the Federal Reserve Bank of Boston, or the Federal Reserve System.

References

Adam, Klaus, and Henning Weber. 2019. "Optimal Trend Inflation." *American Economic Review* 109, no. 2: 702–37.

Alvarez, Fernando, Hervé Le Bihan, and Francesco Lippi. 2016. "The Real Effects of Monetary Shocks in Sticky Price Models: A Sufficient Statistic Approach." *American Economic Review* 106, no. 10: 2817–51.

Amano, Robert, Kevin Moran, Stephen Murchison, and Andrew Rennison. 2009. "Trend Inflation, Wage and Price Rigidities, and Productivity Growth." *Journal of Monetary Economics* 56, no. 3: 353–64.

Andrade, Philippe, Gaetano Gaballo, Eric Mengus, and Benoît Mojon. 2019. "Forward Guidance and Heterogeneous Beliefs." *American Economic Journal: Macroeconomics* 11, no. 3: 1–29.

Andrade, Philippe, Hervé Le Bihan, Jordi Galí, and Julien Matheron. 2020. "Should the ECB Adjust Its Strategy in the Face of a Lower Natural Interest Rate?" Mimeo, Banque de France.

Ascari, Guido, Louis Phaneuf, and Eric R. Sims. 2018. "On the Welfare and Cyclical Implications of Moderate Trend Inflation." *Journal of Monetary Economics* 99:56–71.

Ascari, Guido, and Argia M. Sbordone. 2014. "The Macroeconomics of Trend Inflation." *Journal of Economic Literature* 52, no. 3: 679–739.

Autor, David, David Dorn, Lawrence F. Katz, Christina Patterson, and John Van Reenen. Forthcoming. "The Fall of the Labor Share and the Rise of Superstar Firms." *Quarterly Journal of Economics.*

Ball, Laurence M. 2014. "The Case for a Long-Run Inflation Target of Four Percent." Working Paper 14/92. Washington, D.C.: International Monetary Fund. https://www.imf.org/en/Publications/WP/Issues/2016/12/31/The-Case-for-a-Long-Run-Inflation-Target-of-Four-Percent-41625.

Basu, Susanto, and John G. Fernald. 1997. "Returns to Scale in U.S. Production: Estimates and Implications." *Journal of Political Economy* 105, no. 2: 249–83.

Bernanke, Ben S. 2016. "Modifying the Fed's Policy Framework: Does a Higher Inflation Target Beat Negative Interest Rates?" Blog post, September 13, Brookings Institution. https://www.brookings.edu/blog/ben-bernanke/2016/09/13/modifying-the-feds-policy-framework-does-a-higher-inflation-target-beat-negative-interest-rates/.

Bernanke, Ben S., Michael T. Kiley, and John M. Roberts. 2019. "Monetary Policy Strategies for a Low-Rate Environment." *AEA Papers and Proceedings* 109:421–26.

Bernanke, Ben S., Thomas Laubach, Frederic Mishkin, and Adam S. Posen. 1999. *Inflation Targeting: Lessons from the International Experience.* Princeton, N.J.: Princeton University Press.

Bilbiie, Florin O., Ippei Fujiwara, and Fabio Ghironi. 2014. "Optimal Monetary Policy with Endogenous Entry and Product Variety." *Journal of Monetary Economics* 64:1–20.

Blanchard, Olivier, Giovanni Dell'Ariccia, and Paolo Mauro. 2010. "Rethinking Macroeconomic Policy." *Journal of Money, Credit and Banking* 42, no. S1: 199–215.

Blanco, Julio A. Forthcoming. "Optimal Inflation Target in an Economy with Menu Costs and Zero Lower Bound." *American Economic Journal: Macroeconomics*.

Bodenstein, Martin, Christopher J. Erceg, and Luca Guerrieri. 2009. "The Effects of Foreign Shocks when Interest Rates Are at Zero." *Canadian Journal of Economics* 50, no. 3: 660–84.

Boskin, Michael, Ellen Dulberger, Robert J. Gordon, Zvi Griliches, and Dale Jorgenson. 1996. "Toward a More Accurate Measure of the Cost of Living." Final Report to the Senate Finance Committee.

Brand, Claus, Marcin Bielecki, and Adrian Penalver. 2019. "The Natural Rate of Interest: Estimates, Drivers, and Challenges to Monetary Policy." Occasional Paper 217. Frankfurt: European Central Bank. https://www.ecb.europa.eu/pub/pdf/scpops/ecb.op217.en.pdf.

Burstein, Ariel, and Christian Hellwig. 2008. "Welfare Costs of Inflation in a Menu Cost Model." *American Economic Review* 98, no. 2: 438–43.

Caballero, Ricardo J., and Emmanuel Farhi. 2018. "The Safety Trap." *Review of Economic Studies* 85, no. 1: 223–74.

Carlsson, Mikael, and Andreas Westermark. 2016. "Labor Market Frictions and Optimal Steady-State Inflation." *Journal of Monetary Economics* 78:67–79.

Christiano, Lawrence J., Martin Eichenbaum, and Charles L. Evans. 2005. "Nominal Rigidities and the Dynamic Effects of a Shock to Monetary Policy." *Journal of Political Economy* 113, no. 1: 1–45.

Chung, Hess, Etienne Gagnon, Taisuke Nakata, Matthias Paustian, Bernd Schlusche, James Trevino, Diego Vilán, and Wei Zheng. 2019. "Monetary Policy Options at the Effective Lower Bound: Assessing the Federal Reserve's Current Policy Toolkit." Finance and Economics Discussion Series 2019-003. Washington, D.C.: Board of Governors of the Federal Reserve System. https://www.federalreserve.gov/econres/feds/files/2019003pap.pdf.

Chung, Hess, Jean-Philippe Laforte, David Reifschneider, and John C. Williams. 2012. "Have We Underestimated the Likelihood and Severity of Zero Lower Bound Events?" *Journal of Money, Credit and Banking* 44, no. S1: 47–82.

Clarida, Richard H. 2019. "The Federal Reserve's Review of Its Monetary Policy Strategy, Tools, and Communication Practices." Speech given at the 2019 U.S. Monetary Policy Forum, Initiative on Global Markets, University of Chicago Booth School of Business, New York, February 22.

Clarida, Richard H., Jordi Galí, and Mark Gertler. 1998. "Monetary Policy Rules in Practice: Some International Evidence." *European Economic Review* 42: 1033–67.

Coibion, Olivier, Yuriy Gorodnichenko, and Johannes Wieland. 2012. "The Optimal Inflation Rate in New Keynesian Models: Should Central Banks Raise Their Inflation Targets in Light of the Zero Lower Bound?" *Review of Economic Studies* 79, no. 4: 1371–1406.

Correia, Isabel, Emmanuel Farhi, Juan Pablo Nicolini, and Pedro Teles. 2013. "Unconventional Fiscal Policy at the Zero Bound." *American Economic Review* 103, no. 4: 1172–1211.

Debortoli, Davide, Jordi Galí, and Luca Gambetti. Forthcoming. "On the Empirical (Ir)Relevance of the Zero Lower Bound Constraint." *NBER Macroeconomics Annual 34.*

Del Negro, Marco D., Domenico Giannone, Marc P. Giannoni, and Andrea Tambalotti. 2017. "Safety, Liquidity, and the Natural Rate of Interest." *Brookings Papers on Economic Activity*, Spring, 235–316.

Del Negro, Marco D., Domenico Giannone, Marc P. Giannoni, and Andrea Tambalotti. 2019. "Global Trends in Interest Rates." *Journal of International Economics* 118:248–62.

De Loecker, Jan, and Jan Eeckhout. 2017. "The Rise of Market Power and the Macroeconomic Implications." Working Paper 23687. Cambridge, Mass.: National Bureau of Economic Research. https://www.nber.org/papers/w23687.

Dordal-i-Carreras, Marc, Olivier Coibion, Yuriy Gorodnichenko, and Johannes Wieland. 2016. "Infrequent but Long-Lived Zero-Bound Episodes and the Optimal Rate of Inflation." *Annual Review of Economics* 8:497–520.

Eberly, Janice C., James H. Stock, and Jonathan H. Wright. 2019. "The Federal Reserve's Current Framework for Monetary Policy: A Review and Assessment." Working Paper 26002. Cambridge, Mass.: National Bureau of Economic Research. https://www.nber.org/papers/w26002.

Eggertsson, Gauti B., Neil R. Mehrotra, and Jacob A. Robbins. 2019. "A Model of Secular Stagnation: Theory and Quantitative Evaluation." *American Economic Journal: Macroeconomics* 11, no. 1: 1–48.

Erceg, Christopher J., Dale W. Henderson, and Andrew T. Levin. 2000. "Optimal Monetary Policy with Staggered Wage and Price Contracts." *Journal of Monetary Economics* 46, no. 2: 281–313.

Farhi, Emmanuel, and François Gourio. 2018. "Accounting for Macro-Finance Trends: Market Power, Intangibles, and Risk Premia." *Brookings Papers on Economic Activity*, Fall, 147–250.

Friedman, Milton. 1969. *The Optimum Quantity of Money and Other Essays.* Chicago: Aldine Press.

Fuhrer, Jeff, Giovanni P. Olivei, Eric S. Rosengren, and Geoffrey M. B. Tootell. 2018. "Should the Federal Reserve Regularly Evaluate Its Monetary Policy Framework?" *Brookings Papers on Economic Activity*, Fall, 443–517.

Galí, Jordi. 2015. *Monetary Policy, Inflation, and the Business Cycle: An Introduction to the New Keynesian Framework.* Princeton, N.J.: Princeton University Press.

Golosov, Mikhail, and Robert E. Lucas Jr. 2007. "Menu Costs and Phillips Curves." *Journal of Political Economy* 115, no. 2: 171–99.

Gordon, Robert J. 2015. "Secular Stagnation: A Supply-Side View." *American Economic Review* 105, no. 5: 54–59.

Guerrieri, Luca, and Matteo Iacoviello. 2015. "OccBin: A Toolkit for Solving Dynamic Models with Occasionally Binding Constraints Easily." *Journal of Monetary Economics* 70:22–38.

Gust, Christopher, Edward Herbst, David López-Salido, and Matthew E. Smith. 2017. "The Empirical Implications of the Interest-Rate Lower Bound." *American Economic Review* 107, no. 7: 1971–2006.

Hall, Robert E. 2018. "New Evidence on the Markup of Prices over Marginal Costs and the Role of Mega-Firms in the US Economy." Working Paper 24574. Cambridge, Mass.: National Bureau of Economic Research. https://www.nber.org/papers/w24574.

Hills, Timothy S., Taisuke Nakata, and Sebastian Schmidt. 2016. "The Risky Steady State and the Interest Rate Lower Bound." Finance and Economics Discussion Series 2016-009. Washington, D.C.: Board of Governors of the Federal Reserve System. https://www.federalreserve.gov/econresdata/feds/2016/files/2016009pap.pdf.

Holston, Kathryn, Thomas Laubach, and John C. Williams. 2017. "Measuring the Natural Rate of Interest: International Trends and Determinants." *Journal of International Economics* 108, no. S1: 59–75.

Khan, Aubhik, Robert G. King, and Alexander L. Wolman. 2003. "Optimal Monetary Policy." *Review of Economic Studies* 70, no. 4: 825–60.

Kiley, Michael. 2019. Comment on "The Optimal Inflation Target and the Natural Rate of Interest," by Philippe Andrade, Jordi Galí, Hervé Le Bihan, and Julien Matheron. In the present volume of *Brookings Papers on Economic Activity*.

Kiley, Michael, Eileen Mauskopf, and David Wilcox. 2007. "Issues Pertaining to the Specification of a Numerical Price-Related Objective for Monetary Policy." FOMC memo. Washington, D.C.: Board of Governors of the Federal Reserve System. https://www.federalreserve.gov/monetarypolicy/files/FOMC20070312 memo01.pdf.

Kiley, Michael T., and John M. Roberts. 2017. "Monetary Policy in a Low Interest Rate World." *Brookings Papers on Economic Activity*, Spring, 317–96.

Laubach, Thomas, and John C. Williams. 2016. "Measuring the Natural Rate of Interest Redux." Working Paper 2016–11. Washington, D.C.: Board of Governors of the Federal Reserve System. https://www.frbsf.org/economic-research/files/wp2015-16.pdf.

Lepetit, Antoine. 2018. "The Optimal Inflation Rate with Discount Factor Heterogeneity." Finance and Economics Discussion Series 2018-086. Washington, D.C.: Board of Governors of the Federal Reserve System. https://www.federalreserve.gov/econres/feds/files/2018086pap.pdf.

Levin, Andrew T., Alexei Onatski, John Williams, and Noah M. Williams. 2006. "Monetary Policy under Uncertainty in Micro-Founded Macroeconometric Models." In *NBER Macroeconomics Annual* 20:229–312.

Lindé, Jesper, Junior Maih, and Rafael Wouters. 2017. "Estimation of Operational Macromodels at the Zero Lower Bound." Working paper.

Nakamura, Emi, Jón Steinsson, Patrick Sun, and Daniel Villar. 2018. "The Elusive Costs of Inflation: Price Dispersion during the U.S. Great Inflation." *Quarterly Journal of Economics* 133, no. 4: 1933–80.

Rachel, Łukasz, and Lawrence H. Summers. 2019. "On Falling Neutral Real Rates, Fiscal Policy, and the Risk of Secular Stagnation." *Brookings Papers on Economic Activity*, Spring, 1–76.

Reifschneider, David. 2016. "Gauging the Ability of the FOMC to Respond to Future Recessions." Finance and Economics Discussion Series 2016–068. Washington, D.C.: Board of Governors of the Federal Reserve System. https://www.federalreserve.gov/econresdata/feds/2016/files/2016068pap.pdf.

Schmitt-Grohé, Stephanie, and Martín Uribe. 2010. "The Optimal Rate of Inflation." In *Handbook of Monetary Economics*, vol. 3, edited by Benjamin M. Friedman and Michael Woodford. Amsterdam: North Holland.

Sims, Eric R., and Jing Cynthia Wu. 2019. "Evaluating Central Banks' Tool Kit: Past, Present, and Future." Working Paper 26040. Cambridge, Mass.: National Bureau of Economic Research. https://www.nber.org/papers/w26040.

Summers, Lawrence H. 2014. "U.S. Economic Prospects: Secular Stagnation, Hysteresis, and the Zero Lower Bound." *Business Economics* 49, no. 2: 65–73.

Swanson, Eric T. 2018. "The Federal Reserve Is Not Very Constrained by the Lower Bound on Nominal Interest Rates." *Brookings Papers on Economic Activity*, Fall, 555–72.

Taylor, John B. 1993. "Discretion versus Policy Rules in Practice." *Carnegie-Rochester Conference Series on Public Policy* 39: 195–214.

Traina, James. 2015. "Is Aggregate Market Power Increasing? Production Trends Using Financial Statements." Working Paper 17. Chicago: Chicago Booth, Stigler Center for the Study of the Economy and the State. https://research.chicagobooth.edu/-/media/research/stigler/pdfs/workingpapers/17isaggregate marketpowerincreasing.pdf.

Williams, John C. 2009. "Heeding Daedalus: Optimal Inflation and the Zero Lower Bound." *Brookings Papers on Economic Activity*, Fall, 1–49.

Williams, John C. 2013. "A Defense of Moderation in Monetary Policy." *Journal of Macroeconomics* 38, no. B: 137–50.

Williams, John C. 2016. "Monetary Policy in a Low R-Star World." Economic Letter 2016–23. Federal Reserve Bank of San Francisco. https://www.frbsf.org/economic-research/publications/economic-letter/2016/august/monetary-policy-and-low-r-star-natural-rate-of-interest/.

Woodford, Michael. 2003. *Interest and Prices*. Princeton, N.J.: Princeton University Press.

Comments and Discussion

COMMENT BY
MICHAEL T. KILEY[1] How should central banks adjust their approach to economic stabilization in light of the low level of nominal interest rates among advanced economies? This question is one of the most central facing monetary policymakers, as short-term policy interest rates have been at or below zero for most of the period since 2008 in the United States, the Euro area, and Japan. The challenges associated with the low interest rate environment are one of the considerations motivating the review by the Federal Reserve of its monetary policy framework in 2019.[2]

The paper by Philippe Andrade, Jordi Galí, Hervé Le Bihan, and Julien Matheron confronts this issue head-on through an assessment of the degree to which a decline in the equilibrium real interest rate (r^*) calls for an increase in the inflation target in a New Keynesian dynamic stochastic general equilibrium (DSGE) model. In their analysis, the inflation target affects economic efficiency and activity through two primary channels: the dispersion inflation induces in the distribution of nominal prices and wages and the effect of the level of the inflation target on the likelihood that monetary policy is constrained by its effective lower bound (ELB) and the consequent deterioration in economic stability. Using the welfare function of the representative household as the policymaker's objective function, the model implies that declines in the equilibrium real interest rate, within the 1–3 percent range the authors emphasize, should be accompanied by a nearly equal increase in the inflation target. As a result, they find that a shift in r^* from around 2 percent to 1 percent would increase the optimal

---

1. The analysis and conclusions set forth are those of the presenter and do not indicate concurrence by the Federal Reserve Board or other members of its staff.
2. For a discussion of the Federal Reserve's review, see Clarida (2019).

Figure 1. Outcomes under a Fixed 2 Percent Inflation Target

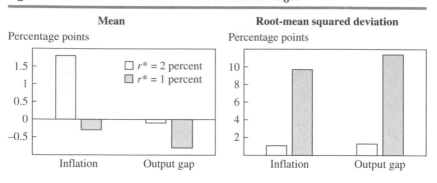

Source: Author's calculations.

inflation target from 2+ percent to 3+ percent. Although the authors do not emphasize the implications for their model of a failure to raise the inflation target when r^* declines, their framework adds to the findings in Kiley and Roberts (2017) that suggest that the effects of the ELB on economic performance absent adjustments in policy strategy are large. To see this, figure 1 presents the mean and root-mean-squared deviation of inflation and the output gap implied by their model assuming an inflation target of 2 percent and r^* equal to either 1 or 2 percent. When r^* is 2 percent, inflation is near the 2 percent target and output is near potential, on average, while economic volatility is low (with root-mean squared deviations from target of about 1 percentage point). If r^* is 1 percent, inflation averages below 0 percent, the output gap averages about −.75 percent, and economic volatility is very high. Indeed, these effects are larger than in Kiley and Roberts (2017), and my remarks will return to the quantitative properties of their model below.

Overall, the analysis is an important extension of earlier work on the optimal inflation target within the New Keynesian framework, including joint consideration of stickiness in nominal prices and wages, estimation of the model to match U.S. macroeconomic dynamics over the period from 1985 to 2008, and consideration of the effects of a low level of r^*.[3] However, a number of important considerations affect interpretation of their results. First, the analysis ignores a range of costs and benefits of inflation

---

3. Earlier similar analyses include Schmitt-Grohé and Uribe (2010) and, most directly, Coibion, Gorodnichenko, and Wieland (2012).

that may be important determinants of the optimal inflation rate. Second, the close link between the New Keynesian microeconomic foundations of the model and the notions of economic welfare underlying the analysis, combined with the assumption that the steady state is efficient, may understate the welfare costs of economic fluctuations. Third, some empirical properties of the model are questionable, including a large role for efficient fluctuations in output and labor input over the business cycle, a steep Phillips curve, and powerful effects of monetary policy forward guidance under their baseline monetary policy rule. Fourth, the analysis appears implicitly optimistic about the level of r^* over the medium term. And fifth, the analysis briefly mentions, but does not emphasize, changes in policy strategy to address ELB risks, such as temporary price level targets or quantitative easing as part of policymakers' systematic reaction function.

THE COSTS AND BENEFITS OF INFLATION In the authors' analysis, the cost/benefit trade-off associated with the choice of inflation target is relatively simple. A higher inflation target lowers costs to economic stability associated with the ELB, as higher nominal interest rates (in the steady state) imply more scope to reduce interest rates during periods of weak economic activity or low inflation. At the same time, a higher inflation target raises costs associated with the inefficient distribution of prices and wages arising from nominal rigidities, which lead to an inefficient distribution of output and labor input and hence lower economic activity and welfare. These mechanisms are quite standard but represent a narrow set of the costs and benefits of inflation that have been discussed in economic research. For example, Kiley, Mauskopf, and Wilcox (2007) review the literature on the costs and benefits of inflation. The costs of positive inflation, beyond those associated with price dispersion, include nominal illusion (the failure of households and firms to understand inflation and make appropriate economic decisions), non-indexation of the tax code and the resulting distortions to investment, redistribution of wealth between borrowers and lenders, and the inflation tax on money balances. The costs of too-low inflation, beyond those associated with ELB risk, include the costs of downward nominal wage rigidity, debt deflation costs, and the loss in government revenue associated with the inflation tax.

In light of these additional costs and benefits of inflation, the New Keynesian tradition's emphasis on costs associated with wage and price dispersion may be overly narrow, and consideration of a broader set of costs and benefits may be desirable. Moreover, Nakamura and others (2018) find limited support for the link between the level of inflation and price dispersion emphasized in the authors' DSGE model.

THE ROLE OF NOMINAL RIGIDITIES IN NOTIONS OF WELFARE The centrality of nominal rigidities in the model's characterization of welfare and economic fluctuations may affect the results, and almost certainly their translation to policy discussions, in other significant ways. It is well known that the New Keynesian welfare function places a large weight on inflation stability relative to stability in economic activity (Coibion, Gorodnichenko, and Wieland 2012). In contrast, policymakers appear to place a large weight on stability of economic activity—as highlighted, for example, by the discussion of optimal policy using a welfare function with equal weights on inflation and unemployment gaps in Yellen (2012). This disconnect may suggest that important considerations are missing from the model.

In addition, the model's steady state is assumed to involve an efficient level of resource utilization through a set of subsidies that undo the inefficiencies associated with monopolistic competition. But the level of resource utilization in the economy is likely not efficient: the effects of monopoly power in product and labor markets are not unwound through subsidies, and distortionary taxation to finance government activities implies that resource utilization falls short of "first-best" levels, to name just two distortions. These real-world complications have important implications. The fact that the typical level of resource utilization is likely lower than the efficient level implies that there are first-order welfare losses associated with the level of economic activity (Benigno and Woodford 2005; Galí, Gertler, and López-Salido 2007). As a result, the asymmetric effects of the ELB, in which severe recessions are deeper than economic expansions and hence the average level of resource utilization is depressed by ELB risk, lead to first-order welfare losses. These effects are ignored by the authors but may well be sizable and thereby have important effects on the optimal level of inflation. For example, figure 1 and Kiley and Roberts (2017) estimate sizable downside skewness in the distribution of economic activity associated with the ELB.

QUANTITATIVE PROPERTIES OF THE MODEL AND THE POWER OF FORWARD GUIDANCE The highly restrictive microfoundations of the model may also contribute to a number of quantitative properties of the model that are questionable, especially among the central banking community. For example, a focus on welfare analysis and the monetary policy rule in the model is a measure of resource utilization based on the deviation of activity from flexible price levels. And the model includes a large role for efficient, flexible price movements in output and labor hours, reflecting the fact that the most important source of fluctuations in output and labor input is a shock to household preferences (which implies that flexible price output and labor input are quite volatile). In contrast, there is a limited role for inefficient sources of fluctuations under flexible prices; for example, the model does not include shocks to financial frictions as a source of economic volatility. These properties may differ from those underlying (some) policy analysis, as policymaker actions appear to point to concern over fluctuations in labor input more generally, perhaps reflecting skepticism regarding the importance of efficient sources of fluctuations in unemployment associated with changes in household preferences.[4]

The large role of efficient shifts in household preferences as a source of economic fluctuations is not the only concern with the quantitative properties of the authors' model. While the authors estimate their model using data from 1985 to 2008 on output, price and wage inflation, and the nominal federal funds rate, estimation does not guarantee a good fit to a broad range of macroeconomic facts, and the model has some properties that call into question the quantitative results. Two noteworthy quantitative properties are the sensitivity of inflation to shifts in monetary policy and the effects of monetary policy forward guidance.

Monetary policy appears to have an outsized effect on inflation in the model. Figure 2 presents the impulse responses of the federal funds rate, inflation (at an annual rate), and output to a (contemporaneous) 100 basis point (annual rate) reduction in the federal funds rate in the dotted lines. Inflation and output respond quickly. More importantly, inflation responds sizably, and by more than output. This response appears inconsistent with research suggesting that the Phillips curve has become quite flat (Kiley 2015; Blanchard 2016) and that this development has important implications for monetary policy (Yellen 2017).

Forward guidance also appears to be very powerful in the authors' model. The solid lines in figure 2 present impulse responses to a 100 basis point reduction in the federal funds rate four quarters into the future, with a commitment to hold the funds rate unchanged prior to the fourth quarter. The effects of forward guidance on output and inflation are several times larger than contemporaneous monetary policy—the model has a forward guidance puzzle.[5] This significantly affects the authors' findings on

4. Kiley (2013) discusses alternative notions of resource utilization within DSGE models.
5. A large body of literature discusses the forward guidance puzzle. Kiley (2016) and McKay, Nakamura, and Steinsson (2016) discuss how the Phillips curve and IS curve affect the forward guidance puzzle. Chung, Herbst, and Kiley (2015) and Bernanke, Kiley, and Roberts (2019) discuss how the power of expectations management affects the efficacy of alternative monetary policy strategies.

Figure 2. Impulse Responses Following Monetary Policy Shocks

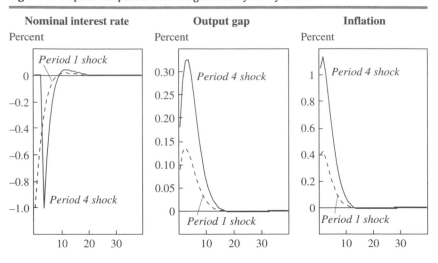

Source: Author's calculations.

the risks associated with the ELB. Specifically (and as the authors discuss clearly), their policy rule embeds a significant amount of inertia/history dependence in monetary policy. Moreover, they emphasize the case in which policymakers keep track of the value of the policy interest rate that would prevail absent the ELB and use this value as the lagged value of the policy rate in the policy rule when determining exit from the ELB. The joint effect of these assumptions is that a sizable degree of forward guidance is provided under their baseline rule, and this sizable amount of forward guidance limits the degree of ELB risk and the size of the optimal inflation rate. While the authors' econometric exercise strongly suggests that inertia is high, the types of policy rules that have been discussed in the Federal Reserve Board's Monetary Policy Report include many without such inertia, it is not clear policymakers have embraced the degree of Odyssean forward guidance associated with shadow rates (Campbell and others 2012), and some work questions the importance of inertia (Rudebusch 2002).

Quantitatively, these issues are very important. For example, if policy inertia equals 0.8, rather than the authors' baseline 0.85, the optimal rate of inflation when r^* equals 1 percent is about 5 percent, far above the 3+ percent obtained under their baseline degree of inertia (authors' figure 15); if a standard Taylor rule, without inertia, is used, the optimal inflation rate for

$r*$ equal to 1 percent is much higher (authors' figure 16). This is because ELB risk is much larger when the policy rule is not as efficient as in the authors' baseline case.

THE LEVEL OF $r*$ The authors focus on values for the steady-state real interest rate ranging from 1 percent to 3 percent or higher. The lower end of this range is linked, in part, to the structural characteristics of their model, as they constrain themselves to consider values of $r*$ linked to the representative household's discount rate or to the trend growth rate of the economy and hence do not consider very low (or negative) values for $r*$. However, the range considered by the authors is arguably too high. For example, the Summary of Economic Projections produced by the Federal Open Market Committee (FOMC) four times a year suggests that FOMC participants generally expect the real federal funds rate over the longer term to lie below 1 percent. This is consistent with model-based estimates of $r*$ for the United States and Euro area; for example, the model by Holston, Laubach, and Williams (2017) suggests $r*$ equals about .5 percent in the United States and lies below zero in the Euro area (figure 3, top panel). Finally, financial instruments suggest such views are widely shared: a simple estimate of the real five-year, five-year forward rate (that is, the real rate for years 5–10 implied by five-year and ten-year inflation-protected securities) has recently been near zero in the United States (TIPS) and has been deeply negative in Germany (iBunds) in recent years (figure 3, bottom panel). While model-based estimates of $r*$ rely on assumptions and real forward rates from inflation-protected securities reflect a range of determinants, these values raise the possibility that $r*$ is below 1 percent.[6] Extrapolation of the relationship the authors find between $r*$ and the optimal inflation rate suggests an optimal inflation target near or above 4 percent for values of $r*$ in the range estimated by policymakers, statistical models, and financial market prices.

SUMMARY ASSESSMENT So what are the key points I glean from the authors' analysis? First, future work may wish to consider a richer set of possible costs and benefits of inflation, as the emphasis on price dispersion in the New Keynesian model may be overdone. At the same time, these additional considerations are likely to affect the optimal inflation target in positive and negative directions. As a result, the authors' conclusion that a decline in $r*$ calls for a nearly equal-sized increase in the optimal inflation target is a reasonable rule of thumb for future work to debate.

---

6. For a discussion of challenges faced in model-based estimates of $r*$, see Kiley (2019, forthcoming).

Figure 3. Estimates of Interest Rates over the Intermediate Term

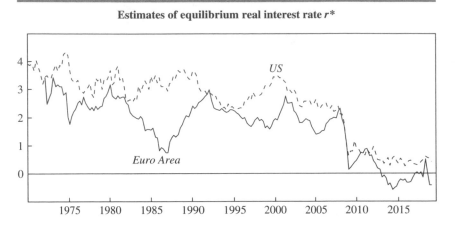

Estimates of equilibrium real interest rate *r**

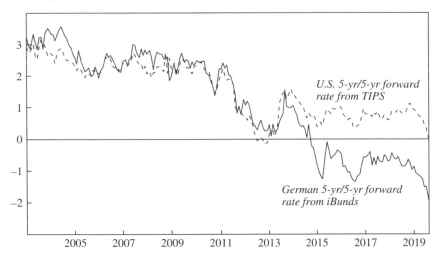

Comparison of inflation-protected securities in the United States and Germany

Sources: Federal Reserve Bank of New York, https://www.newyorkfed.org/research/policy/rstar/overview (*top panel*); author's calculations, U.S. Treasury, and Deutsche Bundesbank (*bottom panel*).

Moreover, I have discussed a number of quantitative properties of the model that are questionable, including the power of forward guidance. A less-powerful degree of forward guidance, as illustrated in the authors' simulations with less monetary policy inertia, is likely to raise ELB risks and the optimal inflation target. Indeed, the authors' example with less forward guidance suggests optimal inflation near 5 percent, a value that makes the suggestion of a 4 percent inflation target in Blanchard, Dell'ariccia, and Mauro (2010) and Ball (2014) appear timid. As a result, the authors' paper should be seen as a spur to further analysis of the optimal level of inflation.

At the same time, a crucial issue—and one largely set aside by the authors—is how changes in monetary policy strategy may lower ELB risk and allow a low optimal inflation rate. Within the DSGE model in the paper, price level targeting is preferable to a higher inflation target, and a credible price level targeting regime implies optimal inflation well below 1 percent. While the extreme power of price level targeting may be overstated owing to the concerns over the power of forward guidance raised above, Bernanke, Kiley, and Roberts (2019) suggest that more limited adjustments, such as simple threshold strategies linked to attainment of the inflation objective, may lower ELB risks even in models with a less powerful role for expectations management.

REFERENCES FOR THE KILEY COMMENT

Ball, Laurence M. 2014. "The Case for a Long-Run Inflation Target of Four Percent." Working Paper 14/92. Washington: International Monetary Fund. https://www.imf.org/en/Publications/WP/Issues/2016/12/31/The-Case-for-a-Long-Run-Inflation-Target-of-Four-Percent-41625.

Benigno, Pierpaolo, and Michael Woodford. 2005. "Inflation Stabilization and Welfare: The Case of a Distorted Steady State." *Journal of the European Economic Association* 3, no. 6: 1185–1236.

Bernanke, Ben S., Michael T. Kiley, and John M. Roberts. 2019. "Monetary Policy Strategies for a Low-Rate Environment." *AEA Papers and Proceedings* 109: 421–26.

Blanchard, Olivier. 2016. "The Phillips Curve: Back to the '60s?" *American Economic Review* 106, no. 5: 31–34.

Blanchard, Olivier, Giovanni Dell'ariccia, and Paolo Mauro. 2010. "Rethinking Macroeconomic Policy." *Journal of Money, Credit and Banking* 42, no. S1: 199–215.

Campbell, Jeffrey R., Charles L. Evans, Jonas D. M. Fisher, and Alejandro Justiniano. 2012. "Macroeconomic Effects of Federal Reserve Forward Guidance." *Brookings Papers on Economic Activity*, Spring, 1–80.

Chung, Hess, Edward Herbst, and Michael T. Kiley. 2015. "Effective Monetary Policy Strategies in New Keynesian Models: A Reexamination." *NBER Macroeconomics Annual* 29: 289–344.

Clarida, Richard H. 2019. "The Federal Reserve's Review of Its Monetary Policy Strategy, Tools, and Communication Practices." Speech given at the Bank of Finland Conference on Monetary Policy and Future of EMU [Economic and Monetary Union], Helsinki, July 1.

Coibion, Olivier, Yuriy Gorodnichenko, and Johannes Wieland. 2012. "The Optimal Inflation Rate in New Keynesian Models: Should Central Banks Raise Their Inflation Targets in Light of the Zero Lower Bound?" *Review of Economic Studies* 79, no. 4: 1371–1406.

Galí, Jordi, Mark Gertler, and J. David López-Salido. 2007. "Markups, Gaps, and the Welfare Costs of Business Fluctuations." *Review of Economics and Statistics* 89, no. 1: 44–59.

Holston, Kathryn, Thomas Laubach, and John C. Williams. 2017. "Measuring the Natural Rate of Interest: International Trends and Determinants." *Journal of International Economics* 108, no. S1: 59–75.

Kiley, Michael T. 2013. "Output Gaps." *Journal of Macroeconomics* 37, no. C: 1–18.

Kiley, Michael T. 2015. "Low Inflation in the United States: A Summary of Recent Research." FEDS Notes 2015-11-23. Washington: Board of Governors of the Federal Reserve System. https://www.federalreserve.gov/econresdata/notes/feds-notes/2015/low-inflation-in-the-united-states-a-summary-of-recent-research-20151123.html.

Kiley, Michael T. 2016. "Policy Paradoxes in the New Keynesian Model." *Review of Economic Dynamics* 21: 1–15.

Kiley, Michael T. 2019. "The Global Equilibrium Real Interest Rate: Concepts, Estimates, and Challenges." Working Paper 2019-076. Washington: Board of Governors of the Federal Reserve System. https://www.federalreserve.gov/econres/feds/the-global-equilibrium-real-interest-rate-concepts-estimates-and-challenges.htm.

Kiley, Michael T. Forthcoming. "What Can the Data Tell Us about the Equilibrium Real Interest Rate?" *International Journal of Central Banking*.

Kiley, Michael T., Eileen Mauskopf, and David Wilcox. 2007. "Issues Pertaining to the Specification of a Numerical Price-Related Objective for Monetary Policy." FOMC memo. Washington: Board of Governors of the Federal Reserve System. https://fraser.stlouisfed.org/title/677/item/23295/content/pdf/fomc20070312memo01/toc/517269.

Kiley, Michael T. , and John M. Roberts. 2017. "Monetary Policy in a Low Interest Rate World." *Brookings Papers on Economic Activity*, Spring, 317–96.

McKay, Alisdair, Emi Nakamura, and Jón Steinsson. 2016. "The Power of Forward Guidance Revisited." *American Economic Review* 106, no. 10: 3133–58.

Nakamura, Emi, Jón Steinsson, Patrick Sun, and Daniel Villar. 2018. "The Elusive Costs of Inflation: Price Dispersion during the U.S. Great Inflation." *Quarterly Journal of Economics* 133, no. 4: 1933–80.

Rudebusch, Glenn. 2002. "Term Structure Evidence on Interest Rate Smoothing and Monetary Policy Inertia." *Journal of Monetary Economics* 49, no. 6: 1161–87.

Schmitt-Grohé, Stephanie, and Martín Uribe. 2010. "The Optimal Rate of Inflation." In *Handbook of Monetary Economics*, vol. 3, edited by Benjamin M. Friedman and Michael Woodford. Amsterdam: North Holland.

Yellen, Janet. 2012. "Perspectives on Monetary Policy." Speech given at the Boston Economic Club Dinner, Boston, June 6. https://www.federalreserve. gov/newsevents/speech/yellen20120606a.htm.

Yellen, Janet. 2017. "Inflation, Uncertainty, and Monetary Policy." Speech given at Prospects for Growth: Reassessing the Fundamentals, 59th Annual Meeting of the National Association for Business Economics, Cleveland, September 26.

COMMENT BY

LUMINITA STEVENS   In this paper, Philippe Andrade, Jordi Galí, Hervé Le Bihan, and Julien Matheron study how the inflation rate targeted by the monetary authority should vary with changes in the natural rate of interest. The authors characterize the (r^*, π^*) relationship in the textbook medium-scale New Keynesian model, augmented with a zero (or effective) lower bound on nominal interest rates. They quantify the following trade-off: a higher inflation target reduces the costs associated with the zero lower bound (ZLB) constraint, but it also entails larger welfare losses from allowing higher permanent inflation. When disciplined by the properties of the modern U.S. economy, the model generates a "hockey stick" relationship between the inflation target and the natural rate, with the slope near −1 for r^* less than 5 percent, when ZLB concerns dominate the welfare analysis, and near zero for r^* larger than 6 percent (roughly), when the probability of hitting the ZLB is effectively zero. In terms of levels, when the natural rate falls below 1 percent, the optimal inflation target exceeds 3.5 percent. The authors conclude by calling for a reassessment of the Federal Reserve's inflation target in light of the recent decline of the real rate.[1]

There is little to quibble with inside the framework set up by the authors: the paper offers an incredibly transparent and comprehensive analysis, with extensive robustness checks. It provides a wide range of valuable results that all future work will be benchmarked against. My discussion approaches the paper's results from the practical question of what the Federal Reserve should do with respect to its inflation target in the current environment. I will push outside the authors' framework to highlight the large uncertainties regarding some key components of the net welfare gains that the model associates with a higher inflation target. In turn, these uncertainties imply a large degree of uncertainty regarding the model's policy prescription.

---

1. For example, in their model of the U.S. economy, Christiano, Eichenbaum, and Evans (2005) target a steady-state real rate of 3 percent, whereas in its 2017 projections, the Federal Reserve's estimate was 1 percent. See Holston, Laubach, and Williams (2017) for a detailed analysis of the recent decline in real rates.

While future research may reduce some of these uncertainties, it may be more prudent for now to embrace strategies that are specific to ZLB episodes, such as makeup policies in the aftermath of ZLB realizations (Yellen 2016; Bernanke 2017). This is especially the case since many of the uncertainties and credibility concerns that critics raise for these alternative policies likely apply to the same extent—if not even more—to the transition to a higher inflation target.

THE SEVERITY OF ZLB EPISODES: THEORY AND PRACTICE The welfare gains of a higher inflation target depend critically on the average severity of ZLB episodes. Given the scarcity of historical ZLB episodes, estimates of the associated output loss are entirely model-based. The standard New Keynesian model generates very strong incentives to avoid the ZLB because of large output losses and the risk of deflationary spirals, as the economy's self-correcting mechanism breaks down: when nominal rates reach zero, if prices continue to fall, real rates rise, demand contracts, prices fall more, and so on.

Key to the severity of ZLB episodes is the formation of expectations by private agents. But what is the empirical evidence of large ZLB contractions? And what are the mechanisms that trigger or dampen any associated deflationary spirals?[2] In practice, large ZLB contractions have not been observed since the Great Depression and did not occur even during the Great Recession. The severity of the Great Recession had more to do with the nature and size of the shocks that hit the economy than with reaching the ZLB per se. By the time the ZLB was reached in December 2008, 70 percent of the output decline and half of the unemployment increase had already occurred.[3] Sustained deflation was avoided despite the large drop in output and the liquidity trap.

A number of explanations have been proposed for the relative stability of inflation during the Great Recession, bearing mixed news for inflation dynamics in future ZLB episodes. Coibion and Gorodnichenko (2015) argue that inflation was stable because the increase in oil prices between 2009 and 2011 kept consumer inflation expectations high. This does not bode well for the future: if expectations respond to oil price changes, then they are not well anchored and hence may spiral next time if an inflationary shock

---

2. Of note, once the ZLB has been reached, the likelihood of converging to the deflationary equilibrium is independent of the inflation target prior to the downturn (Aruoba and Schorfheide 2015).

3. These calculations are peak-to-trough numbers using data from FRED for the monthly seasonally adjusted unemployment rate and quarterly seasonally adjusted real GDP per capita.

does not happen to coincide with the ZLB entry. Countering this concern at least somewhat, Baqaee (forthcoming) documents that household inflation expectations are in fact rigid downward, and he rationalizes this asymmetry with a model of household ambiguity aversion. Wiederholt (2015) points to survey evidence of dispersed and sluggish household inflation expectations and shows that deflationary spirals become less severe in a New Keynesian model with imperfect, dispersed information among consumers. Moreover, the high uncertainty that characterized the Great Recession gave information-constrained firms the incentive to keep prices relatively high, to protect themselves against losses in a volatile environment (Stevens 2019). These mechanisms all work to limit deflationary spirals when decisionmakers are very uncertain about the future. Lastly, controlled laboratory experiments also provide some potentially relevant news: asset market experiments reliably produce overvaluation relative to the rational expectations response in markets with decreasing fundamental values (Smith, Suchanek, and Williams 1988; Stöckl, Huber, and Kirchler 2015).

These theoretical, survey-based, and experimental findings suggest that deviations from the benchmark model—particularly in terms of how expectations are formed and updated—need to be studied much more closely in the context of liquidity traps. For now, it is not clear that we can draw strong conclusions about the costs we are willing to bear to avoid such episodes, if we are not sure how and under what conditions they give rise to large deflation-fueled contractions.

THE PROBABILITY OF ZLB EPISODES VERSUS THAT OF INFLATIONARY PRESSURES The model estimates a probability of at least 10 percent of reaching the ZLB going forward, if the inflation target is kept around 2 percent. One distinguishing feature of the results is that they are based on a model that is estimated on pre–Great Recession data.[4] Such an approach is useful yet subject to the same challenges faced by any attempt to estimate rare events using limited time series, and it comes with large error bands. Another key feature of the model is that it does not incorporate capital, inventories, or housing, all of which significantly affect the likelihood of reaching the lower bound, thus adding to the uncertainty surrounding these estimates.

Whatever its value, the probability of reaching the ZLB should be weighed against the probability of inflationary shocks we face today. The paper presents the trade-offs of higher inflation given historical shocks. However, not just the size of shocks (which the authors experiment with) but also the nature of the shocks may change in the future. First, relative to

4. In contrast, Coibion, Gorodnichenko, and Wieland (2012) calibrate their ZLB model.

the Great Moderation period, increased policy uncertainty regarding fiscal, trade, and monetary policies may be inflationary. There is precedent for such policy uncertainty to raise long-run inflation expectations. Second, more risk taking in a low interest rate environment may increase the likelihood and magnitude of financial shocks in the future. In a controlled lab experiment, Lian, Ma, and Wang (2018, 2108) find that "individuals demonstrate a stronger preference for risky assets when the risk-free rate is low." In turn, more risk taking may fuel more financial cycles and inflation variability. Depending on the mechanism that is active, financial shocks may either raise or lower inflation. But on net, Abbate, Eickmeier, and Prieto (2016) find that in the modern U.S. economy, financial shocks have moved output and inflation in opposite directions.

Inflationary shocks may make it more challenging for the Federal Reserve to control inflation, especially since these challenges rise convexly as inflation rises above 5 percent or so. At the same time, they may limit deflationary spirals that make ZLB episodes so costly, tipping the scales toward a lower inflation target. Overall, an analysis of the desirability of changing the monetary policy regime and increasing inflation expectations should take into account the possibility of such risks going forward.

THE NATURE AND SEVERITY OF PRICING FRICTIONS The cost of having a higher inflation target depends on the severity of inefficient nominal price dispersion and its sensitivity to inflation. The model considered by Andrade and his colleagues generates price dispersion by incorporating nominal price and wage rigidities a la Calvo (1983), augmented with exogenous indexation. The authors estimate the parameters of price and wage rigidities to match time series data on inflation, GDP, wages, and real rates. The estimated values imply low price rigidity. This makes having higher inflation not so costly in normal times, and it also makes deflation more severe in ZLB times. Both of these effects favor higher inflation targets for a given real rate. An alternative would be to estimate the severity of pricing frictions so as to match the degree of monetary nonneutrality implied by the U.S. economy in normal times (Christiano, Eichenbaum, and Evans 2005).

Moreover, the results may be sensitive to the nature of pricing frictions. Calvo frictions do not generate a good approximation of the welfare costs of nominal price rigidities (Sheremirov forthcoming). They underestimate the level of inefficient price dispersion versus the data, and they also generate a sensitivity of inefficient price dispersion to inflation that is at odds with the data. Conversely, a model of information-constrained pricing yields higher price rigidity for a given degree of price dispersion and larger inefficient price dispersion for a given level of inflation (Morales-Jimenez

and Stevens 2019). Both of these forces would push toward a lower inflation target.

A VOLATILE AND UNCERTAIN POLICY? The results imply considerable variation in the optimal inflation target. Optimality would require increasingly
frequent increases in the inflation target in the United States: 1.2 percent
circa 1990, 2.2 percent circa 2005, 3.5 percent circa 2015, and 4.2 percent circa 2020.[5] Another challenge, as illustrated by much of the literature
trying to estimate r^*, is that these estimates are very imprecise, dependent
on the estimation method, and subject to considerable revisions as we accumulate more data (Del Negro and others 2019). This means that not only
is there a risk that what is perceived as a permanent decline in r^* turns out
to be transitory, but there is also the practical difficulty of knowing what
the rate currently is so as to know what the current inflation target should
be. Since the model predicts that the inflation target is very sensitive to
changes in the real rate for rates below 5 percent, it seems it would be a
unstable inflation target. We may prefer instead to solve for a robust policy
in the face of natural rate uncertainty (Orphanides and Williams 2002).

INTERPRETATION, CREDIBILITY, AND EXPECTATIONS How should we expect
private agents to interpret and respond to such a path of the inflation
target? First, private agents could differ in how they update their beliefs—
for example, immediately or in a gradual, adaptive way, resulting in very
different welfare implications. Experiments on the formation of expectations find significant support for gradual adjustment rather than sharp
updating in response to regime changes (Khaw, Stevens, and Woodford
2019). Second, private agents could have one or more interpretations of
a given policy action: they may correctly understand and respond to the
change (either on impact or gradually), they may think that the inflation
target has been abandoned, or, conversely, they may not believe the commitment to a higher target long term at all. In any case, it is quite likely
that any announcement of a potential change in policy regime would result
in increased dispersion in expectations and would increase the probability
of unanchoring long-term expectations. Falck, Hoffmann, and Hürtgen
(forthcoming) show that disagreement about inflation expectations can
result in contractionary monetary policy being inflationary, as agents update
beliefs about the state of the economy. In a similar vein, Andrade and
others (2019) show a decrease in the effectiveness of forward guidance
when private agents have heterogeneous beliefs. More pointedly, Branch

5. I use the figures for the real rate implied by the Laubach and Williams (2003) model
for historical estimates and simple extrapolations for 2020.

and Evans (2017) show how increasing the inflation target can lead to overshooting and instability in the inflation rate when agents have adaptive expectations. In light of this work, the present analysis of the net benefits of a higher inflation target should be extended in the future to include deviations from fully informed rational private agents, allowing for dispersed and sluggish updating of beliefs regarding the state of the economy and the policy regime expected to prevail.

CONCLUSION This paper by Andrade and his colleagues presents a strong conclusion. It pushes us further from Friedman's (1969) optimal disinflation rule, from the complete price stability prescribed by the textbook New Keynesian model (Woodford 2003), and from the 2 percent level that is the current inflation target of the Federal Reserve and the standard among inflation targeting economies. It does so in the context of a well understood and widely used model of the aggregate economy, and hence it serves as both benchmark and launching pad for future work.

More generally, the analysis also makes the point that the target of an inflation-targeting monetary authority is not an invariant constant; rather, it can vary with the economic environment and perhaps other policies. This raises the question of how other structural changes in the economy may affect the optimality of different monetary policy regimes.

In practice, there remain big uncertainties surrounding how deflationary spirals arise, persist, and end. We furthermore face great uncertainties regarding inflationary pressures going forward, the prevailing rate of natural interest and its stability, and the costs in such an environment of targeting higher average inflation. Last but not least, the literature offers virtually no encouraging guidance in terms of how agents' expectations would respond to such a policy change. Along all of these dimensions, departures from the benchmark of fully informed, rational agents consistently push against the results based on full information. To what degree remains an open question, but it seems urgent to incorporate such departures more consistently in basic analyses of monetary policy.

In the meantime, for the purposes of practical policy recommendations, it may be more prudent to focus on ZLB-specific policies such as pursuing a lower for longer policy for the nominal rate upon exiting the ZLB, rather than attempting to implement a higher inflation target uniformly, thus increasing distortions all the time to help deal with infrequent episodes of unknown frequency and severity.[6] While such ZLB-specific policies

---

6. A lower for longer policy was first proposed by Reifschneider and Williams (2000) and more recently discussed by Woodford (2012), Yellen (2016), and Bernanke (2017).

may have credibility issues of their own, they at least do not come with the added cost of additional distortions outside the ZLB. The paper is encouraging on this front. One meaningful deviation to the baseline results is that smaller changes in the inflation target are optimal when the monetary authority implements policies that have this flavor, since these alternatives substantially reduce the costs of the ZLB constraint. I found this deviation encouraging and worthy of future exploration.

REFERENCES FOR THE STEVENS COMMENT

Abbate, Angela, Sandra Eickmeier, and Esteban Prieto. 2016. "Financial Shocks and Inflation Dynamics." Discussion Paper 41/2016. Frankfurt: Deutsche Bundesbank. https://papers.ssrn.com/sol3/papers.cfm?abstract_id=2857845.

Andrade, Philippe, Gaetano Gaballo, Eric Mengus, and Benoît Mojon. 2019. "Forward Guidance and Heterogeneous Beliefs." *American Economic Journal: Macroeconomics* 11, no. 3: 1–29.

Aruoba, S. Borağan, and Frank Schorfheide. 2015. "Inflation during and after the Effective Lower Bound." In *Economic Policy Symposium Proceedings: Inflation Dynamics and Monetary Policy.* Jackson Hole, Wyo.: Federal Reserve Bank of Kansas City.

Baqaee, David Rezza. Forthcoming. "Asymmetric Inflation Expectations, Downward Rigidity of Wages, and Asymmetric Business Cycles." *Journal of Monetary Economics.*

Bernanke, Ben S. 2017. "Monetary Policy in a New Era." In *Proceedings of Rethinking Macroeconomic Policy.* Washington: Petersen Institute for International Economics. https://www.brookings.edu/research/monetary-policy-in-a-new-era/.

Branch, William A., and George W. Evans. 2017. "Unstable Inflation Targets." *Journal of Money, Credit and Banking* 49, no. 4: 767–806.

Calvo, Guillermo. 1983. "Staggered Prices in a Utility-Maximizing Framework." *Journal of Monetary Economics* 12, no. 3: 383–98.

Christiano, Lawrence J., Martin Eichenbaum, and Charles L. Evans. 2005. "Nominal Rigidities and the Dynamic Effects of a Shock to Monetary Policy." *Journal of Political Economy* 113, no. 1: 1–45.

Coibion, Olivier, and Yuriy Gorodnichenko. 2015. "Is the Phillips Curve Alive and Well after All? Inflation Expectations and the Missing Disinflation." *American Economic Journal: Macroeconomics* 7, no. 1: 197–232.

Coibion, Olivier, Yuriy Gorodnichenko, and Johannes Wieland. 2012. "The Optimal Inflation Rate in New Keynesian Models: Should Central Banks Raise Their Inflation Targets in Light of the Zero Lower Bound?" *Review of Economic Studies* 79, no. 4: 1371–1406.

Del Negro, Marco, Domenico Giannone, Marc P. Giannoni, and Andrea Tambalotti. 2019. "Global Trends in Interest Rates." *Journal of International Economics* 118:248–62.

Falck, E., M. Hoffmann, and P. Hürtgen. Forthcoming. "Disagreement about Inflation Expectations and Monetary Policy Transmission." *Journal of Monetary Economics*.

Friedman, Milton. 1969. *The Optimum Quantity of Money and Other Essays*. Chicago: Aldine.

Holston, Kathryn, Thomas Laubach, and John C. Williams. 2017. "Measuring the Natural Rate of Interest: International Trends and Determinants." *Journal of International Economics* 108, no. S1: 59–75.

Khaw, Mel Win, Luminita Stevens, and Michael Woodford. 2019. "Adjustment Dynamics during a Strategic Estimation Task." Working Paper. https://ideas. repec.org/p/red/sed018/1315.html.

Laubach, Thomas, and John C. Williams. 2003. "Measuring the Natural Rate of Interest," *Review of Economics and Statistics* 85, no. 4: 1063–70.

Lian, Chen, Yueran Ma, and Carmen Wang. 2018. "Low Interest Rates and Risk-Taking: Evidence from Individual Investment Decisions." *Review of Financial Studies* 32, no. 6: 2107–48.

Morales-Jimenez, Camilo, and Luminita Stevens. 2019. "Price Rigidity during the Great Recession." Working Paper. http://econweb.umd.edu/~stevens/MJS_ Rigidity.

Orphanides, Athanasios, and John C. Williams. 2002. "Robust Monetary Policy Rules with Unknown Natural Rates." *Brookings Papers on Economic Activity*, no. 2: 63–145.

Reifschneider, David, and John C. Williams. 2000. "Three Lessons for Monetary Policy in a Low-Inflation Era." *Journal of Money, Credit and Banking* 32, no. 4: 936–66.

Sheremirov, Viacheslav. Forthcoming. "Price Dispersion and Inflation: New Facts and Theoretical Implications." *Journal of Monetary Economics*.

Smith, Vernon L., Gerry L. Suchanek, and Arlington W. Williams. 1988. "Bubbles, Crashes, and Endogenous Expectations in Experimental Spot Asset Markets." *Econometrica* 56, no. 5: 1119–51.

Stevens, Luminita. 2019. "Coarse Pricing Policies." *Review of Economic Studies* 87, no. 1: 420–53.

Stöckl, Thomas, Jürgen Huber, and Michael Kirchler. 2015. "Multi-Period Experimental Asset Markets with Distinct Fundamental Value Regimes." *Experimental Economics* 18, no. 2: 314–34.

Wiederholt, Mirko. 2015. "Empirical Properties of Inflation Expectations and the Zero Lower Bound." Working Paper. https://sites.google.com/site/ wiederholtmirko/.

Woodford, Michael. 2003. *Interest and Prices: Foundations of a Theory of Monetary Policy*. Princeton, N.J.: Princeton University Press.

Woodford, Michael. 2012. "Methods of Monetary Policy Accommodation at the Interest-Rate Lower Bound." In *Economic Policy Symposium Proceedings: The Changing Policy Landscape*. Jackson Hole, Wyo.: Federal Reserve Bank of Kansas City.

Yellen, Janet. 2016. Opening Remarks for "The Federal Reserve Monetary Policy Toolkit: Past, Present and Future." In *Economic Policy Symposium Proceedings: Designing Resilient Monetary Policy Frameworks for the Future.* Jackson Hole, Wyo.: Federal Reserve Bank of Kansas City.

GENERAL DISCUSSION   Narayana Kocherlakota found the paper and discussions very helpful. He said that terms like the *effective lower bound* and *zero lower bound* are technical and it is important to remember what they represent. They represent a limit on how far a central bank's policy rate can fall given that banks and households have the option of holding cash, which has a zero return. Therefore, it is important to discuss how valuable cash is to people when thinking about where the zero lower bound is and the costs that the zero lower bound imposes. Kocherlakota also wondered how general the authors' finding of a one-to-one response of the optimal inflation target to changes in r^* is and what aspects of the model are driving this result.

Frederic Mishkin said that the slope of the Phillips curve is a very important issue, and one on which he disagrees with Michael Kiley. While there is a view, supported by regression analysis, that the Phillips curve has become very flat, Mishkin argued that the observed flatness is an artifact of good monetary policy. A central bank that is focused on controlling inflation will respond to positive inflation shocks by tightening monetary policy that would raise the unemployment rate. This endogenous monetary policy induces a positive correlation between the unemployment rate and inflation that masks the underlying negative Phillips curve relationship between the unemployment rate and inflation. Mishkin's interpretation is supported by his own research for the US Monetary Policy Forum and research by McLeay and Tenreyro, he said.[1] Mishkin is therefore less concerned than Kiley that the authors' model features a steep Phillips curve.

Furthermore, Mishkin pointed out that an important implication of the paper, emphasized by Luminita Stevens, is for economists to examine policies that lessen the consequences of the zero lower bound, for instance, policies that no longer let bygones be bygones when it comes to past inflation and policies that make monetary policy more effective at the zero

1. Peter Hooper, Frederic S. Mishkin, and Amir Sufi, "Prospects for Inflation in a High Pressure Economy: Is the Phillips Curve Dead or Is It Just Hibernating?" US Monetary Policy Forum, February 2019, https://research.chicagobooth.edu/igm/usmpf/usmpf-paper (forthcoming in *Research in Economics*); Michael McLeay and Silvana Tenreyro,"Optimal Inflation and the Identification of the Phillips Curve," *NBER Macroeconomics Annual* 34.

lower bound. Mishkin also highlighted that central banks are currently struggling to raise inflation. Economists may need to start thinking outside of the box to solve this issue and may have to think about linking monetary and fiscal policies, he concluded.

Ben Bernanke noted that a key result from the paper is that a Taylor rule performs very poorly in a world where the zero lower bound on interest rates binds frequently. Thus, he remarked, the authors' findings imply that the inflation target should be raised in order to reduce the likelihood of hitting the zero lower bound. Bernanke expressed two concerns about this implication.

First, the paper's one-for-one relationship between r^* and the optimal inflation target indicates that there is no trade-off between policy space and higher inflation, which implies that the marginal cost of inflation in the authors' model must be very low. Bernanke wondered about the realism of this assumption. Second, he noted, it is difficult to change the inflation target in practice as it requires people to change and re-anchor their inflation expectations, which can take years. The Bank of Japan, for instance, has been making announcements about its 2 percent inflation target—first implemented in 2013—for years with little effect. Furthermore, he commented, the authors treat the inflation target like a policy variable that could change again in the future, which would make it even more difficult to re-anchor expectations in practice.

Bernanke pointed out that moving away from a Taylor rule—toward lower for longer, forward guidance, and quantitative easing policies— is an alternative to raising the inflation target. For example, in a recent paper with Kiley and Roberts using the Federal Reserve's model of the US economy—FRB/US—he finds that inflation threshold forward guidance policies and temporary price level targeting can fully compensate for the zero lower bound when real r^* is 1 percent and nominal r^* is 3 percent.[2] Another Kiley paper shows that quantitative easing can offset the zero lower bound as well.[3] Bernanke concluded that changing the way we conduct monetary policy is preferable to raising the inflation target.

John Haltiwanger highlighted a recent paper by Redding and Weinstein that uses item level transaction data to show that conventional price indices

2. Ben S. Bernanke, Michael T. Kiley, and John M. Roberts, "Monetary Policy Strategies for a Low-Rate Environment," *AEA Papers and Proceedings* 109 (2019): 421–26.

3. Michael T. Kiley, "Quantitative Easing and the 'New Normal' in Monetary Policy," Working Paper no. 2018-004 (Washington, DC: Board of Governors of the Federal Reserve System, 2018), https://www.federalreserve.gov/econres/feds/files/2018004pap.pdf.

substantially overstate inflation because they fail to account for rapid product turnover and quality improvements.[4] Haltiwanger pointed out that if inflation is mismeasured, then productivity and output estimates will be wrong as well. He wondered how sensitive the inferences from the paper and the general discussion are to economic mismeasurement, and the mismeasurement of inflation in particular.

William Brainard noted that in the authors' model the costs of inflation reflected the inefficient production of intermediate products because of the price distortions caused by Calvo pricing. Firms face a constant probability of not being able to re-optimize prices. With Calvo pricing the resulting allocation inefficiencies are dominated by the large distortions caused by the prices of firms who have had bad luck, not having had a chance to adjust their price even though there is a great difference between it and its profit-maximizing value. As Robert Lucas has observed, this is implausible and implies that estimates of the welfare cost of price distortions estimated with Calvo prices are a poor measure of their actual cost. They are not well suited to determine the balance between the allocational costs of inflation with the risks of hitting the lower bound.

While Brainard believed that high rates of inflation would be costly, he noted Akerlof, Dickens, and Perry finding that low, but positive, levels of inflation actually improve welfare relative to zero inflation by raising employment rates.[5] Their findings suggest that moving from a 2 percent inflation target to a 3 or 4 percent target might not entail any significant allocation costs. Brainard thought that while 2 percent inflation is low enough that it doesn't factor into most individuals' and firms' behavior, at a much higher rate it would, and high target rates run a risk of triggering an inflationary spiral.

Channeling James Tobin, Benjamin Friedman argued that there are many worse things than 3 percent inflation, yet despite changed economic conditions—specifically, as this paper points out, a lower equilibrium real interest rate—central bankers are becoming increasingly desperate in their attachment to the 2 percent target. He regrets that despite what we have

4. Stephen J. Redding and David E. Weinstein, "Measuring Aggregate Price Indexes with Taste Shocks: Theory and Evidence for CES Preferences," Working Paper no. 22479 (Cambridge, Mass.: National Bureau of Economic Research, 2016), https://www.nber.org/papers/w22479.

5. George A. Akerlof, William T. Dickens, and George L. Perry, "The Macroeconomics of Low Inflation," *Brookings Papers on Economic Activity*, no. 1 (1996), https://www.brookings.edu/bpea-articles/the-macroeconomics-of-low-inflation/.

learned about the importance of avoiding getting stuck at the zero lower bound, the Federal Reserve has ruled out raising its inflation target as part of its ongoing framework review. Their argument is that because they said in the past that the target was 2 percent, it must always remain there. Friedman asked whether when we get to 2016, Federal Reserve policymakers will still say that the target must be 2 percent because that's what they announced in 2012.

Robert Hall pointed out that while this paper focuses on the effect of r^* on the optimal inflation target, it also has implications for the effect of r^* on r—the central bank's policy rate. In a standard Taylor rule, when r^* falls by 1 percentage point r declines by the same amount. If the central bank were to also raise the inflation target by 1 percentage point—the authors' prescribed response—then r would need to fall by more. This is because the inflation target would increase immediately when r^* declines, while actual inflation responds gradually. This slow response creates a gap between actual inflation and the target. Therefore, the authors imply that central banks should respond more aggressively to changes in r^* than under a standard Taylor rule.

In response to Bernanke's point that changing the inflation target is difficult in practice, Jay Shambaugh wondered whether we should also consider fiscal policy as an alternative way of getting away from the zero lower bound rather than focusing on more complicated monetary policy rules. He also wondered what emerging market economies—many of which are still establishing their inflation targets—could learn from the paper. Perhaps as they gradually lower their inflation targets, he reasoned, they should stop at 3 percent, rather than 2 percent.

James Stock pushed back against focusing on either raising the inflation target or unconventional monetary policy, and not both. He noted that there are, after all, limitations to unconventional monetary policies, for example, how long the credibility of forward guidance can persist given the turnover of Federal Reserve board members and the pressures the Federal Reserve is under. In addition, there are political limits to how large the Federal Reserve's balance sheet can get. Stock argued that we should consider unconventional policies in tandem with the possibility of raising the inflation target to reduce the likelihood of hitting the zero lower bound.

David Wilcox suggested that the authors should consider using an asymmetric Taylor rule in their model, akin to the rule used by Chung and others in a recent Federal Reserve working paper, where interest rates are increased gradually during a recovery but cut rapidly in response to negative demand shock.[6] Such an asymmetric rule is a better description of how the Federal Reserve has conducted monetary policy, Wilcox said.

Olivier Blanchard said that despite his support for the idea of a 4 percent inflation target to counteract the 2 percentage point decline in r^* over the past several decades, a comment made by Stanley Fisher at this year's Sintra conference raised a relevant issue. Fisher said that when he was considering raising the inflation target to 4 percent in Israel he was told by the unions that they would respond by demanding wage indexation. Blanchard recognized that people do not care much about inflation when it is at 2 percent but they might care when inflation is 4 percent. This might lead them to react more to actual inflation than they do today, changing again the nature of the Phillips curve relation and complicating the task of the central bank. Blanchard also agreed with Shambaugh that it is important to discuss using fiscal policy to help counteract the zero lower bound and said he would be interested in papers that explore the effectiveness of fiscal policy in an analytical framework similar to the authors' paper.

Philippe Andrade thanked the discussants and audience for their insightful comments. He said that many of the comments are addressed in the paper's robustness checks. He noted that adjusting the labor and goods markets in the model and accounting for parameter uncertainty—for instance, uncertainty about the slope of the Phillips curve—raises the model's optimal inflation target and does not weaken its relationship with r^*. He also emphasized that the model uses an inertial Taylor rule which already implies a lot of forward guidance.

Andrade acknowledged Kiley's suggestion that deviating from the model's assumption of rational expectations would make zero lower bound episodes less costly and therefore reduce the necessity of a higher inflation target. However, he pointed out that deviating from rational expectations would also make alternatives to raising the inflation target—like forward guidance—less effective, strengthening the argument for a higher inflation target. So the effect of relaxing the rational expectations assumption could go either way.

6. Hess Chung, Etienne Gagnon, Taisuke Nakata, Matthias Paustian, Bernd Schlusche, James Trevino, Diego Vilán, and Wei Zheng, "Monetary Policy Options at the Effective Lower Bound: Assessing the Federal Reserve's Current Policy Toolkit," Working Paper no. 2019-003 (Washington, DC: Board of Governors of the Federal Reserve System, 2019), https://www.federalreserve.gov/econres/feds/files/2019003pap.pdf.

In response to comments that argued for changing the monetary policy strategy rather than the inflation target, Andrade accepted that in practice it might be difficult to convince the public of the central bank's commitment to a new target. But he countered that because of the frequency of zero lower bound episodes at the current inflation target, inflation might undershoot 2 percent for long periods, bringing the central bank's commitment to the current 2 percent target into question as well. While he agreed that it might be difficult to build a consensus behind a higher inflation target, he argued that if such a consensus could be achieved, central banks would find it easier to explain than changing the monetary policy rule. This would also be more credible than committing to time-inconsistent policy rules. He therefore believes that there are credibility arguments that both support and counter increasing the inflation target.

In response to comments suggesting a price level target or a similar monetary policy rule to counteract the zero lower bound, Hervé Le Bihan pointed out that such policies imply some overshooting of inflation with respect to the target following a period of below target inflation. He argued that commenters who raised concerns about a higher inflation target triggering an inflationary spiral should have similar concerns about alternative policies that imply some overshooting of inflation.

Le Bihan also addressed concerns about the model's pricing mechanism. He acknowledged that the authors' choice of Calvo pricing was partially motivated by convenience. But he noted a paper by Blanco suggests that alternatives, like a menu-cost model, would make inflation less costly and strengthen the authors' results.[7] Le Bihan also reemphasized that they had been careful to test the robustness of their results to changes in the model.

On the issue raised by Luminita Stevens of estimating of the probability of zero or effective lower bound (ELB) Le Bihan concurred that it was difficult to provide reliable estimates given the current historical record of very rare and long events of ELB. For instance, in the euro area, the relevant policy rate has been negative since 2014 and is currently expected to remain negative for more than seven years according to market-implied data. Such facts however point to the relevance of the ELB constraint and to the need for adjusting the monetary policy strategy.

Jordi Galí took a step back from the specifics of the model and built on the sentiment in Friedman's comment. When central banks chose a 2 percent inflation target several years ago their beliefs about r^* were a key

---

7. Andrés Blanco, "Optimal Inflation Target in an Economy with Menu Costs and Zero Lower Bound," Working Paper. https://sites.google.com/a/umich.edu/andres-blanco/.

component in that choice. Now that r^* has decreased, perhaps permanently, he commented, it makes sense to revisit that choice. Indeed, the decline in r^* necessitates either a change in the inflation target or a change in monetary policy strategy, perhaps combined with fiscal policy, Galí argued. Sticking with a business as usual approach is untenable and is inconsistent with a view of a monetary policy framework built in a more rational, more systematic way, over twenty years ago.

Galí concluded by thanking both the discussants and the audience for their great comments.

KRISTIN J. FORBES

Massachusetts Institute of Technology

Inflation Dynamics: Dead, Dormant, or Determined Abroad?

ABSTRACT   Inflation dynamics have been difficult to explain over the last decade. This paper explores whether a more comprehensive treatment of globalization can help. CPI inflation has become more synchronized around the world since the 2008 crisis, but core and wage inflation have become less synchronized. Global factors (including commodity prices, world slack, exchange rates, and global value chains) are significant drivers of CPI inflation in a cross-section of countries, and their role has increased over the last decade, particularly the role of nonfuel commodity prices. These global factors, however, do less to improve our understanding of core and wage inflation. Key results are robust to using a less-structured trend-cycle decomposition instead of a Phillips curve framework, with the set of global variables more important for understanding the cyclical component of inflation over the last decade but not the underlying slow-moving inflation trend. Domestic slack still plays a role for all the inflation measures, although globalization has caused some "flattening" of this relationship, especially for CPI inflation. Although CPI inflation is increasingly determined abroad, core and wage inflation are still largely domestic processes.

O ver the last decade, the performance of standard models used to understand and forecast inflation has deteriorated. When growth collapsed during the 2008 global financial crisis (GFC), inflation in most

Conflict of Interest Disclosure: The author is the Jerome and Dorothy Lemelson Professor of Management and Global Economics at the Sloan School of Management at the Massachusetts Institute of Technology. Beyond these affiliations, over the last two years the author has received payment for speeches or consulting work with the asset management firm Citadel, the government of Iceland, JPMorgan, and State Street. She is currently not an officer, director, or board member of any organization with an interest in this paper. No outside party had the right to review this paper before circulation. The views expressed in this paper are those of the author and do not necessarily reflect those of the Sloan School of Management or the Massachusetts Institute of Technology.

countries fell less than expected. Since then, as economies have largely recovered and unemployment has fallen—even to record lows in some countries—inflation has not picked up as expected. A burgeoning literature has proposed a range of possible explanations for these puzzles—ranging from claims that the key frameworks are dead, to arguments that the models are alive and well but inflation has been dormant due to temporary factors or a long healing process after the GFC. This paper explores an explanation between these extremes: whether inflation is increasingly determined abroad. The results suggest that globalization has meaningfully affected the dynamics of consumer price index (CPI) inflation over the last decade—but has had a more moderate effect on core inflation and wages. A more comprehensive treatment of globalization can meaningfully improve CPI inflation models, but the dynamics of wage and core inflation are still largely domestic rather than determined abroad.

This question of whether globalization is affecting inflation dynamics is taking on increased urgency as central banks evaluate their ability to continue (or expand) loose monetary policies in the presence of extremely tight labor markets. If inflation is largely determined abroad, a central bank could be less concerned about inflation exceeding its target and more able to pursue a "high-pressure" economy that prioritizes job creation (Yellen 2016). If inflation is largely determined globally and less responsive to domestic conditions, central banks may also need to make larger adjustments to interest rates to stabilize inflation (even ignoring the challenges around starting from lower rates). In the extreme, if inflation has increasingly been determined abroad and the global factors that have dampened inflationary pressures over the last few years reverse (such as movement away from global supply chains), then countries could suddenly experience a sharp increase in domestic inflation and face a difficult trade-off between supporting growth and stabilizing prices.

The debate on how globalization—defined broadly as increased integration between individual countries and the rest of the world—affects inflation dynamics is not new. Soon after the Phillips curve relationship between domestic unemployment and wage inflation gained prominence in the late 1960s, the oil shocks of the 1970s highlighted the need to supplement this framework to account for changes in global oil prices (Gordon 1977, 1985). In the mid-2000s, several prominent policymakers questioned whether globalization, especially increased imports from low-wage economies, was moderating inflationary pressures at that time (Bean 2006; Kohn 2006; Yellen 2006). Research at the Bank for International Settlements (BIS) suggested that global slack was becoming more important than domestic slack in determining inflation (Borio and Filardo 2007). The corresponding discussion and analysis, however, generally concluded that although globalization was an important phenomenon, and may have acted as a temporary supply shock reducing inflation, it had had only limited effects on the underlying inflation process. Ball (2006, abstract) surveyed the evidence at that time on whether the "'globalization' of the U.S. economy has changed the behavior of inflation" and summarized the results as "no, no, and no."

The impact of globalization on inflation received less attention during and after the GFC as most work attempting to explain the "missing disinflation" in this period focused on domestic variables, such as the role of financial frictions (Gilchrist and Zakrajšek 2015; Gilchrist and others 2017). As the recovery progressed, attention shifted to why inflation was slow to recover, and the majority of papers continued to highlight domestic factors. Some prominent explanations are challenges in measuring slack (Albuquerque and Baumann 2017; Hong and others 2018), nonlinearities in the relationship between slack and inflation (Hooper, Mishkin, and Sufi 2019; Gagnon and Collins 2019), the large component of inflation indexes which are not "cyclically sensitive" (Stock and Watson 2018), and the stabilizing role of inflation expectations and central bank credibility (Coibion and Gorodnichenko 2015; Bernanke 2007). Closely related, if central banks target inflation, then inflation should remain around target and be less sensitive to economic slack, as highlighted in McLeay and Tenreyro (2019) and Jordà and Nechio (2018).[1]

Only recently, as inflation has remained muted in many countries, attention has shifted to how globalization may be affecting inflation dynamics (discussed in more detail in section I). One line of research highlights the growing importance of a shared global common factor in inflation dynamics but does not explain what is behind this increased inflation synchronization. Other research highlights specific aspects of globalization, such as structural changes (including increased trade and global supply chains) or larger global shocks (particularly in oil and commodity prices). Ha, Kose, and Ohnsorge (2019) and Obstfeld (2019) provide excellent reviews of this large body of literature, with the former focusing on emerging markets

---

1. This long-standing challenge for estimating Phillips curves has been known since at least Goldfeld and Blinder (1972) and can be addressed through instrumental variables (see Jordà and Nechio 2018) or more disaggregated data, for example, state data used in McLeay and Tenreyro (2019). These issues are attenuated in this paper through its focus on changes over time within countries.

and developing economies and the latter on the United States. Obstfeld (2019) concludes that there are important interactions between the global economy and U.S. inflation (such as through the global neutral interest rate and role of the dollar), but the evidence on whether globalization has affected U.S. inflation dynamics is inconclusive.

Most prominent papers modeling inflation in advanced economies, however, continue to place minimal emphasis on global factors. A generally accepted strategy for modeling inflation in the United States is to control for domestic variables (domestic slack, inflation expectations, and often lagged inflation) and add a control for import prices to capture any international supply or demand shocks. This is perceived to be a sufficient statistic to capture any influences of the global economy on domestic inflation, with no additional benefit from more comprehensive global controls or explicitly modeling global interactions.[2] Also, although there is prominent discussion of how globalization could be flattening the Phillips curve, there have only been limited attempts to test whether global variables are directly affecting the relationship with domestic slack.[3]

This paper assesses whether globalization should play more than this ancillary role in the basic framework for understanding and forecasting inflation. It concludes that a more comprehensive treatment of global variables can meaningfully improve our ability to understand CPI inflation over the last decade but only marginally improve our ability to understand core and wage inflation. More specifically, higher commodity and oil prices, exchange rate depreciations, less world slack, and weaker global value chains are all associated with higher CPI inflation, and the role of these variables (particularly non-oil commodity prices) has increased. Commodity and oil prices and world slack have also been important for understanding the cyclical component of CPI inflation—which has also increased. In fact, when global variables are added to simple models of CPI inflation, the explanatory power of these models recovers to pre-crisis levels. In contrast, core inflation, wage growth, and the trend component of inflation continue to be predominantly driven by domestic variables. Adding global variables provides minimal boost to the ability of simple models to explain these measures, although commodity prices have played a greater role for core inflation over the last decade. Domestic slack plays a role in explaining all measures of inflation, although its role has generally weakened over time, especially for CPI inflation. This flattening of the

2. For a recent prominent example, see Hooper, Mishkin, and Sufi (2019).
3. One exception is Ihrig and others (2010).

Phillips curve for CPI inflation can largely (but not entirely) be explained by increased import exposure, while globalization has had less impact on the relationship between domestic slack and other measures of inflation—particularly wage inflation.

This paper provides new insights on inflation dynamics due to five key elements of the analysis—some of which have been used in other research but not combined simultaneously. First, this paper focuses on multiple channels by which globalization could affect the inflation process, a more granular approach that is important as many global trends are correlated and thereby require multiple controls to identify effects. Second, this paper not only tests whether adding global variables to different models can improve our understanding of inflation but also whether interactions between domestic slack and globalization can explain the flattening of the Phillips curve. Third, this paper explores the dynamics of several inflation measures: the CPI, core CPI, wages, and the short-term cyclical and slow-moving trend components. The results provide a more comprehensive picture of how globalization has had different effects on different price dynamics. Fourth, the paper uses three different empirical frameworks (a trend-cycle decomposition, as well as the more common Phillips curve and principal components models), each of which provides information on different aspects of the inflation process. The combination of approaches ensures that results are not driven by the theoretical construct of a specific model, and several consistent findings across methodologies help build a more convincing picture of the role of globalization—especially given well-known issues with the popular Phillips curve framework. Finally, the paper analyzes a large cross-section of countries, instead of focusing on an individual country, and the combination of the cross-section and time-series dimensions of the data can better identify the role of global factors for inflation dynamics over time.[4]

The analysis begins by discussing changes in the world economy that could cause global factors to have a greater role in inflation dynamics and briefly summarizes the limited literature evaluating any such effects. Increased trade flows, the greater heft of emerging markets and their impact on commodity prices, the greater ease of using supply chains to shift parts of production to cheaper locations, and a corresponding reduction in local worker bargaining power could all affect different inflation measures.

4. New work by Ha, Kose, and Ohnsorge (2019) and Jašová, Moessner, and Takáts (2018) also uses large cross-sections of countries to explore how inflation dynamics have changed over time.

These changes may not be sufficiently captured in inflation models that only control for global influences through a single measure of import prices or ignore the interaction of globalization with domestic slack. Instead, controlling for variables such as world slack, prices of nonfuel commodities (as well as of oil), exchange rates, and global supply chains, as well as interacting domestic slack with a measure of globalization, could all go some way toward better capturing changes in the global economy—even in fairly simple frameworks.

The paper then tests these various channels through which global factors may affect inflation dynamics using three different approaches: principal components, a Phillips curve framework, and a trend-cycle decomposition. Each approach has advantages and disadvantages and encapsulates different aspects of inflation. The principal component analysis focuses on the variance in inflation and finds an important shared global component—but a striking divergence in how this component has evolved over time for different inflation measures. Over the last 25 years the shared global component of CPI inflation in advanced economies has more than doubled (from 27 percent in 1990–94 to almost 57 percent in 2015–17), but for core and wage inflation it has fallen to about half that for the CPI. These patterns are consistent with global factors (such as commodity price volatility) playing a large and increasingly important role for CPI inflation, while having less impact on core and wage inflation. There are other possible explanations, however, and this framework does not address what is driving these patterns.

To better understand this divergence and what these patterns imply for the level of inflation in different countries, the main body of the paper shifts to the most common approach for analyzing inflation—a Phillips curve model. It augments a standard New Keynesian model with a set of global factors: exchange rates, world slack, oil prices, commodity prices, and global value chains. It also interacts domestic slack with a country's import share. When the model is estimated using fixed effects for CPI inflation for a cross-section of countries from 1996 to 2017, all of the domestic and global variables have the expected sign and are significant.[5] This long period, however, masks important changes in these relationships over time. The Phillips curve relationship between CPI inflation and domestic slack is significant throughout the sample but weakens in the last decade, with

5. Results when the model is estimated for individual countries vary, often reflecting different country characteristics. Forbes (2019) provides more information on country-specific estimates using a similar Phillips curve model.

much (but not all) of this flattening explained by increased import exposure. The role of the individual global variables in explaining inflation also increases in the last decade, especially for nonfuel commodity prices (which are insignificant in the pre-crisis window). The increased role of the global variables partially reflects sharp movements during the GFC, as well as greater volatility in commodity prices and a greater elasticity of commodity prices on CPI inflation, but this is only part of the story. The other global variables have also become important since the GFC, including world slack and global value chains.

In order to better understand whether this more comprehensive treatment of globalization meaningfully improves the ability of basic models to explain inflation dynamics, the paper next estimates a series of rolling regressions for CPI inflation in order to allow the relationships between inflation and the different variables to fluctuate over time. The resulting rolling estimates are then used to calculate the error between actual inflation and inflation explained by models incorporating different controls for globalization. The results suggest that CPI inflation has become harder to explain in domestic-focused models, but that adding the more comprehensive global controls meaningfully improves our understanding of inflation dynamics over the last decade—by so much that the model errors fall to pre-crisis levels. More specifically, including the full set of global variables reduces the median prediction error for CPI inflation by about 0.34 percentage points (or 12 percent of median inflation) over the last decade. Including these global variables, however, does much less to improve our understanding of inflation dynamics before 2008, possibly explaining why global variables received less attention in inflation models in the past.

Given the instability in the role of different variables for inflation dynamics over time, and especially given shortcomings of the Phillips curve framework, it is also useful to model inflation dynamics using a less structured approach. The next section of the paper shifts to an atheoretical framework that decomposes inflation into two components: a slow-moving trend and shorter-term cyclical movements. It uses the autoregressive stochastic volatility (ARSV) model developed in Forbes, Kirkham, and Theodoridis (2019), which is grounded in the unobserved component stochastic volatility (UCSV) model developed by Stock and Watson (2007), but allows the deviations in trend inflation to have an autoregressive component. The results suggest that CPI inflation is partially determined by a slow-moving trend, but the cyclical component of inflation has become more volatile and more correlated with global developments—especially world slack and oil and commodity prices. The role of different variables also changes over time, with a more prominent role for commodity prices in cyclical inflation over the last decade but a weaker role for domestic slack—supporting the conclusions from the Phillips curve analysis of CPI inflation.

Next, the paper explores whether these results for CPI inflation and its cyclical component also apply to other inflation measures—core CPI and wage inflation and the slow-moving trend in core inflation (estimated using the ARSV framework described above). Some of the key results are similar across measures, such as a significant negative relationship between each inflation measure and domestic slack and evidence that the relationship has weakened over the last decade for core inflation and the slow-moving trend (even after controlling for interactions with increased import exposure or for the full set of global variables). A few of the global variables are consistently significant—such as the role of commodity prices for core inflation over the last decade—but most of the global variables have fluctuating significance and play a less important role. In fact, including the more comprehensive global variables only provides a minimal improvement in the fit of rolling regression models attempting to explain core and wage inflation, even over the last decade.

This series of results, obtained using very different approaches, helps form a more comprehensive understanding of the role of globalization for different aspects of inflation. The large and growing shared global principal component in CPI inflation supports the increased variance in the cyclical component of CPI inflation, as well as the larger role for global factors in CPI inflation (in the Phillips curve model) and in the cyclical component of inflation (in the trend-cycle decomposition). In sharp contrast, the much smaller and declining shared principal component in core and wage inflation supports the greater role of the trend in core inflation, as well as the more muted role for global factors in core and wage inflation (in the Phillips curve model) and in the slow-moving component of inflation (in the trend-cycle decomposition). Linking these results, the global variables could therefore help explain the growing wedge between CPI inflation and wage inflation, which roughly corresponds to firm margins and profitability, and could therefore help explain the well-documented trend of increased profits and declining labor share in many advanced economies.

A more complete exploration of which aspects of globalization are driving these patterns is an area for future research, but the results in this paper suggest that the changing relationship between prices and the world economy cannot be fully captured by a single variable (such as import prices). The results highlight an important role for world slack, exchange rates, oil prices, nonfuel commodity prices, and global value chains for at least some of the different measures and aspects of inflation. One consistent finding across methodologies is also the greater role of commodity prices over the last decade—for CPI inflation, core inflation, and the cyclical component of inflation. This appears to reflect more volatility in commodity prices combined with nonlinear effects on inflation. This could also result from a greater willingness of central banks to look through inflation driven by commodity prices or from commodity prices increasingly co-moving with other variables that influence inflation (such as growth in emerging markets or the spread of global supply chains). Whichever channels of globalization are most important, however, they do not appear to fully explain the weaker relationship between domestic slack and inflation. This paper confirms previous evidence of the flattening of the Phillips curve (albeit less so for wages than other inflation measures) and finds that although increased import exposure can explain much of this flattening for CPI inflation, it has had a more moderate effect on the slope of the Phillips curve for other inflation measures. Although globalization can make the Phillips curve seem dormant, especially for CPI inflation, this key relationship is not dead.

Finally, while these patterns apply across the sample of advanced economies and several emerging markets, it is important to highlight that the results vary when estimated for individual countries. For some economies, global factors play a dominant role in explaining the variation in inflation, while in other countries domestic variables are more important. Even in the countries for which the global variables are jointly significant, different global factors can drive the joint significance. Exactly which global measures are most important varies based on the period and country characteristics and is an important area for future work.[6] These varied results for different countries could also be one reason why past research, which often focused on an individual country or small set of advanced economies over a shorter period, often found seemingly contradictory results for global variables.

The remainder of the paper is as follows. Section I discusses how globalization could affect inflation dynamics, including a brief literature review. Section II estimates the shared global principal components of different inflation measures and how they have evolved over time. Section III uses

---

6. For recent work, see Forbes (2019) and Ha, Kose, and Ohnsorge (2019).

a Phillips curve framework augmented with global variables and rolling regressions to evaluate the role of different factors, whether their role has changed over time, and whether they meaningfully improve our understanding of inflation dynamics. Section IV breaks inflation into a cyclical component and a slow-moving trend and then evaluates the role of the global factors in the cyclical component. Section V repeats key parts of the analysis for core CPI inflation, wage inflation, and the slow-moving trend component of inflation. Section VI concludes.

I. Globalization and Inflation Dynamics: The Arguments and Previous Evidence

The academic literature modeling inflation—and the many proposals to improve on these frameworks to solve new puzzles—is lengthy.[7] At the core of most models, from the simplest Phillips curve equations to the most complicated dynamic stochastic general equilibrium (DSGE) models, is a central role for domestic slack and inflation expectations. Although many papers and frameworks partially incorporate the rest of the world by adding a control for import prices (and in a few cases by adding a control for global slack or adjusting for import competition in firm markups), domestic variables remain central.[8] Global interactions play a minor, ancillary role—and in some simple models are completely ignored (albeit less so in the DSGE models used by central banks that include a fuller treatment of the international economy).[9] A common justification is that any changes in the global economy should be captured in measures of domestic slack and import prices (if the latter are included), so that these variables are sufficient statistics to control for changes in the global economy.[10] This secondary role for global effects and global interactions is surprising given the extensive literature on globalization and evidence of how increased

---

7. For excellent overviews that capture the key issues, see Stock and Watson (2010); Gordon (2013); Ball and Mazumder (2015); Berganza, Borrallo, and del Río (2018); Miles and others (2017); Blanchard (2018); and Ha, Kose, and Ohnsorge (2019).

8. Papers studying the role of globalization in inflation include Ball (2006); Borio and Filardo (2007); Ihrig and others (2010); Berganza, Borrallo, and del Río (2018); Mikolajun and Lodge (2016); Auer, Borio, and Filardo (2017); Auer, Levchenko, and Sauré (2019); and Borio (2017).

9. One noteworthy exception is Jordà and Nechio (2018), which uses the "trilemma" and how different types of countries were affected by the GFC as an instrument to estimate changes in the Phillips curve during this period.

10. See Eickmeier and Pijnenburg (2013) for an example of this line of reasoning.

integration through trade and capital flows has affected an array of economic variables.

There are, however, a range of channels by which globalization could affect inflation dynamics. This paper focuses on four changes in the global economy that could be relevant: increased trade integration, increased role of emerging markets, increased use of global value chains to divide production across borders, and reduced worker bargaining power. There are other ways in which globalization could affect the inflation process, and many of these changes are related and could interact in important ways, but the channels in this paper provide a useful starting point.[11]

The first of these changes in the global economy—increased trade integration—is well documented. As the share of exports to GDP increases for a given economy, demand in global markets will likely have a greater impact on national income and price setting by domestic firms. Similarly, as shown in Cravino (2019), as the share of imports to GDP increases, domestic inflation will be more affected by import prices (simply due to their higher share in the price basket), and these import prices will at least partially be determined by foreign demand conditions, foreign markups, and foreign marginal costs (assuming incomplete pricing-to-market). Closely related, as the share of traded goods to GDP increases, a given exchange rate movement could have a larger impact on prices—through the effect on the imported component of any domestic inflation index as well as on exporters' competitiveness, margins, and pricing decisions.[12]

A second change in the global economy since the early 1990s has been the increased role of emerging markets. Emerging markets have accounted for over 75 percent of global growth since the GFC and have been the key source of demand for commodities.[13] As a result, global commodity prices have become more tightly linked to growth in emerging markets (particularly China) and more volatile. This could cause more volatility in inflation in advanced economies due simply to the larger price movements, volatility that could be magnified if the effects of commodity price movements on inflation are nonlinear (Hamilton 2011). This would occur in sticky-price

11. See Ha, Kose, and Ohnsorge (2019) for a detailed discussion, including other channels, such as a more common framework for inflation targeting or greater synchronization of financial conditions around the world due to greater financial market integration.

12. Obstfeld (2019), however, highlights that the effect of trade on the Phillips curve relationship is not straightforward if increased import competition drives out smaller domestic firms and thereby increases the market power for remaining firms.

13. See World Bank (2018) and Miles and others (2017).

models in which firms are more likely to adjust prices after larger shocks (Ball and Mankiw 1995). Working in the other direction, however, the reduced reliance of most advanced economies on natural resources as they shift to less commodity-intensive forms of production could lessen the impact of commodity price movements on inflation in these economies.

A third global development that could affect inflation dynamics is greater price competition and pressure on firm markups, resulting from greater ease in purchasing final goods from their cheapest locations or using global supply chains to shift production to where it can be done at the lowest cost.[14] As a result, companies that export or compete with imports must make decisions on markups that take greater account of prices from foreign competitors. Even holding trade flows constant, greater "contestability" from global markets reduces the pricing power of companies and lowers markups, especially in sectors with less differentiated goods (Grossman and Rossi-Hansberg 2008).[15] As it becomes easier to shift activities abroad—even just small stages of the production process—domestic costs will be more closely aligned with foreign costs.[16] A greater use of supply chains could also reduce the sensitivity of prices to exchange rate movements, as more integrated supply chains better allow firms to absorb exchange rate movements at various stages of production without adjusting final prices (Bank for International Settlements 2015).

Finally, each of these changes in the global economy could simultaneously reduce the labor share and bargaining power of workers, dampening the key Phillips curve relationship between domestic slack and wage (and price) inflation.[17] This possibility is clearly modeled in Cravino (2019), which shows that an increase in the import share of GDP could reduce the sensitivity of inflation to domestic slack. There are also other ways in which globalization could affect this Phillips curve relationship. For example, if there is some substitution between labor and energy costs as firms attempt

14. Potentially counteracting this somewhat is the trend toward greater concentration in some markets, especially in the United States. See Guilloux-Nefussi (2018) and Autor and others (forthcoming) for a discussion of how greater concentration may have increased firm pricing power.

15. Also see Sbordone (2010), which models how an increase in traded goods reduces the slope of the Phillips curve.

16. See Auer, Levchenko, and Sauré (2019) and Wei and Xie (2019) for models of these effects of global supply chains on inflation.

17. Blanchard (2016), Ha, Kose, and Ohnsorge (2019), and Jašová, Moessner, and Takáts (2018) provide evidence of the flattening of the Phillips curve over time for different groups of countries. Karabarbounis and Neiman (2013) provide evidence on the decline in the labor share since the 1980s.

to keep margins constant, the greater volatility in commodity prices could weaken the relationship between wage growth and slack (Bean 2006). Increased trade competition could make it more difficult for domestic firms to raise prices in response to tight labor markets and worker demands for higher pay (Auer, Degen, and Fischer 2013), and the increased ease of shifting parts of production to cheaper locations could further reduce the ability of domestic workers to bargain for higher wages (Auer, Borio, and Filardo 2017). Moreover, increased mobility of some workers (such as in the eurozone), or even just the possibility of increased immigration to fill vacancies, could further reduce worker bargaining power. Although there are many other domestic developments that are also likely affecting wage growth and worker bargaining power (such as the increased role of flexible jobs in the sharing economy and greater employer concentration in some industries), these multifaceted changes in the global economy could further weaken the link between domestic slack and inflation.[18]

This range of channels through which globalization could be affecting firm pricing decisions suggests that a more complete treatment of global factors could improve our understanding of inflation dynamics. Simply controlling for domestic slack and import prices does not seem to be a sufficient statistic to capture these multifaceted ways in which the global economy affects price setting. For example, the price of foreign goods and ability to shift production through supply chains may affect pricing even if not incorporated in import prices, as foreign prices may act as a counterweight on domestic pricing decisions even if goods are not traded. Measures of slack in the domestic economy may not capture the expected evolution of slack in other major economies, expectations that could affect firm price setting and therefore inflation. The price of imported oil may fluctuate due to geopolitical events and provide little information about the changes in global demand or other input costs relevant for firm pricing decisions.

Several papers have drawn attention to the increased role of globalization on inflation dynamics, using two very different approaches. This extensive literature is well summarized in Ha, Kose, and Ohnsorge (2019). One approach estimates a global common factor or principal component for inflation in a set of countries. Examples of this approach include Hakkio (2009), Ciccarelli and Mojon (2010), and Neely and Rapach (2011). These

---

18. For evidence on the role of increased employer bargaining power on wage growth, see Benmelech, Bergman, and Kim (2017).

papers generally find a significant common global factor in inflation, but mixed evidence on whether the role of the global factor has increased over time. The major shortcoming of this approach, however, is that it does not identify what drives this common component in inflation across countries. For example, it could reflect a greater role of common shocks (such as from more volatile commodity prices), structural changes (such as increased trade or financial integration), or more similar reaction functions in central banks. Each of these influences would have different implications for forecasting inflation and inflation models.

The other approach for evaluating the role of globalization in inflation dynamics is to add a variable to standard models to capture a specific aspect of globalization. For example, Borio and Filardo (2007) suggest adding global slack and find evidence that it has had a greater effect on inflation over time, even supplementing domestic slack in some cases. This result is supported in some work, but disputed in others.[19] Jordà and Nechio (2018) focus on how the 2008 financial crisis may have had global effects on inflation dynamics in different countries for an extended period. Other papers, usually using industry data, have focused on supply chains (Auer, Levchenko, and Sauré 2019; Auer, Borio, and Filardo 2017). Analyses of U.K. inflation suggest incorporating exchange rates and commodity prices in a Phillips curve framework (Forbes 2015) as well as in a trend-cycle model (Forbes, Kirkham, and Theodoridis 2019). Ihrig and others. (2010) interact key terms with measures of openness to capture how globalization could change relationships between different variables. Mikolajun and Lodge (2016) study the role of globalization in a Phillips curve framework, similar to parts of section III below.[20]

Rather than focusing on one channel, or one framework, by which globalization could affect inflation, this paper takes a more comprehensive approach. It borrows from three methodologies to assess different aspects of globalization and whether their roles have changed in the last decade. While this approach is broad, it is not inclusive and does not address a number of issues that could also influence inflation dynamics—such as the increased commoditization of many goods, changes in market concentration, or improved anchoring of inflation expectations. These topics are important but have received prominent attention elsewhere.

---

19. Ha, Kose, and Ohnsorge (2019) provide an excellent overview of the evidence for and against a role for global slack in Annex 3.1.

20. Mikolajun and Lodge (2016) do not use the other modeling approaches (such as the trend-cycle decomposition) or control for global value chains, but they add a "global inflation" variable which may capture other effects (such as from global pricing competition).

II. First Look: The Global Principal Component of Different Inflation Measures

As an initial look at the role of global factors in inflation, this section estimates the global principal component for inflation based on four price indexes: the consumer price index (CPI), core CPI (excluding food and energy prices), the producer price index (PPI), and private sector hourly earnings (wages). How important is this global component to countries' inflation rates? Has its role changed over time?

The original price indexes for each series are from the Organization for Economic Cooperation and Development (OECD) and the International Monetary Fund (IMF) for as many countries as available from 1990 through 2017, with more information in online appendix A.[21] Each inflation measure is on a quarterly basis, annualized and seasonally adjusted.[22] There are up to 43 countries for each series, listed in online appendix B and divided into advanced economies and emerging markets based on IMF definitions. Data are more limited for some price series—especially for wages and early in the sample. Table 1 reports the first principal component (and first five) for each inflation measure, for the full sample, and then divided into advanced and emerging economies.[23] There is a noteworthy shared global component in CPI and PPI inflation. More specifically, 40 percent of the variance in CPI inflation, and 52 percent for PPI inflation, are explained by a single, common principal component for all countries in the sample. The role of this shared principal component, however, is substantially smaller for core and wage inflation—where the first principal component explains only about 21–26 percent of the inflation variation for the different samples.

As discussed above, however, there have been significant changes in the global economy that could affect inflation dynamics. To test if the role of this shared global component has changed over time, the top graph of figure 1 shows the first principal component for each inflation measure over

---

21. The online appendixes may be found at the *Brookings Papers* web page, www.brookings.edu/bpea, under "Past BPEA Editions."

22. Seasonal adjustment is performed with the X-13ARIMA-SEATS program at: https://www.census.gov/srd/www/x13as/. Data are also adjusted for well-known value-added tax (VAT) increases that caused a one-quarter spike in inflation. The final inflation series is winsorized at the 10 percent level for each tail to remove several periods of extreme inflation (largely in emerging markets).

23. To ensure that differences across inflation measures are not driven by sample changes, the second section of the table repeats the estimates for the smaller sample for which wage data are available.

Table 1. Global Principal Component (PC) of Four Inflation Series

	Percentage of variance accounted for			
	PPI	*CPI*	*Core*	*Wages*
Full sample				
No. of countries	*35*	*43*	*38*	*20*
First PC	51.6	40.2	20.9	22.5
First five PCs	76.0	66.7	51.1	54.1
Sample of countries with wage data				
No. of countries	*19*	*20*	*20*	*20*
First PC	56.3	44.8	26.0	22.5
First five PCs	83.8	74.0	60.6	54.1
Advanced economies				
No. of countries	*29*	*31*	*31*	*18*
First PC	60.5	41.1	25.1	22.7
First five PCs	81.5	69.1	53.2	55.3
Emerging markets				
No. of countries	*6*	*12*	*7*	—
First PC	39.2	25.4	23.2	—
First five PCs	95.7	75.5	85.4	—

Source: Author's calculations.
Notes: PPI is producer price inflation. CPI is consumer price inflation. "Core" is CPI less food and energy. "Wages" is private sector, household hourly wages. All inflation measures are relative to the previous quarter, annualized and seasonally adjusted. See online appendix A for more details on data. Advanced economies and emerging markets are defined according to the IMF as of 2017.

five-year windows since 1990. The graph only includes advanced economies in order to have a more stable sample (as most emerging markets only have data for the later years). While the global component of the PPI has been large and relatively stable over the full period, there is a sharp divergence over time in the role of the shared component for the other inflation measures. This global component of CPI inflation has increased sharply over the sample period—more than doubling from 27 percent in the 1990–94 window to 57 percent in the 2015–17 window. In contrast, the shared global component of core inflation has steadily fallen, from 43 percent at the start of the sample to 26 percent at the end—a pattern mirrored for wage inflation.

One challenge with this principal component analysis, however, is that it does not provide information on what is driving these different patterns across time and inflation measures. An increase in the principal component could be explained by larger common global shocks (greater commodity price volatility), a greater sensitivity of countries to common global shocks (from greater trade or financial integration), or tighter direct linkages

Figure 1. Principal Component of Different Inflation Measures and Commodity Prices for Advanced Economies

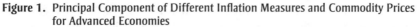

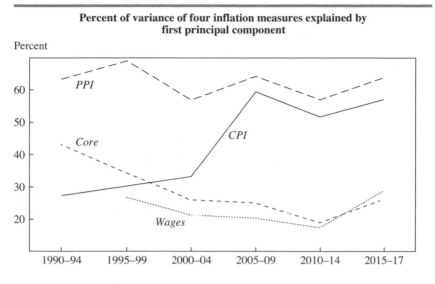

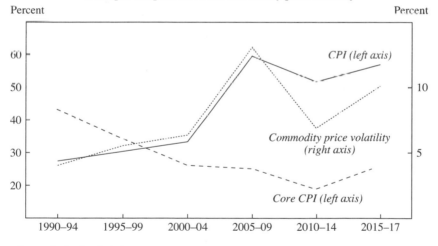

Source: Author's calculations.

Notes: Commodity price volatility measured as the standard deviation over the same windows using the IMF's index of global commodity prices (including fuel). See online appendix A for details on the price series.

between economies (through greater reliance on global supply chains). An increase in the first principal component could also be explained by factors that are not typically included as globalization, such as more central banks adopting inflation targeting and therefore sharing similar reaction functions. This paper will not be able to differentiate between all of these channels but focuses on the more easily quantifiable measures of globalization discussed in section I.

As a preliminary look at one factor that could be contributing to this increased co-movement in CPI inflation (and which is highlighted in the results below), the bottom graph of figure 1 adds the standard deviation of commodity prices to the first principal components of CPI and core inflation.[24] Commodity price volatility moves closely with the shared global component of CPI inflation—with an 89 percent correlation for the advanced economies. This high correlation does not appear to be driven by oil prices, as the correlation between oil price volatility and the first principal component of CPI inflation is only 8 percent.[25] This high correlation between CPI inflation and commodity prices could reflect greater volatility in commodity prices or a greater sensitivity of the CPI to this volatility (such as through shared responses or technological change that increases sensitivity to global developments). It could also reflect omitted factors that simultaneously affect the volatility of CPI inflation and commodity prices—such as global slack and growth in global supply chains (both shown in figure 1 in the online appendix and showing similar trends over time). A more formal empirical analysis that can jointly control for these variables is necessary to better identify the role of at least some of these different global factors.

III. The Role of Globalization in CPI Inflation

To better understand what is driving these different patterns, this section focuses on the most common (albeit also regularly criticized and highly imperfect) framework for analyzing inflation: the Phillips curve. It uses a hybrid version developed in Galí and Gertler (1999) and Galí, Gertler, and López-Salido (2005), which includes domestic slack, inflation expectations, and lagged inflation. This framework is used frequently by central

---

24. Commodity prices are measured using the IMF's index of global commodity prices, including fuel.

25. Oil prices are measured using Datastream's index of Brent crude oil spot world prices in US$.

bankers (Yellen 2017; Powell 2018) and has become a standard starting point for research on monetary policy (Eberly, Stock, and Wright 2019; Hooper, Mishkin, and Sufi 2019). The section begins by discussing the baseline variables and specifications which incorporate global variables, then estimates different variants of the Phillips curve assuming that coefficients are fixed over the full sample period. The following sections allow coefficients to vary over time and then assess how allowing a dynamic role for the global variables improves the fit of the model. The section ends with a summary of a series of sensitivity tests.

III.A. The Framework and Variables

This section develops several specifications that will be used for the different segments of analysis: a domestic version of the Phillips curve model; standard extensions with controls for import or oil prices; the "baseline" version for this paper with more comprehensive global controls; and an extension that also allows the Phillips curve relationship with domestic slack to vary with a country's global exposure.

More specifically, I begin with the standard New Keynesian Phillips curve for CPI inflation, which includes inflation expectations in order to allow for forward-looking behavior:[26]

(1) $$\pi_{i,t} - \beta_1 \pi_{i,t}^e + \beta_2 \pi_{i,t}^L + \beta_3 SLACK_{i,t}^D + \alpha_i + \epsilon_{i,t}.$$

Variables are defined for each country i in quarter t:

— $\pi_{i,t}$ is quarterly CPI inflation, annualized and seasonally adjusted and described in section II.

— $\pi_{i,t}^e$ is inflation expectations, measured by the five-year ahead forecast for CPI inflation from the IMF's *World Economic Outlook*.

— $\pi_{i,t}^L$ is lagged inflation over the previous four quarters (before quarter t).

— $SLACK_{i,t}^D$ is domestic slack, measured as a principal component of seven variables: output gap, participation gap, unemployment gap, and the

---

26. Although some papers only control for inflation expectations or lagged inflation (or use lagged inflation to proxy for inflation expectations), controlling for both has become standard, such as in Blanchard, Cerutti, and Summers (2015); Eberly, Stock, and Wright (2019); Hooper, Mishkin, and Sufi (2019); Jordà and Nechio (2018); and McLeay and Tenreyro (2019). Albuquerque and Baumann (2017) derive a model showing the importance of controlling for lagged inflation and inflation expectations simultaneously if some firms are forward-looking and set prices to maximize profits while others are backward-looking and set prices according to past values.

percent deviation of hours worked, share of self-employed, share of involuntary part-time employed, and share of temporary employment from the relevant average over the sample.

The baseline model is estimated using fixed effects (with robust standard errors clustered by country) in order to focus on the within-country relationships. The baseline model does not constrain the coefficients on inflation expectations and lagged inflation to equal 1, following recent work supporting a more flexible framework (Jordà and Nechio 2018; McLeay and Tenreyro 2019). Sensitivity tests show the key results are robust to random effects and constraining the inflation coefficients to equal 1.

Then I estimate the triangular variant (Gordon 1977, 2013) with supply shocks:

$$(2) \qquad \pi_{i,t} = \beta_1 \pi_{i,t}^e + \beta_2 \pi_{i,t}^L + \beta_3 SLACK_{i,t}^D + \gamma_1 ImpPrices_{i,t} + \alpha_i + \epsilon_{i,t}.$$

All variables are defined as in equation (1) except $ImpPrices_{i,t}$, which is measured as quarterly inflation in the country's import price index from the IMF, relative to quarterly CPI inflation. This variable is only reported for a subset of countries in the sample. Therefore, to compare results with a consistent sample, equation (2) is also estimated replacing world oil prices ($Oil_{i,t}^W$) with import prices.[27]

Next, for the baseline specification, I add a more comprehensive set of global variables to this standard domestic model to better control for changes in the global economy that could affect inflation:

$$(3) \qquad \pi_{i,t} = \beta_1 \pi_{i,t}^e + \beta_2 \pi_{i,t}^L + \beta_3 SLACK_{i,t}^D + \gamma_1 Oil_{i,t}^W + \gamma_2 Comm_{i,t}^W$$
$$+ \gamma_3 ER_{i,t} + \gamma_4 SLACK_t^W + \gamma_5 GVC_t^W + \alpha_i + \epsilon_{i,t}.$$

Definitions for each additional variable are as follows:

— $Oil_{i,t}^W$ is defined above.

— $Comm_{i,t}^W$ is quarterly inflation in an index of world commodity prices (excluding fuel) from Datastream relative to quarterly CPI price inflation, lagged one quarter.

---

27. Also measured as quarterly inflation in the oil price index relative to quarterly CPI inflation. The oil price index is Datastream's index of Brent crude oil spot world prices in US$.

—$ER_{i,t}$ is the percent change in the trade-weighted, real effective exchange rate index based on consumer prices (from the IMF) relative to two years earlier.[28]

—$SLACK_t^W$ is world slack, measured as a weighted combination of the output gap in advanced economies and China.

—GVC_t^W is global value chains, measured as a principal component of four variables: the relative growth in merchandise trade (to global GDP growth), the volume of intermediate trade, the complexity of intermediate trade, and the average change in the dispersion in PPI prices for all countries in the sample.

Finally, I estimate an extension that allows the key Phillips curve relationship between domestic slack and inflation to vary based on a country's exposure to the rest of the world.

$$(4) \qquad \pi_{i,t} = \beta_1 \pi_{i,t}^e + \beta_2 \pi_{i,t}^L + \beta_3 \left(SLACK_{i,t}^D * ImpSh_{i,t}^D \right) + \gamma_1 Oil_{i,t}^W + \gamma_2 Comm_{i,t}^W$$
$$+ \gamma_3 ER_{i,t} + \gamma_4 SLACK_t^W + \gamma_5 GVC_t^W + \alpha_i + \epsilon_{i,t}.$$

Equation (4) is the same as equation (3), except $SLACK_{i,t}^D$ is interacted with the import share to GDP.[29]

Each of these specifications in equations (1) through (4) is estimated with the sample for which all the domestic and global variables for the baseline in equation (3) are available. This yields a sample of thirty-one countries from 1996 through 2017. Online appendix A provides detail on definitions and sources, and section III.E examines robustness. The first three control variables (with coefficients denoted with β) are the "domestic" variables, and the remaining five (with coefficients denoted with γ) are the "global" variables. Although the real exchange rate captures both domestic and global influences, it is usually not explicitly included in Phillips curve regressions (only implicitly in measures of import prices in foreign currency).

These variables are measured using standard conventions in this literature, with three exceptions: domestic slack, world slack, and global value chains.[30] Beginning with domestic slack, researchers such as Albuquerque

28. Relative to two years earlier due to the longer lags by which exchange rate movements pass-through to prices.

29. Results using different interactions between openness and slack (or other variables) are also discussed below.

30. Many of the variables used to create measures of slack (domestic and global) and global value chains are only available annually, so they are interpolated to quarterly frequency.

and Baumann (2017) and Hong and others (2018) have convincingly demonstrated the importance of measuring slack more broadly than simply as the deviation of unemployment from a hard-to-estimate non-accelerating inflation rate of unemployment (NAIRU). This unemployment gap may not capture the discouraged workers—those who are no longer recorded as looking for work—or people who are working part-time or working fewer hours but would prefer to be working full-time or more hours at a company or self-employed. Data on these other aspects of slack, however, are not widely available on a comparable basis across countries. Therefore, I follow the approach suggested by Albuquerque and Baumann (2017) for the United States and estimate a principal component of labor market slack for each country, building on the set of cross-country variables in Hong and others (2018). More specifically, I calculate the principal component using seven measures of slack. The first three are from the OECD: output gap, unemployment gap, and participation gap. I also include a calculated percent gap from the normal level (with "normal" defined as the relevant mean for each country over the sample period) for four measures: hours worked per person employed, the share of involuntary part-time workers, the share of temporary workers, and the share of self-employed workers (with the last three as a share of total employed).[31] Many of these variables are not available for all countries in the sample, in which case I calculate the principal component using as many as are available for each country, ensuring that a consistent set of variables is included throughout the sample period.

Next, in order to measure slack in the global economy, I begin with a measure of the output gap for advanced economies reported by the IMF in the *World Economic Outlook* database. Corresponding estimates of the output gap for other economies are not reported, and the principal components for domestic slack calculated for this paper do not include data on most major emerging and developing economies (including China). Therefore, as a proxy for slack outside the advanced economies, I estimate slack in China based on the deviation in its GDP growth from recent averages.[32] World slack is then estimated as the weighted average of slack in advanced economies and non-advanced economies (proxied by slack in China), with weights varying over time based on IMF estimates of the advanced

31. The hours data from the OECD and data for involuntary workers, temporary workers, and self-employed were all shared by Hong and others (2018). Many are only available annually and are interpolated to quarterly to calculate the principal component.

32. The difference between average GDP growth in China over the previous two years less GDP growth in the current quarter.

economy share of world GDP. The resulting measure of world slack is shown in the top panel of figure 1 in the online appendix, along with the IMF's measure of slack in advanced economies and the OECD's measure of slack in OECD economies.[33] The different series largely move together, but the constructed measure of world slack used in this paper shows more slack during the GFC and a faster reduction after the crisis, as expected given the faster recovery in the emerging markets that are not included in the IMF and OECD measures.

The final variable meriting further explanation is global value chains (GVCs). A range of different statistics on GVCs are available, but many show very different trends over time and are only available for fairly short periods. Therefore, I calculate a principal component of four different statistics. The first three are the relative growth of merchandise trade volumes relative to global GDP, traded intermediate goods as a share of global GDP, and the share of these traded intermediate goods that are complex in the sense that they cross country borders at least twice. All three measures are from Li, Meng, and Wang (2019).[34] The fourth variable in the principal component is the dispersion of PPI inflation across the countries in the sample for which data is available.[35] This measure is used by Auer, Levchenko, and Sauré (2019) and Wei and Xie (2019) to capture how global supply chains have affected PPI indexes by increasing the synchronization of producer prices across countries. The bottom panel of figure 1 in the online appendix graphs the resulting measure of GVCs, with the principal component suggesting that the role of GVCs increased quickly during the early 2000s, collapsed during the 2008 crisis, largely recovered from 2009 to 2011, and then was fairly stable before declining slightly at the end of the sample.

III.B. CPI Inflation with Domestic and Global Variables: First Tests with Fixed Coefficient Estimates

Table 2 reports results for the different variants of equations (1)–(4) for CPI inflation using fixed effects with robust standard errors clustered by country over the full period (1996–2017). These estimates assume that the relationships between CPI inflation and the explanatory variables are stable over time (an assumption revisited below). Columns 2 and 3 report

---

33. The IMF and OECD measures are both of the output gap, which I convert to slack by reversing the sign.

34. These measures were kindly shared by Zhi Wang.

35. Measured as the standard deviation in quarterly PPI inflation, with inflation relative to 4Q earlier to avoid seasonal issues.

Table 2. Phillips Curve Regressions for Quarterly CPI Inflation, 1996–2017

	Different control variables					Different specifications		
	Domestic only (1)	+ Import prices (2)	+ Oil price (3)	+ All global variables (4)	DomSlack × impShare (5)	Only lagged inflation (6)	Random effects (RE) (7)	RE + constraints (8)
Inflation Expectations	0.685***	0.717***	0.656***	0.654***	0.631***		0.708***	0.257***
	(0.105)	(0.161)	(0.108)	(0.101)	(0.104)		(0.065)	(0.036)
Lagged Inflation	0.599***	0.679***	0.626***	0.641***	0.612***	0.716***	0.684***	0.743***
	(0.041)	(0.030)	(0.037)	(0.039)	(0.047)	(0.037)	(0.029)	(0.036)
Domestic Slack	-0.144***	-0.103***	-0.126***	-0.090***	-0.231***	-0.086***	-0.065***	-0.052**
	(0.027)	(0.021)	(0.026)	(0.030)	(0.069)	(0.031)	(0.023)	(0.024)
Import Prices		0.091						
		(0.054)						
World Oil Prices			0.033***	0.029***	0.030***	0.029***	0.030***	0.029***
			(0.003)	(0.003)	(0.003)	(0.003)	(0.003)	(0.003)
World Comm. Prices				0.030***	0.030***	0.028***	0.031***	0.028***
				(0.005)	(0.006)	(0.005)	(0.005)	(0.005)
Real Exchange Rate				-0.029***	-0.031***	-0.025***	-0.028***	-0.022***
				(0.007)	(0.007)	(0.006)	(0.006)	(0.006)
World Slack				-0.153***	-0.160***	-0.149***	-0.158***	-0.158***
				(0.036)	(0.034)	(0.036)	(0.037)	(0.039)
Global Value Chains				-0.055**	-0.052*	-0.108***	-0.037	-0.068***
				(0.026)	(0.028)	(0.030)	(0.024)	(0.025)
Constant	-0.514*	-0.772*	-0.587**	-0.541**	-0.418*	0.710***	-0.776***	0.062
	(0.260)	(0.374)	(0.263)	(0.227)	(0.218)	(0.102)	(0.129)	(0.049)
R^2	0.418	0.498	0.470	0.487	0.458	0.476	0.610	
No. observations	2,635	1,366	2,635	2,635	2,531	2,635	2,635	2,635

Source: Author's calculations.

Notes: See online appendix A for data definitions. Columns 1–6 estimated using fixed effects with robust standard errors clustered by country. Columns 7 and 8 estimated using random effects. Column 8 constrains the coefficients on the two inflation coefficients (inflation expectations and lagged inflation) to equal 1. Column 5 interacts domestic slack with the import share of GDP. ***Significant at the 1 percent level; **significant at the 5 percent level; *significant at the 10 percent level.

variants augmented for supply shocks—with either import or oil prices. The more limited data on import prices reduce the sample by about half, but the other coefficient estimates are very similar when oil prices are used to expand the sample. Column 4 includes the full set of global variables, and column 5 interacts domestic slack with the import share. Columns 6–8 use several different specifications for the baseline in column 4. Column 6 drops inflation expectations and only includes lagged inflation (which often proxies for inflation expectations, as in Ball and Mazumder [2011] and Gordon [2013]). Columns 7 and 8 use random effects (instead of fixed effects), with column 8 constraining the sum of the coefficients on inflation expectations and lagged inflation to equal 1.

In each specification in table 2 the domestic variables central to the Phillips curve model have the expected sign and are significant over the full period. Higher CPI inflation is associated with higher inflation expectations, higher lagged inflation, and less domestic slack. The estimated coefficients on import prices and oil prices also have the expected positive signs (although the coefficient on import prices fluctuates in significance). In the specifications with the full set of global variables in columns 4–8, each of the global variables also has the expected sign and is usually significant at the 1 percent level. More specifically, higher CPI inflation is associated with higher oil prices, higher commodity prices, larger exchange rate depreciations, lower levels of global slack, and weaker global value chains. The magnitudes of the coefficient estimates on the global variables are also fairly stable across specifications (with the only exception the coefficient on global value chains). This suggests that augmenting the standard Phillips curve model with more comprehensive controls for global factors could improve our ability to explain CPI inflation dynamics.[36]

The magnitudes of the estimated coefficients also provide a sense of which variables have a more meaningful impact on inflation in this cross-section of countries. For example, focusing on the baseline results in column 4, the 0.654 coefficient on inflation expectations implies that a 1 percentage point (pp) increase in five-year ahead inflation expectations (that is, from 2 percent to 3 percent) is associated with an increase in annual CPI inflation of 0.65 pp. A 10 percent increase in oil or commodity prices in one quarter is associated with an increase in CPI inflation of about

---

36. The higher R^2 in column 2 relative to columns 3 or 4 reflects the more limited sample size. With a consistent sample, the R^2 is similar when either oil or import prices are included and increases with the full set of global variables.

0.30 pp. A 10 percent depreciation of the real exchange rate relative to two years ago corresponds to an increase in CPI inflation of 0.29 pp per quarter—which if accumulated over eight quarters would imply an increase in the level of the CPI of about 2.3 pp after two years. The coefficients on the different measures of slack are more difficult to interpret given the construction of the underlying variables, but a concrete example helps put them in context. A reduction in domestic slack by 1 percent of GDP (equivalent to the reduction in U.S. slack from 2015:Q3 to 2017:Q4) is associated with inflation 0.09 pp higher in each year.[37] Similarly, a decrease in world slack by 1 percent of global GDP (which occurred from 2014:Q2 to 2017:Q4) is associated with inflation higher by 0.15 pp.[38] These estimates agree with other work suggesting that the relationship between slack and inflation is very flat, but also suggest that world slack, and not just domestic slack, might affect CPI inflation.

It is also worth noting that the coefficient on domestic slack remains highly significant and increases in column 5 when domestic slack is interacted with the country's import share, supporting the hypothesis that globalization contributes to a flattening of the key Phillips curve relationship between domestic slack and inflation.[39] To put these estimates in context, consider a country with the mean import share in this sample of 41 percent. Combining this import share with the estimated β_3 implies that the corresponding Phillips curve slope for just domestic slack is −0.56. If the country's import share was one standard deviation higher (rising to 58 percent), the corresponding Phillips curve coefficient falls to −0.40. This supports the hypothesis that more globalization (at least in the form of more imports to GDP) corresponds to a weaker relationship between domestic slack and inflation, as in Cravino (2019).

37. To further put this in context, this measure of domestic slack increased by 5.05 in the United States from 2008:Q1 through 2009:Q4.

38. To further put this in context, this measure of world slack increased by 4.65 from 2008:Q1 through 2009:Q4.

39. I have also estimated several variants of this interaction. First, when domestic slack is interacted with trade openness (exports plus imports relative to GDP), the β_3 remains significant and increases, but to a smaller extent (to −0.108 for column 5). Second, when an interaction between domestic slack and the import share is added to equation (3) (as suggested in Ihrig and others [2010]), the interaction term is usually negative and significant, but the coefficient on domestic slack is insignificant. Third, when domestic slack is interacted with global value chains, the interaction term is often insignificant. Finally, when all the global variables are interacted with trade openness, most coefficients become insignificant and many have counterintuitive signs.

These results in columns 1 through 6 capture the relationship between inflation and the other variables within countries over time. Even though these are country fixed effects, using the pooled sample of countries is an important advantage of this paper as it helps identify the different variables. The results when estimated for individual countries, however, are more often insignificant and can vary widely, often reflecting country characteristics and different forms of exposure to the global economy.[40] For example, consider two very different European nations: Germany and Iceland. World slack is negatively and significantly associated with CPI inflation for Germany, but not Iceland. Exchange rate movements are significantly associated with CPI inflation for Iceland, but not for Germany. Better understanding these different sensitivities of inflation to global factors in different countries is an important topic for research.[41] This could be one reason why studies that focus on individual countries or smaller samples can find contradicting results (such as for global slack); the composition of countries in the sample can significantly affect results (as well as other differences in methodology, time periods, and specification).

III.C. CPI Inflation with Domestic and Global Variables: Have the Relationships Changed?

The role of different variables in the Phillips curve framework could vary not only across countries but also over time.[42] This could occur due to the changes in the global economy discussed in section I, as well as due to many other factors—such as changes in domestic labor markets or the credibility of central banks. To test if the role of the domestic and global variables in these Phillips curve–based regressions have changed, I re-estimate the basic Phillips curve models in equations (1)–(4) for a pre-crisis window (from 1996–2007) and over the last decade (2008–17).[43]

Table 3 reports results. Beginning with the domestic variables, inflation expectations and lagged inflation both continue to be positively associated with inflation in both periods.[44] Domestic slack continues to be negatively

---

40. See Forbes (2018, 2019) for results for individual countries of Phillips curve models.

41. This is beyond the scope of this paper, but see Ha, Kose, and Ohnsorge (2019).

42. For evidence, see Albuquerque and Baumann (2017), Blanchard, Cerutti, and Summers (2015), IMF (2016), and Mikolajun and Lodge (2016).

43. The sensitivity analysis shows that excluding the period around the GFC has minimal impact on the key results.

44. The coefficient on inflation expectations is insignificant over the last decade, reflecting the lack of variation in most countries. When estimated using random effects, the coefficient on inflation expectations is consistently positive and significant.

Table 3. Phillips Curve Regressions for Quarterly CPI Inflation, 1996–2007 and 2008–2017

	Pre-crisis (1996–2007)					Last decade (2008–2017)				
	Domestic only (1)	+ Import prices (2)	+ Oil prices (3)	+ All global variables (4)	DomSlack × impShare (5)	Domestic only (1)	+ Import prices (2)	+ Oil prices (3)	+ All global variables (4)	DomSlack × impShare (5)
Inflation Expectations	0.663*** (0.169)	0.720*** (0.190)	0.684*** (0.155)	0.741*** (0.163)	0.696*** (0.208)	0.685 (0.425)	0.408 (0.506)	0.508 (0.373)	0.284 (0.274)	0.324 (0.273)
Lagged Inflation	0.556*** (0.065)	0.672*** (0.048)	0.588*** (0.064)	0.589*** (0.067)	0.559*** (0.081)	0.490*** (0.050)	0.431*** (0.070)	0.519*** (0.045)	0.556*** (0.040)	0.556*** (0.037)
Domestic Slack	-0.212*** (0.054)	-0.157** (0.058)	-0.198*** (0.050)	-0.188*** (0.061)	-0.410** (0.155)	-0.154*** (0.034)	-0.112 (0.066)	-0.157*** (0.034)	-0.105** (0.041)	-0.171* (0.088)
Import Prices		0.061 (0.057)					0.136* (0.066)			
World Oil Prices			0.030*** (0.004)	0.030*** (0.004)	0.031*** (0.004)			0.034*** (0.003)	0.026*** (0.003)	0.028*** (0.003)
World Comm. Prices				0.004 (0.013)	0.002 (0.013)				0.031*** (0.009)	0.028*** (0.009)
Real Exchange Rate				-0.027** (0.011)	-0.029*** (0.010)				-0.039*** (0.013)	-0.040*** (0.013)
World Slack				-0.410*** (0.092)	-0.430*** (0.091)				-0.434*** (0.073)	-0.517*** (0.080)
Global Value Chains				-0.258*** (0.068)	-0.253*** (0.072)				-0.357*** (0.078)	-0.407*** (0.086)
Constant	-0.270 (0.380)	-0.700 (0.450)	-0.517 (0.350)	-0.938*** (0.321)	-0.773** (0.351)	-0.370 (0.858)	0.254 (1.150)	-0.063 (0.761)	1.142* (0.606)	1.202* (0.607)
R^2	0.361	0.497	0.394	0.414	0.365	0.252	0.196	0.356	0.419	0.425
No. observations	1,404	769	1,404	1,404	1,350	1,231	597	1,231	1,231	1,181
F-Test: joint significance of global variables				32.38***	36.11***				71.33***	68.09***

Source: Author's calculations.

Notes: See online appendix A for data definitions. Estimated using fixed effects with robust standard errors clustered by country. ***Significant at the 1 percent level; **Significant at the 5 percent level; *significant at the 10 percent level.

associated with CPI inflation, and although this relationship is significant in both periods, it becomes weaker over the last decade. More specifically, the magnitude of this Phillips curve association between domestic slack and CPI inflation falls by about 20–45 percent across periods for the specifications in columns 1–4. The estimates in column 5, when domestic slack is interacted with the import share, however, provide information on whether this apparent flattening of the Phillips curve reflects a higher import share or a weaker underlying relationship between slack and inflation (after controlling for this form of globalization). The magnitude of the coefficient on this interaction term declines over the last period by a large 58 percent, but when the coefficient is evaluated using the mean import share in each period, the underlying Phillips curve elasticity between just domestic slack and CPI inflation falls by only 10 percent.[45] This suggests that globalization has caused much—but not all—of the flattening of the Phillips curve for CPI inflation and that this key Phillips curve relationship is not dead—especially after controlling for globalization.

The global variables are also independently important in both windows, and more tightly linked to CPI inflation over the last decade. More specifically, higher oil prices, higher commodity prices, exchange rate depreciations, less world slack, and weaker global value chains all correspond to higher inflation in both periods. The magnitudes of the coefficients on most of the global variables also increase (in absolute value) over the last decade. All the global coefficients are significant, except on commodity prices, which are only significant over the last decade. The result that this coefficient is insignificant in the pre-crisis window and becomes highly significant (and much larger in magnitude) in the post-crisis window is robust across different specifications (see section III.E). This higher elasticity between commodity prices and CPI inflation implies that a given movement in commodity prices had a greater effect on CPI inflation over the last decade. However, section II (and the bottom panel of figure 1) also showed that commodity price volatility has increased over time and closely mirrors the increased co-movement of CPI inflation rates around the world. This combination of results would be consistent with standard models with menu costs and sticky prices, in which firms adjust prices more quickly in response to larger cost shocks (Hamilton 2011; Ball and Mankiw 1995).

45. The mean import share for the pre-crisis sample is 39 percent and for the last decade is 43 percent. This suggests that the elasticity between domestic slack and CPI inflation (after controlling for the import share) is −1.05 in the earlier window and −0.95 in the later period.

Finally, F-tests of the joint significance of the five global variables (table 3) suggest the global variables are jointly highly significant in both periods. The value of this F statistic, however, roughly doubles in the more recent period. Part of this increase captures the greater role of commodity prices, but an F-test of the four other global variables (excluding commodity prices) is still highly significant (at 30.1 in the last decade for column 4), suggesting that the importance of the global variables does not just reflect the impact of commodity prices. Also, including the global variables leads to a meaningful improvement in the explanatory power of the regressions in the last decade. More specifically, in the baseline specification in column 4, adding the global variables increases the R^2 by only 0.05 in the pre-crisis window but by 0.17 over the last decade (relative to the corresponding estimates with just the domestic variables in column 1).[46] Controlling for commodity prices is about two-thirds of this improvement in the R^2 over the last decade—although given the high correlation between commodity prices and other global developments (such as slack/growth in emerging markets), it is hard to isolate this effect.[47] This series of results supports the hypothesis that global developments are more important for understanding inflation dynamics over the last decade than before the GFC, and that commodity prices are an important part of this, but not the full story.

III.D. How Much Do Global Variables Improve Our Understanding of CPI Inflation Dynamics?

But can the global variables meaningfully improve our ability to understand inflation dynamics—especially some of the puzzles over the last decade? And does the greater role of the global variables simply reflect extreme movements in certain variables or during certain years (such as in commodity prices or during the GFC)? To better understand the evolving relationship between globalization and inflation, I next calculate rolling regressions for CPI inflation over eight-year windows with three model variants: with just the domestic variables (equation 1), the triangle model with import prices (equation 2), and the full set of domestic and global variables (equation 3). The regression windows are rolled forward one quarter at a time so that the number of observations remains constant, and in order

46. No single global variable accounts for the majority of the improved fit in the last decade, and many of the global variables are correlated, so simply adding one variable at a time to equation (1) could bias estimates.

47. Estimating the regression with the domestic variables and only commodity prices for the global variables improves the within-R^2 from 0.25 to 0.33 in the last decade, compared to 0.42 with the full set of global variables.

to maintain a consistent sample across models, I only include observations with the more limited data on import prices. Many of coefficient estimates fluctuate sharply, suggesting that the role of these different variables can also change over time.

Figure 2, top panel, graphs the resulting error between actual inflation and inflation explained using the rolling estimates. The error is calculated as the median absolute value of the deviations of actual from predicted inflation for each country in each quarter, so that a lower value indicates a better model fit (and estimates that are too high or low are equal misses). The graph shows the superior performance of the model with the global variables (darker line relative to that with only the domestic variables (lighter lines) and with the domestic variables plus import prices (striped). Although the errors are similar in some quarters, especially in the first part of the sample, the errors are meaningfully smaller in the global model during most quarters over the last decade. The biggest improvements are during the GFC—when the errors of the domestic models spike—but there are also noteworthy improvements from including the global variables over much of the window from 2011 to 2015.

Figure 2, middle left panel, attempts to better quantify this visual improvement in the global model's performance. It graphs the same errors in predicted inflation for the same three models, averaged over the full period, pre-crisis window, and last decade. Over the pre-crisis window, the median absolute error is 0.90 pp for the model with just the domestic variables and falls to only 0.82 pp with the addition of the five global variables. In contrast, over the last decade, the median error jumps to 1.11 pp for the model with just the domestic variables but falls more meaningfully to 0.77 pp with the addition of the global variables. (Including just import prices instead of the full set of global variables only yields a minor improvement, with the median error falling to 1.05 pp.) The improvement is also meaningful when assessed relative to median inflation rates—with the reduction in errors from adding the global variables equal to 12 percent of median inflation over the last decade (and 5 percent in the pre-crisis window).[48]

These results confirm that Phillips curve models were less successful at explaining inflation over the last decade if they only included domestic variables or limited global controls. They also show, however, that adding

48. Calculated as the reduction in median errors from adding the global variables relative to median inflation in that window. For example, over the last decade median inflation was 2.87 percent, so the corresponding calculation is $(1.11 - 0.77) / 2.87 = 12$ percent.

Figure 2. Gap between Actual and Predicted CPI Inflation in Different Models

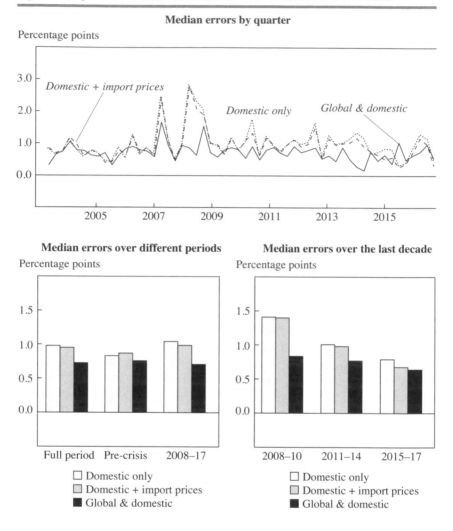

more-comprehensive controls for global factors can reduce the model's errors over the last decade such that the overall explanatory power slightly improves—instead of deteriorating (relative to pre-crisis performance). But how much of this improvement over the last decade occurs during the GFC—when the global model outperforms the other variants by the largest margins in the top panel of figure 2? To test this, figure 2, the middle right panel, breaks down the median errors over the last decade into three

Figure 2. Gap between Actual and Predicted CPI Inflation in Different Models (*Continued*)

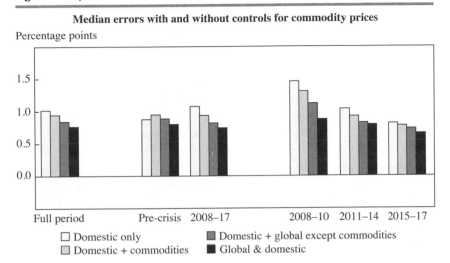

Median errors with and without controls for commodity prices

Percentage points

☐ Domestic only   ■ Domestic + global except commodities
☐ Domestic + commodities   ■ Global & domestic

Source: Author's calculations.

Notes: Median values of the absolute value of the difference between reported and predicted inflation based on coefficients from eight-year rolling regressions. "Domestic Only" is equation (1), which only includes controls for inflation expectations, lagged inflation, and domestic slack. "Domestic + Import Prices" is equation (2), which adds import price inflation. "Global & Domestic" is the full set of domestic variables plus five global variables in equation (3), including world oil prices, world commodity prices, exchange rate movements, world slack, and global value chains. "Domestic + Commodities" is the domestic variables plus commodity (except fuel) prices. "Domestic + Global except Commodities" is the full set of domestic and global variables except commodity prices. The sample size is limited to countries/periods with import price data to maintain a consistent sample.

periods: around the crisis (2008–10) and then 2011–14 and 2015–17.[49] Including the global variables generates a particularly large improvement in the model's fit during the crisis window (reducing the errors from 1.51 pp to 0.90 pp) but continues to meaningfully reduce the errors outside the crisis window (from 1.07 pp to 0.82 pp over 2011–14 and 0.84 pp to 0.68 pp over 2015–17). When these improvements are assessed relative to median inflation rates for each window, they correspond to an improvement of 27 percent during the crisis window, 17 percent over 2011–14, and 18 percent over 2015–17 (when median inflation was only 0.86 percent).

How much of this improved fit from including the five global variables over the last decade reflects the influence of commodity prices? Commodity

49. Breaking out results for the earlier five-year windows in figure 1 show errors similar to the pre-crisis window.

price volatility has increased sharply (section II and the bottom panel of figure 1) and the elasticity of changes in commodity prices to CPI inflation has increased over the last decade (section III.C). Both of these changes could cause commodity prices to explain a larger share of the variation in CPI inflation. To test if the increased role of the global factors is primarily capturing the effects of commodity prices, I re-estimate the rolling regressions for CPI inflation using two variants: only including commodity prices as a global variable, or including all four global variables *except* commodity prices. Figure 2, bottom panel, shows the resulting median errors. Including commodity prices improves the model fit from that with just the domestic variables but only yields part of the error reduction compared to using the full set of global variables. Including the other four global variables (but not commodity prices) yields a larger improvement in each window. This further supports the hypothesis that a more comprehensive treatment of global variables is important—and the key changes in the global economy cannot be captured with a single measure (including just commodity prices).

As a final test, and to better understand the role of these global variables to inflation puzzles over the last decade, figure 3 shows the impact of each of the global variables and domestic slack on U.S. CPI inflation from combining the coefficient estimates from the full global model (used for figure 2) and U.S. data. The global variables have had a meaningful effect on U.S. inflation over some windows. In the period immediately after the peak of the GFC, when U.S. inflation was higher than expected, oil prices, commodity prices, and the dollar's depreciation all contributed to higher inflation. In contrast, over the window 2012–16, global variables such as dollar appreciation, the increased use of global value chains, high levels of world slack, and periods of lower oil and commodity process all contributed to keeping CPI inflation lower than would have been expected given the decline in U.S. slack. The magnitudes shown in figure 3 suggest that the contribution of the global factors changes over time and that although the contributions of individual global variables can be small, their combined effect can be larger than that of domestic slack. The global variables can be important for understanding inflation dynamics, even in a large economy such as the United States that is relatively less exposed to the global economy.

III.E. CPI Inflation, Domestic, and Global Variables: Sensitivity Tests

The key results—that the global variables have played a more important role and domestic slack a weaker (but still significant) role in explaining CPI inflation over the last decade—are based on estimates that required making a number of choices about specification, variable definitions, and

Figure 3. Estimated Impact of Global Variables and Domestic Slack on CPI Inflation in the United States

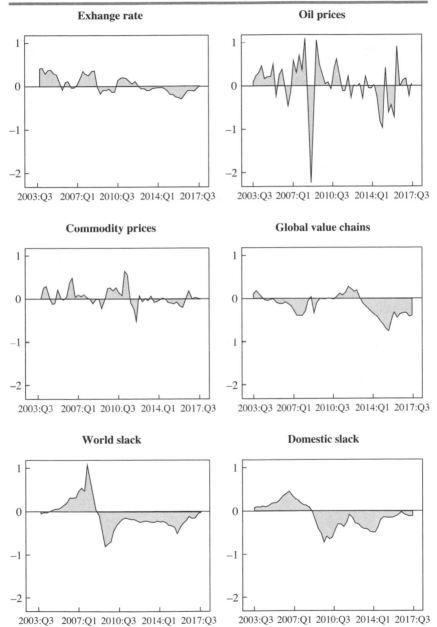

Source: Author's calculations.
Notes: Based on coefficients estimated from equation (3) using rolling eight-year windows and the sample of countries/periods used in figure 2. Variables are defined in online appendix A.

timing conventions. This section summarizes a series of sensitivity tests exploring whether these key results are robust. It focuses on the baseline equation (3), which uses the full set of domestic and global variables and compares the pre-crisis period to the last decade, and performs more than twenty sensitivity tests which can be roughly categorized into three groups:

—*Different variable definitions:* Several papers have highlighted the challenges in measuring the output gap (or slack) and global value chains, so I try several different measures.[50] To measure domestic slack, instead of using a principal component drawing information from up to seven different variables, I simply use the unemployment gap (the difference between unemployment and NAIRU, reported by the OECD) or a simpler principal component which draws information from only three variables—the unemployment gap, output gap, and participation gap (all from the OECD and more consistently available across countries than the larger set of variables). I also interact domestic slack with the variable for global value chains or the country's trade openness (measured as total trade to GDP). Then, instead of using a constructed measure for world slack which incorporates growth in China, I use the IMF measure of global slack (which only includes advanced economies) or the OECD measure of global slack (which only includes OECD members). Finally, instead of using the principal component of several measures to capture the role of global value chains, I use the ratio of traded intermediate goods to GDP or growth in exports from China (over the last four quarters).

—*Different time periods and country samples:* The analysis above highlights how the relationships can change over time, especially during the GFC. Therefore, I re-estimate the model, except I exclude just 2008 or exclude 2008–9. Also, although the sample only includes a few emerging markets due to data availability, I re-estimate the model using only advanced economies.[51]

—*Different specifications:* There is some evidence that the relationship between domestic slack and inflation is nonlinear, so I try three variants proposed by Hooper, Mishkin, and Sufi (2019): a "spline" model (which allows the slope of the Phillips curve to vary when labor markets are tight by adding a dummy variable when slack is negative); a "cubic" model (which includes squared and cubed slack); and a "piecewise quadratic"

---

50. See Albuquerque and Baumann (2017), Hong and others (2018), and discussion in section III.A.

51. The sample of emerging markets is so limited that results for this group are not robust to minor changes in specification.

model (which allows for nonlinearity in countries with less slack by including slack squared when slack is negative).[52] Next, I include the restriction that the sum of the coefficients on inflation expectations and lagged inflation equal 1, or exclude inflation expectations and assume that lagged inflation can proxy for inflation expectations, as in Ball and Mazumder (2011) and Gordon (2013), or use random effects. I also try different combinations of the global variables, such as only including one control for commodity prices (including oil and commodity prices together), or only including world slack. Finally, I experiment with different lag structures and timing conventions for key variables—such as focusing on annual changes in oil and commodity prices (instead of quarterly) or different lengths of time for the pass-through from exchange rate movements to inflation.[53]

Table 1 in the online appendix reports a selection of these sensitivity tests, including those that have received the most attention in other papers or that vary meaningfully from the baseline. Most of the key results discussed above are robust to these changes, and most of these modifications do not improve the model fit, but a few changes are worth noting. In some cases the different variable definitions and specifications matter. For example, when domestic slack is measured with the less comprehensive measure (just the unemployment gap instead of a principal component, in column 1), it is less often significant, as in Hong and others (2018). Similarly, using a narrower measure of world slack that does not include slack in emerging markets (column 2) reduces the magnitude of the coefficient on world slack meaningfully over the last decade. Using different measures for global value chains can affect its sign and significance. The nonlinear specifications for domestic slack also yield mixed results for the coefficients on slack—with significance varying based on exactly where thresholds are set and which nonlinear specification is used—but generally has no effect on the other key variables.

These modifications to the baseline specification suggest that the key results highlighted above are robust to a wide range of definitions, samples, and specifications. More specifically, higher inflation is associated with higher lagged inflation in both periods and with less domestic slack. The Phillips curve relationship between CPI inflation and domestic slack appears to have weakened and often becomes insignificant if the

---

52. For more details on these specifications, see Hooper, Mishkin, and Sufi (2019); see also Gagnon and Collins (2019) for evidence of nonlinearity.

53. Forbes, Hjortsoe, and Nenova (2017, 2018) discuss the challenges in measuring the duration of pass-through from exchange rate movements to inflation.

crisis window is excluded. This flattening persists even when the full set of global controls is included, or when domestic slack is interacted with different measures of openness, although much of this flattening reflects greater import exposure.[54] Global variables are consistently significant in both periods, except global commodity prices, which are only consistently significant over the last decade. An F-test of the joint significance of the global variables (at the bottom of table 1 in the online appendix) indicates that the global variables are jointly significant in all the specifications. This joint significance is not just a crisis-related effect, as the global variables are each still significant over the last decade when 2008 (or 2008–10) is excluded from the sample (column 4).

III.F. CPI Inflation: Summary of Phillips Curve Analysis

The Phillips curve relationship between domestic slack and CPI inflation has flattened (but is not dead), and a meaningful share of this flattening reflects increased import exposure. Global variables are also independently important in explaining CPI inflation, suggesting that a component of inflation is determined abroad, particularly during the last decade. Greater volatility in commodity prices, combined with a greater impact of commodity prices on CPI inflation, is part of the reason for this increased role of global factors. This increased role of commodity prices on CPI inflation could also capture shifts in global demand, especially changes in the growth outlook for emerging markets that are closely linked to commodity demand. But commodity prices are not the full story. The results also suggest that world slack, oil prices, exchange rate movements, and global value chains all play a role and that over the last decade it has become even more important to include a broad set of controls for globalization in order to understand CPI inflation dynamics.

IV. An Alternate Framework to Test for the Role of Globalization: Trend-Cycle Analysis

Although the Phillips curve relationship between slack and inflation is central to most frameworks for thinking about inflation and models such as equations (1) and (2) are frequently used by policymakers and

---

54. Results are not reported, but when domestic slack is interacted with openness, the coefficient is still negative and significant and becomes smaller in absolute value during the last decade; when domestic slack is interacted with GVCs, the coefficient is insignificant in both windows.

academics, this approach has a number of shortcomings. As shown above, parameter instability could limit its ability to explain inflation dynamics in real time and forecast inflation. As also highlighted by McLeay and Tenreyro (2019) and Jordà and Nechio (2018), if monetary policy is endogenous to expected inflation, this could weaken the relationship between inflation and other variables expected to have an impact on inflation (such as domestic slack). Other frameworks can therefore be a useful complement. One such framework is a trend-cycle approach, which separates inflation into a slow-moving, persistent trend and a temporary cyclical component. In this section this approach is used to analyze CPI inflation, evaluate the role of the same domestic and global factors, and test whether their role has changed over time.

IV.A. The Trend-Cycle Model

Although the majority of work analyzing and forecasting inflation has focused on structural relationships grounded in the Phillips curve framework, Stock and Watson (2007) provide an alternate, data-driven, and more atheoretical approach. They propose focusing on the time-series dynamics of price levels to isolate a low-frequency and slow-moving component of inflation (the trend) from deviations around this trend (which I call the "cycle"). Stock and Watson (2007) develop this framework in an unobserved component stochastic volatility (UCSV) model, which inspired a series of papers. Most of these papers have focused on inflation dynamics in the United States, while Cecchetti and others (2007) apply the UCSV model to the G-7 countries and Forbes, Kirkham, and Theodoridis (2019) build on these models to analyze inflation dynamics in the United Kingdom.[55]

This section applies the trend-cycle model developed in Forbes, Kirkham, and Theodoridis (2019) to the larger sample of developed and emerging markets used in this paper. This model is grounded in the UCSV model developed by Stock and Watson (2007) but also allows deviations in trend inflation to follow an autoregressive process, as in the autoregressive unobserved components (ARUC) model developed by Chan, Koop, and Potter (2013), with minimal other assumptions. The resulting ARSV model used below, and discussed in detail in Forbes, Kirkham, and Theodoridis (2019) and in Forbes (2019), can make it more difficult to achieve

55. For examples of papers focusing on the United States, see Stock and Watson (2010), Chan, Koop, and Potter (2013), and Cecchetti and others (2017).

convergence but better captures the inflation dynamics in this paper's more diverse sample of countries (as compared to the U.S. example for which the original UCSV model was developed).

This framework can be used to estimate trend inflation (τ_t) for CPI and core inflation for each of the countries i in the sample, using the quarterly, annualized, seasonally adjusted inflation data from 1990 through 2017 discussed in section II and detailed in online appendix A.[56] The resulting estimates of trend inflation are then subtracted from CPI and core inflation to back out the cyclical component of inflation for each country, with key statistics reported in online appendix table 2.[57] Columns 1 and 2 report the average distance from the 15th to the 85th percentiles of the estimated trends and suggest that there is some imprecision in the estimates (with an average distance of 0.95 and 0.71 for CPI and core inflation, respectively). Columns 3 through 6 show that the median variances of the trends are substantially lower than for the cyclical components, consistent with the trend as a slow-moving and more stable component. Columns 7 and 8 report the percentage of the variation in inflation for each country explained by the trend.[58] Over the full sample period, the trend explains 31 percent of the variation in CPI inflation and 55 percent in core inflation. This suggests that most of the volatility in CPI inflation in advanced economies is driven by short-term cyclical movements (albeit the volatility in the trend still plays a meaningful role), while volatility in core inflation is driven by roughly equal contributions from the cyclical and trend components. Also noteworthy are changes over the two periods, with the variance in the trend falling over the last decade, while the variance in the cyclical component of CPI inflation (but not core) increases in the later period. This would be consistent with greater volatility in commodity prices over the last decade. At the same time, however, the role of the slow-moving trend has increased over the last decade—for both CPI and core inflation.

---

56. The first twelve observations for each country are used to calibrate the prior information, resulting in a trend inflation from 1993 through 2017 for most advanced economies (but limited coverage of emerging markets). Estimates are the (pointwise) median of one thousand draws. If the algorithm did not converge within five hours, the estimation was terminated.

57. Most emerging markets do not have sufficient data to calculate the trend for the longer periods used in this table, and for the few which do, all have periods of very high inflation which skew estimates. See Forbes (2018, 2019) for estimates by country.

58. Calculated as: $\dfrac{\sum_{t=1}^{T}(\tau_t - \bar{\pi}_t)^2}{\sum_{t=1}^{T}(\pi_t - \bar{\pi}_t)^2}$.

IV.B. The Cyclical Component of CPI Inflation: The Role of Domestic and Global Variables

What is the relative importance of the domestic and global variables in this framework? Has their role changed over time? To answer these questions and facilitate a comparison with earlier parts of this paper, this section focuses on the same domestic and global variables as in the Phillips curve analysis in section III. To assess the ability of these variables and the slow-moving trend to explain the cyclical component of inflation, I estimate the following fixed-effects model for the full sample from 1993 through 2017:

$$(5) \qquad\qquad \pi_{i,t} = \alpha_i + \beta\tilde{\tau}_{i,t} + \sum_{k=1}^{7}\gamma_k X_{k,i,t} + e_{i,t}.$$

The $\pi_{i,t}$ is CPI inflation for country i in quarter t (seasonally adjusted and annualized), $\tilde{\tau}_{i,t}$ is the slow-moving trend (estimated in section IV.A), and the $X_{i,t}$ are k additional variables that could help explain the cyclical movements in inflation around this trend. Following the format in section III, the variables in $X_{i,t}$ begin with just domestic variables (inflation expectations and domestic slack), then add a control for oil prices (to focus on a consistent sample).[59] Then the full set of five global variables (world oil prices, world commodity prices, the country's real exchange rate, world slack, and global value chains) is added and this is extended with an interaction of domestic slack with the import share.[60] Each variable in $X_{k,i,t}$ is defined as in the last section, with details in online appendix A.

Columns (1)–(4) of table 4 report results for the full sample period. The coefficients on the trend are highly significant, showing an important role for the trend in CPI inflation (which is not surprising given that the trend is a function of the inflation data). The other variables have the expected sign, and all except the exchange rate are significant in the baseline. As noted above, however, the relationships with inflation could change over time. To test this, table 4 also reports results for the pre-crisis period and last decade. The coefficient on trend inflation increases by roughly 40 percent in the last decade in the baseline.

A comparison of the other estimates for the two different windows yields similar conclusions as for the Phillips curve results in table 3. CPI

---

59. Substituting import prices does not change any of the key results but shrinks the sample by more than half.

60. Lagged inflation is not included due to its high collinearity with the trend.

Table 4. The Cyclical Component of CPI Inflation

	Full period			
	Domestic only (1)	*+ Oil prices (2)*	*+ All global variables (3)*	*DomSlack × impShare (4)*
Trend Inflation	0.641***	0.629***	0.636***	0.749***
	(0.089)	(0.086)	(0.089)	(0.047)
Inflation Expectations	0.172	0.234	0.360**	0.310*
	(0.178)	(0.184)	(0.153)	(0.169)
Domestic Slack	−0.189***	−0.181***	−0.162***	−0.264***
	(0.040)	(0.041)	(0.042)	(0.068)
World Oil Prices		0.025***	0.023***	0.024***
		(0.003)	(0.002)	(0.002)
World Commodity Prices			0.018***	0.017***
			(0.006)	(0.006)
Real Exchange Rate			−0.017	−0.024*
			(0.014)	(0.013)
World Slack			−0.083**	−0.082*
			(0.038)	(0.043)
Global Value Chains			0.065*	0.084***
			(0.035)	(0.028)
Constant	0.565	0.411	0.160	0.007
	(0.298)	(0.318)	(0.301)	(0.331)
R^2	*0.507*	*0.537*	*0.545*	*0.543*
No. observations	*2,456*	*2,456*	*2,456*	*2,355*
F-Test: joint significance of global variables				

Source: Author's calculations.

Notes: Estimated using fixed effects with robust standard errors clustered by country. See online appendix A for variable definitions and section V for estimation of the trend. ***Significant at the 1 percent level; **significant at the 5 percent level; *significant at the 10 percent level.

inflation is associated with less domestic slack, and this relationship is meaningfully weaker over the last decade, although slack continues to be significant. When domestic slack is interacted with the import share, the underlying Phillips curve relationship between just domestic slack and cyclical inflation still declines, although by less, and the decline is still meaningful even after adjusting for changes in the import share.[61] The global variables usually have the expected sign and are often (but not

---

61. More specifically, after adjusting for the increase in the import share from 38 percent to 42 percent across the two periods in this sample, the underlying Phillips curve coefficient evaluated at the sample means declines by 16 percent.

	Pre-crisis (1996–2007)				Last decade (2008–2017)		
Domestic only (5)	+ Oil prices (6)	+ All global variables (7)	DomSlack × impShare (8)	Domestic only (9)	+ Oil prices (10)	+ All global variables (11)	DomSlack × impShare (12)
0.550***	0.548***	0.542***	0.715***	0.841***	0.797***	0.781***	0.772***
(0.099)	(0.099)	(0.099)	(0.059)	(0.148)	(0.135)	(0.145)	(0.145)
0.465**	0.539**	0.635***	0.491	0.076	0.045	−0.026	0.021
(0.209)	(0.212)	(0.183)	(0.229)	(0.454)	(0.417)	(0.371)	(0.371)
−0.282***	−0.277***	−0.238***	−0.355***	−0.178***	−0.196***	−0.165***	−0.329**
(0.061)	(0.061)	(0.070)	(0.097)	(0.053)	(0.050)	(0.055)	(0.152)
	0.023***	0.023***	0.024***		0.026***	0.023***	0.024***
	(0.003)	(0.003)	(0.003)		(0.003)	(0.003)	(0.003)
		−0.008	−0.007			0.024**	0.021**
		(0.011)	(0.010)			(0.009)	(0.009)
		−0.011	−0.017			−0.033	−0.034
		(0.014)	(0.012)			(0.021)	(0.022)
		−0.392***	−0.384***			−0.266***	−0.329***
		(0.122)	(0.124)			(0.046)	(0.046)
		−0.170*	−0.127			−0.075	-0.109
		(0.091)	(0.088)			(0.071)	(0.073)
0.091	−0.148	−0.562*	−0.652	0.468	0.621	1.141	1.163
(0.328)	(0.348)	(0.320)	(0.475)	(0.926)	(0.829)	(0.698)	(0.703)
0.474	0.494	0.506	0.500	0.384	0.444	0.471	0.476
1,313	1,313	1,313	1,259	1,143	1,143	1,143	1,096
		16.55***	15.53***			42.74***	44.00***

always) significant. Higher oil prices and less world slack are significantly correlated with higher CPI inflation in both periods, and higher commodity prices are only significant in the later period. Real exchange rate depreciations are not significantly correlated with this component of CPI inflation—although any such effects may now be captured by the slow-moving trend since the pass-through effects of exchange rates on inflation tend to be prolonged. Global value chains are also usually not significant at the 5 percent level.

The bottom of table 4 provides final evidence on the role of the global variables for the cyclical component of CPI inflation and how their role has changed. F-tests suggest that the global variables are jointly significant in the pre-crisis period but add minimal explanatory power.

In the last decade, however, the F statistics of the joint significance of the global variables are much larger, and adding the global variables increases the R^2 by about three times. As also found for CPI inflation, the explanatory power of the domestic models falls over the last decade, but including the full set of global variables can improve the model's fit to around pre-crisis levels (at least as assessed by the R^2). Also, once again, much of this improvement—but not all—comes from including world commodity prices.[62] This supports the conclusion in the last section that more comprehensive controls for global variables have become more important for understanding inflation dynamics in the last decade and that commodity prices are part, but not all, of the story. A series of the same sensitivity tests reported in the last section supports each of these conclusions.

V. The Role of Globalization in Core Inflation, Wage Growth, and the Trend

Over the last decade, CPI inflation and the cyclical component of CPI inflation have had a weaker relationship with domestic slack (partly explained by increased import exposure) and a stronger relationship with global variables—especially commodity prices. Do these patterns apply to other measures of inflation—such as core CPI, wages, and the slow-moving trend—all of which might be more tightly linked to domestic developments and less sensitive to global factors?

V.A. Core and Wage Inflation: The Role of Domestic and Global Variables

To begin, I return to the Phillips curve model discussed in section III and repeat the analysis for core CPI and wage inflation (defined in online appendix A), measured quarterly, seasonally adjusted, and annualized. I continue to report four specifications for each inflation measure: with only domestic variables, adding import (or oil) prices, adding the full set of global controls (the baseline), and an extension that interacts domestic slack with the import share. I make three changes from equations (1)–(4) to more closely follow the literature: First, instead of including oil and commodity (ex-fuel) prices separately, I just include one broader commodity

---

62. When commodity prices are dropped from the set of global variables, the F statistic from a joint test of the global variables is 52.5 and the R^2 is almost unchanged at 0.47 for the period covering the last decade.

price index.[63] Second, I drop real exchange rate movements in the model of wage growth (which would capture Balassa-Samuelson effects). Finally, I add a control for productivity growth to some models of wage growth.

Table 5 reports results for core inflation over the full period, the pre-crisis window (1996–2007), and last decade (2008–2017). Some of the results are similar to those for CPI inflation. Higher core inflation is positively correlated with higher inflation expectations (which is more consistently significant across windows), higher lagged inflation, and less domestic slack, and the elasticity with domestic slack has weakened in the last decade. Results when slack is interacted with the import share, however, suggest that most of this flattening reflects a weaker underlying relationship between domestic slack and core inflation, even after controlling for the import share.[64] Adding the global variables has less impact, and they are less often significant. Commodity prices continue to be positively and significantly associated with inflation in the last decade but not the pre-crisis window, and the magnitude of the estimated effect is more muted (about half that for CPI inflation). The other global variables are usually insignificant over the last decade (with the significance of exchange rates and world slack fluctuating across specifications). Not surprisingly, adding the global variables leads to a much more muted improvement in the explanatory power of the regression in all the windows.[65] More specifically, even though an F test suggests that the global variables are jointly significant in each period, adding the global variables only improves the R^2 by 0.01 for the full sample and by 0.02 for the last decade (compared to 0.07 and 0.17, respectively, for CPI inflation).

To check the robustness of these results, I repeat the same series of more than twenty sensitivity tests reported for the CPI regressions in section III.D. A sample of estimates are in table 3 in the online appendix. The results highlighted above are robust; the association between core inflation and domestic slack is still usually significant but has weakened

---

63. If oil prices are included separately (as in the CPI regressions), the coefficient is usually insignificant. I lag the broader measure of commodity prices by one period to allow for slower pass-through to core and wage inflation.

64. More specifically, when the coefficient on domestic slack is adjusted for the increase in the mean import share across periods (from 39 percent to 43 percent), this still implies a decline in the underlying Phillips curve coefficient of about 39 percent.

65. The significance of the coefficient on world slack fluctuates based on what other variables are included and the specification. For example, when domestic slack is measured using the nonlinear specifications, or if domestic slack is interacted with GVCs or trade openness, the coefficient on world slack often becomes significant.

Table 5. Phillips Curve Estimates for Core CPI Inflation, 1996–2017

	Full period				
	Domestic only (1)	+ Import prices (2)	+ Oil prices (3)	+ All global variables (4)	DomSlack × impShare (5)
Inflation Expectations	0.501***	0.434***	0.503***	0.515***	0.543***
	(0.054)	(0.080)	(0.054)	(0.054)	(0.058)
Lagged Inflation	0.646***	0.711***	0.647***	0.664***	0.639***
	(0.039)	(0.046)	(0.039)	(0.039)	(0.043)
Domestic Slack	−0.115***	−0.082***	−0.113***	−0.094***	−0.216***
	(0.018)	(0.019)	(0.018)	(0.018)	(0.041)
Import Prices		0.032*			
		(0.017)			
World Oil Prices			0.005***		
			(0.002)		
World Comm. and Oil Prices				0.009***	0.008***
				(0.003)	(0.003)
Real Exchange Rate				−0.017***	−0.018***
				(0.005)	(0.005)
World Slack				−0.078***	−0.080***
				(0.022)	(0.021)
Global Value Chains				−0.003	−0.002
				(0.018)	(0.019)
Constant	−0.353***	−0.350**	−0.369***	−0.390	−0.397
	(0.111)	(0.162)	(0.113)	(0.088)	(0.091)
R^2	0.507	0.531	0.508	0.515	0.495
No. observations	2,636	1,374	2,636	2,636	2,532
F-Test: joint significance of global variables					

Source: Author's calculations.

Notes: See online appendix A for data definitions. Estimated using fixed effects with robust standard errors clustered by country. ***Significant at the 1 percent level; **significant at the 5 percent level; *significant at the 10 percent level.

over the last decade, and increased import exposure only plays a minor role in explaining this flattening. Global variables usually have the expected sign but are less often significant, with the noteworthy exception of commodity price inflation, which is more tightly linked to core CPI inflation over the last decade. Exchange rate depreciations can be significantly associated with higher core inflation, especially in the precrisis window and over the last decade when the peak year of the crisis (2008) is excluded.

Table 6 reports the comparable results for wage inflation. The sample size is meaningfully smaller, so results are not as comparable across inflation measures. With this caveat, wage inflation is less strongly correlated with inflation expectations or lagged inflation but continues to be negatively and significantly associated with domestic slack. This Phillips curve relationship does not appear to have weakened over the last decade (with

	Pre-crisis (1996–2007)					Last decade (2008–2017)				
	Domestic only (6)	+ Import prices (7)	+ Oil prices (8)	+ All global variables (9)	DomSlack × impShare (10)	Domestic only (11)	+ Import prices (12)	+ Oil prices (13)	+ All global variables (14)	DomSlack × impShare (15)
	0.467***	0.472***	0.466***	0.483***	0.498***	0.580***	0.487	0.527***	0.522***	0.596***
	(0.085)	(0.074)	(0.085)	(0.092)	(0.120)	(0.165)	(0.299)	(0.157)	(0.165)	(0.173)
	0.630***	0.682***	0.630***	0.653***	0.641***	0.458***	0.390***	0.461***	0.474***	0.466***
	(0.061)	(0.077)	(0.061)	(0.059)	(0.070)	(0.050)	(0.062)	(0.050)	(0.051)	(0.053)
	−0.165***	−0.148***	−0.165***	−0.170***	−0.327***	−0.127***	−0.089*	−0.128***	−0.116***	−0.223***
	(0.037)	(0.043)	(0.037)	(0.042)	(0.108)	(0.026)	(0.044)	(0.026)	(0.027)	(0.068)
		−0.002					0.071***			
		(0.020)					(0.018)			
			0.000					0.007***		
			(0.002)					(0.002)		
				−0.001	−0.002				0.015***	0.013***
				(0.006)	(0.006)				(0.004)	(0.004)
				−0.026***	−0.027***				−0.013	−0.013
				(0.006)	(0.006)				(0.009)	(0.009)
				−0.124**	−0.129**				−0.038	−0.070
				(0.059)	(0.062)				(0.056)	(0.059)
				−0.069	−0.056				0.077	0.052
				(0.043)	(0.045)				(0.062)	(0.065)
	−0.209	−0.378*	−0.207	−0.360	−0.356	−0.215	0.066	−0.110	−0.164	−0.245
	(0.138)	(0.182)	(0.136)	(0.111)	(0.146)	(0.276)	(0.612)	(0.257)	(0.324)	(0.332)
	0.475	*0.505*	*0.475*	*0.488*	*0.456*	*0.224*	*0.162*	*0.235*	*0.243*	*0.241*
	1,402	*766*	*1,402*	*1,402*	*1,348*	*1,234*	*608*	*1,234*	*1,234*	*1,184*
				*6.58****	*6.92****				*5.71****	*6.44****

or without the interaction between domestic slack and the import share)—even when the full set of global controls is included. It is worth highlighting that these results partially reflect the focus on within-country changes through the fixed-effects specification. When the model is estimated with random effects (shown in the sensitivity tests), inflation expectations and lagged inflation are more often significant, while domestic slack is weaker and often insignificant. Higher wage growth is also positively correlated with higher productivity growth in the pre-crisis window (as expected), but this relationship seems to reverse over the last decade. Including productivity growth also shrinks the sample size, so I focus on results without this control. The global variables have the expected signs and are often significant for the full period but not for the shorter windows. This suggests that global variables may play a role in explaining differences in wage growth over longer periods but not shorter ones.

Table 6. Phillips Curve Regressions for Wage Inflation, 1996–2017

	Full period			
	Domestic only (1)	*+ Product growth (2)*	*+ All global variables (3)*	*DomSlack × impShare (4)*
Inflation Expectations	0.535***	0.183	0.472**	0.504***
	(0.175)	(0.322)	(0.172)	(0.160)
Lagged Inflation	0.244***	0.141	0.217	0.216
	(0.075)	(0.156)	(0.064)	(0.065)
Domestic Slack	−0.273***	−0.246***	−0.153***	−0.326**
	(0.050)	(0.056)	(0.047)	(0.114)
Productivity Growth		0.512		
		(0.305)		
World Comm. and Oil Prices			0.002	0.003
			(0.006)	(0.006)
World Slack			−0.351***	−0.352***
			(0.092)	(0.086)
Global Value Chains			−0.144**	−0.154**
			(0.066)	(0.067)
Constant	1.863***	2.299**	2.167***	2.085***
	(0.286)	(0.802)	(0.326)	(0.315)
R^2	*0.122*	*0.069*	*0.150*	*0.152*
No. observations	*1,660*	*1,148*	*1,660*	*1,643*
F-Test: joint significance of global variables				

Source: Author's calculations.

Notes: Wages are private-sector household wages. See online appendix A for data definitions. Estimated using fixed effects with robust standard 0errors clustered by country. ***Significant at the 1 percent level; **significant at the 5 percent level; *significant at the 10 percent level.

To check the robustness of these results, I repeat the same series of more than twenty sensitivity tests described in section III.D. Key results are in table 4 of the online appendix. The one consistent result is that most variables are not consistently significant. The most robust finding is that higher levels of domestic slack are correlated with lower inflation, although this relies on using a fixed-effects model. When the cross-country dimension is included (such as column 7), the relationship between domestic slack and wage inflation often weakens and becomes insignificant. There is also stronger evidence of a nonlinear relationship between wages and slack than for the other inflation measures. These results suggest a more limited role for the global variables in wage inflation than for CPI or core inflation. This is supported by the *F*-tests of the

| | Pre-crisis (1996–2007) | | | | Last decade (2008–2017) | | |
Domestic only (5)	+ Product growth (6)	+ All global variables (7)	DomSlack × impShare (8)	Domestic only (9)	+ Product growth (10)	+ All global variables (11)	DomSlack × impShare (12)
0.030	−0.536	0.052	0.030	0.233	0.866	0.235	0.428
(0.197)	(0.731)	(0.202)	(0.196)	(0.595)	(0.588)	(0.638)	(0.637)
0.241***	0.199*	0.237***	0.254***	−0.036	0.003	−0.026	−0.008
(0.062)	(0.105)	(0.058)	(0.062)	(0.111)	(0.179)	(0.104)	(0.112)
−0.213***	−0.195**	−0.197***	−0.320**	−0.369***	−0.227**	−0.306***	−0.574***
(0.069)	(0.081)	(0.066)	(0.124)	(0.088)	(0.079)	(0.092)	(0.144)
	1.035***				−0.847**		
	(0.322)				(0.388)		
		0.005	0.006			0.006	0.007
		(0.013)	(0.013)			(0.008)	(0.008)
		−0.230	−0.227			−0.233	−0.230
		(0.178)	(0.181)			(0.167)	(0.147)
		−0.126	−0.117			−0.066	−0.046
		(0.107)	(0.107)			(0.093)	(0.084)
3.307***	3.664**	3.100***	3.112***	2.807**	1.211	3.052**	2.512*
(0.415)	(1.583)	(0.438)	(0.425)	(1.244)	(1.119)	(1.332)	(1.328)
0.061	0.049	0.065	0.057	0.052	0.039	0.059	0.056
878	601	878	871	782	547	782	772
		1.21	1.25			1.13	1.36

joint significance of the global variables (bottom of the table) which suggest that the global variables are rarely significant (unlike for CPI and core inflation). Wage inflation is still primarily a domestic phenomenon and does not appear to be determined abroad.

As a final test of whether the global variables can improve our understanding of core CPI and wage dynamics, and especially if the role of these variables has changed over time, I return to the analysis with rolling regressions from section III.D. I estimate rolling regressions for core and wage inflation over eight-year windows for the different models in tables 5 and 6 and then calculate the error between actual inflation and inflation explained by the model in each quarter. The resulting errors for the different models are shown in figure 4. The simple model is far more successful

Figure 4. Gap between Actual and Predicted Inflation for Core CPI and Wages
in Different Models

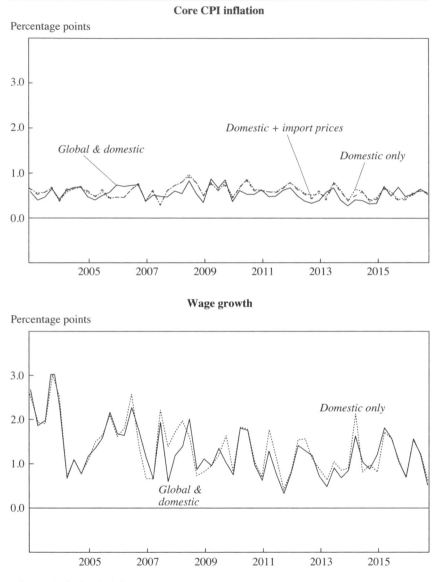

Core CPI inflation

Percentage points

Global & domestic

Domestic + import prices

Domestic only

Wage growth

Percentage points

Domestic only

*Global &
domestic*

Source: Author's calculations.
Notes: Median values of the absolute value of the difference between reported and predicted inflation
based on eight-year rolling regressions. "Domestic only" is equation (1), which only includes controls
for inflation expectations, lagged inflation, and domestic slack. "Domestic + import prices" is equation
(2), which adds relative import price inflation. "Global & domestic" is the full set of domestic variables
plus global variables, including an index of world oil and other commodity prices, world slack, and
global value chains. The regressions for core CPI also include exchange rate movements. The sample size
is limited to countries and periods with import price data to maintain a consistent sample.

at explaining core inflation than wage inflation, with not only lower errors but much less variation over time. The graphs also suggest that adding the global variables does little to reduce the errors for either core or wage inflation—with the lines for the different models very close to each other.

To more formally capture differences in the explanatory power of the different models, figure 5 reports summary statistics of the estimated errors. The graphs are a sharp contrast to the same analysis for CPI inflation. There is no meaningful reduction in the errors from adding the global variables over any period for core inflation (with the largest improvement only 0.12 pp during the 2008–10 window). There are slightly more modest improvements for wage inflation over the last decade (such as the median error falling by 0.17 pp during the 2008–10 window and by 0.13 pp from 2011–14) but no improvement in 2015–17. When these errors are assessed relative to median core and wage inflation, the improvements are also much more modest than for CPI inflation, with the global variables only improving the fit by 2.9 percent and 2.6 percent for core and wage inflation, respectively, as compared to 11.8 percent for CPI inflation, over the last decade.[66]

V.B. Trend Inflation: The Role of Domestic and Global Variables

To further explore the role of globalization for other measures of inflation, I return to the trend-cycle decomposition from section IV. Global factors had become more important for the cyclical movements in CPI inflation around its trend, but what explains this slow-moving trend? Are global factors less important for this more persistent component of inflation—just as they seem to be less important for the slower-moving core and wage inflation than the CPI?

To better understand the slow-moving trend—especially for core inflation where the global variables play a less important role—this section uses the estimates of trend core inflation (from section IV.A) and follows Cecchetti and others (2017) and Forbes, Kirkham, and Theodoridis (2019) to examine its correlates:

$$(6) \qquad \Delta\tilde{\tau}_{i,t} = \alpha_i + \sum_{k=1}^{7} \gamma_k \Delta X_{k,i,t} + e_{i,t},$$

66. Calculated as the reduction in the median error from adding the global variables relative to median inflation in that window. Median core and wage inflation over the last decade are 2.64 percent and 3.82 percent, respectively.

Figure 5. Summary Statistics: Gap between Actual and Predicted Inflation for Core CPI and Wages in Different Models

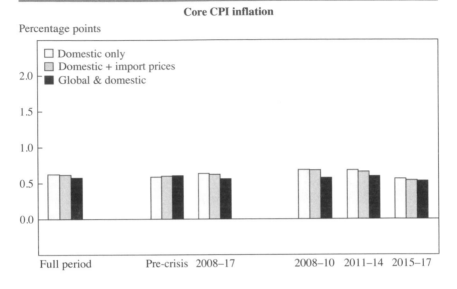

Core CPI inflation

Percentage points

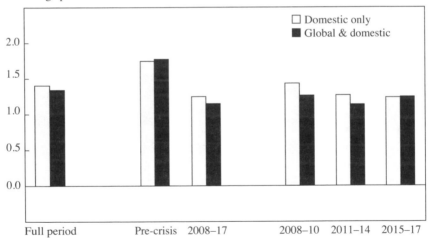

Wage growth

Percentage points

Source: Author's calculations.

Notes: Median values of the absolute value of the difference between reported and predicted inflation based on eight-year rolling regressions. "Domestic only" is equation (1), which only includes controls for inflation expectations, lagged inflation, and domestic slack. "Domestic + import prices" is equation (2), which adds relative import price inflation. "Global & domestic" is the full set of domestic variables plus global variables, including an index of world oil and other commodity prices, world slack, and global value chains. The regressions for core CPI also include exchange rate movements. The sample size is limited to countries and periods with import price data to maintain a consistent sample.

where all variables are defined above, except now expressed in first differences.[67] As explained by Cecchetti and others (2017), it is necessary to estimate the equation in first differences due to the assumption that the trend is a random walk (equation 5), so that the level of inflation is nonstationary.

Table 7 reports results from these panel regressions of trend core inflation on similar groups of variables as in equations (1)–(4).[68] Domestic slack continues to be negatively correlated with inflation, and this relationship continues to weaken over the last decade (including when slack is interacted with the import share). The flatter Phillips curve relationship over the last decade is only partially due to increased import exposure, with a meaningful decline that does not appear to reflect globalization (through the interaction term or other global controls).[69] The global variables show noteworthy differences relative to the comparable regressions for the cyclical component of CPI inflation, but results are closer to the estimates for core and wage inflation (as would be expected). Most of the global variables are not significantly correlated with inflation. The only global variable significant at the 5 percent level (in the earlier period and sometimes the later window) is exchange rates—the global variable that was not significantly correlated with the cyclical component of inflation in table 4. This suggests that exchange rates have more persistent effects on inflation than the other global variables. The global variables are not jointly significant, however, and the overall fit of these regressions is fairly low—with the within-R^2 only 0.02 with the full set of global variables in the last decade. While global variables can meaningfully improve our ability to understand CPI inflation and the cyclical component of CPI inflation over the last decade, they only have limited ability to improve our understanding of the dynamics of the underlying slow-moving trend in inflation, and they do not appear to have become more important over the last decade.

---

67. The change in the trend is relative to the previous quarter. The change in the other variables is relative to one year ago for the base case in order to allow for lagged effects on trend inflation. Sensitivity tests show that using different lag structures does not affect the key results. The current approach reduces concern about seasonality.

68. I use the full set of control variables but exclude lagged inflation, which is highly correlated with the trend.

69. The Phillips curve coefficient falls from −0.35 to −0.10 across the two periods when evaluated at the mean import shares.

Table 7. The Trend in Quarterly Core Inflation

	Full period			
	Domestic only (1)	*+ Oil prices (2)*	*+ All global variables (3)*	*DomSlack × impShare (4)*
Inflation Expectations	0.105**	0.108**	0.113**	0.078***
	(0.039)	(0.039)	(0.043)	(0.025)
Domestic Slack	−0.029**	−0.033**	−0.036***	−0.075**
	(0.011)	(0.012)	(0.012)	(0.033)
World Oil Prices		0.001		
		(0.001)		
World Comm. and Oil Prices			0.003	0.003
			(0.002)	(0.002)
Real Exchange Rate			−0.002**	−0.001**
			(0.001)	(0.001)
World Slack			−0.014	−0.019
			(0.012)	(0.011)
Global Value Chains			−0.018**	−0.012*
			(0.008)	(0.007)
Constant	−0.028***	−0.028***	−0.024***	−0.020***
	(0.001)	(0.001)	(0.002)	(0.001)
R²	*0.009*	*0.015*	*0.022*	*0.022*
No. observations	*2,260*	*2,260*	*2,165*	*2,067*
F-Test: joint significance of global variables				

Source: Author's calculations.

Notes: Estimated using fixed effects with robust standard errors clustered by country. See online appendix A for variable definitions and section V for estimation of the trend. ***Significant at the 1 percent level; **significant at the 5 percent level; *significant at the 10 percent level.

VI. Summary and Conclusions

The global economy has changed in many ways over the last twenty years—including through increased trade and financial integration, a greater role for emerging markets in driving global growth and commodity price fluctuations, and the increased use of global supply chains to shift segments of production to cheaper locations. These forms of globalization could all affect inflation dynamics. They could also simultaneously weaken the role of domestic factors in inflation models, explaining the recent flattening in the Phillips curve relationship between domestic slack and inflation in many economies.

This paper uses three different approaches (principal components, a Phillips curve framework, and a trend-cycle decomposition) to evaluate

	Pre-crisis (1996–2007)				Last decade (2008–2017)			
	Domestic only (5)	+ Oil prices (6)	+ All global variables (7)	DomSlack × impShare (8)	Domestic only (9)	+ Oil prices (10)	+ All global variables (11)	DomSlack × impShare (12)
	0.109**	0.109**	0.120***	0.092***	0.059*	0.047	0.034	0.035
	(0.042)	(0.042)	(0.042)	(0.032)	(0.033)	(0.034)	(0.028)	(0.028)
	−0.058***	−0.058***	−0.067***	−0.131*	−0.014	−0.024**	−0.023*	−0.041*
	(0.018)	(0.018)	(0.023)	(0.067)	(0.011)	(0.011)	(0.012)	(0.024)
		0.000				0.002		
		(0.000)				(0.002)		
			0.001	0.001			0.003	0.003
			(0.001)	(0.001)			(0.003)	(0.003)
			−0.004**	−0.003			−0.001	0.000
			(0.002)	(0.002)			(0.001)	(0.001)
			0.005	−0.008			−0.026*	−0.030**
			(0.029)	(0.026)			(0.013)	(0.014)
			−0.010	−0.004			−0.017*	−0.016*
			(0.011)	(0.010)			(0.009)	(0.008)
	−0.044***	−0.044***	−0.041***	−0.033***	−0.017***	−0.014***	−0.010*	−0.011**
	(0.003)	(0.003)	(0.009)	(0.009)	(0.002)	(0.003)	(0.005)	(0.004)
	0.042	0.042	0.052	0.051	0.001	0.014	0.020	0.020
	1,197	1,197	1,102	1,051	1,063	1,063	1,063	1,016
			1.62	1.32			1.76	1.84

the role of global factors for the dynamics of different inflation measures (CPI, core CPI, wages, the cyclical component, and slow-moving trend) and assess if the role of the global factors has changed over time or can explain the flattening of the Phillips curve. The rich set of results helps form a more comprehensive picture of how globalization has influenced different price dynamics. Global factors play a significant and increasingly important role in the dynamics of CPI inflation and the cyclical component of inflation. Part of this reflects increased volatility in commodity prices— but not all. Global factors have played a more muted role but can still be significant for core inflation, wage inflation, and the slow-moving trend in core inflation, with little evidence that their role has increased for any of these inflation measures over the last decade. The relationship between most measures of inflation and domestic slack has weakened over the last decade, even after interacting domestic slack with a country's exposure to the global economy or including more comprehensive controls for globalization that are often cited as causing the flattening of the Phillips curve. This does not mean, however, that the traditional domestic factors are no longer relevant for inflation; domestic slack continues to play a significant role (albeit often smaller) for many specifications and inflation measures, especially for core and wage inflation. Moreover, the weaker relationship between domestic slack and the different measures of inflation may reflect central banks being more attentive to slack and more willing to look through changes in inflation that result from other factors, such as commodity price movements, which have had a stronger relationship with CPI inflation over the last decade.

The results in this paper also raise a number of new questions. Are the changes in the relationships between the global factors and CPI inflation that have occurred over the last decade long lasting? If these developments have contributed to higher margins, a higher profit share, and reduced labor share, are they sustainable? If global variables have dampened CPI inflation over the last few years, could inflation quickly rebound if increased tariffs reduce the use of global supply chains? Which country characteristics determine the role of these different global variables for individual countries? And could other aspects of globalization be affecting inflation dynamics—such as changes in global capital flows or the "superstar" effect that is leading to increased company concentration in some industries? Finally, given the key result that global variables have become more important for understanding CPI inflation dynamics, but not wage inflation, could these patterns help improve our understanding of the factors behind the declining labor share in global income?

While this paper leaves many questions for future work, it makes some progress in understanding recent inflation puzzles. Simple frameworks for understanding inflation dynamics are not dead, and even though inflation has been dormant, some of the puzzling patterns in CPI inflation can be explained by CPI inflation being more determined abroad. In fact, the explanatory power of basic models for CPI inflation can be meaningfully improved over the last decade with the addition of the global variables discussed in this paper. This does not mean, however, that there is no longer a role for central banks or domestic developments in inflation dynamics. Even though CPI inflation is increasingly affected by globalization, and most inflation measures move less tightly with domestic slack, domestic variables are still important determinants of inflation dynamics.

ACKNOWLEDGMENTS   Special thanks to Javier Cravino, Ayhan Kose, and Jim Stock for detailed comments and suggestions on this draft, to Kostas Theodoridis for joint work on the trend-cycle analysis used in this paper, to Gee Hee Hong, Zsóka Kóczán, Weicheng Lian, and Malhar Nabar for kindly sharing their labor market data, and to Zhi Wang for sharing his data on global value chains. Additional thanks to participants at the Brookings Panel on Economic Activity held in Washington, D.C., on September 6, 2019, and to Simon Gilchrist, Carlos Viana de Carvalho, and other participants at the 17th BIS Annual Research Conference held in Zurich on June 22, 2018, for comments on initial work on this topic. Author contact information: kjforbes@mit.edu.

References

Albuquerque, Bruno, and Ursel Baumann. 2017. "Will US Inflation Awake from the Dead? The Role of Slack and Non-Linearities in the Phillips Curve." Working Paper 2001. European Central Bank. https://www.ecb.europa.eu/pub/pdf/scpwps/ecbwp2001.en.pdf.

Auer, Raphael A., Claudio Borio, and Andrew Filardo. 2017. "The Globalisation of Inflation: The Growing Importance of Global Value Chains." Working Paper 602. Basel: Bank for International Settlements. https://www.bis.org/publ/work602.pdf.

Auer, Raphael A., Kathrin Degen, and Andreas M. Fischer. 2013. "Low-Wage Import Competition, Inflationary Pressure, and Industry Dynamics in Europe." *European Economic Review* 59: 141–66.

Auer, Raphael A., Andrei A. Levchenko, and Philip Sauré. 2019. "International Inflation Spillovers through Input Linkages." *Review of Economics and Statistics* 101, no. 3: 507–21.

Autor, David, David Dorn, Lawrence F. Katz, Christina Patterson, and John Van Reenan. Forthcoming. "The Fall of the Labor Share and the Rise of Superstar Firms." *Quarterly Journal of Economics.*

Ball, Laurence M. 2006. "Has Globalization Changed Inflation?" Working Paper 12687. Cambridge, Mass.: National Bureau of Economic Research. https://www.nber.org/papers/w12687.

Ball, Laurence M., and N. Gregory Mankiw. 1995. "Relative-Price Changes as Aggregate Supply Shocks." *Quarterly Journal of Economics* 110, no. 1: 161–93.

Ball, Laurence M., and Sandeep Mazumder. 2011. "Inflation Dynamics and the Great Recession." *Brookings Papers on Economic Activity,* Spring, 337–81.

Ball, Laurence M., and Sandeep Mazumder. 2015. "A Phillips Curve with Anchored Expectations and Short-Term Unemployment." Working Paper 15/39. Washington, D.C.: International Monetary Fund. https://www.imf.org/en/Publications/WP/Issues/2016/12/31/A-Phillips-Curve-with-Anchored-Expectations-and-Short-Term-Unemployment-42735.

Bank for International Settlements (BIS). 2015. "Another Year of Monetary Policy Accommodation." *85th Annual Report,* 65–82. https://www.bis.org/publ/arpdf/ar2015e4.pdf.

Bean, Charles. 2006. "Globalisation and Inflation." *Quarterly Bulletin* Q4. Bank of England.

Benmelech, Efraim, Nittai Bergman, and Hyunseob Kim. 2017. "Strong Employers and Weak Employees: How Does Employer Concentration Affect Wages?" Working Paper 24307. Cambridge, Mass.: National Bureau of Economic Research. https://www.nber.org/papers/w24307.

Berganza, Juan Carlos, Fructuoso Borrallo, and Pedro del Río. 2018. "Determinants and Implications of Low Global Inflation Rates." In *International Macroeconomics in the Wake of the Global Financial Crisis,* edited by Laurent

Ferrara, Ignacio Hernando, and Daniela Marconi. Cham, Switzerland: Springer International Publishing.

Bernanke, Ben S. 2007. "Inflation Expectations and Inflation Forecasting." Speech given at the Monetary Economics Workshop of the National Bureau of Economic Research, Cambridge, Mass., July 10.

Blanchard, Olivier. 2016. "The U.S. Phillips Curve: Back to the 60s?" Policy Brief 16-1. Washington, D.C.: Peterson Institute for International Economics. https://www.piie.com/publications/policy-briefs/us-phillips-curve-back-60s.

Blanchard, Olivier. 2018. "Should We Reject the Natural Rate Hypothesis?" *Journal of Economic Perspectives* 32, no. 1: 97–120.

Blanchard, Olivier, Eugenio Cerutti, and Lawrence Summers. 2015. "Inflation and Activity: Two Explorations and Their Monetary Policy Implications." In *Proceedings of the ECB Forum on Central Banking: Inflation and Unemployment in Europe*. Sintra: European Central Bank.

Borio, Claudio. 2017. "Through the Looking Glass." OMFIF City Lecture, September 22.

Borio, Claudio, and Andrew Filardo. 2007. "Globalisation and Inflation: New Cross-Country Evidence on the Global Determinants of Domestic Inflation." Working Paper 277. Basel: Bank for International Settlements. https://www.bis.org/publ/work227.htm.

Cecchetti, Stephen G., Michael E. Feroli, Peter Hooper, Anil K. Kashyap, and Kermit L. Schoenholtz. 2017. "Deflating Inflation Expectations: The Implications of Inflation's Simple Dynamics." Paper prepared for the U.S. Monetary Policy Forum, New York, March 3. https://papers.ssrn.com/sol3/papers.cfm?abstract_id=2941510.

Cecchetti, Stephen G., Peter Hooper, Bruce C. Kasman, Kermit L. Schoenholtz, and Mark W. Watson. 2007. "Understanding the Evolving Inflation Process." Paper prepared for the U.S. Monetary Policy Forum, Washington, D.C., March 9. http://people.brandeis.edu/~cecchett/Polpdf/USMPF2007.pdf

Chan, Joshua C. C., Gary Koop, and Simon M. Potter. 2013. "A New Model of Trend Inflation." *Journal of Business and Economic Statistics* 31, no. 1: 94–106.

Ciccarelli, Matteo, and Benoît Mojon. 2010. "Global Inflation." *Review of Economics and Statistics* 92, no. 3: 524–35.

Coibion, Olivier, and Yuriy Gorodnichenko. 2015. "Is the Phillips Curve Alive and Well After All? Inflation Expectations and the Missing Disinflation." *American Economic Journal: Macroeconomics* 7, no. 1: 197–232.

Cravino, Javier. 2019. Comment on "Inflation Dynamics: Dead, Dormant, or Determined Abroad?," by Kristin Forbes. In the present volume of *Brookings Papers on Economic Activity*.

Eberly, Janice C., James H. Stock, and Jonathan H. Wright. 2019. "The Federal Reserve's Current Framework for Monetary Policy: A Review and Assessment." Paper prepared for the Conference on Monetary Policy Strategy, Tools, and Communication Practices, Federal Reserve Bank of Chicago, June 4–5. https://www.chicagofed.org/conference-sessions/session-1.

Eickmeier, Sandra, and Katharina Pijnenburg. 2013. "The Global Dimension of Inflation—Evidence from Factor-Augmented Phillips Curves." *Oxford Bulletin of Economics and Statistics* 75, no. 1: 103–22.

Forbes, Kristin. 2015. "When, Why, and What's Next for Low Inflation? No Magic Slippers Needed." Speech given at the London School of Economics, London, June 17. https://www.bankofengland.co.uk/speech/2015/when-why-and-whats-next-for-low-inflation-no-magic-slippers-needed.

Forbes, Kristin. 2018. "Fixing the Astrolabe: Global Factors and Inflation Models." In *Proceedings of the ECB Forum on Central Banking: Price and Wage Setting in Advanced Economies*. Sintra: European Central Bank. https://www.ecb.europa.eu/pub/pdf/sintra/ecb.forumcentbank201810.en.pdf.

Forbes, Kristin. 2019. "Has Globalization Changed the Inflation Process?" Working Paper 791. Basel: Bank for International Settlements. https://www.bis.org/publ/work791.htm.

Forbes, Kristin, Ida Hjortsoe, and Tsvetelina Nenova. 2017. "Shocks versus Structure: Explaining Differences in Exchange Rate Pass-Through across Countries and Time." Working Paper 50. London: Bank of England. https://www.bankofengland.co.uk/external-mpc-discussion-paper/2017/explaining-differences-in-exchange-rate-pass-through.

Forbes, Kristin, Ida Hjortsoe, and Tsvetelina Nenova. 2018. "The Shocks Matter: Improving Our Estimates of Exchange Rate Pass-Through." *Journal of International Economics* 114: 25–275.

Forbes, Kristin, Lewis Kirkham, and Konstantinos Theodoridis. 2019. "A Trendy Approach to UK Inflation Dynamics." *The Manchester School* (special issue): 1–53.

Gagnon, Joseph E., and Christopher G. Collins. 2019. "Low Inflation Bends the Phillips Curve." Working Paper 19-6. Washington, D.C.: Peterson Institute of International Economics. https://www.piie.com/publications/working-papers/low-inflation-bends-phillips-curve.

Galí, Jordi, and Mark Gertler. 1999. "Inflation Dynamics: A Structural Econometric Analysis." *Journal of Monetary Economics* 44, no. 2: 195–222.

Galí, Jordi, Mark Gertler, and J. David López-Salido. 2005. "Robustness of Estimates of the Hybrid New Keynesian Phillips Curve." *Journal of Monetary Economics* 52, no. 6: 1107–18.

Gilchrist, Simon, Raphael Schoenle, Jae Sim, and Egon Zakrajšek. 2017. "Inflation Dynamics during the Financial Crisis." *American Economic Review* 107, no. 3: 785–823.

Gilchrist, Simon, and Egon Zakrajšek. 2015. "Customer Markets and Financial Frictions: Implications for Inflation Dynamics." In *Economic Policy Symposium Proceedings: Inflation Dynamics and Monetary Policy*. Jackson Hole, Wyo.: Federal Reserve Bank of Kansas.

Goldfeld, Stephen M., and Alan S. Blinder. 1972. "Some Implications of Endogenous Stabilization Policy." *Brookings Papers on Economic Activity*, no. 3: 585–640.

Gordon, Robert J. 1977. "World Inflation and Monetary Accommodation in Eight Countries." *Brookings Papers on Economic Activity,* no. 2: 409–68.

Gordon, Robert J. 1985. "Understanding Inflation in the 1980s." *Brookings Papers on Economic Activity,* no. 1: 263–99.

Gordon, Robert J. 2013. "The Phillips Curve Is Alive and Well: Inflation and the NAIRU during the Slow Recovery." Working Paper 19390. Cambridge, Mass.: National Bureau of Economic Research. https://www.nber.org/papers/w19390.

Grossman, Gene M., and Esteban Rossi-Hansberg. 2008. "Trading Tasks: A Simple Theory of Offshoring." *American Economic Review* 98, no. 5: 1978–97.

Guilloux-Nefussi, Sophie. 2018. "Are Monopolies a Danger to the United States?" Blog post, February 2, Banque de France, Paris. https://blocnotesdeleco.banque-france.fr/en/blog-entry/are-monopolies-danger-united-states.

Ha, Jongrim, M. Ayhan Kose, and Franziska Ohnsorge. 2019. *Inflation in Emerging and Developing Economies: Evolution, Drivers, and Policies.* Washington, D.C.: World Bank. https://www.worldbank.org/en/research/publication/inflation-in-emerging-and-developing-economies.

Hakkio, Craig S. 2009. "Global Inflation Dynamics." Working Paper 09-01. Federal Reserve Bank of Kansas City. https://papers.ssrn.com/sol3/papers.cfm?abstract_id=1335348.

Hamilton, James D. 2011. "Nonlinearities and the Macroeconomic Effects of Oil Prices." *Macroeconomic Dynamics* 15, no. S3: 364–78.

Hong, Gee Hee, Zsóka Kóczán, Weicheng Lian, and Malhar Nabar. 2018. "More Slack than Meets the Eye? Wage Dynamics in Advanced Economies." Working Paper WP/18/50. Washington, D.C.: International Monetary Fund. https://www.imf.org/en/Publications/WP/Issues/2018/03/09/More-Slack-than-Meets-the-Eye-Recent-Wage-Dynamics-in-Advanced-Economies-45692.

Hooper, Peter, Frederic S. Mishkin, and Amir Sufi. 2019. "Prospects for Inflation in a High Pressure Economy: Is the Phillips Curve Dead or Is It Just Hibernating?" Paper prepared for the U.S. Monetary Policy Forum, Chicago, February 22. https://research.chicagobooth.edu/igm/usmpf/usmpf-paper.

Ihrig, Jane, Steven B. Kamin, Deborah Lindner, and Jaime Marquez. 2010. "Some Simple Tests of the Globalization and Inflation Hypothesis." *International Finance* 13, no. 3: 343–75.

International Monetary Fund. 2016. "Global Disinflation in an Era of Constrained Monetary Policy." In *World Economic Outlook: Subdued Demand Symptoms and Remedies,* October. Washington.

Jašová, Martina, Richhild Moessner, and Elod Takáts. 2018. "Domestic and Global Output Gaps as Inflation Drivers: What Does the Phillips Curve Tell?" Working Paper 748. Basel: Bank for International Settlements. https://www.bis.org/publ/work748.htm.

Jordà, Òscar, and Fernanda Nechio. 2018. "Inflation Globally." Working Paper 2018–15. Federal Reserve Bank of San Francisco. https://www.frbsf.org/economic-research/publications/working-papers/2018/15/.

Karabarbounis, Loukas, and Brent Neiman. 2013. "The Global Decline of the Labor Share." *Quarterly Journal of Economics* 129, no. 1: 61–103.

Kohn, Donald L. 2006. "The Effects of Globalization on Inflation and Their Implications for Monetary Policy." Speech given at the Federal Reserve Bank of Boston 51st Economic Conference, Chatham, June 16. https://www.federal reserve.gov/newsevents/speech/kohn20060616a.htm.

Li, Xin, Bo Meng, and Zhi Wang. 2019. "Recent Patterns of Global Production and GFC Participation." In *Global Value Chain Production Report 2019*. Geneva: World Trade Organization.

McLeay, Michael, and Silvana Tenreyro. 2019. "Optimal Inflation and the Identification of the Phillips Curve." *NBER Macroeconomics Annual* 34.

Mikolajun, Irena, and David Lodge. 2016. "Advanced Economy Inflation: The Role of Global Factors." Working Paper 1948. European Central Bank. https://www.ecb.europa.eu/pub/pdf/scpwps/ecbwp1948.en.pdf.

Miles, David, Ugo Panizza, Ricardo Reis, and Ángel Ubide. 2017. *And Yet It Moves: Inflation and the Great Recession.* London: Centre for Economic and Policy Research.

Neely, Christopher J., and David E. Rapach. 2011. "International Comovements in Inflation Rates and Country Characteristics." *Journal of International Money and Finance* 30, no. 7: 1471–90.

Obstfeld, Maurice. 2019. "Global Dimensions of US Monetary Policy." Working Paper 26039. Cambridge, Mass.: National Bureau of Economic Research. https://www.nber.org/papers/w26039.

Powell, Jerome H. 2018. "Monetary Policy and Risk Management at a Time of Low Inflation and Low Unemployment." Speech given at Revolution or Evolution? Reexamining Economic Paradigms, National Association for Business Economics, Boston, October 2.

Sbordone, Argia M. 2010. "Globalization and Inflation Dynamics: The Impact of Increased Competition." In *International Dimensions of Monetary Policy*, edited by Jordi Galí and Mark J. Gertler. Chicago: University of Chicago Press.

Stock, James H., and Mark W. Watson. 2007. "Why Has U.S. Inflation Become Harder to Forecast?" *Journal of Money, Credit, and Banking* 39, no. 1: 3–33.

Stock, James H., and Mark W. Watson. 2010. "Modeling Inflation after the Crisis." In *Economic Policy Symposium Proceedings: Macroeconomic Challenges—The Decade Ahead.* Jackson Hole, Wyo.: Federal Reserve Bank of Kansas City.

Stock, James H., and Mark W. Watson. 2018. "Slack and Cyclically Sensitive Inflation." In *Proceedings of the ECB Forum on Central Banking: Price and Wage Setting in Advanced Economies.* Sinta: European Central Bank. https://www.ecb.europa.eu/pub/pdf/sintra/ecb.forumcentbank201810.en.pdf.

Wei, Shang-Jin, and Yinxi Xie. 2019. "The Wedge of the Century: On the Divergence between CPI and PPI as Inflation Gauges." Working Paper 24319. Cambridge, Mass.: National Bureau of Economic Research. https://www.nber.org/papers/w24319.

World Bank. 2018. "The Role of Major Emerging Markets in Global Commodity Demand." In *Global Economic Prospects*. Washington, D.C.: World Bank.

Yellen, Janet L. 2006. "Monetary Policy in a Global Environment." Speech given at The Euro and the Dollar in a Globalized Economy Conference, University of California, Santa Cruz, May 27. https://www.frbsf.org/our-district/press/ presidents-speeches/yellen-speeches/2006/may/monetary-policy-in-a-global-environment/.

Yellen, Janet L. 2016. "Macroeconomic Research after the Crisis." Speech given at the Elusive "Great" Recovery: Causes and Implications for Future Business Cycle Dynamics, 60th Annual Economic Conference, Boston, October 14. https://www.federalreserve.gov/newsevents/speech/yellen20161014a.htm.

Yellen, Janet L. 2017. "Inflation, Uncertainty and Monetary Policy." Speech given at Prospects for Growth: Reassessing the Fundamentals, National Association for Business Economics, Cleveland, September 26. https://www.federalreserve. gov/newsevents/speech/yellen20170926a.htm.

Comments and Discussion

COMMENT BY

JAVIER CRAVINO
In "Inflation Dynamics: Dead, Dormant, or Determined Abroad?" Kristin Forbes argues that inflation dynamics have changed since the global financial crisis (GFC). She notes two important changes: first, the Phillips curve has become flatter, that is, large changes in the unemployment rate have been associated with small changes in inflation; second, inflation dynamics since the GFC have been difficult to explain using existing empirical models. Forbes asks whether globalization is behind these changes and shows how empirical models of inflation can be extended to better account for global factors.

The idea that foreign factors can affect domestic inflation has a long tradition in economics.[1] The main premise in the paper is that globalization can affect CPI inflation beyond its effect on import prices. Forbes argues that to properly control for the effects of globalization, it is important to introduce a broad set of global variables into the workhorse empirical models of inflation.

The paper highlights three main empirical findings. First, it shows that CPI inflation has become more synchronized since the GFC, while core and wage inflation have not. Second, it shows that workhorse empirical models of inflation lose explanatory power after the GFC. However, the models maintain their explanatory power if they are extended to include global variables. Finally, the paper argues that much of the flattening of the Phillips curve can be accounted for by an increase in the share of imported goods in the CPI.

---

1. For a modern treatment of the Phillips curve in open economies, see Galí and Monacelli (2005) and the literature that followed.

Forbes's extensions to the existing models flexibly control for global variables in a way that is loosely grounded in theory. One drawback of this approach is that the mapping of the results to existing theories of inflation is not always straightforward. This discussion attempts to interpret the results of the paper in light of a standard (though highly stylized) open economy model of the Phillips curve.

The discussion is organized as follows. First, I present a small open economy model to guide the discussion on how foreign factors can affect domestic inflation. I then use this model to evaluate how changes in these factors affect the slope of the Phillips curve. Finally, I use the model to evaluate how adding foreign variables can increase the explanatory power of the Phillips curve.

THE PHILLIPS CURVE IN A STYLIZED SMALL OPEN ECONOMY MODEL This section provides a stylized small open economy model to illustrate how globalization can affect domestic inflation. The ingredients of the model intend to capture the main mechanisms described in Forbes's paper: the economy consumes commodities and non-commodities and imports intermediate inputs and final goods, firms' desired markups are variable, and nominal prices are sticky.[2] Since Forbes does not emphasize how globalization affects inflation expectations, I abstract from dynamic decisions and focus on a two-period economy to facilitate the exposition.

Environment. Consider a small open economy that lasts for two periods, $t = 1,2$. The consumption basket in the economy contains commodities and non-commodities. The (log) aggregate price index in period t is

$$(1) \qquad\qquad p_t = \omega p_t^{Core} + [1 - \omega] p_t^{Com},$$

where p_t^{Core} and p_t^{Core} are, respectively, the core and the commodity price indexes, and ω is the share of non-commodities in the consumption basket. All variables are denoted in logs. The core price index is

$$(2) \qquad\qquad p_t^{Core} = \mu p_t^{D} + [1 - \mu] p_t^{M},$$

2. Another mechanism mentioned in the paper is that globalization may reduce workers' bargaining power. Changes in workers' bargaining power should be reflected in a change in the slope of the wage Phillips curve (that is, the relation between wage inflation and unemployment or domestic slack). Forbes notes that the slope of the wage Phillips curve has not changed since the GFC. I will thus assume that this slope is constant and not model this mechanism explicitly.

where p_t^D and p_t^M are the price indexes for domestic and imported goods respectively, and μ is the share of domestic goods in the core price index. Commodity and import prices are determined in world markets and are exogenously given.

Domestic goods are produced by a continuum of monopolistically competitive producers. These producers would like to set prices equal to

$$(3) \qquad \bar{p}_t^D = [1 - \alpha]w_t + \alpha p_t + \bar{\rho},$$

in each period t. The desired price $\bar{p}_t^D$ depends on the nominal wage and the aggregate price index, w_t and p_t, up to a constant $\bar{\rho}$. The parameter α captures the extent to which the price that a domestic producer would like to set depends on the prices set by other producers in the economy. This dependence may arise from strategic complementarities in either production or demand.[3]

All producers know w_1 and p_1 before choosing prices in period 1 and thus set prices equal to $p_1^D = \bar{p}_1^D$. I introduce nominal price rigidities by assuming that only a fraction θ of producers know w_2 and p_2 before setting prices in period 2. These producers set prices equal to $\bar{p}_2^D$. The remaining producers $1 - \theta$ price according to their expectations of w_2 and p_2. I assume that these producers expect wages and prices in period 2 to equal those in period 1 and thus set prices equal to $\bar{p}_1^D$ in the second period. Note that the parameter θ controls the fraction of prices that adjust in the second period.

The aggregate price index for domestic goods is thus given by

$$(4) \qquad p_2^D = \theta \bar{p}_2^D + [1 - \theta]p_1^D.$$

Combining equations (1)–(4) and denoting aggregate inflation by $\pi_t \equiv p_2 - p_1$, we obtain

$$(5) \qquad \pi_t = \frac{\mu[1 - \alpha]\omega\theta}{1 - \mu\alpha\omega\theta}\pi_t^w + \frac{[1 - \mu]\omega}{1 - \mu\alpha\omega\theta}\pi_t^M + \frac{1 - \omega}{1 - \mu\alpha\omega\theta}\pi_t^{com},$$

where π_t^w, π_t^M, and π_t^{com}, respectively, denote wage, import, and commodity price inflation.

---

3. For example, strategic complementarities in production can arise if production uses intermediate inputs produced by other firms in the economy. Strategic complementarities in demand can arise if the producer's desired markup depends on the prices set by its competitors. Blanco and Cravino (forthcoming) show how various models of strategic complementarities can be mapped to equation (3).

Globalization and slope of the Phillips curve. Equation (5) can help us understand how globalization affects the relationship between the aggregate inflation rate and the slack of the domestic economy. Since import and commodity prices are exogenous, domestic slack affects aggregate inflation only through its effect on nominal wage inflation, π_t^w. Forbes highlights that the relationship between wage inflation and domestic slack has not changed since the GFC. I will thus assume that this relationship is constant and focus on how globalization may have affected the slope between aggregate price and wage inflation, which is given by

$$\beta \equiv \frac{\mu[1 - \alpha]\omega\theta}{1 - \mu\alpha\omega\theta}.$$

Import share. Forbes highlights that one way in which globalization can reduce the slope of the Phillips curve is through increased trade integration. This is indeed the case in the model, where the slope β depends positively on the share of domestic goods in the core price index μ. Intuitively, inflation is more responsive to domestic wages (and domestic slack) the larger the share of domestic goods in the price index.

Commodity prices and nominal price rigidities. Forbes also highlights that the increased role of emerging markets in the global economy has made commodity prices more volatile, which can affect inflation dynamics. Note that while the slope β depends on the share of non-commodities in the CPI ω, it does not depend directly on the volatility of commodity prices.

Forbes argues that increased volatility of commodity prices can affect inflation dynamics indirectly if firms change prices more frequently in the presence of large commodity price shocks. However, in the model laid out above, the slope of the Phillips curve becomes steeper, not flatter, as we increase the fraction of firms that adjust prices, θ.[4] Thus, while greater commodity price volatility may affect inflation dynamics, it is unclear how it can flatten the Phillips curve.

Variable markups and global value chains. Finally, Forbes notes that globalization could affect inflation dynamics by putting pressure on markups via foreign competition and on costs via global supply chains. Indeed, in the model, the slope β depends on the degree of strategic complementarities α. The higher the strategic complementarities, the lower the slope of the Phillips curve. The degree of strategic complementarities depends on both the cost share of intermediate inputs and the curvature of the demand function. It is not obvious that globalization affects either of

---

4. This is a common feature of New Keynesian models; see, for example, Galí (2008).

these things directly. Instead, the effects mentioned in Forbes are likely to arise from the interaction between the degree of complementarities and the import share, $1 - \mu$. In particular, in the presence of complementarities, domestic prices depend more on foreign markups and costs (and less on domestic wages) the higher the import share.[5]

In sum, equation (5) validates Forbes's point that globalization can affect inflation beyond its effect on import prices. It also reveals that increased trade integration can flatten the slope of the Phillips curve.

Connection with the empirics. The discussion above highlights that to evaluate how globalization affects the slope of the Phillips curve, one must evaluate how it affects the parameters μ, α, θ, and ω. It is important to note that these effects cannot be gauged simply by adding global variables to the existing Phillips curve framework.

If we abstract from the strategic complementaries, $\alpha = 0$, the slope is given by $\beta = \mu\omega\theta$. In this case, if the change in inflation dynamics following the GFC was driven by globalization, and globalization did not affect ω, θ, or the slope of the wage Phillips curve, a regression of the form $\pi_t = b \times [\mu \times slack_t] + \varepsilon_t$ should yield a slope b that does not change after the GFC.

Forbes runs a version of the Phillips curve model in which the dependent variable is an interaction between the import share and the domestic slack.[6] This is somewhat different from what the theory suggests, since slack is interacted with the share of imports rather than with the share of domestic goods. Setting this difference aside, Forbes shows that the coefficient b falls after the GFC, from –0.41 to –0.17. Taken at face value, these numbers suggest that the decline in the slope of the Phillips curve since the GFC was not simply due to the mechanical effect of an increase of the share of imports on the CPI. Instead, the evidence indicates that one of the following pertains:

1. Globalization somehow affected the slope of the Phillips curve through the share of commodities in the CPI ω, the degree of price stickiness θ, the slope of the wage Phillips curve, or through channels not considered in this model.

---

5. To see this, note that combining equations (1)–(4) we obtain domestic inflation given

as $\pi_t^D = \dfrac{\theta[1 - \alpha]}{1 - \theta\alpha\omega\mu}\pi_t^w + \dfrac{\theta\alpha\omega[1 - \mu]}{1 - \theta\alpha\omega\mu}\pi_t^M + \dfrac{\theta\alpha\omega[1 - \omega]}{1 - \theta\alpha\omega\mu}\pi_t^{Com}$. Thus, the relation between domestic inflation and wages is increasing in μ.

6. This is equation (4) in the paper, which also has controls for inflation expectation and other global variables. In the notation of this discussion, equation (4) in the paper corresponds to running $\pi_t = b \times [[1 - \mu] \times slack_t] + \varepsilon_t$.

2. The change in the slope of the Phillips curve was not driven solely by increased globalization.

3. The nonlinear effects of μ on the slope of the Phillips curve that arise from the strategic complementarities are not well captured by this specification.

While further research is needed to disentangle these explanations, it is hard to conclude from the evidence given by Forbes that globalization was the main cause for the decline in the slope of the Phillips curve. In contrast, the evidence in the paper speaks more directly to the effect of globalization on the explanatory power of the Phillips curve.

Globalization and the explanatory power of the Phillips curve. Equation (5) underscores how globalization may affect the explanatory power of the Phillips curve. In particular, this model's version of equation (1) in the paper is given by

$$(6) \qquad \pi_t = \tilde{\beta} slack_t + \varepsilon_t,$$

where $\tilde{\beta} \equiv \beta \Gamma$ and Γ is the elasticity of wage inflation with respect to economic slack (which is assumed to be constant). The error term is given by

$$\varepsilon_t \equiv \frac{[1-\mu]\omega}{1-\mu\alpha\theta\omega}\pi_t^M + \frac{1-\omega}{1-\mu\alpha\theta\omega}\pi_t^{Com}.$$

The equation states that if import and commodity prices are omitted from the regression, they will be captured by the error term. Globalization can increase the variance of the error term by increasing $1-\mu$ or by increasing the volatility of import and commodity prices or both. Clearly, augmenting equation (5) to control for π_t^M and π_t^{Com} should increase the explanatory power of the regression. While high trade integration (high $1-\mu$) is one consequence of globalization, further research is needed to pin down the relation between commodity price volatility and the growth of emerging markets.

REFERENCES FOR THE CRAVINO COMMENT

Blanco, Andrés, and Javier Cravino. Forthcoming. "Price Rigidities and the Relative PPP." *Journal of Monetary Economics.*

Galí, Jordi. 2008. *Monetary Policy, Inflation and the Business Cycle: An Introduction to the New Keynesian Framework.* Princeton, N.J.: Princeton University Press.

Galí, Jordi, and Tommaso Monacelli. 2005. "Monetary Policy and Exchange Rate Volatility in a Small Open Economy." *Review of Economic Studies* 72, no. 3: 707–34.

COMMENT BY

M. AYHAN KOSE[1]   It is difficult to think of a more important question for the design and conduct of monetary policy than the one this paper focuses on: Have the forces of globalization changed our understanding of inflation? The paper also has all the hallmarks of Kristin Forbes's work: after starting with a well-defined, topical, and policy-relevant question, she attacks the question with a comprehensive empirical analysis. She then concludes with a set of clear results and carefully crafted policy messages.

After posing her question and summarizing earlier work, Forbes presents a rich empirical exercise. She employs three different empirical frameworks: a simple factor model (principal component analysis); an augmented Phillips curve model with global variables; and a model with trend-cycle decomposition. For the latter two frameworks, she uses a series of panel regressions. The data set has a total of forty-three countries (thirty-one advanced economies and twelve emerging markets) and covers the period 1996–2017.

Forbes has a basic conclusion: globalization plays an increasingly more important role in driving the dynamics of domestic consumer price index (CPI) inflation, but its role is somewhat less important in the case of core inflation and wage inflation. Domestic forces are still relevant in driving inflation, but their roles have evolved over time and differ across measures of inflation. For example, domestic slack remains important, but it has become less so over time, especially for CPI inflation. These findings push the frontiers of our understanding of the drivers of inflation. They also lead to several new research avenues to explore.

I begin my comments with a brief analysis of the evolution of inflation over the past 50 years to put the motivation behind the paper in a broader context. I then focus on two specific questions to highlight some future areas of research. First, what are the potential factors explaining the behavior of inflation over time? Second, how important is the global factor in driving fluctuations in inflation? I conclude with a couple of observations that also require additional analytical work in light of Forbes's findings.

1. World Bank, Prospects Group; Brookings Institution; CEPR, and CAMA; akose@worldbank.org. I thank my coauthors, Jongrim Ha, Alain Kabundi, Peter Nagle, Franziska Ohnsorge, and Naotaka Sugawara, for many discussions on the links between globalization and inflation. Some of my comments here are based on joint work with Jongrim Ha and Franziska Ohnsorge. The findings, interpretations, and conclusions expressed in this report are entirely those of the author and should not be attributed to the World Bank, its executive directors, or the countries they represent.

Figure 1. Evolution of CPI Inflation

Percent, year-on-year

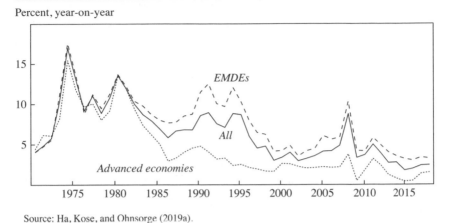

Source: Ha, Kose, and Ohnsorge (2019a).
Note: Median year-on-year consumer price inflation for thirty advanced economies and 125 emerging market and developing economies (EMDEs).

EVOLUTION OF INFLATION Forbes starts with a simple observation about the poor performance of standard models in forecasting inflation during the past decade. It is useful to put this observation in a longer historical context because of the remarkable decline in inflation since the early 1970s (figure 1). The collapse of inflation has been highly synchronized across groups of countries. For example, advanced economies saw their median annual national CPI inflation drop from its highest (15 percent in 1974) to its lowest level (0.4 percent in 2015) in more than 60 years. Since then, it has risen somewhat but remains below the median inflation target of advanced-economy central banks. After 2008, below-target inflation and, in some cases, deflation became pervasive across advanced economies: for example, at some point in 2015, inflation was negative in a number of advanced economies. Some central banks have struggled to lift inflation back to their inflation targets over the past decade.

Emerging market and developing economies (EMDEs) have also experienced a significant decline during the same period: median inflation went down from a peak of 17.5 percent in 1974 to 3.2 percent in 2018. Disinflation over recent decades has been broad-based across many regions. For example, disinflation occurred across all EMDE regions, including those with a history of persistently high inflation, such as Latin America and sub-Saharan Africa (Ha, Kose, and Ohnsorge 2019a).

POTENTIAL SOURCES OF THE SYNCHRONIZED DECLINE IN INFLATION The highly synchronized nature of the decline in inflation points to the possibility of some global factors driving inflation in many countries. In light of this observation, Forbes motivates her exercise by documenting some prominent changes in the world economy that could affect the dynamics of inflation: "increased trade flows, the greater heft of emerging markets and their impact on commodity prices, the greater ease of using supply chains to shift parts of production to cheaper locations, and a corresponding reduction in local worker bargaining power could all affect different inflation measures."

There is no question about the first-order importance of these changes, and it is natural that Forbes focuses on these given the well-known measurement and data challenges with some other changes. However, there is a wide range of sources for the synchronized decline in inflation that will require a much broader examination. These include shocks, similar policy frameworks (and responses), and structural changes (Ha, Kose, and Ohnsorge 2019a).

Shocks. Inflation synchronization could be driven by common shocks that spread across countries or by country-specific shocks that spill over from one country or a subset of countries to others. Commodity price shocks, internationally correlated productivity shocks, other cost-push shocks, and real demand shocks could all affect national inflation rates and often in the same direction, which would represent inflation synchronization.

Similar policy responses/frameworks. Correlated or coordinated monetary policies could also be an important source of inflation co-movement, especially among advanced economies. Even if there is no deliberate coordination of policies, similar monetary policy frameworks can trigger similar policy responses to global shocks. This policy synchronicity would then translate into inflation synchronicity. For example, a growing number of countries have introduced inflation-targeting monetary policy frameworks that in turn potentially lead to similar policy responses to shocks.

Structural changes. Over the past five decades, the degree of global integration in trade and financial markets has grown rapidly. These structural changes have often strengthened cross-country spillovers of real and nominal shocks, which have in turn led to more synchronized movements in inflation. Stronger trade linkages and rapidly expanding global supply chains increase an economy's exposure to external shocks, as Forbes notes. Some also argue that greater international competition has made domestic inflation less sensitive to domestic output gaps, flattening Phillips curves. Increased international financial integration has been accompanied by greater synchronization of financial conditions across countries. As financial stress spreads (or recedes) across global financial markets, it tightens (or loosens) credit and financial conditions in a large number of countries.

Figure 2. Inflation by Country Characteristics

Percent

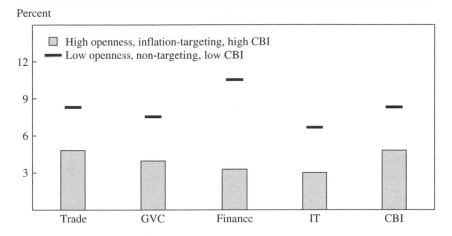

Source: Ha, Kose, and Ohnsorge (2019a).

Note: Columns indicate median inflation rates in country-year pairs with trade-to-GDP ratios ("Trade"), global value chain integration ("GVC"), financial assets and liabilities relative to GDP ("Finance"), or central bank independence and transparency index ("CBI") in the top quartile of 175 economies during 1970–2017 or with inflation targeting monetary policy regimes ("IT"). Horizontal lines denote median inflation rates in the bottom quartile or with monetary policy regimes that are not inflation-targeting. Differences are all statistically significant at the 5 percent level. Inflation-targeting regimes are defined as in Caceres, Carrière-Swallow, and Gruss (2016) and the IMF *Annual Report on Exchange Arrangements and Exchange Restrictions*. Central bank independence is measured by the index independence and transparency, taken from Dincer and Eichengreen (2014). GVC is based on the sum of backward and forward participation in global value chains. See Ha, Kose, and Ohnsorge (2019a) for more details on the definitions of country characteristics.

As a result, movements in domestic demand and disinflationary or inflationary pressures are also synchronized across countries. Technological changes, in addition to deepening supply chains, can also help globalize markets for nontradable service sectors. This may extend and deepen the impact of global forces on domestic inflation.

Preliminary empirical analysis supports the relevance of some of these channels. For example, inflation has typically been lower in economies with greater trade and financial openness (figure 2). Compared with other monetary policy regimes, inflation-targeting regimes were also associated with lower inflation, and countries with more independent and transparent central banks tend to experience lower inflation.

Forbes briefly discusses some of these channels but omits most of them in her empirical exercise. In order to have a more complete understanding of the dynamics of inflation, future work needs to capture the roles of these channels and their interactions with the globalization-related variables.

For example, it would be useful to examine how the interactions between stronger trade linkages and changes in monetary policy frameworks translate into inflation outcomes in more integrated economies.

HOW IMPORTANT IS THE GLOBAL FACTOR IN DRIVING INFLATION? Forbes employs a simple principal component analysis (PCA) to estimate the importance of a global factor in driving inflation. The PCA identifies the common movements in the cross-sectional inflation data without imposing any additional model structure. Forbes considers the first principal component estimated by the PCM as the global factor. She examines four measures of inflation: CPI, core CPI (excluding food and energy prices), the producer price index (PPI), and private sector hourly earnings (wages). The data set for the PCA covers forty-three countries over the 1990–2017 period.

It is useful to extend this exercise by employing a richer empirical framework with a much larger and longer data sample. I estimate a dynamic factor model to study the role of common factors in driving inflation. Dynamic factor models are designed to extract a few unobservable common elements from a large number of (observable) variables. In the context of inflation, the dynamic factor I consider here also imposes a much richer structure than the PCA in the paper. Specifically, the model has two types of factors: a global inflation factor that captures common elements in inflation fluctuations across countries and a group-specific factor that accounts for common elements in inflation fluctuations in advanced economies and EMDEs (Ha, Kose, and Ohnsorge 2019b). The presence of group factors allows the model to account for the large differences in country characteristics between advanced economies and EMDEs. In addition, the model includes idiosyncratic factors that cannot be attributed to the other factors. The analysis is based on annual headline CPI inflation data for ninety-nine countries—twenty-five advanced economies and seventy-four EMDEs—for 1970–2017.

The results suggest that during this period, the global inflation factor accounted for a sizable share of inflation variance in advanced economies and EMDEs (figure 3). In the median country, the global factor accounted for 12 percent of inflation variation, but its role varied widely across and within country groups. For example, the contribution of the global inflation factor was much greater in the median advanced economy (24 percent) than in the median EMDE (10 percent). The group-specific factors have also played an important role in driving inflation. For example, in the median advanced economy, the group-specific factor accounted for 8 percent of inflation variation.

Figure 3. Contribution of Global and Group Factors to Inflation Variation

Percent

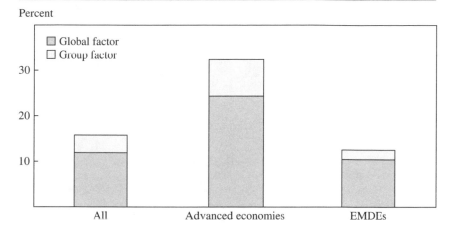

Source: Ha, Kose, and Ohnsorge (2019a).
Note: The contribution of global and group factors to inflation variance is estimated with the dynamic factor model over 1970–2017. The sample includes ninety-nine countries (twenty-five advanced economies and seventy-four EMDEs). The means or medians are unweighted. See Ha, Kose, and Ohnsorge (2019b) for more details on model estimation and results.

A critical feature of the international inflation experience of the past five decades has been the emergence of a global inflation cycle. This is reflected in a growing contribution of the global factor to the variation in country-level inflation rates (figure 4). In order to illustrate this, it is useful to consider estimates of the model for three approximately equal subperiods: 1970–85, 1986–2000, and 2001–17. The first period overlaps with the Great Inflation of 1965–82; the second was a period of widespread disinflation; and the third was a period of low but typically stable inflation.

The contribution of the global factor to inflation variation has grown over time: since 2001, it has more than doubled from the earlier period (1986–2000) and now accounts for 22 percent of inflation variation. It has explained about one-fifth and one-quarter of EMDE and advanced economy inflation variation, respectively, since 2001. Over the past five decades, an EMDE-specific factor has also become more prominent. The rising importance of these global and group-specific factors indicates that inflation synchronization has indeed become more broad-based over time.

These findings suggest three important avenues for future research. First, it is useful to examine the importance of the global factor over a

Figure 4. Contribution of Global Factor to Inflation Variation over Time

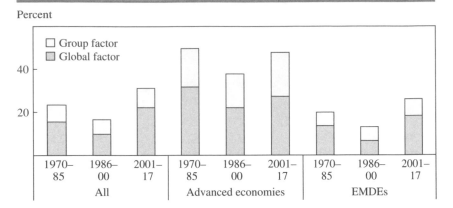

Percent

Source: Ha, Kose, and Ohnsorge (2019a).

Note: The contribution of global and group factors to inflation variance is estimated with the dynamic factor model over three subsample periods. The sample includes ninety-nine countries (twenty-five advanced economies and seventy-four EMDEs). Means or medians are unweighted. See Ha, Kose, and Ohnsorge (2019b) for more details on model estimation and results.

longer time period. Forbes reports that the global factor has become more important in explaining the CPI inflation over time by focusing on the post-1990 period. The results here indicate that in the first period (1970–85), the global factor was quite important probably because of multiple common shocks the world economy experienced. In the case of advanced economies, the global factor played even a more important role in the first period than it did in the last period, which witnessed much stronger global linkages.

Second, the importance of the global factor differs across country groups. The global factor plays a more important role in driving inflation in advanced economies than it does in EMDEs. This implies that one needs to take into account differences between country groups when studying the sources of inflation synchronization. In addition, it is important to consider the role of group-specific inflation cycles (cycles specific to advanced economies and those specific to EMDEs) to get a better understanding of the drivers of inflation. One interpretation of this finding is that China could be playing an increasingly more important role in driving inflation in other EMDEs because of its dominant role in commodity markets.

In this context, there is a need to have a stronger connection between the PCA exercise and the other two empirical frameworks used in the paper. The PCA is all about the variance of inflation but the other two frameworks are about the level of inflation. The results from the PCA suggest that the global factor has become more important over time in explaining the variance of CPI inflation but less important in the cases of core inflation and wage inflation. If the objective is to understand the variance share of inflation attributable to the global factor, then a different empirical framework should be set up in a way that the dependent variable is this variance share (and one can think of a number of explanatory variables).

However, Forbes takes a different approach by focusing on the level of inflation (in the last two frameworks) after presenting a rough connection between commodity price volatility and the fraction of inflation variance due to the global factor. It would be useful to conduct an empirical exercise to study the roles of globalization-related variables in explaining the inflation variance due to the global factor.

WHAT IS NEXT? Forbes provides a set of intriguing findings that will likely trigger future research in multiple directions. In addition to the specific items I discussed above, there are two additional areas for future work.

Understanding the roles played by country-specific features. Forbes presents a rich cross-country panel exercise. From the perspective of an individual country, these panel-based results are useful, but the big question, of course, is whether they are relevant for an individual country's own domestic inflation process. Future work can usefully consider some basic questions on the importance of country-specific characteristics in driving some of the headline findings in the paper: Do we see a larger impact of global variables in economies with inflation targeting? Do we see a larger impact of the global factors in commodity importers? How do the forces of globalization affect cross-border spillovers of inflation in different groups of countries (advanced economies versus EMDEs)?

Explaining divergence. Forbes presents a truly striking finding: global factors have become more important for CPI inflation over time but have not become important for core inflation, with mixed evidence for wage inflation. It would be useful to explore the divergence of these results across different inflation measures in future work.

REFERENCES FOR THE KOSE COMMENT

Caceres, Carlos, Yan Carrière-Swallow, and Bertrand Gruss. 2016. "Global Financial Conditions and Monetary Policy Autonomy." IMF Working Paper 16/108.Washington: International Monetary Fund. https://www.imf. org/en/Publications/WP/Issues/2016/12/31/Global-Financial-Conditions-and-Monetary-Policy-Autonomy-43943.

Dincer, N. Nergiz, and Barry Eichengreen. 2014. "Central Bank Transparency and Independence: Updates and New Measures." *International Journal of Central Banking* 10, no. 1: 189–259.

Ha, Jongrim, M. Ayhan Kose, and Franziska L. Ohnsorge. 2019a. *Inflation in Emerging and Developing Economies: Evolution, Drivers, and Policies.* Washington: World Bank. https://www.worldbank.org/en/research/publication/inflation-in-emerging-and-developing-economies.

Ha, Jongrim, M. Ayhan Kose, and Franziska L. Ohnsorge. 2019b. "Global Inflation Synchronization." Working Paper 8768. Washington: World Bank. http://documents.worldbank.org/curated/en/733211551994244422/pdf/WPS8768.pdf.

GENERAL DISCUSSION   Eswar Prasad suggested an analysis using subindexes of the Consumer Price Index (CPI). The subindexes related to traded goods should capture more of the effects of globalization than service price indexes. He acknowledged that disaggregated data might be more inaccurate, as in the case of Argentina, but noted that nonetheless disaggregating and looking at the subindexes might uncover some useful insights. He wondered whether the co-movement of inflation is only seen when inflation is falling. He questioned how big of a role the characteristics of a country play into the results of the paper, specifically, the role of commodity prices in larger economies. He suggested weighted regressions to control for the role that commodity prices might play in the economies of large and advanced countries.

Peter Henry echoed some of the comments in Ayhan Kose's discussion to expand the framing to include policy shocks. He referenced a paper by Dornbusch and Fischer which found that policy shocks are important in understanding inflation dynamics, particularly for emerging markets in the last 30 years.[1] He noted that it would be useful to include country-specific time series around global policy shocks such as shocks to the global value chain. This addition would help to analyze the transmission mechanism through specific variables, considering that countries have different policy regimes and react differently to various shocks.

Ben Bernanke noted that in 2008 oil prices were very high before falling. Considering this, he asked Forbes what the motivation and narrative was for her results around the financial crisis period. The results showed that international factors were important in 2008 and 2010. He asked Forbes whether she was motivated by the idea that inflation did not

---

1. Rudiger Dornbusch and Stanley Fischer, "Moderate Inflation," *World Bank Economic Review* 7, no. 1 (1993): 1–44.

fall as much as the recession metrics suggested. Next Bernanke questioned Kose on whether disinflation in the United States in the 1980s influenced inflation globally, and if so, how. After a trend of high inflation, the United States saw disinflation in the 1980s under Volcker. There was then a decline in inflation globally.

Frederic Mishkin stated that one of the most interesting results in the paper is that global factors are less important for core inflation, given that central banks—in particular the Federal Reserve—have focused more on core inflation. The implication of this specific result is that the Federal Open Markets Committee's (FOMC) frameworks—which do not place much importance on global factors—are correct. Second, he noted that a theory is needed when evaluating whether the Phillips curve is "alive or dead." Many people recently, including participants of the FOMC, have argued that the Phillips Curve is dead or flat. Mishkin argued that the curve is alive and well but just hidden. The main cause of a hidden curve, he reasoned, is that monetary policy in recent years has been doing its job properly and has stabilized inflation.

Mishkin stated that when monetary policy is stabilizing inflation, then when there is a positive shock to inflation, central banks will tighten monetary policy. This will cause the unemployment rate to go up and create an upward bias in estimates of the slack coefficient, resulting in an estimated slack coefficient that is biased toward zero. He noted that when monetary policy is not doing its job properly and is not stabilizing inflation, as in the late 1960s and 1970s, this bias won't be present and then the estimated slack coefficient is large and negative. On the other hand, when the Federal Reserve moved toward a focus on stabilizing inflation in the mid-1980s and afterward, the bias toward zero would become large, so these large coefficients disappear. Thus the fact that estimated slack coefficients were large and negative before the mid-1980s and then declined to near zero afterward strongly suggests that the Phillips curve still exists.

Mishkin remarked that Phillips curve estimates for wage inflation, in comparison with price inflation, are less likely to be biased toward zero because the endogeneity of monetary policy affects wages much less than it affects prices. The fact that wage Phillips curves have larger, more negative slack coefficients than price Phillips curves provides further evidence that the Phillips curve is not dead. In addition, when evaluating state and local data there are limited endogenous effects of monetary policy; thus the finding that the slack variable on the subnational level is significant and does not change much with policy also provides support

for the Phillips curve being alive. For international factors, these endogeneity effects are less likely to be less present. All in all, this evidence
suggests that the Phillips curve is still active. Mishkin cautioned that
believing that the Phillips curve is dead could lead to serious monetary
policy mistakes.

Jordi Galí noted that it is understandable that the channels through
which global factors affect energy inflation or imported inflation differ
from those that affect core domestic inflation. The real challenge and the
need for analysis is to understand the latter. When evaluating how global
factors affect core domestic inflation, he commented, it is not optimal
to look only at the core inflation defined in Forbes's analysis as this measure includes imported goods. In addition, he suggested that Forbes think
carefully about the measure of slack used in her analysis. For example, he
remarked, in models with monopolistic competition and price rigidities,
the driver of inflation is markup misalignment—the gap between average
markups and desired markups. Alternative measures of slack that focus
on markups can be useful in interpreting the results and understanding
the channels through which global factors operate.

Narayana Kocherlakota recommended looking at the models that
central banks use to make policy. In these models, the endogenous
response of policy to inflation is stripped out of the equation. In the
model of the U.S. economy constructed by the Federal Reserve (the FRB/
US model) the Phillips curve is very flat. When analyzing the policy
choices and errors that have resulted from these models, it can be argued
that the Phillips curve should be even flatter than presented in the FRB/
US model. Similarly, it can be argued that the FRB/US model does not
consider global factors. One can then ask about the ramifications of
incorrectly using global factors in the FRB/US model's calculations
of the Phillips curve. For example, he wondered whether such incorrect specifications have led to monetary policy mistakes. Similarly, he
pondered whether inflation would have been closer to target or farther
away from target. Lastly, he questioned whether there would have been
different outcomes had those constructing the FRB/US model considered
global factors.

Justin Wolfers focused on a table in the appendix which contained the
list of countries used in the analysis. He noted that the sample of countries
includes thirty-one advanced countries and twelve emerging countries.
He commented that although Forbes describes the paper as "the world," the
small amount of emerging market economies in the sample is not representative. Furthermore, of the thirty-one advanced counties, twenty-four

are European countries. He remarked that because the sample is largely European it is not surprising that the results show common factors affecting inflation during this period. For example, sixteen of the thirty-one countries use the euro, and within this group five of them adopted the euro over the sample period. He commented that this sample choice explains why there are common factors in the analysis that gain importance over time.

John Haltiwanger commented that the volatility of commodity prices might play a bigger role than stated. The commodities that have high volatility are basic industrial inputs and metals. Although commodities may not be the whole story, the endogenous transmission of commodity prices may be reflected in other variables.

Richard Cooper stated that Western macroeconomics did not pay much attention to inflation in the '50s, '60s, and early '70s. Starting in the '80s, inflation was brought down, mainly attributable to Volcker. Cooper wondered how this experience has influenced the thinking in governments and central banks about inflation. He noted that this question can be investigated by evaluating how the International Monetary Fund's (IMF) Article IV consultations have changed over time. The same analysis can be completed with the World Bank's advice about inflation to emerging markets and developing countries. Cooper hypothesized that the results of doing such an analysis would show that since the late 1970s there has been greater emphasis on inflation targeting and the independence of central banks when compared with the earlier periods.

Olivier Blanchard urged Forbes to consider further analysis of heterogeneity across countries. There would be different transmission mechanisms for countries depending on if they had fixed or variable exchange rates. Blanchard also emphasized Kose's suggestion to use a measure of openness in the analysis.

James Stock recommended the Goldfeld and Blinder paper that discusses how the flattening of the Phillips curve could be a result of endogenous policy.[2]

Forbes thanked the participants for their comments and intended to follow up with the commenters on those comments she would not have time to address. On Stock's recommendation of the Goldfeld and Blinder paper, Forbes noted that it is impressive how many Brookings papers there are on many of these topics. At one point, she was referred to a

2. Stephen M. Goldfeld and Alan S. Blinder, "Some Implications of Endogenous Stabilization Policy," *Brookings Papers on Economic Activity*, no. 3 (1972): 585–640.

Gordon paper on inflation in a certain year but there were multiple papers by Gordon on inflation in that same year.[3]

Addressing a major theme in the comments about identifying country variation within the results, Forbes noted that she had looked at aspects of this through her sensitivity analyses. In one set of tests, she controls for openness by country and interacts openness with some of the elastic variables. She noted that the empirical analysis of these sensitivity tests would require its own paper. If such a further paper were to be written, she noted, it should include how the country-specific characteristics change the results and interact with the channels described.

Forbes acknowledged Wolfers's comment about the sample containing a majority of advanced economies. Forbes performed sensitivity tests without euro countries and the results remained consistent. She noted that it is difficult to focus on emerging market economies due to the lack of data for those countries. She remarked that when focusing on only emerging markets the results are inconsistent. Because of this, she did not focus on them in her paper or discussion. Forbes recommended some of Kose's work on developing countries because it includes a larger sample of emerging markets.

Responding to comments about the Phillips curve, Forbes noted that her analysis both shows that the Phillips curve still exists and shows evidence of nonlinearity. She commented that because there are already several papers providing evidence of this nonlinearity, she does not focus on it in her analysis.

Lastly, Forbes touched on the results for wages where she found that globalization was not as important. She had found these results surprising, and other empirical work has found mixed evidence that globalization matters for wage dynamics. She noted that there may be other techniques and models that could be helpful, such as evaluating different channels of globalization. There could also be lagged inflation effects that might not be captured. Regardless, she observed that it is important to acknowledge the non-results for wages as that might have an impact on the central banks' response to the various inflation metrics.

---

3. The specific paper she was referred to is Robert J. Gordon, "World Inflation and Monetary Accommodation in Eight Countries," *Brookings Papers on Economic Activity*, no. 2 (1977): 409–68.

FEDERICO STURZENEGGER
Universidad de San Andrés

Macri's Macro: The Elusive Road to Stability and Growth

ABSTRACT   This paper reviews the various macroeconomic stabilization programs implemented during the Macri government between 2015 and 2019. After an initial success, each program was discontinued because of a distinct form of fiscal dominance: as pensions are indexed with a lag and represent a large portion of spending, quick disinflations jeopardize fiscal consolidation. Thus, lack of progress on the fiscal front was the fundamental reason why the objective of macroeconomic stability remained elusive.

> Whenever I visit a country, they always say: "You don't understand, Professor Dornbusch, here it is different . . ." Well, it never is.
> —Professor Rudi Dornbusch to his students, as recalled by the author

O n December 10, 2015, Mauricio Macri was sworn in as president of Argentina. Macri was an unexpected character for such a position: an outsider coming from Argentina's business elites who had left that coveted world to become first the president of a popular soccer team and later the mayor of the city of Buenos Aires. His own personal story of change symbolized what he wished for his country: a change that was expected to reverse Argentina's decades-long decline.

Note: The events in this paper are based on the recollection of the author, who served as the governor of the Central Bank of Argentina from December 2015 until June 2018.

Conflict of Interest Disclosure: The author served as governor of the Central Bank of Argentina from December 2015 until June 2018 and is professor of economics at Universidad de San Andrés and an adviser for Latus View, an investment firm. Beyond these affiliations, the author did not receive financial support from any firm or person for this paper or from any firm or person with a financial or political interest in this paper. He is currently not an officer, director, or board member of any organization with an interest in this paper. No outside party had the right to review this paper before circulation. The views expressed in this paper are those of the author and do not necessarily reflect those of Universidad de San Andrés or Latus View.

339

Macri's presidency sparked interest worldwide. The soft-spoken Macri, emphasizing moderation, empathy, and democratic values, had dethroned a 14-year hold on power by the Peronist party. His fight had been that of a kind word against an aggressive state machine with plenty of resources, David versus Goliath. As Argentina slid closer to becoming a more authoritarian left-wing populist country, the world gazed on in awe. Argentina, a member of the G-20, could transform the political spectrum throughout the region. Thus, Macri's triumph, which reversed course, was received with a sense of relief.

The same sense of relief and quiet optimism was shared by Argentina's population, as well as by Macri's team. The program they had set up envisioned a baseline annual growth rate of 3 percent, though deep down they believed this was a conservative number. Inflation would gradually come down, and they expected it to be around 5 percent by the end of Macri's first term. As a result of this combination, real wages would have increased and populism would have been proven wrong.

Yet by the end of Macri's presidency, things had turned out very differently. Output had actually decreased by more than 4 percent (close to 8 percent in per capita terms), and inflation had added nearly 300 percent to the price level. By the end of the term, nobody could help feeling a sense of frustration. Should things not have turned out much better? Did things work out so badly because necessary measures were too painful and were not tackled? Was what happened the result of external factors? Was it the result of self-inflicted mistakes? Was it an unavoidable consequence of the situation the government had inherited? Or was it confirmation that Argentina is a lost cause and will never overcome its problems? This paper attempts to shed some light on these questions.

The paper proceeds as follows. Section I begins with an analysis of the initial conditions. My conclusion is that the starting point was worse than expected and perceived at the time. Section II discusses the main components of the initial plan: a gradual fiscal adjustment, inflation targeting, and a floating exchange rate, together with the reasons why this plan was chosen. Section III, the core of the paper, discusses the first two years of the program, when inflation targeting was implemented. The results, on the one hand, were a consistent disinflation driven by expectations, at a pace that was comparable with other experiences but slower than expected and slower than the preestablished targets. Fiscal policy, on the other hand, suffered a large initial worsening relative to the plan. The subsequent efforts at fiscal consolidation were not enough and led to a collision with the stabilization program. This collision was not the result of an attempt to secure more resources from the Central Bank (BCRA) but rather the result of a disagreement with the speed of disinflation: its fast pace jeopardized fiscal convergence because half of government spending is indexed backward. Section IV discusses the unraveling of the program, which started with changing the inflation targets at the end of 2017, leading to a series of successive crises that lasted until the elections, almost two years later. Section V endeavors to draw some lessons. My main conclusion is that the program failed because an excessively lax fiscal policy led to a conflict with the Central Bank that resulted in weaker monetary institutions, which, in turn, sent the economy into turmoil. In a paradoxical twist, it was the embracing of populist fiscal policy that undermined the administration's efforts to prove populism wrong.

I. Initial Conditions

Perhaps a good way to start is to review the conditions inherited by the incoming government at the end of 2015. The inheritance included four years of stagnation, a large and growing budget deficit, persistent high inflation, exchange rate controls that had led to a black market exchange rate trading at a large premium relative to the official rate, utility prices that had been frozen in spite of high inflation, and lack of reliable statistics. On the positive side, the current account deficit was not too large, though it had been growing. Table 1 shows the starting points of these variables, among others.

The issue of debt levels requires discussion, given that it was the centerpiece of the debate on the legacy left by the previous government. The previous administration argued that it had managed to achieve a dramatic reduction in the level of debt-to-GDP and, particularly, in the debt owed to private creditors. This was supported by official data as shown in figure 1 ("Gross debt with private creditors as defined by the government") and in table 1 ("Official debt").

Yet, I believe that some adjustments should be made, as some of the changes in debt levels came hand in hand with changes in the government's assets or liabilities, creating a different dynamic on the government's net worth. For example, in 2014 the government issued about US$ 6.2 billion in government bonds to purchase a 51 percent equity stake in the oil company (YPF).[1] However, this debt increase came with a simultaneous growth

1. Resolution 26/2014 of the Secretariat of Finance (Ministry of Finance). The purchase of 51 percent of YPF occurred when the price of West Texas intermediate (WTI) was US$ 101 per barrel. Five years later, the market value of that 51 percent was just US$ 3.7 billion.

Table 1. Initial Conditions

Variable	Inflation (%) Var: y/y[a]	GDP growth (%) Var: y/y[a]	Primary fiscal result % GDP	Current account % GDP	Official debt % GDP	Adjusted debt % GDP	Central Bank's net worth USD Bn[b]	Black market FX Premia Annual average
2011	22.80	6.00	0.20	-0.80	20.20	24.20	-32,642	5.90
2012	24.40	-1.00	-0.20	-0.20	19.00	23.00	-47,000	32.50
2013	27.80	2.40	-0.70	-2.00	20.00	27.00	-54,465	56.50
2014	40.20	-2.50	-0.80	-1.40	19.50	30.00	-70,552	38.20
2015	24.80	2.70	-3.80	-2.50	22.50	40.00	-92,971[c]	41.50[d]

Sources: Provincial Statistical Institutes and Congress CPI, INDEC, Ministry of Finance, BCRA, Bloomberg.

Notes: Inflation for 2011 and the first half of 2012 is an average between the San Luis Province CPI and Congress CPI; from the second half of 2012 to the end of 2015, an average between San Luis Province CPI and CABA CPI is used; CPI Dec/Dec variation. GDP growth is computed using the GDP measured in 2004 constant pesos. Fiscal result does not include Social Security Fund (FGS) and Central Bank transfers to the Treasury. Official debt refers to public debt with private creditors and international agencies. Adjusted debt is the author's elaboration; it is calculated as the official debt plus FGS's sovereign bonds, GDP warrants, debt with holdouts, and the Central Bank's securities, minus the Central Bank's net international reserves and the value of the shares held by the national government of the oil company YPF (nationalized in 2014).

[a] Year-on-year variation

[b] End of period

[c] As of December 9, 2015

[d] Until the liberalization of FX market

Figure 1. Adjusted Net Debt with Private Sector

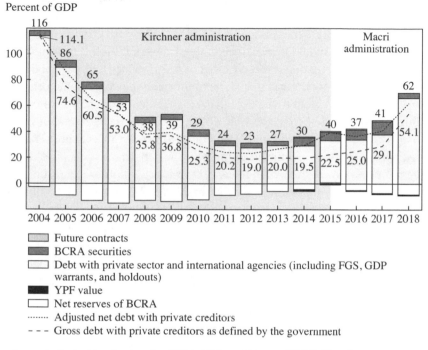

Percent of GDP

Future contracts
BCRA securities
Debt with private sector and international agencies (including FGS, GDP warrants, and holdouts)
YPF value
Net reserves of BCRA
······· Adjusted net debt with private creditors
- - - Gross debt with private creditors as defined by the government

Source: Author's elaboration based on BCRA, Ministry of Finance, INDEC, Bloomberg.

in assets and as such does not alter the government's net worth. In contrast, when the government nationalized the pension system, it absorbed the government debt that pension firms had accumulated over the previous decade, generating a sharp reduction in debt owed to third parties. But at the same time the government took over the liabilities with pensioners that this debt was supposed to finance. As a result, there was no change in net indebtedness (only a conversion from contractual debt into a government spending obligation). A third relevant adjustment to be considered is the role of the Central Bank's net reserves. If the government cancels debt using Central Bank reserves, it reduces both debt and assets, without a change in net worth. In fact, other countries report debt only net of Central Bank reserves.

Adjusting these changes in assets and liabilities is a difficult task. How should some of these liabilities be measured? For example, what is the net present value (NPV) of the future pensions that the government took over when it nationalized the pension system? Can they be defaulted more easily or less easily than contractual debt? Does this affect the value of this liability?[2]

In order to address these issues, I have made five corrections to the official account that should be relatively uncontroversial. First, I net out Central Bank net international reserves. Second, I consider that the liabilities assumed by the government at the time of the nationalization of the pension system were equivalent to the debt that was nationalized (and its rollover). Third, I add the debt from the U.S. dollar future contracts issued in 2015 (using the actual cost paid in 2016). Fourth, I net out the value of YPF's assets. And finally, I include an estimate of the debt to holdouts (also using the numbers agreed on in 2016 to cancel these obligations). The results are shown in the column "Adjusted debt" in table 1 and the different components are identified in figure 1.

These corrections show that, until 2012, there was a substantial reduction in debt as a result from a restructuring in 2005, economic growth, fiscal surpluses, and the appreciation of the real exchange rate. Yet starting in 2012 debt began to creep up again. In fact, between 2012 and 2015, the debt-to-GDP ratio had increased from 23 percent to 40 percent. In conclusion, while the levels of debt remained low, they had increased significantly in the four years prior to the change in government.

Even more striking is the evolution of the Central Bank's balance sheet. During the previous years, the government had systematically paid back debt using Central Bank reserves. In exchange, the government stashed U.S. dollar-denominated *letras intransferibles*, that is, nonnegotiable notes, in the Central Bank. These notes paid a below market rate and had a ten-year maturity. The first was due in 2016, although the budget law enacted in 2015 had extended this maturity an additional decade.[3] In short, the NPV of this bill was minimal at most and had zero liquidity. As a result, the quality of the Central Bank's balance sheet deteriorated very rapidly. Netting out the *letras intransferibles* and the domestic credit account (*adelantos transitorios*), the net worth of the Central Bank took a nosedive between 2006 and 2015, as shown in figure 2.

2. For a detailed discussion about this topic, see Levy-Yeyati and Sturzenegger (2007).
3. Law no. 27198.

Figure 2. Net Worth—Central Bank of Argentina

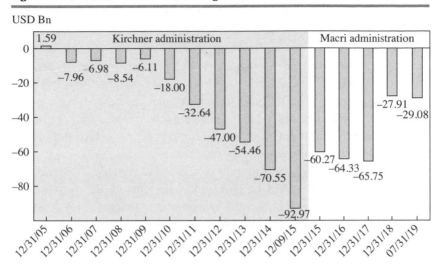

Source: BCRA.

II. The Plan and the Cleaning Up Phase

II.A. The Plan

During the year prior to taking office, a group of economists, businesspeople, and government officials gathered by Fundación Pensar, a think tank sponsored by Macri's political party, started working on a program in case Macri won the election. Only one constraint was imposed on the group: the reduction of the fiscal deficit had to be gradual. Beyond that limitation, the candidate left the team free to design the program as it seemed fit.

The definition of a "gradual" adjustment (*gradualism*, as it later became known) had both an economic and a political motivation. On the economic front, the consensus was that, as government debt was low, Argentina would be able to access international funding and that it is always better to smooth over economic adjustments.[4]

---

4. An early such approach was Thatcher's program of macroeconomic stabilization. Sargent (2013, 14) says: "A hallmark of Mrs. Thatcher's publicly announced strategy is gradualism . . . her government did not propose to execute any abrupt or discontinuous changes in aggregate government variables. . . . Instead, the Conservatives proposed to carry out a preannounced and gradual tightening of monetary and fiscal policies over a five-year period."

But the main goal was political. The Macri administration carried the stigma of being a right-wing or center-right party, and as such it was anticipated that it would kick off its government with a large fiscal and monetary adjustment. However, the political team thought it was essential to remove this stigma. The argument was that if the Macri administration was seen as a different political object, this would build political capital which would allow greater policy flexibility in turbulent times. In other words, while gradualism entailed the risk of increasing the level of debt during the initial years, it was also argued that not taking this path involved the risk of weaker political support later on.[5]

Despite this mandate, the program (summarized in table 2) envisioned an initial budget correction of 1.5 percent to 2 percent of GDP, mostly from a reduction of subsidies (universally considered too large), with a slowly declining deficit thereafter. The program envisaged an annual growth rate of about 3 percent. With a tax burden of the national government of around 20 percent (Argentine Ministry of Treasury 2018), this entailed a 0.6 percent of GDP increase in fiscal resources each year. Thus, to the extent that real expenditure remained constant, the government could expect to keep the deficit relatively stable, as the resources derived from growth would allow the absorption of the biggest fiscal challenge facing the government: the fact that, as inflation decelerated, the real value of pension spending would grow as a result of backward indexation. At any rate, the team expected growth to be faster, so a sense of (maybe unwarranted) easiness regarding fiscal results was transmitted.

On the monetary front, the team selected an inflation targeting regime. The speed of disinflation, however, was determined by the need to coordinate monetary and fiscal policy, and therefore constrained by the agreement that part of the fiscal deficit would be monetized to diminish the need for debt financing during the transition to a healthier fiscal result. (In addition, it was believed that the money printing agreed upon to finance the deficit should not be sterilized, given the weakness of the Central Bank's balance sheet.) Naturally, this led to the idea of establishing multiyear inflation targets that were set on the basis of the resources to be transferred in each year. In all, the program assumed that, over the four years of Macri's administration, inflation would add up to 73 percent (table 2), though it was expected to be below 5 percent toward the end of his term.

---

5. The previous center-right experience, the de la Rúa presidency, had indeed started with a quick attempt at fiscal consolidation, which had met universal criticism. De la Rúa resigned just two years into his term.

Table 2. The Predictions of the Fundación Pensar Team in June 2015

Variable	Units		2015	2016	2017	2018	2019
GDP growth	%	Effective	2.7	-2.1	2.7	-2.5	-2.3
		Projected	2.0	1.0	4.0	3.0	3.0
Inflation	yoy average (%)	Effective	26.0	39.3	25.7	34.3	53.5
		Projected	28.5	38.2	12.5	6.9	4.1
Nominal exchange rate	USD vs. Arg $	Effective	9.3	14.8	16.6	28.1	48.2
		Projected	9.3	15.6	16.0	16.9	17.0
Primary deficit	% GDP	Effective[a]	-3.8	-4.2	-3.8	-2.6	-0.4
		Effective[b]	-3.8	-5.4	-4.1	-2.6	-0.4
		Projected	-4.6	-2.5	-2.5	-2.4	-2.2
Monetary base growth	Arg $ Mn	Effective	161,325	197,775	179,449	407,864	313,528
		Projected	163,600	94,972	81,508	59,337	43,527
Monetary base growth	%	Effective	40.5	26.6	24.7	36.0	28.9
		Projected	35.4	15.3	11.3	7.4	5.1
Financial assistance of Central Bank to the Treasury	Arg $ Mn	Effective[c]	158,524	159,997	150,000	30,500	394,245
		Effective[d]	158,524	136,098	122,526	-21,285	317,000
		Projected[c]	158,524	94,972	81,508	59,337	43,527
Financial assistance of Central Bank to the Treasury	% GDP	Effective[c]	2.7	1.9	1.4	0.2	1.8
		Effective[d]	2.7	1.7	1.2	-0.1	1.5
		Projected[c]	2.8	1.2	0.9	0.6	0.4
Official reserves of the Central Bank	USD Mn	Effective	25,563	39,308	55,055	65,806	43,785
		Projected	25,766	27,888	38,198	51,339	66,084
Nonmonetary liabilities of the Central Bank	% GDP	Effective	7.0	8.5	10.9	5.0	4.6
		Projected	7.0	7.6	9.1	11.1	12.8
Current account	USD Mn	Effective	-17,622	-15,105	-31,598	-28,002	-7,500
		Projected	-7,605	-11,958	-12,363	-16,289	-22,361

Source: Author's elaboration based on INDEC, BCRA, and Ministry of Finance. Data for 2019 for the year, except reserves, monetary growth, and nonmonetary liabilities of the Central Bank, which go through December 15, 2019, the end of Macri's term.
[a] Primary deficit including resources obtained from tax amnesty
[b] Primary deficit excluding resources obtained from tax amnesty
[c] Gross financial assistance to the Treasury
[d] Financial assistance to the Treasury net of the interest generated by the government bonds held by the BCRA

It was also agreed that Argentina would pursue a floating exchange rate regime. The consensus on this was a legacy of Argentina's trauma over the final period of convertibility, a fixed exchange rate regime that had lasted a decade, between 1991 and 2001. While very successful in its initial years, its inability to adjust relative prices after the 1998 Russian default had plunged the economy into a four-year-long crisis that ended with a banking crisis and a dramatic fall in output. In addition, international experience had enshrined floating rates as the agreed upon standard, due to their ability to smooth out external shocks and deliver higher growth and lower volatility in output.[6]

In all, table 2 shows what the program envisioned at the start of the government (in italics), and what actually happened. The rest of this paper attempts to explain why the divergence was so big.

II.B. Capital Controls Liberalization

At the outset, the government faced significant challenges: net international reserves were negative, there were no liquid reserves to tap, and, as the government had campaigned on the promise to unify the exchange rate, both the market and exporters were expecting a depreciation of the currency, so exports had decreased sharply.[7] Any attempt to delay a solution would have just postponed facing the issue, while the government would lose momentum and renege on one of its fundamental campaign promises. D-day was decided for a week later, December 17.

The relaxation of capital controls was not only a matter of economic freedom but also of economic efficiency. It eliminated a heavy burden on exporters and normalized their trade relationships: since they were not forced to convert their foreign proceeds into local currency almost immediately, they were able to offer credit to their clients abroad.

It was decided that capital controls would be lifted not suddenly but gradually. Two main reasons supported the view that a gradual relaxation should be undertaken. First, there was no clear idea of how money demand would react after four years of capital controls and forced peso savings.

---

6. There is extensive literature on the relative benefits of fixed versus floating rates. See, for example, Levy-Yeyati and Sturzenegger (2001, 2003, 2005, 2007, 2016), Di Giovanni and Shambaugh (2008), Schmitt-Grohé and Uríbe (2012), and Calvo and Reinhart (2002).

7. On December 10, 2015, the first day of the new government, the Board of the Central Bank was about to approve a bank and exchange rate holiday, a move that was quickly averted by the incoming (not yet appointed) authorities. Commercial banks agreed to operate as a de facto exchange rate rationing mechanism until the controls could be dismantled. This allowed for a transition without disruptions in the functioning of the financial sector.

Second, there was allegedly a large stock of pending import payments and dividend distributions to be made. Nobody was sure to what extent this was true or not, or how real these requests were, but they posed a latent risk. In addition, to make the whole picture complete, net reserves were negative (see figure 9, panel b).

The desired impact on expectations would be achieved with two features: all commercial flows would be freed immediately and no authorization would be required to buy foreign exchange (FX) for up to US$ 2 million per month. This number was so unexpected (some analysts expected the government to allow buying in the tens of thousands) that the team believed it would create the perception of a substantial change. Requests to pay for previous imports would be authorized gradually over time and were queued according to the original request day. The freeing of the demand for this purpose was expected to be fully completed by midyear.

At the same time, the Central Bank forced banks to sell their net FX exposure to the Central Bank on December 16, the day prior to the unification, allowing them to repurchase this exposure on December 17, only after the jump in the exchange rate. This implied a gain of about 7 billion pesos (1.2 percent of the money base) and served to compensate, at least partially, the losses the Central Bank was expecting from a large stock of dollar future liabilities accumulated in the previous administration.[8] Simultaneously, floors in deposit rates and ceilings in lending rates were removed.

D-day was December 17. The night before, the Central Bank made an agreement with the People's Bank of China for an immediate disbursement of a US$ 3.1 billion loan by converting the equivalent amount of yuan from a currency swap into U.S. dollars.[9] In addition, grain exporters (who had hoarded grain in expectation of the exchange rate unification) had offered to sell US$ 330 million per day on the market for three weeks, a very significant amount considering that the FX market operated at only about double this amount.[10]

Net reserves were negative, and liquid resources available to the Central Bank that day were just a mere US$ 400 million. The market opened at 13.90 ARS/USD and closed at ARS 13.30, a price between the

8. See the BCRA's balance sheet for 2016, note 4.23.11.
9. See BCRA communication P50675.
10. See press conference https://www.youtube.com/watch?v=1RcVAMJAjMM and also https://www.lanacion.com.ar/politica/el-gobierno-elimina-el-cepo-y-anticipa-una-devaluacion-del-orden-del-40-nid1854962.

previous official price of ARS 9.83 and the black market price of approximately ARS 15.[11] The Central Bank did not intervene that day, nor in the following days, when the exchange rate moved freely around this value. In all, this was regarded as an unexpected first success of the government.

II.C. Futures, Holdouts, and Initial Steps in Monetary Policy

The Central Bank also faced the challenge that the previous government had sold a sizable number of future contracts falling due throughout June 2016 at off-market prices. The Central Bank's short position on FX futures was approximately US$ 17,400 million, which, when comparing the fixing price and the informal exchange rate, delivered an expected cost of 62,750 million pesos (11.2 percent of the monetary base).[12]

Two things alleviated the burden. On the one hand, ROFEX, which was the market that traded these contracts, unilaterally decided to change the terms of contracts signed after September 29, 2015 (it was assumed that after this date participants had engaged only for "speculative reasons").[13] This reduced the cost by about 11,085 million pesos. The cost of operations conducted over the counter by banks was partially compensated by purchasing the banks' FX position described above, which saved an additional 6.9 billion. All in all, the costs were reduced by nearly 18,000 million pesos, and the total effective cost of these futures for the BCRA ended at 53,719 million pesos (9.6 percent of the monetary base).[14]

At the same time, the government set out to solve the long-pending issue of Argentina's default. The saga had reached a dead end a few years earlier with a ruling in favor of the holdouts on the basis of a pari passu clause that precluded payments to current debt if payments were not made in full to holdouts. This had motivated the previous administration to default on the entire debt. The Treasury started working on this issue and reached an agreement in April. Given the complexity of this negotiation, the details are deferred to online appendix 1 of this paper. The overall

---

11. See https://www.ambito.com/economia/primera-operacion-el-mulc-se-negocio-1390-us-1-millon-n3920252.

12. See BCRA (2016c, exhibit 8).

13. See Rofex Comunicación, no. 657. https://www.rofex.com.ar/upload/comunicaciones/Comunicaci%C3%B3n%20657%20-%20Declaraci%C3%B3n%20emergencia%20art%C3%ADculo%204%C2%B0%20Reglamento%20DLR.pdf.

14. See the BCRA's balance sheet for 2016, note 4.23.11, and BCRA (2016c, exhibits 7 and 8).

payment to settle with the holdouts amounted to US\$ 9.3 billion. Together with the removal of capital controls and the resolution of the futures issue, this entailed a significant normalization of the economy.

The Central Bank kicked off with a strongly contractionary monetary policy to ensure a managed removal of capital controls. Money demand was uncertain after four years of capital controls, but money supply also became difficult to pin down. At the end of each year, reserve requirements in Argentina were averaged for the period December–February. However, in December, banks had stockpiled an unusually large amount of liquidity in anticipation of a run on deposits (BCRA 2015). These resources had not been used, given that the transition was smoother than expected, so they found themselves covering most of the reserve requirements through February. The result was that money supply in January and February could grow significantly, as the unused excess reserves in December could be allowed to run down reserve requirements in the following two months.

Somewhat unaware of this, in January and February, the Central Bank absorbed significant amounts of money at decreasing interest rates, misreading the fall in interest rates, while contracting the monetary base, as an improvement in credibility. So, while the Central Bank absorbed 25 percent of the money base, it allowed the interest rate to fall significantly (from 38 percent to 30.25 percent). The result was an immediate reaction of the exchange rate, which moved from 13.55 to 15.91.[15] Attempts to smooth the exchange rate spike by using reserves (which had started to grow since the relaxation of exchange rate controls) were not successful and were quelled only when interest rates were increased to 38 percent at the beginning of March.

By then, the real amount of money had fallen by 16 percent, substantially more than what the government had anticipated. In hindsight, monetary policy should have been significantly tighter in these first months (yet this mistake in the initial months of the year would be repeated again in 2017, 2018, and 2019!). At any rate, the difficulties of these first months convinced the authorities that assessing money demand and supply movements would be too difficult and that a mechanism should be quickly implemented to smooth out these large swings.

During those initial months, inflation rates registered an increase of 5.0 percent in December, 3.8 percent in January, 3.4 percent in February,

---

15. Data for the exchange rate can be found at http://www.bcra.gov.ar/Pdfs/Publicaciones Estadisticas/com3500.xls.

3.2 percent in March, and 5.2 percent in April, this last spike the result of the government having decided to bundle most tariff adjustments in April.[16] Only after this did inflation decelerate.

III. The Inflation Targeting Regime

As a result of the difficulties of those first months, in March the Central Bank announced a convergence process to an inflation targeting (IT) regime. I organize the discussion of the regime around four main questions. First, was there a rationale for using inflation targeting in Argentina? Second, were the preconditions met to launch an IT regime? Third, what was the adequate speed of disinflation and how was it chosen? And finally, what were the results? On this last point, I discuss both the transmission mechanism and the policy response. I then briefly discuss the evolution of fiscal accounts and the Central Bank's balance sheet—two factors that built up tensions which ended up being relevant in the program's eventual undoing.

III.A. A Framework to Assess Inflation Targeting

A disinflation program requires a mechanism to coordinate expectations along the disinflation path. While consistent monetary and fiscal policies cannot be avoided, the alternatives include a plethora of possibilities: using the exchange rate as an anchor, using income policies, reverting to monetary aggregates targets, or the more conventional (at least at the time) framework of inflation targeting with floating exchange rates.

Recent experience shows that the instruments chosen vary across countries. Of the twenty-one countries that, having experienced inflation rates above 20 percent, implement an IT regime with a floating rate today (including Argentina at the time), nine chose to disinflate with a floating exchange rate, while twelve used an additional anchoring mechanism on the convergence path. This second group always used the exchange rate as an anchor; with a few exceptions like Israel (Bufman and Leiderman 1998; Frenkel 1996; Maman and Rosenhek 2008) and Iceland (Guðmundsson and Kristinsson 1997; Matthiasson 2008) that also resorted to income policies (wage and price freezes) and the Slovak Republic (Beblavy 2002; Nagy 2016) which also targeted

---

16. Due to lack of official statistics at the federal level, these numbers are derived from the average between the consumer price indexes (CPIs) of the City of Buenos Aires and San Luis Province.

monetary aggregates targeting. Interestingly, all programs implemented after 2000, with the exception of Kazakhstan, were implemented using a floating regime. (See online appendix 2 for a detailed description.)

Consistent with the diversity of experiences, there is extensive literature discussing the merits and benefits of each alternative. Exchange rates typically help to quickly coordinate expectations, something that had already been tested in many successful stabilization episodes in the 1980s and early 1990s (convertibility in Argentina, the Plano Real in Brazil, or Israel's stabilization program).[17] In addition, a large body of literature suggests that exchange rate–based stabilizations lead to initial booms (Calvo and Végh 1993), thus helping build political support for reforms. Fixed exchange rates also provide a sign of commitment as well as an enforcement mechanism for fiscal discipline.

Barring the fact that using the exchange rate as an anchor requires holding sufficient reserves (or allowing a large initial depreciation), it also implies forgoing the exchange rate as a shock absorber, a trade-off between credibility and flexibility well understood in the literature on optimal currency areas and second generation currency crisis models. In fact, as countries improved the credibility of their macro frameworks, they increasingly relied on exchange rate flexibility as a shock absorber (Levy-Yeyati and Sturzenegger 2016). Thus, the question is to what extent policymakers were willing to forgo the initial benefits of exchange rate anchoring to build this adjustment mechanism. Tornell and Velasco (2000) turn on its head the notion of exchange rate anchoring as a credibility device. According to them, floating rates signal unsustainable policies earlier on, therefore providing stronger commitment incentives.

In the case of Argentina, I acknowledge, in Sturzenegger (2016a), these trade-offs and argue that it was worth paying the short-term costs of not having the initial boom and an easier coordination of expectations in order not to forgo the use of the exchange rate as a shock absorber, which was perceived as necessary to build a more resilient framework. Of course, the protracted recession of 1998–2001 under a fixed exchange rate weighed heavily in this conclusion. It was also believed that credibility would be enhanced by using a framework that was mainstream. This was also the reason why the use of incomes policies was discarded. In addition to the fact that among recent stabilization experiences it had

---

17. See, for example, Bruno and others (1988), Calvo and Végh (1999), and Fischer (2001).

been used only in two cases (one of which was Iceland, whose output performance had been poor; see figure 4). In addition to not being standard practice, incomes policies had been the bread and butter of recurrently failed populist experiences of yesteryear, making them an unattractive option.[18] The government also believed that it would dilute its power if it had to sustain an ongoing debate with the traditional political establishment at the decision table, more so if that decision table were to implement policies similar to those implemented by the previous administration, from which the current administration wanted to differentiate itself. Important in this assessment was that wage indexation, one of the main issues tackled by incomes policies, was forbidden, so wage negotiations could be forward-looking and, in fact, ended up being so (see footnote 33). At any rate, inflation and inflation expectations fell very quickly at the beginning of the program. Therefore, to the extent that incomes policies are suggested as a mechanism to help coordinate expectations, it seems this was not the main difficulty faced by the stabilization effort.[19]

Barring the use of the exchange rate and incomes policies, the team faced the alternative of using monetary aggregates or inflation targets as anchors (the latter implemented by using an interest rate policy). Frankel, Smit, and Sturzenegger (2008) help to understand some of the trade-offs involved. Consider an output equation that depends on demand and supply shocks (d and s), as well as on monetary shock ($m - m^d$):

$$y = d + s + \beta(m - m^d)$$

and an inflation equation, which also depends on the same three shocks:

$$\pi = m - m^d - \omega s + vd.$$

Here all shocks have zero mean, so the issue at stake is volatility (β, ω, and v are response parameters). Let us assume two possibilities: an

---

18. See Dornbusch and Edwards (1991) for a survey.

19. One point, however, where it may have helped, was that half of government spending was indexed to past inflation, therefore some sort of agreement as to how to deal with the impact of disinflation on actual spending would have been useful. This effect was disregarded.

IT regime where m is chosen to make $\pi = 0$, and another possibility—monetary aggregates—where $m = 0$. Under inflation targeting (assuming all covariances are equal to zero) we have:

$$\sigma_\pi^2 = 0$$

$$\sigma_y^2 = \sigma_d^2 (1 - \beta v)^2 + \sigma_s^2 (1 + \beta \omega)^2 ,$$

while under monetary aggregates, these volatilities are:

$$\sigma_\pi^2 = \sigma_{m^d}^2 + \omega^2 \sigma_s^2 + v^2 \sigma_d^2$$

$$\sigma_y^2 = \sigma_d^2 + \sigma_s^2 + \beta^2 \sigma_{m^d}^2 .$$

Inflation targeting delivers a more stable inflation, obviously, but output volatility depends on the relative strength of supply shocks (which an IT regime amplifies) and demand and money demand shocks (which an IT regime smoothes).

I confront this basic framework with the data in the following way. In order to identify the volatility in money demand, I look at periods of constant interest rates in various IT regimes. Given that money supply is endogenous, changes in money stock can only be associated with changes in money demand, so this procedure provides a valid identification mechanism for money demand shocks.[20] In order to avoid volatility arising from seasonality, I take the period in which this identification can be made in Argentina and compare it to similar periods for other countries where this condition is also met. For supply shocks, I use the volatility in the prices of regulated goods, assuming that this is a valid proxy for changes in the supply conditions of these goods. The results are summarized in table 3, which shows that Argentina exhibits an unusually high volatility both in money demand and in supply shocks.

The fact that *both* shocks are larger in Argentina means that we cannot reach a conclusion on the relative benefits of either regime, though this makes clear that dealing with the volatility of money demand presents a

---

20. While there are several estimates of money demand—see, for example, Benati and others (2016), Gay (2005), Aguirre, Burdisso, and Grillo (2006), Ahumada and Garegnani (2002)—we believe this approach avoids the need to side with a specific specification.

Table 3a. Money Demand Volatility Compared across Countries

$\sigma_{Ln(M_2/P)}$	Country	Years
0.0431	Argentina	2016–17
0.0416	Peru	2011–12
0.0325	Peru	2004–5
0.0285	Chile	2012–13
0.0282	Chile	2002–3
0.0223	Chile	2017–18
0.0186	U.S.	2010–11
0.0180	Brazil	2015–16
0.0177	Peru	2012–13
0.0160	Chile	2014–15
0.0159	Colombia	2014–15
0.0158	Mexico	2009–10
0.0157	Mexico	2010–11
0.0119	Mexico	2014–15
0.0105	U.S.	2011–12
0.0102	Mexico	2011–12
0.0081	U.S.	2012–13
0.0080	U.S.	2013–14
0.0076	U.S.	2014–15
0.0059	U.S.	2009–10

Source: Author's elaboration based on the statistical institutes and central banks of the respective countries.

Notes: The table compares the standard error of M_2/P across different Latin American countries and the United States for comparable periods of stable monetary policy rate since 2000. The comparison is established for the same months in which the monetary policy rate was fixed in Argentina, that is, from December 2016 to March 2017 and from May 2017 to October 2017.

Table 3b. Regulated Price Volatility Compared across Countries, 2016–18

	$\sigma_{Ln(Reg. Prices/CPI)}$	
Country	Housing, water, electricity, gas, and other fuels	Transport
Argentina	0.1307	0.0428
Brazil	0.0596[a]	0.0087
Peru	0.0319[a]	0.0091
Mexico	0.0198	0.0412
Chile	0.0155	0.0136
U.S.	0.0095	0.0178
Colombia	0.0081	0.0227

Sources: National statistical institutes of the respective countries.

Notes: The table compares the volatility in the ratio of regulated prices to the headline consumer price index for the same countries from 2016 to 2018. It uses the COICOP standardized division in the countries in which it is available; for the cases of Brazil and Peru, the categories used are fuels and transport, as defined by their national statistical institutes.

[a] Only fuels

particular challenge in Argentina.[21] Regarding supply shocks, they were very high in 2016 but were about half as much in 2017, when they were more in line with those of other countries.[22] The large size of supply shocks and the challenge they posed to the IT framework were mentioned repeatedly.

While the benefits of smoothing over monetary shocks are clear, a drawback of an IT regime is that the inflation rate is not under full control of the authorities, so transitory shocks that deviate inflation from the trajectory have a more detrimental effect on credibility than in a monetary aggregates regime, as it is more difficult to assess if monetary authorities are sufficiently committed to fighting inflation.[23] This credibility effect would later turn out to be a drawback.

Another weakness of the regime arises from the fact that money supply is endogenous, so if expectations are not tamed, the inflation process remains unanchored unless there is a strong policy reaction.[24] While inflation expectations declined almost constantly during the IT regime and signaled disinflation going forward, they also remained above the inflation targets, undermining credibility.

III.B. Preconditions for Inflation Targeting

The challenges of implementing IT starting at high inflations are not unknown and in fact have been the source of much debate. Mishkin and Schmidt-Hebbel (2002) discuss at length the mitigating factors for the risk of credibility losses, which are likely to occur during the disinflation path. In particular, they suggest four ways of dealing with these issues: (a) a gradual formalization of inflation targeting over time, (b) a path of disinflation with multiyear targets, (c) avoiding a range in the inflation targets,

---

21. Money demand is particularly volatile in Argentina because twice a year, salaries receive a 50 percent extra payment, leading to large seasonal swings, and public sector deposits are a relatively large fraction of the financial sector and exhibit substantial volatility. Financial innovation, incentivized by the Central Bank itself, led to a sizable fall in the demand for cash, compounding the volatility in base money demand.

22. During the first four months of 2016, electricity prices were increased by 250 percent, natural gas prices by 195 percent, water distribution by 300 percent, and transportation by 100 percent (BCRA 2016a).

23. An alternative view is that inflation targeting must be understood as "flexible inflation targeting," meaning that an inflation shock does not need to be reversed later on. In this case, supply shocks need not elicit the reaction assumed in the previous model, as a deviation arising from a supply shock is just explained and not necessarily undone, tilting the balance even more so in favor of inflation targeting. However, if these shocks are larger than expected and require permanent explanations for the deviation from targets, they eventually undermine credibility, a feature that was underestimated.

24. See Sargent and Wallace (1975), Cochrane (2011), and Neumeyer and Nicolini (2011).

and (d) having a reasonable pace of disinflation. The Central Bank tried to take into consideration these recommendations by initially allowing for a transition to IT, though it was announced it would be short (less than a year), and by setting multiyear targets with a pace associated to the agreed upon transfers to the Treasury.[25] Contrary to the recommendation, a range was established, which in fact became useless, as expectations converged on the upper bound (this was changed briefly in 2018).[26]

There is extensive literature that also discusses the conditions required for effective inflation targeting.[27] Among these, the typical five pillars are the absence of other nominal anchors, an institutional commitment to price stability, the absence of fiscal dominance, Central Bank autonomy, and policy transparency and accountability.[28]

The team believed that to coordinate expectations it was necessary for the Central Bank to take ownership of the fight against inflation and to be totally committed to that objective. Regarding the absence of other nominal anchors, there is substantial consensus that this works well once economies have reached their long-term inflation objectives (Agénor and Pereira da Silva 2019), but as to the need to use another anchor during the disinflation phase, opinions are divided. As discussed in the previous section, there were roughly as many countries that deemed it necessary to have an additional anchor (typically the exchange rate) as countries that did not share this view. In the case of Argentina, this debate lingered throughout the IT regime, particularly because of the relevant role that was ascribed to the exchange rate in setting prices and inflation expectations. The Central Bank argued the opposite: that in order to lower pass-through levels it was important for the Central Bank to state that it did not care about the exchange rate at all (Sturzenegger 2016b). I will confront these two views with the data below.[29]

25. The Central Bank of Argentina announced in detail the transition to IT in a conference on April 28, 2016; see http://www.bcra.gov.ar/Pdfs/Prensa_comunicacion/Presentacion PoliticasMonetarias2016.pdf.

26. One issue was specific to Argentina: when the program was launched, there were no official inflation statistics, as the inflation numbers had been significantly tampered with and the new authorities were trying to relaunch a credible inflation statistic. The first available number came in May. Prior to that, the inflation rate of the City of Buenos Aires and San Luis Province were used.

27. See Masson, Savastano, and Sharma (1997), Mishkin (2000), and Mishkin and Savastano (2001).

28. For a recent review of these issues, see Agénor and Pereira da Silva (2019).

29. There is also literature on the role of FX in the reaction function. See Morón and Winkelried (2005), Céspedes, Chang, and Velasco (2014), De Paoli (2009), Garcia, Restrepo, and Roger (2011), and Pourroy (2012).

By allowing a floating rate and committing to inflation as the main priority of the Central Bank while implementing policy transparency and accountability (well-defined targets, prescheduled communiqués, and press conferences), the authorities thought most of the preconditions were met. Fiscal dominance was contained by anticipating a path for transfers from the Central Bank to the government, and while these announcements initially met little credibility, it built up pretty quickly as the government stuck to the framework. One important flaw, which would eventually turn lethal, was that the regime lacked Central Bank independence, as the president could easily remove the Central Bank governor. The team believed that an institutional framework was not enough to offer protection from the lack of consistent fiscal and monetary policies, so they relied on delivering results to strengthen their independence, postponing an institutional improvement to a later time when it would also be more sustainable (I will argue below that this was a mistake).

What can be said regarding two hotly debated issues: that Argentina started its disinflation program with a relatively high inflation rate and that it should have used the exchange rate as an alternative anchor?

Figure 3 tries to shed light on these questions.[30] It shows all countries that implemented IT or eventually converged to IT but had inflation rates above 20 percent at least once since 1990. For each country, the figure shows disinflation from the last time inflation was above 20 percent, and for those coming from higher rates, from the time they reach a 45 percent yearly inflation rate. In short, the sample attempts to illustrate the final phases of disinflation in each case.

The reason why the graph includes a period prior to the formal launch of IT is that the denomination of the regime changed over time. In the 1990s and 2000s, many central banks focused on disinflation by implementing most of the features of IT regimes but only named their regime as such later in the process, when the denomination became popular. If we focused on the later part, we would be missing most of the picture. Furthermore, once

---

30. The countries were selected from the IMF report (IMF 2019). The Slovak Republic was included because of having adopted an IT framework before joining the euro area in 2009; see Novák (2011). Data were retrieved from the International Financial Statistics (IFS) of the IMF. The classification of floating regimes and nominal anchor regimes was established with a case-by-case narrative analysis (see online appendix 2). Using a de facto classification of exchange rate regimes, such as that in Levy-Yeyati and Sturzenegger (2016), Israel, Colombia, the Czech Republic, and Poland would be classified as floats. The Russian Federation and Kazakhstan would also be classified as floats at the beginning of the disinflation process.

Figure 3. The Path of Disinflation in Countries that Implemented IT

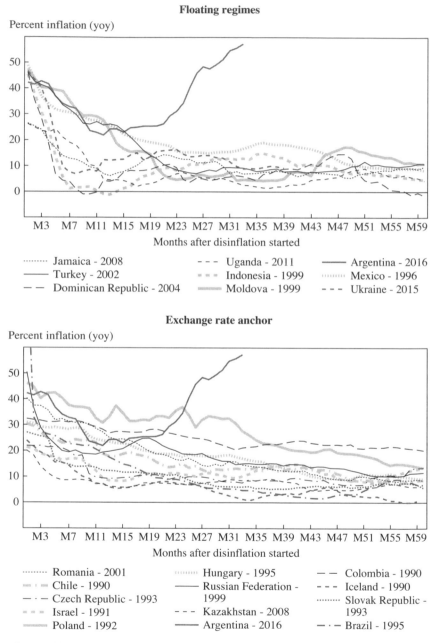

Floating regimes

Percent inflation (yoy)

M3 M7 M11 M15 M19 M23 M27 M31 M35 M39 M43 M47 M51 M55 M59

Months after disinflation started

········ Jamaica - 2008   – – – Uganda - 2011   ——— Argentina - 2016
——— Turkey - 2002   ▪ ▪ ▪ Indonesia - 1999   ········· Mexico - 1996
– – Dominican Republic - 2004   ——— Moldova - 1999   – – – Ukraine - 2015

Exchange rate anchor

Percent inflation (yoy)

M3 M7 M11 M15 M19 M23 M27 M31 M35 M39 M43 M47 M51 M55 M59

Months after disinflation started

········ Romania - 2001   ········ Hungary - 1995   – – Colombia - 1990
▪ – ▪ Chile - 1990   ——— Russian Federation -   – – – Iceland - 1990
– · – Czech Republic - 1993   1999   ········· Slovak Republic -
▪ ▪ ▪ Israel - 1991   – – – Kazakhstan - 2008   1993
——— Poland - 1992   ——— Argentina - 2016   – · – Brazil - 1995

Sources: IMF, San Luis Statistical Office, Buenos Aires Statistical Office, INDEC.

the name started to be used, many countries split the disinflation process into two: a pre-inflation targeting period and a full-fledged inflation targeting. However, this did not cause a relevant change in policies; it simply allowed a larger degree of initial flexibility. Leaving out this initial period would also be a methodological mistake.

The graph does distinguish those cases that implemented disinflation through a pure float and those that used some sort of exchange rate anchor during the initial phases of the disinflation period (in this latter group, I include Iceland, Israel, and the Slovak Republic, which used other anchors as well).

Figure 3 shows that countries choosing either a floating regime or alternative anchors engineered consistent disinflations (online appendix 2 provides a case-by-case analysis). Those that opted for a floating rate started typically at inflation rates similar to those of Argentina. Countries with lower inflation rates used the exchange rate tool but, contrary to the idea that exchange rate–based stabilization achieved faster disinflation, they had slower stabilizations, probably because the gradual adjustment in the exchange rate conditioned the rate of disinflation. In some cases, by enabling sharp appreciations, the float made it possible to accelerate stabilization, as in the case of Indonesia, where the rupiah appreciated from 14,900 to approximately 7,000 per U.S. dollar, or the Dominican Republic, where the Dominican peso appreciated from 48.67 to 28.55 per U.S. dollar.

III.C. The Discussion on Speed and Other Implementation Details

The speed of disinflation embedded in the inflation targets was, somewhat surprisingly, the source of much debate. Some argued that it would have been better to finance a larger share of the deficit through money printing and inflation to avoid a debt buildup; others argued that the targets were too aggressive for Argentina, given its history of inertia and chronic inflation, and would lead to output costs.[31]

---

31. Di Tella (2019), in his comments on this paper, defines aggressiveness as the ratio between the inflation rate at the launch of formal IT and the target set for the first year. I believe this is misguided on two counts. First, this definition excludes the initial phases of disinflation as discussed in the previous section. Second, by looking arbitrarily at yearly inflation at the time of the launch, Di Tella may include shocks that may be irrelevant to inflation dynamics when the IT regime is implemented. Argentina is an obvious case. At the beginning of 2017, year-on-year inflation was close to 40 percent, but this was due to the large transitory shock that took place a year earlier, when capital controls were removed. If the six-month period before the launch had been chosen, when inflation had already fallen to 18.5 percent (the annualized inflation of the second half of 2016), the Argentine program would have been classified as one of the *least* aggressive. Similar caveats can be applied to Indonesia and Ukraine.

Uribe (2016) provides a normative analysis. In his perfect foresight infinitely lived agent model, the optimal policy is to aim directly for the long-run inflation rate, even if this implies a higher sterilization effort and a higher steady-state inflation.[32] Yet the weakness in the balance sheet of the Central Bank made this tax smoothing approach too risky. Therefore only part of the fiscal deficit was financed with money printing (full financing would have led to very high inflation rates), but then none of these transfers was sterilized. Thus the amount of financing to the deficit would determine how much the money base would grow in each year, and this, in turn, would roughly determine what the target should be. Barring big changes in money demand, inflation should align with this number (only a 10 percent fall in money demand was expected in the first year, according to Fundación Pensar estimates). For example, the first year the Central Bank would transfer the equivalent of 25 percent of the money base; the second year, 17 percent, then 12 percent, and then 6 percent, roughly in line with the upper bound of the inflation targets.[33] Matching exactly the targets with the Central Bank's money transfers did, however, reduce to a minimum the Central Bank's margin to improve its balance sheet throughout the process. This would eventually become a heavy burden.

The upper limits of the path (25 percent/17 percent/12 percent/ 6.5 percent) appeared to be quite in line with those of other disinflation experiences starting at similar rates. Among them were the cases of Chile (20 percent/16 percent/12 percent), Mexico (42 percent/20.5 percent/ 15 percent), Turkey (35 percent/20 percent/12 percent), and Ukraine, which, starting at 25 percent, set its initial targets at 12 percent/8 percent, leaving the first year undefined (see online appendix 2).

Figure 4 addresses another issue that was hotly debated: the output cost of stabilization. It shows what could be expected in terms of output

---

32. The long-run inflation rate is a version of the tax smoothing principle of Barro (1979). Manuelli and Vizcaino (2017) provide a similar model with incomplete credibility.

33. A point of contention was the targets for 2016. The team anticipated a fall in the demand of money that would take the inflation rate initially to the 40 percent range, thus a commitment of 25 percent for the year seemed too aggressive and risked undermining the credibility of the Central Bank from the start. The Central Bank suggested that the inflation targets should be set once money demand was stabilized in April or May. However, the executive announced the targets in January. Eventually, the Central Bank did not endorse the 2016 target and just announced that it would try to approximate it as much as possible. However, considering that the targets for the following years matched those announced, the Central Bank suffered in terms of credibility, as it could never reverse the idea that it had committed to a 25 percent target for the first year.

Figure 4. The Output Effect of Disinflations

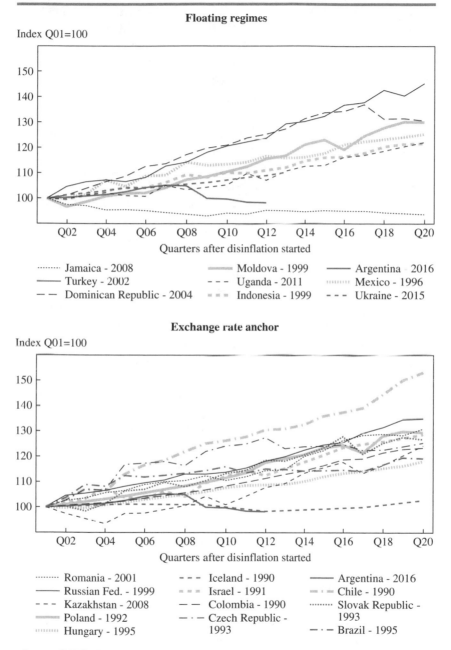

Floating regimes

Index Q01=100

Quarters after disinflation started

Jamaica - 2008	Moldova - 1999	Argentina 2016
Turkey - 2002	Uganda - 2011	Mexico - 1996
Dominican Republic - 2004	Indonesia - 1999	Ukraine - 2015

Exchange rate anchor

Index Q01=100

Quarters after disinflation started

Romania - 2001	Iceland - 1990	Argentina - 2016
Russian Fed. - 1999	Israel - 1991	Chile - 1990
Kazakhstan - 2008	Colombia - 1990	Slovak Republic - 1993
Poland - 1992	Czech Republic - 1993	Brazil - 1995
Hungary - 1995		

Sources: IMF, World Bank, INDEC, Eurostat.

from similar disinflation experiences. Splitting the sample between floaters and non-floaters, the graph again delivers a uniform message: disinflations implemented within (or on the way to) the IT framework are simultaneous with sustained economic recoveries (Iceland and Jamaica being the only two outliers), rendering the debate on the costs of stabilization rather moot. Argentina would fit this mold, as the disinflation of the first two years came with a sustained recovery in economic activity, which reversed only when the program was abandoned.

However, two decisions concerning the targets became a problem. The first was to use overall inflation and not core inflation as the objective. As we will see later, core inflation declined smoothly over the first year and a half of the program, while overall inflation had larger fluctuations. At the time, some countries, such as Thailand, had moved away from core to overall inflation arguing that this is a measure more easily identified by the population (IMF 2017, box 2). Yet large disinflations that need considerable changes in relative prices may be better served by using core inflation (the Czech Republic, where authorities created a special index where all regulated prices were excluded, is perhaps the clearest example; see Adrian, Laxton, and Obstfeld 2018). So, while overall inflation is a more palpable measure for the target, it is more volatile, which makes it more difficult to control and to build credibility.

In addition, setting targets for a fixed calendar year also becomes a problem. If the initial months of the year were above target, this represented a drag throughout the year, inflicting a loss of credibility if the Central Bank was not willing to undershoot its target in order to compensate for past deviations. Maybe a better system would have been to look at twelve-month forward expectations, more in line with the current view that central banks should target inflation expectations and not inflation per se or have a rolling target (many countries set targets on a yearly basis). However, Gibbs and Kulish (2017) provide a model of disinflation in an inflation target framework with imperfect credibility. Their findings suggest that announcing a path of disinflation reduces the sacrifice ratio even at low levels of credibility. At a minimum, having an institutional mechanism to set and even review the targets would have avoided sending out such a negative signal if the targets at any point were changed. Alternatively, the targets could have been interpreted more loosely (as a projection rather than an objective), thus reducing their coordination power but diluting the credibility costs in case they were not reached. All these issues suggest that implementing targets requires meticulous attention.

III.D. Results of the Inflation Targeting Regime

In March 2016, the Central Bank announced a transition to an IT regime that would start the following year, with inflation targets of 12 to 17 percent for 2017, 8 to 12 percent for 2018, and 3.5 to 6.5 percent for 2019. After launching the program, inflation came down quickly, and inflation expectations started at relatively low levels, that is, the program started with a substantial amount of credibility. After many years with inflation ranging between 23 and 40 percent, the first measurement of inflation expectations in June 2016 reported an expected inflation of 19 percent for 2017 and 15.7 percent for two years ahead. In October 2016, when the Central Bank survey asked for a multiyear inflation expectation, the results were 19.7 percent for 2017, 14.8 percent for 2018, and below 10 percent for 2019.[34] Figure 5 shows that twelve-month forward inflation expectations decreased systematically.[35]

Month-over-month inflation was 5.2 percent in April, 4.2 percent in May, 3.1 percent in June, 2.0 percent in July, and 0.2 percent in August, when some of the April tariff hikes were temporarily reversed.[36] Inflation remained subdued in the second half of the year, amounting to 8.9 percent, averaging 1.4 percent per month. Inflation in December and January was 1.2 percent and 1.6 percent.

Disinflation met with continuous criticism from the Treasury regarding interest rates. This discussion was particularly serious between March and May, when the interest rate stood at 38 percent, but disagreements did not abate even after the Central Bank started reducing interest rates more sharply in the second half of the year. In addition, in July the Treasury managed to secure a presidential decree requesting US$ 4 billion from Central Bank reserves, which the Central Bank blocked.[37] In all, these conflicts helped the Central Bank gain credibility and reaffirm its independence and commitment to lowering inflation.

---

34. BCRA Market Expectations Survey, June 2016, p. 2; http://www.bcra.gov.ar/Pdfs/PublicacionesEstadisticas/REM160630%20Resultados%20web.pdf.

35. Due to the lack of a national (core and general) price index at the beginning of Macri's administration, the reported series uses the expected inflation for the metropolitan area of Buenos Aires until June 2017 and the national expected inflation from July 2017 to the present. Data retrieved from BCRA Market Expectations Survey (REM).

36. If the effect of the tariff reversal had not been considered, headline inflation of August would have been 0.9 percent (as explained in BCRA 2016b, section titled "Prices").

37. Decree 834/2016; see http://servicios.infoleg.gob.ar/infolegInternet/anexos/260000-264999/263233/norma.htm.

Figure 5. The Economy during the IT Phase

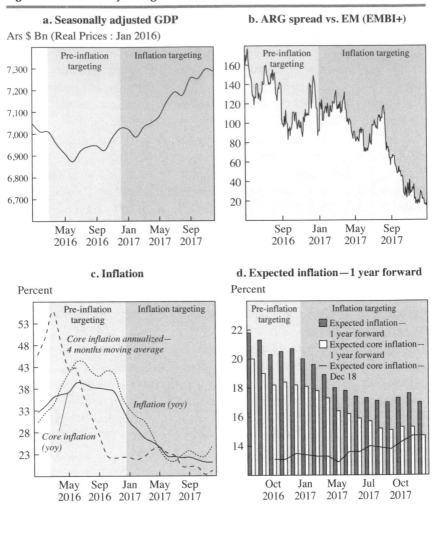

a. **Seasonally adjusted GDP**

Ars $ Bn (Real Prices : Jan 2016)

b. **ARG spread vs. EM (EMBI+)**

c. **Inflation**

d. **Expected inflation—1 year forward**

Figure 5. The Economy during the IT Phase (*Continued*)

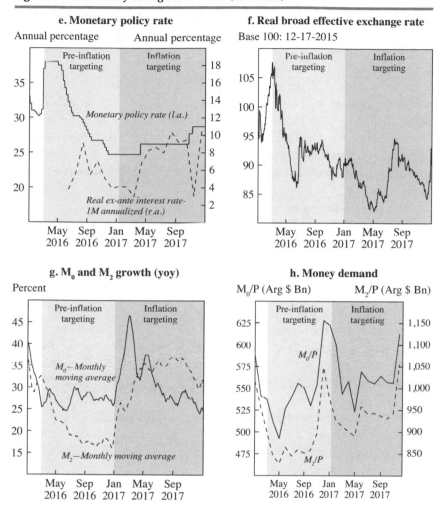

e. Monetary policy rate

Annual percentage   Annual percentage

Pre-inflation targeting / Inflation targeting

Monetary policy rate (l.a.)

Real ex-ante interest rate–1M annualized (r.a.)

f. Real broad effective exchange rate

Base 100: 12-17-2015

Pre-inflation targeting / Inflation targeting

g. M_0 and M_2 growth (yoy)

Percent

Pre-inflation targeting / Inflation targeting

M_0–Monthly moving average

M_2–Monthly moving average

h. Money demand

M_0/P (Arg $ Bn) M_2/P (Arg $ Bn)

Pre-inflation targeting / Inflation targeting

M_0/P

M_2/P

Sources: INDEC, BCRA, JP Morgan, San Luis Statistical Office, Buenos Aires Statistical Office.

During this period, the Central Bank pushed for a further opening of the capital account. In fact, in April 2016, ahead of schedule, the U.S. dollar demand for past imports and dividend payments was fully freed.[38] In addition, in May 2016 the US$ 2 million cap for FX purchases was increased to US$ 5 million and eliminated altogether in August.[39]

In September 2016, the Central Bank announced the formal launch of the inflation targeting regime starting in 2017. In fact, not much would change, except that the policy instrument would stop being the 35-day Lebacs and would become the midpoint of the 7-day repo rate. This change attempted to align the operational framework of the Central Bank with that of standard procedures in central banking and build a more direct link with rates in the financial sector.

The fall in inflation during this period had an impact in output and the bond market. Figure 5 shows that the economy started growing in the third quarter and country risk continued to fall. In October 2016, Argentina placed US$ 8.3 billion in peso bonds at five, seven, and ten years at nominal annual rates of 18.2 percent, 16 percent, and 15.5 percent, which showed confidence in the stabilization program. This issue would have been unimaginable a few months earlier.[40]

Despite the fears of inertial inflation, the fall in inflation was rather quick, though year-on-year numbers remained big due to the big spike of earlier months. Perhaps the only sour spot in this process was that core inflation did remain somewhat higher, at 10.8 percent, in the second half of 2016 (1.7 percent monthly).[41]

WHAT WAS THE DISINFLATION MECHANISM? Despite the fall in the inflation rate, a debate ensued on whether the interest rate was enough to reduce inflation and on the role of utility price adjustments, inertia, and the FX in the inflationary process.

Due to the lack of data, little research in Argentina has focused on the role of expectations in the inflation process. As shown in figure 6, prices, expectations, the FX, and regulated prices all move together. Thus, it is easy to see how any of these variables could be interpreted as fueling

38. BCRA communication A5955; http://www.bcra.gov.ar/Pdfs/comytexord/A5955.pdf.

39. See BCRA communication A5963, http://www.bcra.gov.ar/Pdfs/comytexord/A5963. pdf, and BCRA communication A6037, http://www.bcra.gov.ar/Pdfs/comytexord/A6037. pdf, respectively.

40. See, for example, http://www.telam.com.ar/notas/201610/166886-bonos-gobierno-nacional-financiamiento-secretaria-de-finanzas.html, https://www.ambito.com/economia/inedito-bono-10-anos-pesos-salio-tasa-fija-del-155-anual-n3958711, or http://www.telam.com.ar/notas/201609/165084-bonos-financiamiento-ministerio-de-hacienda-y-finanzas.html.

41. IPC-GBA INDEC, the only core inflation index available until 2017.

Figure 6. The Co-movement of Prices and Expectations

Log sep-16=0

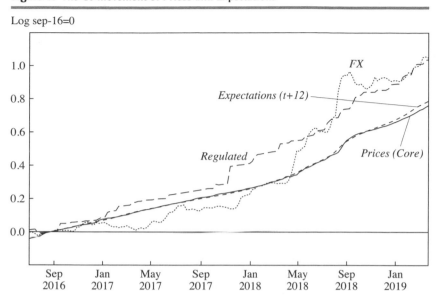

Sources: Pricestats, Elypsis, BCRA, INDEC.

inflation. But how does each variable play out when taking the others into account? In particular, is it true that the FX has such a determinant role in price dynamics as is typically believed?

I address this question by running a vector error correction model (VECM) of weekly core prices, FX, regulated prices, and inflation expectations, not with the intention to provide a model for inflation but to check how these variables interact and react to each other. Online appendix 3 describes the methodology. Table 4 shows the coefficients of the cointegrating regression.[42] In the first column for each sample period, only FX and regulated prices are taken into account, while the second and third columns include inflation expectations at a one-month and a twelve-month horizon. The results show that during the IT period, once expectations are included,

42. All the regressions start in August 2016 because that is the first month in which the BCRA reported core inflation expectations in its Market Expectations Survey (REM). The first time period ends in November 2017 because December 2017 expectations were collected after the conference on December 28. The second time period ends in March 2018, the month before the sudden stop of capital flows began (it began on April 25, when the BCRA had to sell US$ 1.5 billion in order to prevent the currency from depreciating). The last time period ends in April 2019, the last data point available when these calculations were carried out.

Table 4. VEC Model for Inflation in Argentina: Cointegrating Vector

Period	August 2016–November 2017			August 2016–March 2018			August 2016–April 2019		
	Weekly			Weekly			Weekly		
Frequency of data	(I)	(II)	(III)	(I)	(II)	(III)	(I)	(II)	(III)
Prices	1	1	1	1	1	1	1	1	1
FX	−0.3566**	−0.0268	−0.0194	−0.3268	−0.0235*	−0.0233*	−1.1840**	−0.0822**	−0.1831**
	(0.1270)	(0.0153)	(0.0157)	(0.3692)	(0.0111)	(0.0109)	(0.4395)	(0.0263)	(0.0478)
Reg	−0.7186**	0.0275	0.0030	−0.6434**	−0.0006	−0.0373	0.0753	−0.0612	−0.1759*
	(0.0812)	(0.0574)	(0.0521)	(0.2322)	(0.0167)	(0.0201)	(0.4764)	(0.0451)	(0.0815)
Exp (t+1)		−1.0356**			−0.9978**			−0.7991**	
		(0.0784)			(0.0244)			(0.0774)	
Exp (t+12)			−1.014**			−0.9517**			−0.5739**
			(0.0728)			(0.0286)			(0.1380)
Constant	Yes	Yes	Yes	Yes	Yes	Yes	Yes	Yes	Yes

Sources: CPI reported by Pricestats. FX: ARS/USD exchange rate reported by com.A3500 of BCRA. Reg: regulated prices reported by com.A3500 of BCRA. Reg: regulated prices reported by Elypsis. Inflation expectations reported by BCRA.

Notes: Standard deviation in parentheses. Exp (t+1): core inflation expectations one month forward. Exp (t+12): core inflation expectations twelve months forward. Cointegration of Johansen test (maximum eigenvalue test). Each equation is cointegrated at 1 percent of significance.

*Significant at 5 percent; **significant at 1 percent.

the statistical relationship between prices with FX and utility prices virtually disappears. This result reverses if the sample is extended to 2019, when the inflation process had become unanchored and inflation targeting was abandoned. These results also apply to the short-run pricing behavior (results in online appendix 3). Noticeably, during the IT regime, shocks to the FX had no effect on pricing behavior, a result that also reverted once the regime was abandoned. These results show that pass-through coefficients typically considered large had been quickly reduced (actually eliminated) as a result of the new monetary regime. Figure 7 shows the variance decompositions and portrays the same results from a different angle. It shows that inflation has an inertial component, but again, for the IT period, expectations appear to have been the fundamental driver of price dynamics while the exchange rate became relevant only when the regime was abandoned. Other results (see online appendix 3) show that during the IT regime, while moot in the long run, jumps in regulated prices did affect pricing in the short run.[43]

The estimation is not without problems, and the samples are small, as discussed in online appendix 3, but the result is relatively robust for different econometric specifications. These results are included here to note that it is necessary to include expectations as a relevant driver of the inflationary process, something that has been lacking in the empirical work on inflation in Argentina. Certainly, further research on this topic is required.

These estimates address the fundamental question of the transmission mechanism to achieve disinflation in the IT regime. It appears that expectations coordination played a fundamental role in the disinflation process and that the traditional channel from exchange rates to inflation expectations and pricing behavior had weakened, if not altogether disappeared, indicating a quick adjustment to the new monetary regime. These results were probably aided by the fact that Argentina has no formal indexation of contracts, which reduces inertia. In fact, wage negotiations were quite forward looking. For example, consider the transition from 2016 to 2017. Inflation ended at 36.1 percent in 2016, and the Central Bank inflation target for 2017 focused on the upper limit of 17 percent. Wage negotiations ended in the 20 to 25 percent range, which was consistent with the inflation target.[44] Thus, to some extent, the inflation target acted as a substitute for income

---

43. A result found also in Navajas (2019) and consistent with Alvarez and others (2018).
44. See BCRA (2016b), where it is shown that in a disinflation process wage negotiations that keep the real wage constant equal the average of the next year inflation and the past year inflation, thus reaching a higher value than the future inflation rate.

Figure 7. Variance Decompositions (using Cholesky factors)

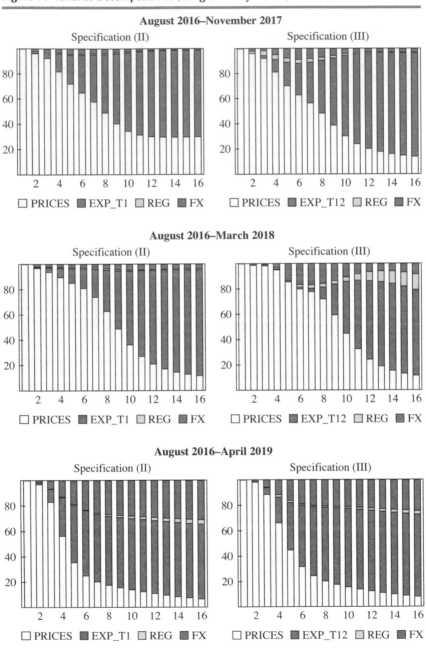

Source: Author's elaboration based on Pricestats, Elypsis, BCRA, INDEC.

policies. On the other hand, inflation expectations remained consistently around 5 percent above the upper limit of the inflation targets in every year, a result reminiscent of a Barro-Gordon bias: as if players expected the Central Bank to be willing to tolerate a deviation from its target, which expectations anticipated.[45]

THE POLICY REACTION The quick fall in the inflation rate triggered a gradual reduction in the policy rate. By the end of 2016, the rate had been cut from 38 percent (in May) to 24.75 percent. In January 2017, when the transition to a formal IT regime was made, a technical problem emerged. Repos paid a local city tax which the Lebacs did not, and as the policy rate was kept constant at the previous Lebac rate, this led to an abrupt fall in the Lebac rate that had neither been anticipated nor desired by the authorities. The Central Bank delayed a solution, allowing a de facto easing of monetary policy.

In addition, in January 2017 a new Treasury minister eliminated the last remaining vestiges of capital controls: a four-month minimum holding period on peso investments. The four-month stay imposed a sizable amount of currency risk on any bet on the Argentine peso. The Treasury decided to collapse this period to zero, thus freeing all capital flows in practice. The Central Bank seconded this move, as it allowed eliminating the last vestiges of capital controls, which consisted of a required registration (needed to be able to track this four-month period).[46] As a result, capital flows started to increase, thus resulting in a moderate peso appreciation. The Central Bank read the ensuing real appreciation as a consolidation of the disinflation of the second half of 2016. For a second time, reading inflation signals at the beginning of the year turned out to be difficult.

In February, as the government resumed utility price adjustments, inflation picked up again, signaling the Central Bank that easing had gone too far.[47] In fact, by the end of February, inflation seemed to be above the levels needed to attain the 17 percent target for the year. Thus, in late February the Central Bank started tightening monetary conditions

---

45. See, for example, http://www.bcra.gov.ar/PublicacionesEstadisticas/Relevamiento_Expectativas_de_Mercado.asp; http://www.bcra.gov.ar/PublicacionesEstadisticas/Relevamiento_Expectativas_de_Mercado_i.asp; and http://www.bcra.gov.ar/Pdfs/PublicacionesEstadisticas/REM161229%20Resultados%20web.pdf.

46. BCRA communication A6150; http://www.bcra.gov.ar/Pdfs/comytexord/A6150.pdf.

47. Electricity prices were increased by 90 percent, natural gas prices by 30 percent, and water distribution by 20 percent between February and April (BCRA 2017a).

by pushing the Lebac curve upward and then in April moving the policy rate upward.[48]

Inflation increased somewhat in the February–April period, but by mid-2017 monetary tightness appeared to be working again and inflation started abating pretty quickly. By July, yearly inflation had fallen to 21.4 percent, the lowest in seven years, while wholesale prices had increased 13.9 percent in the previous year. In the second half of 2017, while overall disinflation stalled, core inflation continued to decrease. Core inflation, which had been 1.7 percent monthly in the second half of 2016, fell to 1.5 percent in the second half of 2017, and fell further to 1.4 percent in the last quarter. For 2018, the expected core inflation was just 14.9 percent. However, overall inflation, which had been 1.4 percent in the second half of 2016, was 1.8 percent in the second half of 2017 (1.6 percent if excluding the large increase in December resulting from a large regulated price jump engineered after the midterm elections). Inflation expectations for 2018 had increased 2.3 percentage points (pp) in the previous fourteen months, which, considering that the target for 2017 would be missed, led to continued doubts about the success of the disinflation program.

Throughout this period, as inflation decreased, output recovery had been quite consistent and had strengthened in 2017, which ended with a growth rate of 4 percent (figure 5, panel c), capping seven quarters of sustained growth. Credit growth had also accelerated in 2017, reaching 20 percent growth in real terms by the end of the year, allowing investment to grow at double digits. The growth in credit responded to a series of deregulation measures taken to improve the operation of the financial sector. The question of whether this in turn jeopardized the disinflation process was again disregarded at the time by the Central Bank on the argument of the endogeneity of money, although it may also have played a role in somewhat slowing the disinflation path. The combination of high growth and falling inflation worked to sharply bring down poverty levels. The end result was a landslide victory for the government during the midterm elections.

---

48. Monetary growth had also picked up at the end of the previous year, hand in hand with a tax amnesty for nondeclared capital abroad which required funneling tax payments through the financial sector. This, combined with an abnormal reduction in the money base in February of the previous year, briefly propelled the year-on-year money growth rate to nearly 50 percent (see figure 5, panel g), before normalizing at a 34 percent year-on-year rate by the end of May. The Central Bank disregarded these numbers under the argument that money demand was endogenous, but this nonetheless stirred renewed criticism against the Central Bank for carrying out a monetary policy that was considered inconsistent with the disinflation path.

After the midterm elections, even though core inflation had decreased, as inflation remained above the target, the Central Bank implemented a significant monetary policy tightening—with two hikes, one of 150 basis points (bps) and one of 100 bps two weeks later. Its intention was to keep the disinflation process moving ahead. What the Central Bank did not know is that, by doing so, it had triggered resistance to its policies within the government, which would shortly after unravel the program.

III.E. The Evolution of Fiscal Accounts

So far, we have focused on monetary policy, but to understand why disinflation eventually conflicted with fiscal policy, we need to discuss the evolution of fiscal accounts. As mentioned, the government inherited a large fiscal problem and expected some fiscal convergence, initially from a reduction in subsidies, but was not ambitious (see table 2). However, even this lax plan got quickly off track for three main reasons: output did not grow as expected, taxes were cut, and expenditures were increased beyond what had been planned.

That the fiscal situation would be challenging became clear when, a few days before taking office, the Supreme Court granted a favorable ruling to three provinces on a tax dispute (which the government later extended to other provinces).[49] Galiani (2018) estimates that there was an impact of 1.6 percent of GDP on the government's accounts between 2016 and 2018, and a steady state annual impact of 1 percent. In addition, export taxes were eliminated across the board, followed by a series of other tax cuts, such as those to small and medium-sized enterprises and to the automobile industry. Toward the end of 2016, the government also increased the minimum income required to pay the income tax and indexed this amount. This cost an additional 0.6 percent of GDP. In all, tax reductions added up to 2.2 percent of GDP (Galiani 2018).

In addition to the weakening of the income stream the government implemented an increase in pension payments to settle litigation for the lack of indexation of pensions during the years 2002–2006. This added an annual expense of about 1 percent of GDP to government spending, plus the obligation to repay the accumulated debts with pensioners

---

49. Argentine Supreme Court ruling 338:1356, November 24, 2015. (https://sjconsulta. csjn.gov.ar/sjconsulta/documentos/verDocumentoByIdLinksJSP.html?idDocumento=72682 92&cache=1579496165473).

Figure 8. The Evolution of Fiscal Accounts

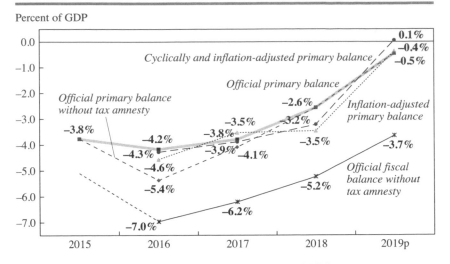

Percent of GDP

Source: Author's elaboration based on Ministry of Finance, BCRA, INDEC.

originating from that absence of indexation, which added an additional stock of 1.4 percent of GDP.[50]

While utility price adjustments provided additional resources, rather than decreasing, the deficit actually *increased* from 3.8 percent to 5.4 percent (figure 8)! The 2016 tax amnesty provided some relief, but just enough to avoid a marked deterioration of the fiscal situation (it added 1.2 percent of GDP in 2016 and 0.3 percent in 2017).[51]

Before moving on, we need to point out a critical feature of fiscal accounts in Argentina: the backward indexation of pensions and social expenditure. As Argentina returned to high inflation in the 2000s after a decade of stability, it was forced to reindex pensions that had been frozen during the convertibility period. However, at the time, there were doubts about the reliability of inflation statistics, so the government indexed pensions to a combination of tax collection and nominal wages.[52] In reality, this represented

50. According to the figures reported by the Fondo de Garantía de Sustentabilidad (FGS) in its accountability report to the Congress in October 2016 and official information provided by Casa Rosada retrieved from www.casarosada.gob.ar/36439-programa-nacional-de-reparacion-historica.

51. See the monthly reports made by the Treasury Ministry: https://www.argentina.gob.ar/sites/default/files/presentacion-metas-2018-vfinal.pdf and https://www.argentina.gob.ar/sites/default/files/seguimiento-resultado-diciembre-2018.pdf.

52. Law no. 26417.

an indexation of pensions to nominal GDP, thus triggering an unsustainable dynamic, particularly if Argentina were to start growing again.

Thus, in order to analyze the evolution of fiscal performance during this period more objectively, it is useful to implement two adjustments. The first is aimed at correcting the cyclical movements of the economy.[53] The second adjustment corrects the fact that pension and social aid are formally indexed backward so that their real value is reduced when inflation accelerates and increases in a context of disinflation. A rough estimate is that the budget improves (deteriorates) about 0.4 percent for each increase (fall) of 10 percent in yearly inflation. Thus, a relevant concept in Argentina is the cyclically adjusted inflation-constant budget deficit. Figure 8 shows the results (online appendix 4 discusses the methodology).

With this estimation at hand, we can see that in 2017, after a new Treasury minister took over, the government started tackling the fiscal imbalance. In fact, in the inflation-constant measure, the budget improved by 1.1 percent in 2017. This was a significant reduction. However, the headline budget deficit moved only from a 4.2 percent deficit to 3.8 percent: disinflation had increased the real value of pensions, undoing most of the fiscal effort. It was this divergence which prompted the Treasury to attempt to slow down the disinflation process in order to avoid a repeat of these dynamics in 2018.

Confident that the government would strengthen after the elections later that year, the markets did not appear overly concerned with the slow pace of fiscal improvement, and country risk continued to fall despite the large deficits (figure 5, panel b). Indeed, after its success in the midterm elections, the government made additional moves at fiscal consolidation by passing a tax and pension reform as well as by hiking up utility prices (December 2017 saw the largest increase in regulated prices for the whole period; see figure 6). But the tax reform, while improving the efficiency and distributive impact of taxes, implied a *reduction* of taxes going forward.[54] The only

---

53. We follow the standard methodology detailed in Escolano (2010). See also Girouard and André (2005), Daude, Melguizo, and Neut (2010), Larch and Turrini (2010), and Fedelino, Ivanova, and Horton (2009).

54. The tax reform included a reduction in corporate income tax (though increasing taxes on the distribution of dividends), the introduction of a tax on financial investment income, and a tax-exempt minimum income, which reduced the incidence of labor taxes for the lower half of the income distribution. A tax on bank movements would progressively be considered as a withholding of income tax. The provinces agreed to reduce the maximum rates of the turnover tax (though some provinces which were below these maximum rates used the opportunity to increase taxes). In all, the tax reform anticipated a gradual reduction of the tax burden, which would reach 2.9 percent of GDP by 2022 (Argentine Ministry of Treasury 2018).

cost-saving features came from the pension reform.[55] One of the law's provisions was that workers were to be allowed to stay an extra five years in their jobs if they so decided. As this was voluntary, it did not create much controversy. In practice, it extended the working age approximately three years (women were previously allowed to retire at between 60 and 65 years old, and the average retirement age was 63). The other provision was that the government pushed for a change in the indexation formula, which attempted to move it to a more sustainable dynamic, increasing the weight of prices and shortening the adjustment lags. This change, however, met fierce resistance and significant union mobilization, which cast doubts on the ability of the government to push further with other reforms.

To summarize, figure 8 shows that the government tried to move in the direction of fiscal consolidation in 2017, but the effort was undermined by disinflation, which led the Treasury to become a strong advocate of slowing the stabilization program. In fact, the data for 2018, when inflation accelerated, show the opposite dynamic. At a constant inflation rate, there was no progress in the fiscal numbers (the devaluation forced the government to increase energy and transportation subsidies), but the acceleration of inflation made a sharp reduction in the real value of pension and social programs, which allowed for a reduction of 1.2 percent in the headline primary deficit. It was only in 2019 that all measures coincide to signal a significant reduction in the deficit.

The lack of adjustment in the fiscal accounts (for whatever reasons) in the first two years, plus a reduction in the private sector's savings, led to a significant deterioration of the current account. By the end of 2017, there were growing concerns regarding the external imbalance. With political power consolidated in the midterm elections, the markets considered that the time had come for the government to start delivering on the fiscal front, but nobody was prepared for what was about to happen.

III.F. The Central Bank's Balance Sheet and the Issue of Lebacs

The program started with a weak Central Bank (figure 2), with a mind-boggling negative net worth of US$ 93 billion, net of *letras intransferibles* and *adelantos transitorios*. The Central Bank balance carried remunerated liabilities for 5.6 percent of GDP in Lebacs and repos, a number that grew

---

55. Law no. 27426.

to 6.9 percent in March 2016, when the Central Bank sterilized the bulk of issuance arising from dollar futures liabilities and at least part of the monetary overhang.[56]

After the agreement with the holdouts, the economy started experiencing a capital inflow process from two sources. One was the external financing of the budget deficit (of both the national government and provinces), which was primarily financed abroad. The second was private sector inflows. While the Central Bank removed the Euroclearibility of Lebacs early on in an attempt to fend off private speculative capital inflows, once the Treasury removed the stay period on local investments at the beginning of 2017, inflows increased.[57]

Panels g and h in figure 9 show the relative importance of both sources of capital inflows, making it clear that the lion's share was the government's sector indebtedness. Private sector flows were nonexistent in 2016 and relatively small in 2017. In 2018, the private sector outflows were larger than the inflows of the two previous years, as a large portion of these outflows were from residents. In summary, and contrary to what is believed, the challenge posed by capital flows had more to do with government indebtedness than with hot money (hot money flows were probably contained due to the fact that the exchange rate floated).

The Central Bank confronted government sector indebtedness with an aggressive program of reserves accumulation, buying reserves that were sterilized by issuing peso liabilities (Lebacs).[58] By doing so, the currency mismatch of the consolidated government balance sheet and the exchange rate appreciation resulting from the inflows were both reduced, but the inflation objective was made conditional on an exchange rate objective.

56. In the first weeks, the Central Bank and the Treasury agreed to exchange US$ 16 billion of *letras intransferibles* for marketable government bonds (see the BCRA's press note, December 28, 2015, http://www.bcra.gob.ar/Pdfs/Prensa_comunicacion/Nota_Prensa_28-12-15.pdf), somehow compensating part of the deterioration in the balance sheet of previous years (see figure 2). However, there was an agreement that this debt would not be used for open market operations. As a result, while it significantly improved the balance sheet, it did not preclude the need to issue Central Bank securities for monetary policy.

57. Resolution E 1/2017 of the Ministry of Treasury. The transfer of Lebacs to Euroclear was banned in May 2016.

58. For a justification for reserve accumulation by comparing reserves to those of other Latin American countries, see Sturzenegger (2019). The Central Bank decided to buy these reserves as the government required, not timing the purchases to the developments of the FX market. As a result, these purchases were not disruptive of the functioning of the FX market, which made it possible to sustain a floating exchange rate regime despite large FX purchases.

Figure 9. The Parallel Growth of Reserves and Central Bank Liabilities

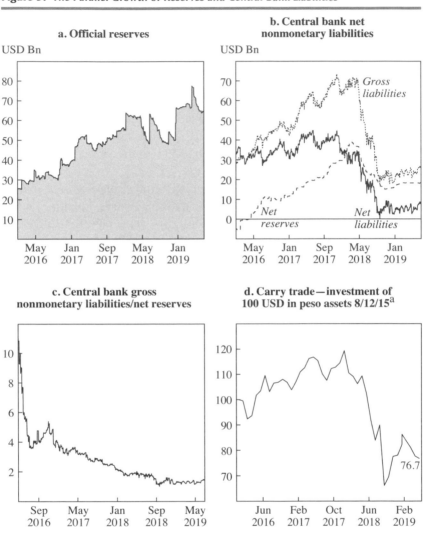

a. Official reserves

b. Central bank net nonmonetary liabilities

c. Central bank gross nonmonetary liabilities/net reserves

d. Carry trade—investment of 100 USD in peso assets 8/12/15[a]

Figure 9. The Parallel Growth of Reserves and Central Bank Liabilities (*Continued*)

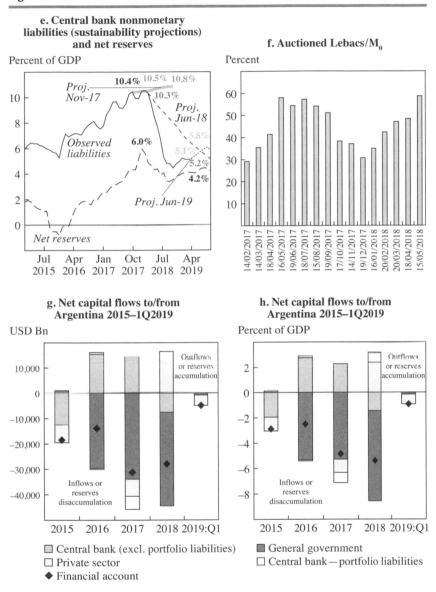

e. Central bank nonmonetary liabilities (sustainability projections) and net reserves

f. Auctioned Lebacs/M₀

g. Net capital flows to/from Argentina 2015–1Q2019

h. Net capital flows to/from Argentina 2015–1Q2019

☐ Central bank (excl. portfolio liabilities)   ■ General government
☐ Private sector   ☐ Central bank—portfolio liabilities
◆ Financial account

Sources: BCRA, INDEC.
ᵃ Based on an investment of USD 100 in 35-day Lebac from 12/18/2015 to 11/30/2018 and in LECAP (30-day constant maturity) since then.

The growth in Lebacs had its counterpart in the accumulation of reserves, but a debate emerged regarding the growth in the Central Bank's balance sheet, even though, as shown in figure 9, panel c, the ratio of FX backing of Central Bank interest-bearing liabilities improved steadily throughout the process. The debate heated up when the real exchange rate appreciated, as this resulted in the Central Bank paying a cost (ex post) in terms of carry that increased the larger the reserves. Figure 9, panel d, shows that, by the end of 2017, the cumulative ex post return in dollars paid to sterilize reserves reached a maximum of about 20 percent for the two-year period.

There is extensive literature on reserve accumulation, even when reserves are borrowed, as in this case. Rodrik (2006) argues that the cost is not large relative to the insurance benefits, while Levy-Yeyati (2006, 2019) argues that the costs are smaller because of their positive effect in country risk. Additionally, historical evidence (de la Torre, Levy-Yeyati, and Pienknagura 2013) suggests that central banks typically gain from such purchases because they tend to buy reserves at moments of FX appreciation and to sell in moments of turbulence, so that the cost is further decreased by a natural timing to the market of purchases and sales.

In this case, however, given that the financing for reserves was denominated in pesos and not in U.S. dollars, the discussion was whether the stock was unsustainable or whether it was sustainable only in a high inflation/ devaluation scenario, along the lines of Calvo (1988, 1991). Alternatively, the discussion was framed as if the interest on Lebacs were a source of inflation itself. According to this view, if the growth in the Lebacs became "money," it could trigger an increase in the inflation rate, as in interest peg runs discussed by Bassetto and Phelan (2015).

Three arguments suggest that the eventual reduction of these Central Bank liabilities needed not be done through inflation. Firstly, central banks' balance sheets do not acknowledge their strongest asset: the net present value of future seigniorage. An estimate of this seigniorage by the Central Bank (BCRA 2017b) placed it at 30 percent of GDP, much larger than the stock of Lebacs (which reached 11 percent at its maximum). Second, assuming no further purchases of reserves and using market expectations for interest rate, growth, and inflation, the stock of Lebacs had stabilized by the end of 2017 (as shown in figure 9, panel b), which suggested a rollover was feasible. Finally, the reserves themselves could be used to cancel these liabilities. For these reasons, the Central Bank considered that the situation was sustainable, a view that was shared by the markets but not by most analysts. Of course, even if inflation were not a foregone result, there was still a latent risk that at some point the government may *decide* to pay for them with inflation.

The question of whether Argentina would have fared better if these reserves and liabilities were not accumulated is not a settled issue. We will come back to this in the final section of this paper.

A final but relevant point refers to the maturity of Central Bank liabilities. During the second half of 2017, concerned with rollover risk, the Central Bank had extended maturities by increasing long rates on Lebacs (see figure 9, panel f, which shows that Lebacs maturing each month had fallen from around 60 percent to around 30 percent of the money base).[59] A long body of literature, starting with Cole and Kehoe (1996) and including the Greenspan-Guidotti rule, pays attention to the relationship between short-term debt and reserves as key for avoiding multiple equilibria.

IV. The Unraveling of the Program

IV.A. The Change in Targets and Start of the Crisis

In July 2017, inflation was decreasing relatively quickly, prices had risen by 21 percent in the previous year (a fall of more than 15 pp relative to six months before) and wholesale prices had increased just shy of 14 percent. Because of backward indexation of half of government expenditure, this quick reduction in inflation represented a challenge to fiscal accounts as explained above; hence, the Treasury started pushing for setting inflation targets higher to ensure a slower disinflation path.[60] In addition, the Central Bank had tightened monetary policy in the aftermath of the midterm election, which rallied other actors who believed monetary policy was too tight against the Central Bank. As 2017 was coming to an end, the Ministry of Finance started doubting whether Argentina would be able to finance the stubborn deficit abroad. The Central Bank's effort to extend maturities and reduce rollover risk had come at the price of increasing longer rates, which made local financing more expensive. By the end of the year, most voices (the Treasury wanting slower disinflation for fiscal reasons, the Ministry of Finance wanting cheaper domestic financing, and other members of the cabinet wanting lower interest rates) were challenging the Central Bank's policy.

59. This strategy was also followed with success by Chile in 2003, reducing exposure to rollover risk. For an analysis of the maturity of central bank securities, see Mohanty and Turner (2005) and Gray and Pongsaparn (2015).

60. It was unclear who determined the inflation targets. But, as in 2015 the executive had announced the initial targets, the Treasury believed it could unilaterally change them again.

Toward the end of the year, the executive decided to move ahead and change inflation targets, even though the leitmotiv at the Central Bank had been "to change a target is to have no target" (BCRA 2017a). The president had decided to fire the governor if necessary. The change was a risky gamble. At the time, inflation expectations were 17 percent for 2018 (with expectations of core inflation at 14.9 percent) and 11 percent for 2019, so the disinflation program was pretty consolidated. In fact, the province of Cordoba had concluded the first wage agreement of 2018 with an 11 percent annual increase.[61] Economic growth also was expected to continue, with an expected growth rate of about 3 percent for both 2018 and 2019.[62] Before the change, the economic outlook for the remainder of Marci's presidency was positive.

The change was announced on December 28, 2017, in a relatively bizarre twist, as that is the day Argentina celebrates Fools' Day. To communicate the change, the government staged a press conference where it announced that it wanted *more* inflation.[63] In an attempt to counter the impact on credibility, the executive also announced a 50 percent reduction in transfers from the Central Bank to the Treasury in 2019 and to the equivalent of seigniorage starting in 2020.

Many countries repeatedly miss their targets (Colombia and Mexico, for example, did not attain their targets during the first six years of their stabilization programs), particularly during disinflation episodes. Yet the targets operate as an anchor for expectations regardless of whether they are achieved or not. In recent times, there are three cases of increases in inflation targets: Indonesia in 2005, Brazil in 2003, and Turkey in 2008.[64] The cases of both Indonesia and Brazil occurred after a large devaluation that had gotten the inflation process off track, causing a significant increase in inflation relative to the previous year. In the case of Indonesia, inflation went up from 6.4 percent in 2004 to 17 percent in 2005, so the targets for 2006 and 2007 were moved upward while keeping the 5 percent

---

61. See https://www.infobae.com/politica/2017/12/21/cordoba-cerro-la-primera-paritaria-de-2018-11-de-aumento-para-estatales-y-clausula-gatillo-por-inflacion/.

62. BCRA Market Expectations Survey, November 2017; http://www.bcra.gov.ar/Pdfs/PublicacionesEstadisticas/REM171130%20Resultados%20web.pdf.

63. The press conference can be seen at https://www.youtube.com/watch?v=9_ccA9XonWk.

64. See OECD economic surveys for the cases of Indonesia (OECD 2008a, 32) and Turkey (OECD 2008b, 112). For the case of Brazil, see de Campos Meirelles (2003), which is a letter to the minister of finance explaining the deviations from the inflation target, and Garcia (2006). For additional information about Turkey, see Kara (2008, 2017). Romania in 2018 might be considered an additional case, but the change was not significant, so in practice it is not comparable to these cases.

longer-run objective fixed. In Brazil, inflation had moved from 5 percent in 2000 to 12.6 percent in 2002 (when the target was 3.75 percent); thus the target was adjusted for 2003. In neither case was there a change in monetary policy. While Indonesia converged to its long-term inflation relatively unscathed, Brazil struggled to reach its targets later on (twelve years later, inflation was still above 10 percent). The case of Turkey is similar to that of Argentina because the inflation target was changed in the middle of a successful disinflation program. Turkey started its disinflation program with inflation running at 70 percent, when it set an initial target of 35 percent, and three years later it had inflation below 10 percent. But the target of 4 percent after 2007 became difficult to reach. Thus, the target was reset for 2009, almost doubling it from 4 percent to 7.5 percent. The targets for 2010 and 2011 were also raised to 6.5 percent and 5.5 percent. The change tried to make the targets more realistic while signaling a continued commitment to stabilization. The result was the opposite: this change had a lasting negative impact on credibility, and Turkey is struggling with a two-digit inflation rate still today.

In summary, the precedents for such a move were not auspicious. Thus, it was not surprising that the market's initial response was one of disbelief. When two weeks after the December 28 announcements the Central Bank reduced the interest rate by 75 bps, from 28.75 percent to 28 percent, the news was received with a sense of relief, as it was sufficiently moderate to be read as an affirmation of the independence of the Central Bank. The peso appreciated, spreads stabilized, and the government managed to squeeze what would be its final bond issue for US$ 9 billion in international markets (BCRA 2018a, 12).

However, when the Central Bank implemented an additional reduction of 75 bps two weeks later, arguing it was the natural response to a softening of the targets, the market reacted as if there had been a large institutional shift. The peso depreciated, and the spread on dollar-denominated government bonds increased. By the end of January the spread of Argentine debt relative to emerging markets had quadrupled. Inflation expectations for 2018, which at the end of 2017 stood at 17.4 percent, jumped to 19.4 percent in January, a bigger increase than that of the previous 14 months combined. In fact, even when no further cuts in interest rates were implemented, core inflation continued to increase, and the spread on government bonds continued to climb. The loss of credibility had become a permanent shock.

Figure 10 shows how prices and expectations became unanchored after December 28. It also shows that country risk started escalating after the

Figure 10. Main Variables after December 28, 2017

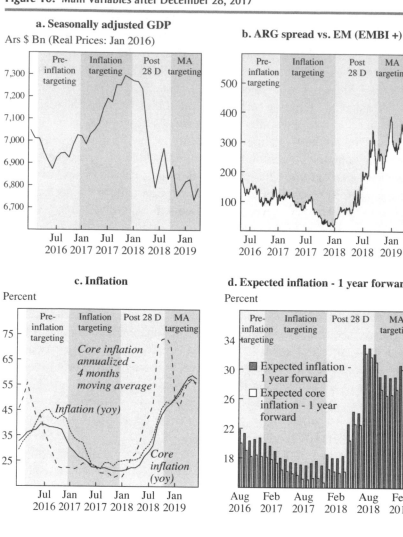

a. Seasonally adjusted GDP

Ars $ Bn (Real Prices: Jan 2016)

b. ARG spread vs. EM (EMBI +)

c. Inflation

Percent

d. Expected inflation - 1 year forward

Percent

Figure 10. Main Variables after December 28, 2017 (*Continued*)

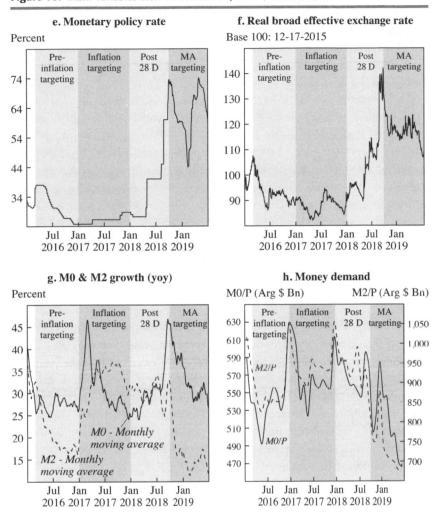

e. Monetary policy rate

Percent

f. Real broad effective exchange rate

Base 100: 12-17-2015

g. M0 & M2 growth (yoy)

Percent

h. Money demand

M0/P (Arg $ Bn)   M2/P (Arg $ Bn)

Sources: INDEC, BCRA, JP Morgan, CPI CABA, and CPI San Luis.

change in targets, indicating that the announcement had been read as a change in both fiscal and monetary policy. The markets had been willing to finance the government while it built political support, but with the midterm elections behind, there were no excuses for further procrastination. The announcement then cast doubts on the intentions of the government to pursue fiscal consolidation.

On December 28, the Central Bank reduced the interest rate on longer Lebacs (also as a result of the softening of the targets) and in April announced that it would not issue Lebacs with a maturity longer than five months.[65] Both facts started piling up the maturities in the short end, reversing the liability management that the Central Bank had achieved in the second half of 2017 and increasing the rollover risk of Lebacs. As can be seen in figure 9, panel f, Lebac auctions had been reduced from about 60 percent of the money base to about 30 percent by December 2017, but this process was fully reversed in the first months of 2018. This would turn out to be a costly mistake. In fact, while this had been a policy decision, market participants believed it could only be the response to difficulties in rollover, which worsened market sentiment.

Facing dwindling credibility, the Central Bank and the executive decided to try to restore it by focusing on the objective that wage negotiations should close in line with the new 15 percent inflation target, as well as containing the exchange rate, which it perceived as having now a stronger impact on price dynamics, leading to intervention in the FX market during most of March. The Central Bank hoped that the market would read the support of the exchange rate as a precommitment on future monetary policy. However, after two years of almost free floating, the interventions only added to the confusion about the monetary regime. In fact, expectations continued to anticipate a significant loosening of monetary policy. Rates remained unchanged, but this was not enough to change this view.

As uncertainty on the economic program mounted, worries grew on Argentina's ability to roll over its debt. Most indebtedness had been incurred in external debt denominated in dollars, thus making the fiscal situation itself vulnerable to a large devaluation. In this unfavorable context, on April 24 a new tax on financial income, approved as part of the fiscal reform at the end of the previous year, came into effect.[66] The first

---

65. BCRA communication P50902; https://www.bcra.gob.ar/Pdfs/comytexord/P50902.pdf.
66. National Tax Agency's General Resolution 4227/2018; http://servicios.infoleg.gob.ar/infolegInternet/anexos/305000-309999/308760/norma.htm.

tranche was a tax on nonresidents, on all instruments, including Central Bank securities. The result was a massive exit from government paper and Lebacs. The Central Bank interpreted this as a specific portfolio shift and decided to redeem the Lebacs in exchange for dollars, avoiding an exchange rate jump. The Central Bank sold US$ 1.5 billion on April 25 and US$ 5.3 billion in the first week of the crisis.[67] The stock of Lebacs fell by 137 billion pesos, roughly an equivalent amount.

Concerned with the inflationary process, the initial sales were made at the ongoing exchange rate. The Central Bank argued that the peso had depreciated significantly relative to other currencies since the end of 2017, so it was not clear that a further adjustment would be necessary. In this view, the sale of reserves was a way of accommodating the portfolio shift, avoiding excessive volatility in the exchange rate. It took less than a day for the Central Bank to realize that much more was at stake, as other currencies, particularly the Brazilian real and the Turkish lira, also came under attack, probably in response to tightening interest rates in the United States.

This put the Central Bank in a bind: it was using the exchange rate as a substitute anchor, given that its credibility had been worn out by the December 28 announcements, but that conflicted with the need to adjust the exchange rate in a deteriorating context, where two exogenous factors became more visible—a severe drought, the worst in 70 years, coupled with the hike in interest rates in the United States.[68] Therefore, the Central Bank moved to a strategy of leaning against the wind in an attempt to smooth the exchange rate market, while not necessarily going against an adjustment of the real exchange rate that it would not be able to put off. Simultaneously, along the way, it would use the sale of reserves as a way of canceling Central Bank liabilities. This strategy continued until October, when the Central Bank exited the FX market. By then, it had sold US$ 13.5 billion of reserves and reduced its Lebac stock by 617 billion pesos (figure 9, panel b), about half the stock that the Central Bank had a few months earlier.

The combination of the peso depreciation, the increase in country risk, and the drought led to a sharp contraction in economic activity.

67. See BCRA daily statistics; www.bcra.gov.ar/Pdfs/PublicacionesEstadisticas/seriese.xls.

68. See the Rural Society of Rosario, press note, February 19, 2018; https://rural rosario.org/detalle/10599/Comunicado-de-Prensa-19-02-18-La-sequia-mas-importante-de-los-ultimos-70-anos.html.

By May 2018, as the exchange rate continued to search for a new equilibrium, the sudden stop was aggravated. The lack of clarity in exchange rate policy did not help align expectations. With the access to markets cut off, as was made clear by a couple of unsuccessful government debt auctions, the government acted swiftly and sought help from the International Monetary Fund (IMF). Yet the announcement of this move did little to calm the market.

In the meantime, the policy rate was increased to 40 percent with only partial success. During this time, the Central Bank continued to sell dollars against Lebacs. In the weeks that followed, however, the climate continued to deteriorate, and the rollover of Lebacs became a source of concern. In order to calm expectations, on May 14 the Central Bank committed US$ 5 billion at a rate of 25 ARS/USD (a value more than 40 percent above the level of mid-December), thus imposing an upper band to the exchange rate.

This commitment brought some relief and allowed for a new issue of US$ 3 billion in peso-denominated bonds on May 16, which were mostly bought by foreign investors. It was decided that the dollars thus obtained would be sold by the Treasury rather than bought by the Central Bank, as had been the case throughout the first two years. But these resources quickly dwindled, while the authorities of the Central Bank tried to bridge the time gap to an agreement with the IMF minimizing Central Bank FX intervention.

Two sources of concern started mounting, both related to the ongoing discussions with the IMF. First, it was believed that the IMF thought a much higher exchange rate was needed to deal with the sudden stop; second, it was understood that the IMF would constrain the use of Central Bank reserves. In that context, it was believed that the policy of redeeming Lebacs with reserves could be discontinued. Both ideas increased the run on Lebacs and the pressure on the FX market in anticipation of the IMF deal.

While the Central Bank had piled up reserves, a concern had been that reserves may be used for purposes other than the backing of the Lebacs, forcing the Central Bank to monetize its liabilities. In reality, the opposite occurred. A strong social and media pressure developed to "protect" the reserves, as if society preferred to reduce its liabilities through inflation rather than relinquishing this asset. Thus, as the Central Bank continued to reduce the stock of Lebacs against the sale of reserves, it received growing criticism. This added to the arguments suggesting that the Central Bank may eventually stop selling reserves and accelerated the run. Paradoxically, the accumulation of reserves did not serve to ease fears of potential instabilities, but neither did the reduction in the liabilities that were the source of concern in the first place.

IV.B. The IMF Program

The IMF believed that Argentina had suffered a sudden stop as a result of slow fiscal consolidation, together with an institutional deterioration in monetary institutions as a result of the December 28 announcements. Thus, naturally, the focus was placed on improving fiscal accounts and recovering the Central Bank's credibility.

The agreement with the IMF led to relatively timid adjustments in fiscal numbers (primary deficits of 2.7 percent of GDP in 2018 and 1.3 percent in 2019 were allowed, only reaching equilibrium in 2020), while transfers from the Central Bank would be forbidden. To avoid further interference with the Central Bank, a new bill enshrining the independence of the Central Bank would be sent to Congress. In addition, the government committed to buying back some of the debt issued to the Central Bank to strengthen its balance sheet. The expected impact on the evolution of Lebacs is shown in figure 9, panel e.

The program was sufficiently large to allow Argentina to roll over most of its debt and finance its transitory deficit, and it became the largest program in the IMF's history, committing US$ 50 billion. It maintained the main tenets of the macro framework: inflation targeting and floating rates. However, given the acceleration of inflation, as in the case of Ukraine, no inflation target was established for the first year of the program. The target for 2019 would be 17 percent, the original upper bound of the 2017 target. There would be minimal intervention in the exchange rate market, and if needed, it would be implemented through transparent auctions.

The Central Bank intervened sporadically to keep the exchange rate in check until the program was launched, then at the start it eliminated the cap on the exchange rate at 25 pesos per dollar and exited the exchange rate market. The exchange rate experienced a significant jump that day, which was considered unacceptable to the executive and led to the governor's replacement.

IV.C. Monetary Experiments

The new governor had two views. The first was that the exchange rate could be placed at whatever level the authorities desired, irrespective of monetary policy or expectations. All that was required was a smart way of intervening in the market, squeezing the shorts out of their positions and disciplining traders with surprise interventions. His second belief was that the government could aid in the sterilization efforts so that, with appropriate coordination, Lebacs could be paid back in pesos and replaced by government debt.

There is extensive literature on exchange rate interventions, and there is evidence that intervention through reserve accumulation affects the real exchange rate in the short and medium term.[69] It has also been shown that intervention may help reduce the volatility of exchange rate fluctuations. Carstens (2019) provides a recent review. But there is little literature, if any, that focuses on intraday intervention, which was the tool the Central Bank argued would be used to affect exchange rate dynamics.

In fact, interventions became somewhat self-defeating: the irruption of the Central Bank as an additional player tended to dry liquidity, as market participants retrenched until they could better assess what this "large" player intented to do. In fact, to avoid this, the IMF argued that interventions should occur through auctions, since transparent interventions would be less disruptive to the market.

In order to address the run on Lebacs, the Central Bank increased interest rates further, eliminated the upper band of the repo corridor, and increased reserve requirements (3 pp on June 21, 3 pp on July 2, and 2 pp on July 18). In addition during 2018 the government partially honored its commitment to cancel some of its debt with the Central Bank (39.4 billion pesos).[70]

However, the turning point occurred in August, when the Central Bank designed an ill-conceived strategy to reduce the stock of Lebacs.[71] The idea was that the government would issue debt to "sterilize" the money printed, as Lebacs were paid out at a preestablished pace (the strategy was ill-conceived because government debt does not sterilize increases in money supply). The Central Bank was ready to sell dollars if necessary to contain money supply growth. In addition, banks were not allowed to renew their Lebac holdings, forcing them to move to Leliqs, another Central Bank liability, although these had a seven-day maturity and could only be held by financial institutions.[72]

---

69. A good survey of literature on exchange rate interventions is Chamon and others (2019); see also Agénor and Pereira da Silva (2019).

70. See the BCRA's sheet "Base Monetaria," column F; www.bcra.gov.ar/Pdfs/PublicacionesEstadisticas/seriese.xls.

71. BCRA press note, August 13, 2018; https://www.bcra.gob.ar/Institucional/DescargaPDF/DownloadPDF.aspx?Id=756.

72. From then onward, investments in pesos had to be done through financial institutions, which later bought the Leliqs. This implied that the volatility of carry trade was transferred to the financial sector. Toward the end of the term, this became a source of concern.

On August 15, the Central Bank allowed 100 billion pesos (US$ 3.3 billion) to mature, but then sold only US$ 1 billion in the FX market to compensate the monetary effect. The released stock of pesos represented a jump in the monetary base of 16 percent that day, which shortly after fueled a run on the exchange rate, jumped from 30 ARS/USD to 39.60 ARS/USD in the month, and further unanchored prices (see figure 10, panel c). The end result was a reduction in the real value of Lebacs through an inflation shock.

As the FX depreciated, the value of Central Bank liabilities in dollars decreased from about US$ 70 billion to about US$ 20 billion in December. This resulted from a reduction in the sale of reserves (US$ 15.9 billion) and from the devaluation itself (US$ 35.4 billion). The combination wiped out the full stock of unbacked liabilities, as seen in figure 9, panel b, dramatically improving the balance sheet of the Central Bank (see figure 2).

As a result of the large monetary shock, inflation moved a step upward. It had been higher than 3 percent since June but reached 6.5 percent in September and 5.4 percent in October. The combination of the de-anchoring of prices, the jump in the exchange rate, and continued discretionary interventions in the FX market in violation of the agreement with the IMF led to the ousting of the governor, as the government realized it needed to implement a new revision in the program with the IMF to calm expectations. However, the decision to reduce the burden of peso liabilities through a significant jump in prices would create a lingering cost: by undermining credibility, the market requested extremely high nominal and real interest rates going forward, thus thwarting any possibility of economic recovery.

IV.D. The IMF II Program

The new program with the IMF agreed on a faster disbursement of funds, in exchange for tighter monetary and fiscal policy. The target for the primary fiscal result for 2019 was improved from −1.3 percent to 0 percent, which would come mostly from tax hikes.[73] On the monetary side, the program fixed monetary aggregates. As discussed in section II, fixing monetary aggregates faces the challenge of dealing with the volatility in money demand, which appears to be exceptionally high in the case of Argentina.[74] These uncertainties imply that any program focused on stabilizing monetary aggregates could face substantial deviations in terms of its objective to achieve disinflation.

73. See, for example, the IMF first review under the standby arrangement; https://www.imf.org/~/media/Files/Publications/CR/2018/cr18297-ArgentinaBundle.ashx.
74. See table 3.

The program was marketed as one where base money growth would be zero, but it started immediately after the big shock in money supply in August and allowed an additional increase in money supply in December for seasonal reasons, which need not be reversed later on. Therefore, the initial monetary conditions turned out to be relatively lax. The program nevertheless was an initial success. Inflation dynamics not only stabilized but reversed, as reflected by a sharp drop in running weekly inflation, as well as in inflation expectations (figure 10, panels c and d). According to weekly data, inflation in November was only slightly above 1 percent (considering a comparison between the end of November and the end of October).[75] At the same time, the interest rate, now endogenous, jumped above 70 percent when the program was implemented. As the economy persisted in its deep recession, the conditions for quick disinflation were in place.

A wide band was established within which exchange rate fluctuations would be allowed, but with a monthly depreciation trend of 3 percent.[76] For a couple of weeks, the government seemed to buy into the program by stating that wage negotiations would be free but that agents should take into consideration the fact that the money supply would not grow the following year. However, shortly after, it started suggesting wage negotiations in the 20–25 percent range, inconsistent with the monetary target. In fact, Central Bank officials commented that after the November disinflation, the Treasury had asked the Central Bank to increase the inflation rate to avoid the lagged effect on pensions that could compromise the fiscal objective (a discussion on the speed of disinflation reminiscent of the one that led to the change in inflation targets a year before). Thus, the Central Bank extended the high rate of depreciation for the first quarter of the year (2 percent monthly).[77] The confirmation of this large expected depreciation into 2019 was very detrimental to expectations (see figure 10), as it implied that the Central Bank itself did not believe disinflation was possible.

The large jump in money supply in August and December was not reversed in January and February, when money demand usually falls. The

---

75. Elypsis; http://elypsisweb.com/en/.

76. See the speech by Guido Sandleris, governor of the BCRA, on September 26, 2018, when this new program was launched; https://www.bcra.gob.ar/Institucional/DescargaPDF/DownloadPDF.aspx?Id=799.

77. Monetary Policy Committee (COPOM) decision on January 2, 2019; http://www.bcra.gov.ar/Noticias/Comunicado-2-enero-2019.asp.

Figure 11. Seasonally Adjusted Monetary Base

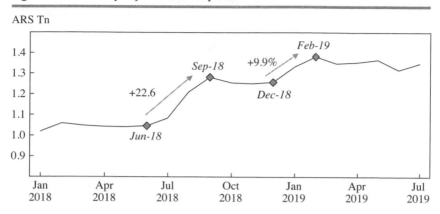

ARS Tn

Source: BCRA; seasonal adjustment by the author.

fact that the Central Bank allowed the interest rate to plunge (it fell from 59.25 percent at the end of 2018 to 44.21 percent on February 15, 2019) implied that it did not absorb this overhang, leading to a sharp increase in money supply (deseasonalized) in January and February (see figure 11). The result was a sharp depreciation in March and April and a very steep increase in inflation, which reached 4.7 percent in March. This caused a political earthquake and seriously compromised the government's prospects for an election that was now only six months away.

By early March, and as political uncertainty increased, the Central Bank realized that its monetary targets were too lax and started contracting the money supply and increasing the interest rate regardless of the target. In April, it froze the exchange rate bands through the rest of the year, while committing to freeze the money supply until December.[78] At the same time, it started sustaining a more stable path for the interest rate. Within a few months the Central Bank had come back full swing to a program with exchange rate targeting and interest rates as its primary policy instrument.

However, the exchange rate remained unstable. On April 29, the Central Bank announced that it had obtained a waiver from the IMF and had been allowed to intervene within the exchange rate band. However, the Central

78. Monetary Policy Committee (COPOM) decision on March 14, 2019; http://www.bcra.gov.ar/Noticias/Comunicado-140319.asp.

Bank made sure that no intervention was necessary by keeping rates high. As inflation remained high, the resulting increase in money demand clashed with a program that required keeping the money supply constant. In June, the Central Bank reacted by reducing reserve requirements.[79] This allowed it to keep compliant with the program (which only fixes base money), though easing monetary policy. At the beginning of July, it further reduced reserve requirements to deal with the high positive seasonality of money demand but simultaneously committed to reducing the monetary targets by an equivalent amount two months later.[80] However, when it was unable to meet the monthly target, it announced that the target would become bimonthly.[81] Later, it increased the target for September and October. These permanent changes in the monetary framework hindered the recovery of credibility and, as a result, interest rates remained very high. The open primaries in August delivered a heavy blow to the government and increased uncertainty. With that, the end of the four-year term was marked by an abandonment of monetary restraint, unchecked monetary printing, a sharp depreciation of the peso, and accelerating inflation, which forced the government, in an almost ironic turn of events, to resort again to capital controls and a default on local debt.

V. Lessons Learned

In a nutshell, the Macri administration implemented a lax fiscal program financed with short-term external debt, together with an IT program with a flexible exchange rate. While the inflation targets had been set to be consistent with fiscal needs, fiscal consolidation lagged and disinflation compromised further improvements in fiscal results as lagged indexation of about half the spending entailed an increase in real spending. This led to a conflict between the Central Bank and the Treasury that was settled with a change in inflation targets. The uncertainties this created in the macroeconomic framework coincided with a tightening of rates in the United States and a severe drought. Combined, these factors produced the ingredients for a sudden stop that led to a sharp recession and an abrupt adjustment of the exchange rate, while the government, slowly at first, but decidedly in 2019, tackled fiscal consolidation. While the consolidation of fiscal policy

79. BCRA communication A6703, http://www.bcra.gov.ar/Pdfs/comytexord/A6703.pdf, and BCRA communication A6706, http://www.bcra.gov.ar/Pdfs/comytexord/A6706.pdf.

80. Monetary Policy Committee (COPOM) decision on July 1, 2019; http://www.bcra.gov.ar/Noticias/Decisiones-del-Comite-de-Pol%C3%ADtica-Monetaria-010719.asp.

81. Monetary Policy Committee (COPOM) decision on July 22, 2019; http://www.bcra.gov.ar/Noticias/Decisiones-del-Comite-de-Pol%C3%ADtica-Monetaria-220719.asp.

provided a chance at stabilization, lax monetary policy and the withdrawal of political support in the primary elections, combined with doubts about the policies of the future government, precipitated the economy again into turmoil toward the end of Macri's presidency.

From a policy perspective, these four years pose a number of questions. Was fiscal gradualism a mistake? Was fiscal policy adequate? Was IT too fast and aggressive? Was the change in targets justified? Was aiming for a floating rate a mistake? Was the accumulation of reserves (and Lebacs or Leliqs) excessive? Was the financing structure of fiscal deficits correct? Was the reaction to the sudden stop adequate? Were the poor results derived from domestic or external factors, or were they just a product of bad luck? This paper has tried to provide evidence and an analysis with these questions in mind. In what follows, I summarize possible answers to these questions.

Was gradualism a mistake? As mentioned, gradualism was more of a political choice than an economic one. The risks of gradualism—higher debt and a larger risk of a credit event—were well understood. The goal of gradualism was to build political capital, which could be handy in times of need. The markets approved the strategy, and country risk actually decreased throughout the first two years, reaching a minimum after the midterm elections. Thus, gradualism provided a feasible path for reform. Yet, after the midterm elections, when the political thesis had been proven correct, the government relaxed both fiscal and monetary policies. This led to a quick reversal of expectations, which was responsible for the turn-around, not gradualism per se.

Was fiscal policy adequate? Even if gradualism may have been the correct strategy, fiscal policy was shown to have actually moved in the opposite direction. Rather than implementing a gradual deficit reduction, the deficit initially *increased* (with unclear political and economic ben-efits). Even though markets were complacent with this situation, it built significant risks. It not only required stronger actions down the road, but the sustained weakness in fiscal policy was ultimately responsible for the change in inflation targets, undermining the credibility of the whole program. Fiscal dominance regarding monetary policy was contained by fixing the transfers to be received from the Central Bank, yet a different sort of fiscal dominance emerged: the need for a slower path of disinflation to avoid a large fiscal effect from backward indexation. The inconsistency between the speed of disinflation and fiscal needs led to a reversal of the two stabilization programs: first in the form of a change in the inflation targets, and second, after the IMF II, by setting a large rate of depreciation.

In this sense, lack of progress on the fiscal front played a key role in undermining stabilization attempts. In short, it is difficult not to point to fiscal policy as the main reason for the program's collapse.

Was inflation targeting too fast and aggressive? The analysis of section III addresses this issue. Other countries implemented IT or a path to IT at inflation rates similar to those of Argentina, and the path of disinflation chosen was very much in line with the international experience. A framework with floating rates (the norm after the 2000s) in some cases even accelerated the disinflation by allowing large appreciations.

Some analysts have suggested that IT was too aggressive because interest rates were too high, leading to an exchange rate appreciation that meant that the successful disinflation of 2016–2017 was unsustainable. But this view is contradictory with inflation expectations for 2018 and 2019, which, prior to the change in targets, suggested the disinflation (and growth) process would continue into the future.[82]

I did, however, point out several drawbacks in implementation. Three-digit utility price adjustments spiked inflation, which led to continuously missing the target and undermining credibility, particularly when overall inflation, rather than core inflation, had been chosen. There was no institutional framework to correct the inflation targets, and while disinflation was steady, monetary policy ended up being not as tight as required to achieve the targets, leading to deviations. Trying to show its commitment to disinflation, the Central Bank focused on these misses, without realizing that, in doing so, it was eroding its own credibility.

A point not to be missed is that IT regimes in particular, and disinflation in general, presuppose central banks' independence and a lack of fiscal dominance. In fact, had the Central Bank been independent, the turnaround in policies and unanchoring of expectations following December 28 would not have occurred, and the turmoil of the final months of the administration would have also been avoided as nobody would have thought that there would be big changes in monetary policy as a result of an election outcome. However, the failed experiences of these two disinflation attempts do not seem to have convinced the general public regarding the need for an independent Central Bank.

Therefore, one possible conclusion is not that the inflation program was excessively ambitious but that neither the fiscal nor the institutional

---

82. This also holds for inflation expectations computed from bond prices. Corso and Matarrelli (2019) show that by end of 2017, inflation expectations for 2019 were close to 10 percent, similar to that of analysts.

preconditions were present. Of course, this does not mean that another disinflation program would have performed better. It simply indicates that those preconditions should have been addressed more forcefully. In fact, in our opinion, the main lesson from this experience going forward is that it is key to create a much stronger institutional framework for macroeconomic policy: an independent Central Bank and some sort of fiscal rule, perhaps along the lines of the structural fiscal surplus that Chile implemented in the 1990s.

Was the change in targets justified? Much of this paper's analysis placed the change in targets as central to the turnaround in expectations, as it meant a debasement of the Central Bank's credibility. This debasement, in turn, unanchored the disinflation process and, sooner rather than later, required higher interest rates, aborting the economic recovery and opening the room for multiple equilibria. Of course, had fiscal consolidation not occurred, the program would eventually have had to face a financing reckoning. But the change of targets virtually exhausted any remaining buffer that the market was willing to provide, thus precipitating the crisis.

Was aiming for a floating rate a mistake? An issue of much discussion was whether a floating exchange rate was an appropriate choice, particularly in a country with such a long history of inflation and dollarization. I discussed this from different perspectives. On the one hand, other countries floated their exchange rates in disinflation processes similar to that of Argentina, which typically helped accelerate disinflations. On the other hand, I demonstrated that the exchange rate played a limited role in price dynamics, particularly during the IT regime period, when expectations drove most of the process. This can be considered a success of the IT framework and confirms that Argentina is normal in all possible ways: faced with a credible monetary policy, pricing behavior immediately changed, even relative to decade-long practices.

At the same time, a floating rate may have provided a buffer both in the period of capital inflows and in the sudden stop. In fact, toward the end of the term, employment was growing, even amid a protracted recession, thus suggesting that the depreciation was helping reduce the impact of the shocks in the labor market. While my analysis suggests that seeking a floating rate may not have been an unreasonable choice, by implementing a floating rate, the government also gave away the benefits of an economic boom it could have profited from with an exchange rate–based stabilization. Whether this boom would have provided more room for implementing reforms or accelerating fiscal convergence remains an open question. However, this idea can be turned upside down, arguing that the problem was that the government did not implement a *sufficiently* floating rate. If the Central Bank had not purchased reserves in the face of the inflows driven by the fiscal deficit, the exchange rate would have plunged; this could have provided a quicker success on the inflation front, which may have also helped provide political support for reforms.

Before moving on, it is worth mentioning another relevant advantage of flexible rates: the flexibility it provides is not only economic, but also institutional. A fixed exchange rate, being a government commitment, creates a sense of obligation to compensate losers if a devaluation occurs, which is not present with floating rates. Thus, it is much easier to adjust to shocks "without changing the rules of the game" with floating rates than with fixed rates. Argentina was able to go through a large sudden stop in 2018 and 2019 without fundamentally changing contracts, something that may help build confidence and reduce risks going forward.

Was the accumulation of reserves (and Lebacs) excessive? During the initial phase of the program, the Central Bank acquired the dollars bought by the government to finance its deficit, issuing short-term Central Bank paper to sterilize the monetary effect of these purchases. Was this a mistake? While prima facie it would seem obvious that without reserves some should be accumulated, the fact that they were purchased with short-term peso debt increased the temptation of an inflationary dilution. Calvo (1988, 1991) provides a simple specification. In his model, government finances debt in local currency. In the absence of a precommitment the market chooses the interest rate and the government decides whether to default or not on the debt. His main idea is that there are multiple equilibria, depending on how the government internalizes costs and benefits for default. At low interest rates, the cost of servicing the debt is low, and the unique equilibrium is no default. At very high rates, taxes required to service the debt are larger, and the government may find an incentive to default.

During 2018, several developments increased the possibility of a bad equilibrium. On the one hand, the size of reserves and debt had increased; on the other, the December 28 announcements had broken the precommitment equilibrium by signaling that the government assigned a lower cost to inflation than previously expected. As a result, the private sector asked for a higher rate ex-ante, and the higher rate increased the incentives to default. In that sense, the initial increase in the interest rate to 40 percent (and subsequent increases) was a double-edged sword. It was necessary to reduce the required sales of reserves, but it also created multiple equilibria.

The accumulation of reserves also hindered a quicker disinflation. Had the Central Bank not intervened, would a larger appreciation and maybe a faster disinflation have occurred? Would this have allowed for more political support and a faster convergence to a low inflation equilibrium? Would it have allowed the Central Bank to achieve its inflation target, thus improving credibility and easing the disinflation process? We will never know the answer to these counterfactual exercises. Regarding the incentives for fiscal imbalance, had the Central Bank not purchased the reserves, the government probably would have found a limit to its indebtedness earlier on. This may have pushed for faster fiscal consolidation and, through that channel, it may have induced a better outcome.

Is this enough to conclude that the process of reserve accumulation was too large or inconvenient? This remains an open question. The reserve accumulation reduced vulnerabilities, and the possibility of facing the sudden stop without reserves would also have to be evaluated, and the prospect of such a scenario appears daunting. The accumulation of international reserves also contained the exchange rate appreciation resulting from the government deficit, reducing the current account deficit, which even *with* the intervention was considered a source of concern.

While it is difficult to assess the relative benefits and costs, toward the end of the presidential term everything seemed to hinge on the availability of reserves, thus suggesting that accumulating them earlier on may have provided a valuable insurance mechanism.

Was the financing structure of fiscal deficits correct? The financing of the deficit was done with short-term external debt in foreign currency, which led to substantial vulnerabilities: a larger real exchange rate appreciation, a bigger current account deficit, a currency mismatch in case of a real exchange rate depreciation, and high rollover risk. While the Central Bank tried to reduce the currency mismatch by accumulating dollars (a policy that worked as expected, producing a significant reduction in its liabilities in 2018 and 2019), the reversal of its 2017 strategy to extend maturities on Central Bank paper added to the rollover risk of the consolidated public sector debt. While the Treasury attempted some domestic currency issues, these became unfeasible as instability mounted, and there were no serious attempts to reprofile the debt, including some obvious alternatives, such as transforming debt owned by the public sector into peso-indexed debt with longer maturities and lower rollover risk. In all, the financing structure added significant volatility. And, as mentioned above, focusing on the domestic market would have shown the limits to debt financing earlier on and would have led to more fiscal discipline.

Table 5. Effects of Sudden Stops

	Dependent var.: $GDP_t - GDP*$			Dependent var.: $GDP_t - GDP*$	
OLS	(1)	(2)	*OLS*	(1)	(2)
Floating	0.0196**	0.0186**	Floating	0.0301***	0.0291***
	(0.0078)	(0.0080)		(0.0093)	(0.0094)
Deposit rate	−0.0017***	−0.0016***	Deposit rate	−0.0016***	−0.0016***
	(0.0002)	(0.0002)		(0.0002)	(0.0003)
World exports	0.0719**	0.0710**	World exports	0.0846**	0.0861**
	(0.0311)	(0.0321)		(0.0366)	(0.0390)
Terms of trade	0.0963**	0.0971**	Terms of trade	0.0953**	0.0949**
	(0.0379)	(0.0397)		(0.0432)	(0.0460)
Openness	0.0131	0.0125	Openness	0.0121	0.0115
	(0.0083)	(0.0100)		(0.0085)	(0.0101)
Regional dummies	No	Yes	Regional dummies	No	Yes
Observations	81	81	Observations	64	64

Sample: Countries that experienced a financial account contraction (yoy) larger than one standard error below its sample mean and larger than 3 percent of GDP and an adjustment of the current account of more than 2 percent of GDP in the same year, the following year, or accumulated between those two years.	Sample: Countries that experienced a financial account contraction (yoy) larger than one standard error below its sample mean and larger than 5 percent of GDP and an adjustment of the current account of more than 2 percent of GDP in the same year, the following year, or accumulated between those two years.

Sources: IMF and World Bank.

Notes: "$GDP_t - GDP*$" stands for variation of real GDP (yoy) minus the long-run trend of real GDP from 1970 to 2018. "Floating" indicates the dummy variable = 1 in countries with floating exchange rate regime, as defined in Levy-Yeyati and Sturzenegger (2016) for 2001–13, and IMF (2019) for 2014–18. "Deposit rate" is the annual change in the interest rate of deposits. "World exports" is the year-on-year variation. "Terms of trade" are logarithmic difference of terms of trade. "Regional dummies" are the regions considered: Latin America, Africa, Asia, and "others" (which includes countries of the Pacific Ocean, Eastern Europe, and the Middle East). Robust standard errors.

*Significant at 10 percent; **significant at 5 percent; ***significant at 1 percent. Standard deviation in parentheses.

Was the reaction to the sudden stop the adequate one? Once faced with the sudden stop, it is necessary to decide the best way to deal with it.[83] Table 5 shows performance in a sudden stop as a result of policy responses. The dependent variable is the change in output, and the explanatory variables are global growth, terms-of-trade shocks, interest rates, openness, and the exchange rate regime.[84] The results here are relatively

83. See Cavallo (2019) for a recent review.
84. See Guidotti, Sturzenegger, and Villar (2004).

standard. Floating rates and lower interest rates provide the best recipe for dealing with the sudden stop, in line with Ortiz and others (2009); the ability to implement countercyclical fiscal and monetary policy in those events improves output performance.[85]

How do these results help us understand Argentina's experience? Once the sudden stop began, because prices had become unanchored due to the December 28 announcements, the Central Bank initially did not allow the exchange rate to fully float and sharply increased the interest rate. This policy response was suboptimal. The first IMF program was thought to provide room for a better response: to avoid an excessively procyclical fiscal policy and to recover credibility as a way of allowing the exchange rate to do its job. But the program failed to deliver this change of expectations. In 2019, fiscal policy became very contractionary and, while its effects were somewhat buffered by the floating exchange rate, the economy could not recover.

Finally, were the poor results derived from history, self-created mistakes, external factors, or just bad luck? While the macroeconomic heritage received by the government was not ideal, it is difficult to blame the results on it. The start of the program was relatively successful, and the economy experienced healthy growth in the first two years. In fact, by the end of the second year, growth expectations were solid at 3 percent per year for the remaining two years.[86] If heritage did not hinder such a positive start, why would it constrain what happened afterward? Luck played its role, primarily in the guise of a large drought that shaved off 2 percent of GDP in early 2018 (BCRA 2018b, 28), which in turn coincided with a tightening of external conditions due to the interest rate hikes associated to the reversal of quantitative easing policies in the United States. However, this shock was limited in size and affected many countries without the same consequences. Thus, it is difficult to associate the bad performance with luck or external conditions.

In the end, the blame resides in the policies that were introduced: fiscal policy deterioration at the beginning of the administration and betting on short-run growth, even at the expense of monetary institutions and inflation. Slackening the fight against inflation appears to have been a costly and obvious political mistake in a country that rewards stabilization

85. For an analysis of the effects of the exchange rate policy, see Levy-Yeyati (2019); for an analysis of sudden stops dynamics, see Calvo (1998).
86. BCRA Market Expectations Survey, December 2017, p. 13; http://www.bcra.gov.ar/ Pdfs/PublicacionesEstadisticas/REM171228%20Resultados%20web.pdf.

in the polls. This mistake seems paradoxical for a team that had showed significant professionalism in its evaluation of political risks and benefits and had seen the political benefits of disinflation in the midterm elections of 2017.

At the end, quite ironically, Macri's presidency failed from an excess of populism: lax fiscal policies and an inability to build macroeconomic institutions, in particular, weakening the Central Bank. It is somewhat paradoxical that it was this excess of populism that undermined Macri's attempt to prove populism wrong. In the end, the experience suggests that institutional buildup is an essential prerequisite for a successful stabilization and growth process. Even in this basic lesson Argentina is conventional.

ACKNOWLEDGMENTS Paper prepared for the Fall 2019 Brookings Papers on Economic Activity Conference. I thank Alberto Ades, Daniel Artana, Santiago Barraza, Nicolas Catena, Domingo Cavallo, Eduardo Cavallo, Marcelo Delmar, Florencia Gabrielli, Corso Galardi, Ricardo Lopez Murphy, Lucas Llach, Mauricio Macri, Andy Neumeyer, and seminar participants at Johns Hopkins, Universita Bocconi, IADB, the Peterson Institute, Universidad de San Andrés, and UTDT, as well as Janice Eberly, Rafael Di Tella, and Andres Velasco for their useful comments.I also thank Federico Forte, Santiago Cesteros, and Tomás Vilá for their useful research assistance. I also thank Luciano Cohan and Alberto Cavallo for making high-frequency price data available. Any remaining errors are mine.

References

Adrian, Tobias, Douglas Laxton, and Maurice Obstfeld. 2018. *Advancing the Frontiers of Monetary Policy*. Washington, D.C.: International Monetary Fund.

Agénor, Pierre-Richard, and Luiz A. Pereira da Silva. 2019. *Integrated Inflation Targeting: Another Perspective from the Developing World*. Basel: Bank for International Settlements.

Aguirre, Horacio, Tamara Burdisso, and Federico Grillo. 2006. "Hacia una estimación de la demanda de dinero con fines de pronóstico: Argentina, 1993–2005" [Toward an estimation of money demand with forecasting purposes: Argentina 1993–2005]. *Ensayos Económicos* [Essays in Economics] 45: 7–44.

Ahumada, Hildegart, and María Lorena Garegnani. 2002. "Understanding Money Demand of Argentina: 1935–2000." Paper prepared for Seventh Conference on Monetary and International Economics, National University of La Plata, La Plata, Argentina, May 2002.

Alvarez, Fernando, Martin Beraja, Martín Gonzalez-Rozada, and Pablo Andrés Neumeyer. 2018. "From Hyperinflation to Stable Prices: Argentina's Experience with Menu Costs." *Quarterly Journal of Economics* 134, no. 1: 451–505.

Argentine Ministry of Treasury. 2018. *La Reforma Tributaria Argentina de 2017* [The 2017 tax reform of Argentina]. Secretariat of Economic Policy.

Banco Central de la República Argentina (BCRA). 2015. *Monetary Policy Report*. December. http://www.bcra.gov.ar/PublicacionesEstadisticas/Informe_macroeconomico_y_de_politica_monetaria i.asp.

Banco Central de la República Argentina (BCRA). 2016a. *Monetary Policy Report*. May. http://www.bcra.gov.ar/Pdfs/PoliticaMonetaria/IPM_Mayo_2016_i.pdf.

Banco Central de la República Argentina (BCRA). 2016b. *Monetary Policy Report*, October. https://www.bcra.gob.ar/Pdfs/PoliticaMonetaria/IPOM_Octubre_2016_i.pdf.

Banco Central de la República Argentina (BCRA). 2016c. *Monetary Policy Report*, July. http://www.bcra.gov.ar/Pdfs/PoliticaMonetaria/IPOM_Julio_2016_i.pdf.

Banco Central de la República Argentina (BCRA). 2017a. *Monetary Policy Report*, April. http://www.bcra.gov.ar/Pdfs/PoliticaMonetaria/IPOM_April_2017_i.pdf.

Banco Central de la República Argentina (BCRA). 2017b. *Monetary Policy Report*, July. https://www.bcra.gob.ar/Pdfs/PoliticaMonetaria/IPOM_July_2017_i.pdf.

Banco Central de la República Argentina (BCRA). 2018a. *Monetary Policy Report*, January. http://www.bcra.gov.ar/Pdfs/PublicacionesEstadisticas/IPOM_Enero_2018_i.pdf.

Banco Central de la República Argentina (BCRA). 2018b. *Monetary Policy Report*, October. http://www.bcra.gov.ar/Pdfs/PoliticaMonetaria/IPOM1018_i.pdf.

Barro, Robert J. 1979. "On the Determination of the Public Debt." *Journal of Political Economy* 87, no. 5: 940–71.

Bassetto, Marco, and Christopher Phelan. 2015. "Speculative Runs on Interest Rate Pegs." *Journal of Monetary Economics* 73: 99–114.

Beblavy, Miroslav. 2002. "Exchange Rate and Exchange Rate Regime in Slovakia: Recent Developments." Working Paper 5. International Center for Economic Growth.

Benati, Luca, Robert E. Lucas Jr., Juan Pablo Nicolini, and Warren Weber. 2016. "International Evidence on Long Run Money Demand." Working Paper 22475. Cambridge, Mass.: National Bureau of Economic Research. https://www.nber.org/papers/w22475.

Bruno, Michael, Guido Di Tella, Rudiger Dornbusch, and Stanley Fischer, eds. 1988. *Inflation Stabilization: The Experience of Israel, Argentina, Brazil, Bolivia, and Mexico*. Cambridge, Mass.: MIT Press.

Bufman, G., and L. Leiderman. 1998. "Monetary Policy and Inflation in Israel." Working Paper 04/1998. Bank of Israel.

Calvo, Guillermo A. 1988. "Servicing the Public Debt: The Role of Expectations." *American Economic Review* 78, no. 4: 647–61.

Calvo, Guillermo A. 1991. "The Perils of Sterilization." *IMF Staff Papers* 38, no. 4: 921–26.

Calvo, Guillermo A. 1998. "Capital Flows and Capital-Market Crises: The Simple Economics of Sudden Stops." *Journal of Applied Economics* 1, no. 1: 35–54.

Calvo, Guillermo A., and Carmen M. Reinhart. 2002. "Fear of Floating." *Quarterly Journal of Economics* 117, no. 2: 379–408.

Calvo, Guillermo A., and Carlos A. Végh. 1993. "Exchange-Rate Based Stabilisation under Imperfect Credibility." In *Open-Economy Macroeconomics*, edited by Helmut Frisch and Andreas Wörgötter. London: Palgrave Macmillan.

Calvo, Guillermo A., and Carlos A. Végh. 1999. "Inflation Stabilization and BOP Crises in Developing Countries." In *Handbook of Macroeconomics*, edited by J. B. Taylor and M. Woodford, edition 1, volume 1, chapter 24, pages 1531–1614. Amsterdam: Elsevier.

Carstens, Agustín. 2019. "Exchange Rates and Monetary Policy Frameworks in Emerging Market Economies." Lecture given at the London School of Economics, London, May 2.

Cavallo, Eduardo A. 2019. "International Capital Flow Reversals (Sudden Stops)." In *Oxford Research Encyclopedias, Economics and Finance*. New York: Oxford University Press.

Céspedes, Luis Felipe, Roberto Chang, and Andrés Velasco. 2014. "Is Inflation Targeting Still on Target? The Recent Experience of Latin America." *International Finance* 17, no. 2: 185–208.

Chamon, M., David Hofman, Nicolás E. Magud, and Alejandro Werner, eds. 2019. *Foreign Exchange Intervention in Inflation Targeters in Latin America*. Washington, D.C.: International Monetary Fund.

Cochrane, John H. 2011. "Determinacy and Identification with Taylor Rules." *Journal of Political Economy* 119, no. 3: 565–615.

Cole, Harold L., and Timothy J. Kehoe. 1996. "A Self-Fulfilling Model of Mexico's 1994–1995 Debt Crisis." *Journal of International Economics* 41, nos. 3–4: 309–30.

Corso, Eduardo A., and Constanza Matarrelli. 2019. "Expectativas de Inflación Implícitas en la Curva de Rendimientos: Argentina 2017–2018" [Implicit inflation expectations in the yield curve: Argentina 2017–2018]. Technical Note 3/2019. Buenos Aires: Banco Central de la República Argentina. https://www.bcra.gob.ar/Pdfs/PublicacionesEstadisticas/NotasTecnicas/Nota_Tecnica_n3.pdf.

Daude, Christian, Ángel Melguizo, and Alejandro Neut. 2010. "Fiscal Policy in Latin America: Countercyclical and Sustainable at Last?" Working Paper 291. Paris: Organisation for Economic Cooperation and Development. https://www.oecd-ilibrary.org/development/fiscal-policy-in-latin-america_5km8zdcp7j41-en.

de Campos Meirelles, Henrique. 2003. "Como é do conhecimento de Vossa Excelência" [Mr. Minister, As you know . . .]. Letter from the governor of Banco Central do Brasil, to the minister of finance, January 21. https://www.bcb.gov.br/htms/relinf/carta2003.pdf.

de la Torre, Augusto, Eduardo Levy-Yeyati, and Samuel Pienknagura. 2013. "La desaceleración en América Latina y el tipo de cambio como amortiguador" [The slowdown in Latin America and the exchange rate as a buffer]. *LAC Informe Semestral* [LAC Semiannual Report], October. Washington, D.C.: World Bank. https://www.worldbank.org/content/dam/Worldbank/Feature%20Story/lac/AM_LAC_es.pdf.

De Paoli, Bianca. 2009. "Monetary Policy and Welfare in a Small Open Economy." *Journal of International Economics* 77, no. 1: 11–22.

Di Giovanni, Julian, and Jay C. Shambaugh. 2008. "The Impact of Foreign Interest Rates on the Economy: The Role of the Exchange Rate Regime." *Journal of International Economics* 74, no. 2: 341–61.

Di Tella, Rafael. 2019. Comment on "Macri's Macro" by Federico Sturzenegger. In the present volume of *Brookings Papers in Economic Activity*.

Dornbusch, Rudiger, and Sebastian Edwards, eds. 1991. *The Macroeconomics of Populism in Latin America*. Chicago: University of Chicago Press.

Escolano, Julio. 2010. "A Practical Guide to Public Debt Dynamics, Fiscal Sustainability, and Cyclical Adjustment of Budgetary Aggregates." IMF Technical Notes and Manuals 10/02. Washington, D.C.: International Monetary Fund, Fiscal Affairs Department.

Fedelino, Annalisa, Anna Ivanova, and Mark Horton. 2009. "Computing Cyclically Adjusted Balances and Automatic Stabilizers." IMF Technical Notes and Manuals 09/05. Washington, D.C.: International Monetary Fund, Fiscal Affairs Department.

Fischer, Stanley. 2001. "Exchange Rate Regimes: Is the Bipolar View Correct?" *Journal of Economic Perspectives*, American Economic Association, 15, no. 2: 3–24, Spring.

Fondo de Garantía de Sustentabilidad (FGS). 2016. *Accountability Report to the Congress*. October.

Frankel, Jeffrey, Ben Smit, and Federico Sturzenegger. 2008. "Fiscal and Monetary Policy in a Commodity-Based Economy." *Economics of Transition* 16, no. 4: 679–713.

Frenkel, Jacob. 1996. "Israel's Experience with Inflation." In *Economic Policy Symposium Proceedings: Achieving Price Stability.* Jackson Hole, Wyo.: Federal Reserve Bank of Kansas City.

Galiani, Sebastian. 2018. "La herencia y el esfuerzo fiscal" [The inheritance and fiscal effort]. Blog post, December 7, Foco Económico. http://focoeconomico.org/ 2018/12/07/la-herencia-y-el-esfuerzo-fiscal/.

Garcia, Carlos J., Jorge E. Restrepo, and Scott Roger. 2011. "How Much Should Inflation Targeters Care about the Exchange Rate?" *Journal of International Money and Finance* 30, no. 7: 1590–1617.

Garcia, Márcio. 2006. "Inflation Targeting in Brazil: Evaluation and Policy Lessons for Latin American Countries." Working Paper. http://www.economia. puc-rio.br/mgarcia/Artigos/Infl_Targ_Brazil_MGarcia_060113%20v02.pdf.

Gay, Alejandro. 2005. "Money Demand in an Open Economy Framework: Argentina (1932–2002)." Paper prepared for Tenth Conference on Monetary and International Economics, National University of La Plata, La Plata, Argentina, May 12–13, 2005.

Gibbs, Christopher G., and Mariano Kulish. 2017. "Disinflations in a Model of Imperfectly Anchored Expectations." *European Economic Review* 100: 157–74.

Girouard, Nathalie, and Christophe André. 2005. "Measuring Cyclically-Adjusted Budget Balances for OECD Countries." Working Paper 434. Paris: Organisation for Economic Cooperation and Development. https://www.oecd-ilibrary.org/ economics/measuring-cyclically-adjusted-budget-balances-for-oecd-countries_ 787626008442.

Gray, Simon, and Runchana Pongsaparn. 2015. "Issuance of Central Bank Securities: International Experiences and Guidelines." Working Paper 15/106. Washington, D.C.: International Monetary Fund. https://www.imf.org/external/pubs/ft/wp/ 2015/wp15106.pdf.

Guðmundsson, Már, and Yngvi Örn Kristinsson. 1997. "Monetary Policy in Iceland during the Nineties." In *Monetary Policy in the Nordic Countries: Experiences since 1992.* Basel: Bank for International Settlements.

Guidotti, Pablo E., Federico Sturzenegger, and Agustín Villar. 2004. "On the Consequences of Sudden Stops." *Economia* 4, no. 2: 171–214.

International Monetary Fund (IMF). 2017. *Thailand: 2017 Article IV Consultation—Press Release; Staff Report; and Statement by the Executive Director for Thailand.* Washington, D.C.: Author. https://www.imf.org/en/Publications/CR/ Issues/2017/05/31/Thailand-2017-Article-IV-Consultation-Press-Release-Staff-Report-and-Statement-by-the-44948.

International Monetary Fund (IMF). 2019. *Annual Report on Exchange Arrangements and Exchange Restrictions.* Washington, D.C.: Author. https://www.imf.org/ en/Publications/Annual-Report-on-Exchange-Arrangements-and-Exchange-Restrictions/Issues/2019/04/24/Annual-Report-on-Exchange-Arrangements-and-Exchange-Restrictions-2018-46162.

Kara, A. Hakan. 2008. "Turkish Experience with Implicit Inflation Targeting." *Central Bank Review* 1: 1–16.

Kara, A. Hakan. 2017. "Turkish Experience with Inflation Targeting." Presentation prepared for the International Financial Congress, St. Petersburg, July 12–14. http://ibcongress.com/upload/iblock/593/593f1c9dabf32e0c5ee5babc2bb50dac.pdf.

Larch, M., and Alessandro Turrini. 2010. "The Cyclically Adjusted Budget Balance in EU Fiscal Policymaking: Love at First Sight Turned into a Mature Relationship." *Intereconomics* 45, no. 1: 48–60.

Levy-Yeyati, Eduardo. 2006. "The Cost of Reserves." Working Paper 2006-10, Universidad Torcuato Di Tella.

Levy-Yeyati, Eduardo. 2019. "Exchange Rate Policies and Economic Development." In *Oxford Research Encyclopedias, Economics and Finance*. New York: Oxford University Press.

Levy-Yeyati, Eduardo, and Federico Sturzenegger. 2001. "Exchange Rate Regimes and Economic Performance." *IMF Staff Papers* 47: 62–98.

Levy-Yeyati, Eduardo, and Federico Sturzenegger. 2003. "To Float or to Fix: Evidence on the Impact of Exchange Rate Regimes on Growth." *American Economic Review* 93, no. 4: 1173–93.

Levy-Yeyati, Eduardo, and Federico Sturzenegger. 2005. "Classifying Exchange Rate Regimes: Deeds vs. Words." *European Economic Review* 49, no. 6: 1603–35.

Levy-Yeyati, Eduardo, and Federico Sturzenegger. 2007. "A Balance-Sheet Approach to Fiscal Sustainability." Working Paper 150. Boston: Center for International Development at Harvard University. https://www.hks.harvard.edu/centers/cid/publications/faculty-working-papers/cid-working-paper-no.-150.

Levy-Yeyati, Eduardo, and Federico Sturzenegger. 2016. "Classifying Exchange Rate Regimes: 15 Years Later." Working Paper 319. Boston: Center for International Development at Harvard University. https://www.hks.harvard.edu/centers/cid/publications/faculty-working-papers/classifying-exchange-rate-regimes.

Maman, Daniel, and Zeev Rosenhek. 2008. "The Contested Institutionalization of Policy Paradigm Shifts: The Adoption of Inflation Targeting in Israel." *Socio-Economic Review* 7, no. 2: 217–43.

Manuelli, Rodolfo E., and Juan I. Vizcaino. 2017. "Monetary Policy with Declining Deficits: Theory and an Application to Recent Argentine Monetary Policy." *Federal Reserve Bank of St. Louis Review* 99, no. 4: 351–75.

Masson, Paul R., Miguel A. Savastano, and Sunil Sharma. 1997. "The Scope for Inflation Targeting in Developing Countries." Working Paper 97/130. Washington, D.C.: International Monetary Fund. https://www.imf.org/en/Publications/WP/Issues/2016/12/30/The-Scope-for-Inflation-Targeting-in-Developing-Countries-2356.

Matthiasson, Thorolfur. 2008. "Spinning Out of Control: Iceland in Crisis." *Nordic Journal of Political Economy* 34, no. 3: 1–19.

Mishkin, Frederic S. 2000. "Inflation Targeting in Emerging-Market Countries." *American Economic Review* 90, no. 2: 105–9.

Mishkin, Frederic S., and M. A. Savastano. 2001. "Monetary Policy Strategies for Latin America." *Journal of Development Economics* 66, no. 2: 415–44.

Mishkin, Frederic S., and Klaus Schmidt-Hebbel. 2002. "A Decade of Inflation Targeting in the World: What Do We Know and What Do We Need to Know?" In *Inflation Targeting: Design, Performance, Challenges*, edited by Norman Loayza and Raimundo Soto. Santiago: Banco Central de Chile.

Mohanty, M. S., and Phillip Turner. 2005. "Intervention: What Are the Domestic Consequences?" In *Foreign Exchange Market Intervention in Emerging Markets: Motives, Techniques, and Implications*. Basel: Bank for International Settlements.

Morón, Eduardo, and Diego Winkelried. 2005. "Monetary Policy Rules for Financially Vulnerable Economies." *Journal of Development Economics* 76, no. 1: 23–51.

Nagy, László. 2016. "From Independent Slovakian Central Bank Policy to the Monetary Policy of the Euro Area." *Public Finance Quarterly* 1: 49.

Navajas, Fernando. 2019. "High-Frequency Data on Prices: Do Worry, Don't Be Happy." Presentation given at Argentina's 2019 Economic Outlook with FIEL Chief Economists, New York, May 2. 'https://www.as-coa.org/events/argentinas-2019-economic-outlook-fiel-chief-economists.

Neumeyer, Pablo A., and Juan Pablo Nicolini. 2011. "The Incredible Taylor Principle." Slides.

Novák, Zsuzsanna. 2011. "Alternative Monetary Strategies before EMU Membership in Central Europe." *Global Business and Economics Anthology* 2, no. 2: 414–24.

Organisation for Economic Cooperation and Development (OECD). 2008a. *OECD Economic Surveys: Indonesia 2008: Economic Assessment*. Paris: Author.

Organisation for Economic Cooperation and Development (OECD). 2008b. *OECD Economic Surveys: Turkey 2008: Economic Assessment*. Paris: Author.

Ortiz, Alberto, Pablo Ottonello, Federico Sturzenegger, and Ernesto Talvi. 2009. "Monetary and Fiscal Policies in a Sudden Stop: Is Tighter Brighter?" In *Dealing with an International Credit Crunch: Policy Responses to Sudden Stops in Latin America*, edited by Eduardo Cavallo and Alejandro Izquierdo. Washington, D.C.: Inter-American Development Bank.

Pourroy, Marc. 2012. "Does Exchange Rate Control Improve Inflation Targeting in Emerging Economies?" *Economic Letters* 116, no. 3: 448–50.

Rodrik, Dani. 2006. "The Social Cost of Foreign Exchange Reserves." *International Economic Journal* 20, no. 3: 253–66.

Sargent, Thomas J. 2013. "Stopping Moderate Inflations: The Methods of Poincaré and Thatcher." In *Rational Expectations and Inflation*. Princeton, N.J.: Princeton University Press. Originally published May 1981.

Sargent, Thomas J., and Neil Wallace. 1975. "'Rational' Expectations, the Optimal Monetary Instrument, and the Optimal Money Supply Rule." *Journal of Political Economy* 83, no. 2: 241–54.

Schmitt-Grohé, Stephanie, and Martín Uribe. 2012. "Pegs and Pain." Working Paper 16847. Cambridge, Mass.: National Bureau of Economic Research. https://www.nber.org/papers/w16847.

Schmidt-Hebbel, Klaus, and Matías Tapia. 2002. "Inflation Targeting in Chile." *North American Journal of Economics and Finance* 13, no. 2: 125–46.

Sturzenegger, Federico. 2016a. "Los primeros 100 días de un Banco Central que vuelve a ocuparse de sus objetivos primordiales" [The first 100 days of a Central Bank that returns to its primary objectives]. Speech given at the Bloomberg Argentina Summit 2016, Buenos Aires, April 5. http://www.bcra.gob.ar/Pdfs/Prensa_comunicacion/Disertaci%C3%B3n_de_Sturzenegger_en_Bloomber-Argentina%20Summit.pdf.

Sturzenegger, Federico. 2016b. Speech given at the 13th Conference of Monetary and International Economy, National University of La Plata, La Plata, Argentina, August. http://www.bcra.gov.ar/Pdfs/Prensa_comunicacion/Sturzenegger_UNLP.pdf.

Sturzenegger, Federico. 2019. "Reserve Management: A Governor's Eye View." In *HSBC Reserve Management Trends 2019*, edited by Nick Carver and Robert Pringle. London: Central Banking.

Tornell, Aaron, and Andrés Velasco. 2000. "Fixed versus Flexible Exchange Rates: Which Provides More Fiscal Discipline?" *Journal of Monetary Economics* 45, no. 2: 399–436.

Uribe, Martín. 2016. "Is the Monetarist Arithmetic Unpleasant?" Working Paper 22866. Washington, D.C.: National Bureau of Economic Research.

Comments and Discussion

COMMENT BY
RAFAEL DI TELLA   Sturzenegger's paper details Argentina's transition to an orthodox, center-right government that employed experts like himself to stabilize the economy following 13 years of populist administrations. Four years later, and with inflation about twice the level inherited from the populists, there is widespread disappointment with Macri's handling of the economy. What went wrong? According to Sturzenegger, the key mistake was the change in the inflation target in the middle of a "successful disinflation program." While this is an intriguing claim, the paper does not explain why Macri and other members of the government failed to appreciate all this progress and changed course. It would be ironic if all we could conclude from this episode is that Macri's Achilles' heel was, in the end, just old-style populist shortsightedness.

A more plausible explanation is that Argentina's macroeconomic performance was poor, that there was no significant disinflation relative to where the Kirchners left off, and that Sturzenegger's surprising program failed to convince the skeptics. In brief, his plan embraced simultaneously fiscal gradualism and a pure form of inflation targeting (IT) that promised to keep the exchange rate freely floating at all times. The plan covered three distinct periods: an initial "informal" phase when restrictions on capital flows would be lifted, relative prices would be adjusted, and inflation would actually go up; a second phase when there would be disinflation to "normal" levels; and a third and final stage when economic cycles would take place around a rate of inflation that was lower than the one inherited from the Kirchners. The plan can be described as surprising because pure IT, with a floating exchange rate and no room for the use of other tools, such as income policies, is an extremely unusual approach to stabilization (phase two) and because absence of fiscal dominance is a well-known precondition for IT. The plan can be seen as unconvincing because it made assumptions that went against conventional wisdom (for example, contrary to what most Argentines believe, Sturzenegger's plan assumed that there was no pass-through from the exchange rate to local prices). This simpler explanation would certainly be consistent with the rest of the information presented in this paper.

It is worth starting out by noting how unexpected Sturzenegger's plan really was. Table 1 suggests that Argentina had a reasonable fiscal performance in the years leading to the 2015 presidential election, registering a primary fiscal deficit of less than 0.4 percent per year on average for 2011–14. Then, during Cristina Kirchner's last year it jumped to 3.8 percent. Sturzenegger and his team expected (in June 2015) this deficit to shrink to 2.5 percent during 2016, which appears reasonable given that one-year changes might not be costly to undo. Some may see the projected adjustment as insufficient, but this is not obvious since, as emphasized by Sturzenegger at the time, a case could be made that debt levels were not large. A more pertinent observation is that larger adjustments might have been feasible, particularly if we note that government spending under the Kirchners had dramatically increased relative to historic levels. But overall, I don't see the proposed fiscal path as obviously unsustainable, even if not particularly amenable to a pure IT regime. Indeed, the absence of fiscal dominance is a well-known precondition for effective IT, and the paper explains that the expectation was to contain it "by anticipating a path for transfers from the Central Bank to the government." The question of how successful such containment was likely to be in practice given Argentina's context is moot because a series of highly visible "gifts" (income tax reductions, increases in pensions, and so on) soon turned fiscal gradualism into a robust fiscal *expansion* that took the 2016 primary deficit to 5.4 percent of GDP (or 4.2 if one includes the revenues from the one-off tax amnesty). It is reasonable to expect that Argentines, having lived through hyper-inflations and several episodes of debt default, give considerable weight to the consistency of fiscal plans in deciding whether to believe the monetary authority. Thus, Sturzenegger's plan to use IT in the presence of fiscal gradualism seems initially risky and, by the end of 2016, hard to justify.[1]

---

1. The paper's epigraph is a quote from Dornbusch dismissing explanations that are specific to particular countries, which is strange given the number of specific explanations that are later included in the paper, starting with the volatility of money demand in Argentina. A more relevant Dornbusch passage criticizes stabilization plans with inconsistent fiscal policy, explaining that there are "many thousand years of failed experiments" (4) since Diocletean, and calls "poets" and "magicians" those that implement programs "without paying attention to the *sine qua non* of fiscal correction" (Dornbusch and Simonsen 1987, 4, emphasis in the original).

Sturzenegger states that fiscal gradualism was a constraint decided by the political authority.[2] Even if one accepts this, there are two ways to read it. One is that it reflects a political rationale that is exclusively attached to the fiscal deficit by some deus ex machina and that there is not much else to discuss. The second is more natural and simply assumes that Sturzenegger is referring to a broad set of political constraints facing a weak government, and he provides some hints in this direction when he explains that fiscal gradualism would help the government avoid the stigma of being right-wing. But this opens up more questions. For example, were there any political gains when the first year's projected fiscal adjustment turned into a strong expansion? Was there a plan to spend this political capital in ways that supported the economic program? The paper doesn't explain. Furthermore, the rest of the program included many nongradual policies, such as the decision to reduce the income tax or to allow a sharp increase in regulated prices (see below). Are we supposed to view these policies as left-wing? Or is it that political constraints are irrelevant at the time of making these decisions? Political constraints in Sturzenegger's paper are a bit like the Cheshire cat in *Alice in Wonderland*: now you see them, now you don't.

The decision to embrace a pure version of IT for the three periods ahead was particularly surprising given the country's historical love affair with the dollar. As is well known, macroeconomists have extensively explored the pros and cons of exchange rate–based stabilization programs, and the class of problems they address differs drastically from the class of problems discussed in models of IT. To my knowledge, work on IT does not offer answers to the central challenges addressed in the stabilization literature, including the fact that sometimes changes in the price of the dollar represent much more than just a change in a relative price or the presence of considerable inflation inertia (through contracts or other formal and informal institutions). A key challenge in stabilization episodes is to keep the real interest rate low as inflation levels fall, and the use of IT seems to introduce forces pulling in the opposite direction, making it less credible.

---

2. Given the centrality of fiscal weakness in Sturzenegger's account of the crisis, it is a pity that this claim is not well documented. One insider's account of Macri's campaign directly contradicts it, portraying Sturzenegger's optimism as an exogenous enabler of the gradualist approach. He cites a meeting where Sturzenegger rejects the need for privatizations, cuts in pensions, cuts in social subsidies, and cuts in other items and notes that Marcos Peña, Macri's future chief of staff, seemed "pleasantly surprised" (quoted in Iglesias Illa 2016, 152–53, author's translation).

The paper does not really answer the critics who argued in favor of income policies, exemplified by the temporary freeze in wages, pensions, and prices observed during several successful stabilization episodes.[3] After dismissing these policies as not mainstream and part of old politics, Sturzenegger concludes that they weren't needed because "inflation expectations fell very quickly." Since he doesn't discuss the role of the appreciation of the exchange rate in this part of the paper, it is hard to evaluate this particular claim.

Similarly, the paper does not offer a clear response to critics who advocated including the dollar in the Central Bank's objective function.[4] Of course, there are limits to what the monetary authority can achieve with very few reserves at hand, but that is a different argument. Besides, there were several episodes of intervention in the market for dollars that, without some framework or guideline, appeared haphazard, and one wonders how they affected credibility. Sturzenegger does mention the inconvenience of fixing the exchange rate following the experience of the convertibility plan, and he has emphasized, both now and in the past, that there are no theoretical reasons to expect pass-through (Sturzenegger 2016). He has also offered empirical exercises demonstrating low pass-through. This is a very lucky coincidence, but, given that there is lots of evidence suggesting otherwise, one wonders if optimism is not playing a role here.[5] At a minimum, I note that the assumptions that the program employed are at the top range of the distribution of optimism regarding macroeconomic constraints. And this opens up a broader question in political economy, namely, the selection of optimists and pessimists into public office (and perhaps also into the different political parties).

Perhaps the paper's most extreme claim concerns the suitability of IT to engineer a disinflation process in Argentina in 2015. Two aspects stand out. The first is that the mechanism through which IT was supposed to work is never spelled out. There is no place in the paper where we get an explanation of the channels through which an increase in the

---

3. See, for example, the discussion in Dornbusch and Simonsen (1987), where they emphasize the requirements of consistent fiscal plans.

4. Sturzenegger states: "The Central Bank argued the opposite: that in order to lower pass-through levels it was important for the Central Bank to state that it did not care about the exchange rate at all," which is perhaps relevant during phase three but seems to have the priorities backward during a stabilization phase.

5. See Cavallo, Neiman, and Rigobon (2019), who find extremely high levels of pass-through in Argentina.

interest rate could be expected to moderate prices in tandem with the available evidence, either during the initial disinflation phase or later on. The paper emphasizes that "expectations coordination played a fundamental role in the disinflation process." The challenge is to square it with the evidence that was becoming available. In June 2015 Sturzenegger's team expected growth to be 2 percent for the year and 1 percent for 2016 as inflation was expected to come down. Growth by the end of 2015 was somewhat higher at 2.7 percent, but for 2016 it was *negative* 2.1 percent. Of course, rapid reductions in inflation without Phillips curve costs have long been known to be possible in models with rational expectations. Sargent (1981) defends their applicability to "moderate" inflations, but he explains how changes in regime have to be widely accepted and understood if they are to be effective. This seems to differ drastically from the context in which Sturzenegger's costless disinflation was supposed to happen, so there is a question of the applicability of these ideas in a politically divided context.[6] And when negative growth numbers came in for 2016, the authorities presumably had evidence that it was common knowledge that any convergence on lower inflation expectations was the result of other, more traditional channels (real exchange rate appreciation, recession, and so on) and that we were more in Thatcher's world rather than Poincaré's. This is not to claim that one cannot find particular slices of the sample period where there is growth, and Sturzenegger engages in this activity.[7] But the point here is that it became clear early on that the costless disinflation mechanism envisaged in Sargent (1981) was not in play and that monetary policy was very contractive. In brief, it was soon clear that any disinflation observed was taking place through other, costlier, channels than what was claimed by the Central Bank, and one wonders how this affected its credibility.

6. Sargent (1981, 7) describes how the stabilization of the French franc in 1926 took place after it was "universally recognized the country was in trouble again and all political parties, except the socialists and communists, gathered behind Poincaré. Five former premiers joined the government. There was a political truce." In Sturzenegger's case, it is precisely political weakness that is behind the only gradual fiscal adjustment constraint. Note also the strength of political support for the populists (in the 2015 ballotage they had obtained 49 percent versus Macri's 51 percent) and the fact that Macri's administration rejected calls for broadening the government coalition.

7. I stay with the data presented in the paper, both for simplicity and because they are likely to be the ones that are relevant for forming expectations. I note that seasonal adjustments or other partitions of the sample period, for example, yield slightly different magnitudes, without affecting the conclusions.

The second controversial aspect is Argentina's very high initial rate of inflation. Well-known examples of countries with a successful IT framework achieved disinflation through other means and only then adopted a full-fledged IT framework. One good example is the United Kingdom, a country where the big disinflations were achieved through a combination of monetarism during Thatcher and exchange rate targeting (the European Exchange Rate Mechanism in 1990–92, after inflation revived from the mid-1980s).[8] In other words, it wasn't that IT was used to bring down inflation, but rather that IT was a way of cementing in the fall in inflation that was achieved through other, more painful mechanisms. In contrast, Sturzenegger claims that his strategy of stabilizing through IT is standard and presents data on a sample of countries that "implemented IT or eventually converged to IT." In the current version of the paper he divides countries into floaters and fixers and doubles down on his stand, claiming that "countries with lower inflation rates used the exchange rate tool" and that they had slower disinflations. Sturzenegger makes the interesting methodological point that we should look at the policies in place, regardless of the name given to the regime.

I have three different reactions to this. First, countries judged by Sturzenegger to be purely floating in the period that precedes IT used other policies during the disinflation.[9] Thus, these countries cannot be used to describe Sturzenegger's approach as standard. Second, it is informative to separate the period leading to IT from the full IT regime. Thus, I repeat Struzenegger's exercise in figure 1, but I include countries only from the time that they focused exclusively on IT, and compare them to Argentina in January 2017 when Argentina's Central Bank adopted full-fledged IT. For example, in the case of Mexico, this date is 2001, five years later than the date Sturzenegger uses. This picture tells a very different story: looking at countries only from when they rely only on IT, Argentina's inflation rate is about 3.6 standard deviations higher than the mean of the other countries. Third, it is possible to derive a measure of

8. De Gregorio (2019) makes the point that IT is not a useful disinflation strategy. There is the question of whether applying IT at high levels of inflation is just unhelpful or if it is itself a significant source of new problems. Argentina seems to be an example of the latter. There is a parallel with the use of IT when inflation is below its steady-state level; see Pill (2019) for a discussion.

9. For example, the same source used by Sturzenegger to classify Turkey as purely floating states that "incomes policy will continue to play an important role in the program" and "any other intervention in the foreign exchange market will be strictly limited to the smoothing of short-term fluctuations" (Dervis and Serdengeçti 2001, n.p.).

Figure 1. Disinflation in Countries That Implemented IT (5-Year Horizon)

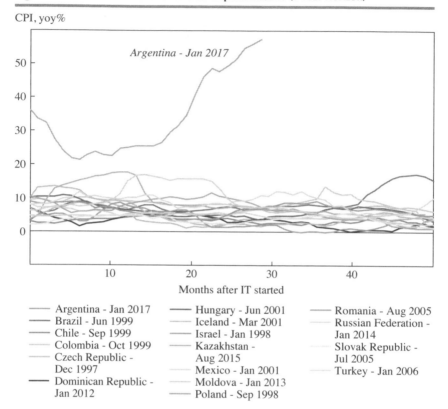

CPI, yoy%

Months after IT started

—— Argentina - Jan 2017	—— Hungary - Jun 2001	—— Romania - Aug 2005
—— Brazil - Jun 1999	—— Iceland - Mar 2001	—— Russian Federation -
—— Chile - Sep 1999	—— Israel - Jan 1998	Jan 2014
—— Colombia - Oct 1999	—— Kazakhstan -	—— Slovak Republic -
—— Czech Republic -	Aug 2015	Jul 2005
Dec 1997	—— Mexico - Jan 2001	—— Turkey - Jan 2006
—— Dominican Republic -	—— Moldova - Jan 2013	
Jan 2012	—— Poland - Sep 1998	

Sources: IMF and national statistical institutes.

Note: The chart plots inflation trajectories for the countries included in figure 3 in the paper from the moment they enter an inflation targeting regime. Sturzenegger has them entering earlier because he considers a pre-IT period.

how aggressive the initial policy stand was by subtracting the target from the initial rate of inflation. This is presented in figure 2. It reveals that Argentina's policy stand was about 3.5 standard deviations more aggressive than the average of the countries considered in Sturzenegger's original sample.[10] Figure 3 repeats these two exercises using an expanded sample

10. This underestimates the initial aggressiveness of Sturzenegger's plan because it uses the 2017 target announced by Alfonso Prat-Gay (and later endorsed by the Central Bank) and the effective annual inflation rate for December 2016. This yields 22.3 percent. If we use the team's anticipations (presented in table 2 in the paper), the projected inflation rate for 2016 is 38.2 percent while that for 2017 is 12.5 percent, for an aggressiveness of 25.7 percent.

Figure 2. Aggressiveness of Inflation Target at Adoption

Aggressiveness

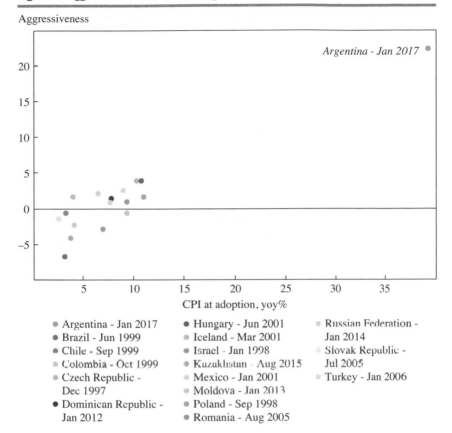

CPI at adoption, yoy%

- Argentina - Jan 2017
- Brazil - Jun 1999
- Chile - Sep 1999
- Colombia - Oct 1999
- Czech Republic - Dec 1997
- Dominican Republic - Jan 2012

- Hungary - Jun 2001
- Iceland - Mar 2001
- Israel - Jan 1998
- Kazakhstan - Aug 2015
- Mexico - Jan 2001
- Moldova - Jan 2013
- Poland - Sep 1998
- Romania - Aug 2005

- Russian Federation - Jan 2014
- Slovak Republic - Jul 2005
- Turkey - Jan 2006

Sources: IMF and national statistical institutes.
Note: "Aggressiveness" is the difference between the yoy% CPI target at the adoption of the inflation targeting regime and yoy% CPI in the month before the adoption took place. If the target was a range, the upper band was taken into account.

and reaches a similar conclusion. In other words, Argentina's context was nothing like the context of other countries relying exclusively on IT and Sturzenegger's plan on this dimension was also anything but standard.

Returning to the mismatch between the speed of fiscal adjustment determined by the politicians (gradual) and the speed of adjustment along other margins decided (or tolerated) by Sturzenegger and his team, I note that it is extreme in the case of regulated prices. There was a lot of anticipation about the approach that the monetary authority would take, as some of these prices were obviously lagging, and prior studies had

Figure 3. Expanded Sample

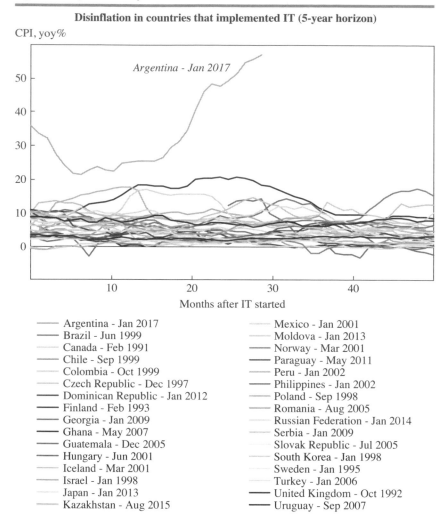

Disinflation in countries that implemented IT (5-year horizon)

CPI, yoy%

Argentina - Jan 2017

50

40

30

20

10

0

10   20   30   40

Months after IT started

Argentina - Jan 2017   Mexico - Jan 2001
Brazil - Jun 1999   Moldova - Jan 2013
Canada - Feb 1991   Norway - Mar 2001
Chile - Sep 1999   Paraguay - May 2011
Colombia - Oct 1999   Peru - Jan 2002
Czech Republic - Dec 1997   Philippines - Jan 2002
Dominican Republic - Jan 2012   Poland - Sep 1998
Finland - Feb 1993   Romania - Aug 2005
Georgia - Jan 2009   Russian Federation - Jan 2014
Ghana - May 2007   Serbia - Jan 2009
Guatemala - Dec 2005   Slovak Republic - Jul 2005
Hungary - Jun 2001   South Korea - Jan 1998
Iceland - Mar 2001   Sweden - Jan 1995
Israel - Jan 1998   Turkey - Jan 2006
Japan - Jan 2013   United Kingdom - Oct 1992
Kazakhstan - Aug 2015   Uruguay - Sep 2007

Sources: IMF and national statistical institutes.
Notes: These charts repeat the exercises in figures 1 and 2 but include the maximum number of
countries with monthly data available.

provided estimates warning of a substantial short-term impact on inflation
(Navajas 2015). Sturzenegger lists four of these increases, ranging from
100 percent to 300 percent, in the first months of 2016. Economists had long
argued that any direct impact on inflation in the short run could be moderated
by the subsequent improvement in the fiscal accounts. But, unfortunately,
as it soon became public knowledge, a large fraction of the increase went

Figure 3. Expanded Sample (*Continued*)

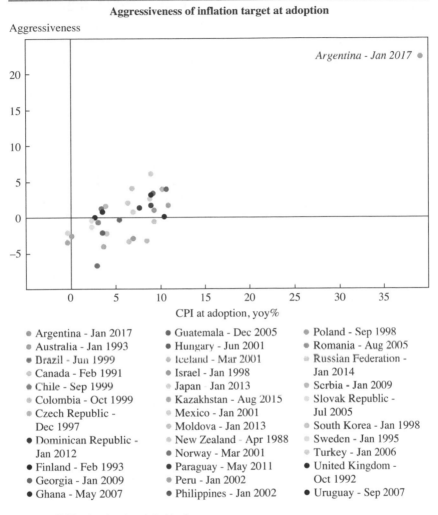

Sources: IMF and national statistical institutes.

Notes: These charts repeat the exercises in figures 1 and 2 but include the maximum number of countries with monthly data available.

to recover the profitability of energy sector firms, with a more muted effect on fiscal accounts. As I have alluded above, it is hard to understand what political rationale guided these adjustments: it is far more likely that they would fuel the "stigma of being . . . right-wing" than a simple fiscal adjustment. It is true that the starting point was extremely low and, even after these large increases, may fall short of the level that would help finance investment. But the impact on inflation—Sturzenegger's main policy objective—was consistently dismissed as an "adjustment to relative prices" (Sturzenegger 2016, 3, author's translation).[11] While this is certainly a possibility, changes that are so large and that take place in so many products, so close in time, and so clearly as a result of government action might have a different impact on inflation, perhaps because there is a signaling dimension to them (as compared to, say, the change in the price of one type of lightbulb).

One possibility, of course, is that Sturzenegger and his team were concerned about all this but accepted the government's aversion to having one person centralize power over economic decisions (a so-called superminister). This would then be another political constraint accepted by Sturzenegger that made his job much more difficult than necessary, and it is a pity we do not get his opinions on the trade-offs involved, including whether so much deference to political constraints might, in the end, have undermined the perception of independence of the monetary authority.

Regardless of one's take on these political constraints, it is still hard to square Sturzenegger's position on pass-through, which appears to play a key role in his decision to embrace IT, with his early projections. Indeed, the team's June 2015 projections have inflation for 2016 *increasing* to 38.2 percent (from a 2015 inflation rate of 26 percent under Kirchner). The challenge is figuring out how they arrived to that number without any pass-through. As noted above, the obvious channels involving pass-through from the devaluation and hikes in energy prices are ruled out (Sturzenegger 2016). It is difficult to justify the 38.2 percent through money growth because the plan projected a drastic reduction in monetized deficits (both because the primary deficit was expected to drop and because they were expecting to issue more debt). Perhaps Sturzenegger and his team were making an extreme assumption regarding the change in the Central Bank's credibility a few months after their arrival (but not immediately after) and, in turn, extreme assumptions regarding the impact of the regime's credibility on pass-through. Or perhaps the team simply used a model with

---

11. Sturzenegger (2016) explains how "rigorous reasoning" grounded in "general equilibrium" is enough to dismiss critics of his program who expect an impact of the adjustments in regulated prices (or of the dollar) on inflation. Even if one disagrees with Sturzenegger's view, one has to accept that it is consistent with some of his other claims (for example, that there was a "successful disinflation" led by expectations anchored by an increasingly credible Central Bank). Surprisingly, on page 31 he contradicts this claim by writing that the increases in the inflation rate during 2017 originate in the increases in regulated prices that took place during that year and that the increase in 2016 was due to the lifting of capital controls (see footnote 31).

standard assumptions regarding pass-through to make the 2016 projections and then they changed it when they had to think about the benefits of IT. If this is the case, and given that they actually hit that projection, one wonders why the economic team did not continue using the standard model.

The second part of the paper refers to the way rivals within the government interfered and convinced the president to change the target on December 28, 2017. These forces followed different logics and went on unappreciated by a political team that Sturzenegger himself describes in favorable terms. Take the conspirators from the Treasury. The idea is that, because pensions were indexed on past inflation, a "different sort of fiscal dominance" led to demands for *slower* disinflation and the changing of the target. This sounds strange, in part because Sturzenegger himself writes that in the second half of 2017 "disinflation stalled" and that inflation expectations for "2018 had increased 2.3 percentage points in the previous 14 months, which, considering that the target for 2017 would be missed, led to continued doubts about the success of the disinflation program."

There is also a short discussion of how unusual and unhelpful changing the targets might be, independently of how much results differ from the target.[12] The Central Bank's leitmotiv was "to change a target is to have no target" (BCRA 2017), but, presumably, there is a point beyond which retaining targets that have been repeatedly missed lowers credibility. Unfortunately, the paper doesn't comment on this possibility. There is also little discussion of the decision to lower nominal rates soon after. Following the change in the targets, survey-based inflation expectations went up substantially, which lowered the real rate, and this was followed by a reduction in the nominal rate that stabilized the market (allowing a large bond issue). This presumably reduced the pressure on the Central Bank, so it is difficult to understand why it was soon followed by a second lowering of the nominal rate, one that triggered the increase in dollar-denominated government bond spreads. Sturzenegger has written before about this and, in the

12. The upper bound for the inflation target for 2016 was announced at 25 percent on January 12, 2016, by Prat-Gay, in charge of the Treasury. He also announced 17 percent for 2017, 12 percent for 2018, and 6.5 percent for 2019. At that time, the statistical office (INDEC) was not yet able to produce CPI data following years of intervention by the Kirchners. So these numbers were likely to be interpreted as tentative. The targets were soon ratified by the Central Bank on April 28, 2016. Argentina's inflation exceeded the target by 14.3 percentage points in 2016 and by 8.7 in 2017. Sturzenegger calls the first year a "transition" period, and he claims to have tried only to "approximate" the target for 2016 and "did not endorse" it. He laments the coincidence between the targets for 2017–18–19 announced by the Treasury in January and those adopted by the Central Bank in April as it could have suggested more commitment to the 2016 target.

current version, explains that it was the "natural response to a softening of the targets," without referring to the fact that the real rate had already dropped considerably. Perhaps Sturzenegger did explain this in detail to the political authorities and they were simply insatiable. In that case, we should revise our view of who are the populists in Argentina.

At one level, this is an easy paper on which to comment: it explains that it is standard to use IT for disinflation purposes and I see this as anything but standard. Sturzenegger also explains that he and his team were aware of the fact that absence of fiscal dominance is a precondition for effective IT but that they insisted on relying on IT, even in early 2017 when it was clear that the fiscal position had worsened. While the paper makes many valuable points, it doesn't explain whether Sturzenegger was concerned over this, and if he was, why he failed to transmit this constraint to the political authorities or why he insisted on applying such a pure version of IT, with a floating exchange rate and unchanging targets. The relationship between politicians and economists in government is always complicated. Most of the time, politicians explain the constraints within which economists must design their policies. But occasionally, economists are able to convince politicians of the benefits of avoiding certain paths. What is striking in this paper, if one accepts its basic premise of an exogenously mandated gradual fiscal adjustment, is how little Sturzenegger was able to shape the environment in which he and his team had to work, and how optimistic he remained as he interpreted the rest of the constraints he faced.

Sturzenegger ends his paper with some lessons. They differ from my own, which are relatively straightforward.

1. The use of inflation targeting with a floating exchange rate to stabilize the economy is nonstandard. The usual approach is to use IT as a way of cementing in the fall in inflation achieved through other means. While this certainly doesn't mean it couldn't work as a matter of principle, it does suggest that the paper's portrayal of the use of IT as mainstream is incorrect.

2. A credible fiscal path can help anchor expectations during a stabilization program. It is likely a precondition, particularly in countries with a history of fiscal indiscipline as most participants monitor the fiscal accounts. Under a "pure" version of IT with a floating exchange rate, it is particularly important because the relatively easy and immediate substitution of local price expectations by the (exogenous) process determining foreign price expectations that is offered by a traditional peg has been forgone.

3. Income policies and exchange rate interventions are reasonable instruments, at least in principle, so one should not accept political or ideological constraints on their use.

4. It seems that it wasn't easy for Sturzenegger to derive credibility from appearing tough or overambitious. I wonder if one can derive credibility from appearing to be reasonable. For example, after missing the target, I wonder about the effects of recognizing it publicly in an effort to rally support for the new targets. In that sense, changing targets that one has missed might be more credible than appearing stubborn.

5. It can be useful to calibrate each of the assumptions of a program on an optimism scale. If most or all of them are on the optimistic side, relative to other assumptions that can be made, then one should wonder about its robustness and probably rethink it. At a minimum, if one cannot convince the members of one's own government of the virtues of the program, the margin for error is small, so a case can be made for leaning toward policies that are seen as reasonable by most, rather than as the best by a few.

6. While some key elements of the economic program put together by Sturzenegger and his team depart from those observed in prior successful stabilization attempts, my main criticism is that the political authorities do not seem to have been aware of the nonstandard nature of the plan and the uncertainties involved. We do not have many experiments in macroeconomics so most of our knowledge comes from historical narratives and simplified models. Thus, it is good to let the clients (politicians and voters) know the large margins of error within which macro policymakers work. Pretense of knowledge is unlikely to help build credibility and may even fuel resistance to experts, even amongst no-populist voters in Argentina.

REFERENCES FOR THE DI TELLA COMMENT

Banco Central de la República Argentina (BCRA). 2017. *Monetary Policy Report*, April. http://www.bcra.gov.ar/Pdfs/PoliticaMonetaria/IPOM_April_2017_i.pdf.

Cavallo, Alberto, Brent Neiman, and Roberto Rigobon. 2019. "Real Exchange Rate Behavior: New Evidence from Matched Retail Goods." Working Paper 20–040. Cambridge, Mass.: Harvard Business School. https://www.hbs.edu/faculty/Publication%20Files/20-040_237cc084-3e63-4376-bb58-50043cd281fb.PDF.

De Gregorio, Jose. 2019. "Inflation Targets in Latin America." Working Paper 19–19. Washington: Peterson Institute for International Economics. https://www.piie.com/sites/default/files/documents/wp19-19.pdf.

Dervis, Kemal, and Süreyya Serdengeçti. 2001. Letter to Horst Kohler, Managing Director of the IMF. https://www.imf.org/external/np/loi/2001/tur/03/index.htm.

Dornbusch, Rudiger, and Mario Henrique Simonsen. 1987. "Inflation Stabilization with Incomes Policy Support: A Review of the Experience of Argentina, Brazil and Israel." Working Paper 2153. Cambridge, Mass.: National Bureau of Economic Research. https://www.nber.org/papers/w2153.

Iglesias Illa, Hernán. 2016. *Cambiamos: Mauricio Macri Presidente* [We Changed: Mauricio Macri President]. Buenos Aires: Sudamericana.

Navajas, Fernando. 2015. "Subsidios a la energia, devaluación y precios" [Energy subsidies, devaluation and prices]. Working Paper 122. Buenos Aires: Fundación de Investigaciones Económicas Latinoamericanas. http://www.fiel. org/publicaciones/Documentos/DOC_TRAB_1431636145020.pdf.

Pill, Huw. 2019. "Monetary Policy: 'Whatever It Takes within Our (New?) Mandate.'" In *Renewing Our Monetary Vows: Open Letters to the New Governor of the Bank of England,* edited by Richard Barwell and Jagjit S. Chadha. London: National Institute for Economic and Social Research.

Ramos-Francia, Manuel, and Alberto Torres García. 2005. "Reducing Inflation through Inflation Targeting: The Mexican Experience." Working Paper 2005-01. Banco de México. https://www.banxico.org.mx/publications-and-press/banco-de-mexico-working-papers/%7B7F3073DE-937B-4393-1C77-6C77A661A348 %7D.pdf.

Sargent, Thomas J. 1981. "Stopping Moderate Inflations: The Methods of Poincaré and Thatcher." Working Paper. Federal Reserve Bank of Minneapolis. https:// www.minneapolisfed.org/research/working-papers/stopping-moderate-inflations-the-methods-of-poincare-and-thatcher.

Sturzenegger, Federico. 2016. "El uso del concepto de equilibrio general en su aplicación a la política monetaria." Speech given at the Academia Nacional de Ciencias Económicas, March 16. http://www.bcra.gob.ar/Pdfs/Prensa_ comunicacion/Distertaci%C3%B3n_Sturzenegger_Academia_NCE.pdf.

COMMENT BY

ANDRÉS VELASCO   I learned a great deal from reading this paper. One finds novel or illuminating observations at almost every turn. But it is not an easy paper to discuss. Sturzenegger is the author of the paper and also one of the authors of the 2016 Argentine stabilization plan the paper analyzes. My task is therefore twofold: to discuss the plan itself and at the same time to discuss the paper's interpretation of the plan and what went wrong.

Let me say first of all that all postmortems are painful, but this is a particularly painful one. It is by now a cliché of international economics that Argentina is the impossible-to-explain outlier, the country that was about as rich as Canada and Australia around a century ago yet has stagnated ever since. Mauricio Macri, coming to power after a particularly inept and corrupt administration and enjoying good will at home and (initially at least) propitious economic conditions abroad, had a unique opportunity to make Argentina a normal country again. Today, that aspiration lies in tatters as the economy contracts and careens toward yet another debt default, while the polity appears bitterly divided into irreconcilable camps.

FISCAL POLICY Macri's "gradual adjustment" approach to fiscal policy was based on two arguments: one economic and one political. The economic argument was that the fiscal situation allowed for gradual consolidation because initial debt levels were low (that is one advantage of a default). The political argument was that all previous experiences with fiscal shock treatments had failed in Argentina, often for political reasons. I will discuss the economic argument first and save the politics for the closing portion of my comment.

A useful contribution of the paper is to show that, once all necessary adjustments to the data are performed, the initial debt burden was 40 percent of GDP, not 23 percent. To that one should add the Central Bank's gaping equity hole, amounting to some $93 billion. So the initial position of the consolidated public sector, including the BCRA, was much worse than headlines suggested.

Moreover, the gradual fiscal adjustment went off course for three reasons: tax cuts were large, equal to 2.2 percent of GDP; economic growth, and therefore revenue, was smaller than initially planned; and adverse political shocks materialized, among them a Supreme Court decision that raised the federal deficit by 1 percent of GDP. There was a fourth reason the paper does not emphasize: the removal of energy subsidies did happen, but more slowly than government projections initially envisioned.

So rather than going down, however gradually, the fiscal deficit actually *increased*. Not counting the temporary revenue produced by a tax amnesty, the primary deficit rose from 3.8 percent of GDP in 2015 to 5.4 percent in 2016. Fiscal adjustment was limited until early in 2019. By then, it was too late.

This all prompts an inevitable question: Why did the authorities, when confronted with this reality, not implement an early course correction? Why did the Macri team not do what it had to do, say, in late 2016? One possible answer is that it was not politically feasible to adjust more. Another is that the base case scenario for fiscal policy was worse than expected but sustainable and therefore no major adjustment was required. What happened instead, the paper suggests, is that the shocks kept coming, and they eventually caused the fiscal program to go off course.

This argument, again, is not fully convincing because it raises issues about the reasonable degree of risk aversion. Engineers do not build bridges to withstand all kinds of earthquakes, but they do build bridges that will remain upright, say, 99 percent of the time. The more seismic is the country in question, the stronger the bridges will have to be to meet this standard. Argentina is a financially seismic country. Shocks have occurred in the past and will recur in the future. Given all of this, shouldn't the fiscal bridge have been stronger?

One last point on fiscal policy. The paper makes a great deal of the impact of changes in inflation on the real value of expenditures and revenues, and therefore on the fiscal deficit. In particular, it argues that because pensions were indexed backward, a sharp disinflation would have actually worsened fiscal accounts. This, the paper argues, caused the fiscal authority to exert pressure on the BCRA to slow down the disinflation process.

Surely unexpected inflation shocks can have real and unwanted effects. If the expenditure side of the budget was built with the expectation of 20 percent inflation, and then inflation surprisingly reached only 15 percent, then the real value of expenditure will be too large and so will the deficit. But in this case, inflation often surprised on the upside, not on the downside. Moreover, the effects of backward indexation were perfectly predictable. Why did the authorities not take this into account when designing the initial fiscal and monetary strategy? Or why did they not spend more political capital early to obtain the congressional support needed to tweak the indexation formula? Perhaps the answer is that they tried but it was not politically possible. If so, then something else (perhaps taxes) had to give.

MONETARY POLICY As for price stability, Argentina followed conventional wisdom and quickly adopted an inflation targeting (IT) regime. The paper stresses that core inflation fell throughout Sturzenegger's tenure as governor. But headline inflation was volatile, reflecting utility price increases and a very erratic exchange rate. Pass-through from the exchange rate to prices fell but remained high (Cavallo, Neiman, and Rigobon 2019), and every time headline inflation targets were missed (which happened often), credibility took a hit.

IT has worked well in countries where inflation was already low. But to get there, countries that were successful at inflation targeting like Chile, Israel, and Poland initially employed some combination of currency pegs, dual exchange rates, income policies, or all of the above. The Argentine authorities, by contrast, ruled out a currency peg because of the traumatic experience with the one-to-one dollar peg two decades ago. And income policies would have required negotiating prices and wages with union bosses regarded as political adversaries.

The question is whether all the bells and whistles of IT, including a floating exchange rate, should have waited until inflation was lower (say, 20 percent). Sturzenegger takes a firm stance on this, arguing that this is mostly a labeling issue, in the sense that successful countries began doing IT de facto long before they officially called it that. I am not sure I agree with that characterization. One reason many countries did not adopt the label (Chile is an example) is precisely because they were using crawling pegs or exchange rate bands to aid the initial disinflation.

Yes, there is a handful of countries—the experiences of Indonesia and the Dominican Republic are stressed in the text—where disinflation starting at high levels of inflation occurred under a float. But neither of these was a country with chronic inflation (and therefore widespread indexation) like Argentina. And, as the paper shows, they both underwent sharp nominal and real appreciations that would have been hard to sustain in the Argentina of 2016, where export growth was a priority.

Under standard inflation targeting the central bank, having decided to control the interest rate, is supposed to let the exchange rate float. But, in fact, the BCRA often intervened in foreign exchange (FX) markets, buying dollars in order to have more international reserves ready for a rainy day. Sturzenegger is quite enthusiastic—and persuasive—in arguing that the reserve buildup was necessary. Of course, after the fateful Southern Hemisphere summer of 2017, the BCRA also attempted to use intervention and the resulting exchange rate appreciation as a source of anti-inflation credibility.

So if FX intervention was both necessary and desirable, does this not raise the question of whether IT with a "cleanly" floating exchange rate was the right policy for Argentina? Or was perhaps some kind of modified or flexible IT, one that allowed for reserve accumulation and decumulation at some predefined junctures, preferable? These are general issues that go far beyond the implementation of IT in the particular case of Argentina, but they take on especial importance there given the attention that is always lavished to Central Bank purchases or sales of foreign exchange.

There is a case to be made for occasional sterilized intervention, even in the context of the IT framework; the Bank for International Settlements, led by Agustín Carstens and drawing on important work by Hyun Song Shin, has been making that case recently (Carstens and Shin 2019). But if a central bank is willing to buy reserves in an orderly manner, it should also be prepared to sell them in an orderly manner when the need arises. In Argentina there was no such rule, and when the crunch came Central Bank decisions—whether to sell dollars or to stop selling them—were not understood by the market and tended to be more destabilizing than stabilizing. Sturzenegger is candid about this failure: "after two years of almost free floating, the interventions only added to the confusion about the monetary regime."

Last but not least, successful inflation targeting assumes prudent fiscal policy and central bank autonomy. As Sturzenegger makes clear in the paper, Argentina met neither prerequisite. In December 2017, the president's political enforcers pressured the Central Bank to raise its inflation target and, a few weeks later, to cut interest rates twice, by a cumulative 150 basis points.

It was the beginning of the end. While other inflation targeting countries have relaxed targets without dire consequences, they did not suffer from Argentina's combination of weak underlying conditions and limited government credibility. Investors headed for the exits, the peso depreciated, and country risk spreads soared. Because debt was dollar-denominated, as the exchange rate weakened from 20 to 40 pesos to the dollar, the debt-to-GDP ratio doubled almost overnight. Soon enough, Argentina was asking the International Monetary Fund for a bailout.

Late 2017 was a strange time for President Macri to lose his cool. He and his coalition, called Cambiemos, had triumphed over the Peronist Justicialist Party in that October's legislative and gubernatorial elections, even in the Peronists' traditional stronghold of Buenos Aires Province. If ever there was a time to put Argentina's fiscal house in order and pursue disinflation, this was it. Instead, for reasons that remain unknown, Macri browbeat the Central Bank into a mistimed monetary loosening.

STERILIZATION, SHORT-TERM BONDS, AND MULTIPLE EQUILIBRIA I found the discussion of this issue one of the most interesting portions of the whole paper. It is fascinating, beyond the features of the Argentine experience, because it points to a fundamental tension. While sterilized intervention can be effective, its quasi fiscal costs are often sizeable, and the presence of a large stock of short-term domestic liabilities, whether issued by the Central Bank or by the Treasury, opens the door to rollover risks and self-fulfilling crises.

The probability of a self-fulfilling attack depends on two factors the paper discusses in some detail (the size of the debt and its average maturity) and one that the paper only touches in passing: the degree to which amortizations are bunched. Having allowed maturities to shorten was only one of the sins committed in Argentina in late 2017 and early 2018; the other was to have permitted a huge bunching of amortizations in 2018:Q2.

The story unfolded as in the textbook account. At first, longer maturity issues by the Central Bank were avoided so as to make room for the Treasury in that segment of the yield curve. But this shift set in motion a series of perverse changes in expectations: "while this [the decision to shorten maturities] had been a policy decision, market participants believed it could only be the response to difficulties in rollover, which worsened market sentiment." Soon enough, in late April, there was a massive run-out of short-term BCRA paper, which also became a run on the peso.

POLITICAL ECONOMY Sturzenegger argues that Macri spent fiscal and credibility capital in order to build up another kind of asset: political capital. By choosing not to begin its administration with a shock treatment, the argument goes, the Macri administration showed it was not like all the other center-right (or, in most cases, extreme right) administrations in recent Argentine history.

I have some sympathy for this argument. Showing that Macri had little to do with Carlos Menem, and even less to do with the likes of Generals Videla and Galtieri, who led Argentina's military dictatorships in the 1970s and 1980s, was important. But the point should not be exaggerated.

While Macri was right to steer away from shock treatment, he likely had more political capital than he thought: voters backed his coalition in October 2017 even though utility prices had gone through the roof, inflation remained high, and slow growth persisted. In the two years since, Macri has presided over a balance of payments crisis, repeated devaluation episodes, an inflation spike, a deep recession, two IMF bailouts, and a deep (though late) fiscal adjustment. And nonetheless, contravening many forecasts of impending electoral collapse, he received over 40 percent of the vote in the October 2019 presidential election.

Perhaps Mauricio Macri could have spent more of that political capital on a gradual—but substantial—fiscal adjustment, cut taxes by a smaller amount, dismantled capital controls more slowly, used a wider set of tools to fight inflation, and pushed sooner for pension reform. On the political front, to avoid the stigma of being called right-wing he could have tacked left on issues like human rights and abortion, where, as an avowed liberal, he should have been less timid.

But he did not. It may be a long time until Argentina gets another chance to be a normal country.

REFERENCES FOR THE VELASCO COMMENT

Carstens, Agustín, and Hyun Song Shin. 2019. "Emerging Markets Aren't Out of the Woods Yet." *Foreign Affairs*, March 15. https://www.foreignaffairs.com/articles/2019-03-15/emerging-markets-arent-out-woods-yet.

Cavallo, Alberto, Brent Neiman, and Roberto Rigobon. 2019. "Real Exchange Rate Behavior: New Evidence from Matched Retail Goods." Working Paper 20-040. Cambridge, Mass.: Harvard Business School. https://www.hbs.edu/faculty/Publication%20Files/20-040_237cc084-3e63-4376-bb58-50043cd281fb.PDF.

GENERAL DISCUSSION   Eswar Prasad began by comparing the session to a postmortem of a corpse that is not yet cold. In his view, Sturzenegger's analysis was sobering and persuasive. However, he pointed out that Sturzenegger's conclusion that the exchange rate regime worked better than anticipated seemed to be based solely on an analysis of the inflation outcomes. However, the literature on exchange rate regimes, balance sheet effects, or the dominant currency shows that other measures matter as well. Therefore, he wondered whether this result still held in the context of the regime's ability to absorb shocks in the context of broader macroeconomic outcomes.

Echoing comments made by both discussants, Frederic Mishkin turned the focus toward the risks of pursuing pure inflation targeting in the context of high initial inflation. He drew two key lessons from this analysis: One was that in the context of fiscal dominance, it is crucial to discuss commitments at the very beginning so that monetary and fiscal policy can work consistently to bring down inflation. Second, in the context of high initial inflation, a central bank needs to make use of other tools such as exchange rate stabilization policies, which he believed would have been the most sensible approach for Argentina. Of course, this approach also poses its own risks when central banks do not have a clear exit strategy at the outset. He noted that Argentina's convertibility law is a classic example of this.

Even with an exit strategy, however, Mishkin remarked that outlining an exit strategy is not foolproof. For example, he observed that despite intending to pursue inflation targeting with an exit strategy, Chile's economy went into crisis following the Russian 1998 crisis, and it made a mistake by focusing too much on the exchange rate. Still, having an exit strategy was useful as it helped Chile eventually get rid of the peg and transition toward a pure inflation targeting regime.

Mishkin concluded by restating his belief that exchange-based stabilization was the right way to go but emphasized the importance of having a clear exit strategy. Otherwise, he argued, stabilization might appear to be successful at first but lead to a disaster later on, as happened during the 1998–2002 Argentine great depression.

Olivier Blanchard found the paper and discussion both fascinating. In terms of the consistency of the initial monetary policy framework, he recalled that Sturzenegger had said that the Central Bank had to give some of the seigniorage to the central government such that the money supply would grow enough to cover it. In principle, he remarked, this can conflict with using an interest rate instrument, which Sturzenegger had also said he used when he was president of the Central Bank. Therefore, Blanchard wondered how he had approached this potential contradiction.

Peter Henry discussed the gradualist approach through the lens of the literature on reductions of moderate inflation in emerging markets. In 2002, he published a paper which showed that there is no evidence that rapid disinflation can be done without cost from moderate levels.[1] Therefore, he noted that even moderate disinflations pursued gradually could have some upward costs.

Moreover, Henry added that fiscal adjustment is still necessary for disinflation to succeed. Although the discussants mentioned the case of Venezuela, he pointed out that another disinflation program in the Caribbean basin received much less attention. In his view, Jamaica is probably the most surprising macro story of the last three or four decades. Its debt-to-GDP ratio, over 120 percent less than four years ago, is forecasted to decline to roughly 90 percent in the fiscal year 2019–20, and its inflation rate has fallen to less than 5 percent under two different governments that were consistent in their fiscal adjustment. Henry optimistically asserted that if it can be done in Jamaica, it can be done elsewhere, albeit with some leadership sacrifice.

Henry concluded by asking about the decision-making process around monetary adjustment. One alternative, he noted, would have been to tighten monetary policy and force a recession to do the adjustment on the monetary side instead of the fiscal side. Therefore, he asked Sturzenegger to comment on his decision-making process and other alternatives that he considered.

Kristin Forbes flipped Velasco's question on whether Sturzenegger had changed the inflation target without lowering interest rates and asked what would have happened if he had refused to change the inflation target but

1. Peter Blair Henry, "Is Disinflation Good for the Stock Market?," *Journal of Finance* 57, no. 4 (2002): 1617–48.

lowered interest rates. Brazil took this approach around this time, and in general, it seemed to have stabilized inflation without running into the problems Sturzenegger encountered in Argentina.

Lastly, she said she would like to hear more about the decisions Sturzenegger made on financing the debt. She wondered whether these debt-financing decisions had more of an impact on Argentina's economic problems than the mistakes emphasized in the paper. In particular, she noted, given that Argentina's debt financing is mainly in dollars, then whenever there is any shock to confidence, its currency depreciates and its debt skyrockets to quickly become unsustainable, which is what has happened now. Forbes wondered whether Sturzenegger could have financed more of the debt in local currency or with growth-indexed debt—which investors have made money in—when it was relatively cheap to finance debt. She asked if this approach would have cost much more at the time in terms of making the fiscal numbers look worse but may have been worth it in the current situation by preventing the debt from rapidly increasing due to exchange rate movements.

Jeromin Zettelmeyer wondered whether Sturzenegger or the discussants could say something about the last 18 months, which were not the main focus of the presentation. Sturzenegger's explanation, he observed, contained a puzzle: on one hand, the initial success of the disinflation program was surprising given that the monetary strategy was relatively risky, and the fiscal policy was not collaborating. In other words, inflation unraveled despite a lack of fiscal support. However, in the last 18 months, Argentina has pursued a drastic fiscal adjustment by about 3 points of GDP, but inflation has stayed high. With this said, he asked whether this puzzle was an unavoidable consequence of the waning credibility of the program, which unfolded by early 2018 or if it had something to do with the execution of monetary policy. Furthermore, he wondered what lessons we should draw for future monetary policy in Argentina.

John Lipsky followed up on Zettelmeyer's point by adding that Argentina has been the beneficiary of the most extensive IMF stabilization program ever. The IMF's loan, he pointed out, ballooned from $50 billion originally to around $57 billion, and currently about $50 billion has been disbursed. Therefore, he questioned whether the program was flawed at the outset on technical grounds and asked Sturzenegger if he could comment on why it has failed so catastrophically despite unprecedented actual disbursement of funds.

Sturzenegger started by responding to Prasad's and Mishkin's question on the role of inflation targeting without exchange rate support. He admitted that perhaps he failed to mention an important constraint at the beginning of his term, that the Central Bank's net reserves were around minus $5 billion. Therefore, he noted, targeting the exchange rate could have been done in theory, but in practice it was off the table.

On the point made by Di Tella that Argentina's fiscal reforms were only selectively gradualist given harsh increases in utility prices, he claimed that the public understood an adjustment had to be done there. He stated that he believed that the population knew very well that although prices had increased ten times over the previous ten years, utility prices had not moved. Therefore, some dimensions of fiscal adjustments were feasible while maintaining the perception of following a gradualist path.

With regards to the questions on monetary policy he argued that Di Tella's belief that the program was too harsh can be put to rest by just checking that during 2016 and 2017 inflation fell and output grew. All these gains were swept aside once the executive decided to change the targets, weakening the commitment of the government to disinflation.

Specifically, he noted that the de-anchoring of inflation expectations unraveled once the market understood this following the second interest rate reduction in January. For this reason, he said he believed that the big lesson to draw from this experience is that the institutional framework is very relevant because if the Central Bank had been independent, this event would not have happened. While he acknowledged that because Argentina has changed course many times, Central Bank independence may be less effective as investors would fear that this might change in the future, he posited that the story still would have been different in his view, particularly because the program had worked until that change.

On Forbes's question about Argentina's external financing and its effects on the exchange rate, Sturzenegger said that they had discussed the benefits to moving to domestic-denominated debt or even to domestic inflation-denominated debt, but that it was difficult to understand how serious this was—especially since the economy grew around 4 percent in 2017. Hence, he said that it was not evident at the time that real exchange appreciation was a real problem. In retrospect, he argued, one reason this may not have been so clear was that despite how lax fiscal policy was, the market gave them a surprising amount of credit during the first two years. However, he noted that eventually, governments must deliver concrete results, and fiscal policy should have been less lax. In fact, the tax reform of late 2017 went in the opposite direction, relaxing fiscal policy even further. He concluded that the form of external financing exacted a significant toll once the time came, and the government failed to deliver because then the short-term dollar-denominated debt led to a currency and maturity mismatch.

On Zettelmeyer's and Lipsky's puzzle, it all points to the institutional story again. With little help from fiscal policy, inflation came down because there was credibility. Once the credibility was undermined by the government itself, even a fiscal contraction or tighter money conditions were not enough to compensate and inflation increased.

EMMANUEL SAEZ
University of California, Berkeley

GABRIEL ZUCMAN
University of California, Berkeley

Progressive Wealth Taxation

ABSTRACT   This paper discusses the progressive taxation of household wealth. We first discuss what wealth is, how it is distributed, and how much revenue a progressive wealth tax could generate in the United States. We try to reconcile discrepancies across wealth data sources. Second, we discuss the role a wealth tax can play to increase the overall progressivity of the U.S. tax system. Third, we discuss the empirical evidence on wealth tax avoidance and evasion as well as tax enforcement policies. We summarize the key elements needed to make a U.S. wealth tax work in light of the experience of other countries. Fourth, we discuss the real economic effects of wealth taxation on inequality, the capital stock, and economic activity. Fifth, we present a simple tractable model of the taxation of billionaires' wealth that can be applied to the Forbes list of the four hundred richest Americans since 1982 to illustrate the long-run effects of concrete wealth tax proposals on top fortunes.

Income and wealth inequality have increased dramatically in the United States over the last decades (Piketty and Saez 2003; Saez and Zucman 2016; Piketty, Saez, and Zucman 2018). A long-standing concern with wealth concentration is its effect on democratic institutions and policymaking.[1]

Conflict of Interest Disclosure: Emmanuel Saez holds the Chancellor's Professorship of Tax Policy and Public Finance and directs the Center for Equitable Growth at the University of California, Berkeley; Gabriel Zucman is an assistant professor of economics at the University of California, Berkeley. Beyond these affiliations, the authors did not receive financial support from any firm or person for this paper or from any firm or person with a financial or political interest in this paper. They are currently not officers, directors, or board members of any organization with an interest in this paper. No outside party had the right to review this paper before circulation. The views expressed in this paper are those of the authors and do not necessarily reflect those of the University of California, Berkeley. The authors have advised several presidential campaigns recently on the issue of a wealth tax.

1. See, for example, Mayer (2017) and Page, Seawright, and Lacombe (2018). Political contributions, for example, are extremely concentrated with 0.01 percent of the population accounting for over a quarter of all contributions (Drutman 2013).

The view that excessive wealth concentration corrodes the social contract has deep roots in America—a country founded in part in reaction against the highly unequal, aristocratic Europe of the eighteenth century. Before 1776, the northern American colonies already taxed wealth, including financial assets and other personal property, instead of land only as in England (Saez and Zucman 2019a, chapter 2).

In the first part of the twentieth century, the United States invented very progressive income and estate taxation, combined with heavy corporate taxation.[2] This led to a large and sustained reduction in income and wealth concentration that reversed after tax progressivity went away (Saez and Zucman 2019a). There is a renewed political demand to use progressive taxation to curb the rise of inequality and raise revenue. A wealth tax is a potentially more powerful tool than income, estate, or corporate taxes to address the issue of wealth concentration as it goes after the stock rather than the flow.

Two major U.S. presidential candidates have proposed wealth taxes in 2019. In January 2019, Elizabeth Warren proposed a progressive wealth tax on families or individuals with net worth above $50 million with a 2 percent marginal tax rate (3 percent above $1 billion). In September 2019, Bernie Sanders proposed a similar wealth tax starting at $32 million with a 1 percent rate and with substantially more progressivity within the billionaire class (with marginal tax rates growing from 5 percent for billionaires up to 8 percent for decabillionaires). Such a tax would impose a much heavier burden on billionaires than all existing income, estate, and corporate taxes combined (Saez and Zucman 2019a). The key difference relative to earlier proposals or existing wealth taxes in other countries is the high exemption thresholds proposed. Less than 0.1 percent of U.S. families would be liable for the Warren or Sanders wealth tax (Saez and Zucman 2019b, 2019c). The United States has never implemented a progressive wealth tax before, but other countries have. What do economists have to say about the merits and demerits of wealth taxation and how it compares with other tax tools?

We first discuss what wealth is, how it is distributed, and how much revenue a progressive wealth tax could generate in the United States. Wealth tax revenue depends on how much wealth there is at the top (which

---

2. The United States was the first country—in 1917, four years after the creation of the income tax—to impose top marginal tax rates as high as 67 percent on the highest incomes. It was also the first country, starting in the 1930s, to impose high top tax rates (of 70 percent or more) on wealth at death. No European country ever imposed similarly high top inheritance tax rates (Scheve and Stasavage 2016).

in turn depends on the amount of aggregate household wealth and the distribution of wealth) and on enforcement (the fraction of their wealth the rich could hide). Aggregate household wealth has increased from about three times the annual national income around 1980 to about five times the national income in 2018. This increase has been driven by a rise in asset prices rather than capital accumulation, as the replacement-cost value of the capital stock has remained constant relative to national income. Meanwhile, wealth has become more concentrated. The share of wealth owned by the top 0.1 percent has doubled, from less than 10 percent in 1980 to almost 20 percent today. According to Forbes, the share of wealth owned by the four hundred richest Americans has almost quadrupled from 0.9 percent in 1982 to 3.3 percent in 2018 (Zucman 2019). We discuss recent estimates of U.S. wealth inequality, why they differ, and how to reconcile them.[3] We show that the wealth tax base above the 99.9th percentile is large, about $12 trillion in 2019 (about 60–70 percent of national income). With perfect enforcement, a 1 percent marginal tax on the top 0.1 percent would thus raise about $120 billion (about 0.6 percent–0.7 percent of national income). A well-enforced wealth tax has also significant revenue potential.

Second, we discuss the role a wealth tax can play in the overall progressivity of the U.S. tax system. A well-enforced wealth tax would be a powerful tool to restore progressivity at the top of the U.S. income and wealth distribution. It would increase the tax rate of wealthy families who can currently escape progressive income taxation by realizing little income relative to their true economic income. Despite the rise of inequality, the U.S. tax system has become less progressive in recent decades. The three traditional progressive taxes—the individual income tax, the corporate income tax, and the estate tax—have weakened. The top marginal federal income tax rate has fallen dramatically, from 70 percent or more between 1936 and 1980 down to 37 percent in 2018. Corporate taxes (which are progressive in the sense that they tax corporate profits, a highly concentrated source of income) as a share of corporate profits have declined from about 50 percent in the 1950s and 1960s to 16 percent in 2018 (Saez and Zucman 2019a). Estate taxes on large bequests now raise little revenue due to a high exemption threshold, many deductions, and

---

3. In particular, we show that taking into account the rising life expectancy differential between the very rich and the rest of the population (Chetty and others 2016) goes a long way toward reconciling wealth concentration estimates obtained from estate tax data with other sources.

weak enforcement. As a result, when combining all taxes at all levels of government, the U.S. tax system now resembles a giant flat tax. All groups of the population pay rates close to the macroeconomic tax rate of 28 percent, with a mild progressivity up to the top 0.1 percent and a significant drop at the top end, with effective tax rates of 23 percent for the top four hundred richest Americans (Saez and Zucman 2019a, chapter 1).

Third, we discuss the empirical evidence on wealth tax avoidance and evasion, as well as tax enforcement policies. Several recent and well-identified empirical studies cast light on these issues. We discuss lessons learned from the experience of other countries. The specific form of wealth taxation applied in a number of European countries had three main weaknesses. First, they faced tax competition (moving from Paris to London extinguished the French wealth tax immediately) and offshore evasion (until recently there was no cross-border information sharing). Second, European wealth taxes had low exemption thresholds, creating liquidity problems for some moderately wealthy taxpayers with few liquid assets and limited cash incomes. Third, European wealth taxes, many of which had been designed in the early twentieth century, had not been modernized, perhaps reflecting ideological and political opposition to wealth taxation in recent decades. These wealth taxes relied on self-assessments rather than systematic information reporting. These three weaknesses led to reforms that gradually undermined the integrity of the wealth tax: the exemption of some asset classes such as business assets or real estate, tax limits based on reported income, or a repeal of wealth taxation altogether.

A modern wealth tax can overcome these three weaknesses. First, offshore tax evasion can be fought more effectively today than in the past, thanks to a recent breakthrough in cross-border information exchange, and wealth taxes could be applied to expatriates (for at least some years), mitigating concerns about tax competition. The United States, moreover, has a citizenship-based tax system, making it much less vulnerable than other countries to mobility threats. Second, a comprehensive wealth tax base with a high exemption threshold and no preferential treatment for any asset classes can dramatically reduce avoidance possibilities. Third, leveraging modern information technology, it is possible for tax authorities to collect data on the market value of most forms of household wealth and use this information to prepopulate wealth tax returns, reducing evasion possibilities to a minimum. We also discuss how missing market valuations could be obtained by creating markets. In brief, the specific way in which wealth was taxed in a number of European countries is not the only possible way, and it is possible to do much better today.

Fourth, we discuss the real economic effects of wealth taxes on wealth inequality, the capital stock, entrepreneurial innovation, top talent migration, family structure, and charitable giving. For many of these aspects, there is relatively little empirical evidence to draw on, and we flag the most important avenues for future research.

Fifth, we present a new tractable model of wealth taxation of billionaires that can be applied to the Forbes 400 data since 1982. The model can be used to illustrate the long-run effects of concrete wealth tax proposals such as those put forth by the Warren and Sanders campaigns on top fortunes and wealth concentration.

I. Wealth Inequality and Tax Potential

A progressive wealth tax is an annual tax levied on the net wealth that a family (or an individual) owns above an exemption threshold. Net wealth includes all assets (financial and nonfinancial) net of all debts. The tax can be levied at progressive marginal tax rates above the exemption threshold. For instance, the wealth tax proposed by Senator Warren in January 2019 would be levied on families (defined as a single person or a married couple with dependents, if any) with net wealth above $50 million. The marginal tax rate is 2 percent above $50 million and 3 percent above $1 billion. A family with $50 million in net wealth would owe no tax, a family with $100 million would owe $1 million (2 percent of $50 million), and a family with $2 billion would owe $49 million (3 percent of $1 billion plus 2 percent of $950 million).

Wealth tax potential revenue depends on the wealth tax base, which obeys the simple informal equation:

$$\text{tax base} = \text{total wealth} \times \text{top wealth share} \times (1 - \text{evasion rate}),$$

where total wealth is total aggregate wealth in the economy, the top wealth share measures the share of aggregate wealth held by the wealthy that would be targeted by the wealth tax, and the evasion rate measures the fraction of their true wealth that the wealthy could hide from taxation. Based on this basic equation, it makes sense to look at each of the three factors.

I.A. What Is Wealth?

The standard and broadest measure of household wealth includes all financial and nonfinancial assets valued at their prevailing market prices, net of debts. Assets include all property that is marketable or, even if not directly marketable, whose underlying assets are marketable.[4] Financial assets include fixed-claim assets (checking and saving accounts, bonds, loans, and other interest-generating assets), corporate equity (shares in corporations), and noncorporate equity (shares in noncorporate businesses, for instance, shares in a partnership). Financial assets can be held either directly or indirectly through mutual funds, pension funds, insurance companies, and trusts. Nonfinancial assets include real estate, that is, land and buildings.[5] Debts primarily include mortgage housing debt, consumer credit (such as auto loans and credit card debt), and student debt. Assets owned by businesses, such as a headquarters building or a patent, contribute to household wealth through their effect on share prices. Net wealth does not include "human capital," such as future wages and pension rights that have not yet been accrued.[6] Wealth also excludes the present value of future government transfers (such as future Social Security benefits or health benefits), which are not marketable.

Private wealth includes household wealth plus the wealth of nonprofit institutions (university and foundation endowments, church buildings, and so on). The frontier between household and nonprofit wealth is sometimes fuzzy, as in the case of private foundations controlled by wealthy individual donors, such as the Bill and Melinda Gates Foundation. Our statistics exclude nonprofit wealth.[7] Private wealth is not the same as national wealth, which also includes the assets owned by the government such as public land and infrastructure (net of government debt). In the

4. For example, claims on a defined benefit plan may not be sold but the underlying assets in the defined benefit plan (typically corporate stock and bonds) can. A trust might not allow beneficiaries to sell the underlying assets but the underlying assets (again typically corporate stock and bonds) generally are marketable.

5. We exclude consumer durable goods (such as cars, jewelry, collectibles) from our wealth statistics. In aggregate, cars are the largest item, and this item is evenly and widely distributed. Contrary to popular belief, jewelry, collectibles, and private planes and boats are very small at the top relative to other forms of wealth, as shown by the Survey of Consumer Finances. A well-functioning wealth tax, however, would have to include these assets (at least above some threshold) to prevent tax avoidance. A wealth tax that does not tax art collectibles could produce an art collectible price boom.

6. It is only in slave societies that human capital can constitute marketable wealth. From the point of view of slave owners, the value of slaves was a large component of U.S. wealth before the Civil War (Piketty and Zucman 2014).

7. As we shall discuss below, to limit tax avoidance opportunities it might be desirable to include wealth that is still controlled by the initial owner in the wealth tax base, even if this wealth has been pledged for charitable giving.

Table 1. Aggregate Household Wealth and Its Composition, 2018

	Amount ($ trillion)	Percentage of total net worth	Percentage of national income
Total net worth	**88.7**	**100**	**503**
Assets	**107.7**	**121**	**611**
Housing	32.4	37	184
Business assets	9.7	11	55
Equities (direct holding)	18.6	21	105
Publicly listed	13.6	15	77
Privately listed	4.9	6	28
Fixed income assets	16.1	18	91
Interest-bearing	14.9	17	84
Deposits and currency	1.2	1	7
Pensions and insurance	30.9	35	175
DB and DC pensions	17.0	19	96
IRAs	8.8	10	50
Life insurance	5.1	6	29
Liabilities	**19.0**	**21**	**108**
Mortgages	14.3	16	81
Student loans	1.6	2	9
Other consumer credit	2.5	3	14
Other	0.7	1	4

Source: Piketty, Saez, and Zucman (2018), aggregate series appendix table TB1 updated to 2018.
Note: Aggregate statistics on household wealth in 2018 are averaged over the four quarters. Housing and mortgages include both owner-occupied and tenant-occupied housing. Equities and fixed income assets exclude those held indirectly through pension and insurance funds.

United States, public wealth is about zero on net: public debt is about as large as public assets (Alvaredo and others 2018).[8]

Table 1 displays the value of total U.S. household wealth and its composition by asset class in 2018. The data come from the U.S. financial accounts published by the Federal Reserve Board. Total U.S. household wealth reaches about $90 trillion, or about five times the national income (or about 4.5 times GDP). The wealth tax base is thus potentially large.

8. In official balance sheets, public assets only include assets that can be sold. Natural resources and the environment are not included but there are efforts to try to incorporate them. Note that a country with a large public debt held by residents can have high private wealth and negative public wealth, and may have to devote significant fiscal resources to service the debt. In recent decades, public debt has increased in the United States, but a large fraction of this extra debt is held by foreign central banks as reserves (U.S. Department of the Treasury 2018). The interest rate paid on public debt is currently low, limiting interest payments.

Wealth arises from capital accumulation and price effects (changes in asset prices absent any net saving). Capital accumulation takes many forms: improved land, residences and buildings, equipment and machinery, intangible capital such as software. Capital accumulation is made possible by savings that are invested in growing the capital stock. The national accounts provide a measure of the capital stock—the replacement cost of capital, sometimes called wealth at book value—reflecting only past saving poured into the capital stock, net of the depreciation of capital and adjusted for general price inflation. This measure does not take into account changes in asset prices (such as increases in real estate prices or stock prices). By contrast, the measure of household wealth at market value published in the financial accounts captures such price effects.

The top panel of figure 1 compares the evolution of household wealth at market value to the evolution of the replacement cost of private capital, both expressed as a percent of national income. Strikingly, the ratio of household wealth to national income has almost doubled from about 270 percent in the mid-1970s to more than 500 percent in 2018, the most recent year available. By contrast, the replacement cost of the private capital stock has not increased since the mid-1970s and has remained around 250 percent of national income over the last four decades. This means that the rise in aggregate wealth relative to income is primarily due to price effects.[9]

While more capital is valuable (since capital makes workers more productive), a higher market value for private wealth is not necessarily desirable. A higher market value for private wealth is a positive economic development if the market value of wealth reflects expectations about the future income (or utility) stream that assets will generate. For instance, if businesses become more efficient, the value of corporate equity will rise even if the replacement cost of capital does not. But a rise in the market value of wealth can also reflect an increase in the capacity of property owners to extract economic resources at the expense of other groups of the population. This extractive power is constrained by regulations and can increase when regulations are removed. For example, a monopoly that can set its price freely is more valuable to its owners than the same monopoly whose price setting is regulated. But the higher value of the unregulated monopoly comes at the expense of consumers (with typically

---

9. In principle, the discrepancy between the replacement cost of the private capital stock and the market value of household wealth could also be due to nonprofit capital and to net foreign private assets. Both, however, are relatively small.

Figure 1. U.S. Aggregate Household Wealth and Capital Income

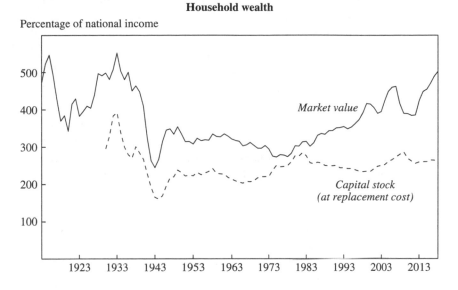

Household wealth

Percentage of national income

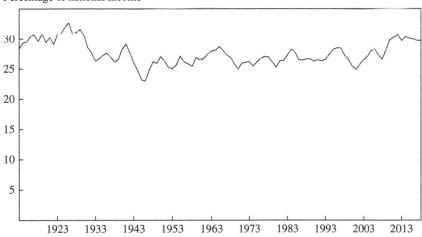

Share of capital income in national income

Percentage of national income

Source: Piketty, Saez, and Zucman (2018), updated to 2018.

Notes: Aggregate household wealth is calculated as assets minus liabilities. The replacement cost of capital value of the U.S. capital stock includes all residential structures, but not land, and capital assets, including the value of intangible assets such as patents and copyrights, valued at replacement cost.

negative distributional implications) and at the expense of overall efficiency (monopoly prices are too high). When antitrust becomes more lax, private wealth can rise despite the fact that the economy becomes less efficient and less equal. Similarly, a patent generates wealth for its owner at the expense of the users of the technology. When a patent expires, the private wealth associated with the ownership of the patent goes to zero, but production becomes cheaper. Like antitrust, patent regulation affects the market value of wealth.

The value of businesses can also increase when owners more aggressively pursue profits by cutting workers' pay or increasing prices. The business of private equity firms is precisely to increase shareholder value by any means: productive improvements but also squeezing existing stakeholders such as workers, suppliers, or customers (Appelbaum and Batt 2014).

The relative share of for-profit and not-for-profit organizations also affects the market value of wealth. For-profit businesses represent wealth for their shareholders while nonprofits do not have shareholders. A country with privatized for-profit education and health care will typically have a higher market value of private wealth than a country where education and health are provided by the government or nonprofit institutions.[10] Yet there is no particular reason to presume that this extra wealth is socially valuable. Whether private for-profit, private not-for-profit, or government provision is best (even from a pure efficiency perspective) depends on the situation. To give one example from the financial sector where profit motives are generally thought to be crucial for incentives, consider the case of mutual funds. One of the largest for-profit mutual funds, Fidelity, managed $1.4 trillion for its clients in 2018 (Morningstar 2019). Fidelity stock has a substantial value (over and above the funds it manages on behalf of its clients). The founding Johnson family made a fortune of about $40 billion from Fidelity and still owns about half of the company. But there is an even larger not-for-profit mutual fund, Vanguard, which manages $4.2 trillion in 2018 but has no stock value (over and above the funds it manages on behalf of its clients). Vanguard developed the model of low-cost index funds, perhaps one of the most valuable inventions of the financial sector in recent decades. This invention created social value but hardly any marketable wealth. Vanguard's founder, John Bogle, had an

---

10. One example economists are familiar with is the example of scientific journals. Some journals are not-for-profit and priced low while others, most notably those published by Elsevier, are for-profit and priced high. For-profit journals create wealth for shareholders but at the expense of university budgets.

estimated fortune of less than $100 million, four hundred times less than Fidelity founders. This example is particularly relevant for the analysis of wealth taxes, since mutual fund and pension fund fees constitute a significant privatized wealth tax for the middle class and upper-middle class. The average tax rate is 0.48 percent on $17 trillion in assets, that is, $90 billion (Morningstar 2019).[11]

Ideally, one would like to know what part of the rise in the market value of private wealth (relative to the replacement cost of private capital) owes to expected extra future income streams due to real economic progress (expected new products or more efficient ways to produce) and what fraction owes to rent extraction from property owners at the expense of other stakeholders (workers, consumers, or governments). It can be tempting, as a first-order approximation, to treat the difference between the replacement cost of private capital and the market value of private wealth as an estimate of rent extraction. We stress, however, that such a naive computation is too simplistic and that more research is needed in this area.[12]

I.B. The Distribution of U.S. Household Wealth

How is U.S. household wealth distributed? There are four main sources to estimate the distribution of wealth in the United States: (1) the Survey of Consumer Finances (SCF), (2) named lists of wealthy individuals such as the Forbes 400, (3) estate tax data using the estate multiplier technique, and (4) income tax data using the capitalization technique. The capitalization method infers wealth from capital income by assuming a constant rate of return by asset class and year (estimated from macro data). The estate multiplier method reweighs each estate by the inverse probability of death (estimated by age times gender cells) to recover the distribution of wealth in the full population. Each source and method has limitations, and hence

11. The tax rate is slowly going down (it was about 0.94 percent in 2000) as the middle class slowly learns how to avoid this "tax." Absent Vanguard, the strongest force driving down fees on index funds, it is likely that for-profit mutual funds would charge more. See Malkiel (2013, 97–98) for an overview of the industry. Without calling it a tax, he says: "the increase in fees is likely to represent a deadweight loss for investors" and "the major inefficiency in financial markets today involves the market for investment advice" (108).

12. One difficulty involves the measurement of intangible capital. Estimates of the replacement cost of private capital include some intangibles (software, research and development assets, and artistic originals) but not others (for example, brand-name organizational capital). Another difficulty involves the treatment of privatization: part of the increase in household wealth reflects sales of public assets at potentially low prices (thus at the expense of government), but macroeconomic balance sheets do not reveal what the "right" price is (as government assets are typically valued at their current replacement cost).

triangulating among sources is useful. The best source would be a well enforced and comprehensive wealth tax in the same way that the development of the income tax created a crucial tool to measure the concentration of income in the United States.[13] Zucman (2019) discusses the methodologies and sources in detail.[14]

Because the SCF by design excludes the Forbes 400, it is natural to add the wealth of the Forbes 400 to the wealth reported in the SCF when estimating top wealth shares. The Forbes 400 data are not perfect but they are the best estimates we have of wealth at the very top.[15] The wealth of large shareholders of publicly traded companies (for example, Amazon's Jeff Bezos) is probably well measured. In 2018, twelve of the fifteen richest Americans were shareholders of large public companies (see table 4).[16] Forbes might miss diversified wealth coming from inheritance (Piketty 2014) and might not value private businesses accurately. Famously, Donald Trump misrepresented his wealth to reporters to get onto the Forbes list in the 1980s.[17]

The top panel of figure 2 depicts the evolution of the top 0.1 percent wealth share according to SCF data (with the Forbes 400 added); the estate multiplier method from Kopczuk and Saez (2004), updated in Saez and Zucman (2016), smoothed out after 2000, adjusted for more accurate mortality differentials by wealth groups in recent decades (Chetty and others 2016), and using tax units (instead of individual adults) as units of observation; and the capitalization method of Saez and Zucman (2016),

---

13. Before the start of the income tax in 1913, there were some estimates of how much revenue an income tax would bring, but these estimates were imprecise.

14. Kopczuk (2015), Bricker and others (2016), and Kennickell (2017) also discuss discrepancies between the SCF and estimates based on tax data.

15. Refusing to use the Forbes 400 amounts to saying we should not make any empirical statement about billionaires, a nihilistic attitude we reject, although we recognize that the data are imperfect.

16. The three exceptions were Charles and David Koch and Michael Bloomberg.

17. Kopczuk (2015) further notes that debt and wealth controlled through charities are not well measured. But private foundation wealth is public information and can be linked to founders. Except for the Bill and Melinda Gates Foundation, we have found that such private foundation wealth is negligible relative to the wealth held by the Forbes 400. Estate tax data show that debt is small among top wealth holders. According to Kopczuk and Saez (2004), debt represented 6.1 percent of wealth for the top 0.01 percent on average in 1991–2000. For estates filed in 2017, the latest year available, debt is 6.25 percent of gross estates for estates above $50 million (data available online at https://www.irs.gov/statistics/soi-tax-stats-estate-tax-statistics-filing-year-table-1).

Figure 2. U.S. Wealth Inequality and Its Evolution

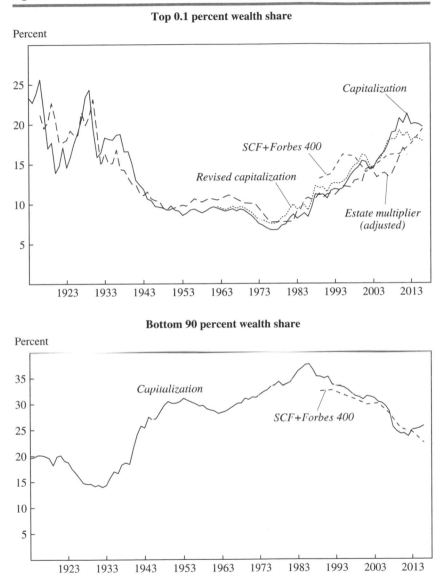

Top 0.1 percent wealth share

Bottom 90 percent wealth share

Source: Authors' calculations based on the Survey of Consumer Finances (SCF) and the Forbes 400 rich list, with estimates from Piketty, Saez, and Zucman (2018), Kopczuk and Saez (2004), and Saez and Zucman (2016).

updated to 2016 in Piketty, Saez, and Zucman (2018).[18] All three series are based on taking 0.1 percent of all tax units (not individual adults).[19] Both the estate multiplier and capitalization series show that wealth concentration was high in the 1910s and 1920s, with a particularly fast increase in the second half of the 1920s. The top 0.1 percent wealth share peaked at close to 25 percent in 1929. It then fell abruptly in the early 1930s (in the context of the Great Depression) and continued to fall gradually from the late 1930s to the late 1940s (in the context of the New Deal and the war economy). After a period of remarkable stability in the 1950s and 1960s, the top 0.1 percent wealth share reached its low watermark in the 1970s. Since the 1980s, all series show a marked increase in wealth concentration, although there is some variation across sources in the magnitude of the increase. The capitalization method suggests an increase from 7.5 percent in the late 1970s up to 20 percent in recent years. The estate multiplier method suggests an increase from 7.8 percent to 16 percent over the same period. In the shorter period from 1989 to 2016, the top 0.1 percent wealth share estimated using SCF data increases from 13 percent to 20 percent. In 2016, both the capitalization method and the SCF (plus Forbes 400) have the same 0.1 percent wealth share of about 20 percent. The top 0.1 percent wealth share is 16 percent in the estate tax data for 2011–12, the latest years available.

SENSITIVITY OF CAPITALIZATION ESTIMATES As noted in Saez and Zucman (2016) and the subsequent literature, there are a number of potential

---

18. See figure 4 for a step-by-step decomposition of the adjustments to the estate multiplier method. Three improvements were made relative to Saez and Zucman (2016): First, the series is updated to reflect the latest version of the macroeconomic household balance sheet published in the Financial Accounts of the United States. Second, the series includes a better treatment of wealth that does not generate taxable income, based on a more systematic use of the SCF. Third, it fixes an error in the computation of top wealth shares in the early 1930s; the new estimates show that wealth concentration fell more rapidly in the early 1930s than was originally reported. See Zucman (2019) for more details.

19. In the SCF, we select not the top 0.1 percent of the 130 million households present in the survey but 0.1 percent of the total 175 million tax units in the United States. So we select effectively the top 0.135 percent of SCF households. There are fewer households than tax units because households may include more than one tax unit (for example, adult children living with their parents). Typically, the SCF captures the wealth of the "economically dominant" tax unit in the household and misses wealth (or debt) from secondary tax units. This explains, for example, why the SCF captures only 70 percent of total student loan debt (for 2016:Q2, the SCF has $0.96 trillion in student loans while the Financial Accounts have $1.37 trillion). The sampling at the top for the SCF is made using tax data, and hence selecting the top 0.1 percent of tax units (rather than households) provides the most accurate comparison across sources for top groups.

Figure 3. Interest Rate by Wealth Class, 2000–2016

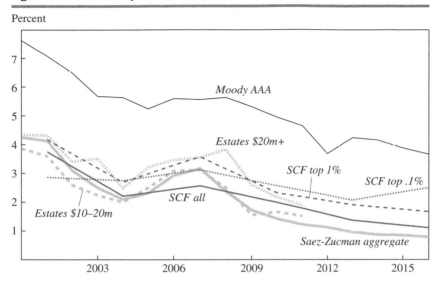

Source: Authors' computations based on the Survey of Consumer Finances (SCF) and Saez and Zucman (2016).

limitations with the capitalization method. Two issues are particularly noteworthy. In this paper, we present modified capitalized income top 0.1 percent wealth shares that account for these two issues.

Interest Rate by Wealth Class Interest rates may be heterogeneous across the distribution. If the rich own assets generating higher interest rates (such as risky corporate bonds), the capitalization method overestimates fixed-income assets at the top. This could be particularly problematic in recent years, in a context of low overall interest rates.[20]

Figure 3 displays how the interest rate on fixed-claim assets (savings and checking accounts, taxable bonds) varies over time and by wealth class using linked income and wealth data sources: linked estate and income tax data and the Survey of Consumer Finances (SCF). The figure displays the aggregate rate of return economy-wide used in the baseline Saez and

20. This issue is pointed out in Kopczuk (2015). More recently, Bricker and others (2016), Bricker, Henriques, and Hansen (2018), and Smith, Zidar, and Zwick (2019) estimate top wealth shares using the capitalization method and assign higher interest rates to the rich. Bourne and others (2018) link estate and income tax data and make the reverse point that the very wealthy report low capital income relative to their wealth.

Zucman (2016) series. The figure depicts the interest rate using estate tax returns matched to prior year income tax returns for nonmarried filers from internal tax data for large estates over $20 million and between $10 and $20 million (Saez and Zucman 2016, fig. 5b).Figure 3 also depicts the interest rate observed in the SCF in aggregate and for the top 1 percent and top .1 percent wealth holders. Overall, while somewhat noisy, the SCF data confirm the estate income tax data which shows that the interest rate for the wealthy tracks pretty closely the aggregate interest rate but is slightly higher. When interest rates are very low, as in recent years, this small difference translates into a significant difference in capitalization factors. Therefore, we revise the capitalization method to incorporate these empirical findings as we did in the earlier sensitivity analysis presented in Saez and Zucman (2016, 547–51 and appendix tables B41, B41b, and B41c). As in the Saez and Zucman (2016) appendix B41c series, we apply higher interest rates to the top 0.1 percent to match the interest rate differential observed in matched estate income tax returns for estates above $20 million. Concretely, this correction reduces the fixed-income claims owned by the top 0.1 percent by a factor of about two in recent years, consistent with the more recent SCF evidence depicted in figure 3.

Finally, figure 3 depicts the Moody AAA rate of return on corporate bonds used by Smith, Zidar, and Zwick (2019) revised capitalization method. The AAA rate is much higher (by about 3 points) than the empirical interest rate earned by the wealthy from income to estate-linked tax data and from SCF data throughout the period. In recent years with low interest rates, using this AAA rate for capitalizing interest greatly underestimates fixed-claim assets at the top and hence underestimates top wealth shares.[21]

Value of Pass-Through Businesses A second known issue is that the official Federal Reserve Financial Accounts provide a low value for the value of private (that is, unlisted) corporations. Innovatively, Smith, Zidar, and Zwick (2019) value the stock of S-corporations and other pass-through businesses (partnerships, sole proprietorships) using a formula based on profits, book value of capital, and sales that replicates what is done by financial analysts trying to value private equity. Switzerland also applies

---

21. This reconciles our findings with Smith, Zidar, and Zwick (2019). We think that using the AAA return overstates the interest rate at the top because most of the bonds held by mutual funds are Treasury, agency, and foreign sovereign bonds (about 60–70 percent versus about 30–40 percent for domestic and foreign corporate bonds in recent years; see Financial Accounts of the United States, table L.122), and the yield on sovereign and quasi-sovereign debt is lower than on private AAA bonds (about half as low in recent years).

a similar method to administer its wealth tax. We follow their adjustment and increase the value of the pass-through businesses owned by the top 0.1 percent by a factor of 1.9 (adjusting the total wealth denominator accordingly). We apply the same 1.9 correction factor over time since 1962.[22]

As shown by figure 2, the adjustments for the higher interest rate of the rich and the higher value of pass-through businesses offset each other, except in recent years when the interest rate adjustment slightly dominates. The benchmark Saez and Zucman (2016) top 0.1 percent wealth share, updated in Zucman (2019), is 19.6 percent in 2016. In the modified capitalized income series presented in this paper, the top 0.1 percent share is 17.8 percent. In the SCF (with the Forbes 400 added) it is 19.3 percent, closer to the original Saez and Zucman (2016) series (in all three cases statistics are for tax units, similarly defined). The main difference is in terms of wealth composition. The share of fixed-income assets in the top 0.1 percent in 2016 decreases from 42 percent in the original Saez and Zucman (2016) series to 26 percent in the modified series. Meanwhile, the share of pass-through business wealth increases from 18 percent to 34 percent, which is more in line with what is observed in the SCF.

CORRECTING ESTATE MULTIPLIER ESTIMATES The capitalized income estimates of Saez and Zucman (2016) and the raw estate multiplier estimates of Kopczuk and Saez (2004), updated in Saez and Zucman (2016), track each other well from 1916 to 1985 but diverge thereafter. The raw estate multiplier estimates for recent decades are depicted in the bottom panel of figure 4. They show a modest increase in the top 0.1 percent wealth share from 7.5 percent in the early 1980s to around 10 percent in recent years. A top 0.1 percent wealth share around 10 percent is similar to Denmark (Jakobsen and others 2019, fig. 2B), a country with one of the most equal distributions of wealth on earth (Alvaredo and others 2018). How could the United States have the most unequal income distribution among advanced economies (Alvaredo and others 2018) and the most equal wealth distribution? Something is wrong with the raw estate multiplier estimates.

As discussed in detail in Saez and Zucman (2016, sect. VII.B), there are two main potential explanations for the diverging trends in recent decades. First, there might have been an increase in estate tax evasion. Second, the

---

22. Smith, Zidar, and Zwick (2019) also implement two other changes: capitalizing equity using dividends and capital gains but putting a lower weight on capital gains (Saez and Zucman [2016] also conducted such a sensitivity analysis) and capitalizing property taxes using state specific multipliers (this has a minor effect on top wealth shares but is a useful innovation for creating state-specific estimates).

Figure 4. Correcting Estate Multiplier Estimates

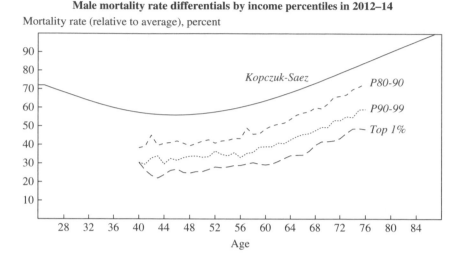

Male mortality rate differentials by income percentiles in 2012–14

Mortality rate (relative to average), percent

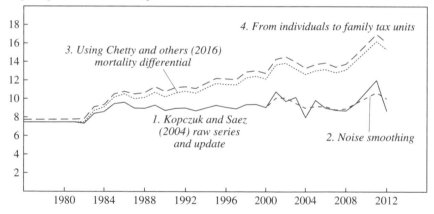

Correcting estate multiplier estimates

Top 0.1 percent wealth share, percent

Source: Authors' computations based on Chetty and others (2016), Kopczuk and Saez (2004), and Saez and Zucman (2016).

Notes: In the top panel income is measured two years earlier or at age 61, whichever is less. The panel also depicts the mortality rate advantage for top wealth holders assumed by Kopczuk-Saez estate multiplier series, from an estimate of the college graduate mortality differential in the 1980s created by Brown, Liebman, and Pollet (2002). The bottom panel shows a step-by-step correction of estate multipliers in four steps: (1) we start from the raw estimates from Kopczuk and Saez (2004), updated to 2012 in Saez and Zucman (2016); (2) we smooth the series after 2000 to reduce noise; (3) we use the mortality differential from the top 1 percent from Chetty and others (2016) in 2012 and the Kopczuk-Saez differential in 1980 (with a linear phased-in adjustment for years between 1980 to 2012); and (4) we convert the individual adult estimates coming from estates into tax unit family-based estimates, using the same ratios of individual adult versus tax unit from the Piketty, Saez, and Zucman (2018) top wealth share series.

estate multiplier estimates of Kopczuk and Saez (2004) fail to incorporate the longevity gains of the rich (relative to average).

Longevity Gains by the Wealthy The estate multiplier method blows up estates by the inverse probability of death. Mortality rates by age, gender, and year for the full population exist, but the wealthy are likely to live longer. Kopczuk and Saez (2004) assume that the mortality rate advantage of the wealthy is the same as the mortality rate advantage of college graduates in the 1980s (Brown, Liebman, and Pollet 2002). The correction factors of Kopczuk and Saez (2004) are depicted in the top panel of figure 4 (for males). Male college graduates in their forties have mortality rates only around 55 percent of the population average (for males of the same age). The Kopczuk and Saez series uses the same correction factors for all years, thereby ignoring the rising life expectancy differential by income groups documented for recent decades by Waldron (2007) and Chetty and others (2016).

Chetty and others (2016) provide precise and granular mortality rates by income percentiles, age, and year. The top panel of figure 4 depicts the mortality rates of upper income groups relative to average by age (for males) in 2012–14.[23] We depict three groups: the top 1 percent, the next 9 percent, and the next 10 percent (percentile 80 to 90). Two findings are worth noting. First, there is a strong mortality gradient within the top 20 percent. This suggests that it is not enough to consider the relative mortality advantage of large groups such as college graduates when applying the estate multiplier method. More granular corrections are required. Second, the mortality rate for the top 1 percent is only about half of the mortality rate of college graduates used in Kopczuk and Saez (2004).

The data in Chetty and others (2016) also provide a short time series, from 2001 to 2014. The time series shows that the mortality rate of the top 1 percent (relative to average) decreased from 40.6 percent in 2001–3 to 30.7 percent in 2012–14 (for individuals age 40 to 63). Using Social Security data, Waldron (2007) shows that the life expectancy difference between males in the top half versus bottom half of the lifetime earnings distribution at age 60 was only 1.2 years for the 1912 cohort but 5.8 years for the 1941 cohort. Therefore, the mortality differential between the wealthy and the rest was likely pretty small in 1980. Based on these data, it makes sense to use the Kopczuk and Saez (2004) mortality advantage up to

---

23. Income is measured two years earlier or at age 61, whichever is less. Income is measured at age 61 at the latest because income falls substantially after that age due to retirement.

1980 but then assume that the mortality rate advantage increases (linearly) from 1980 to 2012 up to the level of the top 1 percent from Chetty and others (2016). The data in Chetty and others (2016) imply that Kopczuk and Saez (2004) overstate mortality at the top by a factor of 1.9 on average.[24]

As noted by Kopczuk (2015), using a mortality rate that is too high by a factor $1 + x$ lowers the estimated top wealth share by a factor of $(1 + x)^{1/a}$ where a is the Pareto coefficient of the wealth distribution, equal to 1.5 based on the Kopczuk and Saez (2004) estimates for recent years.[25] If we assume that the top 0.1 percent wealthiest Americans have the same mortality rate as the top 1 percent income earners from Chetty and others (2016), then the mortality rate in Kopczuk and Saez (2004) is off by a factor of $1 + x = 1.90$. This implies that the wealth shares in Kopczuk and Saez (2004) should be inflated by a factor of $(1 + x)^{1/a} = 1.9^{2/3} = 1.53$ in recent years. Concretely, instead of around 10 percent in recent years, the top 0.1 percent wealth share should be around 15.3 percent.

The bottom panel of figure 4 shows a step-by-step correction of the estate multiplier series. First, we start from the raw estimates from Kopczuk and Saez (2004), updated to 2012 in Saez and Zucman (2016). Second, we smooth the series after 2000 to reduce noise.[26] Third, we use the mortality differential of the top 1 percent from Chetty and others (2016) in 2012 and the differential in 1980 in Kopczuk and Saez (2004), with a linear adjustment between 1980 to 2012. Fourth, we convert the individual adult estimates coming from estates into tax unit–based estimates using the same ratios of individual adult versus tax unit top wealth as in Piketty, Saez, and Zucman (2018). The mortality adjustment (step 3) has a very large impact on the series.

In sum, improving the estate estimates with more accurate mortality rates has the potential to close about half of the gap between estate-based

---

24. To compute this average, we weight each age and gender by their weight in the top 1 percent distribution from Chetty and others (2016). Chetty and others (2016) do not provide data for ages below 40 (who hold 4 percent of the top 0.1 percent wealth according to SCF) and for ages above 76 (who hold 11.5 percent of the top 0.1 percent wealth). For those below age 40, we assume the same ratio as for ages 40–41, namely 2.41 (as the small wealth there is in this group is likely concentrated among those close to age 40). For those above 76, we assume that the ratio is 1.27, which is the average of the age 75–76 ratio (1.54) and 1 (as the mortality advantage of the rich has to disappear for the very old). In net we have $.040 \times 2.41 + (1 - .04 - .115) \times .675/.343 + .115 \times 1.27 = 1.905$.

25. The reasoning is the same as for the effect of tax evasion that we spell out below.

26. As explained in Saez and Zucman (2016), Steve Jobs, who died at age 56 in 2011, has a weight of 200, which means that his $7 billion wealth (from the Forbes 400) would weigh $1.4 trillion, or 3 percent of aggregate wealth—enough to explain the 2011 spike.

and capitalized income estimates. It is important to note that the mortality of the super wealthy might not be the same as the mortality of high earners, as illness might reduce labor income (a flow) faster than wealth (a stock). Future work using internal IRS data could directly estimate mortality rates by capital income or capitalized income year by year. Since 2000, population-wide data would allow for precise and granular estimates, as in Chetty and others (2016). From 1979 to 1999, mortality rates could be estimated more roughly, as in Saez and Zucman (2016). Conditioning mortality rates on marital status would also likely improve accuracy.

Estate Tax Evasion One simple way to measure the growth in estate tax evasion is to assume that this evasion is captured by the residual (growing) gap between the adjusted estate-based top 0.1 percent wealth share and the other series depicted in the top panel of figure 2. While some forms of estate tax avoidance have always existed (Cooper 1979), it is likely that tax avoidance has increased substantially since the 1980s, as the political will for enforcement of the tax declined (Saez and Zucman 2019a, chapter 3). For example, in 1975, the IRS audited 65 percent of the 29,000 largest estate tax returns filed in 1974. By 2018, only 8.6 percent of the 34,000 estate tax returns filed in 2017 were audited.[27] Researchers in the tax administration found that the wealth reported by decedents from the Forbes 400 richest Americans on their estate tax returns is only half the wealth estimated by *Forbes* magazine (Raub, Johnson, and Newcomb 2010). In 2017, estate taxes raised only $20 billion, or about 0.13 percent of the wealth of the top 0.1 percent richest households (in spite of a 40 percent tax rate above the $5.5 million exemption threshold, which doubles to $11.4 million in 2019). In 1976, the top 0.1 percent paid the equivalent of 0.7 percent of its wealth in estate taxes, primarily because of fewer deductions (especially no marital deduction), higher rates, and better enforcement.

I.C. Revenue Projections

As mentioned above, revenue projections for a wealth tax depend on three key elements: aggregate wealth, the share of aggregate wealth that the rich own, and finally what fraction of their wealth they could shelter from the tax. We will discuss in section III the issue of tax evasion. Our main conclusion is that evasion depends on the design of the wealth tax and the

27. These auditing statistics are published by the IRS annually and available online in U.S. Department of the Treasury (2019, table 9a) for the year 2018 and U.S. Department of the Treasury (1976, table 2, p. 89) for the year 1975.

strength of enforcement. It is a policy choice.[28] In this section, we consider various scenarios for enforcement.

PARETO DISTRIBUTION AND REVENUE It is useful to estimate the tax base of the top 1 percent, top 0.1 percent, and top 0.01 percent richest Americans. We also consider the tax base above fixed nominal cutoffs of $10 million and $50 million. The advantage of percentiles is that they are not tied to a specific nominal value or currency.

As is well known since Vilfredo Pareto noted it in 1896 (Pareto 1965), the top tail of the wealth distribution is well approximated by a Pareto distribution. Let p be a fractile (such as the top 1 percent) and w_p the wealth at threshold p. The fraction of people with wealth above w is given by a power law of the form $1 - H(w) = p \cdot (w_p/w)^a$ where a > 1 is the Pareto parameter. The Pareto law relates two fractiles p and q and their corresponding wealth thresholds w_p, w_q as follows: $p/q = (w_q/w_p)^a$ or $\log(p) - \log(q) = a \cdot [\log(w_q) - \log(w_p)]$.

A Pareto distribution has the property that the average wealth above a given threshold w is given by $b \cdot w$, where $b = a/(a - 1)$ is a constant. Empirically the U.S. wealth distribution has a thick tail with a coefficient $a \simeq 1.4$ (Saez and Zucman 2016) and hence $b \simeq 3.5$. Denoting by N the size of the population, the tax base above wealth threshold w_p (corresponding to percentile p) is $W_p = N \cdot p \cdot (b - 1) \cdot w_p = (N \cdot p \cdot b \cdot w_p)/a$ or $1/a$ times the total wealth of people with wealth above w_p. With $a = 1.4$, we have $1/a = 0.714$, or roughly 70 percent. Concretely, if the wealth share of the top 0.1 percent is 20 percent, then the tax base above the top 0.1 percent wealth threshold is 70 percent of 20 percent, or 14 percent of aggregate wealth, that is, $13 trillion in 2019.

EVASION RATE AND REVENUE How does tax evasion affect these computations? Suppose the rich can hide a fraction h of their wealth. We consider two polar scenarios: (1) *homogeneous evasion*: everybody hides a fraction h of wealth, and (2) *concentrated evasion*: a fraction h of taxpayers hide their entire wealth while a fraction $1 - h$ reports truthfully. The real world is in between these two polar cases.

For a wealth tax on the top fractile p, the tax base is scaled down by a factor $1 - h$ when evasion is homogeneous, as the share of reported wealth at the top relative to true total aggregate wealth falls by a factor $1 - h$. When evasion is concentrated, the tax base is scaled down by less than $1 - h$.[29]

---

28. This is also the main conclusion from the analysis of tax evasion in the income tax context (Slemrod 1994; Slemrod and Kopczuk 2002).

29. With a Pareto distribution, the factor is $(1 - h)^{1/a} = (1 - h)^{0.7}$. For example, with $h = 0.2$, the scale-down factor is 0.85 (instead of 0.8).

For a wealth tax above a fixed threshold w^*, the tax base is scaled down by a factor $1 - h$ when evasion is concentrated, as a fraction $1 - h$ of people with more than w^* vanish. When evasion is homogeneous, the tax base is scaled down by more than $1 - h$.[30]

Therefore, a rough rule of thumb is that hiding a fraction h of wealth reduces revenue by a fraction h as well. If the exemption threshold is adjusted to always capture a given fractile, the fraction of revenue lost will be somewhat less than h. If the exemption threshold is kept fixed, the fraction of revenue lost will be somewhat higher than h.

REVENUE PROJECTIONS We project wealth tax revenue using the various wealth data sources depicted in the top panel of figure 2. The unit is always the family tax unit, not the individual adult.[31] Table 2 presents the results. Columns (1) to (3) present estimates of the base above specific percentiles (top 1 percent, top 0.1 percent, top 0.01 percent). The percentiles are defined relative to the total number of family tax units in the economy (173 million in 2019). For example, the top 1 percent represents the top 1.73 million families. The statistics are reported assuming no tax evasion (over and beyond tax evasion in the raw wealth data source). Columns (4) and (5) display the base above fixed nominal amounts (in 2019 dollars): $10 million and $50 million.

The latest capitalized income and SCF statistics are for the year 2016. We extrapolate them to 2019 assuming no change in the distribution and using the Federal Reserve Financial Accounts aggregates for 2019. Estates-based estimates are the average from years 2009–12, corrected for differential mortality from Chetty and others (2016), converted to tax units, and extrapolated to 2019 (assuming again no change in distribution).[32]

The bottom rows show by how much the tax base would shrink if taxpayers can hide a fraction of their wealth (10 percent or 50 percent). We assume that tax evasion comes half and half from intensive and extensive margins. We assume that the percentile thresholds would be adjusted to always capture the same fraction of the population. In contrast, the nominal thresholds ($10 million and $50 million) are not adjusted, explaining why the revenue loss is larger. The last row shows the implied estate

---

30. With a Pareto distribution, the factor is $(1 - h)^a = (1 - h)^{1.4}$. For example, with $h = 0.2$, the scale-down factor is 0.73 (instead of 0.8).

31. Recall that we converted estate multiplier estimates into family-based estimates.

32. For estates-based estimates, the wealth denominator is about 10 percent lower because it excludes annuitized wealth (for example, defined benefits pensions) that disappears at death. We conservatively assume that such annuitized wealth is negligible among top wealth holders.

Table 2. Wealth Tax Base Estimates, 2019

	Top 1 percent cutoff (1)	Top .1 percent cutoff (2)	Top .01 percent cutoff (3)	$10 million cutoff (4)	$50 million cutoff (5)
Capitalized incomes					
Threshold (2019 $ millions)	5.9	30.8	171.8	10.0	50.0
Base above threshold (2019 $ trillions)	25.9	13.0	6.3	21.3	10.9
As a percentage of aggregate wealth	27.7%	13.9%	6.8%	22.8%	11.6%
As a percentage of national income	140%	70%	34%	115%	59%
Revised capitalized incomes					
Threshold (2019 $ millions)	5.3	28.0	156.2	10.0	50.0
Base above threshold (2019 $ trillions)	23.6	11.8	5.8	18.4	9.4
As a percentage of aggregate wealth	25.2%	12.6%	6.2%	19.7%	10.1%
As a percentage of national income	127%	64%	31%	99%	51%
SCF plus Forbes 400					
Threshold (2019 $ millions)	9.0	40.6	172.3	10.0	50.0
Base above threshold (2019 $ trillions)	27.5	11.5	5.5	24.8	9.7
As a percentage of aggregate wealth	29.4%	12.2%	5.9%	26.5%	10.3%
As a percentage of national income	148%	62%	30%	134%	52%

Estates with multiplier

Threshold (2019 $ millions)		25.5	123.6	10.0	50.0
Base above threshold (2019 $ trillions)		8.9	4.3	14.2	6.8
As a percentage of aggregate wealth		9.5%	4.6%	15.1%	7.2%
As a percentage of national income		48%	23%	76%	37%

Base reduction with tax evasion

Strong enforcement: 15% evasion rate	13.0%	12.9%	12.7%	17.7%	17.7%
Weak enforcement: 50% evasion rate	44.6%	44.4%	43.8%	56.1%	56.2%
Estate tax implied evasion: 33%		31.6%	32.2%	33.5%	37.8%

Source: Authors' computations.

Notes: This table reports statistics on the wealth tax base above specific thresholds from various data sources. The unit is always the family tax unit, not the individual adult (estate multiplier individual-based estimates are converted into family-based estimates). For the percentiles thresholds (top 1 percent, top .1 percent, top .01 percent), percentiles are defined relative to the total number of family tax units in the economy (173 million in 2019). The top 1 percent represents the top 1.73 million families, and so on. The statistics are reported assuming no tax evasion (over and beyond the raw source, estates estimates are lower primarily because of tax avoidance/evasion). Capitalized incomes and Survey of Consumer Finances statistics are for year 2016 extrapolated to 2019 (assuming no change in distribution and using financial accounts aggregate wealth for 2019). Estates are the average from years 2009–2012, corrected for differential mortality (from Chetty and others 2016), converted to tax units, and extrapolated to 2019. The bottom rows show by how much the tax base would shrink if taxpayers can hide a fraction of their wealth (10 percent or 50 percent). We assume that tax evasion comes half and half from intensive and extensive margins. We assume that the percentile thresholds would be adjusted to always capture the same fraction of the population. In contrast, the nominal thresholds ($10 million and $50 million) are not adjusted, explaining why the revenue loss is larger. The last row shows the implied estate tax evasion rate that would fully explain the gap between the tax base from the capitalized incomes estimates at the top and the tax base from the estate multiplier estimates at the bottom.

tax evasion rate that would fully explain the gap between the tax base from the capitalized income estimates and the tax base from the estate multiplier estimates.

The tax bases are quite close across the first three sources. For example, the tax base above $50 million is $10.9 trillion according to the Saez and Zucman (2016) capitalized income series, $9.4 trillion is the revised capitalized income series, and $9.7 trillion is the SCF. The tax base is about a third lower for the estate-based estimates ($6.8 trillion). Above the $10 million cutoff, the SCF tax base estimate is larger than capitalized incomes ($25 trillion instead of around $20 trillion). The SCF (after adding the Forbes 400) has slightly fewer superrich than the capitalized income estimates but it has more merely rich—rich but not superrich—households in the $10 million to $50 million range. With a top 0.1 percent wealth share of around 20 percent, a wealth tax with an exemption threshold at the 99.9th percentile has a base of 14 percent of aggregate wealth, which is $13 trillion in 2019 (assuming perfect enforcement). Top 0.1 percent wealth share from estate tax statistics is only 15 percent, suggesting that the evasion/avoidance rate for estate tax purposes is approximately 33 percent today. The estates-based wealth tax base is approximately 35 percent lower as well.

RECONCILIATION WITH SUMMERS AND SARIN Summers and Sarin (2019a, 2019b) argue that the wealth tax base above $50 million would only be $1.25 trillion (so that a 2 percent tax would raise only $25 billion). All the estimates in table 2, including the estates-based estimates, are much larger. The SCF and the capitalized income estimates deliver estimates about eight times larger than the Summers and Sarin estimates. Even the estates-based estimates deliver estimates around 5.4 times larger than Summers and Sarin. The Forbes 400 alone represent (according to Forbes) a tax base of $2.9 trillion in 2018, already more than twice the Summers and Sarin estimate. In other words, based on capitalized income or SCF (plus Forbes 400) data, Summers and Sarin's calculations amount to assuming an evasion/avoidance rate of around 85 percent.[33]

Why do Summers and Sarin project such low revenue? They obtain their $25 billion revenue estimate by noting that the estate tax collected only $10 billion from estates above $50 million in 2017 with a nominal tax rate of 40 percent (above $10 million). They assume that one out of fifty rich

---

33. Even if one takes the wealth estimates coming out of the raw estate multiplier method of Kopzcuk and Saez (2004) at face value, one would still find a tax base about three times larger than what Summers and Sarin find.

people die in a given year, so a wealth tax of 40 percent on the living population (instead of decedents only) would collect fifty times what the estate tax does. Hence a wealth tax at the rate of 2 percent (1/20 of 40 percent) would collect 50/20 times what the estate tax does, that is, $25 billion.

The methodology in Summers and Sarin (2019a, 2019b) underestimates the revenue potential of a wealth tax for two main reasons. First, taxable estates are only one-third of the net worth of decedents, due to the full exemption of spousal and charitable bequests.[34] But such deductions would not apply for an annual wealth tax, which means that the Summers and Sarin estimate needs to be multiplied by a factor of three. Second, Summers and Sarin assume that one out of fifty rich people die in a given year. This multiplier of 50 approximately corresponds to the mortality rate used in Kopczuk and Saez (2004). But we have seen that the mortality rate of the rich is lower than this by a factor of 1.9. Using the correct multiplier would further increase the Summers and Sarin estimate by about 90 percent, and combining these two corrections increases their revenue projection by a factor of 5.7 (3 × 1.9). This is enough to approximately reconcile the Summers and Sarin revenue estimate with our estimate based on estate tax data in table 2.[35]

II. Role in Overall Tax Progressivity

In this section, we examine the impact of wealth taxes on the progressivity of the tax system.

II.A. Tax Progressivity

Wealth taxes are very progressive because net wealth is more concentrated than income. Wealth taxes are more progressive than property taxes because property taxes are only levied on real estate, which is more equitably distributed than net wealth (Saez and Zucman 2016). Wealth taxes also more closely track ability to pay than property taxes because they allow

---

34. For estates filed in 2017, total deductions are 67.9 percent of the net estate for gross estates above $50 million. Out of the 67.9 percent, 40 points come from the spousal bequest deduction and 20 points from charitable bequests (online at https://www.irs.gov/statistics/soi-tax-stats-estate-tax-statistics-filing-year-table-1).

35. There are other smaller differences. Summers and Sarin implicitly score a wealth tax on individual (not family) wealth above $50 million, which mechanically reduces the base by about a quarter according to SCF data for 2016. They use 2016 numbers and do not adjust to 2019; nominal aggregate wealth has grown by about 25 percent from 2016 to 2019. Conversely, the estate tax applies starting at a lower threshold of $10 million so there is an infra-marginal tax below $50 million that should not be counted.

people to deduct debts. The progressivity of a wealth tax depends on how high the exemption threshold is and on whether a graduated rate schedule is applied among taxpayers.

Saez and Zucman (2019a) estimate effective tax rates (including all taxes at the federal, state, and local levels) by income groups using the data developed by Piketty, Saez, and Zucman (2018). We can use the same data on the joint distribution of income and wealth to estimate the effect of the wealth tax on the overall progressivity of the current U.S. tax system.

TAX RATE ON THE FORBES 400 One justification for a wealth tax is to increase the effective tax rate on the very wealthiest Americans who may not realize much income and hence may pay low effective tax rates today. Indeed, the two wealth tax proposals by Warren and Sanders target specifically billionaires (and multibillionaires) with higher rates.

As shown in table 4, the top of the Forbes 400 list includes founder-owners of large companies (Amazon's Jeff Bezos, Microsoft's Bill Gates, Berkshire Hathaway's Warren Buffett, and Facebook's Mark Zuckerberg). Of these four companies, only Microsoft pays dividends. As long as Bezos, Buffett, and Zuckerberg do not sell their stock, their realized income is going to be minuscule relative to their wealth and true economic income. For example, Buffett disclosed that his fiscal income—defined as adjusted gross income reported on his individual income tax return—is in the tens of millions. Since his wealth is in the tens of billions, the realized return on his wealth is on the order of 0.1 percent.[36] Bezos's, Buffett's, Zuckerberg's, and Gates's companies are also multinational companies which can book a substantial share of their profits in tax havens to reduce their corporate income tax (Zucman 2015).

How much the top four hundred wealthiest Americans report in fiscal income—and hence pay in income taxes—is a central question for the desirability of a wealth tax. Absent direct evidence on the income taxes paid by the Forbes 400, we need to triangulate using various sources. We use three sources which turn out to provide consistent results. Table 3 summarizes the computations.

First, the IRS provides statistics on linked estate and income tax data. Bourne and others (2018) study the link between wealth on the estate tax

---

36. Buffett's fiscal income was $63 million in 2010 when his wealth was $45 billion and $12 million in 2015 when his wealth was $62 billion. Some billionaires do report substantial incomes (relative to wealth). In August 2019, candidate Tom Steyer disclosed that he reported on average $133 million in annual income from 2009 to 2017 (for a total of $1.2 billion) which is 8.3 percent of his $1.6 billion wealth according to Forbes 400.

Table 3. Reported Income Relative to True Income for Top Wealth Holders

	Estates above $100 million (linked to income tax) (1)	SCF top .001 percent wealth holders (2)	SCF top .01 percent wealth holders (3)	Forbes 400 (combined with IRS top 400) (4)
Year	2007	2016	2016	2014
Wealth ($ millions)	313	951	365	5,725
Reported income ($ millions)	9.4	30.5	11.6	159
Reported income/wealth	3.0%	3.2%	3.2%	2.8%
Average macro return on wealth	5.9%	6.4%	6.4%	6.8%
Percentage true income reported	**51%**	**50%**	**50%**	**41%**
Sample size	116	86	465	400

Source: Authors' calculations.

Notes: This table reports statistics on how much income top wealth holders report on their individual tax returns relative to their true economic income using various sources of publicly available data (across columns). Column (1) uses data from Bourne and others (2018); the sample is all estates above $100 million for 2007 decedents. The source in columns (2) and (3) is the 2016 Survey of Consumer Finances (SCF household unit). Column (4) combines the Forbes Top 400 with the IRS top 400 highest income earners. Wealth and reported income on the individual tax return are averages. Average macro return on wealth is total capital income to total household wealth economy-wide. The percentage of true income reported on individual tax returns assumes conservatively that the rich get the same rate of return as the macro-average. In column (1), average wealth is estimated as 3.14 times the $100 million threshold (based on estate tax statistics for 2007 decedents). The reported income of the Forbes 400 is estimated as 50 percent of the reported income of the IRS Top 400 (as SCF top .001 percent wealth holders have reported income of 50 percent of the SCF top .001 percent income earners in 2016).

return for 2007 decedents and fiscal income over the last five years preceding death (2002–6). In the highest wealth category they consider—$100 million and above—reported capital income (averaged over 2002–6 and expressed in 2007 dollars) is 3 percent of 2007 wealth (Bourne and others 2018, fig. 4). In national and financial accounts, the ratio of aggregate capital income in 2002–6 to aggregate wealth in 2007 is 5.9 percent. This suggests that reported capital income of the wealthiest decedents is only 51 percent of their true income (assuming conservatively that the wealthy obtain a return on their wealth equal to the aggregate return). One objection is that the wealthy may avoid realizing capital gains toward the end of their life, since unrealized capital gains benefit from the step-up of basis at death. Bourne and others (2018, fig. 2), however, show that realized capital gains are very large in their sample, on average 45 percent of capital income.

Second, the SCF provides information on the joint distribution of wealth in year t and reported income in $t − 1$. In 2016, the ratio of reported income to wealth was 3.2 percent for the top 0.001 percent wealthiest Americans (wealth above $650 million, 86 records in the public SCF) and 3.2 percent for the top 0.01 percent (wealth above $190 million, 465 records). This 3.2 percent rate of return is only 50 percent of the 6.4 percent aggregate capital income-to-wealth ratio in 2016. Earlier waves of the SCF provide similar results, which is reassuring given the small sample sizes. These SCF results are very similar to the IRS linked estate and income tax results and not subject to the issue that realized capital income might be particularly low within a few years before death.

Third, the IRS provides statistics on the top four hundred highest earners, a group we call the IRS top 400. In 2014, the latest year available, the IRS top 400 had an average fiscal income of $318 million. The Forbes 400 wealthiest have, by definition, less fiscal income than this on average. How much less? To address this question, we relate the fiscal income of top income earners to the fiscal income of top wealth holders in the SCF. In the 2016 SCF, the top 0.001 percent income earners (sample of 64) reported fiscal incomes that were 6.7 percent of the wealth of the top 0.001 percent wealth holders. This is approximately twice the income of the top 0.001 percent wealth holders mentioned above. Averaged across all SCF years from 1998 to 2016, this ratio is 2.3 on average.[37] This result shows that there is indeed substantial re-ranking in wealth versus reported income. Based on this finding, we estimate that the Forbes 400 wealthiest Americans have a reported income of $159 million ($318 million divided by the ratio of 2). In 2014, the average wealth of the Forbes 400 was $5.725 billion. So the fiscal income of the Forbes 400 was 2.77 percent of their wealth (2.77 percent × $5.725 billion = $159 million), which is only 41 percent of the 6.77 percent economy-wide return on wealth in 2014. If we make the conservative assumption that the return on wealth for the Forbes 400 is the same as the economy-wide return, fiscal income for the Forbes 400 is only 41 percent of their true economic income.[38]

In sum, using three different sources and methodologies, we find that top wealth holders have a fiscal income that is about or slightly less than half of their true economic income (defined as wealth times the average macroeconomic return to wealth). In what follows, we assume that the Forbes 400 have a ratio of fiscal income to true economic income of 45 percent; population-wide, this ratio is around 70 percent (Piketty, Saez,

---

37. For the top 0.01 percent (instead of top 0.001 percent), this ratio is 2.0 on average from 1998 to 2016.
38. Similar estimates would be obtained for other years using the same methodology.

and Zucman 2018).[39] The super wealthy do not realize as much income as the average person, but on average they realize substantially more than what Warren Buffett publicly disclosed.

Naturally, our 45 percent estimate of reported income relative to full economic income is based on triangulating the best available sources, and it could be refined in future work. We have applied this 45 percent ratio to estimate taxes paid by the top four hundred retrospectively to all years since 1950 in Saez and Zucman (2019a).[40] We are fully aware that this triangulation is an approximation, but it is the best approximation we could create using public sources. Given the importance of the policy question— How much do billionaires really pay in taxes?—we view it as important to mobilize internal data to provide better estimates.[41]

EFFECTS OF WEALTH TAXATION ON OVERALL TAX PROGRESSIVITY Figure 5 depicts the average tax rate by income groups in 2018, the year following the passage of the Tax Cuts and Jobs Act. All federal, state, and local taxes are included. Taxes are expressed as a fraction of pretax income, a comprehensive measure of income before government taxes and transfers (other than Social Security) that add up to total national income (Piketty, Saez, and Zucman 2018). P0-10 denotes the bottom 10 percent of adults, P10-20 the next 10 percent, and so on. The economy-wide average tax rate is 28 percent. Tax rates in the bottom seven deciles are slightly lower than average (25 percent instead of 28 percent). Tax rates between percentiles 80 and 99.9 are very slightly higher than average (around 29 percent). The tax rate peaks at 33 percent for P99.9-99.99 (that is, the bottom 90 percent of the top 0.1 percent). The tax rate then falls above P99.99 and is lowest for the top four hundred at 23 percent. Taking all taxes together, the U.S. tax system looks like a giant flat tax with similar tax rates across income groups but with lower tax rates for billionaires.

A wealth tax such as the one proposed by Elizabeth Warren would have a large impact on progressivity within the top 0.1 percent. To illustrate

39. In the Piketty, Saez, and Zucman (2018) micro-files, the ratio is about 65 percent for the top four hundred in recent years. It is too high because wealth is imputed based on realized fiscal income. We plan to address this issue in future research.

40. In earlier decades when the corporate tax was particularly large, the direct computation from the micro tax data generates ratios of reported income to actual income that are lower than 45 percent, in which case we do not adjust down reported income.

41. For example, linking the Forbes 400 to income tax data would allow for a direct estimation of the fiscal income of the four hundred richest. Similar linking for research purposes has already been done in the context of estate tax data by Raub, Johnson, and Newcomb (2010). A well-enforced wealth tax would be an even better source to study this question in depth and make sure the Forbes 400 estimates are themselves accurate.

Figure 5. The Effects of Wealth Taxation on Overall Tax Progressivity

Percentage of pretax income

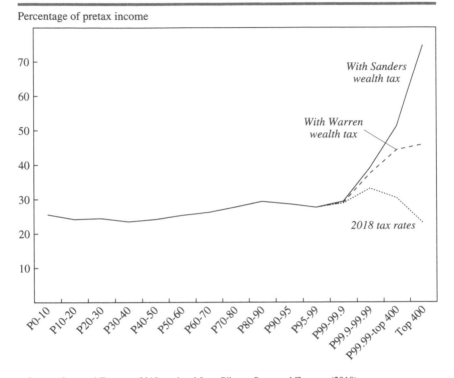

Source: Saez and Zucman (2019) updated from Piketty, Saez, and Zucman (2018).

Notes: The figure depicts the average tax rate by income groups in 2018. All federal, state, and local taxes are included. Taxes are expressed as a fraction of pretax income. P0-10 denotes the bottom 10 percent of adults, P10-20 the next 10 percent, and so on. The figure depicts how adding the wealth taxes proposed by Elizabeth Warren and Bernie Sanders would affect the progressivity of the overall tax system. The Warren wealth tax has a 2 percent marginal tax rate above $50 million and a 3 percent marginal tax rate above $1 billion; the Sanders wealth tax has a 1 percent marginal tax rate above $32 million, 2 percent above $50 million, 3 percent above $250 million, 4 percent above $500 million, 5 percent above $1 billion, 6 percent above $2.5 billion, 7 percent above $5 billion, 8 percent above $10 billion.

this point, we use the capitalized income wealth estimates and assume that the wealthy would hide 15 percent of their wealth. The tax rate on the top 0.1 percent excluding the top 0.01 percent would increase modestly by 4 points. The tax rate in the top 0.01 percent would rise by 14 points. Among the top four hundred, the tax rate would double from 23 percent to 46 percent. A wealth tax with a high exemption threshold ($50 million) and a marginal tax rate of 2 percent (3 percent above $1 billion) would have a major impact on progressivity. It would restore tax progressivity at the top to levels last observed in 1980 (Saez and Zucman 2019a, chapter 7).

II.B. Alternatives

Several alternatives to increase tax progressivity have been proposed.

TAXING REALIZED CAPITAL GAINS BETTER There is widespread recognition that capital gains are not taxed systematically.[42] The step-up of basis at death is the largest and most inefficient loophole (charitable giving of appreciated property is another). Conversely, the fact that price inflation is not taken into account when computing realized gains adds a "wealth tax" rate layer (equal to the rate of inflation times the tax rate on realized gains). But it is a capricious wealth tax that varies with the inflation rate and hits only gains eventually realized. Most economists agree that closing the step-up of basis loophole and adjusting gains for inflation would be a good idea. This would make the tax base less elastic (as everybody eventually dies or disposes of assets), allowing for an increase in the capital gains rate and possibly an alignment with ordinary tax rates. The key remaining issue would be that the tax might come with substantial delay for very wealthy individuals who are still fairly young and do not need to sell their stocks (for example, Mark Zuckerberg).

TAXING CAPITAL GAINS ON ACCRUAL One solution to remedy the delayed realization problem is to tax capital gains on accrual (or mark-to-market taxation).[43] The main difficulty is that there is a lot of year-to-year fluctuation in assets prices.[44] An appreciation of 20 percent (which is not uncommon) taxed at 40 percent could amount to a very large wealth tax of 8 percent. The tax would be particularly heavy on entrepreneurs. For example, Zuckerberg has experienced a 40 percent annual growth in wealth since 2008; a mark-to-market tax at 40 percent would amount to a 16 percent annual wealth tax. Taxing capital gains on accrual means a heavy tax on entrepreneurs growing a successful business and building up wealth. In contrast, the wealthy rentier or heir who is invested in bonds or mature stock might not be taxed much. This is in contrast with a wealth tax which is based solely on wealth and not returns.

MERGING WEALTH TAXATION AND CAPITAL GAINS TAXATION Taxing realized capital gains only means that the tax is delayed. Taxing capital gains

42. See Batchelder and Kamin (2019) for a recent detailed discussion.

43. See Weisbach (1999) for a detailed proposal.

44. For hard to value assets, such as private equity, generally, the mark-to-market tax is applied only when the asset is sold retrospectively. The tax can be computed as if a tax had been owed each year, what is called "retrospective taxation," an idea originally proposed by Auerbach (1991). See Batchelder and Kamin (2019) for a recent discussion and Kleinbard and Evans (1997) for the practical difficulties it can generate.

on accrual means capricious taxation based on the ups and downs of volatile financial markets. An intermediate solution would be to track unrealized capital gains and have a prepaid withholding tax kick in whenever such unrealized gains exceed a chosen amount. For example, unrealized real capital gains above $1 million would face a recurring annual tax of 2 percent, but the tax would be credited back when capital gains are realized. The withholding tax could be made progressive with higher tax rates on very large amounts of unrealized gains.[45] Such a tax would ensure more timely payment, and since it is a withholding tax, the issue of imperfect or imprecise valuation is less critical. In practice, such a withholding tax on unrealized capital gains would look quite similar to a wealth tax (except that the withholding tax is refundable upon realization and does not hit large wealth holdings with no unrealized gains).[46] This tax would be particularly useful for state income taxes that are based on residence (the current capital gains tax can be avoided by leaving a high-tax state such as California and becoming, for example, a Florida resident before realization).

CONSTITUTIONALITY: THE WEALTH TAX AS A MINIMUM INCOME TAX The key advantage of the wealth tax is that it hits the implicit return on wealth even if the realized return on the individual income tax is low. This can also be achieved through an income tax based on the presumptive income from wealth defined as a fixed return on wealth, as in the Netherlands. Colombia's income tax is based on the maximum of reported income and presumptive income defined as 3 percent of wealth (Londoño-Vélez and Avila 2020). The advantage of this system is that such a tax would clearly be constitutional.[47] In this system for example, if Warren Buffett's wealth is $65 billion, then his presumptive income would be $1.95 billion, much higher than his actual reported income, and hence his income tax would be computed based on presumptive income and not reported income.

---

45. And the tax would apply only if cumulative tax paid is below the tax owed upon realization of all gains.

46. Such a tax could also be integrated with the estate tax by making it creditable for estate tax purposes as well so that it also represents a prepayment on the estate tax that comes late by definition.

47. The constitutionality of a straight wealth tax is debated among legal scholars and hence would effectively depend on the makeup of the Supreme Court (Ackerman 1999).

III. Tax Enforcement

In this section, we analyze the issue of enforcement of the wealth tax.

III.A. Tax Avoidance and Evasion

A natural starting point to think about tax avoidance is the experience of the many countries that have implemented a wealth tax.

OVERALL RESPONSES A number of studies estimate the response of reported wealth to a change in the wealth tax rate. Note that such estimates do not directly tell us how much tax avoidance or evasion there is overall but instead how changes in the tax rate affect the level of wealth reported. Short-run responses likely capture tax avoidance and evasion (as real responses are expected to take longer).

Bunching Studies A wealth tax above a given threshold creates incentives to report (or reduce) wealth to just below the threshold to avoid the tax. Hence, there should be bunching in the distribution of wealth at the exemption threshold. The amount of bunching is proportional to the size of the behavioral response and can be used to recover the elasticity of reported wealth with respect to the tax rate.[48] Seim (2017) finds clear evidence of bunching at the exemption threshold for the Swedish wealth tax. This implies that there is a behavioral response to the wealth tax but it is quantitatively small: a 1 percent marginal wealth tax rate reduces reported wealth by 0.2 percent only. The response comes from self-reported assets suggesting that it is driven by avoidance and evasion rather than real response. Jakobsen and others (2019) also use a bunching design in the case of the Danish wealth tax and find even smaller elasticities. Londoño-Vélez and Avila (2020, also using bunching methods, find larger avoidance and evasion responses: a 1 percent marginal wealth tax rate reduces reported wealth by about 2–3 percent in Colombia, where third-party reporting is much less developed than in Sweden or Denmark. In both cases, the bunching methodology provides very compelling evidence of behavioral responses but perhaps not its full magnitude. If many filers ignore the exact details of the tax system but still respond to the overall tax, the total response could be much larger.[49]

---

48. See Kleven (2016) for a survey of this bunching methodology.

49. This issue affects bunching studies in income tax contexts as well, as discussed in Kleven (2016).

Diff-in-Diff Studies In Denmark, where third-party reporting is extensive, Jakobsen and others (2019) also use a difference-in-differences approach and find estimates substantially larger than their bunching estimates. In particular, they find a growing effect of wealth taxes on reported wealth (possibly through a combination of avoidance and real responses). In Switzerland, where there is no third-party reporting of financial wealth (due to bank secrecy), Brulhart and others (2016) find very large responses to wealth taxation: a 1 percent wealth tax lowers reported wealth by 23–34 percent. This extremely large estimate is extrapolated from very small variations in wealth tax rates over time and across Swiss cantons and hence is possibly not as compellingly identified as the other estimates based on larger variations in the wealth tax rate.

EXPLOITING ASSET EXEMPTIONS Wealthy taxpayers can take advantage of asset exemptions to avoid the wealth tax. Alvaredo and Saez (2009) provide a striking illustration in the case of the Spanish wealth tax which exempted closely held stock when the business owner was substantially involved in the management and owned at least 15 percent of the company stock (but such exempted stock remained reportable). In 1994, the first year the exemption was introduced, exempted stock represented only about 15 percent of total closely held stock reported by the top 0.01 percent of wealth holders. By 2002, the fraction had grown to 77 percent. The time series from 1993 to 2002 shows stability in the value of taxable plus exempt closely held stock among top wealth holders, implying that the behavioral response comes from shifting from taxable to nontaxable closely held stock rather than a supply side effect of more business activity (Alvaredo and Saez 2009, 1159, fig. 10). This example shows that exempting assets can seriously undermine the wealth tax.

HIDING ASSETS ABROAD Wealthy individuals can try to hide assets abroad to evade income and wealth taxes. Zucman (2013, 2015) and Alstadsæter, Johannesen, and Zucman (2018) provide evidence on the amount of wealth held in tax havens for each country in aggregate. They estimate that U.S. residents hold about 9 percent of U.S. national income in offshore wealth or about 2 percent of total U.S. household wealth.

Recent evidence from customer lists leaked from offshore financial institutions matched to administrative wealth tax records (in Scandinavia and Colombia) shows that offshore tax evasion is highly concentrated among the rich. Alstadsæter, Johannesen, and Zucman (2019) show that in Norway about 75 percent of wealth hidden offshore is owned by the top 0.1 percent. This implies high rates of tax evasion at the top: the wealthiest 0.01 percent of households evade about 25 percent of their taxes through offshore tax evasion. Londoño-Vélez and Avila 2020) show a rise in the use of offshore entities following the reintroduction of wealth taxation in Colombia. The use of offshore accounts is also extremely concentrated in Colombia. Interestingly, the Panama Papers leak generated a 800 percent surge in the use of a voluntary disclosure amnesty scheme. All in all, 40 percent of individuals in the top 0.01 percent used the amnesty scheme, implying that offshore tax evasion is very high but also very responsive to policy enforcement in Colombia.

Extrapolating these findings to the United States would imply that, of the 2 percent of total U.S. household wealth hidden in tax havens, about 1.5 points are owned by the top 0.1 percent, which would increase their wealth share from 20 percent to 21.1 percent (= 21.5/1.02). This implies that all our previous tax base estimates already factor in this baseline offshore evasion of about 7.5 percent for the top .1 percent (= 1.5/20).

Wealth concealment is a serious enforcement concern. However, just like legal avoidance, illegal evasion depends on policies and can be reduced through proper enforcement. Key to reducing evasion are (1) the collection of comprehensive data, (2) sanctions for the suppliers of tax evasion services (the countries and financial intermediaries that facilitate it), and (3) proper resources for auditing. In terms of data collection, the United States has taken an ambitious path forward with the 2010 Foreign Account Tax Compliance Act (FATCA) which requires all foreign financial institutions to identify and report their U.S. customers to the IRS. Future research will analyze whether FATCA has had a significant impact on compliance.

EXPATRIATION Another way to avoid taxes is to expatriate. There is some evidence that residential decisions of the wealthy are sensitive to taxes on wealth. Moretti and Wilson (2019) show that the Forbes 400 residential decisions are sensitive to state-level inheritance taxes (using as identification the repeal in 2004 of the federal estate tax credit for state inheritance taxes that made state-level taxes relevant after 2004). Martinez (2017) shows, in the Swiss context, that a sharp decrease in income tax progressivity in the canton of Obwalden in 2006 did increase the share of rich taxpayers in the canton by 20–30 percent relative to neighboring countries. There is a recent body of work showing that the residential decisions of high earners—football players in the EU, innovators, and highly skilled workers—are sensitive to taxes.[50] In all cases where large responses are

50. See Kleven and others (forthcoming) for a recent survey.

found, however, three conditions are met: mobility is easy (such as across Swiss cantons or U.S. states), mobility is allowed (EU football players did not move much in response to tax differentials before teams were freely allowed to hire foreign players; Kleven, Landais, and Saez 2013), and mobility reduces taxes. These conditions may be affected by policy, especially the last one.

In particular, avoiding taxes through residential mobility is particularly difficult for U.S. citizens because it requires renouncing U.S. citizenship, since U.S. citizens living abroad are liable for U.S. taxes (with credits for foreign taxes paid). The United States also currently has an exit tax to deter expatriation by individuals with over $2 million in net worth. Individuals renouncing their citizenship are required to pay income tax on all their unrealized capital gains. Building on the existing exit tax, Senator Warren's proposal would introduce an exit tax of 40 percent of net worth above $50 million, which would greatly reduce incentives to expatriate for tax reasons. Therefore, the threat of expatriation is primarily a policy variable.

III.B. Why Have Wealth Taxes Been Abandoned in a Number of European Countries?

As pointed out in the recent study of progressive wealth taxation by the OECD (2018), twelve OECD countries (all of them in Europe) had progressive wealth taxes in 1990, but only four still had wealth taxes in 2017 (Switzerland, Spain, France, and Norway). As of 2019, four OECD countries levy a progressive wealth tax on individuals.[51] The decline of wealth taxation abroad is one of the main arguments from skeptics in the U.S. debate (Summers and Sarin 2019a, 2019b). It is important to understand why wealth taxes have been repealed in a number of European countries.

MOBILITY In the European public debate, the concern that the rich or their wealth will flee abroad is the most frequently used argument by opponents. For example, France's President Macron transformed the French wealth tax into a real estate property tax in 2018, arguing that real estate cannot move abroad while people or financial wealth can (Rose 2017). The rich can evade the wealth tax by putting their wealth in offshore tax havens (for example, Switzerland), which do not share information with foreign tax authorities. This is evasion, since wealth taxes are based on the global wealth of residents regardless of the location of the assets or the financial

---

51. France has eliminated its progressive wealth tax (and replaced it with a real estate property tax), and Belgium has introduced a modest wealth tax.

institutions managing the assets. The rich can also avoid the wealth tax by moving their residence to a foreign country, as wealth taxes are generally based on residence. These two issues are potentially serious in the European context. There is clear tax competition across EU countries, which try to attract high earners or wealthy residents from other countries with special tax breaks. Most of these tax breaks are focused on high earners but some are focused on high-wealth individuals.[52] For example, Switzerland works out customized deals with wealthy individuals. Portugal and Italy provide income tax breaks for retirees (which is most valuable for high-pension retirees).[53]

In the public debate, mobility of the wealthy versus mobility of their bank accounts versus mobility of the capital they ultimately own is often confused. Because progressive wealth taxes are based on the worldwide wealth of individual residents, wealth taxes do not generate incentives to move capital abroad. Hiding wealth abroad does reduce taxes, but this is tax evasion and in general the underlying assets (stocks and bonds) can be the same whether the wealth is held through offshore versus domestic bank accounts.

However, the central point is that this "European context" is not a law of nature but results from policy choices (or non-choices). Other choices could lead to radically different outcomes in terms of tax evasion and tax competition.

First, EU efforts at curbing offshore tax evasion have been weak. As shown, for example, by Johannesen and Zucman (2014), halfhearted tax enforcement efforts can be easily circumvented and end up having minimal effects on tax evasion. In contrast, the United States took a bold step toward enforcement in 2010 with FATCA, which imposes steep penalties on foreign financial institutions that fail to report accounts of U.S. residents to the U.S. tax authorities (Zucman 2015). It is possible to curb offshore tax evasion because such evasion is done through large and sophisticated financial institutions that keep records and know the ultimate owners of the accounts (even if such accounts are held through offshore shell corporations to make it more difficult for tax authorities to link the accounts to owners). As the recent leaks from HSBC, UBS, and the Panama Papers have shown, such financial institutions maintain the names

52. See OECD (2011) for a description of such tax breaks.
53. Since 2009, Portugal exempts foreign pensions from taxation for ten years. Starting in 2019 in Italy, new immigrants who receive foreign pensions benefit from a special low tax rate of 7 percent only for their first six years of residence in some regions in Italy.

of their clients. Such data can easily be linked to tax data.[54] The multiplicity of leaks also shows that clients are at risk of seeing their accounts disclosed.

FATCA follows the route of policing foreign financial institutions directly but with the difficulty that the U.S. tax authorities have less power to audit foreign financial institutions effectively than home financial institutions. Another route is to get foreign governments to share the information they can collect from their financial institutions. The second route is best in the long run but likely more difficult to establish, as it requires international cooperation.[55]

Second, the degree to which residential decisions of the wealthy are affected by taxation is also heavily dependent on policy. The EU is organized to foster such tax competition. Individual income and wealth taxation depends solely on current residence. Hence, when France had a progressive wealth tax before 2018, moving from Paris to London would immediately extinguish progressive wealth tax liability (except for domestic real estate assets). Contrast this with U.S. policy: U.S. citizens remain liable for U.S. income taxes for life and regardless of residence (but with full credit for foreign income taxes paid). The only way to escape the U.S. income tax is to renounce U.S. citizenship and even then, the United States imposes a substantial exit tax. The exit tax, formally known as the expatriation tax, is essentially a tax on all unrealized capital gains upon expatriation. It applies to high-income (incomes over \$160,000) and high-wealth (wealth above \$2 million) expatriates. It applies to citizens who renounce citizenship and also to long-term residents who end their U.S. resident tax status.[56] While the EU and the United States are the two polar opposites along this tax competition dimension, midway solutions are possible and probably preferable.[57] For example, movers could remain tax liable in their country of origin (but with full foreign tax credit) for a certain number of

54. Indeed this is what the recent research studies by Alstadsæter, Johannesen, and Zucman (2019) and Londoño-Vélez and Avila (2020) have done.

55. At the level of the EU, it is almost impossible to make progress on this front as any change requires unanimous agreement of all EU countries, some of which are net beneficiaries of lax enforcement.

56. See the IRS website's page on expatriation tax (https://www.irs.gov/individuals/international-taxpayers/expatriation-tax) for a description of the expatriate tax regulations. The Sanders and Warren wealth tax plans further strengthen the exit tax with a 40 percent wealth tax on expatriates' assets.

57. The U.S. system imposes a lifetime tax filing burden on U.S. citizens who have lived abroad sometimes for decades and who might not be very rich.

years (for example, five years). This would essentially negate the effects of special, often temporary schemes set up to attract high-income foreigners.

While countries in the EU generally have bigger governments, more social spending, and more regulations than the United States, the EU super-structure actually promotes policies constraining subcentral governments more than in the United States. This is true for tax competition but also for government deficits and monetary policy.

FAIRNESS Opposition to the wealth tax also arises from a feeling of unfairness: "the wealth tax aggravates millionaires without bothering billionaires."[58] The aggravated millionaires are taxpayers wealthy in illiquid assets (or at least wealthy enough to be above the exemption threshold) but poor in cash. As a result, such taxpayers feel the wealth tax as a heavy and unjust burden. In France, for example, some retired farmers on Île de Ré living on a small pension but owning very valuable land, due to the real estate boom for secondary residences, became liable for the wealth tax. In Denmark, there were complaints that owners of historical castles were liable for the wealth tax but had no income to pay it (Henrik Kleven, personal communication). The United States does not have a progressive wealth tax but has a long experience with real estate property taxes. The property tax also generates strong opposition when rapid tax appreciation leads to increasing property tax bills hitting people on fixed incomes (such as retirees or widows) hard.[59] A classic complaint against the U.S. estate tax is that it can force the sale of family businesses or farms that have high market value but little in liquid assets.

Obviously, to an economist, such complaints do not make sense, since wealth is by definition marketable, and credit markets are supposed to function well when there are collateral assets. But humans often do not behave as the standard, perfectly rational economic model predicts: people may not want to sell family estates or businesses or even borrow against them. Such behavioral effects have consequences and need to be taken into account for policymaking.

Indeed, in practice, stories of aggravated millionaires can fuel successful lobbying against wealth taxation. This leads to three types of reforms of the wealth tax that undermine the integrity of the wealth tax.

58. This statement was made by Dominique Strauss-Kahn in 1997 when he was minister of the economy, finance and industry in the French center-left government of Lionel Jospin: "l'impôt sur la fortune embête les millionnaires sans gêner les milliardaires."

59. Wong (2019) shows that indeed property tax increases following reappraisals increase financial hardship measures such as delinquencies on mortgages.

Limitations Based on Fiscal Income First, a number of countries have introduced tax limitations whereby the sum of the wealth tax and the income tax cannot exceed a certain percentage of total fiscal income. As we discussed above, this precisely defeats the main purpose of the wealth tax, as the ultrarich can find ways to report very low fiscal income relative to their true wealth or true income. As a result, this type of tax limitation ends up exempting billionaires.

Base Erosion Second, special treatment is introduced for assets more likely to be illiquid, such as real estate assets and business assets. For example, the French and Spanish wealth taxes exempted business assets when the owner is substantially involved in the business. As mentioned above, when Spain exempted business assets from its wealth tax in 1994, top wealth holders were able to increase sharply the fraction of wealth held in the form of business assets, creating both efficiency costs and reducing the tax progressivity (Alvaredo and Saez 2009). In France, the very richest taxpayers were typically able to incorporate and deduct such assets from wealth taxation (Landais, Piketty, and Saez 2011). In the case of wealth taxation, exempting some asset classes is particularly damaging as marketable wealth can by definition be traded and hence converted into tax-exempt wealth.[60]

Nonmarket Values Third, a number of countries have also used nonmarket values for some asset classes such as real estate. As discussed in Piketty (2014, chapter 15), the early progressive wealth taxes in Prussia and Sweden used assessed values for real estate linked to the land/real estate registries ("cadastral values") and typically not updated with market prices. However, with rapid inflation, such assessed values can quickly lag behind market prices. Spain for example, uses low assessed values for wealth tax purposes (Alvaredo and Saez 2009). While this can provide relief to some of the aggravated millionaires, in the long run this undermines the horizontal equity of the wealth tax. Indeed, the German wealth tax was repealed in 1997 following a ruling by the Constitutional Court that demanded equal taxation of all property. As U.S. states know, there is a tension between using market prices for real estate property taxes versus introducing property tax assessment limits. The use of market prices in a context of fast price increases led to the famous tax revolt Proposition 13 in

---

60. While there can also be income shifting for income tax purposes when some income forms are treated preferentially, such shifting is likely to be more limited than for wealth. Most wage earners, for example, would not be able to transform their income into corporate profits, dividends, or capital gains.

California in 1978 that froze real estate assessment for property taxation to purchasing prices (with only a 2 percent annual adjustment). Four decades later, the property tax in California has huge horizontal inequities: long-term residents may pay one-tenth of what a new resident pays for identical homes. A number of U.S. states have also passed some form of property tax assessment limits, often following ballot initiatives.

The cleanest solution to liquidity issues is to increase the exemption thresholds so that mere millionaires are not liable. This route was followed for the U.S. estate tax. The exemption was increased from $1 million in 2000 to $5 million in 2011. The main argument was that the "death tax" was also killing family businesses and family farms. With the higher exemption threshold, the estate tax is harder to repeal, as this argument is much harder to make. For example, the recent tax reform of the Trump administration, the Tax Cuts and Jobs Act, did not eliminate the estate tax even though this was an initial goal of the reform. Instead, the reform doubled the exemption level to $11.2 million (in 2018). The recent wealth tax proposal by Senator Warren also has a very high exemption level of $50 million—about fifty times higher than typical European progressive wealth taxes (OECD 2018). As a result, the policy debate on the proposal has not emphasized the issue of illiquid wealth and lack of cash.[61]

What lesson do we draw from the decline of progressive wealth taxes in Europe? First, history shows that wealth taxes are fragile. They can be undermined by tax limits, base erosion, and weak enforcement. When wealth taxes were repealed in Europe, it was primarily because policy-makers took the view that tax competition and offshore tax evasion were a given, making a wealth tax too hard to enforce. This somewhat nihilistic view is, however, incorrect: tolerating tax competition and tax evasion is a policy choice. Developing policies to curb evasion and tax competition was hard for a single country in a context where until recently little was done to tame tax competition and offshore evasion at the EU level, but the U.S.

---

61. Another possibility that seems most natural to economists is to provide credit to aggravated millionaires (if markets fail to do so). One simple way would be to allow tax-payers to borrow from the government to pay the wealth tax and repay the loan when the illiquid assets are sold or transferred. For example, the U.S. estate tax allows for spreading payments over fifteen years at low interest for illiquid estates. Some state property taxes also allow tax deferral in special cases (such as elderly or disabled homeowners in Texas). In practice, such tax deferrals are rarely used. Aggravated millionaires or homeowners dislike borrowing to pay taxes, whether borrowing on the private market or from the government (Wong 2019). Therefore, it is probably economists' fantasy to believe that creating credit markets will resolve the issue.

context today is different. European wealth taxes were also undermined because of a poor policy response to complaints by merely rich taxpayers. Instead of increasing the exemption threshold, the responses eroded the base and created tax limitations that benefited billionaires the most. Drawing lessons from this experience, a U.S. wealth tax could avoid this pitfall.[62]

III.C. Enforcing a U.S. Wealth Tax

The key to successful modern income taxation is information reporting by third parties such as employers and financial institutions (Kleven and others 2011). This reporting allows the tax administration to get direct information on most income sources so that self-reporting is reduced to a minimum. The same principle should be followed for the wealth tax. Taxpayers and the IRS would receive information returns from financial institutions showing the value of their assets at the end of the year. For administrative success, it is essential that such third-party reporting cover the widest possible set of assets and debts (just as the income tax is most successfully enforced on the types of income with third-party reporting). A wealth tax also requires policies regarding information reporting, the valuation of assets, and the treatment of trusts, among other design considerations.

INFORMATION REPORTING The most important extension of the current information reporting system would be to require financial institutions to report year-end wealth balances to the IRS. In some cases, this could be combined with existing information reporting for capital income payments, while in other cases it would require new forms. For many types of assets, this information is already stored by third parties (typically financial institutions), so reporting it to the IRS would be straightforward. Information reporting requirements could be readily applied to many types of assets and liabilities including checking and savings accounts and publicly listed stocks, bonds, and mutual funds.

—Interest-bearing assets (deposits, saving accounts, bonds, and so on): information return 1099-INT already provides information on all interest income. It could also report the outstanding balance. This requirement

---

62. If the tax exemption threshold were lowered considerably, complaints from the merely rich would easily arise. In this case, one potential solution would be to provide credits for local property taxes paid, which would effectively protect real estate assets, the most common form of illiquid assets among the merely rich, from the federal wealth tax.

could be extended to noninterest-paying accounts such as zero-interest bank deposits.

—Publicly listed stock: form 1099-DIV for dividend income would report the market value of the corresponding stock holdings (and this requirement could be extended to nondividend-paying stock).

—Assets indirectly held through mutual funds: mutual funds already provide information returns on income earned through mutual funds. It would be easy to add a balance reporting requirement on all mutual funds held by U.S. residents.

—Defined contribution pension assets: the current reporting requirement of IRA balances (form 5498) could be extended to all defined contribution plans such as 401(k)s.[63]

—Defined benefits pension assets: pension distribution form 1099-R could report whether the distribution is an annuity (so as to be able to compute the value of defined benefits pensions for current pensioners).

—Vehicles: states already systematically register vehicles (including luxury vehicles such as boats and planes). Such databases could be used to generate assessed values (based on initial value and standard depreciation schedules).

—Mortgage balances: mortgage interest payments are already reported on form 1098. Mortgage debt balances have been reported on form 1098 since tax year 2017.

—Other debt balances: student loan balances could be reported on form 1098-E (following the model for mortgages). Consumer credit debt is already reported to the credit bureaus, and the IRS could require the credit bureaus to provide information returns on outstanding balances.

—Closely held business ownership: the ownership of closely held businesses organized as partnerships and S corporations is already reported through the schedule K-1 (form 1065) which reports the business income for each partner or shareholder.[64] This ownership reporting requirement should be extended to closely held businesses that are C corporations. The information is already stored in depositories (deposit trust corporations) and could be shared with the IRS.

---

63. Form 5498 in particular already requires valuations of closely held business assets in IRAs.

64. The recent work of Cooper and others (2016) shows that the reporting system for partnerships is not perfect and ought to be improved as they were not able to allocate about 15 percent of income to any final individuals (most likely because of the use of offshore partnerships for tax avoidance).

III.D. Valuation

The general principle guiding valuations should be that all assets should be assessed at their prevailing market value. In the majority of cases, market values are easy to observe by the IRS with proper information reporting. Here we discuss the cases that raise challenges. Two general points should be kept in mind. First, value arises from the expected income stream and expected sale value in the future. The current and past income stream can be observed. Second, values are often eventually revealed by the market when a sale takes place. If the revealed value is significantly different from values used for wealth tax purposes, it is always feasible to apply a retrospective wealth tax correction at the time of sale.[65]

VALUING CLOSELY HELD BUSINESSES As discussed above, it is likely that the share of private businesses among top 0.1 percent wealth holders is fairly large—probably around one-third—and hence the valuation of closely held businesses is very important. It is useful to distinguish between large versus small closely held businesses.

Large Private Businesses For large private businesses, it is possible to draw on the financial system to put market values on many of these assets. Large private businesses (such as Uber or Lyft before their IPOs) are typically valued on secondary markets, and their stock transactions are centrally registered. Making such transactions reportable to the IRS would allow the tax administration to value such stock systematically. More broadly, the financial industry regularly values private businesses (in the context of venture capital funding, mergers and acquisitions, or share issuance). These valuations could be made reportable to the IRS for the purpose of administering a wealth tax and could be used to value assets retrospectively.[66] More ambitiously, in case of disagreement about valuation for large private businesses between the IRS and the owners, owners should pay in stock, and the government can then create the missing valuation market when selling back the stock. A defining feature of modern capitalism is precisely the ability to divide business ownership with dispersed shareholding. Creating a valuation market is the best solution, since any asymmetry in treatment between comparable publicly traded corporations versus private corporations would create incentives to

---

65. Various cantons in Switzerland use such retrospective corrections, which are called "supplementary net wealth tax[es]" (Lehner 2000, 670).

66. Of course, taxpayers have an incentive to undervalue their business for tax purposes. This is why the IRS should use systematically existing valuations for business purposes.

game the system and, in particular, to remain private if private equity gets preferential treatment.[67]

Small Private Businesses For smaller businesses for which no information exists within the financial industry, there already exists a section of the Internal Revenue Code (409A) that values private businesses for the purpose of taxing stock options or valuing IRAs.[68] These valuations can be perfected based on best international practices. Switzerland is the best example of a country that has successfully taxed equity in private businesses by using simple formulas based on the book value of business assets and multiples of average profits in recent years. The IRS already collects data about the assets and profits of private businesses for business and corporate income tax purposes, so it would be straightforward to apply similar formulas in the United States. Smith and others (2019) give a recent example of how to use administrative data to systematically create valuations for S corporations using formulas based on profits, book value, and sales.

This means that when the business is owned by a very wealthy individual above the exemption threshold, the business faces a higher tax through the wealth tax that takes the form of a profits surtax, a property surtax, and a sales surtax. The important point is that no costly valuation would be required each year, as the calculation would be entirely formula based. Also note that few small businesses are owned by the 75,000 families with net worth above $50 million, meaning that such surtaxes would apply only to a small fraction of small businesses.[69]

A number of intangible assets (such as property rights on patents and trademarks, royalty rights for books) are owned directly by individuals. In this case, the simplest approach would be to consider such ownership as a business (producing income) and value it using the standard formula. Some closely held businesses, especially large ones, own financial assets. For example, the largest private businesses, such as Bloomberg LP or Koch Industries, own large chunks of publicly traded stock. In this case, it seems

67. Allais (1977) and Posner and Weyl (2018) have a more radical proposal where the government can buy any asset at its reported value (plus some premium), which sharply reduces incentives to underreport but would likely generate backlash (as many people do not want to be bought out even at prices above market).

68. The IRS issued Ruling 59-60 (in 1959) as guidance on how to credibly value a closely held business. This ruling has in turn influenced private valuations.

69. Based on our estimates (Piketty, Saez, and Zucman 2018), families with wealth above $50 million receive only 1.7 percent of total schedule C (sole proprietorship) income. They receive 19 percent and 25 percent of partnership and S corporation income, respectively.

desirable to value financial assets separately at the value of the underlying securities. This effectively shuts down the ability to mask the value of underlying assets by using intermediate shell corporations.

WEALTH HELD THROUGH INTERMEDIARIES Some assets are held through intermediaries such as trusts, holding companies, partnerships, and so on. Current estate tax enforcement allows taxpayers to claim valuation discounts for assets repackaged into such intermediaries. But this opens the door to widespread avoidance.[70] The model to follow is the income tax model where dividends, realized capital gains, and interest paid by stocks and bonds flow through intermediaries (trusts, partnerships, mutual funds) to the individual income tax return of the ultimate beneficiary. Third-party reporting of balances like the third-party reporting of income would enable the same procedure for the wealth tax. Trust income distributed to beneficiaries is considered income for beneficiaries and taxed as such. Trust income that is retained within the trust is taxed directly at the trust level with very narrow brackets so that the top tax rate is quickly reached.[71] The rationale is to deter progressive tax avoidance through splitting one's wealth into many smaller trusts.

WEALTH CONTROL VERSUS BENEFITS In contrast to income, there can be a separation between who controls wealth and who benefits from wealth. For example, private foundations are often controlled by their wealthy funders (the Bill and Melinda Gates Foundation is the most prominent recent example), but the funds can only be used for charitable causes.[72] Foundations often survive their funder and operate as independent entities. A trust allows for separating who controls the fund, who receives the income stream, and who might be the ultimate recipient of the fund (when the grantor dies, for example). How should such trusts and foundations be treated for wealth tax purposes?

To prevent tax avoidance, there need to be clear rules that allocate such wealth to the individuals who control or benefit from it. For example, the Sanders plan assigns trust wealth to the original funder. Assigning wealth in priority to the wealthiest person involved (such as the funder if that person retains control over the use of funds) and with lowest priority to nontaxable entities (such as a charitable organization, which may use the

---

70. Repetti (2000, 613) notes, "These devices currently result in valuation of interests in the partnership that are approximately 30% to 40% less than the value of the partnership's underlying assets."

71. In 2018, trust income above $12,500 is taxed at the top tax rate of 37 percent.

72. On a smaller scale, donor-advised funds function in the same way.

funds or will eventually be able to use the funds) is the best way to curb tax avoidance. In all cases and to avoid liquidity issues, the wealth tax liability created by the trust should be paid nominally out of the trust fund itself.

More broadly, a progressive wealth tax (like a progressive income tax) raises the issues of using straws—individuals who legally own the wealth but who do not control or benefit from it in practice. This issue looms larger in developing countries where property rights are not as clearly established as in advanced economies.

VALUING REAL ESTATE Local governments maintain registers of real estate property for the administration of local property taxes. Such property taxes are based on assessed value. In most states, assessed values closely follow market value. Commercial websites such as Zillow have also developed systematic methods to estimate real estate values. Therefore, the technology to systematically obtain reliable real estate values exists, and these values could be reported to the IRS. This would also help improve local governments' assessments for property tax purposes, which are often highly imperfect and hence discriminatory (Avenancio-Leon and Howard 2019).

WORKS OF ART AND OTHER VALUABLES Valuables such as works of art are often mentioned as hard-to-value assets. In reality, they are quantitatively small, and they are most often insured, which generates a valuation. There are also systematic catalogs of the most valuable art and other collectibles.

VALUING DEFINED BENEFIT PENSION ASSETS In the case of defined benefit pensions not yet in payment, the value of assets could be apportioned in proportion to the accrued benefits of each worker using simple formulas based on current salary, tenure, and age. The key requirement is that the total current value of each defined benefit fund should be distributed across beneficiaries.[73]

IV. Economic Effects

All economists agree that, to the extent that it would not be entirely avoided, a progressive wealth tax would have real economic effects.

---

73. Most pension wealth is owned on a pretax basis, which means that pension contributions were exempt from income taxation, but pension benefits are taxed at withdrawal. As a result, the government has a claim on such pension wealth (in contrast to wealth owned outright or posttax pensions such as Roth IRAs). Some downward adjustment to pretax pension wealth could be made to restore balance. Pension assets are small at the top (Saez and Zucman 2016), but this issue could become significant in the case of a wealth tax with a lower exemption threshold.

IV.A. Optimal Tax Theory

A significant body of work has analyzed the problem of optimal capital taxation. In a basic model with homogeneous return r on all assets, a capital tax at rate τ_K is equivalent to a wealth tax at rate $\tau_W = r\tau_K$ as both result in the same net of tax return $\bar{r} = r(1 - \tau_K) = r - \tau_W$.

ZERO CAPITAL TAX RESULTS Two famous zero capital tax results have been highly influential.

In the Atkinson and Stiglitz (1976) life-cycle model where people earn and save when young and consume their savings when old, the optimal capital tax is zero because there is no heterogeneity in wealth, conditional on labor income: any combination of labor and capital taxes can be replaced by a more efficient tax on labor income only that leaves everybody better off (Kaplow 2006; Laroque 2005). In the real world however, there is enormous heterogeneity in wealth, conditional on labor income history. Such heterogeneity arises because of inheritances, heterogeneous rates of returns, and preferences for wealth accumulation. In this case, taxing capital becomes desirable (Piketty and Saez 2013; Saez and Stantcheva 2018).

In the Chamley (1986) and Judd (1985) model, the optimal capital tax is zero in steady state because long-run capital supply is infinitely elastic. As is well known, taxing infinitely elastic bases is not desirable. However, the infinite elasticity assumption is not backed up by empirical evidence. Introducing finite elasticities in the Chamley-Judd model leads to positive taxes on capital income that follow classical inverse elasticity rules (Saez and Stantcheva 2018).

In basic models, taxing consumption is equivalent to taxing labor income and initial wealth but exempting capital income. Therefore, the zero capital tax recommendation is often expressed as "we should only tax consumption." Concrete policy proposals have been made in this direction.[74] On normative grounds, there is a long-standing philosophical debate (at least since Hobbes) over whether it is better to tax consumption or income. Empirically, savings are concentrated at the top of the distribution (Saez and Zucman 2016). Therefore, taxing consumption allows the income-rich to defer taxation (relative to an income tax). For example, Jeff Bezos's recently accumulated fortune may not be consumed before decades or even longer if wealth is bequeathed across generations. Is it fair that Bezos pays low taxes if his personal consumption is low?

---

74. See the flat tax proposals by Hall and Rabushka (1985) and, more recently, Carroll and Viard (2012).

For the ultra wealthy, personal consumption is likely to be modest relative to economic power and hence seems almost beside the point when thinking about their proper tax burden. The progressive wealth tax goes after accumulated wealth before consumption takes place or even sometimes before income happens (for example, when a start-up is created and expected to be lucrative in the future).

WEALTH IN THE UTILITY FUNCTION Carroll (2002) notes that it is a challenge to explain wealth accumulation at the very top with standard preferences that depend only on consumption. Saez and Stantcheva (2018) show that wealth in the utility function can be microfounded in several ways. It can arise from bequest motives, from a utility flow of running a business, or from direct service flow from wealth (such as housing services or liquidity value). Adding wealth in the utility function changes dramatically the analysis of optimal capital taxation as shown by Saez and Stantcheva (2018). In this case, the response of wealth accumulation with respect to the net of rate of return is finite, and a capital tax would be desirable if society puts low social marginal welfare weights on wealth holders and follows the standard inverse elasticity optimal tax rules.

HETEROGENEOUS RETURNS Guvenen and others (2019) consider a model with heterogeneous returns on wealth where wealth taxation differs from capital taxation. A wealth tax bears more heavily on low-return assets (such as low-yield bonds or unused land) than a capital income tax. Under capital income taxation, entrepreneurs who are more productive, and therefore generate more income, pay higher taxes. Under wealth taxation, entrepreneurs who have similar wealth levels pay similar taxes regardless of their productivity, which expands the tax base, shifts the tax burden toward unproductive entrepreneurs, and raises the savings rate of productive ones. In a calibrated model, Guvenen and others (2019) show that replacing the capital income tax with a wealth tax in a revenue-neutral fashion increases aggregate productivity and output (7.5 percent in consumption-equivalent terms). They conclude that wealth taxation has the potential to raise productivity while simultaneously reducing consumption inequality.[75]

IV.B. Effects on Wealth Inequality

A well-enforced wealth tax would reduce wealth concentration. That seems to be a consensus view among economists: in the IGM poll on wealth

---

75. This idea of the greater efficiency of wealth taxation had been considered informally for a long time, at least since the 1940s, by Maurice Allais Allais 1977) and more recently by Posner and Weyl (2018).

taxes, 73 percent of economists agreed and only 12 percent disagreed with such a statement (results weighted by self-reported expertise).[76]

The reason is simple: if the rich have to pay a percentage of their wealth in taxes each year, it makes it harder for them to maintain or grow their wealth. Changes in consumption versus saving can exacerbate this effect. With a wealth tax, wealthy taxpayers may decide to spend more today and save less (this is the substitution effect: consuming now rather than later becomes relatively cheaper). Changes in consumption versus saving could conversely dampen this effect if the wealthy decide to spend less to preserve their wealth (this is the wealth effect, as the wealth tax reduces economic resources of the taxpayer). In any case, the wealth of people subject to the tax is expected to rise more slowly after the introduction of the wealth tax than before. There is relatively little empirical work evaluating whether a progressive wealth tax can reduce wealth concentration. One recent exception is Jakobsen and others (2019), who exploit compelling identification variation with the Danish wealth tax and find that the long-run elasticity of wealth with respect to the net-of-tax return is sizable at the top of the distribution.

IV.C. Effects on the Capital Stock

A potential concern with wealth taxation is that by reducing large wealth holdings, it may reduce the capital stock in the economy—thus lowering the productivity of U.S. workers and their wages. This conclusion certainly arises from the standard economic model where savings decisions are driven by rational intertemporal maximization and are therefore very sensitive to the after-tax rate of return on capital, as in the Chamley-Judd model discussed above. However, these effects are likely to be dampened in the case of a progressive wealth tax for several reasons.

First, the United States is an open economy and a significant fraction of U.S. saving is invested abroad, while a large fraction of U.S. domestic investment is financed by foreign saving. Therefore, a reduction in U.S. savings does not necessarily translate into a large reduction in the capital stock used in the United States. In the extreme case of a small open economy model, a reduction in domestic saving has no effect on domestic investment (as it's fully offset by an increase in foreign investment).

Second, calibrated models that add heterogeneity, risk, and finite life can shrink the response of capital to capital taxation (Conesa, Kitao, and

---

76. See Chicago Booth IGM Forum, "Wealth Taxes," April 9, 2019, http://www.igmchicago.org/surveys/wealth-taxes.

Krueger 2009). Therefore, in the end, the response of the capital stock to wealth taxation has to be an empirical question.

Last, even if the empirical response is large, increased savings from the rest of the population or the government sector could possibly offset any reduction in the capital stock. This argument does not make sense in a fully rational model where each actor saves optimally, but there are strong reasons to believe that society plays a big role in savings decisions that standard models do not capture.

A large body of recent academic work in behavioral economics has shown that institutions and nontax policies can have major effects on middle-class saving (Thaler and Sunstein 2008). Middle-class wealth consists primarily of pensions, housing (net of mortgage debt), consumer credit debt, and student loans. Each of these components has historically been directly affected by government regulations. Government-sponsored thirty-year mortgages increased home ownership rates and provided an effective tool to save over a lifetime. Regulations encouraged employer-provided pensions in the post–World War II period. Student loans are affected by public funding for higher education. Changes in government regulations since the 1980s have contributed to the decline in middle-class saving. The rise in middle-class debt took place in a context of financial deregulation and decline in the public funding of higher education. The surge in mortgage refinancing before the Great Recession was associated with equity extraction (refinancing into a larger mortgage) and amortization extensions (starting a new thirty-year mortgage), both of which reduce saving (Saez and Zucman 2016).

The recent behavioral economics literature has shown compellingly that behavioral nudges such as changing default choices for pension savings, or commitment choices, are much more effective ways to encourage retirement savings than traditional tax incentives exempting returns on pension funds from taxation. Madrian and Shea (2001) showed extremely large and persistent effects of default choices on 401(k) pension contributions for new hires. Chetty and others (2014) showed that defaults in Denmark not only change retirement savings but also affect overall savings, as individuals do not adjust their nonretirement savings; in contrast, the traditional policy of exempting returns from taxation has minimal effects on overall savings, as (sophisticated) individuals just shift nonretirement savings into retirement savings.

In the standard economic model, where people maximize intertemporal utility, most of the institutional forces affecting saving would be offset by individual decisions (barring corner solutions). In modern societies, however, government is always heavily involved in the key consumption smoothing decisions: education for the young, retirement benefits for the old and disabled, health benefits for the sick, and insurance for the unemployed. It looks like societies know better than individuals how to smooth consumption. Economists mistakenly assume that individuals should know equally well how to smooth consumption.

IV.D. *Effects on Entrepreneurial Innovation*

A wealth tax would reduce the financial payoff of extreme business success (we will illustrate this quantitatively in section V) and hence could potentially discourage innovation. Smith and others (2019) show that typical top earners derive most of their income from human capital, not financial capital. The Forbes 400 list also shows that many of the top wealth holders built up their fortunes through entrepreneurship.

There are many calibrated models that can capture the effects of wealth taxation on entrepreneurship and wealth accumulation (Cagetti and De Nardi 2006, 2009) but unfortunately little direct evidence on whether wealth taxation dampens incentives to start a firm in the first place. The key parameter we would like to estimate is the elasticity of entrepreneurship with respect to the wealth tax rate.

There is, however, a larger body of work on the effects of business income taxation on entrepreneurship.[77] There is clear evidence that credit constraints affect entrepreneurship. For example, inheriting wealth increases the likelihood to become an entrepreneur (Holtz-Eakin, Joulfaian, and Rosen 1994). But a wealth tax with a high exemption threshold by definition spares the credit constrained.

There is also evidence that innovators move to avoid taxation. Akcigit, Baslandze, and Stantcheva (2016) find that superstar top 1 percent inventors are significantly affected by top tax rates when deciding in which country to locate. Akcigit and others (2018) exploit variation in state tax policies and find that higher personal and corporate income taxes negatively affect the quantity and quality of inventive activity and shift its location. Business stealing from one state to another is important but does not account for all of the effect. Both papers also find that concentrated activity due to agglomeration effects dampens the effects of taxes on location choices. This suggests that a wealth tax in a large country with worldwide taxation

---

77. See Rosen (2005) for a survey.

based on citizenship like the United States is likely to have much smaller effects than a wealth tax in a small jurisdiction with residency-based taxation (such as a state or a small European country).

It is harder to evaluate whether high taxes on success (such as a wealth tax) would discourage young innovators to start with. The literature has found conflicting results on the effect of progressive income taxes on risk taking; for example, Gentry and Hubbard (2005) find negative effects while Cullen and Gordon (2007) find the reverse.[78] Therefore, more empirical and well-identified research is needed to resolve this key question.

To foster innovation, it is key to encourage young—and not yet wealthy—people to become entrepreneurs. Bell and others (2019a) have shown that exposure to innovation during childhood has significant causal effects on children's propensities to become innovators themselves later in life. Building on these results, Bell and others (2019b) present a stylized model of inventor career choice. The model predicts that financial incentives, such as top income tax reductions, have limited potential to increase aggregate innovation in a standard intertemporal expected utility model. In contrast, increasing exposure to innovation (for example, through mentorship programs) could have substantial impacts on innovation by drawing individuals who produce high-impact inventions into the innovation pipeline.

Established businesses typically devote a lot of their resources to protect their dominant positions by fighting new competition. A progressive wealth tax hits wealthy owners who have already established their businesses, while it does not immediately affect emerging businesses. Other policies, like antitrust, should also play a major role in leveling the playing field. Large businesses with diluted ownership can also be anticompetitive (even if the rents accrue to a large number of middle-class owners rather than a few superwealthy owners). Antitrust was typically thought of as a market efficiency policy blind to distributional considerations. In practice, monopoly rents are concentrated at the top of the wealth distribution, and therefore the bad distributional consequences of monopoly power are likely more important than the efficiency consequences. The antitrust movement of the early twentieth century was famously fueled by anger at the robber barons.

---

78. Theoretically, taxation makes the government a shareholder in the business venture (and cushions failure with more generous transfers) so that entrepreneurs might be willing to take more risk.

IV.E. Charitable Giving

A wealth tax that does not apply to private foundations or public charities could spur an increase in charitable giving among the extremely wealthy. This increase would reflect both an acceleration in the timing of donations that would otherwise have been made later in life and an increase in the overall level of charitable giving. This increase in charitable giving would also reduce wealth concentration.

To prevent abuse, donor-advised funds or funds in private foundations controlled by funders should be subject to the wealth tax until the time that such funds have been spent or moved fully out of the control of the donor. For example, assets in the Bill and Melinda Gates Foundation should be counted as part of the wealth of Bill and Melinda Gates. If the foundation receives funding from others, such as Warren Buffett, this wealth would also be part of the Gateses' wealth. More generally, how to treat wealth held in foundations not controlled by the original funder (who may have passed away) is a difficult question. To the extent that the foundation is controlled primarily by one person or family (as opposed to a board that rotates), such wealth constitutes concentrated individual power, and it makes sense to make such wealth taxable. At the same time, because such wealth is pledged to charitable giving, it could arguably receive preferential treatment. Currently, private foundation wealth is slightly above 1 percent of total U.S. wealth, so this is small relative to the 20 percent owned by the top 0.1 percent.[79]

Charities no longer related to a living founder, such as universities or older foundations, can also accumulate wealth. Indeed, their long life puts them at an advantage to patiently accumulate and take advantage of the high rate of return on expertly managed assets. This type of accumulation can snowball, as explained by Piketty (2014). A wealth tax is a potential tool to curb this risk. Allowing charities to pay in-kind in the form of giving some control rights to society is an avenue to explore. For example, instead of paying 2 percent of its wealth in cash, a charity could instead cede 2 percent of its board seats to representatives of the public.[80]

IV.F. Inter Vivos Giving

A progressive wealth tax could also accelerate giving to children. However, gifts trigger gift tax liability and result in a real deconcentration

---

79. According to Saez and Zucman (2016), 1.2 percent in 2012.
80. Similar proposals have been made in the corporate context to give workers stakes on the board of their companies.

of wealth, thus generating tax revenues while achieving one of the goals of the wealth tax—reducing wealth concentration. In some situations, it is possible that such splitting could be done on paper while not changing how wealth is controlled or used. For example, a business founder could give parts of his or her wealth to children while effectively running and controlling the business. The wealth of minor children should be added to the wealth of their parents.[81] Adult children may waste the wealth away, a significant concern of wealthy parents. Indeed, in the U.S. estate tax context, Poterba (2001) shows that only about 45 percent of the wealthy take advantage of the opportunity for tax-free inter vivos giving.

The exemption levels for married versus single families can also create tax arbitrage (either toward marriage or toward divorce). The Warren tax proposal has the same brackets for singles and married, creating a marriage penalty (splitting wealth through divorce reduces taxes). The Sanders wealth tax halves the brackets for singles, creating a marriage subsidy (a wealthy single gains by marrying a poorer spouse). It is well known that a tax cannot be progressive, marriage neutral, and family-based. Resolving this impossibility requires a move to individual taxation (instead of family taxation). Absent this, some average of the Warren and Sanders treatment of couples can reduce marriage penalties or subsidies on average and is, for example, how the U.S. individual income tax traditionally operates (singles brackets are less than, but more than half of, the married brackets).[82]

IV.G. Other Effects

In this section, we examine the effects of the wealth on two additional dimensions.

EFFECTS ON TOP TALENT MIGRATION Would a wealth tax deter the talented from coming to the United States? This issue looms large in the public debate but there is scant empirical evidence on this issue. Many factors affect the migration of top talent. Top universities and research centers are a key factor in attracting and retaining talented foreign students. The number of skilled foreign workers is regulated through immigration and visa policies. The United States is currently restricting top talent migration

---

81. Children's trust funds that are still controlled by parents should also be taxed with parental wealth.

82. Some countries with wealth taxes (such as France before it repealed its wealth tax) treat cohabiting partners in a nonmarital relationship as a single tax unit for wealth tax purposes to avoid couples splitting wealth through divorce.

through its immigration policy with strict quotas in H1B visas. In principle, a change in any of these policies could reverse any adverse effect of steeply progressive wealth taxation on immigration in the United States.

MACROECONOMIC STABILIZATION A wealth tax would be procyclical as the stock of wealth is more procyclical than income (see the top panel of figure 1). Furthermore the most procyclical component of wealth is corporate equity, which is even more concentrated than overall wealth. Therefore, a wealth tax would add to automatic macro stabilizers.[83]

V. Optimal Billionaire Taxation

In this section, we would like to consider the specific problem of optimal taxation of billionaires' wealth. This has the advantage of addressing a pressing issue, the surge of large fortunes, for which there are actually data created by *Forbes* magazine's lists of the wealthy. It is important to keep in mind that the Forbes 400 data are far from perfect, but they are the best we have for billionaires (while waiting for a well-enforced wealth tax). Another advantage is that, when talking about billionaires, it is immediately obvious that issues of consumption smoothing are irrelevant, forcing us to depart from the traditional model of intertemporal utility maximization.

V.A. Basic Positive Model

Forbes magazine has created a useful panel of the four hundred richest Americans since 1982 that tracks their net worth year after year. The data offer a fascinating, almost four-decade-long view of how billionaires arise, how their wealth can grow explosively as they create new corporate behemoths (like Google, Amazon, and Facebook), how their wealth matures as their businesses remain dominant (for example, Microsoft), and how it is split among heirs (for example, Walmart and Mars).

Suppose person i has the (real) wealth trajectory $W_{i1}, \ldots W_{it}, \ldots$ W_{iT} from time $t = 1$ to time $t = T$, absent the wealth tax. Let us denote by $1 + r_{it} = W_{it+1}/W_{it}$ real wealth growth from t to $t + 1$. The variable r_{it} captures the full return of wealth (price effects and income) net of any consumption (or transfers to heirs or charities). For billionaires, it is likely that consumption is small relative to wealth.

---

83. Corporate profits and, especially, realized capital gains are highly procyclical, even more so than wealth. This cyclicality raises issues for states that have balanced budget requirements. In this context, a wealth tax construed as a prepayment on future realized capital gains might be helpful to reduce tax revenue cyclicality.

Suppose that at time 1, we introduce a wealth tax at average tax rate $\tau > 0$ on individuals with net worth above \$1 billion. We assume that the tax rate applies to total wealth (and not just wealth above \$1 billion), as in the Colombian wealth tax analyzed in Londoño-Vélez and Avila (2020). Let us denote by $W_{i1}^\tau, \ldots W_{it}^\tau, \ldots W_{iT}^\tau$ the wealth trajectory of person i under the billionaire wealth tax at rate τ.

Absent tax evasion and avoidance, in the first year of the tax, billionaire i pays τW_{i1} reducing wealth by a factor $1 - \tau$ so that $W_{i1}^\tau = W_{i1} \times (1 - \tau)$. For example, if Bill Gates held 10 percent of Microsoft in year 1, with a tax of $\tau = 1$ percent, he would hold only 9.9 percent of Microsoft after the tax in year 1.

Let us make the simple assumption that the wealth tax does not affect the return r_{it} on wealth after the tax has been paid in period t and before the tax has to be paid in period $t + 1$. In the case of Bill Gates, this amounts to assuming that the Microsoft stock price evolves in the same way with or without the tax: Bill Gates makes the same executive decisions, and the wealth tax rate is small enough that it does not affect Bill Gates's ability to remain CEO and chair. This also amounts to assuming that Bill Gates scales down by a factor $1 - \tau$ his consumption, giving, and hence savings decisions due to his reduced wealth. For billionaires, consumption decisions are likely small relative to the stock of wealth. Giving could potentially be affected by the tax in a nonproportional form. If giving only happens at the end of life, the proportional assumption holds. It is conceivable that Bill Gates could accelerate giving to avoid the tax. He could also slow down giving if his goal is to keep ownership control of Microsoft longer. Therefore, the proportionality assumption seems like a natural benchmark to start with.

If we carry these assumptions up to year t, wealth in year t is going to be $W_{it}^\tau = W_{it} \times (1 - \tau)^t$. Hence, t years of taxation at rate τ reduce wealth by a factor $(1 - \tau)^t$. The reduction is exponential with time. If person i is exposed only t' years to the tax over the t year period (because the person might not be a billionaire for the full period), then wealth would be $W_{it}^\tau = W_{it} \times (1 - \tau)^{t'}$.

It is important to note that the simple multiplicative assumption makes sense for billionaires but would break down for less wealthy individuals. For people of more modest wealth, savings is driven to a much larger extent by labor income rather than returns from wealth. As a result, it is likely that the wealth tax would have less than a proportional impact on savings. For example, a homeowner whose wealth is only home equity is likely to pay for the property tax out of labor income (and reduced consumption) rather than downsizing the home.

Hence, the elasticity of the individual billionaire with respect to the net-of-tax rate $1 - \tau$ is simply the number of years exposed to the tax. The wealth of a young billionaire, like Zuckerberg, is less elastic than the wealth of a more mature billionaire, like Buffett. For heirs, for example, members of the Walton family, the elasticity is not only the number of years they have faced the tax but also includes the number of years their parents have been exposed to the wealth tax as well.

In sum, young billionaires' wealth is inelastic and affected less by the wealth tax, as it has not been exposed long to the tax, while old billionaires' and their heirs' wealth is very elastic, as the wealth tax has had more time to erode wealth.

Let us denote by B the set of billionaires in year T and by $W^A(1 - \tau)$ their collective wealth under a tax at rate τ since time 1. Let $T(i)$ be the number of years that billionaire i has been exposed to the wealth tax from year 1 to year T. We have

$$W^A(1 - \tau) = \sum_{i \in B} W_{iT} \times (1 - \tau)^{T(i)}.$$

Therefore, the elasticity e_T of the billionaire tax base with respect to the net-of-tax base after T years of taxation is given by:

$$e_T = \frac{1 - \tau}{W^A} \frac{dW^A}{d(1 - \tau)} = \frac{\sum_{i \in B} T(i) \times W_{iT} \times (1 - \tau)^{T(i)}}{\sum_{i \in B} W_{iT} \times (1 - \tau)^{T(i)}}.$$

The parameter e_T is simply the average number of years billionaire fortunes have been exposed to the wealth tax (weighting each billionaire by wealth).[84]

This average length of exposure e_T is less than T and grows with T. Presumably, it converges to some long-run e_∞. If wealth rankings were frozen, as in the standard dynastic model with no uncertainty, then $e_\infty = \infty$. That is, the progressive wealth tax would eradicate all billionaires in the long run, a point made by Piketty (2003) and Saez (2012). In contrast, with uncertainty, there would always be new billionaires arising and hence the tax base would not shrink to zero and $e_\infty < \infty$. In other words, a country

---

84. This computation is an approximation because it assumes that a marginal change in τ does not affect $T(i)$ nor the set B. We ignore such issues for simplicity of exposition. The rigorous way to obtain this formula would be to consider a continuum with a smooth wealth density and assume that the wealth tax applies to all individuals above a fixed percentile (in this case reshuffling due to a marginal tax change has only second-order effects, as people falling below percentile p are replaced by people with approximately the same wealth.

where billionaires come from old wealth will have a large e_∞ and hence a very elastic billionaire tax base. Conversely, a country where new billionaires constantly arise and replace older ones will have a low e_∞ and hence a fairly inelastic billionaire tax base.

With the Forbes 400 data, it is possible to simulate the path of wealth under a billionaire at rate τ starting in year 1982 and trace out the effect on the tax base to compute the elasticity e_T. In the Forbes 400 data, 2018 billionaires have been on the list for fifteen years on average, implying that $e_T = 15$ for $T = 36$.

Here, we have considered a single average tax rate τ, but it is possible in simulations to consider more-complex tax systems with several brackets. More-complex tax systems, however, do not lend themselves to simple analytical expressions.

V.B. Revenue Maximizing Tax Rate

What is the wealth tax rate τ that maximizes wealth tax revenue? In our basic setting, this is a very simple question to answer. Wealth tax revenue is given by $R = \tau W^A (1 - \tau)$. A small increase $d\tau$ generates a change in revenue dR given by:

$$dR = W^A d\tau - \tau \frac{dW^A}{d(1 - \tau)} d\tau = \left[1 - \frac{\tau}{1 - \tau} \times e_T \right] \times W^A d\tau,$$

which is the classic expression from tax theory: the mechanical revenue effect is reduced by the behavioral response effect. The revenue-maximizing rate τ^R is such that $dR = 0$, that is, the mechanical and behavioral response effect cancel out. It is given by $e_T \times \tau/(1 - \tau) = 1$, which can be rearranged into the standard inverse elasticity rule:

$$\text{revenue-maximizing billionaire wealth tax rate: } \tau^R = \frac{1}{1 + e_T}.$$

In words, the revenue-maximizing wealth tax rate for billionaires is the inverse of one plus the average number of years billionaires have been subject to the tax.

Naturally, with a new tax, the revenue-maximizing wealth tax rate is large. It is actually 100 percent in the first year of operation of an (unexpected) wealth tax. In the long run, τ^R converges to $1/(1 + e_\infty)$. If, as in the United States, billionaires have been around for about fifteen years on average, the long-run revenue-maximizing (annual) wealth tax would be around 6.25 percent, which is higher than the Warren tax proposal of 3 percent on billionaires and in the ballpark of the Sanders tax proposed with graduated rates from 5 percent to 8 percent for billionaires and multibillionaires.

Several points are worth noting. First, we are computing the rate that maximizes revenue from the wealth tax. To the extent that billionaires pay other taxes (such as corporate or individual income taxes), the wealth tax rate that maximizes *total* tax revenue would be lower.[85]

Second, our theory is predicated on the key assumption that savings is in proportion to wealth among billionaires. If billionaires accelerate giving or increase (enormously) their own consumption, then the elasticity would be higher and τ^R correspondingly lower.

Third, we have assumed that the wealth tax can be perfectly enforced. But it is easy to use our simple model of tax evasion or avoidance laid out in section I.C to extend the analysis to take into account tax evasion/avoidance.

EMPIRICAL ILLUSTRATION Table 4 lists the name, source of wealth, and wealth in 2018 of the top fifteen richest Americans (*Forbes* magazine estimates). Columns (2) to (4) show what their wealth would have been if a wealth tax had been in place since 1982. Column (2) considers the Warren wealth tax which has a 2 percent marginal tax rate above $50 million and a 3 percent marginal tax rate above $1 billion. Column (3) considers the Sanders wealth tax, which has a 1 percent marginal tax rate above $32 million, 2 percent above $50 million, 3 percent above $250 million, 4 percent above $500 million, 5 percent above $1 billion, 6 percent above $2.5 billion, 7 percent above $5 billion, 8 percent above $10 billion. Column (4) considers a radical wealth tax with a 2 percent tax rate above $50 million and a 10 percent marginal tax rate above $1 billion. The tax thresholds apply in 2018 and are indexed to the average wealth per family economy-wide in prior years. The wealth tax has a much larger cumulative effect on inherited and mature wealth than on new wealth. Young billionaires like Bezos and Zuckerberg would still be decabillionaires even with a 10 percent tax rate above $1 billion. More mature billionaires like Gates and Buffett would be hit much harder, having faced the tax for over three decades.

---

85. Lower top wealth generates a negative fiscal externality in the public economics jargon (Saez, Slemrod, and Giertz 2012).

Table 4. Effect of Long-Term Wealth Taxation on Top Fifteen Wealth Holders in 2018

	Source	Current wealth ($ billions) (1)	With Warren wealth tax (2)	With Sanders wealth tax (3)	With radical wealth tax (4)
1. Jeff Bezos	Amazon (founder)	160.0	86.8	43.0	24.1
2. Bill Gates	Microsoft (founder)	97.0	36.4	9.9	4.3
3. Warren Buffett	Berkshire Hathaway	88.3	29.6	8.2	3.2
4. Mark Zuckerberg	Facebook (founder)	61.0	44.2	28.6	21.3
5. Larry Ellison	Oracle (founder)	58.4	23.5	8.5	4.0
6. Larry Page	Google (founder)	53.8	35.3	19.5	13.3
7. David Koch	Koch Industries	53.5	18.9	8.0	3.6
8. Charles Koch	Koch Industries	53.5	18.9	8.0	3.6
9. Sergey Brin	Google (founder)	52.4	34.4	19.0	13.0
10. Michael Bloomberg	Bloomberg LP (founder)	51.8	24.2	11.3	5.8
11. Jim Walton	Walmart (heir)	45.2	15.1	5.0	2.0
12. Rob Walton	Walmart (heir)	44.9	15.0	5.0	2.0
13. Alice Walton	Walmart (heir)	44.9	15.0	4.9	2.0
14. Steve Ballmer	Microsoft (CEO)	42.3	18.2	7.5	3.5
15. Sheldon Adelson	Las Vegas Sands (founder)	35.5	18.4	9.3	5.6
Total		943	434	196	111

Source: Authors' calculations.

Notes: Columns (2) to (4) show what the wealth of the top fifteen wealth holders would have been if a wealth tax had been in place since 1982. The Warren wealth tax has a 2 percent marginal tax rate above $50 million and a 3 percent marginal tax rate above $1 billion. The Sanders wealth tax has a 1 percent marginal tax rate above $32 million, 2 percent above $50 million, 3 percent above $250 million, 4 percent above $500 million, 5 percent above $1 billion, 6 percent above $2.5 billion, 7 percent above $5 billion, 8 percent above $10 billion. A radical wealth tax stipulates a 2 percent tax rate above $50 million and a 10 percent marginal tax rate above $1 billion. The tax thresholds apply in 2018 and are indexed to the average wealth per family economy-wide in prior years. The wealth tax has a much larger cumulative effect on inherited and mature wealth than on new wealth.

With a wealth tax, top wealth would look younger and more actively entrepreneurial. This also means that the stake owned by founders (or their heirs) would shrink faster with a wealth tax, and hence they might lose control of the business faster. In principle, founders who remain active managers could be hired as CEOs even if they no longer control their company (like Apple's Steve Jobs, who famously lost control as founder but was later rehired as CEO).[86] On the negative side, separation of control and ownership can create agency costs, but U.S. capitalism has historically resolved the issue of control and ownership separation well (which is not the case in many countries, especially those with developing economies). On the positive side, external CEOs might be more competent than family heirs. Pérez-González (2006) shows that U.S. firms where incoming CEOs are from the family of the departing CEO, founder, or large shareholder underperform relative to firms that promote unrelated CEOs.[87]

What would be the consequences for top wealth concentration? Figure 6 depicts the share of total wealth owned by the top four hundred richest Americans since 1982 from *Forbes* magazine. We adjust for growth in the number of total U.S. families by picking exactly the top four hundred in 2018 but correspondingly fewer rich people in earlier years. As is well known, the share of wealth going to this top group, approximately the top 0.00025 percent richest U.S. families, has increased dramatically from 0.9 percent in 1982 to 3.3 percent in 2018. The figure also depicts what their wealth share would have been if various wealth taxes had been in place since 1982. The Warren wealth tax has a 2 percent marginal tax rate above \$50 million and a 3 percent marginal tax rate above \$1 billion. The Sanders wealth tax has a 1 percent marginal tax rate above \$32 million, 2 percent above \$50 million, 3 percent above \$250 million, 4 percent above \$500 million, 5 percent above \$1 billion, 6 percent above \$2.5 billion, 7 percent above \$5 billion, 8 percent above \$10 billion. The radical wealth tax has a 2 percent tax rate above \$50m and a 10 percent marginal tax rate above \$1 billion.[88] The bracket thresholds apply in 2018 and are indexed to the average wealth per family economy-wide in prior years.

With the Warren wealth tax in place since 1982, their wealth share would have been 2.0 percent in 2018. With the Sanders wealth tax in place since

---

86. Steve Jobs restarted as Apple CEO with no Apple stock. At the end of his life, through CEO compensation, he had accumulated a stake of about 0.1 percent of Apple.

87. Bennedsen and others (2007) confirm this finding in the Danish context using gender of founders' first child as an instrument for family versus external CEO succession.

88. As discussed in Saez and Zucman (2019).

Figure 6. The Effects of Wealth Taxation on Top Wealth Holders

Percent

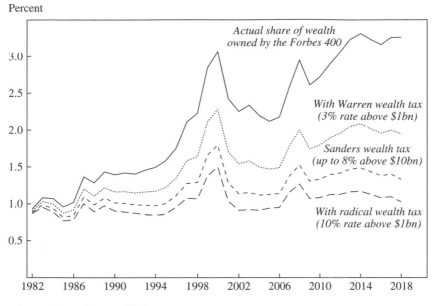

Source: Saez and Zucman (2019).

Notes: The figure depicts the share of total wealth owned by the top 400 richest Americans since 1982 from *Forbes* magazine. The figure also depicts what their wealth share would have been if the Warren, Sanders, or a radical wealth tax had been in place since 1982. The Warren wealth tax has a 2 percent marginal tax rate above $50 million and a 3 percent marginal tax rate above $1 billion. The Sanders wealth tax has a 1 percent marginal tax rate above $32 million, 2 percent above $50 million, 3 percent above $250 million, 4 percent above $500 million, 5 percent above $1 billion, 6 percent above $2.5 billion, 7 percent above $5 billion, 8 percent above $10 billion. The radical wealth tax has a 2 percent tax rate above $50 million and a 10 percent marginal tax rate above $1 billion (as discussed in Saez and Zucman 2019). The bracket thresholds apply in 2018 and are indexed to the average wealth per family economywide in prior years.

1982, their wealth share would have been 1.3 percent in 2018. With a radical wealth tax, it would have been about 1.0 percent in 2018, as in the early 1980s. By 2018, the Warren wealth tax would have raised $49 billion from the richest four hundred families, the Sanders wealth tax would have raised $62 billion, and the radical wealth tax would have raised $66 billion. This confirmed, as our theoretical discussion above showed, that the long-run revenue maximizing tax rate is quite high. Even the Sanders wealth tax with its high 8 percent top tax rate (above $10 billion) remains slightly below the revenue maximizing rate. The radical wealth tax of 10 percent (above $1 billion) is approximately the revenue maximizing tax (it achieves an annual average wealth tax rate of about 7.2 percent on the Forbes 400).

V.C. Normative Discussion

Is the revenue-maximizing rate a good normative criterion for taxing billionaires? For economists who believe in utilitarianism and decreasing returns to consumption, it is natural to assume that the marginal utility of billionaires' wealth is close to zero. As a result, revenue considerations— and consequences on the rest of the economy—should be the only relevant issue from a normative perspective. Another way to arrive at the same conclusion is to note that billionaires are negligible demographically (around nine hundred Americans, or 0.0005 percent of all U.S. families) relative to the wealth they own (around 4–5 percent of total U.S. wealth): billionaires are about ten thousand times more important economically than demographically. The suffering from one multibillionaire losing a billion dollars cannot be ten thousand times worse than the suffering of an ordinary American family losing $100,000. As a result, the revenue consequences of taxing billionaires outweigh the costs on the welfare of billionaires.

There are three main arguments made against higher taxes on the super wealthy. First, such taxes could not be enforced. Second, such taxes would hurt the economy and hence ordinary people. Third, such taxes would undermine respect for property rights and lead to a slippery slope of spoliation: today billionaires, tomorrow millionaires, and then everybody.[89]

In our model old wealth is more elastic than new wealth because the wealth tax has cumulative exponential effects with time. From a revenue-maximizing perspective and applying the classical Ramsey rule that elastic tax bases should be taxed less, this would imply that old wealth should be taxed less than new wealth. Normatively, however, this conclusion feels wrong as old wealth is more likely to come from inheritances than be self-made.

The wealth tax accelerates the process of dispersion of stock ownership for very successful businesses that make their owners-founders billionaires. Dispersed stock ownership has been a feature of U.S. capitalism and is a key reason why taxing wealthy business owners is feasible. Importantly and in contrast to labor income, this dispersion does not mean that economic activity disappears. There might not even be any effect on the wealth stock if the government uses the wealth tax proceeds for public investment, debt reduction, or to create a sovereign fund. The wealth disappears only if the government cannot save the money and cannot encourage middle-class saving.

---

89. Piketty (2019) presents a broad history of such property right–sacralizing ideology.

VI. Conclusion

What can we conclude from our analysis about the prospects for progressive wealth taxation in the United States?

First, the wealth tax is likely to be the most direct and powerful tool to restore tax progressivity at the very top of the distribution. The greatest injustice of the U.S. tax system today is its regressivity at the very top: billionaires in the top four hundred pay less (relative to their true economic incomes) than the middle class. This regressivity is the consequence of the erosion of the corporate and estate taxes and the fact that the richest can escape the income tax by reporting only half of their true economic incomes on their individual income tax returns. A wealth tax with a high exemption threshold specifically targets the richest and could resolve this injustice.

Second, our analysis shows that the wealth tax has great revenue- and wealth-equalizing potential in the U.S. context. Household wealth has grown very large in aggregate (five times annual national income in 2018), and the rich own a growing fraction of it (around 20 percent is owned by the top 0.1 percent of families). The wealth tax, if the tax rates are high enough, is also a powerful tool to deconcentrate wealth. Wealth among the Forbes 400 has grown about 4.5 percentage points faster annually than average since 1982. A wealth tax of 2 or 3 percent per year can put a significant dent in this growth rate advantage. With successful enforcement, a wealth tax must either deliver revenue or deconcentrate wealth.[90] Set the rates low (1 percent) and you get revenue in perpetuity but little (or very slow) deconcentration. Set the rates medium (2–3 percent) and you get revenue for a long time and deconcentration eventually. Set the rates high (significantly above 3 percent) and you get deconcentration quickly but revenue does not last long. Which is best depends on one's objectives.

Can a wealth tax be successfully enforced? Our review of past and foreign experiences in addition to recent empirical work tells us that enforcement is a policy choice. We certainly have plenty of evidence showing that a poorly designed wealth tax generates a lot of avoidance and little revenue. But we have also learned lessons about how to design a wealth tax well. First, cracking down on offshore tax evasion, as the United States has started doing with FATCA, is crucial. Second, taxing expatriates, as the United States currently does, is also very important to

---

90. If neither materializes, it means that enforcement is not successful, or we learn that, in contrast to what all the data sources tell us, U.S. wealth is equally distributed.

prevent the mobile wealthy from avoiding the tax. Third, systematic reporting of wealth balances (instead of relying on self-assessments as for the estate tax) is a necessary condition for good enforcement, as the income tax amply demonstrates. Finally, the issue of valuation of closely held businesses is key for the integrity of the wealth tax. Our view is that the government has to create the currently missing (or highly private) markets for equity of large closely held businesses. It is often the case that accounting rules develop in synergy with the tax system.

As a caveat, it is important to note that progressive wealth taxes are fragile and susceptible to being undermined. The left could undermine its political support by lowering the exemption threshold too much and creating hardship for the illiquid merely rich. The right could then undermine its effectiveness by providing exemptions (and hence loopholes) for certain asset classes or by imposing tax limitations based on income.

ACKNOWLEDGMENTS   Emmanuel Saez, University of California, Department of Economics, 530 Evans Hall #3880, Berkeley, CA 94720, saez@econ.berkeley.edu. Gabriel Zucman, University of California, Department of Economics, 530 Evans Hall #3880, Berkeley, CA 94720, zucman@berkeley.edu. We thank Charles Freifeld, Janet Holztblatt, Edward Kleinbard, Narayana Kocherlakota, Wojciech Kopczuk, Greg Leierson, Greg Mankiw, Thomas Piketty, David Seim, Victor Thuronyi, editors Jan Eberly and Jim Stock, and many conference participants for helpful discussions and comments. Funding from the Center for Equitable Growth at UC Berkeley and the Sandler foundation is thankfully acknowledged. The authors advised (without compensation) several 2020 primary presidential campaigns on wealth taxation. This paper solely reflects the authors' views and not necessarily the views of the campaigns we advised.

References

Ackerman, Bruce. 1999. "Taxation and the Constitution." *Columbia Law Review* 99: 1–58.

Akcigit, Ufuk, Salomé Baslandze, and Stefanie Stantcheva. 2016. "Taxation and the International Mobility of Inventors." *American Economic Review* 106, no. 10: 2930–81.

Akcigit, Ufuk, John Grigsby, Tom Nicholas, and Stefanie Stantcheva. 2018. "Taxation and Innovation in the 20th Century." Working Paper 24982. Cambridge, Mass.: National Bureau of Economic Research. https://www.nber.org/papers/w24982.

Allais, Maurice. 1977. *L'impôt sur le Capital et La Réforme Monétaire* [Capital tax and monetary reform]. Paris: Hermann.

Alstadsæter, Annette, Niels Johannesen, and Gabriel Zucman. 2018. "Who Owns the Wealth in Tax Havens? Macro Evidence and Implications for Global Inequality." *Journal of Public Economics* 162: 89–100.

Alstadsæter, Annette, Niels Johannesen, and Gabriel Zucman. 2019. "Tax Evasion and Inequality." *American Economic Review* 109, no. 6: 2073–2103.

Alvaredo, Facundo, Lucas Chancel, Thomas Piketty, Emmanuel Saez, and Gabriel Zucman. 2018. *World Inequality Report 2018.* https://wir2018.wid.world/files/download/wir2018-full-report-english.pdf.

Alvaredo, Facundo, and Emmanuel Saez. 2009. "Income and Wealth Concentration in Spain from a Historical and Fiscal Perspective." *Journal of the European Economic Association* 7, no. 5: 1140–67.

Appelbaum, Eileen, and Rosemary Batt. 2014. *Private Equity at Work: When Wall Street Manages Main Street.* New York: Russell Sage Foundation.

Atkinson, Anthony B., and Joseph E. Stiglitz. 1976. "The Design of Tax Structure: Direct versus Indirect Taxation." *Journal of Public Economics* 6, nos. 1–2: 55–75.

Auerbach, Alan J. 1991. "Retrospective Capital Gains Taxation." *American Economic Review* 81, no. 1: 167–78.

Avenancio-Leon, Carlos, and Troup Howard. 2019. "The Assessment Gap: Racial Inequalities in Property Taxation." Job Market Paper. https://www.dropbox.com/s/d66yj47ze9h0mg1/Trouppercent20Howardpercent20JMPpercent2Cpercent20Current.pdf?dl=1.

Batchelder, Lily, and David Kamin. 2019. "Taxing the Rich: Issues and Options." Working Paper. SSRN. https://papers.ssrn.com/sol3/papers.cfm?abstract_id=3452274.

Bell, Alexander, Raj Chetty, Xavier Jaravel, Neviana Petkova, and John van Reenen. 2019a. "Who Becomes an Inventor in America? The Importance of Exposure to Innovation." *Quarterly Journal of Economics* 134, no. 2: 647–713.

Bell, Alexander, Raj Chetty, Xavier Jaravel, Neviana Petkova, and John Van Reenen. 2019b. "Do Tax Cuts Produce More Einsteins? The Impacts of Financial Incentives vs. Exposure to Innovation on the Supply of Inventors." *Journal of the European Economic Association* 17, no. 3: 651–77.

Bennedsen, Morten, Kasper Meisner Nielsen, Francisco Pérez-González, and Daniel Wolfenzon. 2007. "Inside the Family Firm: The Role of Families in Succession Decisions and Performance." *Quarterly Journal of Economics* 122, no. 2: 647–691.

Bourne, Jenny, Eugene Steuerle, Brian Raub, Joseph Newcomb, and Ellen Steele. 2018. "More than They Realize: The Income of the Wealthy." *National Tax Journal* 71, no. 2: 335–56.

Bricker, Jesse, Alice Henriques, and Peter Hansen. 2018. "How Much Has Wealth Concentration Grown in the United States? A Re-examination of Data from 2001–2013." Working Paper 2018-024. Board of Governors of the Federal Reserve System. https://www.federalreserve.gov/econres/feds/files/2018024pap.pdf.

Bricker, Jesse, Alice Henriques, Jacob Krimmel, and John Sabelhaus. 2016. "Measuring Income and Wealth at the Top Using Administrative and Survey Data." *Brookings Papers on Economic Activity*, Spring, 261–321.

Brown, Jeffrey, Jeffrey Liebman, and Joshua Pollet. 2002. "Estimating Life Tables That Reflect Socioeconomic Differences in Mortality." In *The Distributional Aspects of Social Security and Social Security Reform*, edited by Martin Feldstein and Jeffrey Liebman. Chicago: University of Chicago Press.

Brulhart, Marius, Jonathan Gruber, Matthias Krapf, and Kurt Schmidheiny. 2016. "Taxing Wealth: Evidence from Switzerland." Working Paper 22376. Cambridge, Mass.: National Bureau of Economic Research. https://www.nber.org/papers/w22376.

Cagetti, Marco, and Mariacristina De Nardi. 2006. "Entrepreneurship, Frictions, and Wealth." *Journal of Political Economy* 114, no. 5: 835–70.

Cagetti, Marco, and Mariacristina De Nardi. 2009. "Estate Taxation, Entrepreneurship, and Wealth." *American Economic Review* 99, no. 1: 85–111.

Carroll, Christopher D. 2002. "Why Do the Rich Save So Much?" In *Does Atlas Shrug? The Economic Consequences of Taxing the Rich*, edited by Joel B. Slemrod. Cambridge, Mass.: Harvard University Press.

Carroll, Robert, and Alan Viard. 2012. *Progressive Consumption Taxation: The X Tax Revisited.* Washington: American Enterprise Institute.

Chamley, Christophe. 1986. "Optimal Taxation of Capital Income in General Equilibrium with Infinite Lives." *Econometrica* 54, no. 3: 607–22.

Chetty, Raj, John N. Friedman, Søren Leth-Petersen, Torben Heien Nielsen, and Tore Olsen. 2014. "Active vs. Passive Decisions and Crowd-Out in Retirement Savings Accounts: Evidence from Denmark." *Quarterly Journal of Economics* 129, no. 3: 1141–1219.

Chetty, Raj, Michael Stepner, Sarah Abraham, Shelby Lin, Benjamin Scuderi, Nicholas Turner, Augustin Bergeron, and David Cutler. 2016. "The Association between Income and Life Expectancy in the United States, 2001–2014." *JAMA* 315, no. 16: 1750–66.

Conesa, Juan Carlos, Sagiri Kitao, and Dirk Krueger. 2009. "Taxing Capital? Not a Bad Idea After All!" *American Economic Review* 99, no. 1: 25–48.

Cooper, George. 1979. *A Voluntary Tax? New Perspectives on Sophisticated Estate Tax Avoidance.* Washington: Brookings Institution Press.

Cooper, Michael, John McClelland, James Pearce, Richard Prisinzano, Joseph Sullivan, Danny Yagan, Owen Zidar, and Eric Zwick. 2016. "Business in the United States: Who Owns It, and How Much Tax Do They Pay?" *Tax Policy and the Economy* 30, no. 1: 91–128.

Cullen, Julie Berry, and Roger H. Gordon. 2007. "Taxes and Entrepreneurial Risk-Taking: Theory and Evidence for the U.S." *Journal of Public Economics* 91, nos. 7–8: 1479–1505.

Drutman, Lee. 2013 "The Political 1 Percent of the 1 Percent in 2012." Blog. Sunlight Foundation, June 24, 2013. https://sunlightfoundation.com/2013/06/24/1pct_of_the_1pct/.

Gentry, William M., and R. Glenn Hubbard. 2005. "Success Taxes, Entrepreneurial Entry, and Innovation." In *Innovation Policy and the Economy*, vol. 5, edited by Adam B. Jaffe, Josh Lerner, and Scott Stern. Cambridge, Mass.: MIT Press.

Guvenen, Fatih, Gueorgui Kambourov, Burhanettin Kuruscu, Sergio Ocampo-Diaz, and Daphne Chen. 2019. "Use It or Lose It: Efficiency Gains from Wealth Taxation." Working Paper 26284. Cambridge, Mass.: National Bureau of Economic Research. https://www.nber.org/papers/w26284.

Hall, Robert E., and Alvin Rabushka. 1985. *The Flat Tax.* Stanford, Calif.: Hoover Institution Press.

Holtz-Eakin, Douglas, David Joulfaian, and Harvey S. Rosen. 1994. "Sticking It Out: Entrepreneurial Survival and Liquidity Constraints." *Journal of Political Economy* 102, no. 1: 53–75.

Jakobsen, Katrine, Kristian Jakobsen, Henrik Kleven, and Gabriel Zucman. 2019. "Wealth Taxation and Wealth Accumulation: Theory and Evidence from Denmark." *Quarterly Journal of Economics* 135, no. 1: 329–88.

Johannesen, Niels, and Gabriel Zucman. 2014. "The End of Bank Secrecy? An Evaluation of the G20 Tax Haven Crackdown." *American Economic Journal: Economic Policy* 6, no. 1: 65–91.

Judd, Kenneth L. 1985. "Redistributive Taxation in a Simple Perfect Foresight Model." *Journal of Public Economics* 28, no. 1: 59–83.

Kaplow, Louis. 2006. "On the Undesirability of Commodity Taxation Even When Income Taxation Is Not Optimal." *Journal of Public Economics* 90, nos. 6–7: 1235–50.

Kennickell, Arthur B. 2017. "Lining Up: Survey and Administrative Data Estimates of Wealth Concentration." *Statistical Journal of the IAOS* 33, no. 1: 59–79.

Kleinbard, Edward D., and Thomas L. Evans. 1997. "The Role of Mark-to-Market Accounting in a Realization-Based Tax System." *Taxes* 75: 788–811.

Kleven, Henrik Jacobsen. 2016. "Bunching." *Annual Review of Economics* 8: 435–64.

Kleven, Henrik Jacobsen, Martin B. Knudsen, Claus Thustrup Kreiner, Søren Pedersen, and Emmanuel Saez. 2011. "Unwilling or Unable to Cheat? Evidence from a Tax Audit Experiment in Denmark." *Econometrica* 79, no. 3: 651–92.

Kleven, Henrik Jacobsen, Camille Landais, Mathilde Munoz, and Stefanie Stantcheva. Forthcoming. "Taxation and Migration: Evidence and Policy Implications." *Journal of Economic Perspectives.*

Kleven, Henrik Jacobsen, Camille Landais, and Emmanuel Saez. 2013. "Taxation and International Migration of Superstars: Evidence from the European Football Market." *American Economic Review* 103, no. 5: 1892–1924.

Kopczuk, Wojciech. 2015. "What Do We Know about the Evolution of Top Wealth Shares in the United States?" *Journal of Economic Perspectives* 29, no. 1: 47–66.

Kopczuk, Wojciech, and Emmanuel Saez. 2004. "Top Wealth Shares in the United States, 1916–2000: Evidence from Estate Tax Returns." *National Tax Journal* 57, no. 2: 445–87.

Landais, Camille, Thomas Piketty, and Emmanuel Saez. 2011. *Pour une révolution fiscale—Un impôt sur le revenu pour le 21e siècle* [Tax revolution: An income tax for the 21st century]. Le Seuil: République des Idées.

Laroque, Guy R. 2005. "Indirect Taxation Is Superfluous under Separability and Taste Homogeneity: A Simple Proof." *Economics Letters* 87, no. 1: 141–44.

Lehner, Moris. 2000. "The European Experience with a Wealth Tax: A Comparative Discussion." *Tax Law Review* 53: 615–91.

Londoño-Vélez, Juliana, and Javier Avila. 2020. "Can Wealth Taxation Work in Developing Countries? Quasi-Experimental Evidence from Colombia." Working Paper. https://sites.google.com/site/julianalondonovelez/research?authuser=0.

Madrian, Brigitte C., and Dennis F. Shea. 2001. "The Power of Suggestion: Inertia in 401(k) Participation and Savings Behavior." *Quarterly Journal of Economics* 116, no. 4: 1149–87.

Malkiel, Burton G. 2013. "Asset Management Fees and the Growth of Finance." *Journal of Economic Perspectives* 27, no. 2: 97–108.

Martinez, Isabel Z. 2017. "Beggar-Thy-Neighbour Tax Cuts: Mobility after a Local Income and Wealth Tax Reform in Switzerland." Working Paper 2017-08. Luxembourg: Luxembourg Institute of Socio-Economic Research (LISER). https://papers.ssrn.com/sol3/papers.cfm?abstract_id=2979275.

Mayer, Jane. 2017. *Dark Money: The Hidden History of the Billionaires behind the Rise of the Radical Right.* New York: Anchor Books.

Moretti, Enrico, and Daniel J. Wilson. 2019. "Taxing Billionaires: Estate Taxes and the Geographical Location of the Forbes 400." Working Paper 26387. Cambridge, Mass.: National Bureau of Economic Research. https://www.nber.org/papers/w26387.

Morningstar. 2019. "U.S. Fund Fee Study for 2018." Chicago: Morningstar Research. https://www.morningstar.com/lp/annual-us-fund-fee-study.

Organisation for Economic Co-operation and Development (OECD). 2011. "The Taxation of Mobile High-Skilled Workers." In *Taxation and Employment.* Paris: OECD Publishing. https://www.oecd-ilibrary.org/taxation/taxation-and-employment/the-taxation-of-mobile-high-skilled-workers_9789264120808-6-en.

Organisation for Economic Co-operation and Development (OECD). 2018. *The Role and Design of Net Wealth Taxes in the OECD*. OECD Tax Policy Studies No. 26. Paris: OECD Publishing. https://doi.org/10.1787/19900538.

Page, Benjamin I., Jason Seawright, and Matthew J. Lacombe. 2018. *Billionaires and Stealth Politics*. Chicago: University of Chicago Press.

Pareto, Vilfredo. 1965. *Ecrits sur la Courbe de la Répartition de la Richesse* [Writings on the distribution of wealth]. Geneva: Droz. Originally published 1896 as *Cours d'économie politique*.

Pérez-González, Francisco. 2006. "Inherited Control and Firm Performance." *American Economic Review* 96, no. 5: 1559–88.

Piketty, Thomas. 2003. "Income Inequality in France, 1901–1998." *Journal of Political Economy* 111, no. 5: 1004–42.

Piketty, Thomas. 2014. *Capital in the 21st Century*. Cambridge, Mass.: Harvard University Press.

Piketty, Thomas. 2019. *Capital et Idéologie* [Capital and ideology]. Paris: Le Seuil.

Piketty, Thomas, and Emmanuel Saez. 2003. "Income Inequality in the United States, 1913–1998." *Quarterly Journal of Economics* 118, no. 1: 1–39.

Piketty, Thomas, and Emmanuel Saez. 2013. "A Theory of Optimal Inheritance Taxation." *Econometrica* 81, no. 5: 1851–86.

Piketty, Thomas, Emmanuel Saez, and Gabriel Zucman. 2018. "Distributional National Accounts: Methods and Estimates for the United States." *Quarterly Journal of Economics* 133, no. 2: 553–609.

Piketty, Thomas, and Gabriel Zucman. 2014. "Capital Is Back: Wealth-Income Ratios in Rich Countries, 1700–2010." *Quarterly Journal of Economics* 129, no. 3: 1255–1310.

Posner, Eric A., and E. Glen Weyl. 2018. *Radical Markets: Uprooting Capitalism and Democracy for a Just Society*. Princeton, N.J.: Princeton University Press.

Poterba, James. 2001. "Estate and Gift Taxes and Incentives for Inter Vivos Giving in the United States." *Journal of Public Economics* 79, no. 1: 237–64.

Raub, Brian, Barry Johnson, and Joseph Newcomb. 2010. "A Comparison of Wealth Estimates for America's Wealthiest Decedents Using Tax Data and Data from the Forbes 400." National Tax Association 103rd Annual Conference on Taxation, November 18–20. https://ntanet.org/wp-content/uploads/proceedings/2010/020-raub-a-comparison-wealth-2010-nta-proceedings.pdf.

Repetti, James R. 2000. "It's All about Valuation." *Tax Law Review* 53: 607–14.

Rose, Michel. 2017. "Macron Fights 'President of the Rich' Tag after Ending Wealth Tax." *World News Reuters*, October 3.

Rosen, Harvey S. 2005. "Entrepreneurship and Taxation: Empirical Evidence." In *Venture Capital, Entrepreneurship and Public Policy*, edited by Vesa Kannianen and Christian Keuschnigg. Cambridge, Mass.: MIT Press.

Saez, Emmanuel. 2012. "Optimal Progressive Capital Income Taxes in the Infinite Horizon Model." *Journal of Public Economics* 97: 61–74.

Saez, Emmanuel, Joel Slemrod, and Seth H. Giertz. 2012. "The Elasticity of Taxable Income with Respect to Marginal Tax Rates: A Critical Review." *Journal of Economic Literature* 50, no. 1: 3–50.

Saez, Emmanuel, and Stefanie Stantcheva. 2018. "A Simpler Theory of Optimal Capital Taxation." *Journal of Public Economics* 162: 120–42.

Saez, Emmanuel, and Gabriel Zucman. 2016. "Wealth Inequality in the United States since 1913: Evidence from Capitalized Income Tax Data." *Quarterly Journal of Economics* 131, no. 2: 519–78.

Saez, Emmanuel, and Gabriel Zucman. 2019a. *The Triumph of Injustice: How the Rich Dodge Taxes and How to Make Them Pay.* New York: W. W. Norton.

Saez, Emmanuel, and Gabriel Zucman. 2019b. "Scoring the Warren Wealth Tax Proposal." Letter to Senator Warren, January 18. https://gabriel-zucman.eu/files/saez-zucman-wealthtax-warren.pdf.

Saez, Emmanuel, and Gabriel Zucman. 2019c. "Scoring the Sanders Wealth Tax Proposal." Letter to Senator Sanders, September 22. http://gabriel-zucman.eu/files/saez-zucman-wealthtax-sanders-online.pdf.

Scheve, Kenneth, and David Stasavage. 2016. *Taxing the Rich: A History of Fiscal Fairness in the United States and Europe.* Princeton, N.J.: Princeton University Press.

Seim, David. 2017. "Behavioral Responses to an Annual Wealth Tax: Evidence from Sweden." *American Economic Journal: Economic Policy* 9, no. 4: 395–421.

Slemrod, Joel. 1994. "Fixing the Leak in Okun's Bucket: Optimal Progressivity when Avoidance Can Be Controlled." *Journal of Public Economics* 55, no. 1: 41–51.

Slemrod, Joel, and Wojciech Kopczuk. 2002. "The Optimal Elasticity of Taxable Income." *Journal of Public Economics* 84, no. 1: 91–112.

Smith, Matthew, Danny Yagan, Owen M. Zidar, and Eric Zwick. 2019. "Capitalists in the Twenty-First Century." *Quarterly Journal of Economics* 134, no. 4: 1–72.

Smith, Matthew, Owen Zidar, and Eric Zwick. 2019. "Top Wealth in the United States: New Estimates and Implications for Taxing the Rich." Working Paper. http://ericzwick.com/wealth/wealth.pdf.

Summers, Lawrence H., and Natasha Sarin. 2019a. "A 'Wealth Tax' Presents a Revenue Estimation Puzzle." *Washington Post*, April 4. https://www.washingtonpost.com/opinions/2019/04/04/wealth-tax-presents-revenue-estimation-puzzle/.

Summers, Lawrence H., and Natasha Sarin. 2019b. "Be Very Skeptical about How Much Revenue Elizabeth Warren's Wealth Tax Could Generate." *Washington Post*, June 28. https://www.washingtonpost.com/opinions/2019/06/28/be-very-skeptical-about-how-much-revenue-elizabeth-warrens-wealth-tax-could-generate/.

Thaler, Richard H., and Cass R. Sunstein. 2008. *Nudge: Improving Decisions about Health, Wealth, and Happiness.* New Haven, Conn.: Yale University Press.

U.S. Department of the Treasury. 1976. *Annual Report of the Commissioner of Internal Revenue 1975.* Washington: Government Printing Office. https://www.irs.gov/pub/irs-soi/75dbfullar.pdf.

U.S. Department of the Treasury. 2014. *Tax Expenditure for Exclusion of Capital Gains at Death*. Office of Tax Analysis, August. https://www.treasury.gov/resource-center/tax-policy/tax-analysis/Documents/Step-Up-Basis-2014.pdf.

U.S. Department of the Treasury. 2018. *Foreign Portfolio Holdings of U.S. Securities*. Washington: Government Printing Office. https://ticdata.treasury.gov/Publish/shla2017r.pdf.

U.S. Department of the Treasury. 2019. *Internal Revenue Service Databook 2018*. Washington: Government Printing Office. https://www.irs.gov/pub/irs-pdf/p55b.pdf.

Waldron, Hillary. 2007. "Trends in Mortality Differentials and Life Expectancy for Male Social Security Covered Workers, by Socioeconomic Status." *Social Security Bulletin* 67, no. 3.

Weisbach, David A. 1999. "A Partial Mark-to-Market Tax System." *Tax Law Review* 53: 95–136.

Wong, Francis. 2019. "The Financial Burden of Property Taxes." Working Paper. https://sites.google.com/view/francisawong/research?authuser=0.

Zucman, Gabriel. 2013. "The Missing Wealth of Nations: Are Europe and the U.S. Net Debtors or Net Creditors?" *Quarterly Journal of Economics* 128, no. 3: 1321–64.

Zucman, Gabriel. 2015. *The Hidden Wealth of Nations: The Scourge of Tax Havens*. Chicago: University of Chicago Press.

Zucman, Gabriel. 2019. "Global Wealth Inequality." *Annual Review of Economics* 11: 109–38.

Comments and Discussion

COMMENT BY

WOJCIECH KOPCZUK   Emmanuel Saez and Gabriel Zucman offer a
discussion of the rationale for introducing wealth taxation in the United
States and its implementation and implications. In my comments, I will
primarily focus on three topics: economic arguments for having this form
of taxation, practical issues in implementing it, and a few aspects of underlying data and assumptions that the authors rely on in evaluating the impact
of this proposal.

A general wealth tax does not exist in the United States. However, the
United States has a highly progressive estate tax, and it taxes capital
income through a mix of personal income taxes on dividends, interest,
capital gains, royalties and business incomes, and corporate taxation. Bases
of all these taxes overlap with the base for wealth taxation, although they
are not economically or administratively identical.[1] Thus, the right question
in my mind is whether a wealth tax is desirable given existence of these
other instruments. In my view, as elaborated below, the case for wealth
taxation over capital income taxation in general is quite weak and rests
on either the desirability of onetime, ideally unexpected, taxation or on
the presence of externalities from wealth concentration (which ideally
should be treated using instruments tailored to specific problems). From
the administrative point of view, even then the challenging and ambitious
solutions that could make wealth tax feasible apply equally well to (otherwise preferred) capital income taxation.

The case that the authors make is not helped by optimistic (from the
point of revenue potential of the tax) empirical assumptions about wealth

---

1. They also may have different legal implications, with some questions about the constitutionality of wealth taxation, which I am not qualified to comment on.

distribution that do not highlight uncertainty, which is likely to run mostly in one direction; that may be a plus for public presentation of the plan but not for an economist. I discuss these issues at the end of the comment.

ECONOMICS OF A WEALTH TAX An individual with this year's stock of wealth W earning the return of r could be subject next year (assuming away any consumption) to a tax that is imposed on either $(1 + r)W$ or rW— a wealth tax or a capital income tax. It is immediately seen that absent any other considerations, a tax of t on wealth is revenue-equivalent to a tax of $\tau = (1 + r)t/r$ imposed on capital income rW. This links the two bases and provides a straightforward comparison of the burden that a wealth tax would impose on capital income. If you consider a safe rate of return of, say, 3 percent, a 3 percent wealth tax is a 103 percent tax on the corresponding capital income and a 6 percent tax rate is a 206 percent tax. Obviously, even though wealth tax rates appear nominally small, they are in fact very heavy taxes on the corresponding streams of income.

Are wealth and capital income taxes economically identical, assuming that rates are adjusted to be revenue-equivalent? A simple way to think about it is to decompose the rate of return into three components:

$$r = \text{normal rate of return} + \text{risk} + \text{rents}$$

where *rents* stand for any extraordinary returns that are not competed away (for example, due to market power, private information, government protection, or, from the tax point of view, any misrepresentation of ordinary income as capital income). A uniform capital income tax collects revenue at a high rate, $(1 + r)/r$ times higher than the wealth tax, from all these components. A wealth tax would collect equivalent revenue from primarily taxing the principal and effectively imposing the same (low) rate on components of the rate of return. Hence, the wealth tax shifts burden from risk and rents toward the normal rate of return (because taxing principal is similar to taxing safe rate of return). Is this desirable?

Paradoxically, given the rhetoric surrounding the wealth tax, shifting taxation from capital income to wealth relieves rents. Rents are the classic argument, going back to Ricardo, for having capital income taxation in the first place. Taxing extraordinary returns is less likely to be distortionary, it has good distributional properties, and it goes after precisely the types of inefficiencies that might give rise to undesirable accumulation. This is the component that wealth tax treats very lightly. If you are worried about monopolies, insider information, or misrepresenting labor as capital, and taxation is your preferred solution to address it, then you should want to tax rents at 20 percent or more (capital income tax) rather than 2 percent (wealth tax).

What about risk? The classic Domar-Musgrave insight is that a symmetric capital income tax (with full deductibility of losses) on a zero-expected value risk component would not change the expected value but would reduce variance, hence encouraging rather than discouraging risk taking. Imposing a tax on the expected return has naturally the opposite effect, and thus the net effect is theoretically ambiguous. Implementing full deductibility of losses is challenging in practice though. From this point of view, a wealth tax has an appealing property: while it heavily taxes expected return, it effectively implements full deductibility. If this effect dominates, it could perhaps encourage risk taking. On the other hand, many countries have experimented with implementing partial or full allowances for the normal rate of return for corporate taxation that mitigates taxation of expected return, therefore also encouraging risk taking, and shifts burden of capital income taxation primarily toward rents—something that is not achievable under wealth taxation.

This basic decomposition suggests that the way to think about the choice between well-implemented capital income and wealth taxation is in terms of trading off taxation of rents versus taxation of normal rate of return. While theoretical arguments for no taxation of capital income in the Chamley-Judd tradition have been recently challenged (Straub and Werning 2020), the case for heavily taxing rents is likely much stronger than the case for taxing normal return.

According to standard theory, there is one natural rationale for wealth taxes. While the Chamley-Judd result is usually presented as solely indicating that capital income tax rates should be zero in the long run, it is usually forgotten that this model involves very high taxation in the short run. Indeed, that framework requires that you restrict the ability to tax capital in the short run: a onetime immediate unexpected capital (or wealth) tax is non-distortionary—swiftly confiscating preexisting wealth is a lump-sum tax. This is the point that I glossed over above by treating tax on principal as the tax on the normal rate of return: it is so when taxpayers have time to adjust, but a onetime, swift, and unexpected tax on principal is qualitatively different because it is non-distortionary. I have some sympathy to this argument, though "unexpected" and "swift" are difficult to execute and "onetime" is hard to commit to. Applying it seriously would require a legitimate reason. Wars (for example, some European countries taxed wealth accumulated during World War II) or ill-gotten gains (Colombia after the drug war) sometimes provided such a reason. Does it apply to the United States in 2019? That is not really an economic question. If you consider past accumulation as an injustice that needs to be fixed, that's a logically coherent, but in my view political and subjective, argument, and I have nothing to say about it as an economist, *de gustibus non est disputandum*.[2] The need for a onetime confiscation of wealth is not an argument that the paper makes explicitly though, even if the rhetoric of past injustice appeals to it. If, instead, one interprets the paper's argument as a call for permanent policy, then the direct comparison to capital income taxation discussed so far strongly suggests that it dominates wealth taxation.

Are there other ways to economically justify a wealth tax? As a permanent policy, a somewhat nonstandard (for an economist) argument in favor of wealth taxation is to target externalities from wealth concentration. On the face of it, this is a plausible argument, and I argued elsewhere (Kopczuk 2013) that this is a reasonable direction for understanding the rationale for estate taxation—in that context, equality of opportunities for the next generation looms large and estate taxation is tied to transfers received from parents. But what is the incremental externality-based case for wealth taxation beyond taxing intergenerational transfers (which we already, albeit imperfectly, do)? First, recall the basic targeting prescription for dealing with externalities: if feasible, you should tax (or target via regulation, property rights, or enforcement) the source of the externality directly rather than its proxies. Is wealth the cause of or a proxy for problems that supporters of wealth taxation bring up? For most arguments that I can think of, it is just a proxy, and alternative feasible direct instruments exist. Monopoly power should be dealt with by antitrust, political power by suitable reforms of political system, dynastic wealth by estate taxation, and misdirected charity by reforming charitable deduction and rules applying to foundations and charities. A wealth tax does not target any of these particularly well and, by familiar logic, it has other undesirable consequences: it encourages earlier spending, including spending on politics and charity; it discourages saving and investment; it endangers control of businesses by founders while shifting control toward outside investors more focused on the short term; and it encourages private rather than public ownership as a

2. There is an alternative argument that builds on the incentive for confiscating existing wealth. Such an incentive gives rise to potential time inconsistency of policy, and relying on capital taxation may weaken that incentive (Farhi and others 2012). This is a variant of an old argument that redistribution is necessary to preserve social peace.

way to game valuation. In fact, the authors do not really make the case that externalities from wealth taxation exist—in the paper they just occasionally assert this without providing much evidence.

EQUITY, EFFICIENCY, SIMPLICITY If wealth taxation does not offer any special advantages in terms of the base or objectives and if it is just a substitute for capital income taxation, then it should be compared to its alternatives on standard equity, efficiency, and simplicity grounds. The comparison of equity implications for taxes that apply primarily to the rich may seem trivial, but even in this case I believe there is something to say. First, there is the relative treatment of savers versus spenders—this concern applies equally to both capital income and wealth taxation, but it is still relevant to note that lavish consumption is a way to reduce tax liability so that any tax of this type is not horizontally equitable in a direction that strikes me as undesirable (punishing thrift). Second, as already discussed, relative taxation of rents versus normal rate of return points in the direction of preferring capital income taxes.

What about efficiency? Is a wealth tax likely to be distortionary? We do not have a lot of evidence on this. Saez and Zucman discuss evidence on tax evasion. I find the studies based on bunching around thresholds of wealth tax are of interest as a way to demonstrate that response is there, but they are of limited quantitative usefulness: targeting the extent of tax evasion to be precisely around the tax threshold in a particular year is unlikely to be the only way to respond, and it is not a particularly practical way to respond to an annual wealth tax that makes the threshold a moving target. Hence, I suspect that the relatively small elasticities (as discussed in the paper) that arise in such contexts are a severe understatement. From that point of view, the study of the Swiss wealth tax (Brulhart and others 2016), which finds much larger effects, is interesting, although I agree with the authors that the mobility response is probably not of major concern in the United States and the high responsiveness to the Swiss wealth tax is probably partially driven by mobility. Jakobsen and others (2019) is the only study so far that directly focuses on longer-term effects of wealth taxation and finds persistent and growing behavioral response of wealth accumulation for Danish taxpayers affected by the wealth tax.[3] There is some related evidence from the estate tax context, which I surveyed a few years ago (Kopczuk 2013). A number of older studies found positive responses to estate taxation in the United States that would be consistent with sizable

---

3. Behavioral rather than simply mechanical, something that's assumed away in the simulations considered by the authors, who instead consider the mechanical case wherein the growth rate of pretax wealth is unaffected by taxation.

wealth tax response.[4] Saez and Zucman note that taxpayers appear not to be making the small inter vivos gifts that are the simplest way to do estate tax planning; however, that evidence is based on taxpayers with estates on the order of $1 million (the level that was taxable in the 1990s). Responses of large gifts to tax reforms are very strong (Joulfaian 2004), and the existence of the estate tax planning industry makes it obvious that avoidance is a real issue, although even in the case of wealthy taxpayers there are indications that the desire to control wealth until death is important (Kopczuk 2007). How important might transfer be? The standard Pareto assumption that the authors rely on implies that 26 percent of the base is between the threshold and two times the threshold (for example, between $50 million and $100 million); this is how much is at stake through the most obvious and simplest type of tax planning strategy for taxpayers with just one child, making gifts up to the tax threshold limit.[5] Harder to evaluate but potentially a very important consideration is the ownership distortion. The authors' "radical" scenario would cut Bezos's wealth by a factor of more than six, and his 2018 Amazon stake from 16 percent to 2.4 percent—which is likely to have a large effect on his ability to control the direction of the firm. If distortions to a founder's ability to direct a business are important, then taxes that are based on realization or taxes that delay payment until a later date would be preferred. A capital gains tax on realization, an estate tax, or accruing a notional tax liability to be settled at realization would all fare better in that respect.

4. Estimated elasticities with respect to the (net of) estate tax rate are of the order of 0.2. Comparing them to estimates of response to the wealth tax is not straightforward—one is a onetime tax with double-digit rates, the other is annual with much smaller rates that when compounded over time would be of the same order of magnitude as the wealth tax. Poterba (2000) suggested multiplying the estate tax rate by the mortality rate to arrive at a measure of annual burden. Using a mortality rate of 1 percent for illustration, a 1 percent estate tax change would then be approximately equivalent to a .01 percent wealth tax change and the elasticity of 0.2 would be equivalent to the elasticity of 20, which is in the same ballpark as estimates by Brulhart and others (2016). Alternatively, compounding the wealth tax over T years would call for scaling the relevant elasticities by a factor of the order of T while accounting for the revenue impact over the whole T years in order to arrive at a comparison to estate taxation. A more recent paper by Goupille-Lebret and Infante (2018) finds quantitatively similar estimates of responsiveness to the French inheritance tax.

5. What cuts against the notion of disincentives due to individual behavioral response is the argument of Guvenen and others (2019) that a wealth tax introduces a (desirable) bias toward better investors. The mechanism for this effect relies on the presence of credit constraints and their interaction with explosive growth. I have doubts whether prospective billionaires are credit constrained nowadays, but under that assumption calibrated gains from a wealth tax are large. Even then though, it is interesting to note that the ideal wealth tax would be imposed on principal, but not the very high realized returns—the whole point of the tax is to bias the distribution toward those able to earn high returns.

IMPLEMENTATION Finally, let me turn to simplicity and implementability of the wealth tax. Saez and Zucman note that "wealth taxes are fragile," but that "tax competition and tax evasion is a policy choice." I agree with the first statement wholeheartedly but with the second only to an extent. Wealth taxes are fragile because they fundamentally rely on information that is not based on observable arm's-length transactions. This is in contrast to the most successful types of taxation. Taxation of labor income relies on transactions between employers and employees. The successful form of consumption taxation—VAT—leverages transactions within supply chain. Arm's-length transactions make information reporting (or third-party reporting) feasible when parties have incentives to comply, either because they are large or because of financial incentives: employers report wages paid to employees, firms report purchases from their suppliers. The same lessons can and are applied in other contexts that involve arm's-length relationships—banks can be required to report information about deposits, brokerages about financial investments. Mechanisms like these are the backbone of modern tax systems that make parts of them work automatically. It is when they are not feasible that problems arise. Examples abound. Transfer pricing in corporate taxation is a problem because cross-border transactions are between parties with shared interest, no arm's-length relationship there. Property tax assessments are problematic because they try to infer value without sale. Taxation of small businesses is an issue when their customers are small or paying in cash. Sales taxes have much narrower revenue potential in practice because retail-level taxation lacks a counterparty with incentives to report.

Successful tax administrations recognize these considerations. There is room for policy: the extent of third-party reporting is a policy choice. But it does not work when there is no third party, and there is usually no third party when what you tax is not an arm's-length transaction and thus there is not a counterparty or an institution that has knowledge about the value of the tax base. Saez and Zucman appeal at times to the insight from Slemrod and Kopczuk (2002) that behavioral elasticities are effectively policy parameters, but the authors ignore two aspects of it. First, there are the administrative and compliance costs of reducing responsiveness. These costs may be worth bearing, but they are not without trade-offs.[6] Second,

---

6. For example, note that the IRS, under an annual wealth tax, would have to deal with roughly 100 times as many taxpayers every year as it deals with in the estate tax context. In particular, valuations are one of the most challenging parts of the process and are costly to both the IRS and taxpayers.

the nature of this trade-off and how high you can push compliance or how low you can drive behavioral elasticities depend on the nature of the base that you tax. Transfer pricing is not realistically solvable by enforcement. Neither is small business taxation as long as we live in the world of cash.

Because wealth taxation fundamentally relies on taxing a base that cannot be fully covered by information reporting, it is bound to have problems. Saez and Zucman read European experience as highlighting the role of unfairness and liquidity issues in the dramatic failure of wealth taxes. While these were issues, they were the consequence of choosing this particular base. My interpretation of the European experience is that unfairness resulted from exempting or treating favorably types of assets that were hard to measure—primarily private businesses but also real estate. These are contexts without third parties. Illiquidity naturally arises in the same places because these are not transactions. Countries with otherwise very progressive policy and with extensive and well-functioning third-party reporting repealed their wealth taxes (for example, Denmark did so in 1996) because third-party reporting does not automatically fix everything if the base is poorly selected.

Saez and Zucman are very optimistic about solving such problems. Why? First, they are right that much of their intended *current* wealth tax base would not be subject to such considerations: publicly traded assets are easy to observe. Second, they note that by making the threshold sufficiently high, the base can be kept relatively clean.

However, just as a given level of tax avoidance and evasion is not the law of nature, neither is the depth of public markets. One might expect that incentives to stay private would be stronger than they are nowadays in the presence of a wealth tax. Even with public markets, ownership through trusts, holding companies, or intermediaries—hedge funds, for example—can be used to make valuation difficult. Saez and Zucman argue that private valuations exist. What they do not note is that they are costly and notoriously speculative (the very recent case of WeWork and many initial public offering cases where trading price departed from offering price, both under- and overvaluations, are obvious examples). Most fundamentally, they ignore the incentives that go in different directions when valuation is done for tax reasons and when it is done for investment purposes.

There are intriguing valuation ideas in the paper. For a theoretically minded economist, the notion of paying in stock and government as a market maker has a certain element of appeal, but practical aspects of it seem daunting both because of the implications of government ownership stake in private companies and because the notion that small stakes in a closely held company are cheaply marketable and correctly valued seems dubious.

An alternative solution the authors offer that could be "perfected" based on international experience is formula-based, involving book value and multiples of profits, as used in Switzerland. Interestingly, Switzerland is a country with evidence of very high responsiveness (Brulhart and others 2016). A simple introspection should also make one immediately skeptical of the implications of this approach for nontrivial tax rates. Say one assumes a profit multiple of 15 and a 2 percent wealth tax rate. This corresponds (for an owner of a closely held business) to a 30 percent profit tax rate, *on top of* any corporate or income taxation.

Returning to the theme of comparison of wealth and capital income taxation, any solution that allows for measuring wealth also automatically allows for measuring wealth *changes* and therefore is of use in addressing deficiencies of the existing system of taxing capital income on realization.

WEALTH AND PROGRESSIVITY MEASUREMENT Although this is not the main focus of the paper, it also provides updates to the Saez and Zucman (2016) and Kopczuk and Saez (2004) estimates of wealth inequality. I commented on these estimates in the past (Kopczuk 2015), so naturally I welcome this effort. Newer work since (Bricker and others 2016; Bricker, Henriques, and Hansen 2018; Smith, Zidar, and Zwick 2019) has revisited the Survey of Consumer Finances (SCF) wealth estimates and offered revisions of capitalization method. The authors attempt to address some of these criticisms by slightly changing the treatment of fixed-income assets and adopting a modified valuation of private businesses but they ignore other adjustments to valuing equity suggested by Smith, Zidar, and Zwick (2019). They also offer a modification of the estate multiplier estimates.

The results are presented in terms of "tax units"—an odd choice if used for illustrating trends in inequality because it is a unit of observation that is motivated by reliance on tax data and economically hard to interpret. It also requires ad hoc conversion of the SCF and estate tax from much more natural and meaningful households or individuals. These choices matter. As Bricker and others (2016) document, adjusting the unit of observation shifts the trend line of inequality in roughly parallel fashion. As a result, given the quite arbitrary nature of these adjustments, I prefer the comparison of changes rather than levels. This preference is further strengthened by systematic differences in coverage of different types of assets in different sources (for example, debt is much better observed in an estate multiplier than in a capitalization approach) that affect the observed level of inequality but may have smaller impact on changes.

Comparing numbers as reported in this paper, an increase in concentration (top 0.1 percent) between 1981 and 2012 (last year of estate tax data) in their capitalized series was 13.1 percentage points; in their revised series it was 9.7 percentage points; in the estate tax series it was 8.3 percentage points. Comparing 1989 and 2016 (years when the SCF is available), their two capitalization series show an increase of 8.5 and 5.8 percentage points respectively, while the SCF plus the Forbes 400 show an increase of 6.1 percentage points, but with a very different time path in between. These are trillion dollar differences that tend to show higher increases using the capitalization approach. When Smith, Zidar, and Zwick (2019) discuss the range of capitalization assumptions for fixed income and equity (which I'll come back to), they find that the range between the original Sacz and Zucman (2016) assumption and the most aggressive adjustment that they consider is $5.8 trillion or 8.6 percentage points as of 2014.

If I can convince the reader of nothing else, I hope I can at least convince that these are highly uncertain numbers that should be presented together with some explicit notion of the magnitude of the measurement error. The headline estimate of an increase in the share of the top 0.1 percent until 2012 has changed by 3.4 percentage points or $2.2 trillion between Saez and Zucman (2016) and this paper. The change was driven by modification of two unknowns—the relevant interest rate that should be applied to high net worth individuals on their fixed-income assets and the conversion factor used to arrive at private business valuations. Both of these are effectively parameters chosen by researchers; one is a unique number for each year, the other one is a single parameter throughout, both relying on very imperfect auxiliary information. All sources of information point to an increase in wealth inequality. Exactly how much is very much uncertain and should not be presented as certain.

These estimates are constructed from the bottom up—ownership of different categories of assets is imputed first and then aggregated, so that compositional problems cannot be just brushed off as issues that have no implications for the total: they are determining the total. The fixed-income part of the revised series was previously included in the appendix to Saez and Zucman (2016). It is unclear why this was not incorporated in the main series to begin with (I suggested that it should be at the time), because the original series makes a clearly unrealistic assumption about very low rate of return on fixed-income assets that is inconsistent with any other source of information about the wealthy, as this work acknowledges.[7] To illustrate compositional changes, I'll focus on the period between 1998 and 2016, when fixed-income adjustments have a bite. Over this period, the original top 0.1 percent capitalization estimate increased from 14.2 percent to 19.6 percent. The part accounted for by equities changed from 7.4 to 7.5 percent (with fluctuations between 6.3 percent and 8.5 percent), while almost the whole growth is explained by fixed-income assets (an increase from 3.3 percent to 8.2 percent). The revised estimates are more modest—an increase in the top share from 14.8 percent to 17.8 percent (note, the revision reduces the growth over that 18-year horizon by 45 percent), with an increase in fixed-income assets from 3 percent to 4.5 percent (note, almost halving relative to their original number by 2016), and little change in equities but compensated by adjustments in business assets by 2 percentage points, which is due to modifications in the approach to valuation of private businesses adopted from Smith, Zidar, and Zwick (2019). The behavior of the revised fixed-income component is closer to realism, although there is still no evidence elsewhere that the rich have rebalanced toward fixed-income assets (Bricker and others 2016; Bricker, Henriques, and Hansen 2018; Smith, Zidar, and Zwick 2019) and the remaining criticism of Smith, Zidar, and Zwick (2019) regarding capitalization of equities is unaddressed.

In contrast to relatively small net adjustments to their headline capitalization estimates, changes to the estate tax multiplier estimates are very large. I argued before (Kopczuk 2015) that assumptions about mortality differentials are likely responsible for the strikingly flat pattern in the wealth inequality series of Kopczuk and Saez (2004): the key assumption there—that we relied on given existing evidence at that time (the estimates until 2000)— was that the relative mortality differential between the top of the wealth distribution and the average has remained constant over time (and that it could be approximated by the difference between a college-educated population and the average). Chetty and others (2016) showed that these differences

---

7. Interest income in tax data does not separate between bonds and banking deposits. The rate of return on the former is larger than on the latter. In a low interest rate environment, the interest rate on deposits is close to zero. Then capitalization of interest income of bond holders (the rich) should be done using a capitalization factor that's much smaller than that implied by the average rate of return. For example, in 2016, the aggregate rate of return on fixed income assets reported by Saez and Zucman is 0.8 percent and the corresponding capitalization factor is 127. The SCF-based rate for the top 0.1 percent is 2.5 and the corresponding capitalization factor is 40. The Moody's AAA rate is 3.67 percent and the capitalization factor is 27. The estimate of fixed-income assets can be reduced by 80 percent by changing this single number.

in recent years, when looking at income distribution, are larger and that they have trended since 2001. Saez and Zucman implement an approach to incorporate these estimates in 2012 and conclude that it increases wealth of the top group by 50 percent. They assume that the original assumption in Kopczuk and Sacz (2004) was correct in 1980 and phase in the change linearly between then and 2012, which introduces a rapid trend rather than a level shift; in particular, it implies an increase by 34 percent or 3 percentage points in 2000, the last year in Kopczuk and Saez (2004).

This is both welcome and pretty uncertain. This calculation relies on the magnitude of the mortality differential between population of the rich and the average and parametric assumption of the Pareto distribution that allows for modifying the original estimates without revisiting original micro data. The mortality levels and differentials should be based on the population of the wealthy, but the estimates are based on the top 1 percent of income distribution. These are not the same, perhaps most importantly because people with high wealth who are approaching death may not have a lot of earnings and very little incentive to realize income. The results are sensitive to the Pareto assumption—it is made here to adjust aggregated estimates rather than revisit directly the confidential micro data. The authors choose to anchor the trend break in 1980, motivated by the comparison between the upper and lower halves of the distribution rather than any evidence that would apply to the rich. If, hypothetically, mortality differentials for the very rich in 1980 were already understated by half of the final adjustment, that would remove 2.1 percentage points in growth from the estate multiplier series.

As with other pieces of evidence, the implicit error bands on these numbers are large. Still, despite heavy uncertainty in these estimates, all of this suggests that the estate tax multiplier estimates of wealth concentration can be reconciled with other methods without appealing to speculative trends in tax evasion as the explanation.

PROGRESSIVITY The final piece is progressivity estimates, which are just the 2018 figures from Saez and Zucman (2019a), with methodology further described in Saez and Zucman (2019b). Splinter (2019) also has a separate discussion that focuses on methodological choices and reconciling these results with estimates in Auten and Splinter (2019). This calculation is based on highly unusual incidence assumptions: it relies on what I would call expert-augmented statutory incidence assumptions. Contrary to the literature and the standard practice, including their own earlier work (Piketty, Saez, and Zucman 2018) that this analysis builds on, it assumes statutory incidence of corporate tax, that is, that the corporate tax is borne by shareholders (nothing on wages, nothing on bonds and other assets). The statutory assumption is not consistently applied elsewhere though—sales tax and payroll tax are assigned to consumers and workers, despite statutory incidence of the former being on sellers and the latter split between workers and employees. Income excludes any transfers other than Social Security and tax liability excludes transfers and refundable portion of tax credits. Despite not including transfers and credits in income, the sales tax burden is calculated based on consumption. At the bottom of the distribution, this implies that incomes are small but tax liability is large because it is partially based on post-transfer consumption and not offset by any other transfers. As a result, at the very bottom of the distribution the implied "tax rates" would be very large—at the extreme of no income, they would be infinite. This problem is "solved" by dropping people below 50 percent of minimum wage annual income—26 million individuals in 2018, over 10 percent of the population, so that what is labeled as the bottom 10 percent in figure 5 is actually closer to being the second decile. The problem is not really solved of course—some transfers are still present higher up in the distribution—but it masks the glaring evidence of problems with this approach to defining tax burden. These choices create the false impression of flat tax liability throughout much of the distribution. Splinter (2019) discusses the more standard approaches, used in Auten and Splinter (2019) and by the CBO and other agencies, that uniformly find that the U.S. tax system is progressive.

What about the top? The statutory incidence assumption assigns the burden of the corporate tax to the shareholders so that drops in corporate tax revenue translate one-to-one into the drop of the effective tax rate paid by shareholders.[8] The paper innovates by separating the top 400 and showing data for 2018. It triangulates tax liability—tax information for Forbes 400 is not available. Finally, it projects to 2018 based on aggregate corporate revenue that has been affected by the 2017 tax reform, assumptions about the impact of individual income tax changes, and assumptions about the extent to which the Forbes 400 is affected by these changes. None of it is certain, but the combined impact is behind the rate at the very top being lower than elsewhere. As with other estimates, it should be taken with a grain of salt.

---

8. Not assigning anything to wages implies that the very top is more sensitive to corporate tax changes. Not assigning anything to assets—bonds predominantly—is more subtle but turns out to matter primarily for the extent of the decline in the burden at the very top that features prominently in Saez and Zucman (2019a) and is in contrast to the findings in Piketty, Saez, and Zucman (2018) that show only a mild decline since the 1950s.

CONCLUSION The paper accompanies political proposals that have been picked up by two of the front-runners in the Democratic primaries at the time. It makes a heartfelt case for a wealth tax that is appealing to many politically. In my view, the economic case for the wealth tax is overstated though. The data that underlie the revenue and progressivity impacts of the proposal have large margins of error. The tax is unlikely to fare well on administrative grounds and, in my view, the economic case for it over a mix of capital income and estate taxation is weak. A much more productive effort would be to focus on feasible and necessary fixes of existing U.S. taxation. My short list of such changes includes the removal of step-up in basis at death; modification of tax treatment of charity (including the ability to transfer unrealized capital gains); moving away from realization and toward accrual taxation, in particular by considering mark-to-market of capital gains where feasible; and reversal of preferences for pass-through businesses introduced in 2017.

REFERENCES FOR THE KOPCZUK COMMENT

Auten, Gerald, and David Splinter. 2019. "Income Inequality in the United States: Using Tax Data to Measure Long-Term Trends." 2019. Working Paper. http://davidsplinter.com/AutenSplinter-Tax_Data_and_Inequality.pdf.

Bricker, Jesse, Alice Henriques, and Peter Hansen. 2018. "How Much Has Wealth Concentration Grown in the United States? A Re-examination of Data from 2001–2013." Working Paper 2018-024. Board of Governors of the Federal Reserve System. https://www.federalreserve.gov/econres/feds/files/2018024pap.pdf.

Bricker, Jesse, Alice Henriques, Jacob Krimmel, and John Sabelhaus. 2016. "Measuring Income and Wealth at the Top Using Administrative and Survey Data." *Brookings Papers on Economic Activity*, Spring: 261–321.

Brulhart, Marius, Jonathan Gruber, Matthias Krapf, and Kurt Schmidheiny. 2016. "Taxing Wealth: Evidence from Switzerland." Working Paper 22376. Cambridge, Mass.: National Bureau of Economic Research. https://www.nber.org/papers/w22376.

Chetty, Raj, Michael Stepner, Sarah Abraham, Shelby Lin, Benjamin Scuderi, Nicholas Turner, Augustin Bergeron, and David Cutler. 2016. "The Association between Income and Life Expectancy in the United States, 2001–2014." *JAMA* 315, no. 16: 1750–66.

Farhi, Emmanuel, Chris Sleet, Ivan Werning, and Sevin Yeltekin. 2012. "Nonlinear Capital Taxation without Commitment." *Review of Economic Studies* 79, no. 4: 1469–93.

Goupille-Lebret, Jonathan, and Jose Infante. 2018. "Behavioral Responses to Inheritance Tax: Evidence from Notches in France." *Journal of Public Economics* 168:21–34.

Guvenen, Fatih, Gueorgui Kambourov, Burhanettin Kuruscu, Sergio Ocampo-Diaz, and Daphne Chen. 2019. "Use It or Lose It: Efficiency Gains from Wealth Taxation." Working Paper 26284. Cambridge, Mass.: National Bureau of Economic Research. https://www.nber.org/papers/w26284.

Jakobsen, Katrine, Kristian Jakobsen, Henrik Kleven, and Gabriel Zucman. 2019. "Wealth Taxation and Wealth Accumulation: Theory and Evidence from Denmark." *Quarterly Journal of Economics* 135, no. 1: 329–88.

Joulfaian, David. 2004. "Gift Taxes and Lifetime Transfers: Time Series Evidence." *Journal of Public Economics* 88, nos. 9–10: 1917–29.

Kopczuk, Wojciech. 2007. "Bequest and Tax Planning: Evidence from Estate Tax Returns." *Quarterly Journal of Economics* 122, no. 4: 1801–54.

Kopczuk, Wojciech. 2013. "Taxation of Intergenerational Transfers and Wealth." In *Handbook of Public Economics*, vol. 5, edited by Alan J. Auerbach, Raj Chetty, Martin S. Feldstein, and Emmanuel Saez. Amsterdam: Elsevier.

Kopczuk, Wojciech. 2015. "What Do We Know about the Evolution of Top Wealth Shares in the United States?" *Journal of Economic Perspectives* 29, no. 1: 47–66.

Kopczuk, Wojciech, and Emmanuel Saez. 2004. "Top Wealth Shares in the United States, 1916–2000: Evidence from Estate Tax Returns." *National Tax Journal* 57, no. 2: 445–87.

Piketty, Thomas, Emmanuel Saez, and Gabriel Zucman. 2018. "Distributional National Accounts: Methods and Estimates for the United States." *Quarterly Journal of Economics* 133, no. 2: 553–609.

Poterba, James M. 2000. "The Estate Tax and After-Tax Investment Returns." In *Does Atlas Shrug? The Economic Consequences of Taxing the Rich*, edited by Joel Slemrod. Cambridge, Mass.: Harvard University Press.

Saez, Emmanuel, and Gabriel Zucman. 2016. "Wealth Inequality in the United States since 1913: Evidence from Capitalized Income Tax Data." *Quarterly Journal of Economics* 131, no. 2: 519–78.

Saez, Emmanuel, and Gabriel Zucman. 2019a. *The Triumph of Injustice: How the Rich Dodge Taxes and How to Make Them Pay.* New York: W. W. Norton.

Saez, Emmanuel, and Gabriel Zucman. 2019b. "The Triumph of Injustice: How the Rich Dodge Taxes and How to Make Them Pay: Online Appendix." https://eml.berkeley.edu/~saez/SZ2019Appendix.pdf.

Slemrod, Joel, and Wojciech Kopczuk. 2002. "The Optimal Elasticity of Taxable Income." *Journal of Public Economics* 84, no. 1: 91–112.

Smith, Matthew, Owen Zidar, and Eric Zwick. 2019. "Top Wealth in the United States: New Estimates and Implications for Taxing the Rich." Working Paper. http://www.ericzwick.com/wealth/wealth.pdf.

Splinter, David. 2019. "U.S. Taxes Are Progressive: Comment on Progressive Wealth Taxation." Working Paper. http://www.davidsplinter.com/Splinter-TaxesAreProgressive.pdf.

Straub, Ludwig, and Ivan Werning. 2020. "Positive Long-Run Capital Taxation: Chamley-Judd Revisited." *American Economic Review* 110, no. 1: 86–119.

COMMENT BY

N. GREGORY MANKIW   I enjoyed reading this paper on the possibility of wealth taxation, especially in light of the recent proposal by Democratic candidate Elizabeth Warren. But I reach a different conclusion about the desirability of this policy. In these comments, I discuss four reasons why I disagree with the authors. Any one of these reasons is sufficient to make one skeptical of this new tax. So count me as quadruply skeptical.

First, Saez and Zucman understate how much redistribution of economic resources occurs under current policy. The problem is that their discussion separates the tax system from the substantial transfers it finances. In other words, the data they present in figure 5 regarding progressivity exclude all transfers, including transfers made through the tax system, such as the refundable part of the earned income tax credit.

Data from the Congressional Budget Office can be used to get a sense of the true amount of redistribution, including all transfers and federal taxes. (The CBO numbers exclude state and local taxes, perhaps because there is so much heterogeneity across states.) My calculations from these data show that the average tax rate for the bottom quintile is about −100 percent. That is, the poorest households receive in transfers (less taxes) about as much as they earn in market income. The second lowest quintile has an average tax rate of about −50 percent. The middle and fourth quintile face average tax rates close to zero. The richest quintile faces an average tax rate of about 25 percent, and the top 1 percent faces an average tax rate of about 33 percent.

In other words, after netting out transfers, the taxes collected by the federal government come almost entirely from the richest fifth of the population. Depending on political philosophy, a reasonable person can still favor more redistribution of economic resources. But it would be a mistake to suggest that there is little redistribution under current policy.

Second, Saez and Zucman understate how difficult it would be to measure wealth to assess the tax. Consider a popular singer like Lady Gaga, whom I presume owns the future royalty rights for her songs. How would the government put a number on that wealth? Sometimes, such intangible assets are sold on markets (Michael Jackson reportedly once bought the rights to Beatles songs), but often there is no market price for them.

A similar situation arises for any family business. When businesses are sold, accountants often attribute substantial value to an intangible asset called "goodwill." To assess a wealth tax, the government would need to estimate the goodwill associated with every business that has not been sold. Saez and Zucman are too cavalier in thinking that the IRS can easily come up with simple formulas to solve this problem. More likely, in the light of the great diversity of circumstances, such formulas would result in significant horizontal inequities. And those disadvantaged by the formulas could well seek remedies through litigation.

Third, I suspect that the wealth tax would induce a substantial rearrangement of assets to avoid the tax and, as a result, raise less revenue than Saez and Zucman suggest. (Here I am referring to legal tax avoidance, not illegal tax evasion.) As described, the Warren wealth tax would provide an incentive for divorce among high-wealth couples: a married couple has a $50 million exemption, whereas the two taxpayers in an unmarried couple can exempt $100 million from the tax. That is, given the 2 percent tax rate, the Warren proposal entails a $1 million per year marriage penalty. (Bernie Sanders's proposal for a wealth tax solves the marriage penalty problem by halving the thresholds for single taxpayers. This approach creates the opposite problem: a sizable marriage bonus, unless the newlyweds initially had equal wealth, and thus also a tax on widows and widowers.)

Gifting money to adult children would also reduce a family's tax liability. A married couple with three adult children could, by divorcing and gifting, exempt a total of $250 million from the Warren tax.

Many wealthy people intend to bequeath much of their wealth to charity. The wealth tax would encourage them to accelerate that giving during their lives. Saez and Zucman suggest taxing private foundations under founder control as if the founder still had the money, but this proposal strikes me as untenable. The Bill and Melinda Gates Foundation is similar in its societal role to the Ford Foundation, even though Bill and Melinda Gates are alive and Edsel Ford is not, and it is hard to make the case for treating these foundations differently for tax purposes. And even if such a distinction were enacted, Mr. and Mrs. Gates would have a large incentive to reform the management of their foundation to avoid the tax.

Finally, if the goal is to achieve a greater redistribution of economic resources, there are better ways to do it. My personal preference would be a progressive consumption tax. That is what occurs in many European countries: a value-added tax finances universal health care and higher education. This combination of taxes and in-kind transfers is effectively a progressive consumption tax.

In the United States, the closest proposal to this now being discussed is that of Democratic candidate Andrew Yang. He advocates a universal basic income financed by a value-added tax.

To see the merits of Yang's proposal over Warren's wealth tax, consider two corporate CEOs, each of whom earns $10 million a year. Spendthrift

Sam spends all his money living the high life. He drinks expensive wine, drives Ferraris, and flies a private jet to lavish vacations. Frugal Frank lives more modestly, saving most his earnings and accumulating a sizable nest egg. He plans to leave some of it to his children and grandchildren and the rest to charity. Ask yourself: Who should pay higher taxes?

The Warren wealth tax hits Frugal Frank hard but leaves Spendthrift Sam without a scratch. By contrast, the Yang proposal hits Sam hard and takes a smaller bite from Frank. Because Frank's behavior confers positive externalities, whereas Sam's does not, I am inclined for conventional Pigovian reasons to favor Yang's method of redistribution over Warren's.

In short, the more one considers the idea of a wealth tax, the less attractive it seems. The tax would target the wrong people, lead to substantial ambiguities and inequities in enforcement, and likely raise less revenue than simple extrapolations suggest. Saez and Zucman point out that many European nations have tried and abandoned taxes on wealth. They think that we can learn from past mistakes, and so this time would be different. But perhaps the right lesson is that the idea itself is ill conceived.

GENERAL DISCUSSION Jason Furman made two economic points. First, he asked the authors whether they were trying to tax the rich in a way that causes the most or the least amount of pain. He said this difference was important and related to whether the authors believe there are negative externalities associated with wealth. If so, he said, the authors might not be trying to maximize revenue while minimizing pain. Second, he asked the authors to comment on whether the United States should increase or reform the capital gains tax. He noted that most economists think that taxing capital gains when they are accrued is better than taxing capital gains when they are realized. He remarked that this opinion has implications for how economists think about a wealth tax. He asked those in the room to assume everyone makes a 4 percent rate every year on their capital. With a 20 percent capital gains rate, a wealth tax of .8 percent a year might be an administratively easier way to implement capital gains as they are accrued. He stated that anyone who thinks accrual is better than realization can't be completely opposed to a wealth tax, although such a tax is a somewhat crude method to implement capital gains that are accrued.

On the political side, Furman noted that a more systematic analysis is required to study the political feasibility of a wealth tax. Furman said that, in fact, it might be counterproductive to support a wealth tax in the absence of such analyses. For example, Furman asked the room to imagine a candidate at a fundraiser who has the seven wealthiest Democrats in New York at their table. Had a wealth tax been in place, the price of this table would decrease, but ultimately the same wealthiest seven Democrats would still be sitting at the table. Furthermore, in his experience on campaigns, candidates spend most of their time talking to the wealthy—those with tens or hundreds of millions of dollars. He argued that those with tens of billions likely affect policy in a different arena. Thus, a wealth tax is not likely to limit such people's ability to access the political system. Other changes to the political finance system in the United States, Furman noted, should be made.

Finally, Furman remarked on how a wealth tax is likely to increase giving. A wealth tax, he explained, reduces the cost of consumption today relative to consumption in the future. If you are wealthy and want to raise your consumption, you won't buy a home, yacht, or art, as these items are all covered by the wealth tax. Instead, such a person is likely to increase their giving to organizations, including political organizations. This increased giving, he noted, might distort the political system even further.

Mark Mazur stated that the paper is an important contribution to the literature regardless of whether one thinks the policy is good or bad. He also noted that in Joel Slemrod's hierarchy of tax responses paper transactions are also important.[1] These types of responses could include putting a family business into an LLC, giving up minority interest to your children, and getting an evaluation discount for a nonmarketable asset. Furthermore, in terms of the mobility problem—where the wealthy might relocate their primary residence to another country—he mentioned that the wealthy could just move to Puerto Rico. In this case, the wealthy would still be U.S. citizens but subject to the Puerto Rico tax system, which does not have a wealth tax. Finally, he remarked that thinking about effective tax rates is important. In the case of Warren Buffett, who has around $85 billion in wealth, a 2 percent wealth tax would raise around $1.7 billion of tax. Mazur remarked that this amounts to a large effective tax rate for Buffett if income is used as a base. This suggests to him that policymakers should rethink the base when computing effective tax rates.

Bob Hall said that the discussion so far has ignored how much wealth taxation exists already. Real estate, for example, is a large part of wealth and is taxed at the state and local levels. In addition, he mentioned, all business income is taxed, which amounts to a prepayment of a wealth tax.

---

1. Joel Slemrod, "A General Model of the Behavioral Response to Taxation," *International Tax and Public Finance* 8, no. 2 (2001): 119–28.

He noted that taxing something at the household level (household wealth), which is already taxed at the source (business income tax) doesn't seem like the best idea. Taxation at the source, he remarked, is a more efficient way to approach taxation. In addition, he pointed out that the calculations that Mankiw presented show that only about the upper 30 percent contribute to the government on net.

Hall expressed the idea that Warren Buffett paid a lot of income tax but that it was prepaid for him by the entities he owns. This prepaid tax means that he has an after-tax claim on his business interests. Thus, Hall stated, it is incorrect to say that Warren Buffett pays almost nothing in taxes; indeed, income tax was prepaid for him by a functioning tax system. In addition, he explained, the Chamley-Judd critique notes that if you pay a tax on a stock over and over, the tax rate compounds and is extremely high further in the future.[2] According to this critique, which he takes seriously, a high compound tax rate equates to a bias against capital formation. This bias puts a substantial burden on the economy. All in all, the Chamley-Judd critique shows that there is an equity efficiency trade-off.

Caroline Hoxby remarked that the paper seemed to fall short on economic or optimal tax motivations. She noticed that the authors' main justification for a wealth tax seemed to be the level of progressivity in wealth taxation in the 1960s, which, to her, wasn't very strong. A stronger justification, she noted, would come from a fundamental notion of what is the best way to tax. She stated that since all wealth is eventually consumed, a wealth tax is a way for policymakers to tax today's consumption rather than taxing future consumption. She said that she didn't see the point of distorting this intertemporal choice, which is fundamental to optimal taxation.

She noted that the wealth tax is taxing the wrong part of returns—which according to normal tax theory, shouldn't be taxed—instead of taxing the normal part of returns, like rents. To her, it is much easier to justify reforming the capital gains or estate tax through optimal tax motivation. Before taxing wealth, she said, policymakers should try to reform these two taxes. Finally, she spoke about the real effect of a wealth tax. The paper shows that such a tax would cause a tremendous reduction in the concentration of wealth. To her, it is not obvious that this reduction in the concentration of wealth is necessarily good. Although there are political economy

2. Christophe Chamley, "Optimal Taxation of Capital Income in General Equilibrium with Infinite Lives," *Econometrica* 54, no. 3 (1986): 607–22; and Kenneth L. Judd, "Redistributive Taxation in a Simple Perfect Foresight Model," *Journal of Public Economics* 28, no. 1 (1985): 59–83.

arguments for reducing the concentration of wealth, there also might be consequences to reducing CEO's stakes in their own companies. For example, she asked the audience to think about whether it would have been a good idea to reduce Steve Jobs's share in Apple while he was still alive.

William Gale praised the authors for elevating the policy debate on taxing affluent households. He remarked, though, that there are other taxes—such as Auerbach's retrospective tax, capital gains taxation at death, and a consumption tax—which are good alternatives to a wealth tax.[3] In terms of the consumption tax, he explained that such a tax functions as a onetime tax on existing wealth. He remarked that although a consumption tax is not quite as redistributionary as the Warren wealth tax, it is non-distortionary, which puts it at an advantage. In addition, he explained that a consumption tax is an implicit tax which means no assessment is required. Finally, he noted that a consumption tax is constitutional.

George Akerlof communicated that there are political externalities associated with such a large concentration of wealth at the top. He specified that the people the authors are proposing to tax have unbelievable amounts of money. With so much money, he noted, a consumption tax will hardly have an effect, as much of their money will likely never be spent. He expressed that one political externality in the large concentration of wealth at the top is that the SEC, the IRS, and various other regulatory agencies are seriously underfunded. This underfunding means that there have been reductions in the ability of agencies to enforce what is in the public interest. For this reason, he said, a wealth tax might be a good idea.

Richard Cooper asked the authors to discuss why wealth taxes have failed in other countries. Specifically, he asked the authors to discuss where these taxes have been flawed and how easy would it be to address these flaws.

Gerald Cohen remarked on a chart the authors presented that showed the ratio of household wealth to national income rising. He explained that since demographics in the United States have been changing (there are many more people of retirement age or approaching retirement), it makes sense that this ratio has increased. A wealth tax, he reflected, might discourage people to save as they age.

Emmanuel Saez thanked the commenters and discussants for their helpful views and said that he would keep his response short as time was running out. He remarked that it seemed like he still had more work to do

---

3. Alan J. Auerbach, "Retrospective Capital Gains Taxation," *American Economic Review* 81, no. 1: 167–78.

before convincing the economic community of the merits of a wealth tax. He remarked that spending a lot of time looking at wealth concentration data, including how much the wealthy pay in taxes—as both he and his coauthor do—draws a person to the fact that a large injustice exists in the United States today. These high-income people's wealth is growing fast, he noted. Moreover, their prepaid income taxes—which he and Zucman spent a lot of time making sure they computed correctly—just don't add up relative to their total income. Together, these two facts mean that it is important—in terms of elementary justice—to reform the tax system. The wealth tax, he remarked, is a powerful tool that can possibly restore this justice. Other tools, he noted, exist as well. He explained that he and Zucman are putting together an online calculator that allows a user to see how changing various taxes affects the shape of the tax distribution.[4] Maybe when some participants in the room use this tool, he reflected, they will become more convinced that something serious must be done and that the wealth tax is an option to consider.

4. Tax Justice Now, http://taxjusticenow.org/.